Predictability, Correlation, and Contiguity

WILEY SERIES ON
ADVANCES IN ANALYSIS OF BEHAVIOUR

Series Editors

Professor **Peter Harzem**
Department of Psychology,
Auburn University

Professor **Michael D. Zeiler**
Department of Psychology,
Emory University

VOLUME 1
Reinforcement and the Organization of Behaviour
Edited by
Michael D. Zeiler and Peter Harzem

VOLUME 2
Predictability, Correlation, and Contiguity
Edited by
Peter Harzem and Michael D. Zeiler

VOLUME 3
Biological Factors in Learning
Edited by
Michael D. Zeiler and Peter Harzem
in preparation

ADVANCES IN ANALYSIS
OF BEHAVIOUR

VOLUME 2

Predictability, Correlation, and Contiguity

Edited by

Peter Harzem   and   **Michael D. Zeiler**
Auburn University   *Emory University*

JOHN WILEY & SONS
Chichester · New York · Brisbane · Toronto

British Library Cataloguing in Publication Data:

Advances in analysis of behaviour.
  Vol.2: Predictability, correlation, and contiguity
  1. Animals, Habits and behavior of
  I. Harzem, P. II. Zeiler, Michael D.
  III. Predictability, correlation, and contiguity
  591.5   QL751   80–40843

ISBN 0 471 27847 5

Photoset by Thomson Press (India) Limited, New Delhi and printed in the United States of America.

Contributors

James Allison, Professor of Psychology at Indiana University, currently a member of the editorial board of *Journal of the Experimental Analysis of Behavior*, holds a Ph.D. from the University of Michigan, an M.A. from Claremont Graduate School, and an A.B. from the University of California at Berkeley. His early work dealt with such topics as acquired fear, ingestive behaviour, frustrative non-reward, and individual differences in animal behaviour. His later work on response deprivation and conservation theory reflects a long standing concern with quantitative models. Like the chapter in the present volume, many of his most recent papers show the influence of a sabbatical leave in 1976–77 devoted to the independent study of economics.

Michael B. Cantor received his Ph.D. in psychology from the University of North Carolina at Chapel Hill in 1970. After a post-doctoral term at the University of Pennsylvania he joined the Psychology faculty at Columbia University and is now at Emory University in Atlanta. His early work involved the problem of electrical brain stimulation as a reinforcer of operant behaviour. This led to an abiding interest in using communication theory to synthesize learning paradigms. His present research program is aimed at the question: What induces satiated rats and humans to ingest? His work has appeared in the *Journal of Comparative and Physiological Psychology*, the *Journal of Experimental Psychology: General, Nutrition in Health and Disease, Chemical Technology, Learning and Motivation*, and *Science*.

A. Charles Catania, Ph.D., Harvard University, is Professor of Psychology at the University of Maryland, Baltimore County. He has served as President of the Society for the Experimental Analysis of Behavior, and of Division 25 of the American Psychological Association. He is a member of the editorial board of *Behaviorism*, and a past editor of the *Journal of the Experimental Analysis of Behavior*. Dr Catania has published articles extensively on basic operant phenomena. He is editor of *Contemporary research in operant behavior* (Scott, Foresman & Co., 1968), and author of *Learning* (Prentice-Hall, 1979).

v

Edmund Fantino received his B.A. in mathematics from Cornell University in 1961 and his Ph.D. in psychology from Harvard University in 1964. After three years as Assistant Professor at Yale University he moved to the University of California, San Diego, where he is Professor of Psychology and a member of the Neurosciences Group. He is author of *Introduction to Contemporary Psychology* (with George S. Reynolds, 1975), *The Experimental Analysis of Behavior: A Biological Perspective* (with Cheryl A. Logan, 1979) and of articles appearing in professional journals and books. He has served as Associate Editor of the *Journal of the Experimental Analysis of Behavior*, on the Board of Directors of the Society for the Experimental Analysis of Behavior, and has been Visiting Professor at the Primate Research Institute, Kyoto University. His principal research interest is in response strength, especially the areas of choice, conditioned reinforcement, and self-control.

I. Gormezano received his Ph.D. from the University of Wisconsin, Madison, in 1958, under the direction of the late Professor David A. Grant. After eight years at Indiana University, Bloomington, where he progressed through the academic ranks traditional to the Department (instructor, assistant, associate, and full professor), he moved to The University of Iowa. Except for Visiting Professorships in 1970 (University of California, Berkeley), 1975 (University of Western Australia), and 1977 (University of California, Irvine), he remains in continuous residence at Iowa, as he puts it 'as the local guru of Pavlovian conditioning'.

Anne L. Harzem holds a doctorate of the University of Wales where, since 1965, she has been a Lecturer in Psychology. There she shared with Peter Harzem the work of founding the Operant Research Laboratory, and since 1969, their private lives. She says the tangible results of such intimate collaboration have been their daughter, the chapter in this volume, and several research papers. At present they are a professional couple commuting across the Atlantic, but plan to return to a less frantic form of living in the near future.

Peter Harzem graduated from the University of London with First Class Honours, and holds a doctorate of the University of Wales. He was a founder-member of the Department of Psychology at the University College of North Wales where he established a laboratory for operant research, and organized the British Experimental Analysis of Behaviour Group. In 1978 he moved to the U.S.A. He is now Professor and Director of Experimental Psychology at Auburn University. He has published numerous research articles and chapters, and he is co-author, with T. R. Miles, of *Conceptual Issues in Operant Psychology* (Wiley, 1978). Recently he has been working on *Human Nature*, a book which, he says, acquired a personality of its own and developed beyond the original plan.

Philip N. Hineline received a B.A. at Hamilton College, followed by a Ph.D. at Harvard University in 1967 under the guidance of R. J. Herrnstein. After three years at the Walter Reed Army Institute of Research he joined the psychology department at Temple University where he is now a Professor, and Director of the Division of Experimental Psychology. His research began in the study of warm-up effects in avoidance, and led to analyses of behaviour in terms of long-term vs. short-term controlling variables. His current research focuses upon the integration of brief events over time, and upon the principle of resonance as it applies to patterns of behaviour. Less active but enduring interests include the psychology of music, the behaviour of the crow, and peculiarities of the language of behaviour analysis. He currently serves on the editorial boards of *Behaviorism* and *The Behaviour Analyst*, and is an Associate Editor for the *Journal of the Experimental Analysis of Behavior*.

E. James Kehoe received his Ph.D. in psychology in 1976, from the University of Iowa. There he worked in the laboratory of I. Gormezano. He is now a Lecturer in Psychology at the University of New South Wales, Australia. His main research interests are in stimulus selection and associative transfer in classical conditioning.

Kenneth J. Keller received his Ph.D. in experimental psychology from New York University, and did postdoctoral work in the experimental analysis of behaviour at the University of Maryland, Baltimore County. At present he is faculty research associate at the Maryland Psychiatry Research Center in Baltimore, where he is studying event-related brain potentials in schizophrenics.

Stephen Lea took a B.A. in natural sciences and a Ph.D. in psychology at the University of Cambridge, and is now a Lecturer in Psychology at the University of Exeter. His main interest is in incentive, though he also works in pattern recognition, and the associated problems of concept formation and semantic memory. His work in incentive chiefly concerns the interrelations between psychology and economics, and he has carried out a number of simulations of economic phenomena using laboratory rats in operant apparatus. In pattern recognition he is mainly interested in the ways in which people and other animals cope with ill-defined or varying stimuli, and this has led him to train pigeons to discriminate letters of the alphabet. Contrary to the belief of the media, he has no plans to teach them to read.

Vincent LoLordo received a B.A. in psychology from Brown University in 1962 and a Ph.D. from the University of Pennsylvania in 1966. He was on the faculty of the University of North Carolina at Chapel Hill for seven years, and is now

Professor of Psychology at Dalhousie University. He has published papers on a variety of topics in conditioning and learning, and at present is the Editor of *Learning and Motivation.*

Alan Randich received B.A. and M.S. degrees in psychology from Syracuse University, and received his Ph.D. from Dalhousie University in 1978. After a year as an NIMH post-doctoral Fellow at Yale University he joined the faculty of the University of Iowa, where he is Assistant Professor of Psychology. He is continuing research on the US pre-exposure effect, the subject of his chapter in this volume.

Robert A. Rescorla received his B.A. in psychology from Swarthmore College in 1962. There he was heavily influenced by S. E. Asch, H. Gleitman, and H. Wallach. He received his Ph.D. from the University of Pennsylvania in 1966. At Penn he worked in the laboratory of Richard Solomon at a time when fellow graduate students were J. B. Overmeier, V. LoLordo, M. E. P. Seligman, and S. Maier. He went directly from the University of Pennsylvania to Yale University where is his presently Professor of Psychology. His research interests have centered on elementary associative learning processes, particularly as exemplified in Pavlovian conditioning.

Contents

About the Series

The purpose of this series of volumes is to provide a forum both for the integration of existing research and for the development of theoretical approaches in the light of that research, in the area of psychology associated with terms such as *learning, operant behaviour, classical conditioning,* and *animal learning*. None of these terms alone is sufficient to identify the area accurately, since this is an area which evolves continually as new perspectives emerge and old classifications are found to need revision. We believe this subject matter is centrally important in understanding behaviour, and warrants, therefore, a continuing series of volumes of the present kind.

Each volume in the series will be organized around a particular topic of contemporary importance. However, this organization will be sufficiently flexible so as to encourage innovation. In this way we hope that these volumes will stimulate new approaches and ideas, as well as organizing existing knowledge and theory.

Peter Harzem
Michael D. Zeiler

Foreword

Inquiry into the sorts of relations that can arise between events in determining behaviour has a long and distinguished history. In recent years this kind of inquiry has again become centrally important in behavioural research. Several questions have been posed, emphasizing different aspects of the problem: Are temporal relations the particularly crucial ones in the control of behaviour? Is what matters the probability with which one event functions as a predictor of another? Do the relations in question involve stimuli, or responses and stimuli? And so on. The chapters of this volume address these issues, and re-examine the empirical evidence from different theoretical perspectives. A broad range of topics is considered, extending from classical conditioning and characteristics of reinforcing events, to economic theory and the behaviour of animals in foraging for food. The volume is intended for the active researcher as well as for the graduate student newly entering the field. Thus it should be suitable for use in graduate seminars.

As with Volume 1 of the series, we wish to thank the authors for the high quality of their contributions. We are grateful to Anne Harzem who, in addition, prepared the index.

Peter Harzem
Michael D. Zeiler
Auburn and Atlanta, 1980

Predictability, Correlation, and Contiguity
Edited by P. Harzem and M. D. Zeiler
© 1981 John Wiley & Sons Ltd.

Chapter 1

Classical Conditioning and the Law of Contiguity

I. Gormezano and E. James Kehoe

Introduction

Over the last 200 years, the Law of Contiguity has formed the keystone of the major philosophical and psychological theories of knowledge, learning, and memory (Boring, 1950; Diamond, 1974; Marx and Hilex, 1973; Robinson, 1932; Warren, 1921). In its most general form, the Law of Contiguity states that if two or more events occur contiguously, the reoccurrence of only one of these events will evoke a 'memory' of the other event(s). However, it would be unwise to regard the Law of Contiguity as a monolithic, invariant proposition since, in response to constant challenges, it has undergone continuous revision and supplementation. Accordingly, it would be more accurate to construe the Law of Contiguity as the name for a family of hypotheses which vary most notably with regard to their specification of the key events required to occur contiguously. The present paper reviews these hypotheses with reference to theoretical accounts of conditioning phenomena, with special emphasis on classical conditioning with animals and, in particular, with the rabbit nictitating membrane response (NMR) preparation. Specifically, our review covers four major developments characterizing the corpus of activity surrounding the Law of Contiguity and classical conditioning. First, we will trace the development of the Law of Contiguity from its philosophical roots in eighteenth and nineteenth century associationistic doctrines to its early, more objective expression by Ebbinghaus (1885), to its strong identification with Pavlov's classical conditioning paradigm. Second, we will review variations in the Law of Contiguity which have been proposed in response to the difficulties posed by the phenomena of successful conditioning under CS–US asynchrony and long-trace intervals between the conditioned stimulus (CS) and the unconditioned stimulus (US). Third, we will review the means by which the Law of Contiguity has been used to account for the action of stimuli at a distance (e.g. goal-directed behaviours). Fourth, and finally, we will discuss supplementations to the Law of Contiguity which have been introduced to account for selective associations among contiguous stimuli (e.g. overshadowing and blocking) and to account for the results of 'contingency' manipulations between the CS and US.

Early Developments

Classical Associationism

As its name implies, the Law of Contiguity states that an associative connection between two events will be formed only if they occur in spatiotemporal proximity to one another. Aristotle, in one of the earliest acknowledged expressions of associationistic principles (*see* Sandiford, 1942), proposed that the similarity and contrast between events, as well as the previous contiguity between events, determined which events would be recalled together. While Aristotle is generally credited with originating the concepts of 'association' and 'contiguity' in his discussion of memory, the writings of the British Empiricists served as the major immediate precursors to psychological interpretations of the formation of associations. For the British Empiricists, who largely rejected the Cartesian proposition of innate ideas, the Law of Contiguity was the fundamental principle by which the association of ideas would be formed and, accordingly, the means by which the experience of individual mental events would leave a permanent imprint on the *tabula rasa* of the mind. Thus, their postulation of association as the 'mental glue' or connective force between mental events (ideas) provided an organizing mechanism for the multitude of simultaneous and successive mental events, and the Law of Contiguity governed which events would become connected.

In elaborating the doctrine of association, the early British Empiricists, viz. Locke, Hume, and Hartley, were not concerned so much with the conditions for association as with the manner in which association provided a mechanism for compounding relatively simple mental events into the more complex mental entities. The concern with the compounding of mental elements characterized British Associationism and led to the 'mental mechanics' of James Mill, the 'mental chemistry' of John Stuart Mill, and ultimately to Structural Psychology. In the attempt to specify composition rules for associations, the Law of Contiguity was largely left in its rudimentary form. However, even in rudimentary form, the Law of Contiguity played the central role in Hume's psychological theory of causation, i.e. the common impression that agents deemed 'causes' somehow 'push', 'pull', or 'act on' their effects. At the risk of gross simplification, Hume argued essentially that there is no special causative relation in the external world but, rather, causation is a subjective impression arising whenever two mental 'objects' occur in 'constant conjunction' with one preceding the other. More specifically, event A would be seen to 'cause' event B whenever three conditions were met: (1) A and B occur in spatiotemporal contiguity; (2) A occurs prior to B; and (3) A and B occur in a 'necessary connection', which Hume reduced to repeated and, perhaps, exclusive contiguity of A and B. Thus, although a single instance of contiguity between A and B may establish an association, repeated instances of contiguity were necessary to establish a cause–effect relation.

While Hume's analysis of causation has been subjected to extensive philosophical analysis and criticism, it has exercised a profound effect on psychology by establishing the correlations of events in time as phenomena of fundamental importance. In particular, Hume proposed that the contiguity of events was the psychologically significant aspect of the temporal flow of events. On the other hand, Hartley's writings are of interest in that they anticipated the modern conceptual link between association and Pavlov's conditioned reflex. Most importantly, Hartley was a psychophysical parallelist to the extent that he recognized that mental events and their associations had counterparts in the nervous system. He speculated that sensation and (physical) motion arose from the waves of vibrations in small particles passing along the nerves, and he argued that, in the brain, there are 'diminutive vibrations, . . . which are the physiological counterparts of ideas'. Accordingly, Hartley framed two parallel laws of association, one for the mental events of sensations and ideas and the other for physiological vibrations and miniature vibrations. Moreover, Hartley's postulation of physiological vibrations gave him a plausible means for accounting for the persistence of a sensation after the removal of the stimulus event. Thus, Hartley appears to have also laid the intellectual foundation of the modern hypothesis of stimulus persistence through the 'stimulus trace'.

Although the early associationists recognized that associations varied in their strength and that not every pair of contiguous events would necessarily become associated, it was the Scottish philosopher, Thomas Brown (1820), who provided the earliest clear statement of the 'Secondary Laws of Association', which would enable the prediction of which events out of a group of contiguous events would become associated and to what degree. Foremost among the secondary laws was the Law of Frequency, which stated that it was the number of repetitions of a contiguous pair of events which determined their subsequent associative strength. In addition to frequency, Brown asserted that the strength of an association would be determined by (1) the duration of the original events, (2) their intensities, (3) the recency of their pairing, (4) the number of other associations in which the two events have been involved, (5) the similarity of the association itself to other, previously acquired associations, and (6) the abilities, emotional state, and bodily state of the person experiencing the events. In the subsequent 200 years, variations on Brown's list have remained a constant feature of theory and research on the determinants of association.

The first empirical substantiation of associative doctrines was carried out by Ebbinghaus (1885). Although his study of 'memory' was phrased in subjective terms, his methods were entirely objective. Ebbinghaus' work is significant in the present context in that he attempted a quantitative examination of the Law of

Contiguity with his methods of derived lists. In classic association doctrine, the Law of Contiguity did not require strict contiguity in the sense of absolute simultaneity among events. In fact, it was common to distinguish between associations among successive events as well as simultaneous events. In any event, associative strength was expected to decline as the temporal separation between successive events increased. Ebbinghaus determined indirectly the strength of 'remote associations' by examining the savings in acquisition for lists in which the adjacent items had, in an earlier learned list, been separated by 0, 1, 2, . . . , 7 intervening items. He found that savings in learning the new list decreased as a smooth function of the separation of the items in the earlier list. Thus, Ebbinghaus' method of derived lists yielded the first empirical contiguity gradient.

The conversion of the Law of Contiguity from a philosophical principle into a testable scientific hypothesis appears to have started with the physiological interpretations by Hartley. Moreover, as described above, Ebbinghaus provided an objective methodology for the study of associations. However, the crucial step in the development of the Law of Contiguity into a fundamental principle of learning and memory came only with the recognition of the parallels between associative doctrine and the conditioned reflex, parallels first clearly stated by Bekhterev (cf. Hilgard and Marquis, 1940, p. 9). In fact, Bekhterev's name for the conditioned reflex was the 'association reflex'. Whereas today 'association' and 'conditioning' are used interchangeably in some quarters, the original acknowledgement of the association–conditioning parallel required not only the development of the conditioning methods but also a major philosophical shift away from Cartesian dualism. Since this shift is still incomplete today, the admixture of philosophies has continually clouded the application of associationism to conditioning and vice versa. Accordingly, these philosophical problems and their consequences for theory and method are worthy of some consideration as the groundwork for subsequent discussion of the Law of Contiguity in its scientific versions.

Dualism

Descartes' (1650) doctrine of dualism has been both the source and bane of modern theories of behaviour. Descartes' fundamental contribution was his introduction of the concept of the 'reflex' to provide a 'mechanical' account of movements in both humans and animals. To do so, Descartes introduced a novel device—the 'stimulus'—a mechanism by means of which he proposed that the 'energy' embodied in external forces (stimuli) flowed into the body and was 'reflected' out from the brain in the form of muscular movements. However, to reconcile the mechanical (deterministic) action of stimuli with the prevailing belief in a free, insubstantial 'soul' (mind) as a determiner of human conduct, Descartes proposed that in humans the 'soul' could intervene at the point of the pineal gland to stop the action of stimuli. In proposing an anatomical reference point, i.e. the pineal gland, for the reflection of stimulus energy and its interaction with the forces of the soul, Descartes provided a theologically acceptable framework which divided psychology from physiology, thereby permitting the concept of association to develop separately from physiology's concept of the reflex.

Whereas the philosophical psychologists progressively expanded the concept of mental association into the primary principle of mental life, the physiologists progressively constricted the character of Descartes' 'reflex'. As described by Descartes, reflex action or reflection of stimuli, being any externally arising energy, governed all movements, simple or complex. The soul or mind itself interacted with the mechanism of reflection but could not, itself, act in the manner of a stimulus. Rather, the mind was a directing agent which determined which stimuli would operate. From Descartes' concept of reflex and its interaction with the mind, physiologists developed a concept of 'reflex' confined to simple stereotyped movements (or glandular secretions) mediated largely by the spinal cord. Moreover, the mind, in the form of 'volition', became a second 'cause' of movement believed to be independent of stimuli, i.e. external forces. These alterations in the concept of the reflex and the role of mind occurred gradually as a result of physiological findings that reflexes present in already decapitated animals could be abolished by destruction of the spinal cord. Such findings led to the conclusion that the 'seat of reflection' was not in the pineal gland but in the spinal cord. Furthermore, it became the practice of physiologists to study reflex phenomena in decapitated or decerebrated animals under the assumptions that (a) consciousness was abolished by destruction of the brain, and (b) the observed absence of spontaneous activity meant that such animals had no 'voluntary' behaviours.

Marshall Hall (1832), formalized the above operating assumptions of physiologists working with spinal preparations and authored the now almost immutable distinction between voluntary and reflex action. Hall described as 'voluntary' any form of movement which was (a) 'spontaneous', and (b) dependent upon the integrity of the brain. Hall reasoned that since the 'spontaneous' movements of organisms disappeared upon removal of the brain, that the brain was essential for volition to operate. However, as Hall used the term 'spontaneity' it described, in effect, only those behaviours (movements) for which no stimulus antecedants had been identified. Accordingly, by defining 'volition' as the hypothetical antecedent of behaviours for which no stimuli had been observed, Hall's definition had the significant property of leaving the domain of volition open to erosion every time it was possible systematically to relate a particular movement of an organism to antedating sensory events.

Physiological investigators of the eighteenth and early nineteenth centuries, in restricting their study of reflexes to spinal preparations, did not necessarily believe that only the spinal cord had reflexes. However, the prevailing dualistic philosophy made it impossible to arrive at an agreed-upon method for studying reflex action of the brain free from the indeterminant influence of an insubstantial mind or will. However, Sechenov, while working in the laboratory of Claude Bernard, produced inhibition of the scratch reflex in the frog by the application of salt solutions and crystals to various parts of the brainstem. Since the scratch reflex had been previously identified as a spinal reflex, Sechenov's observations convinced him that spinal reflexes can be inhibited by 'reflex' action of the cerebral cortex. Accordingly, Sechenov (1863) boldly reasserted Descartes' hypothesis of reflex action of the brain. However, he went beyond Descartes' dualism by totally rejecting the notion of mind or will as having any control over behaviour.

By asserting that the brain operated strictly to mediate a 'reflex process', Sechenov freed the concept of reflex from a dualistic complex, and also recaptured Descartes' original meaning of reflex as a general principle asserting that all behaviour is determined by physical antecedants. Thus, Sechenov's monistic concept of 'reflex' should not be aligned with Hall's dualistic concept of 'reflex', based on the spinal preparation, with its negative connotations of 'involuntary', 'unconscious', and 'automatic'. Within Sechenov's monistic framework, the voluntary–involuntary distinction as specification of the origins of behaviour did not exist; every behaviour was assumed to have discoverable and lawful physical antecedants. Similarly, Sechenov, while not denying subjective states of consciousness, argued that the distinction between consciousness and unconsciousness did not form a boundary line in the determination of behaviour by its stimulus antecedants. Finally, by the thoroughgoing application of reflex to the entire nervous system, Sechenov asserted that all behaviour, simple or complex, was determined by stimulus antecedants.

The Conditioned Reflex

Even while asserting the generality of reflex process, Sechenov distinguished two types of reflex action, the first being innate reflexes, which included spinal reflexes, and the second being 'acquired reflexes', which were presumed to be mediated by the brain and resulted from the previous history of the organism. However, the concept of the acquired reflex lay fallow until Pavlov developed his method of the 'conditioned reflex' as a means for reliably producing and investigating the acquisition of new reflexes (cf. Babkin, 1949). As is well known, in the course of his investigations of digestive processes, Pavlov noted the regular occurrence of salivary secretions prior to the insertion of meat into the dog's mouth. Previously, these secretions were deemed to have a 'psychic' origin; however, Pavlov determined that these psychic secretions regularly followed the distal event of the sight of meat and thus could be deemed to be reflexive under Sechenov's broad concept. In an experiment with puppies, Pavlov determined that the reflexive relation between sight-of-meat and salivation resulted from a previous history of sight-of-meat being followed by insertion of the meat into the mouth. Thus, the sight-of-meat–salivation reflex was acquired rather than innate. Subsequently, Pavlov introduced the terms 'unconditioned reflex' for innate reflex and 'conditioned reflex' to denote the acquired reflex.

While Pavlov developed the method of the conditioned reflex, he regarded it primarily as a tool for the physiological study of brain functioning and, more broadly, for the study of the neural mechanisms by which animals adjusted behaviourally to the exigencies of their individual environments. In contrast, Pavlov's more psychologically oriented contemporary, Bekhterev, was the first to recognize the parallel between the conditioned reflex and the doctrine of association through contiguity. In Bekhterev's own investigations of motor-conditioned reflexes, he went so far as to call them 'association reflexes'. Thus, while Pavlov provided the method, Bekhterev (1913) made the crucial step in linking conditioning to association through contiguity. Later, Pavlov (1927, pp. 88–89) provided data that would cement the linkage; specifically, Pavlov found that the establishment of a conditioned salivary reflex proceeded most rapidly and reliably when the onset of the new stimulus (the conditioned stimulus) preceded the onset of the original stimulus (the unconditioned stimulus) by short intervals of no more than 5 s, whereas at longer intervals the *establishment* of a conditioned reflex was found to be 'difficult if not impossible' (Pavlov, 1927, p. 89). Thus, Pavlov provided the first, albeit crude, contiguity gradient for conditioning.

About the same time that Pavlov was beginning his investigations, Thorndike (1898) began his study of animal intelligence. His subsequent work (Thorndike, 1911, 1913), embodied many of the converging intellectual trends which were later to characterize Watson's Behaviouristic School. Thorndike's methods of investigation were objective in nature, and his Law of Effect summarized his perceived connection between 'habit' (i.e. learned adaptation) and association through contiguity. The relevant portion of the law states, 'Of the several responses made to the same situation, those which are accompanied or closely followed by satisfaction to the animal will, other things being equal, be more firmly connected with the situation so that, when it recurs, they will be more likely to recur. . .'. Although contemporary treatments of effect-type principles in connection with instrumental and operant conditioning methods have tended to concentrate on the relation between the response and 'satisfaction' (reinforcement), Thorndike's Law of Effect is first and foremost a principle of association through contiguity. Specifically, Thorndike's Law of Effect focused on the 'connection' (association) between 'situations' (stimuli) and 'responses', and, thus, paralleled the broad conception of 'acquired reflex' used by Sechenov, Pavlov, and Becheterev. However, the unique aspect of Thorndike's Law of Effect is that it required the contiguity of three events, viz. 'situation', 'response', and 'satisfier', for the formation of an association. The members of the association were the situation and response, and the 'satisfaction' was not itself a member of the association but, rather, a necessary catalyst to its formation. Interestingly, from an historical perspective, Thorndike's stipulation of 'satisfaction' as a necessary condition for association can be seen as aking to Brown's secondary Laws of Association as specifying constraints on the otherwise willy-nilly operation of contiguity.

Behaviourism

During the emergence of behaviourism, the theoretical links between association and the conditioned reflex method became entangled in the broader concerns of the behaviourists with objectivity and habit (learned adaptation). The polemics which attended the spread of behaviourism (and their perpetuation in secondary sources) has had the consequence of frequently burdening present-day conceptions of the Law of Contiguity and classical conditioning with unnecessary connotations. Tentative and partial links between classical conditioning, the Law of Contiguity, objectivity, and learning became enshrined as somehow necessary and exclusive. Least we inadvertently perpetuate that unfortunate tradition, it would seem necessary to distinguish the useful theoretical linkages from the unnecessary linkages as they bear on the Law of Contiguity and classical conditioning.

One of the earliest and still most useful statements in the American literature of the useful relations between classical conditioning methods, association through contiguity, and learning was articulated by Lashley (1916). He stated:

> For an analysis of the mechanism of learning, . . . the study of the conditioned salivary reflex is of the greatest importance. The method of producing it is quite simple, consisting essentially of the simultaneous application of some indifferent stimulus, such as the sound of a bell, with one which excites a direct salivary reflex, such as a gustatory stimulus. *The appearance of salivary secretion following application of the originally indifferent stimulus forms an almost ideal example of an associational as contrasted with a trial-and-error method of learning.* (p. 459; our italics)

Lashley's assertion that the conditioned reflex method was an 'almost ideal example' of associative learning was not mere polemic; he saw it as possessing several methodological advantages over other methods for studying the mechanism of learning:

> Conditions may be so arranged that only two stimuli, and presumably, one reaction are involved. In studies of the effects of the intensity of the stimuli and of the distribution of practice upon the rate of learning this simplification of the problem is of considerable importance, *but its greatest usefulness should be for studies of the temporal relations between the primary*

and associated stimulus necessary for the formation of the association.
(p. 460; our italics)

and,

> The fact that a single reaction is involved is also an advantage. The
> associated reaction either does, or does not, occur and there is no question of
> the elimination of errors or simplification of reaction. This is also true of
> verbal association, but in the latter case there already exists an elaborate
> system of word habits whose influence on experimental studies has not yet
> been determined. (p. 460)

In summary, Lashley noted that the conditioned reflex method permits the
investigator the precision in the control of stimuli and in the measurement of
responding to delineate clearly the effects of important variables on association,
particularly, the variable of CS–US interval.

Subsequent to Lashley's forceful but sound arguments regarding the methodological advantages of classical conditioning, vis-à-vis association through
contiguity, the concept of the conditioned reflex acquired broad theoretical
stature as a fundamental unit of learning. Whereas Lashley had seen the methods
of Pavlov, Thorndike, and Ebbinghaus as all instances of a common 'mechanism
of learning', other authors attempted to present the conditioned reflex itself as a
mechanism of learning. There were some serious, although superficial, attempts
to account for puzzle-box and maze learning results in terms of conditioned
approach and conditioned avoidance reflexes (Frank, 1923; Smith and Guthrie,
1921, p. 122; Wilson, 1924). There were also more extravagent claims: 'Learning
may be studied and accounted for in the same terms that apply to all habit
formation, namely, in terms of the conditioned reflex process' (Frank, 1923; cf.
Razran, 1930). On the other hand, Watson's (1916) initial claims for the
conditioned reflex methods were more modest than those of Lashley (1916), but
in Watson's (1925) book, the conditioned reflex became his central theoretical
construct in a speculative application to virtually the whole range of behaviour.
Such speculative application of the conditioned reflex submerged the more
cautious views of other behaviourists (e.g. Cason, 1922; Woodworth, 1918,
pp. 398–400) regarding the role of the conditioned reflex in theory, and made it
easy for critics to characterize any application of conditioned reflex principles as
simple-minded (e.g. McDougall, 1923).

During the emergence of Behaviourism, the conditioned reflex was also
converted from a clear *example* of association through contiguity to virtually a
substitute for the Law of Contiguity. Specifically, Smith and Guthrie (1921,
p. 253), noting that the laws of the conditioned reflex appeared to parallel those
for the association of ideas, authored the usage of the label 'conditioning' to
denote the objective form of 'associations' said to occur between stimuli and

movements (responses) rather than between ideas (cf. Locke). Furthermore, to avoid some of the surplus meaning and confusion that had come to surround the concept of the reflex, Smith and Guthrie (1921) adopted the term 'conditioned response' instead of 'conditioned reflex'. Most importantly, in their hands conditioning became a general formula for including all that had formerly been treated as associative learning. For them, conditioning was the modern substitute for *contiguity*, the primary law of association. Subsequently, while Guthrie (1930) continued to use 'conditioning' as synonymous with 'association by contiguity', he explicitly distinguished between a theory of learning based on conditioning (i.e. contiguity) and a theory of learning based upon conditioned reflex, which Guthrie saw as connoting a 'stereotyped' unit of behaviour. However, Guthrie's distinction appears to have been too weak to resist the tendency to merge the conditioned reflex with the Law of Contiguity (cf. Holt, 1931).

The initial wave of enthusiasm for classical conditioning ended with the appearance of detailed descriptions of Pavlov's (1927) work and reports of systematic research in the United States which revealed the complexities of classical conditioning (e.g. Cason, 1922; Hilgard, 1931). Moreover, the initial American views of the conditioned reflex as the unit of habit and substitute for association came under strong attack (Hilgard, 1931, 1937; Pavlov, 1932; Robinson, 1932). Thus, although Pavlov (1927) had earlier advocated a view of behaviour as chains of conditioned reflexes, Pavlov's (1932) reply to Guthrie (1930), castigated the use of a single set of identities (conditioning = association = law of contiguity) to account for all behaviour (cf. Hilgard, 1937). Similarly, Robinson's (1932) influential monograph was critical of the same set of identities and, on the positive side, advocated a quantitative approach to the Law of Contiguity as a guide to empirical research using the conditioned reflex methods (Robinson, 1932, p. 77). This climate of intellectual revision coupled with the development of classical conditioning preparations in the United States moved the thrust of the endeavour away from speculative applications of rudimentary conditioning and contiguity principles toward detailed experimentation and greater sophistication in the use of the Law of Contiguity in theories of conditioning and learning.

The Law of Contiguity and the CS–US Interval

CS–US Interval Effects

As a more sober view regarding the role of classical conditioning in psychology took hold, it became clear that the empirical laws regarding the effects of the CS–US interval departed in important ways from a simple Law of Contiguity. These disparities between the empirical findings and the Law of Contiguity are still, today, the source of lively contention. In brief, it has been repeatedly found that conditioning can reliably occur even when the CS and US are temporally separated. This fundamental challenge to any contiguity principle was originally raised by Pavlov's findings to trace conditioning and, more recently, has been resurrected by the extremely long CS–US intervals over which taste aversion learning occurs. A second challenge to a contiguity principle has been the observation that strict simultaneity between a CS and US usually produces little or no conditioning, while asynchronous presentation of the CS and US produces the most reliable conditioning. Accordingly, this section will discuss these crucial findings in more detail and will also review the theoretical responses, including both those formulations which have attempted to retain a contiguity principle as a fundamental determinant of association (Gormezano, 1972; Guthrie, 1935; Hull, 1937, 1943) and those formulations which have attempted to derive the empirical effects of the CS–US interval without postulating a contiguity principle.

Pavlov's (1927, pp. 39–40) trace-conditioned reflex was recognized by early conditioning theorists (Guthrie, 1930; Razran, 1930) as raising difficulties for the Law of Contiguity. In trace conditioning, the offset of the CS antedates the US, leaving an 'empty' interval between them. Furthermore, when a CR occurs, it is usually initiated in the empty interval after CS offset. Thus, there is no aspect of simultaneity between the CS and the US–UR, nor between the CS and CR. To bridge the empty gap between the CS and CR, Pavlov (1927) proposed that the CS event left a 'trace', i.e. a perseverative representation in the central nervous system, and that the portion of the trace immediately antedating the CR was the effective instigator of the response. Since Pavlov's initial reports, the essential features of trace conditioning have been well substantiated in a variety of classical conditioning preparations, including the human eyelid response (Hansche and Grant, 1960), human galvanic skin response (Rodnick, 1937; Switzer, 1933), canine salivary response (Williams, 1965), and rabbit NMR (Schneiderman, 1966; Smith, Coleman, and Gormezano, 1969).

Recently, the problem of action at a distance raised by trace conditioning has, again, been brought into high relief by findings obtained with taste aversion learning. In typical taste aversion studies, the 'CS' arises from the consumption of flavoured water, and the 'US' may consist of an injection of lithium chloride, an injection of apomorphine, or exposure to x-rays (cf. Garcia, McGowan, and Green, 1972). Since the CS fluid is usually removed well before administration of the US, the procedure is a trace-conditioning procedure, although it is often given the misnomer of 'long delay conditioning'. Moreover, the target behaviour is not a UR to the US, as in traditional classical conditioning preparations (cf. Gormezano and Kehoe, 1975), but rather, it is the avoidance of the flavoured water or an increase in the relative preference for an alternative fluid. Nevertheless, with this procedure, conditioning has been obtained when the interval between the CS and US is minutes and even hours long. In particular, studies involving systematic manipulations of the CS–US interval have revealed inverse conditioning functions (i.e. gradients), in which conditioning was maximal when the CS preceded the US by a few seconds but in which some conditioning was evident at 100 min and longer (e.g. Garcia, Ervin, and Koelling, 1966; Revusky, 1968; Smith and Roll, 1967). The extremely long CS–US interval effective in taste aversion learning have been construed as completely beyond the reach of any contiguity-based formulation (Rozin and Kalat, 1971). However, the challenge to the Law of Contiguity by taste aversion learning is only quantitatively more extreme than that posed by trace condition-ing over CS–US interval of several hundred milliseconds with traditional classical conditioning preparations. In both instances, the Law of Contiguity can only be redeemed by identifying hypothetical processes which bring effective representations of the CS and US into simultaneity with one another.

While trace conditioning has repeatedly challenged the Law of Contiguity by raising the prospect of action at a distance, it was the results of early American investigations involving the manipulation of the CS–US interstimulus interval (ISI) which indicated that the Law of Contiguity could not be simply identified with simultaneity of the CS and US. It should be noted, however, that since Pavlov (1927) considered conditioning at CS–US intervals up to 5 s to be 'simultaneous', it is commonly assumed that he found no important differences in ease of conditioning at ISIs from 0 to 5 s. Whether or not this assumption is warranted, it soon became clear to early American investigators that little or no conditioning occurred at ISIs close to zero. Thus, Bernstein (1934) found that in human eyelid conditioning, strict simultaneity of CS and US onsets (ISI = 0 ms) produced no CR acquisition, while ISIs of several hundred milliseconds or more produced substantial CR acquisition. Over the ensuing years, Bernstein's results have been repeatedly confirmed in human eyelid conditioning as well as in a variety of other human and infrahuman classical conditioning preparations (cf. Gormezano and Moore, 1969, p. 136; Hall, 1976, pp. 111–115). Moreover, a number of these studies not only revealed that a forward ISI was superior to an ISI of zero, but that there was a particular ISI which was superior to either shorter or longer intervals. An extensive set of investigations with the rabbit NMR preparation, detail below, documents these two critical outcomes of ISI manipulations.

Schneiderman and Gormezano (1964), investigating the role of the ISI in NMR conditioning, observed that under the delayed conditioning procedure of simultaneous offset of the CS and US and for ISIs of 250, 500, 1000, 2000, and 4000 ms, the percentage of CRs was a monotonic decreasing function of ISI. Schneiderman (1966) extended the investigation by determining the ISI con-ditioning function for ISI values of 250, 500, 1000, and 2000 ms under three conditioning procedures affecting the duration of the CS: two delay conditioning procedures, one with a constant duration tone CS of 3000 ms and the other with simultaneous offset of the CS and US, and the third involved a trace procedure with a CS of 200 ms duration. Schneiderman's results confirmed those of the previous study in finding the percentage of CRs for all three procedures to be a monotonic decreasing function of ISI. Moreover, the study revealed that the trace conditioning procedure produced the lowest level of responding at each ISI with the disparity being least at the 250 ms and greatest at the 2000 ms ISI.

The studies of Schneiderman and Gormezano (1964), and Schneiderman (1966) clearly did not sample the lower limit of the ISI conditioning function for the rabbit NMR. Consequently, Smith *et al.* (1969) conducted a study with the intent of sufficiently spanning the ISI to obtain some indication of a maximum, as well as some minimum in the ISI–NMR conditioning function. Specifically, the ISI manipulation was extended to include groups at more contiguous forward intervals (800, 400, 200, 100, and 50 ms), as well as at simultaneous (0 ms) and backward (− 50 ms) intervals. Moreover, a control group (C) received explicitly unpaired presentations of the CS and US. Figure 1.1 presents the CR frequency data obtained on CS-alone test trials collapsed across acquisition and extinction blocks to reveal the shape of the ISI function. Examination of the figure reveals ISI functions having concave shapes with maxima at 200 ms, little evidence of pseudoconditioning (C), and, despite the large number of conditioning trials (640), no evidence of conditioning at the backward (− 50 ms), simultaneous (0 ms), and shortest forward (50 ms) interval.

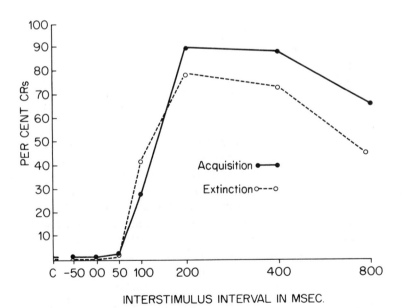

Figure 1.1. The mean percentage of responses in acquisition (test trials) and extinction for groups trained at the various CS–US intervals in msec specified on the abscissa

Theoretical Accounts

Attempts to retain the Law of Contiguity in the face of successful trace conditioning and stimulus asynchrony has led in two directions. One direction may be labelled the 'weak' or 'empirical' Law of Contiguity. At its best, this theoretical tradition accepts the empirical ISI–CR frequency functions, come as they may, and then proceeds to use them in an axiomatic fashion in larger behaviour theories, particularly theories which postulate that hypothetical CRs and their stimulus consequences mediate overt instrumental responses (e.g. Hull, 1943; Sheffield, 1966 *a*, *b*; Spence, 1956). While this theoretical tactic uses the notion of 'CS–US contiguity', it effectively dispenses with the Law of Contiguity as a theoretical principle and substitutes in its place the empirical laws of conditioning. However, since there is no universal ISI–CR frequency but, rather, a variety of functions which can differ for different response systems within the same species (cf. Schneiderman, 1972), it has not been common to tie axiomatic principles to the unique ISI–CR frequency function for a single preparation. For CR mediation theories of instrumental conditioning directed toward original predictions rather than quantitative predictions, a general postulation of a contiguity gradient for the hypothetical CRs is relatively harmless. However, this global specification of ISI effects has been reflected back on theories about classical conditioning itself with the result that 'CS–US contiguity has come to be treated in an all-or-none, qualitative fashion, much in the way that the Law of Contiguity was treated in the 1920s (e.g. Mowrer, 1960). Although such a vague specification of CS–US contiguity was able to evade the problems of trace conditioning and stimulus asynchrony with an implicit close-enough-is-good-enough principle, it has collapsed in the face of the extreme form of trace conditioning seen in taste aversion learning. Thus, in context of theory about classical conditioning, the weak, global formulation of CS–US contiguity has come full circle and led to a reawakened interest in the problems of action at a distance originally posed by Pavlov's trace-conditioned reflex.

The alternative approach to a contiguity-based account of classical conditioning may be labelled a 'strong' or 'theoretical' Law of Contiguity. Accounts of this nature have followed the lead of Pavlov's trace hypothesis by postulating hypothetical stimuli which bridge the gap between the nominal CS and the US–UR (Anderson, 1959; Gormezano, 1972; Guthrie, 1930, 1933, 1935; Hull, 1937, 1943, 1952). Thus, all these accounts have maintained that an association is formed through the strictly simultaneous occurrence of the effective CS with the US–UR. Of course, the cost of such an account is the uncertainty produced by postulating hypothetical stimuli which are assumed to be lawfully related to the nominal CS but yet are not identical in their time course to the objective event. However, it will be shown that these accounts have had enough scope in their deductive consequences to provide considerable indirect but converging evidence for a trace of one sort or another. Guthrie attempted to provide the first strict contiguity account of stimulus asynchrony by postulating that the 'true' CS consists of the kinesthetic and proprioceptive feedback stimuli arising from the subject's postural and orienting responses to the CS. Since there would necessarily be some latency between the nominal CS, the occurrence of the orienting response, and its stimulus feedback, it follows that the most favourable CS–US interval for producing simultaneity between the feedback stimuli and the UR would be one in which the nominal CS precedes the US–UR by a short interval. Hence, according to Guthrie, conditioning with CS–US simultaneity or backward US–CS presentations would only be possible if the UR persisted long enough to coincide with the occurrence of the feedback stimuli.

Although Guthrie's account could explain why forward CS–US intervals would be superior to an ISI of zero, Hull (1937, 1943, 1952) attempted to account for the concave form of the ISI–CR frequency function, as it was then known, and also the temporal characteristics of the CR. The basis for Hull's account and subsequent variants (e.g. Anderson, 1959; Gormezano, 1972) has been Pavlov's concept of the CS trace. All CS trace accounts postulate that CS onset initiates a molar stimulus trace which rises in intensity to a maximum some time after CS onset, after which the trace gradually decays back to a null value. Associative strength is presumed to accrue at the point of contiguity between the CS trace and US/UR initiation, and the increment in associative strength on each trial is presumed to be a direct function of the intensity of the CS trace at the point of CS trace–US/UR contiguity. Thus, the largest increments in associative strength would result from training with those forward CS–US intervals for which the CS trace is at a high or maximum intensity during US/UR occurrence. At shorter or longer CS–US intervals, the CS trace is too weak (or altogether absent) to be able to produce appreciable increments in associative strength. Thus, the form of the ISI–CR frequency function reflects the form of the intensity of the CS trace over time. To explain occurrence of 'anticipatory CRs' during the CS–US interval, trace formulations assume that anticipatory CRs result from generalization along the intensity dimension from the point of CS trace–US/UR contiguity to earlier portions of the trace (Gormezano, 1972). Moreover, as associative strength at the point of contiguity increases, generalization would be expected to extend further along the intensity dimension and, accordingly, the CS trace. In agreement with Hull's predictions, the first CRs have been found to occur near the US, after which the mean CR latency decreases over training toward the onset of the CS in human eyelid conditioning (Ebel and Prokasy, 1963; Suboski, 1967) and in rabbit NMR conditioning (Gormezano, Schneiderman, Deaux, and Fuentes, 1962; Schneiderman, 1966; Schneiderman and Gormezano, 1964; Smith, 1968; Smith et al., 1969).

While the decrease in CR latency is consistent with the hypothesis of generalization of associative strength along a CS trace, there is converging evidence that maximal associative strength is located at the point of contiguity between the CS trace and the US/UR. Specifically, it has been found that the maximal response amplitude, the CR peak, tends to be located around the time of US/UR occurrence. The coincidence of CR peak latency with the temporal locus of the US has been observed in investigations using the rabbit's NMR (Coleman and Gormezano, 1971; Smith, 1968), the dog's salivary response (Colavita, 1965; Ellison, 1964), the human eyelid response (Martin and Levey, 1969), and the galvanic skin response (Kimmel, 1965). Furthermore, the location of the CR peak follows the point of CS trace–US contiguity quite closely. Thus, when for the rabbit NMR preparation the CS–US interval is altered, Coleman and Gormezano (1971) found that the CR peak shifted to the new temporal locus of the US. Furthermore, Millenson, Kehoe, and Gormezano (1977) found that when CS–US pairings were conducted with two randomly alternating ISI values (200 and 700 ms), the CR topography showed two distinct peaks located at 200 and 700 ms after CS onset, respectively. At a minimum, the placement of CR peaks around the temporal locus of the US may be regarded as evidence for a timing mechanism which could be based on a CS trace (Gormezano, 1972; Patterson, 1970). A stronger interpretation, which accounts for the precise characteristics of the CR topography for the NMR, would contend that the momentary CR amplitude is a direct function of generalized associative strength at the corresponding point on the CS trace. Accordingly, the CR's maximal amplitude would fall at the point(s) of maximal associative strength, which for CS trace accounts occur at the point(s) of contiguity between the CS trace and the US/UR.

Although the concept of the 'trace' carries neurophysiological connotations, the form of the trace has been anchored behaviourally to the ISI–CR frequency function obtained in a given preparation under a given set of conditions (cf. Gormezano, 1972). A case-by-case behavioural anchoring of the 'trace' has been necessary since the divergence in ISI–CR frequency functions dashed early hopes that their form would be invariant over species and response system (e.g. Kimble, 1947; McAllister, 1953). However, methods and data are accumulating that may ultimately provide an anchoring for the form of the trace which would be independent of the ISI–CR frequency function. Thus, Patterson (1970) has been able to manipulate the time course of the trace by using electrical stimulation of the rabbit's inferior colliculus as a CS. Such a CS, which bypasses a portion of the afferent system, should reduce the initial recruitment time of the CS trace and, thereby, foreshorten the minimal ISI necessary for conditioning. In fact, Patterson (1970) obtained a substantial level of responding at an ISI of 50 ms, a value which yielded no evidence of conditioning when a conventional tone CS was used by Smith et al. (1969). Patterson's finding cannot be attributed to a greater dynamogenic effect of the intracranial CS relative to a tone CS because, at an ISI of 400 ms, the intracranial CS supported lower levels of responding than the tone CS. An even more promising means of behaviourally anchoring the form of the trace may be found in the 'CS–excitability' function for the rabbit NMR preparation (Ison and Leonard, 1971; Thompson, 1976). In the CS–excitability procedure, animals are presented USs preceded by a tone (or light) CS at various ISI values. The frequency of variable ISI presentations are restricted in number to preclude the appearance of CRs and, hence, permits the URs to be examined. Under the excitability procedure, it has been found that the UR amplitude varies as a function of the ISI and, in terms of the CS trace hypothesis, the effects of the CS on the UR can be construed as reflecting the inherent dynamogenic effects of CS trace intensity at the time of UR occurrence. Moreover, under specific stimulus parameters, the ISI–UR amplitude function has been found by Thompson (1976) closely to parallel the form of the ISI–CR frequency function (Figure 1.1) obtained by Smith *et al.* (1969). If similar parallels can be obtained in other classical conditioning preparations, then it may be possible truly to predict the ISI–CR frequency function for any new preparation as well as to anchor the trace independently of conditioning.

Revusky (1971) has proposed a hypothesis of trace conditioning which is an interesting alternative to the formulations of Guthrie and Hull, in that Revusky does not attempt to save either a weak or strong Law of Contiguity by postulating a transient stimulus trace or short-term memory (Revusky, 1971, p. 159). Instead, he assumes that two events can, in principle, become associated in a forward direction over an unbounded interval. As a basis for deducing the graded and ultimately bounded effect of CS–US interval manipulations on conditioning, Revusky (1971, p. 164) proposes a 'concurrent interference principle'. This principle states that the strength or likelihood of an association between a particular CS and US decreases as a function of the number of other associations in which the CS and US are involved. As a corollary, Revusky (1971, p. 171) states that events which occur between the CS and US are more likely to produce associative interference than events outside the CS–US interval. Accordingly, every increase in the CS–US interval is likely to produce an increase in the number of potentially interfering events. Thus, when increases in the CS–US interval produce progressive decreases in observable conditioning, it is hypothesized that the CS, the US, or both have become associated with intervening events (Revusky, 1971, p. 160).

In Revusky's formulation, not all intervening events between a given particular CS–US coupling will produce associative interference; only 'relevant' events can form associations. Essentially, the proposition of 'relevance' is an empirical 'belongingness' principle, which is based on findings that certain CSs are more readily associated than other CSs with a particular US (Garcia and Koelling, 1966; Revusky, 1971, 1977). For example, taste stimuli are readily associated with an 'illness US', while visual and aural stimuli are not. Consequently, the many visual and aural stimuli which occur during the long CS–US intervals are unlikely to become associated with the illness US and thus are unable to interfere with the establishment of the taste—illness association. In this way, Revusky accounts for the effectiveness of long CS–US intervals used in taste aversion learning. Conversely, the more tightly-bound ISI–CR frequency functions obtained with shock and food USs used in classical conditioning preparations are attributed by Revusky (1971, 1977) to the many demonstrably associable visual, and aural events which can occur in a CS–US interval of even a few seconds or less. By use of the 'relevance' principle, Revusky's (1971, 1977) formulation is able to account for the disparity in CS–US interval effects found in taste aversion learning and classical conditioning preparations.

The most powerful deduction from Revusky's (1971, 1977) formulation is that the effects of CS–US interval manipulations can be altered by experimental manipulations of events during the CS–US interval. In support of this deduction, Revusky (1971, pp. 189–192) found that, in taste aversion learning, the addition of a second flavour between the nominal flavour CS and US reduced the acquired aversion to the nominal CS. Furthermore, the introduction of an additional flavour before the nominal CS also reduced the condition aversion. Thus, there would appear to be mutual interference between two flavour CSs in taste aversion learning. While these results support the hypothesis of concurrent interference, they do not bear directly upon Revusky's hypothesis that associations can be formed over an unbounded interval if relevant interfering events can be eliminated. A more definitive test would require broadening one of the narrow ISI–CR frequency functions by reducing the number of interfering events between the CS and US. However, the classical conditioning preparations which have the narrowest, most well-defined ISI–CR frequency functions (e.g. the rabbit NMR preparation) are characterized by very tight control over extraneous stimulation, particularly within the CS–US interval. Hence, it would seem difficult to identify events which might intervene in the CS–US interval and cause associative interference. However, if Revusky's formulation is taken seriously, it might be possible to lengthen the range of effective CS–US intervals by reducing potentially extraneous receptor inputs (e.g. plugging the ears, deafferentiation, spinal anaesthetic).

Another account of CS–US asynchrony may be found in response-shaping formulations (Boneau, 1958; Prokasy, 1965) which view CS–US asynchrony to be a consequence of the reinforcement process in classical conditioning. These formulations assert that the source of reinforcement in classical conditioning lies in the overlap of the US by the CR. In particular, CR–US overlap is presumed to provide the source of differential reinforcement of CRs through its attenuation of the noxiousness of an aversive US or by enhancement of the 'attractiveness' of an appetitive US. To explain anticipatory CRs and their topographical features (e.g. CR latency and temporal locus of the CR peak), response-shaping hypotheses contend that quantitatively different responses are differentially reinforced according to the degree of US modification that they respectively produce (Kimmel and Burns, 1975; Prokasy, 1965). Furthermore, to account for asynchronous ISI–CR frequency functions, Prokasy and his associates (Ebel and Prokasy, 1963; Prokasy, 1965; Prokasy, Ebel, and Thompson, 1963) have added a time discrimination principle to response-shaping formulations.

Specifically, they have proposed that the maximization of reinforcement through CR–US overlap would be restricted at short ISIs by the minimum reaction time of the CR and at longer ISIs by the increasingly difficult temporal discrimination necessary for appropriate placement of the CR with respect to the US.

Response-shaping theorists have sought to identify on a *post hoc* basis features of the CR which coincide with the US and, thus, could be regarded as reflecting the operation of a differential reinforcement mechanism based on CR–US overlap (cf. Martin and Levey, 1969). The available data suggest that the CR peak is the feature which most consistently coincides with the temporal locus of the US (Colavita, 1965; Coleman and Gormezano, 1971; Ellison, 1964; Kimmel, 1965; Kimmel and Burns, 1975; Martin and Levey, 1969). Furthermore, shifts in the ISI value produce shifts in the CR peak to the new temporal locus of the US (Coleman and Gormezano, 1971), and random mixtures of two ISI values lead to the development of two CR peaks, one located at each temporal locus of the US (Hoehler and Leonard, 1976; Millenson *et al.*, 1977). In contrast to the CR peak, CR initiation does not have a final relation to the US. With a constant ISI, CR onset moves away from the US and toward CS onset (Ebel and Prokasy, 1963; Gormezano, 1972; Suboski, 1967), which is inconsistent with response-shaping theory. After an abrupt shift in ISI from a shorter to a longer value, CR latency has been observed to increase toward US onset in a manner consistent with response-shaping theory, but the shifts in CR placement which regain CR–US overlap have not been accompanied by maintenance of overall CR frequency (e.g. Coleman and Gormezano, 1971; Ebel and Prokasy, 1963; Prokasy and Papsdorf, 1965; Wickens, Nield, Tuber, and Wickens, 1969).

Although CR–US overlap is considered the source of reinforcement in response-shaping theory, relatively little has been done to specify the time-dependent process which controls the placement of CRs. Within the context of the time discrimination hypothesis, some consideration has been given to the psychophysics of time estimation as it applies to classical conditioning. Thus, Ebel and Prokasy (1963) have suggested that the variability of CR peak placement is directly related to the length of the ISI, and Teller, Dieter, and Suboski (1972) found that the accuracy of human judgements of the length of ISIs was indeed a direct function of the ISI. However, CR characteristics indicative of the operation of CR–US overlap have never been precisely specified. Such a lack of specificity may be attributed in part to the response-inferred nature of the CR–US overlap contingency, for response-shaping formulations possess no means for predicting which CR measures should reflect the presumed operation of the differential reinforcement mechanism. Hence, in the absence of a precise definition of a CR–US overlap indicant, response-shaping theorists have had to rely on *post hoc* determinations of the cor-respondence between the expectations of their formulation and a variety of topographical measures, as, for example, CR peak latency. However, the support which such data lend to response-shaping formulations lacks the strength that would accrue if it were possible to manipulate the presumed contingency between the selected CR topographical feature and the degree of US modification (cf. Gormezano and Kehoe, 1975).

Extensions of the Law of Contiguity

At the time that classical conditioning was popularized as an exemplar, if not a substitute, for the Law of Contiguity, it was obvious that the restricted temporal bounds on learning imposed by a contiguity/conditioning mechanism were inconsistent with observations in maze-learning tasks in which animals acquired complicated patterns of behaviour, initiated in response to stimuli which were temporally and spatially remote from the goal-object, e.g. food. Although philosophical associationism contained the doctrine of mediated associa-tion, which contended associations could be linked together in succession (a–b–c–d– . . .), it was not immediately apparent how mediated associations could subserve complex goal-directed behaviour. Watson's polemical assertion that complex behaviour could be considered chains of conditioned reflexes was gratuitous. Even if it had been possible to analyse the behaviour of the animal into component conditioned reflexes (CS–CRs) and to specify their antecedants in the unconditioned responses to food consumption (US–UR), the chaining hypothesis failed to specify a contiguity-based mechanism by which such CRs could be acquired to stimuli so far in advance of the US (food).

An hypothesis of mediated associations began to gain theoretical plausibility when Watson's assumption that all behaviour consisted of chained CRs was replaced by a more cautious approach in which the empirical laws of classical conditioning serve as the source of axioms from which the laws of other behaviour could be deduced (cf. Hilgard, 1937; Hull, 1930, 1931, 1934). Even before the procedural distinctions between classical and instrumental condition-ing were well recognized (cf. Konorski and Miller, 1937; Miller and Konorski, 1928; Schlosberg, 1937; Skinner, 1935, 1937, 1938), American investigators recognized that maze-learning and Thorndikian puzzle-box procedures con-tained the essential requirements for classical conditioning. Specifically, the food reward for an instrumental act elicits a constellation of URs within a specific, albeit relatively complex, stimulus situation and, hence, CRs to stimuli antedating the food reward could be acquired in a collateral fashion (Schlosberg, 1937, p. 385; Skinner, 1935, p. 76).

Although the possibility of collateral CRs was acknowledged by others, it was Hull (1930, 1931, 1934) who first developed the thesis that such collateral CRs serve to modulate overt goal-directed activities. Specifically, Hull argued that the collateral CRs produce feedback stimuli which, in turn, could become cues for the overt instrumental response. In this way, Hull attempted to provide a mechanistic account for the direction of seemingly purposeful and insightful behaviour by the use of axiomatic principles anchored to the empirical laws of classical conditioning as presented by Pavlov (1927). Subsequently, the general proposition that hypothetical collateral CRs can modulate instrumental behaviour has had a major impact on one- and two-process theories of learning (Amsel, 1958; Bindra, 1968, 1972; Konorski, 1948, 1967; Logan and Wagner, 1965; Miller, 1948, 1951, 1963; Mowrer, 1947, 1960; Osgood, 1953; Rescorla and Solomon, 1967; Sheffield, 1966a,b; Sheffield, Roby, and Campbell, 1954; Spence, 1947, 1956; Trapold and Overmier, 1972). Although all these theories commonly use the laws (or what are presumed to be the laws) of classical conditioning to generate axioms, they differ on the mechanism by which the collateral CRs are acquired to stimuli long antedating the reinforcing event. Some theorists have avoided the need to postulate mediated associations by appealing to the laws of stimulus generalization, which base transfer on the physical similarity between stimuli contiguous with the reinforcer and stimuli which are more remote (e.g. Levis and Stampfl, 1972; Osgood, 1953; Spence, 1956). However, other theorists have appealed to higher-order conditioning (Hull, 1951; Sheffield, 1966a) but, oddly enough, none have appealed to the phenomena of sensory preconditioning. Both higher-order conditioning and sensory preconditioning would appear to constitute an empirical counterpart to the philosophical doctrine of mediated associations. Both empirical phenomena are based on pairings of one CS with the US (CS2–US) and pairings of that CS with another CS (CS1–CS2). In higher-order conditioning, the establishment of a CR through CS2–US pairings precedes CS1–CS2 pairings, but in sensory preconditioning, CS1–CS2 pairings precede CS2–US pairings. In either case, final tests of CS1 should produce CRs even though CS1 itself has never been paired with the US.

Despite the use of higher-order conditioning as the empirical basis for an axiom of mediated associations, the empirical laws of higher-order conditioning have been ill-defined and unreliable (cf. Razran, 1955). However, there is now both indirect and direct support for associative mediational processes which could serve to extend CR acquisition to CSs temporally remote to the US, i.e. beyond the bounds of a known ISI–CR frequency function (cf. Gormezano and Kehoe, 1980; Rescorla, 1973, 1977). In particular, Kehoe, Gibbs, Garcia, and Gormezano (1979) found that substantial acquisition of the rabbit's NMR can be obtained to a stimulus temporally remote from the US (CS1) when it is placed in a reinforced serial compound (CS1–CS2–US) in which the second stimulus (CS2) is more contiguous with the US. In their initial experiment, the CS2–US interval was fixed at an optimal value of 350 ms, while the CS1–US interval was varied up to a value of 2750 ms, an ISI which, by itself, yielded an asymptotic level of CRs of less than 25 per cent. In the serial compound, the level of responding to CS1 rose over the course of 6 days (360 trials) to a maximum level near 80 per cent CRs, after which responding to the CS began slowly to decline. Control experiments by Kehoe et al. (1979, Experiments 2 and 3) revealed that the high level of responding to CS1 in the serial compound could not be attributed to direct conditioning brought about by CS1–US presentations, cross-modal generalization from CS2–US training, and/or any synergistic effect of mixed CS1–US and CS2–US training with their respective CS–US intervals intact. Subsequently, another study was undertaken to provide an even more direct demonstration that CR acquisition to CS1 in a serial compound resulted from associations based on CS1–CS2 and CS2–US training (Gormezano and Kehoe, 1980, Experiment 5). In the investigation, a group (P-P) which received both CS1–CS2 and CS2–US pairings, showed CR acquisition to a level that was substantially higher than that of any of the three control groups, viz. Group U-P which received unpaired CS1/CS2 presentations and CS2–US pairings; Group P-U which received CS1–CS2 pairings and unpaired CS2/US presentations; and Group U-U which received all stimuli in unpaired presentations.

Having demonstrated that separate CS1–CS2 and CS2–US pairings could reliably produce CR acquisition to CS1, Cool (Iowa), and Feyer (New South Wales) examined the effects of manipulating the CS1–CS2 intervals. With minor differences, both studies followed the same procedures. Each day of training consisted of 30 CS2–US trials interspersed with 30 CS1–CS2 trials in a Gellerman series with the CS2–US interval being fixed at 400 ms, while the CS1–CS2 interval was manipulated. In the Cool study, separate groups received training at CS1–CS2 intervals of 400, 1400, 2400, 4400, and 8400 ms, respectively, while in the Feyer study, the CS1–CS2 intervals were 400, 800, and 2400 ms, respectively. In both studies, the groups were designated by their respective CS1–CS2 'trace interval' between the offset of CS1 and the onset of CS2. Thus, in the Cool study, the CS1–CS2 trace interval designations were 0, 1, 2, 4, and 8 s, respectively, while in the Feyer study, they were 0, 0.4, and 2 s, respectively. To control for cross-modal generalization from CS2 to CS1 and any non-associative contributions arising from the US, both studies contained a group labelled 'UP', which received 30 unpaired presentations each of CS1 and CS2 interspersed among CS2–US trials. Cool conducted 16 days of training and Feyer conducted 14 days of training.

As seen in Figure 1.2, for the data collected by Cool, CS1 responding was a negative, decelerated function of the CS1–CS2 interval. Specifically, responding to CS1 was highest at the 0 trace interval (400 ms CS1–CS2 interval), and rapidly declined as the CS1–CS2 trace interval increased upto 2 s. For intervals of 2 s and longer, the level of responding was relatively stable at a point higher than that of the unpaired control. The data collected by Feyer also shows a pronounced inverse function over CS1–CS2 trace intervals between 0 and 2 s (i.e. CS1–CS2 intervals between 400 and 2400 ms). Furthermore, responding to CS1 in the paired groups as a whole exceeded that of the unpaired group. In summary, these studies would appear to indicate that CR acquisition to CS1 in a mediated (second-order) association follows a 'contiguity gradient' which is similar, but more extended, than that seen in the ISI–CR frequency functions to single CSs for the rabbit NMR preparation (cf. Gormezano, 1972; Schneiderman and Gormezano, 1964).

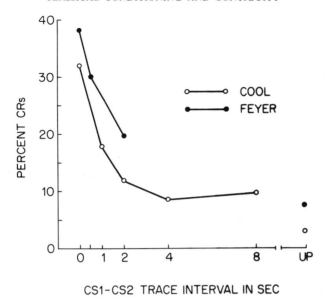

Figure 1.2. The mean percentage of CRs to CS1 on CS1–CS2 paired trials plotted as a function of the CS1–CS2 trace interval

In addition to the finding of mediated associations within the domain of the basic CS–CR classical conditioning paradigm with the rabbit NMR, a large number of demonstrations of second-order conditioning have been obtained with the CS–IR paradigm, that is, classical-instrumental transfer procedures purportedly assessing a covert 'fear' CR through its effects on instrumental responding (e.g. Anderson, Plant, Johnson, and Vandever, 1967; Holland and Rescorla, 1975; McAllister and McAllister, 1964; Rescorla, 1973, 1977; Rizley and Rescorla, 1972; Szakmary, 1979). While all this evidence for mediated association is encouraging, there remains the question as to whether mediated associations can be extended beyond the second order so that lengthy sequences of stimuli antedating a reinforcer could all successively acquire collateral CRs. Pavlov (1927) himself was not confident that higher-order CRs could be readily obtained, for his students were unable to go beyond second-order conditioning based on an appetitive US and were able to obtain only a third-order CR with an aversive US.

As far as we have been able to discern, there are no reports in the Western literature of attempts to obtain third-order conditioning in CS–CR or CS–IR procedures. However, some early Amercian investigators attempted to provide support for higher-order associations by arguing that failure to observe a robust progression of increasingly higher-order CRs in Pavlov's laboratory was tied to the absence of motivational effects of the US rather than any inherent weakness in the higher-order conditioning process *per se* (Brogden, 1939; Brogden and Culler, 1935; Eccher and Culler, 1941; Finch and Culler, 1934, 1935). Hence, during higher-order conditioning phases, 'incentives' were added at the end of the entire sequence of CSs by the administration of thoracic shock to dogs for failing to make a leg-flexion CR (Finch and Culler, 1934) and by the presentation of food for the execution of a flexion CR. Using these procedures, response acquisition was extended out to four and even five orders, although with increasing difficulty. These demonstrations of 'higher-order conditioning' can be faulted for (a) failing to assess the contribution of stimulus generalization, baseline responding, sensitization, and pseudo-conditioning to the measurement of 'higher-order CRs', and (b) introducing instrumental contingencies for the 'incentives'. Nevertheless, their procedures merit consideration and further examination as a means for producing higher-order associations. Their basic procedure, which entailed progressively adding new components to the front of a series of previously established CSs, could be readily adapted to existing serial compound procedures which, up to now, have limited themselves to two CSs (cf. Kehoe et al., 1979).

Constraints on the Law of Contiguity

Challenges to the Law of Contiguity

Few associative theories in philosophy or psychology have specified the contiguity between events as the single sufficient condition for the establishment of a new association. Little thought on the matter is required to conclude that not every pair of sensations, ideas, or events which occur together are necessarily later recalled together. In the philosophical associationistic doctrines, the Law of Frequency acknowledged that a single repetition of a pair of events is not sufficient to establish an association. Furthermore, Brown's Secondary Laws of Association included the proposition that the strength of an association between two sensory events would be modified as an inverse function of the number of other associations in which the sensations to be paired were involved. Clearly, there was a general recognition that the Law of Contiguity was constrained in its operation.

Like the philosophical theories, every theory of classical conditioning includes some constraints on the effectiveness of CS–US contiguity. Moreover, as with the philosophical theories, the most common constraint is the Law of Frequency, which is expressed in the assumption that associative strength grows in an incremental fashion across trials. In this regard, perhaps, the closest thing to an unconstrained Law of Contiguity has been Guthrie's (1930) theory, and its formalized variants (Estes, 1950; Voeks, 1950), in which a single, contiguous S–R pairing was postulated to be sufficient to establish a full-strength association. However, even in Guthrie's theory, extra principles operated to mitigate the behavioural consequences of his all-or-none contiguity principle. For example, to deduce the usual incremental growth in CRs across trials, it was argued that even a simple CS possesses a number of elements and that the likelihood of a CR represents the proportion of those elements that have been associated with the target response. Thus, for Guthrie, a Law of Frequency was a deductive consequence of the Law of Contiguity combined with the postulation of CS elements.

Over the last two decades, it has become clear that previous theoretical constraints on a contiguity principle were insufficient to account for CR acquisition in two types of complex situations. First, research with compound stimuli has produced an accumulation of evidence that CR acquisition to one CS as a result of otherwise effective CS–US pairings may be impaired in lawful ways by the presence of other CSs during training; these findings have been collectively known as 'stimulus selection or 'selective association' phenomena (Gormezano and Kehoe, 1980; Rudy and Wagner, 1975). Second, research in which a CS and US are intermixed but not always paired has revealed that the level of conditioning may vary as a function of the overall 'correlation' or 'contingency' between the CS and US (Prokasy, 1965; Rescorla, 1967, 1972). Although there was some call for major reconceptualizations of classical conditioning theory when both sets of phenomena were delineated (cf. Rescorla, 1967, 1969; Wagner, 1969), the trend of theorizing has been toward formulations which retain an axiomatic contiguity principle but assume that additional processes (competition between stimuli and inhibition) are intimately involved in the formation of associations (cf. Mackintosh, 1975; Rescorla, 1972; Rescorla and Wagner, 1972).

Stimulus Selection

There have been three main classes of stimulus selection phenomena: blocking, overshadowing, and serial stimulus selection. Briefly, the blocking paradigm consists of reinforced training with one stimulus (A) followed by training with a compound of A and a new stimulus (X). After what would otherwise be a sufficient number of trials for X to become conditioned, tests with X alone yield little or no responding in contrast to high levels of responding to A (Kamin, 1968, 1969; Marchant and Moore, 1973). In overshadowing, CR acquisition to an otherwise effective CS is impaired by training in compound with a highly intense CS (Kamin, 1969; Mackintosh, 1976; Pavlov, 1927). In serial stimulus selection, a serial compound (CS1–CS2) is consistently paired with a US, and tests with the individual CSs reveal that responding to CS2 is less than that of the same CS trained by itself (e.g. Kehoe, 1979; Kehoe et al., 1979, Experiment 2). Thus, CR acquisition to a stimulus which is relatively contiguous to the US (i.e. CS2) is impaired by being trained in series with a stimulus which has a more remote temporal relation to the US (cf. Egger and Miller, 1962; Wickens, 1959, 1965, 1973). In all three cases, the results indicate that the laws of response acquisition obtained with repeated CS–US trials were insufficient to predict responding to the individual CSs of a compound stimulus. In this context, the focus of attention has been nominally on the 'sufficiency of CS–US contiguity', which is nevertheless a catchall phrase referring to the range of effective CS–US intervals for a preparation, the number of CS–US trials necessary to establish strong responding, and other conditions of known importance in producing acquisition where a single CS and US are used.

Three major classes of theoretical accounts have emerged regarding stimulus selection phenomena. First, the most radical formulations appear to abandon 'CS–US contiguity' as either necessary or sufficient for conditioning in favour of hypotheses which contend that the relative 'predictive' or 'informational' value of a CS is crucial to acquisition (e.g. Egger and Miller, 1962). Second, the most well-developed formulations have retained 'CS–US contiguity' as a necessary condition but, furthermore, postulate competition between compounded stimuli for associative strength (Rescorla and Wagner, 1972) or attention (e.g. Mackintosh, 1975; Sutherland and Mackintosh, 1971). Third, the most conservative hypotheses have attempted to maintain CS–US contiguity as both a necessary and sufficient condition for CR acquisition and have attempted to attribute stimulus selection effects to a massive stimulus generalization decrement arising from the altered stimulus conditions between compound training and individual component testing (e.g. Borgealt, Donahoe, and Weinstein, 1972; Hull, 1943, 1952; Wickens, 1959, 1965, 1973).

The information hypothesis stems from the initial examination of serial stimulus selection phenomena by Egger and Miller (1962, 1963). They found that, after a CS1–CS2 series had been consistently paired with a food US, CS2 by itself had less secondary reinforcing power for bar-press responding than CS1 by itself. Furthermore, responding produced by CS2 did not exceed the responding produced by a control stimulus that had been explicitly unpaired with food. To account for their findings, Egger and Miller (1962) proposed their information hypothesis which stressed the primacy of CS1 in signalling the impending US rather than the relative contiguity of CS2 to the US. According to the information hypothesis, if CS1 and CS2 are equally reliable 'predictors' of the US, then associative strength will accrue to the initial CS1 and not to the later 'redundant' CS2. To test their hypothesis, Egger and Miller (1962) rendered CS1 as an 'unreliable predictor' of the US by interspersing presentations of CS1 alone among the CS1–CS2–US presentations, thus making CS2 the most reliable predictor of the US. In agreement with expectations of the information hypothesis, CS2 was found to have acquired secondary reinforcing value, even though its relation to the US in the serial compound was unchanged.

The information hypothesis has guided research along two different lines. One line of research which uses simultaneous compound CSs has concentrated on manipulations of the 'relative reliability' or 'validity' a CS in 'predicting' the US (Wagner, 1969; Wagner, Logan, Haberlandt, and Price, 1968). The basic experimental strategy has entailed (a) holding constant the schedule of CS–US pairings for a target stimulus (X), while (b) manipulating the schedule of CS–US pairings for other stimuli (e.g. A_1, A_2, A_3, . . .) with which X was compounded. Like Egger and Miller (1962), it was found that the level of response acquisition to X varied as a function of the relative frequency or consistency with which the A stimuli were paired with the US. However, these findings have contributed less to the development of the information hypothesis and more to the development of the contiguity-based model of Rescorla and Wagner (1972), which is a prominent member of the second class of stimulus selection theories (competitional accounts).

The second line of research originating with the Egger and Miller information hypothesis has continued to examine serial compound stimuli. Here research has indicated that relative CS–US contiguity does play a role in determining conditioning with serial compounds. In a study of secondary punishment, Seligman (1966) found that some associative strength did accrue to CS2, relative to an unpaired control. Consequently, Seligman (1966) proposed a 'weak' information hypothesis which contended that the relative contiguity of CS2 to the US would partially offset the deleterious effects of CS2's redundancy. More recently, Seger and Scheuer (1977) have attributed even greater importance to CS2–US contiguity. Using a conditioned suppression procedure, they repeated previous findings that, within the CS1–CS2 sequence during serial compound training, CS1 produced moderate suppression but CS2 produced even greater suppression (Brahlek, 1968; Scheuer and Keeter, 1969). However, when CS2 was presented alone on interpolated test trials, CS2 produced less suppression than CS1. Seger and Scheuer (1977) concluded that CS2 provides temporal information about 'when shock will occur', but only when CS2 is preceded by CS1. Although Seger and Scheuer's (1977) account grows out of Egger and Miller's information hypothesis, it no longer assumes that a deficit occurs in the acquisition of associative strength to CS2 during serial compound training. Instead, they propose that there is a deficit in the transfer from serial compound training to the testing of CS2 outside the serial compound. In this respect, Seger and Scheuer's account converges with generalization decrement hypotheses which constitute the third class of theories about stimulus selection (cf. Kehoe, 1979).

The most well-developed accounts of stimulus selection phenomena may be labelled 'competitional' accounts and include 'modified continuity' theory (Rescorla and Wagner, 1972; Wagner, 1969) and 'attentional' theory (e.g. Mackintosh, 1975; Sutherland and Mackintosh, 1971). While modified-continuity and attentional theories differ in many respects, their respective accounts of stimulus selection have two common assumption: (a) CS–US contiguity is necessary, i.e. the laws of conditioning obtained with single CS and US are applicable at all times; (b) stimulus selection results from a competitive process between the compounded CSs for associative strength or attention.

In the Rescorla and Wagner model (1972), changes in the associative strength of a CS depend on the existing associative strength of other stimuli concurrently present because there is a fixed amount of associative strength that can be supported by a US on a given trial. Consequently, for two-component compound CSs, the associative strength which accrues to one CS becomes unavailable to the other CS. Under the Rescorla and Wagner model, an account of overshadowing rests on the learning rate parameter for each CS, which is a positive function of that CS's intensity. Accordingly, a relatively intense CS_A would acquire associative strength more rapidly than a less intense CS_X; thereby, CS_A would gain a large portion of the total available associative strength to the relative detriment of CS_X's associative strength. To account for blocking, the Rescorla and Wagner model contends that the pretraining of a CS_A would cause all the available associative strength to accrue to CS_A, leaving none for a new stimulus (CS_X) when added to form a compound.

Attention theory consists of a multitude of formulations with a long history of application in the realm of discrimination learning (cf. Rudy and Wagner, 1975; Sutherland and Mackintosh, 1971). However, in dealing with stimulus selection in compound stimulus conditioning paradigms, attentional theories provide a largely uniform account. In general, attentional accounts assume that, in addition to CS–US contiguity, 'attention' to a CS is necessary for associative strength to be established. Moreover, attentional formulations assume that 'attention' is a positive function of both the physical intensity of the CS and the previous number of CS–US pairings. Accordingly, attentional formulations argue that overshadowing of X in an AX compound occurs because the more intense CS_A attracts more attention to the relative detriment of the less intense CS_X. Similarly, blocking of CS_X is argued to occur because the previously trained CS_S has captured the attention of the subject and, thus, precludes attention to the added CS_X. Most attentional formulations have assumed that there is a fixed amount of attention at any one time (i.e. a limited channel capacity), much in the same manner as the Rescorla–Wagner model assumes that there is a fixed amount of associative strength (cf. Sutherland and Mackintosh, 1971). Recently, Mackintosh (1975) has formalized attentional accounts of stimulus selection and dispensed with the assumption that there is a fixed amount of attention. Nevertheless, Mackintosh (1975) has retained the central proposition that there is a trade-off in the attentional strengths accruing to concurrent stimuli, as a function of their relative associative strengths.

Generalization decrement hypotheses represent the most conservative accounts of stimulus selection phenomena in the sense that they retain CS–US contiguity (the laws of conditioning with a single CS and US) as both necessary and sufficient for CR acquisition. Instead of postulating some competitive constraint on the acquisition of associative strength to a stimulus, generalization decrement hypotheses contend that there is a failure for the associative strength acquired to a stimulus inside a compound stimulus to transfer outside the compound stimulus. Operationally, advocates of a generalization decrement hypothesis note that a test trial for a single stimulus constitutes a change in the stimulating conditions from those during compound stimulus training. Theoretically, generalization decrement hypotheses presuppose that a nominal stimulus produces different effective stimuli depending on whether or not it is presented in the context of other stimuli. This notion that the effective stimulus produced by a CS is context-dependent can be viewed as analogous to hypotheses in the area of human memory research which contend that the encoding of an item will include some representation of surrounding events such that recall and even recognition of the same item will vary in proportion to the presence of the surrounding events at the time of retrieval (Tulving and Pearlstone, 1966; Tulving and Thomson, 1973). In other words, a generalization decrement is analogous to a recognition failure in that both can result from a change in stimulus context between training and testing.

The earliest exposition of a stimulus generalization decrement hypothesis may be found in Hull's (1943) account of overshadowing. As the source for the presumed dissimilarity between a nominal CS's effective stimulus inside and outside the context of the compound, Hull proposed the 'neural afferent interaction' hypothesis, which states that the separate afferent representations of two concurrent CSs mutually modify each other. Hull went on to assume that the more a CS's effective stimulus was modified by concurrent stimuli, the greater would be the generalization decrement when the same nominal CS was presented alone. To account for overshadowing, the modification in an effective stimulus was postulated to be an increasing function of the physical intensity of the concurrent stimuli (Hull, 1943, p. 355). Consequently, a relatively weak CS's effective stimulus would be highly modified by a more intense concurrent CS, while the effective stimulus of the more intense CS would presumably be hardly modified at all. In subsequent single-stimulus testing, the responding to the weaker CS would be expected to suffer a massive generalization decrement, while responding to the stronger CS would undergo little, if any, generalization decrement, thus yielding the overshadowing outcome.

The generalization decrement hypothesis has also been used to account for serial stimulus selection (Borgealt et al., 1972; Kehoe, 1979; Rescorla, 1972; Wickens, 1959, 1965, 1973). Borgealt et al.'s (1972) version simply states that there will be a large generalization decrement from serial compound training to CS2 testing because the animal has never been exposed to CS2 by itself outside the context of the serial compound, in which CS2 is always preceded by CS1. Conversely, responding to CS1 would not suffer a generalization decrement since CS1 is always exposed by itself prior to the onset of CS2. Evidence for a generalization decrement hypothesis may be found in results which indicate that, even when the level of responding to CS2 outside the serial compound is low, the responding during CS2 inside the compound reaches levels comparable to those obtained when the same CS was trained by itself (Kehoe, 1979; Seger and Scheuer, 1977). Not only does responding during CS2 inside the compound reach a high level, CS2's absolute contiguity plays an important role in serial compound conditioning in that the CS2–US interval determines the rate and asymptotic level of CR acquisition to the serial compound as a whole (Kehoe, 1979).

CS/US Contingency and Inhibition

Along with stimulus selection phenomena, the results of manipulating the 'contingency' or 'correlation' between the CS and US have been used to challenge the sufficiency of CS–US contiguity as a determinant of conditioning (Prokasy, 1965; Rescorla, 1967). In particular, Rescorla (1967, 1968, 1969) found with the CS–IR paradigm that the level of responding to a CS varied not only as a function of the previous number of CS–US 'pairings' but also as a function of the overall 'CS–US correlation' as manipulated through the use of CS alone and US alone presentations interspersed among the 'CS–US pairings'. Initially, it was thought that classical conditioning and, more generally, associative learning would have to be reconceptualized in molar terms, in which the statistical relationship between the CS and US is the fundamental determinant of response acquisition (cf. Rachlin, 1976, pp. 80–86, 190–192; Rescorla, 1967). Specifically, Rescorla (1967) proposed a contingency hypothesis which focuses on the degree to which the CS 'predicts' or carries 'information' about the US, as specified in terms of the relative frequency or probability of US occurrence in the presence and absence of the US. Furthermore, the contingency hypothesis assumes that there are symmetric excitatory and inhibitory associative contributions to responding to the CS arising from CS and US presentations. Specifically, if the probability of a US is greater in the presence of the CS than in its absence, a 'positive contingency' would prevail and 'excitatory' associative effects would accrue to the CS. Conversely, 'inhibitory' associative effects would presumably accrue if the probability of a US were higher in the absence of the CS than in its presence to yield a 'negative contingency'. Subsequently, the effects of 'correlational' relationships have been explained in the more molecular terms of the trial-by-trial temporal relations between stimulus events (Rescorla and Wagner, 1972). However, out of the 'correlation' vs. 'contiguity' controversy has come a renewed interest in inhibitory phenomena and their theoretical incorporation into a contiguity-based theory of conditioning (cf. Rescorla and Wagner, 1972).

As a first step in discussing the 'correlation' vs. 'contiguity' controversy, it must be recognized that all descriptions of interstimulus relationships, whether it be CS–US contiguity or correlation, are conventional shorthand notations which draw attention to theoretically important features of the sequence of events to which the organism is exposed. A classical conditioning procedure, taken by itself without theoretical preconceptions, consists of predetermined stimulus presentations and certain types of response measurements (cf.

Gormezano and Kehoe, 1975; Hilgard, 1937). On the stimulus side, any session of classical conditioning can be comprehensively described by the duration of events and intervals between successive events, as is typically done in connection with the actual programming of control apparatus (cf. Millenson, Kehoe, Tait, and Gormezano, 1973; Scandrett and Gormezano, 1980; Tait and Gormezano, 1974). The occurrences of each type of event, i.e. CS and US, can be described separately with respect to a common reference point at the start of the session. As a concrete example, the separate event-marker lines for the CS and US traced on a polygraph chart constitutes a complete record of events presented to an organism under study. Any relationship of 'pairing' or 'correlation' can be seen to be an abstraction of this record.

While both CS–US 'pairing' and 'correlation' are used to describe features of the sequence of stimulus durations and interstimulus intervals in a classical conditioning session, the precise specification of a 'pairing' or value of a 'correlation' for a given preparation requires extensive empirical knowledge as well as the record of events. At a minimum, the distinction between 'pairing' and 'unpairing' of a CS and US requires delineation of the empirical effects of CS–US interval manipulations, i.e. the ISI–CR frequency function. Thus, 'CS–US pairing' denotes the range of CS–US intervals which are efficacious in producing response acquisition. By the same token, what has come to be known as the 'explicitly unpaired' procedure also relies on a delineation of the ISI–CR frequency function for a given preparation. In addition, to provide a full specification of the 'associative' and 'non-associative' determinants of responding, separate CS-alone and US-alone procedures must be used to delineate their respective contributions which are independent of the CS–US interval manipulation (cf. Gormezano, 1966; Gormezano and Kehoe, 1975).

The earliest of the 'correlational' descriptions was based implicitly on a knowledge of the ISI–CR frequency functions for a preparation. Specifically, Prokasy (1965) proposed that, in addition to the CS–US pairings, other 'correlations' between a CS and a US may affect the strength of the CR. To specify these 'correlations', Prokasy proposed that any experimental session be considered divided into equal time units, with each possible event, CS and US, occurring not more than once during the specified time unit. Furthermore, in the event of the joint occurrence of a CS and US in the time unit, a forward pairing restriction would apply. Thus, a 100 per cent reinforcement schedule would be specified as one in which the conditional probability of a US in the presence of a CS is $p(US/CS) = 1.00$ and the conditional probability of a UCS in the absence of a CS is $p(US/\overline{CS}) = 0.00$. Conversely, the 'unpaired' procedure produces a perfectly negative correlation between the CS and US, with $p(US/CS) = 0.00$ and $p(US/\overline{CS}) = 1.00$. Although Prokasy did not specify a precise time unit, it would seem consistent with the spirit of his proposal to assume that a reasonable value for a given preparation could be obtained from the longest CS–US interval producing any substantial CR acquisition. Furthermore, Prokasy did *not* propose that the CS–US correlation as described by conditional probabilities constituted a fundamental molar determinant of conditioning. He left open the possibility that the consequences of the correlational manipulations may represent concatenations of other more molecular processes. For example, a schedule in which $p(US/CS) = p(US/\overline{CS}) = 0.50$ may be recognized as a 50 per cent partial reinforcement schedule combined with a large number of interpolated presentations of US alone.

Prokasy's (1965) 'correlational' description of classical conditioning was clearly based on the temporal intervals between events, but a more radical formulation was Rescorla's (1967) 'CS–US contingency' hypothesis, which viewed the statistical regularities among a sequence of CSs and USs as themselves being the molar determinants of responding (cf. Rachlin, 1976, pp. 190–192; Rescorla, 1972). In most respects, Rescorla's (1967) specification of CS–US 'contingency' parallels that of Prokasy (1965), but Rescorla also entertains the possibility that higher-order temporal and sequential relations between the CSs and USs in a session may have direct consequences for responding. Specifically, Rescorla (1967) argues:

> . . . in order for there to be *no* contingency, the distributions [of events] must be such that CS occurrences do not predict the occurrence of USs at *any* time in the remainder of the session. If the CS predicts the occurrence of a US 30 minutes later in the session, an appropriate random control condition has not been achieved. (p. 74)

With this proposition, Rescorla (1967) departed dramatically from a theory of conditioning based broadly on 'CS–US contiguity' and more specifically on the ISI–CR frequency functions.

Rescorla's (1967) concern with specifying a condition of no contingency, which was associatively neutral, appears to have stemmed from his attempt to introduce a theory of symmetric excitatory and inhibitory processes in conditioning. Accordingly, an explicitly unpaired control condition, in which there is a perfect negative contingency, was regarded as inhibitory in its consequences, not neutral. Similarly, backward conditioning was hypothesized to be inhibitory since the occurrence of the CS 'predicts a period free from the US' (Rescorla, 1967). To provide an associatively neutral condition against which to assess inhibitory conditioning as well as excitatory conditioning, Rescorla (1967) proposed the 'truly random control', which was variously specified in terms of independent programming of the CS and US (Rescorla, 1967 p. 74) or, more precisely, in terms of equal probabilities of US occurrence in the presence and absence of the US (Rescorla, 1967, p. 76). However, subsequent research with truly random control procedures has revealed that it is not invariably zero in its effect on behaviour. In studies using CS–IR procedures, substantial conditioning ('excitatory') effects were obtained depending on the placement of 'chance

CS–US pairings' within the overall schedule of events (Benedict and Ayres, 1972) and on the number of 'chance CS–US pairings' (Ayres, Benedict, and Witcher, 1975; Kremer and Kamin, 1971; Quinsey, 1971). Since these effects demonstrated the substantial consequences of 'CS–US pairings', they provided for accounts based on the molecular description of trial-by-trial interstimulus relations in bounded time units rather than accounts based on molar descriptions of the overall statistical properties of the event sequence. In fact, the Rescorla and Wagner (1972) model provides a molecular account of the effects of 'contingency' manipulations in terms of the net result of excitatory increments and inhibitory decrements in the associative strength of a stimulus.

As we have noted elsewhere (Gormezano and Kehoe, 1975), there are, in addition to the above difficulties, several general theoretical problems with the contingency hypothesis. Specifically, it would appear that the contingency hypothesis assumes a one-to-one correspondence between the experimenter-defined contingency and the 'subjective' (cognitive) contingency which the organism extracts from exposure to CS and US presentations. Moreover, as stated, the contingency hypothesis would apparently require the organism to possess a complex computational apparatus to calculate the CS–US contingency and, since the organism cannot be supplied directly with this contingency, the scope of this hypothesis is largely limited to asymptotic predictions of performance after sufficient time and events have interceded to permit the organism to calculate the CS/US contingency. Taking note of these objections, Rescorla (1972, p. 28) has relegated CS/US contingency from the status of a fundamental variable to the realm of an 'intuitive' guide and derives the asymptotic relations between responding and the correlational variable from the *contiguity-based* hypothesis of excitatory and inhibitory associative effects of the Rescorla and Wagner (1972) model.

While the tenability of molar contingency formulations has been eroded, the concept of symmetric excitatory and inhibitory strengths has been incorporated into the Rescorla and Wanger (1972) model in a way which retains an axiomatic Law of Contiguity. The model's basic equation for any change in the associative strength (dV_i) of some stimulus i follows a linear operator formula:

$$dV_i = a_i \beta_1 (\lambda_1 - V_T),$$

where a_i and β_1 are learning rate parameters between 0 and 1, which are a function of the CS and US intensity, respectively. λ_1 is the asymptotic level of associative strength supported by the US, which is greater than or equal to zero. V_T is the sum of the associative strengths of all stimuli concurrently present at the time of US presentation.

In brief, the Rescorla–Wagner model assumes that associative strength of a given stimulus increments (or decrements) as a proportion of the difference between the asymptotic associative strength (λ_1) and the summated associative strength of concurrent stimuli (V_T) in cases where there is no US, λ_1 takes on a value of zero. If a single previously-reinforced stimulus with a positive associative strength is presented without a US, then the difference $(\lambda_1 - V_T)$ would be negative and, hence, a decrement in the associative strength of the stimulus would occur. Furthermore, any other stimuli present at the same time would also suffer a decrement and, if they had a zero associative strength, their associative strength would be driven into the negative (inhibitory) range of values. The stimuli which enter into the learning process include background, situational stimuli as well as explicit CS events.

To account for the effects of CS–US correlational manipulations, Rescorla and Wagner (1972) argue that the stimuli which can enter into the learning process include tonic background stimuli as well as explicit CS events. Thus, a nominal presentation of US alone is actually a pairing of the background stimuli with the US. Likewise, a nominal CS–US trial contains a compound of the CS and background stimuli. In the case of positive CS–US correlations, positive strength accrues to the CS through its frequent pairing with the US, while any associative strength accruing to background stimuli on CS–US trials is lost during the intertrial interval, which consists of repeated unreinforced 'presentations' of the background stimuli. In the case of negative CS–US correlations, which are presumed to produce a CS with inhibitory strength (Rescorla, 1969), the background stimuli acquire substantial positive strength through their frequent pairings with nominal presentations of US alone. Consequently, on the frequent presentations of CS alone, the decrements in the excitatory background stimuli also produce large decrements in the negligible (or zero) strength of the CS which drives its net strength into the negative range. In this way, the Rescorla–Wagner model can account for the inhibitory effects of negative CS–US contingencies as a special case of the same process which governs a conditioned inhibition paradigm, in which an explicit CS acts in the same role as the background stimuli.

Rescorla and Wagner's (1972) account of inhibitory phenomena represents a formalization of Pavlov's (1927) treatment, which viewed the acquisition of inhibition as dependent upon the prior acquisition of excitatory strength through CS–US pairings. Thus, while the dimension of excitatory and inhibitory strength is perfectly symmetric, the acquisition processes are *asymmetric*. In both Pavlov's theory and the Rescorla–Wagner model, acquisition of excitatory strength is achieved in a straightforward way by means of CS–US contiguity, but acquisition of inhibitory strength to a stimulus can only take place when there is extinction of the excitatory strength of another concurrent stimulus. By tying the acquisition of inhibitory strength to the acquisition and extinction of an excitatory strength of a CS–US association, the Rescorla–Wagner model is able to account for the known behavioural effects of non-reinforcement while avoiding the postulation of an association between a CS and a non-event, the absence of the US (CS–$\overline{US}$). (Had the Rescorla–Wagner model allowed the asymptotic strength to take on a negative value, then the model would be effectively postulating a CS–$\overline{\text{US}}$ association, which entails treating the absence of an event as if it were the functional complement as well as the logical complement to the event in question.)

Although the Rescorla–Wagner model does not postulate inhibitory associations, it does not leave the Law of Contiguity as the sole determiner of changes in excitatory associative strength. The Law of Contiguity governs only the incremental process based on a CS–US contiguity, but there is also the decremental process which comes into operation anytime the summated associative strength of concurrent stimuli exceeds the asymptotic strength supported by the US. Although the decremental process is used to generate extinction curves when a CS with a positive associative strength is presented without the US, the decremental process can also operate when, say, two CSs both with asymptotic associative strengths are combined to form a compound with supra-asymptotic strength. Even if the US is presented on every trial, the associative strength of both CSs in such a compound would presumably decrease until their summated strength falls to the level supportable by the US. Evidence for decrements in associative strength of compound CSs in the face of continued US presentations has been obtained in rabbit eyeblink conditioning (Kinkaide and Walley, 1974) and CS–IR procedures (Rescorla, 1970). Thus, in the Rescorla–Wagner model, an axiomatic decremental process serves along with the competitive process between stimuli as a constraint on the operation of a contiguity-based acquisition process.

As a logical point, it should be noted that the postulation of separate acquisition and extinction processes is useful for the Rescorla–Wagner (1972) model but is not universally necessary. In the past, there have been attempts to explain extinction in terms of a contiguity-based acquisition process. Guthrie (1930) accounted for the loss of responsiveness to a stimulus by postulating the acquisition of a hypothetical competing response to the same stimulus through his contiguity principle. In a similar fashion, Hull (1943) accounted for the relative permanence of extinction by postulating a competing response (essentially one of quiescence) which was reinforced by 'drive reduction' produced by the dissipation of the products of 'fatigue'. In summary, contiguity-based formulations have viewed extinction as a case of counterconditioning. However, the hypothetical nature of the competing response in extinction has limited the testability of such accounts.

Conclusions

If nothing else, the Law of Contiguity is one of the most resiliant principles of philosophical and scientific psychology. From its origins in ancient philosophy, association through contiguity evolved in the hands of the British Associationists from a principle of memory into the source of all cognition and perception. The Law of Contiguity gained its early objectives expression in the experiments by

Ebbinghaus, but it was the strong parallels between the Law of Contiguity and the conditioned reflex methods of Pavlov and Bekhterev that led to its evolution from a principle governing the association of ideas or sensations into a principle governing the association of stimuli with other stimuli or responses. Following its early and largely polemical identification with classical conditioning, the Law of Contiguity has diversified into a family of formulations, each of which contains supplements and constraints necessary to account for the growing body of research findings obtained in both basic and complex conditioning paradigms. In all its modern variants, the Law of Contiguity has served in two paradoxical roles. As a heuristic device, the Law of Contiguity has been eminently testable and easily falsified when forced to stand by itself. In contrast to its 'straw man' role, variants of the contiguity principle have been repeatedly incorporated into theories which have been able to account for conditioning phenomena which would otherwise appear to be violations of an isolated contiguity principle.

Today, there are two major variants of the Law of Contiguity. First there is the 'strong' Law of Contiguity, which requires that the events to be associated must occur simultaneously. As a description of the empirical laws of classical conditioning, the strong Law of Contiguity is wrong, as has been demonstrated by the phenomena of trace conditioning and conditioning at CS–US asynchrony. However, the strong Law of Contiguity has been retained as a theoretical axiom in Guthrie's (1930) theory and, more recently, in CS-trace theories (e.g. Gormezano, 1972; Hull, 1943). The conjunction of the trace hypothesis with a strict contiguity formulation has been able to account for trace conditioning and conditioning at CS–US asynchrony. With the additional hypothesis that anticipatory responding reflects stimulus generalization along the stimulus trace from the point of strict contiguity with the US, it has been possible to account for the topographical features of CR latency and CR peak location (Coleman and Gormezano, 1971; Gormezano, 1972; Millenson et al., 1977). Moreover, the use of intracranial stimulation as a CS (Patterson, 1970) has provided one means for manipulating the time course of the trace, and the discovery of ISI–UR amplitude effects (Ison and Leonard, 1971; Thompson, 1976) offers the possibility of defining the trace for each combination of a CS, US, and response system, thus allowing a trace theory to accommodate the diversity of ISI–CR frequency functions. However, not all theories of CS–US interval effects have attempted to retain the strict Law of Contiguity. These theories include Revusky's (1971) account, which postulates interference among temporally *unbounded* associations, and response-shaping accounts, which postulate a process of time discrimination which affects the accuracy of CR–US overlap (cf. Ebel and Prokasy, 1963; Prokasy, 1965).

The second major varient of the Law of Contiguity is the 'weak' or 'empirical' version. This version takes the known ISI–CR frequency effects as a functional definition for a contiguity principle, even though the empirical effects of CS–US interval manipulations diverge from the strict Law of Contiguity. Specifically, manipulations of the CS–US interval in classical conditioning and other associative procedures (e.g. taste aversion learning) have always obtained at least an inverse function, i.e. a 'contiguity gradient'. However, the diversity in optimal value and breadth of these functions across preparations long ago prevented their incorporation into a single function (Hilgard and Marquis, 1940), and the discovery of the extremely broad functions of taste aversion learning has severely strained even the vague, informal notion of 'contiguity' that has served in lieu of a universal descriptive function for ISI effects. Nevertheless, the empirical contiguity principle has served as an axiom in larger theories directed at explaining CS–CR acquisition (or the lack of it) in relatively complex situations involving compound CSs or 'contingency' manipulations of a single CS and US. In connection with extending CR acquisition to CSs which are temporally remote or never paired at all with a US, the empirical contiguity principle has guided research with serial compound and second-order conditioning procedures. It would appear that CR acquisition through CS–CS presentations in revealing a 'contiguity gradient', follows the same temporal laws as CS–US presentations.

The most dramatic use of an empirical contiguity principle has been its use in sophisticated competitional theories, especially the Rescorla and Wagner (1972) model, which have been developed to account for the phenomena of selective association, contingency manipulations, and conditioned inhibition (cf. Mackintosh, 1975). By including a process of competition between stimuli for associative strength (or attention) and a decremental process based on supra-asymptotic associative strength, the Rescorla–Wagner model retains CS–US contiguity as the necessary condition for association but modulates it in such a way as to produce otherwise paradoxical outcomes. Although these competitional accounts have dealt with stimulus selection phenomena (blocking and overshadowing) only in simultaneous compounds, as a phenomenon of stimulus selection, the demonstration in serial compound conditioning that response acquisition to a component CS relatively contiguous with the US may be retarded by the presence of a preceding, less contiguous CS (Egger and Miller, 1962; Kehoe, 1979; Kehoe et al., 1979; Wickens, 1959, 1965, 1973) would appear to provide a more provocative challenge to the role of contiguity than the blocking and overshadowing phenomena of simultaneous compounds. Specifically, with serial compounds, the variable of interest—that is, the CS–UCS interval of the components—constitutes a direct manipulation along the dimension fundamental to the contiguity principle. Moreover, whereas in blocking and overshadowing, a relatively strong CS (in terms of prior training or physical intensity) suppresses acquisition to a weaker CS, serial CS suppression has involved a relatively weak CS (in terms of CS–UCS contiguity) suppressing acquisition to a relatively stronger (more contiguous) CS. Whether or not these competitional formulations can provide tenable accounts of serial stimulus selection, they do provide examples of the effective use of an empirical contiguity principle in conjunction with constraining principles to account for conditioning phenomena with simple CSs and simultaneous compounds.

Note

The preparation of the manuscript and the research reported was supported by grants from the National Science Foundation to I. Gormezano and grants from the Australian Research Grants Committee to E. James Kehoe.

References

Amsel, A. (1958). The role of frustrative nonreward in noncontinuous reward situations. *Psychological Bulletin*, **55**, 102–119.

Anderson, N. H. (1959). Response emission in time with application to eyelid conditioning. In *Studies in Mathematical Learning Theory* (R. R. Bush and W. K. Estes, eds), pp. 125–134, Stanford University Press, Stanford.

Anderson, D. C., Plant, C., Johnson, D., and Vandever, J. (1967). Second-order aversive classical conditioning. *Canadian Journal of Psychology*, **21**, 120–131.

Ayres, J. J. B., Benedict, J. O., and Witcher, E. S. (1975). Systematic manipulation of individual events in a truly random control in rats. *Journal of Comparative and Physiological Psychology*, **88**, 97–103.

Babkin, B. P. (1949). *Pavlov: A Biography*, University of Chicago Press, Chicago.

Bekhterev, V. M. (1913). *Objektive Psychologie oder Psychoreflexologie. Die Lehre von den Assoziations refflexen*, Teubner, Leipzig.

Benedict, J. O. and Ayres, J. J. B. (1972). Factors affecting conditioning in the truly random control procedure in the rat. *Journal of Comparative and Physiological Psychology*, **78**, 232–330.

Bernstein, A. L. (1934). Temporal factors in the formation of conditioned eyelid reactions in human subjects. *Journal of General Psychology*, **10**, 173–197.

Bindra, D. (1968). Neuropsychological interpretation of the effects of drive and incentive-motivation on general activity and instrumental behaviour. *Psychological Review*, **75**, 1–22.

Bindra, D. (1972). A unified account of classical conditioning and operant training. In *Classical Conditioning II: Current Theory and Research* A. H. Black and W. F. Prokasy, eds), pp. 453–481, Appleton-Century-Crofts, New York.

Boneau, C. A. (1958). The interstimulus interval and the latency of the conditioned eyelid response. *Journal of Experimental Psychology*, **56**, 464–471.

Borgealt, A. J., Donahoe, J. W., and Weinstein, A. (1972). Effects of delayed and trace components of a compound CS on conditioned suppression and heart rate. *Psychonomic Science*, **26**, 13–15.

Boring, E. G. (1950). *A History of Experimental Psychology*, Appleton-Century-Crofts, New York.

Brahlek, J. A. (1968). Conditioned suppression as a function of the number of stimuli that precede shock. *Psychonomic Science*, **12**, 189–190.

Brogden, W. J. (1939). Higher-order conditioning. *American Journal of Psychology*, **52**, 579–591.

Brogden, W. J. and Culler, E. (1935). Experimental extinction of higher order responses. *Amercian Journal of Psychology*, **47**, 663–669.

Brown, T. (1820). *Lectures on the Philosophy of the Human Mind*, Vols I and II, Edinburgh.

Cason, H. (1922). The conditioned eyelid reaction. *Journal of Experimental Psychology*, 5, 153–196.

Colavita, F. B. (1965). Dual function of the US in classical salivary conditioning. *Journal of Comparative and Physioiogical, Psychology* 60, 218–222.

Coleman, S. R. and Gormezano, I. (1971). Classical conditioning of the rabbit's (*Oryctologus cuniculus*) nictitating membrane response under symmetrical CS–US interval shifts. *Journal of Comparative and Physiological Psychology*, 77, 447–455.

Descartes, R. (1650). *Les Passions de l'âme*, Amsterdam. Translated by E. S. Haldane and G. R. T. Ross (1931) in *The Philosophical Works of Descartes*, Cambridge University Press, Cambridge.

Diamond, S. (1974). *The Roots of Psychology: A Source Book in the History of Ideas*, Basic Books, New York.

Ebbinghaus, H. (1885). *Uber das Gedächtnis*, Duncker and Humboldt, Leipzig. Translated by H. A. Ruger and Clara Bussenins (1913) in *Memory*, Columbia University Press, New York.

Ebel, H. C. and Prokasy, W. F. (1963). Classical eyelid conditioning as a function of sustained and shifted interstimulus intervals. *Journal of Experimental Psychology*, 65, 52–58.

Eccher, W. and Culler, E. (1941). Reciprocal facilitation of the conditioned and conditioning mechanisms. *Journal of Comparative Psychology*, 31, 223–231.

Egger, D. M. and Miller, N. E. (1962). Secondary reinforcement in rats as a function of information value and reliability of the stimulus. *Journal of Experimental Psychology*, 64, 97–104.

Egger, D. M. and Miller, N. E. (1963). When is a reward reinforcing? An experimental study of the information hypothesis. *Journal of Comparative and Physiological Psychology*, 56, 132–137.

Ellison, G. D. (1964). Differential salivary conditioning to traces. *Journal of Comparative and Physiological Psychology*, 57, 373–380.

Estes, W. K. (1950). Towards a statistical theory of learning. *Psychological Review*, 57, 94–107.

Finch, G. and Culler, E. (1934). Higher-order conditioning with constant motivation. *American Journal of Psychology*, 66, 596–602.

Finch, G. and Culler, E. (1935). Relation of forgetting to experimental extinction. *American Journal of Psychology*, 47, 656–662.

Frank, L. K. (1923). Suggestion for a theory of learning, *Psychological Review*, 30, 145–148.

Garcia, J. and Koelling, R. A. (1966). Relation of cue to consequence in avoidance learning. *Psychonomic Science*, 4, 123–124.

Garcia, J., Ervin, F. R., and Koelling, R. A. (1966). Learning with prolonged delay of reinforcement. *Psychonomic Science*, 5, 121–122.

Garcia, J., McGowan, B. K., and Green, K. F. (1972). Biological constraints on conditioning. *In Classical Conditioning II: Current Theory and Research* (A. H. Black and W. F. Prokasy, eds), pp. 3–27, Appleton-Century-Crofts, New York.

Gormezano, I. (1966). Classical conditioning. In *Experimental Methods and Instrumentation in Psychology* (J. B. Sidowski, ed.), pp. 385–420, McGraw-Hill, New York.

Gormezano, I. (1972). Investigations of defense and reward conditioning in the rabbit. In *Classical Conditioning II: Current Research and Theory* (A. H. Black and W. F. Prokasy, eds), pp. 151–181, Appleton-Century-Crofts, New York.

Gormezano, I. and Kehoe, E. J. (1975). Classical conditioning: some methodological-conceptual issues. In *Handbook of Learning and Cognitive Processes*, Vol. 2,

Conditioning and Behavior Theory (W. K. Estes, ed.), pp. 143–179, Lawrence Erlbaum Associates, Hillside, N. J.

Gormezano, I. and Kehoe, E. J. (1980). Stimulus selection and associative transfer in classical conditioning to serial compounds: theory and data. In *Conditioning, Cognition, and Methodology: Contemporary Issues in Experimental Psychology* (J. B. Sidowski and H. Hake, eds), Lawrence Erlbaum Associates Hillside, N. J. (in press).

Gormezano, I. and Moore, J. W. (1969). Classical conditioning. In *Learning: Processes* (M. M. Marx, ed), pp. 121–203, Macmillan, Toronto.

Gormezano, I., Schneiderman, N., Deaux, E. G., and Fuentes, I. (1962). Nictitating membrane: classical conditioning and extinction in the albino rabbit. *Science*, **138**, 33–34.

Guthrie, E. R. (1930). Conditioning as a principle of learning. *Psychological Review*, **37**, 412–418.

Guthrie, E. R. (1933). Association as a function of time interval. *Psychological Review*, **40**, 355–367.

Guthrie, E. R. (1935). *The Psychology of Learning*, Harper, New York.

Hall, J. F. (1976). *Classical Conditioning and Instrumental Learning: A Contemporary Approach*, J. B. Lippincott, Philadelphia.

Hall, M. (1832). On a particular function of the nervous system. *Proceedings of the Zoological Society of London*.

Hansche, W. J. and Grant, D. A. (1960). Onset versus termination of a stimulus as the CS in eyelid conditioning. *Journal of Experimental Psychology*, **59**, 19–26.

Hilgard, E. R. (1931). Conditioned eyelid reactions to a light stimulus based on the reflex wink to sound. *Psychological Monographs*, **41**, No. 184.

Hilgard, E. R. (1937). The relationship between the conditioned response and conventional learning experiments. *Psychological Bulletin*, **34**, 61–102.

Hilgard, E. R. and Marquis, D. G. (1940). *Conditioning and Learning*, Appleton-Century-Crofts, New York.

Hoehler, F. K., and Leonard, D. W. (1976). Double responding in classical nictitating membrane conditioning with single-CS dual-ISI training. *Pavlovian Journal Biological Science*, **11**, 180–190.

Holland, P. C., and Rescorla, R. A. (1975). Second-order conditioning with a food unconditioned stimulus. *Journal of Comparative and Physiological Psychology*, **88**, 459–467.

Holt, E. B. (1931). *Animal Drive and the Learning Process*, Henry Holt, New York.

Hull, C. L. (1930). Knowledge and purpose as habit mechanisms. *Psychological Review*, **37**, 511–525.

Hull, C. L. (1931). Goal attraction and directing ideas conceived as habit phenomena. *Psychological Review*, **38**, 487–506.

Hull, C. L. (1934). The rat's speed-of-locomotion gradient in the approach to food, *Journal of Comparative Psychology*, **17**, 393–422.

Hull, C. L. (1937). 'Mind, mechanism, and adaptive behaviors', *Psychological Review*, **44**, 1–32.

Hull, C. L. (1943). *Principles of Behavior*, Appleton-Century-Crofts, New York.

Hull, C. L. (1951). *Essentials of Behavior*, Yale University Press, New Haven, Conn.

Hull, C. L. (1952). *A Behavior System*, Yale University Press, New Haven, Conn.

Ison, J. R. and Leonard, D. W. (1971). Effects of auditory stimuli on the amplitude of the nictitating membrane reflex of the rabbit *(Oryctolagus cuniculus)*. Journal of Comparative and Physiological Psychology, **75**, 157–164.

Kamin, L. J. (1968). Attention-like processes in classical conditioning. In *Miami Symposium on the Prediction of Behavior: Aversive Stimulation* (M. R. Jones, ed.), University of Miami Press, Miami.

Kamin, L. J. (1969). Selective association and conditioning. In *Fundamental Issues in Associative Learning* (N. J. Mackintosh and F. W. K. Honig, eds), Dalhousie University Press, Halifax.

Kehoe, E. J. (1979).The role of CS–US contiguity in classical conditioning of the rabbit's nictitating membrane response to serial stimuli. *Learning and Motivation*, **10**, 23–38.

Kehoe, E. J. Gibbs, C. M., Garcia, E., and Gormezano, I. (1979). Associative transfer and stimulus selection in classical conditioning of the rabbit's nictitating membrane response to serial compound CSs. *Journal of Experimental Psychology: Animal Behavior Processes*, **5**, 1–18.

Kimble, G. A. (1947). Conditioning as a function of the time between conditioned and unconditioned stimuli. *Journal of Experimental Psychology*, **37**, 1–15.

Kimmel, H. D. (1965). Instrumental inhibitory factors in classical conditioning. In *Classical Conditioning: A Symposium* (W. F. Prokasy, ed.), pp. 148–171, Appleton-Century-Crofts, New York.

Kimmel, H. D. and Burns, R. A. (1975). Adaptational aspects of conditioning. In *Handbook of Learning and Cognitive Processes*, Vol. 2, *Conditioning and Behavior Theory* (W. K. Estes, ed.), Lawrence Erlbaum Associates, Hillside, N. J.

Kinkaide, P. S. and Walley, R. C. (1974).Visual evoked potentials during stimulus selection in eyelid conditioning in the rabbit *(Oryctolagus cuniculus)*. *Journal of Comparative and Physiological Psychology*, **87**, 481–494.

Konorski, J. (1948). *Conditioned Reflexes and Neuron Organization*, Cambridge University Press, Cambridge.

Konorski, J. (1967). *Integrative Activity of the Brain*, University of Chicago Press, Chicago.

Konorski, J. and Miller, S. (1937). On two types of conditioned reflex. *Journal of General Psychology*, **16**, 264–272.

Kremer, E. F. and Kamin, L. J. (1971). The truly random control procedure: associative or nonassociative effect in rats. *Journal of Comparative and Physiological Psychology*, **74**, 203–210.

Lashley, K. S. (1916). The human salivary reflex and its use in psychology. *Psychological Review*, **23**, 446–464.

Levis, D. J. and Stampfl, T. G. (1972). Effects of serial CS presentation on shuttlebox avoidance responding. *Learning and Motivation*, **3**, 73–90.

Logan, F. A. and Wagner, A. R. (1965). *Reward and Punishment*, Allyn and Bacon, Boston.

McAllister, D. E. and McAllister, W. R. (1964). Second-order conditioning of fear. *Psychonomic Science*, **1**, 383–384.

McAllister, W. R. (1953). Eyelid conditioning as a function of the CS–UCS interval. *Journal of Experimental Psychology*, **45**, 417–422.

McDougall, W. (1923). *Outline of Psychology*, Scribner, New York.

Mackintosh, N. J. (1975). A theory of attention: variation in the associability of stimuli with reinforcement. *Psychological Review*, **82**, 276–298.

Mackintosh, N. J. (1976). Overshadowing and stimuli intensity. *Animal Learning and Behavior*, **4**, 186–192.

Marchant, H. G., III and Moore, J. W. (1973). Blocking of the rabbit's conditioned nictitating membrane response in Kamin's two-stage paradigm. *Journal of Experimental Psychology*, **101**, 155–158.

Martin, I. and Levey, A. B. (1969). *The Genesis of the Classical Conditioned Response*, Pergamon Press, Oxford.

Marx, M. H. and Hillex, W. H. (1973). *Systems and Theories in Psychology*, McGraw-Hill, New York.

Millenson, J. R., Kehoe, E. J., and Gormezano, I. (1977). Classical conditioning of the rabbit's nictitating membrane response under fixed and mixed CS–US intervals. *Learning and Motivation*, **8**, 351–366.

Millenson, J. R., Kehoe, E. J., Tait, R., and Gormezano, I. (1973). A minicomputer program for control and data acquisition in classical conditioning, *Behavioral Research Methods*, **5**, 212–217.

Miller, N. E. (1948). Studies of fear as an acquirable drive. *Journal of Expimental Psychology*, **38**, 89–101.

Miller, N. E. (1951). Learnable drives and rewards. In *Handbook of Experimental Psychology* (S. S. Stevens, ed.), John Wiley, New York.

Miller, N. E. (1963). Some reflections on the law of effect produce a new alternative to drive reduction. In *Nebraska Symposium on Motivation* (M. M. Jones, ed.), pp. 65–112, University of Nebraska Press, Lincoln, Neb.

Miller, S. and Konorski, J. (1928) Sur une forme particuliere des reflexes conditionnels. *Comptes rendus des séances de la Société de biologie*, **99**, 1155–1157.

Mowrer, O. H. (1947). On the dual nature of learning—a reinterpretation of 'conditioning' and 'problem solving'. *Harvard Educational Review*, **17**, 102–148.

Mowrer, O. H. (1960). *Learning Theory and Behavior*, John Wiley, New York.

Osgood, C. E. (1953). *Method and Theory in Experimental Psychology*, Oxford University Press, New York.

Patterson, M. M. (1970). Classical conditioning of the rabbit's *(Oryctolagus cuniculus)* nictitating membrane response with fluctuating ISI and intracranial CS. *Journal of Comparative and Physiological Psychology*, **72**, 193–202.

Pavlov, I. P. (1927). *Conditioned Reflexes* (Translated by G. V. Anrep, Oxford University Press, London).

Pavlov, I. P. (1932). The reply of a physiologist to psychologists. *Psychological Review*, **39**, 91–127.

Prokasy, W. F. (1965). Classical eyelid conditioning: experimenter operations, task demands, and response shaping. In *Classical Conditioning: A Symposium* (W. F. Prokasy, ed.), pp. 208–225, Appleton-Century-Crofts, New York.

Prokasy, W. F., Ebel, H. C., and Thompson, D. D. (1963). Response shaping at long interstimulus intervals in eyelid conditioning. *Journal of Experimental Psychology*, **66**, 138–142.

Prokasy, W. F. and Papsdorf, J. D. (1965). Effect of increasing the interstimulus interval during classical conditioning of the albino rabbit. *Journal of Comparative and Physiological Psychology*, **60**, 249–252.

Quinsey, V. L. (1971). Conditioned suppression with no CS–US contingency in the rat. *Canadian Journal of Psychology/Revue Canadienne de/psychologie*, **25**, 69–82.

Rachlin, H. (1976). *Behavior and Learning*, Freeman, San Francisco.

Razran, G. H. S. (1930). Theory of conditioning and related phenomena. *Psychological Review*, **45**, 532–538.

Razran, G. (1955). A note on second-order conditioning and secondary reinforcement. *Psychological Review*, **62**, 327–332.

Rescorla, R. A. (1967). Pavlovian conditioning and its proper control procedures. *Psychological Review*, **74**, 71–80.

Rescorla, R. A. (1968). Probability of shock in the presence and absence of CS in fear conditioning. *Journal of Comparative and Physiological Psychology*, **66**, 1–5.

Rescorla, R. A. (1969). Pavlovian conditioned inhibition. *Psychological Bulletin*, **72**, 77–94.

Rescorla, R. A. (1970). Reduction in the effectiveness of reinforcement after prior excitatory conditioning. *Learning and Motivation*, **1**, 372–381.

Rescorla, R. A. (1972). Informational variables in Pavlovian Conditioning. In *The Psychology of Learning and Motivation*, Vol. 6 (G. Bower, ed.), Academic Press, New York.

Rescorla, R. A. (1973). Second-order conditioning: implications for theories of learning. In *Contemporary Approaches to Conditioning and Learning* (F. J. McGuigan and D. B. Lumsden, eds), Winston, Washington, D. C.

Rescorla, R. A. (1977). Pavlovian second-order conditioning: some implications for instrumental behavior. In *Operant-Pavlovain Interactions* (H. Davis and H. M. B. Hurwitz, eds), Lawrence Erlbaum Associates, Hillside, N. J.

Rescorla, R. A. and Solomon, R. (1967). Two-process learning theory: relationships between Pavlovian conditioning and instrumental learning. *Psychological Review*, **74**, 151–182.

Rescorla, R. A. and Wagner, A. R. (1972). A theory of Pavlovain conditioning: variations in the effectiveness of reinforcement and nonreinforcement. In *Classical Conditioning II: Current Theory and Research* (A. Black and W. F. Prokasy, eds), pp. 64–99, Appleton-Century-Crofts, New York.

Revusky, S. H. (1968). Aversion to sucrose produced by contingent x-irradiation: temporal and dosage parameters. *Journal of Comparative and Physiological Psychology*, **65**, 17–22.

Revusky, S. H. (1971). The role of interference in association over a delay. In *Animal Memory* (W. K. Honig and P. H. R. James, eds), pp. 155–213, Academic Press, New York.

Revusky, S. H. (1977). Learning as a general process with an emphasis on data from feeding experiments. In *Food Aversion Learning* (N. W. Milgram, L. Krammes, and T. M. Alloway, eds), Plenum Press, New York.

Rizley, R. C. and Rescorla, R. A. (1972). Associations in second-order conditioning and sensory preconditioning. *Journal of Comparative and Physiological Psychology*, **81**, 1–11.

Robinson, E. S. (1932). *Association Theory To-day*, Century, New York.

Rodnick, E. H. (1937). Characteristics of delayed and trace conditioned responses. *Journal of Experimental Psychology*, **20**, 409–425.

Rozin, P. and Kalat, J. W. (1971). Specific hungers and poison avoidance as adaptive specializations of learning. *Psychological Review*, **78**, 459–486.

Rudy, J. W. and Wagner, A. R. (1975). Stimulus selection in associative learning. In *Handbook of Learning and Cognitive Processes*, Vol. 2 (W. K. Estes), Lawrence Erlbaum Associates, Hillside, N. J.

Sandiford, P. (1942). Connectionism: its origin and major features. In *The Forty-First Yearbook of the National Society for the Study of Education*, Part II, *The Psychology of Learning* (N. B. Henery, ed.), University of Chicago Press, Chicago.

Scandrett, J. H. and Gormezano, I. (1980). Microprocessor control and A/D data acquisition in classical conditioning. *Behavioral Research Methods and Instrumentation*, in press.

Scheuer, C. and Keeter, W. H. (1969). Temporal vs. discriminative factors in the maintenance of conditioned suppression: a test of the information hypothesis. *Psychonomic Science*, **15**, 21–23.

Schlosberg, H. (1937). The relationship between success and the laws of conditioning. *Psychological Review*, **44**, 379–394.

Schneiderman, N. (1966). Interstimulus interval function of the nictitating membrane response in the rabbit under delay versus trace conditioning. *Journal of Comparative Physiological Psychology*, **62**, 397–402.

Schneiderman, N. (1972). Response system divergences in aversive classical conditioning. In *Classical Conditioning II: Current Theory and Research* (A. H. Black and W. F. Prokasy, eds), pp. 341–376, Appleton-Century-Crofts, New York.

Schneiderman, N. and Gormezano, I. (1964). Conditioning of the nictitating membrane of the rabbit as a function of CS–US interval. *Journal of Comparative and Physiological Psychology*, **57**, 188–195.

Sechenov, I. M. (1863). Reflexes of the brain. *Meditsinsk Vestnik*, **3**, 461–484, 493–512.

Seger, K. A. and Scheuer, C. (1977). The informational properties of S1, S2, and the S1–S2 sequence on conditioned suppression. *Animal Learning and Behavior*, **5**, 39–41.

Seligman, M. E. P. (1966). CS redundancy and secondary punishment. *Journal of Experimental Psychology*, **72**, 546–550.

Sheffield, F. D. (1966a). A drive-induction theory of reinforcement. In *Current Research in Motivation* (R. N. Haber, ed.), Holt, New York.

Sheffield, F. D. (1966b). New evidence on the drive-induction theory of reinforcement. In *Current Research in Motivation* (R. N. Haber, ed.), Holt, New York.

Sheffield, F. D., Roby, T. B., and Campbell, B. A. (1954). Drive reduction versus consummatory behavior as determinants of reinforcement. *Journal of Comparative and Physiological Psychology*, **47**, 349–354.

Skinner, B. F. (1935). Two types of conditioned reflex and a pseudo type. *Journal of General Psychology*, **12**, 66–77.

Skinner, B. F. (1935). Two types of conditioned reflex: a reply to Konorski and Miller. *Journal of General Psychology*, **16**, 272–279.

Skinner, B. F. (1938). *The Behavior of Organisms: An Experimental Analysis*, Appleton-Century-Crofts, New York.

Smith, J. C. and Roll, D. L. (1967). Trace conditioning with x-rays as an aversive stimulus. *Psychonomic Science*, **9**, 11–12.

Smith, M. C. (1968). CS–US interval and US intensity in classical conditioning of the rabbit's nictitating membrane response. *Journal of Comparative and Physiological Psychology*, **66**, 679–687.

Smith, M. C., Coleman, S. R., and Gormezano, I. (1969). Classical conditioning of the rabbit's nictitating membrane response at backward, simultaneous, and forward CS–US intervals. *Journal of Comparative and Physiological Psychology*, **69**, 226–231.

Smith, S. and Guthrie, E. R. (1921). *General Psychology in Terms of Behavior*, Appleton-Century-Crofts, New York.

Spence, K. W. (1947). The role of secondary reinforcement in delayed-reward learning. *Psychological Review*, **54**, 1–8.

Spence, K. W. (1956). *Behavior Theory and Conditioning*, Yale University Press, New Haven, Conn.

Suboski, M. D. (1967). UCS intensity and the latency of the classically conditioned eyelid response. *Journal of Experimental Psychology*, **74**, 31–35.

Sutherland, N. S. and Mackintosh, N. J. (1971). *Mechanisms of Animal Discrimination Learning*, Academic Press, New York.

Switzer, S. A. (1933). Disinhibition of the conditioned galvanic skin response. *Journal of General Psychology*, **12**, 78–94.

Szakmary, G. A. (1979). Second-order conditioning of the conditioned emotional response: some methodological considerations. *Animal Learning and Behavior*, **7**, 181–184.

Tait, R. W. and Gormezano, I. (1974). A minicomputer program for stimulus control and analog data for discrete trial paradigms in biological preparations: classical conditioning. *Behavioral Research Methods and Instrumentation*, **6**, 295–300.

Teller, K. J., Dieter, R., and Suboski, M. D. (1972). Time estimation and the interstimulus interval function in classical conditioning. *Journal of Experimental Psychology*, **95**, 445–448.

Thompson, R. F. (1976). The search for the engram, *American Psychologist*, **31**, 209–227.

Thorndike, E. L. (1898). Animal intelligence. An experimental study of the associative processes in animals. *Psychological Monographs*, **2**, No. 8, 1–109.

Thorndike, E. L. (1911). *Animal Intelligence*, Macmillan, New York.

Thorndike, E. L. (1913). *The Psychology of Learning*, Columbia University Press, New York.

Trapold, M.A. and Overmier, J. B. (1972). The second learning process in instrumental conditioning. In *Classical Conditioning II: Current Theory and Research* (A. H. Black and W. F. Prokasy, eds), pp. 427–452, Appleton-Century-Crofts, New York.

Tulving, E. and Pearlstone, Z. (1966). Availability versus accessibility of information in memory for words. *Journal of Verbal Learning and Verbal Behavior*, **5**, 381–391.

Tulving, E. and Thomson, D. M. (1973). Encoding specificity and retrival processes in episodic memory. *Psychological Review*, **80**, 352–373.

Voeks, V. W. (1950). Formalization and clarification of a theory of learning. *Journal of Psychology*, **30**, 341–362.

Wagner, A. R. (1969). Stimulus selection and a 'modified continuity theory. In *The Psychology of Learning and Motivation*, Vol. 3 (G. Bower and J. T. Spence, eds), Academic Press, New York.

Wagner, A. R., Logan, F. A., Haberlandt, K., and Price, T. (1968). Stimulus selection in animal discrimination learning. *Journal of Experimental Psychology*, **76**, 171–180.

Warren, H. C. (1921). *A History of the Association Psychology*, Scribner, New York.

Watson, J. B. (1916). The place of the conditioned reflex in psychology. *Psychological Review*, **23**, 89–116.

Watson, J. B. (1925). *Behaviorism*, Norton, New York.

Wickens, D. D. (1959). Conditioning to complex stimuli. *American Psychologist*, **14**, 180–188.

Wickens, D. D. (1965). Compound conditioning in humans and cats. In *Classical Conditioning: A Symposium* (W. F. Prokasy, ed.), Appleton-Century-Crofts, New York.

Wickens, D. D. (1973). Classical conditioning, as it contributes to the analyses of some basic psychological processes. In *Contemporary Approaches to Conditioning and Learning* (F. J. McGuigan and D. B. Lumsden, eds), John Wiley, New York.

Wickens, D.D., Nield, A. F., Tuber, D. S., and Wickens, C. D. (1969). Strength, latency, and form of conditioned skeletal and autonomic responses as functions of CS–UCS intervals. *Journal of Experimental Psychology*, **80**, 165–170.

Williams, D. R. (1965). Classical conditioning and incentive motivation. In *Classical Conditioning: A Symposium* (W. F. Prokasy, ed.), Appleton-Century-Crofts, New York.

Wilson, W. R. (1924). Selection in 'trial and error'. *Psychological Review*, **31**, 150–160.

Woodworth, R. S. (1918). *Dynamic Psychology*, Columbia University Press, New York.

Predictability, Correlation, and Contiguity
Edited by P. Harzem and M. D. Zeiler
© 1981 John Wiley & Sons Ltd

Chapter 2

Simultaneous Associations

Robert A. Rescorla

Introduction

It has become increasingly popular to view Pavlovian conditioning as the learning of relations among stimulus events in the environment. Those relations are frequently thought to be encoded in the form of learned associations between neutral, conditioned stimuli (CSs) and affective valued unconditioned stimuli (USs). In this context, it is important to describe those relations among events which result in their becoming associated. Although simple contiguity in time has often been offered as a description for the principal relation involved, in the last 10 years that description has received important modification. Many current discussions of Pavlovian conditioning instead emphasize a CS/US relation which might be described as 'informative' or 'predictive'. Such terms seem to apply to a range of phenomena which have recently received extensive experimental investigation (*see*, for example, Rescorla, 1972; Mackintosh, 1974).

Actually, the notion that the CS must provide information about the US for conditioning to occur has been implicit in discussions since Pavlov (1927). For instance, Pavlov emphasized the role of the CS as a signal for the US. That notion of signalling seems to derive primarily from the temporal relation which normally obtains between the CS and US. The observation that conditioning is superior when the CS precedes the US has often been cited as evidence for the adaptiveness of Pavlovian conditioning. More importantly in the present context, it has appeared to support the contention that predictiveness or information value is central to the formation of Pavlovian associations.

But despite the power and attractiveness of describing conditioning in these terms, it seems unlikely that predictiveness exhaustively characterizes the relations among events which organisms learn. The importance of the CS signalling the US seems especially plausible for the most frequently studied Pavlovian situation, in which one, relative neutral, stimulus is presented in relation to another, relatively more valued, stimulus. In that case, the use of the former as a signal for the latter seems to make adaptive sense. However, that intuition is substantially less compelling when we inquire about the learning of relations among stimuli which are more equivalent in value, such as two 'neutral' stimuli. In that case, the organism is less plausibly viewed as needing to use one event to signal the other. In such cases, information value may play a much smaller role and consequently the learning of other relations may be more easily observed. In particular, temporal precedence may play a quite different role in governing associative learning.

It is worth noting that non-Pavlovian discussions of association, which frequently concern stimuli of more equivalent value, have placed considerably less emphasis upon the role of temporal priority. Indeed, many classical discussions suggested that associations are best formed when there is no asynchrony between the events to be associated. For instance, many of the British associationists distinguished between two circumstances which produce association, sequential and simultaneous presentation. A frequent point of discussion concerned the relative importance of these two presentation modes and the possibility that they result in different associative processes. Some authors envisioned sequential stimulus presentation as analogous to learning the relations among two events in the world but simultaneous stimulus presentation as analogous to the organism's learning the properties of the events themselves (*see* Warren, 1921).

This chapter reports results from a research programme exploring the role of this latter, simultaneous, learning in Pavlovian settings. First, we will display some examples which suggest that simultaneous presentation indeed can result in the formation of substantial associations. In line with the previous comments, most of those examples will be from settings which relate stimuli having values comparable to each other. But the results will emphasize the range of paradigms over which such associations are observable. Second, we will provide some empirical comparisons of the success of learning with sequential and simultaneous modes of presentation. We will argue that many past comparisons are flawed in such a way as to favour the observation of superior performance under sequential stimulus presentation; in consequence, we will describe an alternative paradigm which generates a different pattern of results. Finally, we will describe a way of thinking about the learning which occurs with simultaneous presentation which implies a separate, less studied, learning process. Some further experiments will be described which illustrate the usefulness of that alternative view.

Sample Experiment

Historically, most reports of learning associations between simultaneously presented Pavlovian events have yielded only weak positive support, even when neutral events are involved. However, several recently reported experiments using rat subjects have found substantial associative learning among simultaneously presented flavour stimuli. Although, as we will see shortly, the evidence is not confined to those stimuli, it will be convenient to begin with an example using flavours as CSs. That example, reported by Rescorla and Cunningham (1978), will both illustrate the occurrence of such associations and serve as a reference experiment for much of the work described subsequently.

Thirsty rats were given daily 10 min exposures to either water or a flavoured solution. Four different flavours, selected to represent the primary taste qualities, sweet, salt, bitter, and sour, were used as the elementary stimuli. The precise stimuli were 0.1 M sucrose (S), 0.2 M salt (N), 0.00006 M quinine (Q), and 0.005 M hydrochloric acid (H). Each animal initially received four exposures to each of two compound stimuli. Those compounds were constructed by mixing two flavours in the same solution and presenting that solution through a single drinking spout. As indicated in Table 2.1, half the animals received compounds of SH and NQ whereas the other half received SQ and NH. These solutions, although not, of course, entirely neutral, are consumed by thirsty rats in amounts similar to water.

Then each animal was subjected to a procedure intended to reveal the acquisition of any associations between the simultaneously presented components of these compounds. For this purpose the animals in each group received a discriminative conditioning procedure which paired one element of one compound with an illness-inducing agent. For half the animals H was followed twice by 0.5 percent of body weight injection of 0.6 M LiCl, whereas Q was non-reinforced twice; the remaining animals had Q followed by poison but H non-reinforced. Finally, all animals were given simultaneous access to S and N, presented side by side for 10 min in separate tubes. The expectation was that the presence of an association between elements would be revealed by the rejection of that substance which had previously been presented simultaneously with the poisoned element.

Figure 2.1 bears out this expectation. This figure shows the consumptions of S and N as a function of the particular compounds pre-exposed and the particular elements subsequently poisoned. To the left are the results for those animals which received the SH and NQ compounds. In those animals, consumption of S was generally greater than that of N. However, within each flavour, consumption was governed by the treatments of H and Q; that is, S consumption was lower

Table 2.1. Design of Rescorla and Cunningham (1978)

	Phase 1	Phase 2	Test
Group 1	SH, NQ	H +, Q −	S, N
Group 2	SH, NQ	H −, Q +	S, N
Group 3	SQ, NH	H +, Q −	S, N
Group 4	SQ, NH	H −, Q +	S, N

Note: S, sucrose; H, hydrochloric acid; N, salt; Q, quinine; +, toxin; −, non-reinforcement.

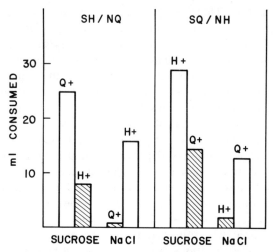

Figure 2.1. Consumption of sucrose and salt after prior exposure to either sucrose–hydrochloric acid (SH) and salt–quinine (NQ) or SQ and NH compounds and poisoning of either H or Q. Consumption of S and N depended upon the treatment of the element with which it had previously been paired. (From R. A. Rescorla and C. L. Cunningham (1978). Within-compound flavor associations. *Journal of Experimental Psychology: Animal Behavior Processes*, **4**, 267–275 Copyright © 1978 by the American Psychological Association. Reprinted by permission)

when H, rather than Q, was poisoned, whereas N consumption was lower in the opposite case. The right-hand panel shows a similar pattern of results for those animals exposed to SQ and NH. Again S was generally flavoured over N, but consumption of either substance was reduced by the poisoning of its paired element. That pattern of results suggests that in this setting substantial levels of simultaneous association were established.

The technique used in this experiment is, of course, a variation on the classical sensory preconditioning design. However, as noted elsewhere (Rescorla and Cunningham, 1978), the present variation has several advantages. The one most relevant in the present context is that of efficiency. A typical sensory preconditioning experiment contains one experimental and two control groups. The experimental group receives paired presentations of S_2 with S_1, then paired presentations of S_1 with a US, and finally a test of S_2 for its ability to elicit a response. The two control groups assess the importance of both these pairings to the observation of responding during S_2, each by destroying one of the pairings while maintaining the other. A control treatment which pairs S_1 with the US but presents S_2 and S_1 in an unpaired fashion is especially important for the conclusion that the relation arranged between S_1 and S_2 influenced learning. But notice that in the present procedure each animal served both as an experimental and a control animal. For instance, animals in Group 1 received an experimental treatment with regard to S (it was paired with H and H was then paired with the poison), but they received a control treatment with regard to N (it was unpaired with H which was subsequently poisoned, and it was paired with Q which was subsequently presented in an unpaired fashion with poison). Thus the present results contain within them the standard comparisons normally demanded for concluding that associative learning is involved, and they do so in a highly efficient manner.

The Generality of this Result

Although the results in Figure 2.1 provide strong evidence that simultaneous associations can occur, one may well wonder about their generality. Under how broad a range of circumstances can we except to observe simultaneous associations? Two kinds of generality seem especially important. The first is generality across different kinds of stimuli and conditioning preparations. The flavour-aversion preparation used in the previous experiment employs CSs to which the animal is especially sensitive and USs which have been claimed to bear special relations to those CSs. It is therefore relevant to ask whether similar results could be obtained with other preparations. The second is generality across different circumstances under which stimuli can be presented simultaneously within a conditioning preparation. Many modren conditioning paradigms involve simultaneous presentation of two or more stimuli, with various reinforcement contingencies. Across what range of such paradigms can we expect simultaneous associations to occur? In this section we explore these two kinds of generality.

Examples from Other Conditioning Preparations

There turns out to be nothing special about the use of illness-inducing agents for the observation of simultaneous associations among flavours. Several authors have recently reported the use of an interesting alternative assessment procedure which does not involve making one flavour aversive by pairing it with a poison. Instead, this procedure makes one flavour especially attractive by inducing a specific hunger for it; that manipulation results in the increased consumption of other flavours which have previously been presented in compound with the needed substance.

Fudim (1978) recently described one example of this manipulation which follows closely the procedure described in Table 2.1. Rats were initially exposed to two compounds, each of which was composed of a target flavour (either banana (B) or almond (A)) together with either sucrose (S) or salt (N). Half the animals received extensive exposure to both BN and AS whereas half received BS and AN. Then all animals were exposed to a combination of a salt-free diet and injections of a formalin solution; this procedure is known to induce a strong specific hunger for salt. Finally, all animals were given a choice test with A and B alone. The issue is whether consumption of A and B would reflect their histories of presentation with the now-desired N. Such an outcome would imply the formation of a simultaneous association.

The major result of Fudim's study is shown in Figure 2.2. That figure shows consumptions of the A and B solutions as a function of the prior compound exposure. It is clear that for the animals receiving BS and AN, salt induction resulted in greater consumption of A; however, the same manipulation produced greater consumption of B in those animals with a history of BN and AS exposure. This outcome pattern is entirely parallel to that observed in Figure 2.1, with one exception. Unlike the Rescorla and Cunningham study, only one substance, N, was changed in value. Presumably, the induction of a specific hunger for sucrose, if possible, would have resulted in a pattern of results opposite to that seen in Figure 2.2. In any case, there is no doubt that simultaneous flavour associations can be detected using this alternative procedure. Similar results have been obtained in a more conventional sensory preconditioning procedure by Rescorla and Freberg (1978).

The rat is especially sensitive to flavour stimuli. Indeed, it is somewhat surprising that so much psychological research has been carried out on rodents using auditory and visual stimuli, since the rat clearly has a much richer perception of flavours. But it should not be thought that results like those reported above are confined to gustatory stimuli. Similar patterns can be found in more conventional Pavlovian conditioning procedures, which use auditory and visual stimuli. Figure 2.3 shows the results of one conditioned suppression

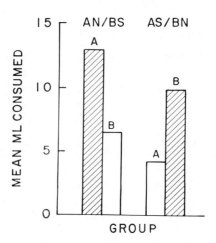

Figure 2.2. Consumption of almond (A) and banana (B) after exposure to either almond–salt (AN) and banana–sucrose (BS) or AS and BN compounds. Consumptions are observed under a salt-deprivation condition, resulting in greater intakes of that substance previously paired with salt. Data are taken from Fudim (1978)

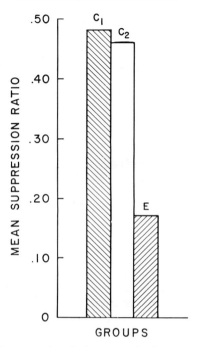

Figure 2.3. Conditioned suppression during a tone in three groups which differed in the relation between light and tone as well as the relation between light and shock. Group E received TL presentations followed by L–shock pairings; Groups C_1 and C_2 were similarly treated except that either the T–L or the L–shock relation was disrupted

experiment recently conducted in our laboratory. These results are from 24 animals which were subjected to a standard sensory preconditioning design. Animals in the experimental groups received 12 30s simultaneous presentations of a 1800 Hz tone and a 6W houselight, presented at a rate of four per session for three 2h sessions. They then received two fear conditioning sessions during each of which the light was presented for 30s and terminated in a 3 mA, 0.5s footshock. Finally they were tested by presenting the tone separately four times. The two control groups were treated similarly, except that one group received the tone and light unpaired during the first phase whereas the other received the light and shock unpaired in the second phase. For 5 days prior to these treatments, and throughout the remainder of the experiment, the animals also received food reinforcement for bar-pressing on a variable interval schedule. Consequently, the index of conditioning was the extent to which the various stimuli interrupted this bar-pressing, as is standard with a conditioned suppression technique. That interruption was calculated by a ratio of the form $A/(A+B)$, where A and B are the rates of bar-pressing during and prior to the stimulus, respectively.

Figure 2.3 shows the results for the final test session with the tone. It is clear that the experimental group showed substantial suppression whereas neither of the control groups changed responding during the tone ($Us < 9$; $p < 0.02$). The dependence of suppression during the tone upon both the history of simultaneous tone–light presentation and the conditioning of the light suggests the presence of a substantial association between the tone and light. Thus simultaneous associations are also formed among relatively neutral auditory and visual stimuli.

It may also be noted that the use of these stimuli does have one advantage not shared by flavours—the experimenter has excellent control over their physical onset and termination. Consequently, the present experiment assists in avoiding the charge that simultaneous presentation inadvertently results in the sequential occurrence of the events. Although we will later see that there is little reason to fear a substantial contribution from that source in the present preparations, this possibility historically has nagged investigations of simultaneous conditioning.

The previous examples illustrate the possibility of simultaneous associations among events which are relatively equal to each other in terms of their affective value. As noted above, the occurrence of simultaneous associations may be especially likely with such stimuli. However, despite the historical emphasis upon the superiority of sequential stimulus presentation with asymetrically valued items, there has for some time been evidence that simultaneous associations also occur with conventional CSs and USs. That observation has been particularly frequent when shock is used as the US. Although emphasizing other aspects of their data, Mowrer and Aiken (1954) were able to observe the acquisition of substantial punishing power by a tone which had its onset simultaneous with that of shock. More recently, Heth and Rescorla (1973) and Heth (1976) have repeated that observation and subjected it to systematic study. Moreover, Burkhardt and Ayres (1978) have reported such learning as a result of a single tone–shock presentation.

Nor are such observations unique to aversive conditioning procedures. For instance, Holman (1975) has recently found that a flavour which has been presented simultaneously with an attractive sucrose flavour will subsequently be consumed in substantial quantities when presented alone. These results suggest that although simultaneous associations are perhaps especially easy to observe with stimuli of equivalent value, they may also occur when one event is stronger than the other. Thus, associations seem to occur in a range of conditioning preparations which arrange for stimuli to occur simultaneously.

Associations Embedded in Other Paradigms

A great many modern Pavlovian conditioning paradigms employ the simultaneous presentation of multiple stimuli signalling a US. In those procedures, the principal interest centres on the degree to which those stimuli become separately associated with that US. But the observations described above suggest that those procedures may also result in the formation of associations among the simultaneously presented CSs. If so, those associations could be quite pervasive and thus greatly complicate our interpretation of the outcomes of many conditioning paradigms. For this reason, it is important to determine whether or not simultaneous associations occur in a variety of compound stimulus paradigms. In this section, we report three studies carried out by Douglas Gillan and Marjorie Speers which implicate simultaneous associations in three commonly employed procedures. All of these studies employed the flavour-aversion procedure, since it permits the use of multiple stimuli which allow more efficient and elegant designs.

The first Gillan–Speers study addressed the question of whether simultaneous associations are formed between stimuli which serve as equivalent signals of an eventual reinforcer. The sensory preconditioning experiments described above found evidence of that learning as a result of presentations of a compound which itself had no substantial consequent. More typically, Pavlovian paradigms employing multiple stimuli follows those stimuli with a reinforcer. This experiment examined the simplest such case, in which two flavours are repeatedly presented and followed by poison. The issue is whether simultaneous associations are still formed among the elements.

The general procedure was modelled after that shown in Table 2.1. Two groups of 16 rats each initially received exposures either to SH and NQ or to SQ and NH. Then either H or Q was followed by a strong poison whereas the other was presented without reinforcement. During this discrimination, one element was followed once by 0.5 per cent of body weight injection of 0.6 M LiCl; the other was presented four times without consequent. Finally, the animals received two test days which provided simultaneous access to S and N for 10 min. The experiment deviated from the one previously described principally in its following each of the compound presentations with a mild poison, 0.5 per cent of body weight injection of 0.06 M LiCl. The question of interest is whether, despite that poisoning, simultaneous accounts are formed. The reason for selecting a mild poison was to generate slow enough conditioning to ensure reasonable levels of consumption (and therefore exposure to the compounds) over multiple trials. Moreover, it permitted the subsequent use of a stronger poison so as to maximize the difference in current values of Q and H at the time of testing S and N.

Figure 2.4 shows the results of various stages of this experiment. To the left are shown the consumptions of the compounds over their three initial conditioning trials. It is clear that even this mild poison produced rapid and substantial flavour aversion to the compound, reducing consumption to about half its initial level by trial 3 (Wilcoxon $T = 0$; $p < 0.01$). The vertical bars show the mean daily consumption of S and N over the two test days, separated according to whether the paired element had been given a strong poison ($S+$ and $N+$) or had received extinction ($S-$ and $N-$). As in Figure 2.1, consumption of S was generally greater than that of N. But within each solution, it is clear that consumption

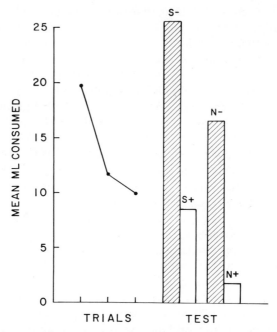

Figure 2.4. Consumption during the training and test phases of a compound flavour experiment. The left portion shows acquisition when S and N in compound with H or Q were poisoned. The test data show consumption of S and N following additional poisoning (+) or extinction (−) with the element which it had been compounded (From Speers, M. A., Gillan, D. J., and Rescorla, R. A., 1980. Within-compound associations in a variety of compound conditioning procedures. *Learning and Motivation, 11*, 135–149. Copyright © 1980 by the Academic Press. Reprinted by permission)

reflected the treatment of the flavour with which it had been compounded. Consumption of S − was greater than that of S + whereas consumption of N − was greater than that of N + ($Us = 13$, $ps < 0.01$). A subsequent test session revealed that, not surprisingly, consumptions of H and Q were governed by their differential treatment, the element paired with a strong poison being consumed with a mean of 1.9 ml and the non-reinforced element being consumed in a mean amount of 18.8 ml.

These results indicate that even when a compound presentation is followed by reinforcing stimulus, simultaneous associations within that compound are readily formed. The fact that those stimuli also signal an event of greater significance does not prevent their becoming associated with each other. Of course these data do not address the issue of whether within-compound learning is reduced by the consequent poison (*see* Cheatle and Rudy, 1978). But they do suggest that, in any conditioning procedure in which two CSs are presented simultaneously so as to be equivalent signals of a US, one must take account of the within-compound associations.

A common variation on experiments which reinforce a compound stimulus is the Kamin blocking procedure (Kamin, 1968, 1969). In that procedure, reinforcement of an AB compound is preceded by the conditioning of A alone. The finding of interest is that such preconditioning of A reduces the amount of conditioning of B which is gained on the subsequent AB + trials. That finding has had great importance for the development of modern theories of Pavlovian conditioning. But the results of such experiments are normally interpreted without reference to the possibility that associations are formed between A and B. Consequently, Gillan and Speers conducted a second experiment which examined the possibility that such associations occur within the context of a blocking procedure.

In its general procedures, this experiment was quite like that just described. Twenty-four thirsty rats received three presentations each either of SH and NQ or of SQ and NH, all followed by the mild LiCl injection. However, prior to this opportunity to learn the simultaneous associations, N and Q had each separately been followed by that same poison on two occassions. That pretreatment of H and Q means that the reinforced compound presentations were embedded in a blocking procedure. Following the reinforced compound presentations, each animal received a single pairing of H or Q with the more substantial poison, embedded in six daily non-reinforced extinction trials with the other element. The intention here, as before, was to maximize the difference in current value of H and Q so as to expose their associations with S and N. Finally, a test session was given during which all animals had simultaneous access to S and N for 10 min. As before, the expectation was that consumption of S and N would reflect the current values of H and Q even though their pairings with those elements took place in the context of a blocking experiment.

Two additional procedural changes were made in order to provide more direct evidence that pairing H and Q with the mild poison was sufficient to condition an aversion. First, 1 hr after each daily exposure to the flavour solutions, the animals received deionized water for 10 min; this procedure more adeqately maintains comparable levels of thirst motivation regardless of the consumptions of the flavoured solutions. That allows a better examination of the acquisition of aversion by those flavours. Second, in a manner orthogonal to the rest of the treatments, each animals received its initial presentation of either H or Q without subsequent poison; then both H and Q received two reinforced presentations. That procedure, together with proper trial sequencing, made it possible to compare, for instance, consumption of H on its second presentation after either H or Q had previously been poisoned once. That comparison of an H previously paired or unpaired with poison allows an inference about the associative consequences of pairing with the poison.

Figure 2.5 shows the results of various stages of this blocking experiment. To the left is shown the acquisition function for H and Q combined. Substantial reduction in consumption resulted from a single poisoning. Furthermore, although not separately displayed here, the mean consumption of a substance

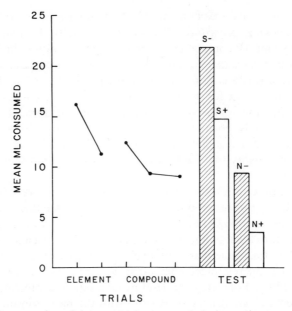

Figure 2.5. Consumption of elements and compounds during various stages of a blocking experiment. To the far left is consumption of H and Q when separately poisoned. The middle portion shows consumption of those elements when S and N were added and poisoning continued. The far right-hand bars show test consumptions of S and N after the element with which they had been compounded was either poisoned (+) or extinguished (−) (From Speers, M. A., Gillan, D. J., and Rescorla, R. A., 1980. Within-compound associations in a variety of compound conditioning procedures. *Learning and Motivation, 11*, 135–149. Copyright © 1980 by the Academic Press Reprinted by permission)

was substantially lower when it, rather than the other substance, had previously received a poisoning trial (10.7 vs. 17.4 ml, respectively; $U = 19, p < 0.05$). Thus the present poison was quite adequate to condition aversion. The addition of S or N to the H and Q elements produced a small disruption in that aversion, but consumption was stable at the end of three compound poisoned trials.

The data of most interest are shown in the vertical bars to the right of this figure. These display separately the consumptions of S and N when the flavours with which they had been presented were either subsequently poisoned (+) or subsequently extinguished (−). As in previous experiments, S was consumed in greater quantities than N. But more importantly, relative consumptions reflected the conditioning histories of H and Q. The consumption of S − was greater than that of S + ($U = 16; p < 0.02$); similarly the consumption of N − was greater than that of N + ($U = 19; p < 0.05$). Consequently, even when their simultaneous presentation takes place in a blocking paradigm, the elements of a compound develop associations with each other. Of course it should be noted that although blocking has been observed in flavour-aversion experiments (Gillan and Domjan, 1977), the present experiment does not contain evidence that blocking actually occurred. However, it does demonstrate that neither the previous conditioning of one element nor the subsequent conditioning of the compound prevent such within-compound learning.

A third theoretically important conditioning paradigm involves the simultaneous presentation of stimuli—the conditioned inhibition paradigm. This paradigm presents to the animal two kinds of conditioning trials, usually in intermixed order: A-alone trials which terminate in reinforcement and AB trials which are non-reinforced. The typical outcome of this precedure is that A develops conditioned excitation, as evidenced by its eliciting a response, whereas B develops conditioned inhibition, as evidenced by its ability to reduce the response which A would normally produce. Together with blocking, this outcome has provoked considerable theoretical attention. However, also as in the case of blocking, that attention has been focused primarily on the nature of the association between B and the reinforcer; relatively less attention has been paid to the potential role of the simultaneous association between A and B. In the experiment to be described, Gillan and Speers explored that possibility.

In its general features, this experiment was quite like those previously described. Thirty-five thirsty rats received two 10 min exposures each with the H and Q solutions, each followed by an injection of 0.5 per cent body weight of 0.06 M LiCl. Over the next 10 days, each animal received four non-reinforced presentations of H and Q each presented jointly with either S or N. For half the animals the compounds were SH and NQ whereas for half they were SQ and NH. In addition, each animal received one trial each of H and Q presented separately and followed by the mild poison. In this procedure H and Q play the roles of two different A stimuli in an $A+/AB-$ conditioned inhibition paradigm. In this experiment the concentrations of the flavours were changed somewhat in an effort to better equate the palatabilities of S and N as well as H and Q. The S was a 0.05 M sucrose, and N a 0.1 M salt, the Q a 0.00003 M quinine and the H a 0.005 M HCl.

To identify whether S and N have associations with their respective excitors, each animal was then given one exposure to either H or Q followed by a strong (0.6 M) LiCl injection; in addition, the other A stimulus was presented three times without reinforcement. Finally S and N were presented simultaneously for 10 min in a test session. The question was whether consumption of the equivalently inhibitory S and N would reflect the differential subsequent conditioning treatment of their respective excitors.

Figure 2.6 shows the data from several stages of this experiment. The first set of bars displays the consumption from the final two trials of the conditioned inhibition training procedure, for both pairs of stimuli combined. The trial sequence was such as to permit this comparison among adjacent trials so as to display the low consumption of A, but the relatively greater consumption of the AB compounds. That difference constitutes one form of evidence that conditioned inhibition developed in this experiment. Although complete comparison conditions were not included, it is relevant to note that this difference developed

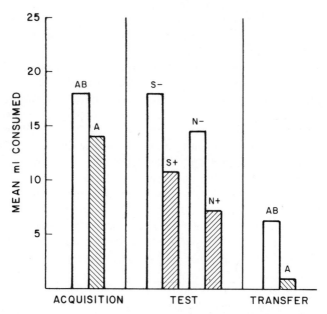

Figure 2.6. Consumption during various stages of a conditioned inhibition experiment. To the left are terminal consumptions of an excitor A (either HCl or quinine) and that excitor in conjunction with an inhibitory B (either salt or sucrose). Subsequent strong poisoning of H or Q depressed intake of that inhibitor which had been paired with the poisoned excitor (S + or N +). The final panel shows the transfer of B's inhibition to the newly poisoned other excitor

over the course of $A+/AB-$ training. The middle two sets of bars show the consumptions of S and N when their excitors either had been given a strong poison (S+ and N+) or had been extinguished (S− and N−). Despite the changed flavour concentrations, consumption of S was still somewhat greater than that of N. But for both stimuli, consumption was greater when its paired excitor had been extinguished, rather than highly poisoned. In both cases that difference was reliable ($Us < 78$; $ps < 0.05$). Thus these results suggest that indeed within-compound associations had been formed between the inhibitors and their respective excitors.

The final set of bars shows the results of an additional test for the inhibitory power of S and N. In this test, each animal was given a choice between two solutions. One solution was the H or Q which had been paired with the strong poison; the other was that same flavour presented in compound with the inhibitor previously paired with the *other* excitor. For instance, an animal which received SH and NQ followed by pairing of H with a strong poison, received in this test a choice between H and NH. The issue is whether NH will be consumed in preference to H. This question is of interest because the procedure assesses the inhibitory power of N against an excitor other than that used to endow it with inhibition. Successful transfer of this sort would speak against an alternative interpretation of the role of S and N solely in terms of configural conditioning (Skinner, 1938). It is clear from the final set of data that indeed this transfer occurred, with consumption of AB exceeding that of A (Wilcoxon $T = 0$; $p < 0.01$). Thus the present experiment suggests that even when a stimulus is an inhibitor with respect to a US, it can enter into an association with its simultaneously presented conditioned excitor.

This set of experiments suggests that the occurrence of simultaneous associations among relatively neutral stimuli is a fairly widespread occurrence. It appears in several conditioning preparations, and, at least within the flavour-aversion preparation, under a wide range of reinforcement circumstances. Such associations occur even when the simultaneous occurrence is followed by a primary reinforcer, when the stimuli are embedding in a blocking paradigm and when one is developing conditioned inhibition based on the other. It is not too speculative to suggest that whenever two stimuli are presented simultaneously there is a reasonable likelihood that they will become associated with each other.

This conclusion could have important implications for the study of Pavlovian conditioning generally. It suggests that not all of the behaviour which one sees during a CS results from its learned relations to the primary reinforcer. As demonstrated in the previous experiments, some of that behaviour depends upon associations with other stimuli which in turn may be associated with the US. This greatly complicates theoretical analysis of compound stimulus paradigms. For instance, the frequent observation that in a blocking paradigm the added element gains some conditioned strength might be due to these simultaneous associations rather than to any incompleteness of the blocking of the association between that element and the US. Similarly, the extensive training often needed to produce a conditioned inhibitor might be partly attributable to its simultaneous association with an excitor which masks the observation of that inhibition. We will see below several procedures which can be used to attenuate the appearance of simultaneous associations, but the present results caution one not to ignore them.

Comparison Between Sequential and Simultaneous Associations

The preceding discussion leaves little doubt about the reality of simultaneous associations. But the Pavlovian conditioning literature is replete with assertions about the inferiority of such associations compared with those formed when stimulus presentation is sequential. Such assertions have been common not only for the associations between CSs and USs but also for those formed between relatively neutral CSs (e.g. Thompson, 1972).

However, an examination of the comparison from which those conclusions are usually drawn raises questions about their adequacy. Consider a typical procedure designed to compare the degree of learning under sequential and simultaneous presentation modes. One might examine two groups, one which receives stimulus A followed by B and another which receives A and B presented simultaneously. Subsequently, perhaps after some additional conditioning manipulations with B, A is presented alone and the response to it examined. The modal outcome is that the response to A is greater if sequential presentation has been used. However, the treatment of A in the two groups differs in a number of ways which are confounded with the difference in A's temporal relation to B. An important additional difference is that during conditioning one group received A presented alone whereas the other did not. That separate presentation might have a number of consequences. For instance, the concurrent presence of B in the simultaneous group might reduce the degree to which A is successfully processed as a stimulus. Relatedly, the presence of B may modify any habituation of A which would otherwise have occurred. Moreover, the test procedure of necessity involves the separate presentation of A; but that constitutes a substantial change in procedure for the simultaneous group, a change which might result in stimulus generalization decrement. These differences may be argued to have a variety of consequences for performance, but whatever their effect, they preclude the attribution of differences in performance during A uniquely to the differences in the temporal relation it bore to B. It is possible that in the absence of these confounded differences, the strength of the association formed between simultaneously presented stimuli would be determined to be as strong or even stronger than that formed between sequentially presented stimuli.

For this reason, we recently attempted to devise a procedure for comparing learning under these two presentation modes which avoids some of these confoundings and therefore provides a more fair comparison. The notion of this procedure was to match the context of presentation of the A stimulus for animals which are subsequently examined for simultaneous and sequential associations. To this end, the procedure presents three stimuli to each animal on each trial. In particular, an AB compound stimulus is followed immediately by the presentation of B'. In this three-stimulus presentation, A bears a simultaneous relation to B but a sequential relation to B'. In order to assess separately the strength of these two associations, some animals subsequently receive conditioning of B and some of B', and finally A is tested. Notice that all animals receive the same exposure to A during the initial learning and test. That is, the context of A's presentations is similar for all animals. They differ only in whether B or B' is subsequently conditioned and thus in whether the A–B or the A–B' association is measured. Under these circumstances, one might hope to measure more purely the importance of the temporal relation.

Our first application of this design employed three groups of eight rats each in a flavour-aversion experiment outlined in Table 2.2. In this experiment, all stimulus presentations were 5 min long and employed the elementary flavours of the previous experiment. Although H and Q were counterbalanced within each treatment group, for ease of exposition that counterbalancing is ignored in Table 2.2. The first two groups (S and F) both received 4 days on which an SH compound was followed immediately by Q alone. On those 4 days, the control group received 5 min of H followed by 5 min of Q. On those intermixed days, the first two groups received 5 min of access to water followed immediately by an

Table 2.2. Design of sequential–simultaneous association experiment

Group	Phase 1	Phase 2	Test
Simultaneous	SH-Q, W-W	H +, Q −	S, W
Forward	SH-Q, W-W	H −, Q +	S, W
Control	S-W, H-Q	H +, Q − or H −, Q +	S, W

Note: S, sucrose; H, hydrochloric acid; Q, quinine; W, water; +, toxin; −, non-reinforcement.

additional 5 min of water. In each case, the solutions were presented through stainless steel tubes inserted into the front of the homecage; the transition between flavours was essentially immediate since the rats drank as soon as the tubes were inserted. The consequence of the first stage of this experiment is that two groups received paired presentation of S with H (simultaneously) and with Q (sequentially) whereas the control animals received unpaired presentations of S with the H–Q sequence. Moreover, all animals received the same total access to the S, H, and Q flavours.

Following this exposure, animals in Group S (simultaneous) received 2 days of 10 min access to H followed immediately by 0.5 percent of body weight injection of 0.6 M LiCl; on 3 intermixed days they received non-reinforced 10 min exposures to Q. Animals in F (forward) were treated identically except that H and Q were interchanged. Half of the animals in the control group received each of these treatments. Finally, all animals were given a single day on which both sucrose and water were simultaneously available for 10 min in separate tubes. For Group S that test assesses the strength of the simultaneous S–H association; for Group F it measures the strength of the forward S–Q association. The control group provides a baseline against which to measure both.

Figure 2.7 shows the consumptions of sucrose and water in each of the three groups. In the control group, sucrose was consumed in greater quantities than was water; the levels found here are consistent with those expected on the basis of available preference data (e.g. Pfaffmann, 1960). Both of the experimental groups showed relatively less consumption of sucrose than did the control. This is particularly striking for the simultaneous group ($U = 8.5$; $p < 0.02$) and, surprisingly, somewhat more marginal for the sequential group ($U = 15$; $p < 0.05$). Indeed, the most striking feature of these data is the substantial difference suggesting more successful formation of simultaneous, compared with sequential, associations ($U = 14$; $p < 0.05$). Consumption of water shows an opposite pattern, suggestive of compensation in total fluid intake. Subsequent repeated one- and two-bottle tests with H followed the course of its extinction but found no differences among the groups in level of aversion. Thus these data suggest that under the present comparison procedure simultaneous associations are stronger than sequential ones. It appears that a relatively less biased assessment procedure can result in a different conclusion than that normally

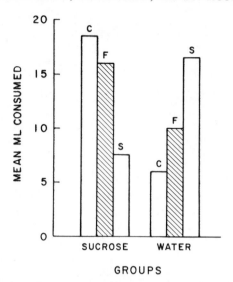

Figure 2.7. Consumption of sucrose and water following poisoning of H or Q. Sucrose had previously been presented in an unpaired (C), forward (F), or simultaneous (S) relation with the poisoned element. (From Rescorla, R. A., 1980. Simultaneous and successive associations in sensory preconditioning. *Journal of Experimental Psychology: Animal Behavior Processes*, **6**, 207–216. Copyright © 1978 by the American Psychological Association. Reprinted by permission)

drawn about temporal relations.

Because of the unusual nature of this outcome, it seemed important to provide additional evidence, particularly with regard to its generality. We will here report two additional experiments which suggest that it may indeed have some generality. The first explores another set of temporal parameters within the flavour-aversion preparation. The second examines an analogous set of manipulations in a conditioned suppression procedure.

One might legitimately be concerned that the forward temporal interval used in the previous study was too long to anticipate the formation of a substantial association. Even though flavour-aversion learning is renowned for its ability to tolerate long time intervals, most available evidence suggests better conditioning with shorter intervals (e.g. Revusky and Garcia, 1970). Moreover, Lavin (1976) has reported good sequential association among flavours with short interstimulus intervals, but little learning with trace intervals of the order of 30 s. Consequently, even though a delayed procedure was used here, it is possible that the 5 min temporal interval between the onset of A and that of B′ was so long that even a simultaneous procedure yielded superior results.

To examine that possibility, the study was replicated using quite short, 10 s, stimulus durations. Sixteen thirsty rats were subjected to the procedures outlined for the first two groups in Table 2.2. On each of 3 days, each animal received four exposures to either SH followed by Q or to SQ followed by H. Within a day, 5 min intervened between trials. Then all animals received 2 days on which either H or Q was presented for 10 min and followed immediately by an injection of 0.6 M LiCl. After 3 additional days of 10 min of drinking water per day, all animals were given 3 days of testing. During the tests, the animals has simultaneous access to sucrose in one tube and water in another.

The results of those test sessions are shown in Figure 2.8. The outcome of primary interest is the greater rejection of sucrose in the simultaneous group. That group consumed both less sucrose ($U = 14$; $p < 0.05$) and more water ($U = 15$, $p < 0.05$) than did the sequential group. Even with these short stimulus durations, sequential presentation apparently generated a weaker association. Although the present experiment did not contain an unpaired control treatment, it is relevant to note that the consumption of sucrose was relatively low in the sequential group. That observation suggests that perhaps with such short stimulus durations, sequential associations are formed, although remaining weaker than simultaneous as ociations.

The use of these short intervals in a flavour-aversion procedure raises one

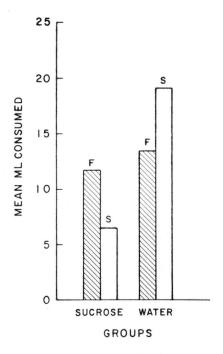

Figure 2.8. Consumption of sucrose which had a forward or simultaneous relation with a subsequently poisoned element. (From Rescorla, R. A., 1980. Simultaneous and successive associations in sensory preconditioning. *Journal of Experimental Psychology: Animal Behavior Processes*, **6**, 207–216. Copyright © 1978 by the American Psychological Association. Reprinted by permission)

difficult interpretative question. It seems likely that these flavours persist in the animal's mouth for a time after a particular solution has been withdrawn. With short time intervals, that persistance may be such that a substantial portion of the second solution is consumed in the presence of the after-effects of the first solution. The result is that a supposedly sequential stimulus presentation may effectively become a simultaneous procedure. Consequently, in the present case, the high level of sequential learning may actually be attributable to unintended simultaneous exposure.

Even though these results are strong, one might still suspect that the case of flavours and the flavour-aversion paradigm is special. As a consequence, we have further compared sequential and simultaneous presentation using a conditioned suppression procedure. This procedure allows the use of auditory and visual stimuli and a shock US, stimuli which permit better temporal control. In general the experiment followed the logic of the previous two experiments. After initial bar-press training for food on a VI schedule, three groups of animals were exposed to trials involving three stimuli, each 30 s in duration: illumination of the houselight (L), presentation of an 1800 Hz tone (T) and presentation of a white noise (N). For one group ($n = 16$), each day contained four trials on which the TL compound was followed immediately by N. For another group ($n = 16$), N and T were interchanged. The third group ($n = 8$) received four separate 30 s presentations each of T, L, and N each day. Following 3 days of this exposure, half the animals in each group received fear conditioning with T and half with N. That conditioning consisted first of 2 days on each of which one auditory stimulus was followed immediately by a 3 mA, 0.5 s footshock whereas the other was presented four times without shock. Then, because of the extensive generalization between T and N, each animal received an additional 4 days on each of which the non-reinforced auditory stimulus was presented alone four additional times. The consequence of this treatment is, as in previous experiments, that for some animals a stimulus presented simultaneously with L was conditioned whereas for others a stimulus which followed L was conditioned. The third group was a control group in which L was never paired with either stimulus. To assess the state of L in the various groups, a single test session presented four non-reinforced lights while the animal engaged in bar-pressing. Finally, to confirm that indeed the auditory stimuli controlled different levels of fear, each animal received a session in which T and N were each presented twice without reinforcement. Throughout, the measure of conditioning was the degree to which the stimuli suppressed the ongoing bar-pressing.

Figure 2.9 shows the mean suppression ratios during the light for the control animals and the various experimental groups. It is clear that in the control animals the light produced no evidence of suppression. However, within each of the experimental groups, those animals which had been fear conditioned with the auditory stimulus presented simultaneously with the lights showed substantial suppression of bar pressing during the light. But those animals with the sequentially-presented auditory stimulus conditioned showed little evidence of

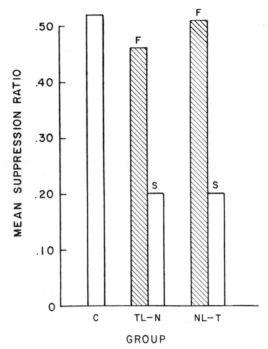

Figure 2.9. Mean suppression ratio during a light (L) following fear conditioning of either a tone (T) or noise (N). In the control (C) animals L, T, and N had been unpaired. Some experimental animals received TL–N and some NL–T presentation; half of each group then received fear conditioning of the element simultaneous (S) with L or the stimulus to which L had borne a forward (F) relation. (From Rescorla, R. A., 1980. Simultaneous and successive associations in sensory preconditioning. *Journal of Experimental Psychology: Animal Behavior Processes*, **6**, 207–216. Copyright © 1978 by the American Psychological Association. Reprinted by permission)

suppression during the light. Overall, suppression attributable to simultaneous associations was greater than that produced either in the control or sequential groups ($Us = 5$, 26; $ps < 0.001$). Subsequent testing of the auditory stimuli confirmed that their differential conditioning had been effective, the reinforced stimulus yielded a mean suppression ratio of 0.05 whereas the non-reinforced stimulus resulted in a ratio of 0.39. There were no differences in the responses to auditory stimuli among the three groups. These results thus confirm, in a conditioned suppression setting, those observed earlier using a flavour-aversion procedure: when compared in the present manner, simultaneous associations can be stronger than sequential ones. This outcome accords with the historical emphasis upon exact simultaneity rather than temporal asynchrony as the primary condition for producing associative learning.

It should be emphasized that these results have all been obtained with stimuli of relatively similar value to each other. It is not clear whether this particular comparison procedure would yield similar outcomes when stimuli differ from each other in value. In that case, of course, the problem of different presentation contexts for A is even more severe, since A either occurs alone or in conjunction with a potent stimulus. But the application of the present three-stimulus procedure to the case of standard CSs and USs may be difficult. It would necessitate having two unconditioned stimuli which evoke detectably different conditioned responses and which provide similar contexts for the presentation of A. Without the former it would be difficult to know whether any conditioning of A resulted from its simultaneous relation to B or its sequential one to B'. Without the latter one could not match the contexts of the presentation of A. Consequently, this issue may be one which is more easily answered with moderately valued stimuli which can then be endowed with differences in value by the experimenter. But these results certainly encourage the exploration of alternative ways of comparing simultaneous and sequential presentation modes in a range of Pavlovian settings.

An Alternative View of Simultaneous Associations

The associationist tradition is so strong in American psychology that it has dominated the study of learning. It proposes a seductive account of the construction of knowledge according to which the organism begins with a few elements and constructs its view of the world in terms of learned relations among those elements. This possibility has been widely applied since the enthusiastic descriptions by the British associationists. It has clearly invaded the study of Pavlovian conditioning. As illustrated by the discussion of the previous sections, students of Pavlovian conditioning also have viewed the organism as beginning with a set of distinguishable elements and learning the relations among them. Various languages have been used to describe the elements associat-ed—sensations, responses, stimuli, ideas—but most students of learning have shared the assumption that learning is primarily a matter of associating given elements.

But throughout the history of the study of learning there has been a less popular counterproposal. According to this alternative view the organism does not start with differentiated elements and construct larger units; rather, it starts with more gross representations of units and learns to differentiate the components. This view has been especially applied to the case in which the organism learns the properties of an event or object. A good characterization of this general view is given by Robbinson (1932):

> One source of error in this situation is the tendency to assume psychological association wherever there is a lack of discrimination between two items of experience or behavior. When the little child sees the whole lamb, are we to assume that head and legs and body and tail of the perceptual ruminant are held together through the operation of the principles of association? Clearly

such an assumption is folly, because it involves the reverse assumption that the disparity of these various members of the lamb was an original condition for the baby. Disparity, however, means some definite kind of isolation and it is rediculous to suppose that the separation of these particular segments was ever a forerunner of their integration. The psychological individual no more makes his start as a perfect analyzer whose analyses must be overcome, than he does as an equally perfect synthesizer (p. 61).

Here Robinson argued that in an important sense the elements which are 'associated' to give the impression of an object do not initially exist as separate elements at all. Rather their identification is itself the product of some learning process. Robinson was neither the first nor the last to suggest such a view. James (1890) articulated this possibility, himself citing earlier authors. Indeed, James gave this possibility a status almost co-ordinate with that of association. For the purpose he employed the term 'dissociation' to indicate the need, through learning, to segregate the parts of an originally unitary stimulus. A similar view of stimulus processing runs through the writings of the Gestalt psychologists. More recently, this alternative has surfaced in the perceptual learning literature with Gibson and Gibson (1955) and more recently Gibson (1969) as the principal advocates.

This view suggests an account of the previously described simultaneous associations which is somewhat different from the traditional explanation. When the organism receives a compound presentation, such as one of SH, instead of analysing it into its component parts and then reassociating those parts, it simply forms a representation of the total SH stimulus. Indeed, in many cases it is difficult to see how, in the absence of other information, the organism could select a particular way to analyse the complex flavour. Certainly there is little compelling reason to expect it to carry out the analysis along the same lines that the experimenter synthesized the flavour. Even in the case where the elements lie in different modalities, such as a light and a tone, the animal may initially treat the TL event as a unit rather than as a stimulus composed of those particular elements.

According to this description, the reason that subsequent poisoning of H and testing of S lead to rejection of S is that both elements are perceptually similar to the SH compound. Consequently, during their initial exposures they reactivate the representation of that compound. When H is poisoned, the reactivation of SH together with the poison results in the conditioning of aversion to the SH unit; when S is then presented, it reactivates that aversive unit and so is consumed in reduced quantities. It is not that S and H are associated but rather that they both are, at least temporarily, mistaken for SH by the organism. This view of 'associative' learning is very similar to that discussed by Asch, Ceroso, and Heimer (1960) in describing learning of the relation between form and mode in visually presented stimuli. They argued that component parts of a figure form a unitary representation rather than separate component representations which are then associated.

Of course, with repeated exposure to the separately presented elements, one would expect the organism also to form representations of those elements, producing what James called dissociation. When that happens, the identified elements might well enter into associations in the way theories normally describe, but they would no longer be mistaken for the compound.

Notice that this discussion centres on simultaneously presented stimuli. It is in that case that the organism cannot readily know how to do the analysis of the stimulus. With sequential stimulus presentation, the inherent separate element occurrence would reduce any such unitary learning and favour the formation of associations among identified elements.

This account is both speculative and vague. Moreover, it may appear to be only verbally different to assert that S and H each reactivate a unitary SH rather than asserting that S and H reactivate each other via an association. However, this description does suggest a number of experimental manipulations which are of interest. For one thing it may help to make sense out of the superiority of the simultaneous mode of presenting stimuli described above. According to this account what we have called simultaneous associations are not really associations at all but something more akin to failures of discrimination. Consequently, especially for materials which may enter into standard associations relatively poorly, such as the neutral events explored here, it may not be surprising that a different process could produce superior results.

Of more potential interest, this account suggests a way to manipulate the magnitude of simultaneous associations. Since it views their appearance as a mistaken identification of the element with the compound, it anticipates that procedures which promote discrimination between the two should sharply reduce the effects described above. Even in its present vague form, this account would anticipate that one way to promote such a discrimination would be to expose the subject to the elements separately. Separate exposure to either S or H should interfere with the ability of a sequence of SH presentation and H poisoning to produce an aversion to S. In what follows we describe some experiments that employ that basic idea in a number of variations. The results follow naturally from this alternative view. They are not always anticipated by an associationist view.

An initial exploration of the importance of separate element exposure was carried out by Rescorla and Freberg (1978) in the form of an 'extinction' experiment. Three groups of thirsty rats were first exposed to the SH compound for 10 min on each of 4 days. Then, in an attempt to destroy the learning so produced, Group S received 6 days of 10 min exposure to S alone and Group H received similar exposure to H alone. A third group (W) received only water on those days. All three groups then received 3 days on which H was followed by a 0.6 M LiCl injection and a final test in which S was given as an alternative to water. That final test was intended to evaluate the status of the SII learning. A fourth group (S/H) was also run, treated identically to Group W except that during the first phase of the experiment S and H were presented in an unpaired fashion.

Figure 2.10 shows the results of the test, displaying consumption of S and W separately. First, notice that Groups W and S/H differed substantially in consumption of S. Those groups constitute the paired and unpaired treatment groups of a standard sensory preconditioning experiment; their difference indicates the presence of substantial SH learning in Group W. More interestingly, exposure to either S or H in the interim between SH exposure and H+ treatment markedly reduced the aversion to S. That outcome suggests that indeed separate presentation of the elements was disruptive, in the manner expected by the dissociation hypothesis.

Of course, there are alternative ways of viewing this disruption. For instance, separate presentation of S and H could have purely non-associative effects, such as the reduction of neophobia of S or the development of latent inhibition to H.

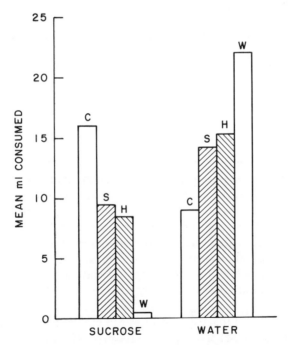

Figure 2.10. Consumptions of sucrose and water after poisoning of H. In Group C, S and H had previously been unpaired. In Groups S, H, and W, SH pairing preceded poisoning of H, but additional presentations of S, H, or water (W) intervened prior to H poisoning. (From Rescorla and Freberg (1978). The extinction of within-compound flavor associations. *Learning and Motivation*, **4**, 411–427. Reprinted by Permission of Academic Press Inc)

Either of those well-documented phenomena would be expected to attenuate aversion to S in the present experiment. However, Rescorla and Freberg (1978) have marshalled evidence that such non-associative processes cannot fully account for the disruptive effects of separate element presentation. Perhaps their most convincing argument is that these effects also occur in the parallel sodium deficiency procedure described earlier. In that procedure, one may identify the occurrence of QN learning through the increased consumption of Q when the animal experiences a sodium deficit. However, the separate presentation of either N or Q between the time of QN exposure and the test of Q sharply attenuates the consumption of Q. Since with this procedure no standard Pavlovian conditioning phase is included, differences in latent inhibition cannot account for the outcome. Moreover, any reduction in neophobia of either N or Q which results from their separate presentation should not in itself lead to reduced consumption of Q during the test. Consequently, this change in consumption with separate element presentation appears to involve more than simply these non-associative processes; instead it depends upon the organism's learning something new about the relation between N and Q.

Of course, an account of simultaneous learning in terms of the simple formation of an association between S and H would also anticipate that separate presentation of S would increase its acceptance during the final test. Such a procedure constitutes an extinction operation for the S–H association. However, somewhat less expected from that view is the decremental effect of separately presenting H following SH or N following NQ. Those outcomes imply a symmetry not normally attributed to Pavlovian associations.

In her dissertation, Freberg (1979) explored the range of circumstances under which separate element presentation disrupts performance. In general, her results suggest that any manner of presenting an element outside of the compound is disruptive. For instance, the presentation of S before SH exposure has much the same effect as does its presentation following SH. Similarly, presentation of S in compound with another flavour, such as Q, attenuates the aversion observed as a result of the SH/H+ sequence. That attenuation also occurs whatever the order of SH and SQ presentation. It is worth noting that this presentation of an element in several contexts was one of the techniques suggested by James (1890) for producing dissociation.

In order to emphasize the rule that any separate presentation of S will disrupt the exhibition of SH learning, Freberg carried out one particularly striking experiment. The idea of that experiment was to present S separately but in close temporal proximity to SH. The design of the experiment is shown in Table 2.3. The first group received, on each of 4 days, a 5 min exposure to SH; in order to match fluid intakes with the other groups, that exposure was preceded by 5 min of water. The second group received the sucrose alone in place of that water. Notice that for this group, S was separately presented but in a close temporal relation to H, in a manner analogous to that of a delayed CS. That procedure is

Table 2.3. Design of Freberg's (1978) separate exposure experiment

Group	Phase 1	Phase 2	Test
1	W-SH	H +	S, W
2	S-SH	H +	S, W
3	SH-S	H +	S, W
4	S-H	H +	S, W
5	S-S/H-H	H +	S, W

Note: S, sucrose; H, hydrochloric acid; W, water; +, toxin; −, non-reinforcement.

normally expected to maximize the formation of a Pavlovian association. The third group received these same events, but in the reverse order. Group 4 provided a conventional sequential presentation for comparison with Groups 1 and 2. Finally, the last group was a control which received two 5 min exposures of S and two 5 min exposures of H, each on half of its exposure days. All groups subsequently received two poisoned exposures to H and were tested for consumption of sucrose and water.

Figure 2.11 shows the results of that consumption test. As before, comparison of Groups 5 and 2 indicates that substantial SH learning occurred in the latter group. However, the separate presentation of S either immediately before (Group 2) or immediately after (Group 3) presentation of the SH compound markedly disrupted the aversive reaction to S ($Us = 8, 15; ps < 0.05$). Finally, Group 4, which received a sequential presentation of S and H, showed no evidence of learning, confirming earlier findings of little sequential association in this preparation with these particular parameters. The consumption of water showed the converse pattern.

These results may best be understood by presuming that all of the SH learning occurred when the two flavours were presented simultaneously. Any separate presentation of S, even that which converts the simultaneous into a delayed procedure, had a deleterious effect. That data pattern seems compatable with the kind of dissociation view described above. The separate presentation of S should facilitate its discrimination from SH.

A further result of separate element presentation provides additional evidence compatable with that view, but less comfortable for a standard associative account. According to the dissociation view, the separate element presentation disrupts performance not so much because it destroys the SH learning, but rather because it allows the organism to discriminate between the SH flavour and its separate S and H elements. Once that discrimination has been made, there is no further reason for the organism to confuse S or H with SH; consequently,

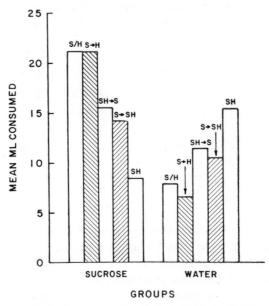

Figure 2.11. Consumption of sucrose and water in animals receiving various treatments with S and H prior to poisoning of H. Group S/H had unpaired presentation. Group S–H, SH–S and S–SH received sequences as indicated by their group designations. Group SH received simultaneous S and H presentation. (From Freberg (1979) by permission of the author)

although the SH representation may still exist, the present procedures do not reveal its presence. The problem is not so much that SH learning has been destroyed as that, following 'extinction', the separate presentations of S and H no longer tap that learning. Consequently, from this viewpoint one would not anticipate that 'extinction' could be reversed by simply presenting SH again; that is, one would not expect retraining to be successful after separate element presentation. That expectation appears to be at variance from one based on an assumption that S and H are associated with one another by a connection which obeys accepted laws of Pavlovian conditioning. If SH presentation establishes an S–H association which separate S presentation extinguishes, then one would expect not only that subsequent SH presentation would retrain the association but also that the retraining would be more rapid than was original learning.

In order to examine these alternatives, Freberg (1979) attempted to retrain the compound learning after its extinction. For this purpose, the sodium deficit procedure was adopted. As noted earlier, that procedure is less sensitive to the non-associative effects of differences in number of flavour presentations which an extinction and retraining procedure necessitates. Three groups of rats initially received four daily exposures to 10 min of QN. Then two of those groups received six daily exposures of Q alone, in order to produce extinction; the third group received water on those days. Six exposures were chosen because prior work had indicated that they would produce a substantial, but incomplete, attenuation in the consumption of Q. It was hoped in this way to maximize sensitivity to the effects of a retraining operation. To attempt retraining, one of the extinguished groups then received on additional 4 days of QN presentation. Previous results had indicated that initial QN learning is asymptotic after four such trials. Finally, all animals had a sodium deficit induced by formalin injection and were tested after being deprived of water for 3 h. The test consisted of 20 min of simultaneous exposure to both Q and water. The experiment also contained a fourth, control, group which had Q and N presented initially in an unpaired fashion and then received neither extinction nor retraining.

Figure 2.12 shows the consumptions of Q and W during the test. First notice that the unpaired control animals (U) consumed little Q. That result is not surprising since this concentration of Q is normally rejected by non-thirsty rats which have a water alternative. However, the group with QN exposure but no extinction showed an intermediate level of performance, which differed from both the untrained control and the unextinguished experimental animals ($Us = 7$, 7; $ps < 0.02$). Of most interest, the retrained group (R) showed a consumption level almost identical to that of the extinguished group. It too differed from the unpaired control and the unextinguished group ($U = 11$, 13;

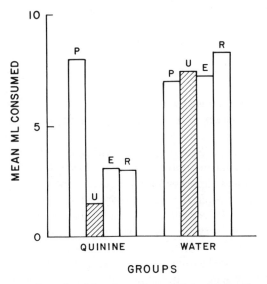

Figure 2.12. Consumption of quinine in sodium deficient rats. Groups P and U had received, respectively, paired and unpaired presentation of quinine (Q) and salt (N). Group E additionally received separate extinction presentations of Q. Group R received both extinction and additional QN presentations to produce reconditioning. (From Freberg (1979) by permission of the author)

$ps < 0.05$), but not from the extinguished group. Water levels in this experiment were not compensatory because the test was conducted under a low level of thirst; salt need was the primary basis for consumption. A final test of the consumption of salt 1 h after the Q test verified the strength and equality of the sodium deficit in the various groups. Mean consumption of salt in a 20 min test varied from 48 to 52 ml, substantial levels indeed.

These results thus replicate the earlier data on the success of separate element presentation in producing 'extinction'. However, they also suggest that the extinction is not subject to retraining by the simple re-exposure to the conditions of original learning. A procedure adequate to accomplish initial learning had no detectable effect as a retraining technique. That outcome seems most compatable with the dissociation view suggested here. Once the organism knows that the separate elements occur, it no longer confuses them with the compound. However, this apparent inability to retrain is not to be expected if extinction has reduces a Q–N association which follows the laws of Pavlovian conditioning.

Finally, it is worth noting that this dissociation view suggests a prescription for maximizing the magnitude of behaviour in a sensory preconditioning experiment. That prescription involves two guidelines which are frequently violated. First, present S_1 and S_2 simultaneously. Presumably simultaneous presentation makes it possible for the organism to use a process like that suggested here. It also permits, of course, the option of standard associations. Second, minimize the frequency of separate S_1 and S_2 presentations. Many investigators violate this second guideline in two ways. First, they pre-expose their stimuli because of a concern that they be 'neutral'. As we have noted, that procedure is harmful. Second, and perhaps less obviously, they carry out extensive conditioning on S_1 after the S_2–S_1 pairings. This is apparently done in the belief that maximizing the response to S_1, will maximize the opportunity to see a response to S_2. However, repeatedly reinforcing S_1 may also have a detrimental effect to the extent that it enables the animal to separate the elements of the S_2–S_1 compound. Notice that in all of the experiments reported here substantial conditioning of S_1 was obtained with a minimum number of separate presentations. Instead of many trials, a potent US was used.

A recent conditioned suppression experiment conducted in our laboratory emphasizes this latter danger. In its general procedures it was like the experiment reported in Figure 2.3. Rats were first trained to bar-press for food reward and then subjected to a sensory preconditioning treatment. First, four groups of animals received 3 days of exposure on each of which four 30 s simultaneous presentations of a 1800 Hz tone and a houselight occurred. A control group received instead four separate presentations each of T and L. Then the four experimental groups received different conditioning treatments with the light and a 3 mA, 0.5 s footshock. Three of the groups received, respectively, one, two, and six L+ trials, administered at the rate of one per session. The fourth experimental group received first four L − and then two L + trials. During this phase the control group received two L − trials. Finally, all animals received four non-reinforced test exposures with T and then repeated extinction testing with L. The issue is how suppression to T will vary with these different treatments of L.

Figure 2.13 shows the test results for the tone and light. Look first at responding during the tone for those animals all of which received two shocked presentations of L. The greater suppression in the experimental group, compared with the control, replicates earlier results. The intermediate suppression in the group which received four non-reinforced lights between TL presentation and its two L+ trials demonstrates that separate element presentation has an effect which is like that reported earlier. However, the results of most interest are those from the three experimental groups which received different numbers of L+ trials; those groups are joined by the solid line. It is clear that although one L + trial was less than completely effective, two L + trials resulted in substantial suppression during the tone. Of most interest, that suppression was less in the animals which received six L + trials ($U = 11$; $p < 0.02$). It is clear that those four additional L + trials hurt, rather than helped, the opportunity to observe sensory preconditioning of the tone. Apparently four L − trials were more disruptive than four L + trials, however, since the six L + group was more suppressed than the group which received four L − and then two L + ($U = 12$; $p < 0.02$). But it is clear that one can carry out too much conditioning of S_1 in a sensory preconditioning experiment.

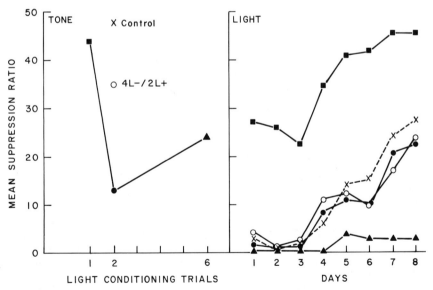

Figure 2.13. Conditioned suppression during a tone which had been presented simultaneously with a light. The light then received one, two, or six pairings with shock. Group 4L − /2L + received four non-reinforced lights prior to two reinforced lights. Group C received L and T unpaired prior to two L + trials

The right-hand side of the figure shows the results of extinction testing with the light. Those results indicate that differences among the groups receiving two L+ trials are not attributable to differences in conditioning of the light. They suggest that the lower suppression during the tone in the group receiving one L+ trials was due to less conditioning of the light; but they also verify that six L+ trials improved fear conditioning of the light at the same time as it attenuated sensory preconditioning with the tone.

This experiment suggests that indeed the prescription given by a dissociation viewpoint is an accurate one. Separate presentation of an element can disrupt our ability to observe sensory preconditioning even when that presentation is done in the service of changing the value of that element.

Conclusion

The intention of this chapter has been to illustrate the existence of substantial learning when relatively neutral stimuli are presented simultaneously with each other. Using principally the flavour-aversion preparation, but employing evidence from other preparations as well, we have displayed powerful examples of such learning. Moreover, we have observed a fairly broad range of conditioning procedures normally carried out with multiple stimuli to have such simultaneous associations embedded within them. We have also suggested that much of the evidence normally taken as showing that simultaneous associations are weaker than sequential ones may depend upon the use of a particular comparison procedure. An alternative procedure yielded quite different results. Finally, we suggested an alternative, perceptual, way of viewing the learning which occurs with simultaneous presentation. Several experiments on the effects of separate element presentation yielded results compatible with that view. Moreover, that view provides a description of the circumstances which maximize the ability to observe sensory preconditioning. As a set, the results reported here suggest that substantial, important, and perhaps qualitatively different, learning occurs when stimuli are presented simultaneously. Whatever its value for arranging out knowledge of between-stimuli learning, the notion of informativeness seems to ignore important instances of within-stimuli learning.

Note

The research reported in this chapter was supported by the National Science Foundation. I wish particularly to thank Chris Cunningham, Laura Freberg, Douglas Gillan, and Marjorie Speers for stimulating discussions and permission to describe their work.

References

Asch, S. E., Ceraso, J. and Heimer, W. (1960). Perceptual conditions of association, *Psychological monographs*, **74**, No. 490, 1–48.

Burkhardt, P. E. and Ayres, J. J. B. (1978). CS and US duration effects in one-trial simultaneous fear conditioning as assessed by conditioned suppression of licking in rats. *Animal Learning and Behavior*, **6**, 225–230.

Cheatle, M. D. and Rudy, J. W. (1978). Analysis of second-order odor-aversion conditioning in neonatal rats: implications for Kamin's blocking effect. *Journal of Experimental Psychology: Animal Behavior Processes*, **4**, 237–249.

Freberg, L. (1979). Evidence supporting a perceptual learning model of the sensory preconditioning of flavours. Ph.D. dissertation, University of California, Los Angeles.

Fudim, O. K. (1978). Sensory preconditioning with formalin-produced sodium need. *Journal of Experimental Psychology: Animal Behavior Processes*, **4**, 276–285.

Gibson, E. J. (1969). *Principles of Perceptual Learning and Development*, Appleton-Century-Crofts, New York.

Gibson, J. J. and Gibson, E. J. (1955). Perceptual learning: differentiation or Enrichment? *Psychological Review*, **62**, 32–41.

Gillan, D. J. and Domjan, M. (1977). Taste aversion conditioning with expected versus unexpected drug treatment. *Journal of Experimental Psychology: Animal Behavior Processes*, **3**, 297–309.

Heth, C. D. (1976). Simultaneous and backward fear conditioning as a function of CS–UCS pairings', *Journal of Experimental Psychology: Animal Behavior Processes*, **5**, 117–129.

Heth, C. D. and Rescorla, R. A. (1973). Simultaneous and backward fear conditioning in the rat. *Journal of Comparative and Physiological Psychology*, **82**, 434–443.

Holman, E. W. (1975). Immediate and delayed reinforcers for flavor preferences in rats. *Learning and Motivation*, **6**, 91–100.

James, W. (1890). *Principles of Psychology*, Holt, New York.

Kamin, L. J. (1968). Attention-like processes in classical conditioning. In *Miami Symposium on its Prediction of Behavior: Aversive Stimulation* (M. R. Jones, ed.), University of Miami, Miami.

Kamin, L. J. (1969). Predictability, Surprise, attention, and conditioning. In *Punishment and Aversive Behaviour* (B. A. Campbell and R. M. Church, eds), Prentice-Hall, Englewood Cliffs, N. J.

Lavin, M. J. (1976). The establishment of flavor–flavor associations using a sensory preconditioning training procedure. *Learning and Motivation*, **7**, 173–183.

Mackintosh, N. J. (1975). A theory of attention: variations in the associability of stimuli with reinforcement. *Psychological Review*, **00**, 000–000.

Mowrer, O. H. and Aiken, E. G. (1954). Contiguity vs. drive-reduction in conditioned fear: temporal variations in conditioned and unconditioned stimulus. *American Journal of Psychology*, **67**, 26–38.

Pavlov, I. P. (1927). *Conditioned Reflexes*, Oxford University Press, London.

Pfaffman, C. (1960). The pleasures of sensation. *Psychological Review*, **67**, 253–268.

Rescorla, R. A. (1972). Informational variables in Pavlovian conditioning. In *Psychology of Learning and Motivation*, Vol. 6 (G. Bower, ed.), Academic Press, New York.

Rescorla, R. A. (1980). Simultaneous and successive associations in sensory preconditioning. *Journal of Experimental Psychology: Animal Behavior Processes*, **6**, 207–216.

Rescorla, R. A. and Cunningham, C. L. (1978). Within-compound flavor associations. *Journal of Experimental Psychology: Animal Behavior Processes*, **4**, 267–275.

Rescorla, R. A. and Freberg, L. (1978). The extinction of within-compound flavor associations. *Learning and Motivation*, **4**, 411–427.

Robinson, J. S. (1932). *Association Theory Today*, Century, New York.

Revusky, S. and Garcia, J. (1970). Learned associations over long delays, In *Psychology of Learning and Motivation*, Vol. 4 (G. Bower, ed.), Academic Press, New York.

Skinner, B. F. (1938). *Behavior of Organisms*, Appleton-Century-Crofts, New York.

Speers, M. A., Gillan, D. J., and Rescorla, R. A. (1980). Within-compound associations in a variety of compound conditioning procedures. *Learning and Motivation*, **11**, 135–149.

Thompson, R. F. (1972). Sensory Preconditioning. In *Topics in Learning and Performance* (R. F. Thompson and J. F. Voss, eds), Academic Press, New York.

Warren, H. C. (1921). *A History of the Association Psychology*, Scribner, New York.

Predictability, Correlation, and Contiguity
Edited by P. Harzem and M. D. Zeiler
© 1981 John Wiley & Sons Ltd.

Chapter 3

Discrimination, Inhibition, and Simultaneous Association of Stimulus Properties: A Theoretical Analysis of Reinforcement [1]

Peter Harzem and Anne L. Harzem

Introduction

In this chapter a different aspect of simultaneous association will be considered: simultaneous association of two different properties of a single stimulus. Specifically, we deal with the properties of reinforcing stimuli.

Whatever else a reinforcer may be, it is, in the first place, a stimulus. It would seem most direct, therefore, to inquire what behavioural effects are observed immediately following presentation of such a stimulus. Under any schedule, reinforcement is followed by a pause from responding: the postreinforcement pause. Normally such a pause is to be expected if the organism has to deal with the reinforcer in some way. The most obvious example is that if the reinforcer is food or water, as it is in most studies using animal subjects, the subject stops responding in order to eat or drink. With other kinds of reinforcers, for example delivery of money, trinkets, or tokens in the case of human subjects, a similar pause is usually observed while the subject stops responding so as to collect the reinforcer from the point of delivery. However, in many cases, and as will be seen, probably in all cases, the duration of the postreinforcement pause exceeds the time taken by the consummatory behaviour. What determines the occurrence of such relatively long postreinforcement pauses?

The most pervasive answer to that question has been that the reinforcer functions as a discriminative stimulus, signalling a period of no further reinforcement, and that for this reason the subject stops responding. An alternative account which suggests that a reinforcer becomes a conditioned inhibitory stimulus arises from exactly the same rationale, with the rider that a negative discriminative stimulus acquires conditioned inhibitory properties. The characteristics of most schedules are such that a discriminative function of this sort can be attributed to the reinforcer. But there are schedules where the probability of reinforcement immediately after a reinforcement is the same as at any other time. The crucial test of the two hypotheses is in seeing whether reinforcement is followed by a pause also in these schedules. The evidence presented in this chapter shows that pausing does, indeed, occur even where there cannot be any discriminative control by the reinforcer. We propose, therefore, that a reinforcing stimulus is an *unconditioned* inhibitory stimulus. The duration of this unconditioned inhibitory effect is relatively brief. However, in those situations where the discriminative control does arise, the unconditioned inhibitory and the discriminative properties are simultaneously associated at each presentation of the reinforcer. Through this association conditioned inhibition develops, extending over the longer periods of non-reinforcement signalled by the reinforcer.

The first two sections review the literature on the discriminative and conditioned inhibitory effects of reinforcers. In the third and fourth sections we argue that a reinforcer is also an *unconditioned* inhibitory stimulus and present evidence in support of the argument. The fifth section briefly reviews the literature on the effects of reinforcer magnitude, and shows that the findings also support the present account. The sixth section presents the formal statements of the theory and discusses them. Finally, in the seventh section, the proposal that a reinforcer is an unconditioned inhibitory stimulus, even though this may result in a lower frequency of reinforcement than might otherwise occur, is examined in a broader context, and the biological utility of such a phenomenon is considered.

Reinforcer as a Discriminative Stimulus

Since presentation of the reinforcer is the event which marks the start of the postreinforcement pause, the reinforcer is the most likely candidate to be implicated in the determination of that pause. The reinforcer, functioning as a discriminative stimulus, may initiate a period of non-responding immediately after its presentation. Regarding such discriminative control by the reinforcer, it may be asked what aspect of the situation is signalled by such a stimulus. Most directly, two possible variables present themselves: the number of responses that occurred prior to reinforcement, and the interreinforcement interval that preceded reinforcement.

Effect of Number of Responses

It would seem plausible that presentation of a reinforcer signals the response requirement for the next reinforcement. Such a function would necessarily be based on the relationship previously experienced between responses and reinforcement, extending over one or more of the preceding occasions when reinforcement occurred. In almost all schedules of reinforcement, with the notable exception of the fixed ratio (FR) schedule, the number of responses that occurred prior to reinforcement varies. Postreinforcement pause durations also vary. Is there a relationship between these two sets of variations? For example, it might be that a long pause occurs after a large number of responses, and a shorter pause after a smaller number of responses. This would at least be consonant with the intuition that the more the work done, the longer might be the rest period.

In a study directly concerned with this possibility, Neuringer and Schneider (1968) found that the number of responses did not affect the duration of the postreinforcement pauses of pigeons. They compared the postreinforcement pauses that occurred under fixed interval (FI) and FR schedules. Under the FR schedule they manipulated the interreinforcement interval while holding the number of responses constant. This was done by presenting brief blackouts after each response and manipulating the duration of the blackout. Under the FI schedule they held the interreinforcement interval constant but varied the number of responses by means of blackouts after each response. In the FI schedule changing the number of responses had no effect on the postreinforcement pause, whereas in the FR schedule the pauses did vary with variations in the interreinforcement intervals. In an earlier experiment with rats, Farmer and Schoenfeld (1964) added a differential reinforcement of low rate (DRL) requirement to an FI schedule so that reinforcement occurred if either a fixed interval elapsed since previous reinforcement (FI schedule), or a minimum interval elapsed since previous response (DRL schedule). Performance consisted of postreinforcement pauses followed by a 'run' of responses where the rate was lower than it would be under the same FI schedule without the additional DRL requirement. However, the occurrence of lower response rates had no effect on the durations of the postreinforcement pauses. Other experiments have also found that the number of responses does not affect the postreinforcement pause. For example, adding an FR requirement to the end of a schedule closely resembling FI (Killeen, 1969); delivering a reinforcer at the end of a fixed interval provided a single response occurred at any point in the course of the interval (Shull, 1970a); and taking a fixed number of responses rather than a single response as the 'response unit' under FI schedules (Shull, Guilkey, and Witty, 1972) all had effects on the response rate but left the postreinforcement pause unaffected.

It appears, then, that variations in the number of responses do not affect the pause duration. At this point some caution is necessary. The number of responses can, under some conditions, nevertheless affect the postreinforcement pauses. Barrett (1976) used a conjunctive FI adjusting FR schedule with pigeons. At the start of each fixed interval (3 min for one group and 6 min for another group) and FR requirement (90–600) was also in operation. Provided that the subject did not respond, the number of responses required for reinforcement decreased linearly, reaching 1 at the end of the interval. If a response occurred in the course of the interval, as it almost always did, then reinforcement occurred when both the ratio remaining at that point and the remainder of the interval were completed. The duration of the postreinforcement pause (during which the ratio decreased) was an increasing function of the size of the FR prevailing at the start of the interval. This relationship was observed up to FR 300; above that the ratio resulted in shorter pausing but also 'disrupted responding' (Barrett, 1976, p. 157). It appears that the number of responses can affect the postreinforcement pause in special circumstances. In this case it is possible that pausing was 'reinforced' since longer pausing resulted in lower ratio requirements for reinforcement. For example, Harzen, Lowe, and Spencer (1978) have reported that under FI schedules the duration of postreinforcement pauses was controlled over a wide range by appropriately reinforcing the response that terminated the pause. Finally, under multiple FR schedules, if the interreinforcement interval was held constant the postreinforcement pause was longer when the subjects had to emit a fixed number of responses for reinforcement than when, instead, they were placed in a blackout ('time-out') lasting as long as the emission of the responses lasted (Crossman, Heaps, Nunes, and Alferink, 1974).

Effect of Temporal Distribution of Reinforcers

The suggestion that the reinforcer may function as a temporal discriminative stimulus was first made with reference to the pattern of responding that typically develops under the FI schedule. Under this schedule reinforcement is followed by a relatively long pause, occupying approximately one- to two-thirds of the fixed interval. Ferster and Skinner (1957) have suggested that because reinforcement is never immediately followed by another reinforcement, its *presence* sets the occasion for not responding.

It is important to note that the discriminative function that is being described is that of S^Δ, i.e. the reinforcer is said to set the occasion for *not* responding. In fact, throughout this discussion we will be concerned with this S^Δ function of the reinforcer. Although S^D and S^Δ are sometimes thought to be exact counterparts, one setting the occasion for responding and the other the occasion for not responding, there may be important differences between the effects of the two. There is considerable evidence that extinction, i.e. non-reinforcement of a previously reinforced response, has emotional and frustrative effects (Amsel, 1958; Keller and Schoenfeld, 1950; Mowrer, 1960; Mowrer and Jones, 1943). These effects may be associated with S^Δ but not, of course, with S^D.

Under the FI schedules the duration of the postreinforcement pause is an increasing function of the schedule value; the longer the fixed interval the longer the postreinforcement pause (Harzem, 1968; Lowe, Harzem, and Spencer, 1979; Schneider, 1969; Sherman, 1959). This does not present a problem as far as FI schedules are concerned, because under these schedules reinforcement is evenly distributed in time. But we may ask whether, and in what ways, the discriminative function of the reinforcer would be affected if the interreinforcement intervals were not all of the same duration. Given variations in the temporal distribution of reinforcers, this period of pausing initiated by the reinforcer may be related to the longest interreinforcement interval, the shortest interreinforcement interval, or to some averaging process.

Under FR schedules the interreinforcement intervals vary as a result of the variations that occur in the durations of successive postreinforcement pauses, as well as the variations in the rate at which the subject responds following a pause. Both of these variations are small, however, so that the interreinforcement intervals under an FR schedule do not differ greatly from those under an FI schedule. Killeen (1969) found that the postreinforcement pauses of a group of pigeons under an FR schedule were not different from the pauses of another group under an FI-like schedule. The latter was a schedule which operated like an FI schedule (i.e. only the first response was reinforced in each of successive intervals) but the durations of the intervals varied to the extent that they were the same as the interreinforcement intervals produced by the FR group. The variations that occurred in the intervals of the FI-like schedule did not disrupt or notably reduce the postreinforcement pauses. Berryman and Nevin (1962) compared the durations of the postreinforcement pauses under FR, FI, and four 'intermediate' interlocking FR FI schedules. The postreinforcement pause was related to the time that elapsed between reinforcements. In a more extensive study, Lund (1977) used a mixed variable interval (VI) FI schedule, manipulating the probability of occurrence of the VI and FI components. In this way the mixed schedule ranged between being like a VI schedule and being like an FI schedule. The response pattern that occurred following reinforcement indicated that 'temporal control' (i.e. effect of the interreinforcement interval) was maximal when the schedule approximated FI, and it was minimal when it approximated VI. In a second experiment Lund manipulated the minimum and maximum interreinforcement intervals of a VI schedule while holding the mean interval constant at 100 s. Here, too, temporal patterning was a function of the extent to which the schedule approximated an FI schedule (i.e. where the difference between the minimum and maximum interreinforcement intervals was small). All the results showed that 'changes in the temporal pattern of responses were systematically related to changes in the temporal distribution of reinforcements' (Lund, 1976, p. 155).

Interreinforcement intervals were varied in a different way by Lattal and Bryan (1976), who delivered additional reinforcers, distributed at variable intervals, in the course of fixed intervals. The response rate declined as the frequency of reinforcer delivery increased. Lattal and Bryan's data consisted of response-rate measures in successive 1 min segments of the FI 5 min schedule. However, it is likely that the decrease in the response rates was largely due to the pauses that occurred following each presentation of the reinforcer (cf. Harzem *et al.*, 1978). The decline occurred when the additional reinforcers were delivered independently of responses when delivered at the same variable intervals but; however, contingent on responses, responding was maintained at a relatively high rate. Such response-contingent reinforcement at variable intervals is, of course, the same as introducing a VI schedule, and it is known that the VI schedule maintains high rates of responding.

Given that the postreinforcement pause varies with variations in the interreinforcement interval, which value of the interreinforcement interval determines the duration of the postreinforcement pause? Although one suggestion is that this may be the arithmetic mean of the interreinforcement intervals (Berryman and Nevin, 1962; Nevin, 1973), subsequent research has shown that the *shortest* interreinforcement interval has a distinct effect on the postreinforcement pause. Catania and Reynolds (1968), using pigeons as subjects, randomly mixed the individual intervals of two FI schedules. One (long) interval was always 240 s, and the other (short) interval was 30, 90, 150, and 210 s. Although the results were presented in terms of 'local' response rates occurring in successive 10 s periods following reinforcement, inspection of the data clearly shows that the duration of the postreinforcement pause (the period when the response rate was zero) was determined by the short FI interval. This was so even when the short interval was presented only once in a daily experimental session. Recently, Harzem *et al.* (1978) reported a series of experiments which provide further evidence of the phenomenon. With rats responding under an FI schedule, they *additionally* reinforced the response that terminated the postreinforcement pause, provided that this pause exceeded a criterion of minimum duration. In different experiments they systematically varied the duration of this criterion, and the parameter of the FI schedule. In all cases the duration of the postreinforcement pause[2] was in the region of the criterion for the reinforcement of the response terminating the postreinforcement pause. This was so even when the criterion was 20 s and the FI parameter was 480 s. On the basis of this evidence Harzem *et al.* (1978) concluded that

> where more than one temporal contingency is in operation, the pause is not the result of some averaging process; what prevails is the contingency controlling the shortest pause. (p. 269)

An exception to the above findings should be noted. This is the variable interval (VI) schedule under which many different interreinforcement intervals occur, so that no particular interreinforcement interval could be singled out as a separate 'temporal contingency'. The postreinforcement pauses that occur under this schedule have not been studied in detail. However inspection of the data presented by Lachter (1971, p. 210, Table 2) shows that under such a schedule the duration of the pauses was an orderly increasing function of the mean interreinforcement interval.

We have so far concentrated mainly on the FI schedule because this is the schedule in which the discriminative effect of reinforcement and the determination of the postreinforcement pause have been largely studied. Another schedule in which such temporal control can be observed is the DRL.

Under this schedule a low response rate does in fact develop; the greater the schedule parameter (i.e. the minimum pause since previous response, required for the reinforcement of a response) the lower is the response rate (Wilson and Keller, 1953; Zimmerman and Schuster, 1962). The relative frequency distribution of interresponse times (IRTs) is usually found to be bimodal; a large number of very short IRTs occur, but also the duration of a large number of IRTs is in the region of the minimum IRT that is reinforced (Sidman, 1956; Harzem, 1969). If IRTs are classified according to the event initiating them (i.e. reinforcement or an unreinforced response), considerably more IRTs that meet the schedule criterion are found to occur following reinforcement than following unreinforced responses (Kelleher, Fry, and Cook, 1959; Malott and Cumming, 1964). Farmer and Schoenfeld (1964) have shown, in a detailed study, that under a DRL schedule, the probability of a sequence of two reinforced responses is greater than a sequence of two responses where only the second response is reinforced. This is strong evidence that reinforcement functions as a discriminative stimulus for pausing for a period approximating the schedule criterion. Since such pausing also occurs following unreinforced responses, although with a lower frequency than following reinforcement, it appears that unreinforced responses do, also, have a discriminative function under this schedule. We may ask, however, why reinforcement apparently has a 'better' discriminative function than the unreinforced responses. This is an important question from the point of view of this chapter, and it will be considered again. For the present, the study to be discussed next provides further evidence of distinct discriminative control by reinforcement and unreinforced responses.

The studies that have been discussed so far have all presented data in terms of means calculated across one of several experimental sessions. Such mean values do, of course, summarize repeated measurements of a variable, and together with a measure of variability, they may be all that is needed. Sometimes, however, the question asked in the research may be such that seeing the successive individual changes that take place in successive observations of a variable may be particularly informative. Showing such individual changes in IRTs, a study by Harzem, Lowe, and Davey (1975a) provided convincing evidence of the distinct discriminative function of reinforcement and of unreinforced responses. These data are reproduced here in Figure 3.1. Harzem et al. (1975a) devised a two-component DRL schedule in which the reinforcement criterion, i.e. the minimum pause duration required for reinforcement, was set separately for pauses following reinforcement and pauses following unreinforced responses. For example, in a DRL 20 s, 60 s schedule a response terminating a pause was reinforced if the pause duration, provided that the pause *started from a reinforcement*, exceeded 20 s; a pause which *started from an unreinforced response* terminated in reinforcement if its duration exceeded 60 s. Several values of these components were studied with rats as subjects. Figure 3.1 shows the successive

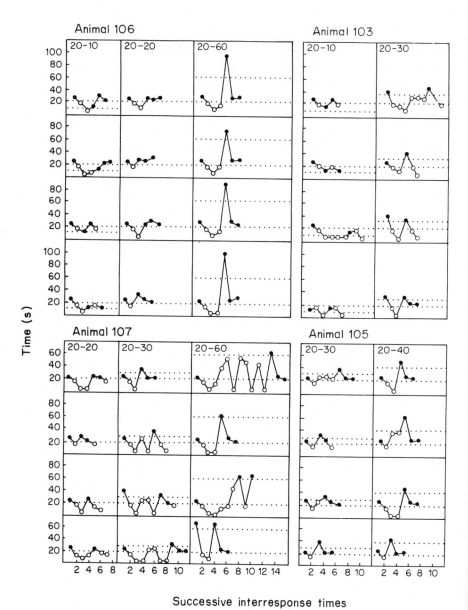

Figure 3.1. Durations of successive IRTs under various two-component DRL schedules. Filled circles show IRTs that ended in reinforcement, and open circles the IRTs that were too short for reinforcement. Note that following a reinforcement the next IRT was in the region of the minimum duration required for the reinforcement of an IRT that started from reinforcement; following non-reinforcement the next IRT was either very short ('response burst') or in the region of the minimum duration required for the reinforcement of an IRT that started from non-reinforcement. (From Harzem *et al.*, 1975a, Two-component schedules of differential reinforcement of low rate. *Journal of the Experimental Analysis of Behavior*, **24**, 33–42. Copyright © 1975 by the Society for the Experimental Analysis of Behavior)

IRTs that occurred at the end of the last session, when responding was stable. Each IRT was appropriate to, i.e. was in the region of, the minimum pause duration required by each component. (There were also some response-bursts, i.e. very short IRTs, following unreinforced but not reinforced responses.) When an IRT was initiated by an unreinforced response, that IRT approximated the duration required following unreinforced responses; when an IRT was initiated by reinforcement, that IRT approximated the duration required following reinforced responses. Since there was no stimulus change in the experimental situation other than the occurrence of responses and reinforcement, these two types of event were responsible for the differential pausing. As well as showing that reinforcement functioned as an S^Δ, this study also provided evidence that individual responses can function as discriminative events for the subsequent behaviour of the same organism.

Discriminative Control by Different Reinforcers

Given that a reinforcer functions as a discriminative stimulus, it would be expected that two or more different reinforcers might serve as different discriminative stimuli, initiating pauses of different durations. Two studies provide evidence of such differential control.

Cruse, Vitulli, and Dertke (1966) reinforced a single rat under a multiple FR 30, FI 3 min schedule, using two different types of reinforcers: a food pellet and a sucrose pellet. The schedule which operated following reinforcement by a food pellet was FR 30, and the schedule following sucrose was FI 3 min. For example, successive FR components ended in food pellet reinforcement except for the last component, which ended in reinforcement by a sucrose pellet. Thus sucrose signalled that thereafter the FI schedule was in operation, until another change in the reinforcer. The response pattern following each type of reinforcer was characteristic of the schedule signalled by that reinforcer; after food pellets the postreinforcement pauses were relatively short, and after sucrose pellets they were considerably longer.

Harzem et al. (1978) provided further evidence of differential discriminative control by two different reinforcers. Under an FI 60 schedule the response that terminated any postreinforcement pause exceeding 30 s was additionally reinforced. For one group of 4 rats the additional reinforcer was the same as the FI reinforcer (a food pellet); for a second group of four rats the additional reinforcer was different (a solution of condensed milk in water). For the group whose reinforcers were the same, the durations of the pauses following reinforcement were approximately the same following the FI reinforcement and the additional reinforcement that depended on the duration of the postreinforcement pause. With different reinforcers, however, the animals produced a long postreinforcement pause following FI reinforcement and a short pause following the pause-dependent reinforcement.

There is another aspect of the results that should be noted. The group experiencing first the condition where the same reinforcer was used nevertheless behaved differently following FI reinforcement and additional reinforcement. Although both pauses were long, the pause after FI reinforcement was longer than the pause after additional reinforcement; i.e. a degree of discrimination occurred, based on cues other than characteristics of the reinforcer. However, there was no difference between the two types of pauses for the group experiencing this condition after the condition where the reinforcers were different. It seems likely that this was an example of the 'blocking' described in studies of discrimination, when the learning of one discrimination retards the learning of another discrimination (cf. Mackintosh, 1974).

Postreinforcement Pause in Ratio Schedules:
A Problem for the Discrimination Account

The above conclusion answers only a part of the question as to the determination of the postreinforcement pause. In the studies considered so far the occurrence of reinforcement was either unaffected by the postreinforcement pause (in the FI schedule) or was actually facilitated by the pauses (in the DRL schedule). In other words, pausing either enhanced reinforcement frequency or kept it at its maximum possible level. Under ratio schedules, however, a contrary relationship operates. The sooner the next number of responses is emitted, the sooner the next reinforcement occurs. Thus there is an inverse relationship between the duration of the postreinforcement pause and frequency of reinforcement. Nevertheless, appreciable postreinforcement pauses are observed under ratio schedules.

Under an FR schedule the duration of the postreinforcement pause was positively related to the ratio (Boren, 1961; Felton and Lyon, 1966; Ferster and Skinner, 1957; Powell, 1968). Moreover, reinforcement frequency was not kept constant by means of compensating increases in response rate. With increased ratios the response rates declined (although in a less orderly way than the changes occurring in the postreinforcement pauses), thus further contributing to a decline in reinforcement frequency.

The postreinforcement pauses that occur under variable ratio (VR) schedules have not attracted much attention. It is generally assumed that under this schedule, which generates high and constant response rates, no consistent pauses occur (e.g. Nevin, 1973; Staddon, 1972). However, one study (Farmer and Schoenfeld, 1967) did find that the postreinforcement pauses occurring under this schedule, although brief, were nevertheless an increasing function of the mean ratio.

A schedule under which surprisingly long postreinforcement pauses occur is a variant of the FI schedule with the addition of a minor ratio requirement. Under this schedule the fixed interval starts not from reinforcement (or the end of the preceding interval), but from the response terminating the postreinforcement pause. Under these conditions maximum reinforcement frequency depends on responding soon after reinforcement. This is the tandem FR 1 FI schedule. Chung and Neuringer (1967) found that under this schedule pigeons nevertheless paused after reinforcement. When the FI parameter was increased from 1 to 15 s, the postreinforcement pause also increased. Shull (1970b) studied the effects of five different FI parameters between 3.75 s and 60 s with pigeons; the postrein- forcement pause duration was an increasing function of the FI parameter. Lowe, Davey, and Harzem (1974) reported similar results. For example, with the FI at 60 s, pauses were in the region of 70–80 s. Harzem, Lowe, and Bagshaw (1978) have reported experiments with adult humans where pauses sometimes were two to three times as long as the FI parameter. Of course any ratio involves an interreinforcement interval, and for a given fixed ratio there must be a minimum interreinforcement interval set by the fastest response rate. General consensus appears to be that it is the inevitable occurrence of the interreinforcement intervals which result in the occurrence of postreinforcement pauses, although these pauses reduce the frequency of reinforcement (cf. Staddon, 1972).

This is, at first sight, plausible. However, there remain a number of questions that are not answered by such an explanation. First, the postreinforcement pause generated under the tandem FR1 FI schedule is longer than the pause that occurs under a comparable FI schedule. Inspection of Shull's (1970b) data shows, for example, that when the FI parameter was 60 s, the pause under tandem FR1 FI schedule was in the region of 70–80 s; the human subjects of Harzem *et al.* (1978) paused two to three times as long as the FI parameter. The difference cannot be accounted for in terms of interreinforcement intervals, since it is not clear how such an account would explain the fact that the postreinforce- ment pauses under tandem FR1 FI schedules are so much longer than in comparable FI schedules. Second, under any schedule of reinforcement the postreinforcement pauses develop gradually, in the course of training. When they develop under an FI schedule they have no consequence with regard to reinforcement. Under ratio schedules, however, the pauses delay reinforcement Why do long pauses nevertheless *develop*, resulting in long intervals? Third, even when stable responding, including long pauses, has developed, the duration of individual postreinforcement pauses is not perfectly constant but varies after each reinforcement. Thus, the subject is exposed to the contingency of short pauses being followed by earlier reinforcement. It is a well-established fact that the shorter the delay of reinforcement the stronger is the related behaviour. Why do not the postreinforcement pauses become shorter?

In summary, the essential point of the problem is as follows. In a schedule such as tandem FR1 FI there are two main contingencies that operate: (i) pausing delays reinforcement, and (ii) reinforcement signals a period of non- reinforcement. What prevents the first of these from affecting behaviour? Note that there are no appreciable pauses at the start of training; the interreinforcement intervals *increase* to an asymptote. Thus, what is observed here is not the dynamic process described by Zeiler (1979).

We suggest that the reinforcer, as well as being a discriminative stimulus, also actively *inhibits* responding. It will next be considered whether this is the case.

Reinforcer as a Conditioned Inhibitory Stimulus

Until the 1960s the possibility that inhibitory processes might be involved in operant behaviour attracted little attention. This was probably mainly due to Skinner's (1938) view that the concept of inhibition is unnecessary in accounting for operant phenomena, and that it has no experimental basis. Hearst, Besley, and Farthing (1970) suggested that 'the greatest obstacle to the study of inhibitory phenomena has been the lack of objective, unambiguous, and relatively direct methods for their detection and measurement' (p. 374). These difficulties are especially great in investigating the possibility that reinforcers may be inhibitory stimuli.

Hearst *et al.* (1970) defined an inhibitory stimulus as follows:

an inhibitory stimulus is a stimulus that *develops during conditioning* the capacity to decrease response strength below the level occurring when that stimulus is absent. (p. 376; our italics)

This summarizes clearly the conditions necessary for demonstrating inhibition, and is representative of the generally held view of the term. Of course, the mere absence of responding is not a sufficient reason for believing that stimuli present at that time were inhibitory; in other words, there is a difference between not responding, and one's responses being inhibited. The important point is this: in order to demonstrate its inhibitory property, a stimulus must be added to a situation in which, without that stimulus, the response occurs with a given strength or frequency. If the addition of the stimulus results in a decline in responding then the stimulus can be said to be inhibitory. With reference to reinforcers, the fact that the reinforcing and the possible inhibiting functions are combined in the same stimulus presents a special experimental problem: the 'inhibitory' part of the reinforcing stimulus cannot be presented independently of its 'reinforcing' part.

A stimulus acquires its inhibitory property when it functions as an S^Δ (or S^-). Therefore it is sometimes *assumed* that a reinforcer is also an inhibitory stimulus simply on the grounds that it has an S^Δ function. Staddon (1970a) has pointed out that several phenomena, in particular the fact that when a regularly occurring reinforcer is omitted the following response rate is elevated for a time, can be explained in terms of an inhibition hypothesis (i.e. reinforcement inhibits responding, and that when reinforcement is omitted responses are now not inhibited; they simply occur). Staddon claims, rightly, that 'one desirable consequence of this analysis' (i.e. that reinforcement is inhibitory) 'is that it does not require postulation of special "consummatory" inhibition, demotivation, satiation, even "salience" effects of reinforcement' (Staddon, 1972, pp. 233–234). There is, however, still a problem. Unparsimonious postulations of this kind could be eliminated by referring only to the discriminative effect of reinforcement. In other words it is not clear, on this showing, what the notion of conditioned inhibition adds to the simple statement that reinforcement has an S^Δ function, so that when reinforcement is omitted responses occur. If we are to take the notion of conditioned inhibition seriously in this context, what is necessary is evidence of this phenomenon *independently* of the evidence of discrimination.

There is, in fact, some *indirect* evidence that phenomena associated with inhibition may be observed in the periods following reinforcement. It is known that inhibition in classical conditioning, and possibly in operant behaviour, dissipates when a novel stimulus is presented (disinhibition); that it results in emotional activity such as aggression; and that it has aversive properties so that a subject will respond to escape from it. Under FI schedules presentation of a novel stimulus during the postreinforcement pause results in a shorter pause than without that stimulus, and the subsequent response rate is elevated (Flanagan and Webb, 1964; Hinrichs, 1968; Singh and Wickens, 1968). Kello, Innis, and Staddon (1975) exposed pigeons to a 'cyclic' multiple FI schedule, where a sequence of 12 short intervals (1 min each) and a sequence of four long intervals (3 min each) alternated. Once in each sequence a novel stimulus (they termed this an 'eccentric stimulus') was presented, the colour of the response key changed from green to white, and three vertical or horizontal bars were projected on it. The novel stimulus lasted for the duration of one interval, i.e. 1 min or 3 min, in each sequence. In the sequence with the short intervals, the effect was elevation of the response rate in the presence of the novel stimulus. There was no such effect in the sequence with long intervals. The elevation of response rate appears to be an instance of disinhibition, and the experimenters speculate that the absence of an effect in the long interval sequence may be a function of relative reinforcement frequency. Kello *et al.* (1975) conducted another experiment with the same pigeons where this time the long interval was 1 min, and the short interval was 20 s. The novel stimulus resulted in higher response rates in the 20 s interval, but not in the 1 min interval. In yet another experiment the effect disappeared altogether when the 'eccentric' stimulus was not novel (i.e. when the background stimulus and the eccentric stimulus were interchanged). Disinhibition appears to have been demonstrated, although it is curious why it did not occur in the longer intervals—especially in view of the fact that inhibition, given that it is inhibition, lasts longer in longer fixed intervals; i.e. the postreinforcement pause is longer. It might be thought that more inhibition builds up with greater frequency of reinforcement; but this would be a *post hoc* explanation leaving unanswered, in turn, the question of why postreinforcement pauses are longer with lower frequency of reinforcement.

Disinhibition by the presentation of a novel stimulus has also been studied under DRL schedules. Contrucci, Hothersall, and Wickens (1971), using rats as subjects under a DRL 20 s schedule, occasionally sounded a buzzer lasting 4 s, either 4 or 12 s after a reinforcement. Responses occurring at those times were more frequent when the buzzer sounded than when it did not. Brimer (1972) used a longer stimulus, a light lasting 3 min. Rats were trained under a DRL 120 s schedule and the light was presented either 16 min or 51 min after the start of each experimental session. The response rate in the presence of the light was higher than in comparable periods without the light. Davis and Iriye (1973), with rat subjects under DRL schedules of 10, 20, and 30 s, occasionally presented a brief tone lasting 0.5 s after both reinforcement and unreinforced responses. In both cases, the IRT following the tone was shorter than comparable IRTs without the tone.

Aggressive behaviour occurs in the course of responding under a schedule of reinforcement. Hutchinson, Azrin, and Hunt (1968) found that during FR responding squirrel monkeys attacked a rubber hose placed near them by biting it. The attacks were confined to postreinforcement pauses and the early part of the ratio, the frequency of attacks being an increasing function of the fixed ratio. Gentry (1968) found that pigeons, also responding under an FR schedule, attacked a restrained pigeon placed in the experimental box. Again, the attacks occurred mostly during the postreinforcement pauses, and almost every reinforcement was followed by such attacks. In control sessions where no reinforcement occurred, no attacks were observed. With pigeons, too, the rate of attack is an increasing function of the ratio size (Cherek and Pickens, 1970; Knutson, 1970). However, attacks did not occur if the restrained pigeon was introduced after prior training under the schedule (Knutson, 1970); and they occurred only when the ratio was increased from a low to a high value, but not when it was decreased from a high to a low value (Cherek and Pickens, 1970). Same types of attacks by pigeons have been also observed under FI schedules (Richards and Rilling, 1972) and VI schedules (Dove, Rashotte, and Katz, 1974). Again the attacks occurred mostly during the postreinforcement pause. In the early sessions, under VI schedules where normally postreinforcement pauses are very brief, the attacks occurred soon after reinforcement, resulting in the *development* of postreinforcement pauses; and, as the number of daily sessions increased, the attack rates first also increased, and then decreased (Dove *et al.*, 1974).

During extinction, also, attacks of this kind have been observed (Azrin, Hutchinson, and Hake, 1967; Knutson, 1970). It appears that this type of aggressive behaviour may be generated by inhibition present both during the periods following reinforcement and in extinction, associated in both situations with the non-availability of reinforcement.

Inhibition and absence of reinforcement are thought to have aversive properties. If so, and if inhibition is present during postreinforcement pauses, a subject would be expected to respond so as to 'escape' from that situation, given the opportunity. Brown and Flory (1972) reinforced pigeons under FI schedules. Each response on a second key resulted in an 'escape' period during which the stimuli associated with the FI schedule were changed, and the reinforcement contingency stopped operating. The subjects responded on this key, 'escaping' from the schedule of reinforcement. The escape responses occurred mostly following reinforcement, and the total escape period in a session was an increasing function of the duration of the fixed interval; i.e. the longer the postreinforcement pauses, the longer was the time spent in escape.

Finally, an experiment by Wilkie (1974) provides evidence than an inhibitory effect is present following reinforcement. Pigeons were trained under FI 3 min and FI 6 min schedules. Successive intervals were separated by 1 min blackouts. During training a vertical line was projected on the response key throughout each interval. After stable responding was established, tests of stimulus generalization were carried out by presenting the line at different angles (with reference to the vertical, at angles of $-45°$, $-22.5°$, $0°$, $+22.5°$, and $+45°$). The data were response rates occurring in successive thirds of each fixed interval. In the first third of the interval, U-shaped generalization gradients were obtained; i.e. the fewest responses occurred in the presence of the training stimulus, and the most responses in the presence of the stimulus least like the training stimulus ($\pm 45°$). In the last third of the interval, inverted U-shaped generalization gradients were obtained, so that most responses occurred in the presence of the training stimulus, and the least number in the presence of the stimulus least like it. The curves obtained characterize inhibitory and excitatory generalization gradients. Indeed, according to Terrace (1966) a U-shaped generalization gradient serves to define an inhibitory stimulus operationally.

Unfortunately, Wilkie's (1974) evidence is not conclusive. What has been demonstrated is that the *stimulus* presented acquired an inhibitory property (in the early part of the fixed interval). In the absence of that stimulus, introduced by the experimenter, in other words in a conventional FI schedule, what is the stimulus that is inhibitory? Wilkie speculates as to the effects of an 'FI stimulus'; but, as he acknowledges, this is a hypothetical entity, and cannot be manipulated in the same way as the vertical line was in order to test its properties. In any case, with regard to the main interest of this chapter, the reinforcer, unlike the stimulus used by Wilkie, is a brief stimulus which does not last long into the interval.

Nevertheless, in the light of the evidence, it seems very likely that where reinforcement occurs an inhibitory effect of some kind, whatever its source and nature, operates. In all the literature considered so far, it is assumed that if there is an inhibitory effect, it must be a *conditioned* inhibitory effect, i.e. with reference to the reinforcer it must be one that is *acquired* through the discriminative (S^Δ) function of the reinforcer. Hearst et al. (1970), for example, in their review of inhibition, wrote 'throughout this article, our discussion is confined to stimuli that develop inhibitory properties *as a result of conditioning*' (1970, p. 374; their italics). However, there is a different possibility which has been almost totally disregarded: a reinforcer may have an *unconditioned* inhibitory effect, analogous to the 'external inhibition' of Pavlov. The main proposition of this chapter is that a reinforcer functions as an unconditioned inhibitory stimulus.

Reinforcer as an Unconditioned Inhibitory Stimulus

If a reinforcer becomes an inhibitory stimulus through its discriminative function, then another stimulus presented in exactly the same way as the reinforcer should also function as a discriminative stimulus and also acquire, to the same extent, inhibitory properties. This possibility has been investigated in a number of experiments by Staddon and his associates (e.g. Kello, 1972; Staddon, 1974; Staddon and Innis, 1966, 1969; *see also* Staddon, 1972). In each session the reinforcer was omitted on some occasions, being replaced by another (presumed 'neutral') stimulus. Thus the stimulus, as well as the reinforcer, signalled the beginning of periods in which reinforcement was not available, and developed discriminative control. That is, pauses occurred following the presentation of the stimulus (post-stimulus pauses), similar to postreinforcement pauses. In each experiment, however, the post-stimulus pauses were shorter than the postreinforcement pauses. Kello (1972), with pigeons responding under an FI 2 min schedule, occasionally replaced the reinforcement by either a blackout, or a blackout plus the switching on of the food magazine. Also, on some occasions, reinforcement was omitted but not replaced by a stimulus. The pauses that occurred when reinforcement was omitted were shortest without any stimulus presentation, and longest following blackout and magazine light, but none was as long as the postreinforcement pause. In another experiment, with pigeons responding under an FI schedule (Starr and Staddon, 1974), reinforcement and a blackout occurred with equal frequency but the probability of a fixed interval beginning *and* ending with blackout was, in one condition, 0.9 and in another condition 0.1. The important point is that under the $p = 0.9$ condition the blackout predicted better than reinforcement that the interval would *not* end in reinforcement, i.e. that the next interreinforcement interval would be at least twice as long as the FI parameter. Therefore, under this condition, the post-blackout pause would be expected to be longer than the postreinforcement pause. In fact, although the post-blackout pause was longer in the $p = 0.9$ condition than in the $p = 0.1$ condition, the postreinforcement pause was always the longest. Starr and Staddon aptly ask,

> if the pause-producing effect of reinforcement is attributable to its signal properties, as all the available evidence suggests, why does not the blackout come to have the same effect? (Starr and Staddon, 1974, p. 536)

Staddon (1972) has suggested that this is due to the 'memorability' of the reinforcer, because of its greater significance for the organism. Such an explanation, however, suffers from major defects. First, it is *post hoc*, without any evidence from outside the situation to which it is intended to apply. For the same reason, secondly, it merely involves a verbal shift by which the phenomenon to be explained is given a new name (memorability) so that the 'explanation' is illusory. Third, it reintroduces the unparsimony which, it will be recalled, the conditioned inhibition hypothesis was claimed to have eradicated. Finally, it might be inquired why, for example, an organism better remembers (pauses longer) under an FI 5 min schedule than it does under an FI 1 min schedule.

A simpler and more direct proposition is that a reinforcer has an *unconditioned* inhibitory effect. If this is correct the questions raised earlier concerning the occurrence of postreinforcement pauses under ratio schedules can be answered: postreinforcement pauses occur under such schedules despite the reinforcement-delaying effect simply because responding is *inhibited* by the unconditioned inhibitory property of the reinforcer. Further, under DRL schedules the occurrence of longer pauses following reinforcement than following unreinforced responses can also be explained in this way. What facilitates longer pausing after reinforcement is the inhibitory effect, *in addition* to the discriminative property which both reinforcement and unreinforced responses acquire under this schedule. As Starr and Staddon (1974) have pointed out in the above quotation, (almost) all the available evidence to date suggests that the pause-producing effects of reinforcement are due to its signal properties. This, however, may not be the whole truth. In other words the relationship between the signalling and pause-producing effects of reinforcement may in part be artefactual because the relationship has only been examined in those situations where the reinforcer does have a signal property. If this discriminative property is the sole factor in producing postreinforcement pauses, then pauses should not occur in situations where the reinforcer cannot act as a discriminative stimulus. Situations of the latter kind are those where the probability of reinforcement immediately following reinforcement is the same as at any other time.

Only one published study investigated the postreinforcement pauses under conditions of constant probability of reinforcement. Harzem, Lowe, and Priddle-Higson (1978), using rats as subjects, manipulated the magnitude of a reinforcer (the concentration of a condensed milk solution) under a constant probability VI schedule. They found that under these conditions too, the duration of the postreinforcement pause, although brief, was nevertheless an increasing function of reinforcer magnitude. Since in this schedule the postreinforcement pause cannot be attributed to any discriminative control, it can be persuasively argued that the reinforcer was an unconditioned inhibitory stimulus, and that the increases in the pause duration were due to increases in the intensity of that stimulus. Unfortunately, however, this evidence is not conclusive. The constant probability VI schedule used by Harzem *et al.* (1978) had an interval of 4 s as its shortest interval. Therefore, although the probability of reinforcement was constant beyond 4 s after reinforcement, below 4 s it was zero; and the duration of the shortest pause was in the region of 4 s.

Experiments: The Postreinforcement Pause in the CRF schedule

We have previously reported a series of experiments, conducted in our laboratory, on the effects of varying the magnitude of a reinforcer upon the postreinforcement pause (Harzem, Lowe, and Davey, 1975b; Harzem et al. 1978; Lowe et al., 1974; Lowe, Davey, and Harzem, 1976). Over a wide variety of schedules the effects were uniform: the postreinforcement pause duration was an increasing function of reinforcer magnitude. With the exception of the constant probability VI schedule, all of the schedules studied had one characteristic in common: the schedule parameter determined a minimum interreinforcement time either directly, as in interval schedules, or indirectly, as in ratio schedules, where the minimum interreinforcement time would relate to the maximum speed with which a subject can respond. Thus, in every case, the possibility existed that the reinforcer functioned as an S^Δ, signalling a period of non-reinforcement, and consequently resulting in the postreinforcement pause. The CRF schedule is almost unique in this respect since it is one of only three schedules (the others being the constant probability VI and VR schedules) where the reinforcer cannot have such an effect. In CRF the probability of reinforcement remains 1.0 at all times.

Experiment 1

In this experiment we used the same procedure as in our previous studies. Four rats were trained under the CRF schedule in five daily sessions. The reinforcer was 0.05 ml of 40 percent sucrose solution (weight by volume), and 60 reinforcements occurred in each session. Three test sessions were then conducted with reinforcer concentrations of 10, 20, 30, 40, 50, and 60 percent being presented in random order in each session.

Figure 3.2 shows the median durations of the postreinforcement pauses for each animal as a function of the preceding reinforcer concentration. The interquartile ranges of these data are given in Table 3.1. The higher the reinforcer concentration, the longer was the pause following the presentation of that reinforcer. The regularity of the functions was best in the last test session.

If, as we proposed above, the phenomenon observed here is unconditioned inhibition, it should be possible to find in these data features that are characteristic of the phenomenon of inhibition. One such feature is that inhibition is thought to be cumulative. Thus, the inhibitory effect, if any, would be expected to increase across two or more presentations of the reinforcer. Since in this experiment reinforcer magnitude varied randomly, a second-order analysis, i.e. analysis of the postreinforcement pause durations following a given

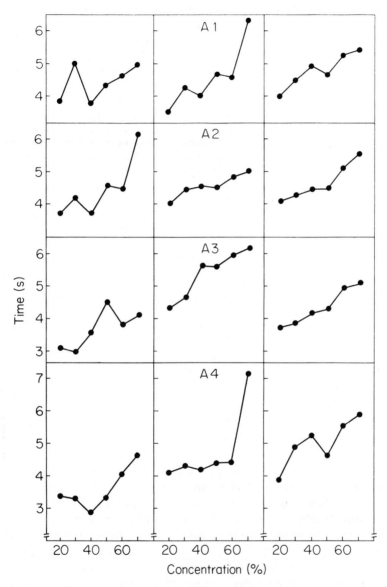

Figure 3.2. Experiment 1. Median duration of postreinforcement pauses as a function of the concentration of the reinforcer initiating the pause, in the three test sessions. The order of sessions is left to right. Each row gives the data from one animal

Table 3.1. Experiment 1. Interquartile ranges of the postreinforcement pause durations as a function of the preceding reinforcer concentration. Data are given for individual animals separately for each of the three test sessions

Animal	Concentration (%)	Test sessions		
		1	2	3
A1	20	3.55–4.17	3.22–3.78	2.68–4.32
	30	4.24–5.93	4.12–4.85	4.06–4.81
	40	3.69–4.72	3.35–4.58	4.80–7.13
	50	3.92–4.06	4.18–5.40	3.81–5.15
	60	3.12–5.04	3.76–5.20	4.68–5.72
	70	2.70–5.74	4.82–7.31	2.32–5.82
A2	20	3.46–4.14	3.59–4.73	3.84–4.75
	30	2.55–4.31	4.12–4.80	4.02–4.60
	40	3.01–4.51	4.90–5.10	4.18–4.63
	50	3.00–4.92	4.68–5.34	4.06–4.90
	60	4.12–4.61	4.91–5.72	4.77–5.67
	70	5.88–6.54	5.50–6.40	5.27–5.57
A3	20	2.98–3.46	3.52–4.93	3.43–4.02
	30	2.68–5.15	4.45–5.56	3.75–4.27
	40	3.30–3.96	5.01–9.04	3.89–4.43
	50	3.49–6.46	3.77–5.39	2.44–4.70
	60	3.45–5.14	5.32–6.25	4.60–5.35
	70	3.38–6.94	5.44–6.70	3.77–6.08
A4	20	3.18–3.80	3.91–4.34	3.75–4.72
	30	2.15–5.40	4.12–5.77	4.52–7.83
	40	1.52–3.59	4.16–4.54	4.89–6.00
	50	3.70–4.06	4.09–5.14	4.02–5.04
	60	3.33–4.32	3.56–5.18	4.28–6.41
	70	4.06–5.54	4.36–23.58	5.66–6.20

concentration as a function of the penultimate reinforcer concentration, would reveal any cumulative effect that might have been present.

Figure 3.3 shows the results of such an analysis. Although there was considerable variability between subjects, as well as in the functions for each subject, a trend can nevertheless by discerned. Especially the pauses following the 20 and 70 percent concentrations appeared to increase as a function of the penultimate reinforcer concentration. This evidence was not entirely convincing, but it was sufficient to encourage further investigation.

Experiment 2

This experiment differed from the previous one in that the animals were trained more extensively prior to the collection of data. Six rats were trained to

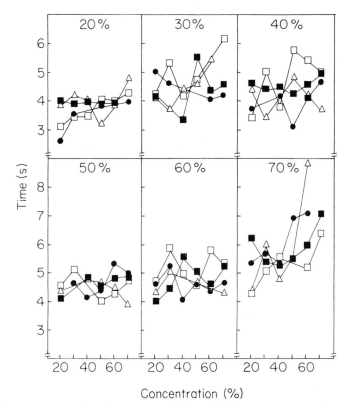

Figure 3.3. Experiment 1. Cumulative effects of reinforcer concentration. Median duration of postreinforcement pauses following a given reinforcer concentration are shown as a function of the concentration of the *preceding* reinforcer; i.e. the pause durations are given in relation to the penultimate reinforcer concentration. The symbols indicate the different subjects. Note that data points do not represent equal numbers of pauses. Data were not included in those cases where the number of pauses for a given concentration was less than four

lever press with 0.05 ml of 50 percent concentration of Nestlé's condensed milk[3] (volume by volume). Nine sessions were then conducted with reinforcer concentrations of 20, 40, 60, and 80 percent, changing randomly within each session. Sixty reinforcements occurred in a session. Data were collected in the last five sessions.

As this experiment was mainly concerned with second-order relations, the first-order relations are shown only for one of the animals, in Figure 3.4. The median duration of postreinforcement pauses was an increasing function of reinforcer concentration. Interquartile ranges of these data are given in Table 3.2. These results confirm the findings of Experiment 1, and are representative of the data from the other animals.

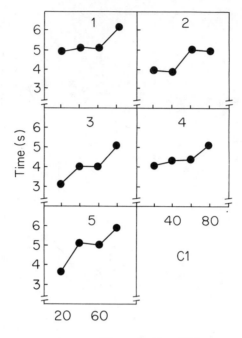

Figure 3.4. Experiment 2. Median duration of the postreinforcement pauses as a function of the concentration of the preceding reinforcer in five daily sessions. The number in each square is the session number. The figure shows data from one of the animals (C1)

Similarly consistent positive functions emerged in second-order relations. Figure 3.5 shows the relationship between the mean duration of the postreinforcement pause that occurred following a given concentration and the concentration of the penultimate reinforcer. These data are based on the last four occasions when each reinforcer concentration occurred; i.e. the last four times

Table 3.2. Experiment 2. Interquartile ranges of the postreinforcement pauses as a function of reinforcer concentration. Data are from one animal, and are representative of other animals' data

| Session | Concentration (%) | | | |
	20	40	60	80
1	4.70–5.87	4.23–5.26	4.87–6.17	5.40–7.07
2	3.50–4.41	3.58–4.36	4.30–5.44	4.23–6.98
3	2.91–3.58	3.69–4.67	3.57–5.63	4.38–6.87
4	3.76–4.48	3.07–4.84	3.73–5.09	4.70–6.76
5	3.46–4.28	4.84–5.65	4.71–5.67	4.89–6.58

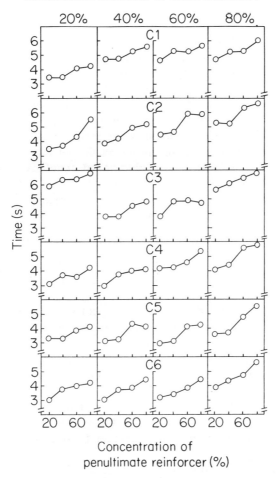

Figure 3.5. Experiment 2. Mean duration of the postreinforcement pauses following a given reinforcer, as a function of the concentration of the preceding reinforcer. Each row shows data from one animal, as indicated in the centre top part of the row. The percentage figures at the head of each column indicate the concentration of the ultimate reinforcer

when 80 percent was preceded by 20 percent, by 40 percent, and so on. The functions provide strong evidence that the pause-producing effect of reinforcer magnitude is cumulative. When the concentration of the reinforcer initiating the pause was the same, the duration of that pause increased as a function of the concentration of the penultimate reinforcer. This effect cannot be related to any discriminative control by the reinforcer, or to activities such as chewing and mouth cleaning. The most direct conclusion appears to be that reinforcers have an inhibitory property.

Experiment 3

There are, of course, yet more ways of testing whether a reinforcer has an inhibitory effect. If inhibition that results from reinforcement is cumulative, then introduction of a change into the reinforcement situation should act as a disinhibitor, and result in the dissipation of any inhibition that has been built up. Occasional omission of the reinforcer in the CRF schedule, for example, should function in this way. There is evidence of such an effect in classical conditioning. Hovland (1936) found that when conditioning trials were 'massed', i.e. occurred closely in time, the magnitude of the galvanic skin response was greater in the second trial where the unconditioned stimulus was omitted than in the first trial. He attributed this to dissipation of 'inhibition of reinforcement' in the first trial. Hilgard and Marquis (1935) have also noted, with reference to the first extinction trial, that, 'This unexpected ommission may act as a disinhibitor, and result in a larger response on the second trial' (p. 48).

The above observations were with reference to extinction where reinforcement, once withdrawn, is not restored. If reinforcement were occasionally withheld, but restored after omission, the converse of the effect would be expected. Thus, in such a situation, two predictions can be made. First, after disinhibition the inhibitory effect of reinforcement will once again build up, so that the second of the first two post *reinforcement* pauses following omission will be longer than the first. Second, when two or more omissions occur consecutively, unlike Hovland's (1936) findings, there will be no systematic difference between the post-omission pauses. The first omission will dissipate inhibition, but no inhibitory effect is to be expected on the second post-omission pause as the reinforcer is not present. In Hovland's (1936) experiment it was, of course, the response, and not the postreinforcement pause that increased in amplitude, i.e. recovered in the second extinction trial, following the dissipation of inhibition.

Seven rats were reinforced under the CRF schedule, one group (P2, P3, and P4) with 0.05 ml of 60 percent Nestlé's condensed milk solution, and another group (P5, P6, P7, and P8) with 0.05 ml of 60 percent sucrose solution. Nine daily sessions were followed by six further sessions in which 50 percent of reinforcements were omitted at random. In omission the reinforcement mechanism operated but the reinforcer cup was empty.

Mean durations and standard deviations of the post-omission and postreinforcement pauses are given in Table 3.3. In almost every case (exceptions were sessions 2 and 3 for P7 and session 3 for P8; all these exceptions were from animals reinforced with sucrose) the well-known omission effect occurred: the animals responded sooner after omission than after reinforcement. The main interest in this study was in comparing the first and second consecutive postreinforcement pauses to occur after an omission. Table 3.4 shows the number of occasions when the second of these pauses was longer and shorter

Table 3.3. Experiment 3. Mean durations and standard deviations of post-omission and postreinforcement pauses for each animal in each session

Animal	Session	Omission		Reinforcement	
		Mean	S.D.	Mean	S.D.
P2	1	4.02	3.28	5.18	1.74
	2	4.41	4.45	8.36	6.64
	3	2.65	1.93	5.60	3.33
	4	2.76	1.52	3.34	2.08
	5	2.87	0.96	5.33	2.94
	6	3.10	1.33	4.85	1.29
P3	1	8.02	7.55	8.79	3.50
	2	5.95	5.44	8.12	3.44
	3	9.03	7.85	12.31	8.78
	4	5.70	5.97	8.08	3.80
	5	5.12	3.02	7.60	2.35
	6	3.11	0.88	6.60	1.28
P4	1	4.16	4.03	4.46	2.18
	2	4.13	3.34	4.93	1.60
	3	5.17	4.10	6.01	3.74
	4	3.00	1.72	5.09	1.77
	5	4.78	2.83	8.59	6.66
	6	2.74	0.73	4.30	1.16
P5	1	3.82	1.34	5.92	3.83
	2	4.58	2.92	4.78	1.08
	3	5.89	3.78	7.50	7.05
	4	5.51	3.73	6.10	3.91
	5	4.79	3.69	4.89	1.88
	6	3.12	0.81	4.48	1.54
P6	1	3.57	2.67	4.26	2.05
	2	2.87	1.36	4.44	1.87
	3	4.03	2.02	5.95	3.34
	4	4.24	2.63	4.47	1.97
	5	3.34	1.36	4.13	1.47
	6	3.41	1.94	4.16	2.96
P7	1	4.51	3.36	4.56	3.07
	2	3.84	2.83	3.46	1.32
	3	8.55	7.35	7.68	8.07
	4	4.37	3.77	4.42	3.21
	5	3.18	0.89	3.37	0.91
	6	3.21	1.84	3.46	2.23
P8	1	4.60	3.93	5.50	4.63
	2	4.67	3.13	7.11	3.04
	3	5.43	7.22	4.71	2.94
	4	4.32	4.50	4.39	5.35
	5	3.36	1.34	5.52	2.89
	6	2.96	0.85	4.13	1.72

Table 3.4. Experiment 3. The number of times the second of first two postreinforcement pauses following an omission was longer and shorter than the first. The difference between these scores, and totals of all sessions for each animal, are also given

Animal	Session	Increase	Decrease	Difference
P2	1	5	1	4
	2	7	2	5
	3	6	0	6
	4	4	1	3
	5	6	0	6
	6	5	1	4
	Total	33	5	28
P3	1	6	0	6
	2	5	1	4
	3	6	0	6
	4	5	1	4
	5	3	2	1
	6	6	2	4
	Total	31	6	25
P4	1	5	1	4
	2	4	1	3
	3	5	2	3
	4	8	1	7
	5	4	2	2
	6	6	0	6
	Total	32	7	25
P5	1	6	3	3
	2	7	2	5
	3	7	1	6
	4	5	1	4
	5	7	1	6
	6	4	2	2
	Total	36	10	26
P6	1	3	1	2
	2	7	0	7
	3	5	2	3
	4	8	1	7
	5	5	2	3
	6	7	1	6
	Total	35	7	28
P7	1	5	3	2
	2	3	3	0
	3	5	3	2
	4	1	4	−3
	5	5	3	2
	6	3	2	1
	Total	22	18	4

Table 3.4. (*Contd.*)

Animal	Session	Increase	Decrease	Difference
P8	1	4	2	2
	2	5	4	1
	3	3	5	−2
	4	4	1	3
	5	5	4	1
	6	3	3	1
	Total	25	19	6

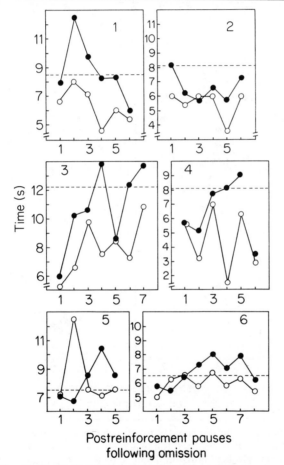

Postreinforcement pauses
following omission

Figure 3.6. Experiment 3. Durations of the first (open circles) and second (solid circles) postreinforcement pauses that occurred following omission of reinforcement. The data are from one animal. Broken horizontal line indicates the mean duration of the postreinforcement pause for that session. Note that abscissa is not in equal units: successive pairs of postreinforcement pauses following each omission are shown in the sequence of their occurrence in a session

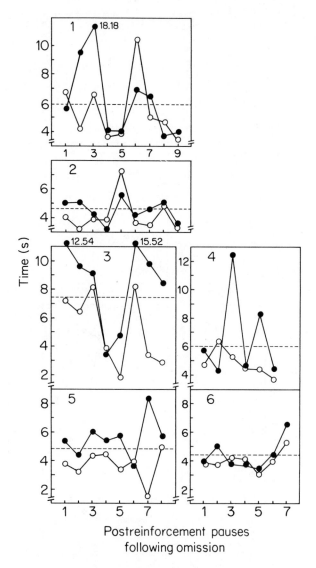

Figure 3.7. Experiment 3. Durations of the first (open circles) and second (solid circles) postreinforcement pauses that occurred following omission of reinforcement. The data are from one animal. Broken horizontal line indicates the mean duration of the postreinforcement pause for that session. Note that abscissa is not in equal units: successive pairs of postreinforcement pauses following each omission are shown in the sequence of their occurrence in a session

than the first pause, and also the difference between these two scores. The results confirmed our first prediction: on most occasions the second postreinforcement pause was longer than the first. The durations of these pairs of postreinforcement pauses are shown, for two animals, in Figures 3.6 and 3.7. These are representative of the results of the other animals. A further aspect of these data is worth noting. Even though there were exceptions, generally both first and second pauses were shorter than the mean duration of all postreinforcement pauses in a session. Thus, the increase in postreinforcement pause duration following omission continued beyond the second pause; in our terms, the inhibitory effect cumulated across more than two consecutive pauses.

The second prediction was also confirmed. Table 3.5 shows the number of times the second of two consecutive post omission pauses was longer and shorter than the first. Taking the total number of times for all sessions, the second post-omission pause was longer than the pause for four animals, and it was shorter for three animals.

The finding that when reinforcement is omitted the following response increases in speed, or the following pause decreases in duration, is a well-documented one (*see* for example, Scull, 1973, for a review of the literature). It has generally been assumed that these two changes in the two measures (response speed and pause duration) reflect the same phenomenon. This phenomenon has been thought to be one where responding increases *either* due to the energizing effect of reinforcer omission (e.g. Amsel, 1958, 1962) *or* due to the absence, in omission, of a conditioned inhibitory effect that would have been present had reinforcement occurred (e.g. Staddon, 1970*b*). Thus, when omission occurs the level of responding maintained by reinforcement is said either to *increase* above that level, or *return* to that level, having previously been inhibited. (Note that the latter hypothesis could not, in any case, apply to the present experiment since it asserts that the inhibitory effect is solely dependent on the reinforcer having a discriminative function. According to Staddon (1970*b*), for example, where the reinforcer cannot have a discriminative function the omission effect should not occur.)

In the light of the present results, and of previous findings in our laboratory (Harzem, *et al.*, 1978) we take a different position. Reinforcement omission affects differently (i) the postreinforcement pause, and (ii) the rate or speed of responding, *once responding has commenced*. The postreinforcement pause becomes shorter in omission because the inhibitory effect of reinforcement is absent. The response rate, on the other hand, when measured after excluding the postreinforcement pauses, is elevated following reinforcer omission. The present experiment does not provide any evidence on the latter point. However, Harzem *et al.* (1978) found that, when the reinforcer was omitted, the 'local' rate of responses, i.e. responses in successive 8.5 and 11 s intervals following reinforcement or omission, increased under an arithmetic VI schedule but not under a constant probability VI schedule. They therefore concluded that

Table 3.5. Experiment 3. The number of times the second of first two post-omission pauses was longer and shorter than the first. The difference between these scores, and totals for all sessions for each animal, are also given

Animal	Session	Increase	Decrease	Difference
P2	1	2	5	−3
	2	3	4	−1
	3	3	5	−2
	4	3	4	−1
	5	2	6	−4
	6	7	3	4
	Total	20	27	−7
P3	1	4	3	1
	2	1	6	−5
	3	3	3	0
	4	3	4	−1
	5	7	1	6
	6	5	2	3
	Total	23	19	4
P4	1	5	2	3
	2	4	3	1
	3	1	5	−4
	4	4	1	3
	5	4	4	0
	6	6	1	5
	Total	24	16	8
P5	1	3	1	2
	2	3	6	−3
	3	6	3	3
	4	2	5	−3
	5	3	3	0
	6	5	2	3
	Total	22	20	2
P6	1	6	4	2
	2	3	6	−3
	3	5	3	2
	4	3	4	−1
	5	1	5	−4
	6	3	2	1
	Total	21	24	−3
P7	1	5	1	4
	2	2	4	−2
	3	2	4	−2
	4	5	2	3
	5	4	1	3
	6	3	4	−1
	Total	21	16	5

Table 3.5 (contd.)

Animal	Session	Increase	Decrease	Difference
P8	1	4	5	− 1
	2	3	2	1
	3	3	4	− 1
	4	2	7	− 5
	5	4	1	3
	6	3	4	− 1
	Total	19	23	− 4

elevation of response rate following reinforcement omission is observed when the reinforcing stimulus signals a period of nonreinforcement . . . but not when the reinforcer has no such predictive significance (p. 9).

Thus the evidence points to a difference in the effects on responding and pausing. Omission affects the pauses regardless of whether the reinforcer is predictive or not, but it affects responding only when it is predictive. Most studies of the frustration effect have used runways. In these situations and, indeed, in operant studies that have only measured the overall response rate, the effects on the pauses and response rates that occur following the pauses have been confounded. The present account would suggest that the divergence in some of the findings that have proved difficult for any of the theories of frustration effect (cf. Scull, 1973) might be resolved if the data were analysed with regard to the difference between pausing and responding.

Reinforcer Magnitude and Behaviour

Implicit in the account we have presented so far is the assumption that increasing the magnitude of a reinforcer increases its strength as a stimulus, and for this reason its inhibitory effect is enhanced. It will not have escaped notice, however, that the results we have reported from experiments with the CRF schedule are contrary to some of the previous literature on the relationship between reinforcer magnitude and response rate. The CRF schedule is unique in one respect. As in this schedule there are no unreinforced responses, three different measures are expressions of the same measure. The postreinforcement pause duration and IRT are identical; and the mean IRT reflects the same measure as response rate, one being the reciprocal of the other. Thus, to say that postreinforcement pause duration *increased* as a function of reinforcer magnitude is the same as saying the response rate *decreased* as a function of reinforcer magnitude. This would seem to go against one's common-sense expectation, at least at first sight. For this reason, and also because the existing literature provides further support for our thesis, we briefly consider in this section the effects of reinforcer magnitude.

The literature has been reviewed in detail by the present authors (Harzem and Harzem, 1981). Previous reviews of the same literature (Bolles and Moot, 1972; Kling and Schrier, 1971) have shown that the evidence is complex and often contradictory. Increasing the magnitude of a reinforcer has been found to (i) increase the rate of responding; (ii) increase and then decrease the rate of responding (non-monotonic relationship); (iii) have no systematic effect on the rate of responding; and (iv) decrease the rate of responding. These apparently irreconcilable findings are based not on a few superficial studies, but arise from a large amount of research. Kling and Schrier (1972) have commented:

> It therefore comes as something of a shock to some students of behavior when they discover that amount of reinforcer frequently is quite an ineffective variable when manipulated in laboratory studies, and that there is considerable discrepancy between the results of studies which appear to be equally well designed and organized. (p. 630)

Re-examination of the literature has shown, however, that these contradictions are only apparent, and that they can be accommodated within a single conceptual scheme (Harzem and Harzem, 1981). What is needed is to take into account the distinct control of the postreinforcement pause. Measures of response rate have typically ignored this distinction; in other words, in calculating the response rate the time parameter includes the time taken by the pauses. Since postreinforcement pauses develop gradually in the course of acquisition, the extent to which the pauses contribute to the rate measure would depend on at what point in the experiment the rate data are collected. The studies reporting a positive relationship between reinforcer magnitude and response rate have obtained their data in the course of acquisition, before the postreinforcement pauses made any appreciable contribution to the measure of response rate; those studies reporting an inverse rate–magnitude function have obtained their data after responding and pausing stabilized. These two kinds of relationships represent the two ends of a continuum. When data are collected late in acquisition, in the course of transition from acquisition to stable performance, a function containing elements of the two is obtained: it is non-monotonic, increasing with lower magnitudes and decreasing with higher magnitudes. The fact that greater reinforcer magnitude results in faster development of stable behaviour is the factor that contributes to the transition from increasing function to decreasing function that is seen when the overall function is non-monotonic. Averaging of data across acquisition and stable performance has a similar effect.

When stable responding has been established with two or more reinforcer magnitudes, the picture that emerges is quite different. Under those schedules that typically produce long postreinforcement pauses, which therefore make a substantial contribution to the overall response rate, the rate–magnitude function is inverse. On the other hand, unsystematic rate–magnitude relationships are seen when a balance occurs between the postreinforcement pause

Table 3.6. Summary of the main research findings on the effect of reinforcer magnitude upon response rate and postreinforcement pause duration under FI schedules. Total amount of time in training (*) and effect on response rate (×) are shown. Plus sign indicates that the magnitude–pause duration function was positive. Note that the first two columns showing duration of training are in 5 h steps, and the remainder in 10 h steps. Two or more signs in a row indicate that all these durations or all these results occurred in the experiment

Study	Duration of training (h)					Rate–magnitude function				
	0–5	6–10	11–20	21–30	31+	Positive	Non-monotonic	Unsystematic	Negative	Pause
Guttman (1953)	*					×				
Hutt (1954)	*					×				
Collier and Myers (1961)										
Experiment 1	*					×				
Experiment 2	*					×				
Collier and Willis (1961)	*					×				
Collier (1962)										
Experiment 2	*					×				
Experiment 6	*					×				
Collier and Myers (1961)										
Experiment 3		*							×	
Collier (1962)										
Experiment 1		*				×	×			
Experiment 3			*				×			
Experiment 4		*	*			×	×		×	
Experiment 5		*	*				×			
Stebbins, Mead, and Martin (1959)			*							
Collier and Siskel (1959)				*		×	×			
Meltzer and Brahlek (1968)					*				×	+
Meltzer and Brahlek (1970)					*				×	+
Staddon (1970a)					*					
Lowe et al. (1974)					*				×	+
Davey, Harzem, and Lowe (1975)					*				×	+

and the running rate (calculated after excluding the pauses), so that increases in the pause duration are more or less compensated by increases in the running rate. The result is either little difference in the overall rate with different magnitudes or changes in either direction, depending on this balance.

Table 3.6 summarizes the studies of the effect of reinforcer magnitude upon response rate under FI schedules. This is the most frequently studied schedule, and illustrates best the relations described above. In almost every case the type of result obtained was directly related to the extent of training. The literature on the effects of reinforcer magnitude provides strong support for the present account of the postreinforcement pause. However, although this support is substantial, evidence of a change from a positive rate – magnitude function in the early stage of an experiment to an inverse function in the later stage of the same experiment would be even more convincing.

Two studies have provided evidence of this sort. Van Hartesveldt (1973) reinforced rats with different volumes of water under the CRF schedule. Three groups of rats were used, one with lesions in the hippocampus (which is thought to be involved in internal inhibition; e.g. Douglas, 1967, Kimble, 1968); another group with cortical lesions; and a third, sham-operated group. For half of the rats in each group the reinforcer was 0.08 ml water, and for the other half it was 0.01 ml. For all three sub-groups the speed of acquisition, i.e. the number of

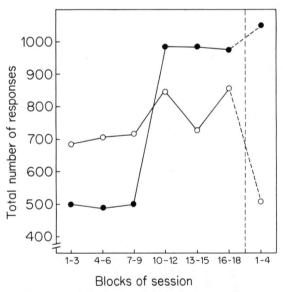

Figure 3.8. Total number of responses emitted in three-session blocks with 8 per cent (solid circles) and 32 per cent (open circles) sucrose solutions as reinforcers. Other experimental manipulations intervened before the final block of four sessions. (Redrawn from Hurwitz et al., 1965)

20 min sessions required to reach a criterion of 50 responses in a 20 min session, was greater when the reinforcer volume was 0.08 ml. Five further sessions were conducted with the rats who received the 0.08 ml water, and then the volume was reduced to 0.04 ml for five sessions, and to 0.01 ml for five more sessions. In all three sub-groups the response rate was inversely related to reinforcer volume. Hurwitz, Walker, Salmon, and Packham (1965) have reported similar results, obtained under an FR schedule. The reinforcer for two groups of six rats was sucrose solution of 8 and 32 percent respectively. Five 30 min sessions were conducted under the CRF schedule, followed by 18 sessions under FR 20 schedule. Figure 3.8 shows the total number of responses in successive three-session blocks. In the early sessions the response rate of the group receiving 32 percent sucrose solution was higher. After the ninth session, however, this relationship was reversed so that the 8 percent group emitted more responses. After several other manipulations, the conditions described above were restored in a final phase of four sessions. The last data points in Figure 3.8 show that the inverse relationship was preserved in this final phase.

In summary, the existing evidence shows that the effect of reinforcer magnitude upon response rate depends on whether, under a given schedule, stable responding has been established. This dependence largely reflects the extent to which the postreinforcement pauses have developed. At least two important questions remain: (i) what determines the occurrence and duration of the postreinforcement pauses? and (ii) given that postreinforcement pauses and the running rate of responses are observed separately, what determines the running rate? We now turn, once again, to the first question.

A Theory of Reinforcement: Stimulus Effects of Reinforcers

The theory we propose contains the following statements:

(i) Any stimulus that functions as a reinforcer is also an unconditioned inhibitory stimulus.

(ii) This inhibitory effect is specific to the response that is associated with the reinforcer.

(iii) The inhibitory effect is observed in the pause which occurs after every reinforcement.

(iv) In those situations when the reinforcer has a discriminative function, signalling that for a period another reinforcement will not occur, the reinforcer will become a conditioned inhibitory stimulus. This takes place through the simultaneous occurrence (pairing) of discriminative and unconditioned inhibitory effects, as might occur if two different stimuli were paired (cf. Rescorla, Chapter 2 in this volume).

(v) The amount of inhibition produced by a reinforcer is a direct function of the magnitude of that reinforcer.

(vi) The inhibitory effect is cumulative over successive presentations of the reinforcer, varying according to the time that elapses between reinforcements.

The term inhibition is used in the same sense as it was used by Pavlov (1927) and in subsequent studies of classical conditioning, except that it does not imply a cortical process, as suggested in Pavlov's theory. Thus, 'inhibition' refers to absence of a response or a decrease in response strength which results from the presentation of a stimulus when, without that stimulus, the response would occur or would be stronger. Pavlov distinguished 'internal' and 'external' inhibition, the former being the result of the presentation of a conditioned stimulus, and the latter, the result of an extraneous stimulus (cf. Kimble, 1961). Here the term 'unconditioned inhibition' is used to emphasize that the particular stimulus has an inhibitory property not due to any prior conditioning procedure. It is assumed that phenomena associated with inhibition, such as disinhibition and cumulation, also occur in the present case.

The notion that reinforcement may inhibit responding is not new. It was first put forward by Hilgard and Marquis (1935), to explain the fact that in the extinction of classically conditioned responses sometimes, but not always, the magnitude of the response is greater in the second extinction trial than in the first. They suggested that this may be due to dissipation of the inhibition built up during acquisition, by the first extinction trial. The altered conditions of that trial would act as a disinhibitor. Hovland (1936) followed up this suggestion, and showed that the rise in the extinction curve at the second trial occurred when the conditioning trials were massed, thus enabling cumulation of inhibition, but not when they were spaced. The term 'inhibition of reinforcement' was used, indicating the inhibition effect of an unconditioned stimulus. More recently Catania (1963), with specific reference to performance under concurrent schedules, has proposed that reinforcement may be 'self-inhibiting', affecting all of the responses an organism may emit. The present suggestion is that the inhibitory effect is specific to the class of responses associated with the particular reinforcer, and that the effect is on the postreinforcement pause and not on the response rate.

A reinforcer has at least two effects on behaviour: inhibition, and the more obvious 'reinforcing' or 'excitatory' effect. From the present of point of view, under partial reinforcement schedules these two effects are manifested in two distinct features of performance; namely, the postreinforcement pause and the 'run' of responses. The excitatory effect is seen early in training, since responding occurs from the start, even if with some variability, but the pauses develop gradually. In CRF schedules both the excitatory and inhibitory effects are on the responses that are followed by postreinforcement pauses, since there are no unreinforced responses. In these conditions the excitatory effect might be the dominant one at the start of training, before the establishment of stable pauses. This would account for the positive rate–magnitude function in early sessions, and for the change to inverse function in later sessions.

If the above account is correct, it would be expected that the running rate, as well as the postreinforcement pause duration, would be positively related to reinforcer magnitude. Although effects of reinforcer magnitude upon running rate have not been studied extensively, there is considerable indirect evidence bearing on this relationship; for example, in studies of preference where a choice is given between two or more reinforcer magnitudes. In most of these studies it is found that subjects allocate more time to responses that result in the greater magnitude, or more of such responses are made (e.g. Balsam, Brownstein, and Shull, 1978; Bitterman, 1976; Brownstein, 1971; Collier, Vogel, and Rega, 1966; Collier and Rega, 1971; Walker, Schnelle, and Hurwitz, 1970).

Generality of the Theory

An advantage of the present account appears to be that it embraces a broad range of phenomena, for which separate explanations have previously been offered. It incorporates an explanation of the postreinforcement pause with an explanation of the varied effects of reinforcer magnitude.

If reinforcers have an inhibitory property that is unconditioned, then this property should play a part in a wide range of studies involving problems that are usually considered separately. This should be the case in runway experiments as well as experiments conducted in the Skinner box. One difficulty with runway studies, however, is that ordinarily they exclude the postreinforcement pause; only the behaviour up to the entry into the goal box is observed and recorded. An exception to this is the double runway, where behaviour that occurs after reinforcement in the middle goalbox can be observed without intervention by the experimenter. Results of the experiments that have been conducted in that apparatus may have an important bearing on the account outlined here, as comparison of the start times from the middle box when food was present and absent (and after different amounts of food) would give measures of the postreinforcement pause.

Biological Utility of Inhibition

The notion that a reinforcer may inhibit the type of response that produced it appears, at first, to violate common sense. This type of inhibition has, in fact, an important biological function. Several examples of it have been observed in ethological studies, although the phenomenon has been interpreted in several different ways. Thorpe (1963), for example, has used the term 'action specific exhaustibility'. One example is to be found in the behaviour of the male Grayling butterfly, which flies upwards to a female. If a 'dummy' female, suspended by a thread, is held above the male it will fly up towards it. However, when the dummy was presented at intervals of less than 20 s, the percentage of positive responses declined as a function of number of presentations. (From an account by Thorpe,

1963, of observations made by Tinbergen and his associates.) A similar effect was observed by Sevenster (1973) in the behaviour of male sticklebacks. Each time they swam through a ring an opaque screen was lifted so that a female stickleback, behind glass, could be seen, and the male could perform a courting dance. The response of swimming through the ring was acquired slowly, but thereafter occurred many times. On the other hand, a different response, that of biting a rod, was acquired quickly as the fish in any case perform this action spontaneously, from time to time. In contrast, after acquisition a large number of responses was never achieved, and many responses were abandoned before completion. Performance of the courting dance and/or sight of the female appeared to inhibit the biting response. When the 'reinforcer' was changed to sight of a rival male, the biting response increased in frequency. Thus, events associated with courting inhibited biting, but events associated with fighting did not (*see also* Eibl-Eibesfeldt, 1975; Dunham, 1977). Yet another example, rather more similar to studies of the reinforcing effects of sugar solutions, is seen in the behaviour of the blowfly (Dethier, 1966). The blowfly 'pumps in' sugar solution through its proboscis. The higher the concentration, the more rapidly there is a decline in pumping. Once pumping stops, it will start again if a stronger concentration of sucrose is provided, to be followed by a decline. These phenomena have been interpreted in terms of sensory adaptation. The important point is that there are processes which slow down the behaviour related to stimuli that are nevertheless biologically important for the organism.

Other examples of an inhibitory effect appear in ethological studies. It is not, of course, suggested that all of these are instances of the inhibitory effect of *reinforcers*. But the generality of inhibition, or phenomena like inhibition, is impressive and suggests the question of what may be their biological utility. The following attempt at an answer is entirely speculative, and relates only to the effects of reinforcers.

Reinforcement has a powerful effect on behaviour. A given repetitive response can be maintained, over many hours and even days, by occasional reinforcement with very small amounts of food. Such a strong hold on behaviour has, however, dangers for the organism, especially in the natural environment. Let us consider, for example, a foraging hungry animal. When it comes upon food it may become engrossed in eating, at the expense of attending, from time to time, to other events in the environment. Thus it may miss an even richer source of food, or it may fail to sample a variety of sources, thereby failing to get the range of nutrition it requires. Even more importantly, it may not notice approaching danger. Considerable evidence in the operant literature shows that when two or more responses are available, changing from one to the other occurs most often during the postreinforcement pause. Thus, the postreinforcement pause provides opportunities for switching between different activities, and for relating behaviour to different aspects of the environment. It is, in this way, a biologically important characteristic of behaviour.

Postscript

Bishop Butler (1726), in his sermons opposing hedonism, argued that if man was made continuously to seek pleasure, the unchecked pleasures would emaciate him and lead to his destruction. God, thought Bishop Butler, would never have created such a man. In a sense he was right. One mechanism for putting an end to incessant gratification is well known. Whatever the source of pleasure, ultimately it leads to satiation, long before the danger of destruction approaches. (It may be as well to note that it is not unknown for some men to pit against this another of their faculties: to use their ingenuity to circumvent this useful mechanism.) A second way of averting excess lies in the fact that increasing the intensity of stimulation, whatever the pleasure, culminates in pain. And there is, apparently, a third mechanism. It enters the picture long before the other two make their effects felt. From the outset, each reinforcement carries with it an inhibitory effect, specifically upon the behaviour that brought about that reinforcement. This is a mechanism that gives to an organism an opportunity to break away, before being engulfed in preoccupation with just one sort of activity.

Bishop Butler's concern with hedonism is, of course, a far cry from the inhibitory effect of reinforcement. But it helps to make the point. Inhibition by a reinforcer, although it may at first seem paradoxical—why inhibit a reinforcer-producing response?—has a biologically useful function. It enables a hungry organism to switch to other stimuli while feeding, and so to avoid the dreadful consequences of, say, oblivion to a fast-approaching predator. And looking up at the end of a delightful passage in the book one is reading helps one to reduce the chances of missing the train. The train is, of course, sometimes missed, and predators are successful enough to survive. No inhibitory effect may be sufficient to save the pigeon from pecking a circular disc at high speed, for hours on end. But ordinarily the mechanism works quite effectively: pigeons and rats are more likely to switch to other activities just after reinforcement than at other times. Judging by casual observations, so are people.

Notes

1. The ideas expressed in this chapter developed in discussions over many years. Their present form was arrived at, and main parts of the chapter were written, when Peter Harzem was on a year's leave from Auburn University. He wishes to thank the University. Anne Harzem wishes to thank Professors L. R. Reid and A. Summerfield for encouraging and helpful comments on the ideas expressed here. We are also grateful to Marion Ellis and Carol Griffith at the University of Wales for help with running the experiments and drawing the figures, and Rita Dauber at Auburn University for typing the final manuscript.
2. Strictly speaking there were two different postreinforcement pauses in this experiment, one following the FI reinforcement and the other following the reinforcement of the response terminating the pause. For the present purpose, the term 'postreinforcement pause' is used here to refer to the pause relevant to the FI schedule—i.e. following the FI reinforcement.

3. We have conducted a large number of experiments with sucrose and condensed milk as reinforcer, and found that sucrose produces rather more variable results than condensed milk. Other researchers have also observed that sucrose is rather a 'finicky' reinforcer (cf. Mackintosh, 1974). We know of no explanation as to why there is such a difference between the two reinforcers that are, basically, not unlike each other.

References

Amsel, A. (1958). The role of frustrative nonreward in noncontinuous reward situations. *Psychological Bulletin*, **55**, 102–119.

Amsel, A. (1962). Frustrative nonreward in partial reinforcement and discrimination learning: some recent history and a theoretical extension. *Psychological Review*, **69**, 306–328.

Azrin, N. H., Hutchinson, R. R., and Hake, D. F. (1967). Attack, avoidance and escape reactions to aversive shock. *Journal of the Experimental Analysis of Behavior*, **10**, 131–148.

Balsam, P. D., Brownstein, A. J., and Shull, R. L. (1978). Effects of varying the grain duration in automaintenance. *Journal of the Experimental Analysis of Behavior*, **29**, 27–36.

Barrett, J. E. (1976). Conjunctive schedules of reinforcement: III. A fixed-interval schedule. *Journal of the Experimental Analysis of Behavior*, **25**, 157–164.

Berryman, R. E. and Nevin, J. A. (1962). Interlocking schedules of reinforcement. *Journal of the Experimental Analysis of Behavior*, **5**, 213–223.

Bitterman, M. E. (1976). Incentive contrast in honey bees. *Science*, **192**, 380–382.

Bolles, R. C. and Moot, S. A. (1972). Derived motives. *Annual Review of Psychology*, **23**, 51–72.

Boren, J. J. (1961). Resistance to extinction as a function of the fixed-ratio. *Journal of the Experimental Psychology*, **61**, 304–308.

Brimer, C. J. (1972). Disinhibition of an operant response. In *Inhibition and Learning* (R. A. Boakes and M. S. Halliday, eds), pp. 205–227, Academic Press, London.

Brown, T. G. and Flory, R. K. (1972). Schedule induced escape from fixed-interval reinforcement. *Journal of the Experimental Analysis of Behavior*, **17**, 395–403.

Brownstein, A. J. (1971). Concurrent schedules of response-independent reinforcement: duration of a reinforcing stimulus. *Journal of the Experimental Analysis of Behavior*, **15**, 211–214.

Butler, J. (1726). *Fifteen Sermons Preached at the Rolls Chapel and a Dissertation Upon the Nature of Virtue*, London (reprinted by Bell, London, 1958).

Catania, A. C. (1963). Concurrent performances: a baseline for the study of reinforcement magnitude. *Journal of the Experimental Analysis of Behavior*, **6**, 299–300.

Catania, A. C. and Reynolds, G. S. (1968). A quantitative analysis of the responding maintained by interval schedules of reinforcement. *Journal of the Experimental Analysis of Behavior*, **11**, 327–383.

Cherek, D. R. and Pickens, R. (1970). Schedule-induced aggression as a function of fixed-interval value. *Journal of the Experimental Analysis of Behavior*, **14**, 309–311.

Chung, S. H. and Neuringer, A. J. (1967). Control of responding by a percentage reinforcement schedule. *Psychonomic Science*, **8**, 25–26.

Collier, G. (1962). Some properties of saccharin as a reinforcer. *Journal of Experimental Psychology*, **64**, 184–191.

Collier, G. and Myers, L. (1961). The loci of reinforcement. *Journal of Experimental Psychology*, **61**, 57–66.

Collier, G. and Rega, F. (1971). Two-bar sucrose preference. *Learning and Motivation*, **2**, 190–194.

Collier, G. and Siskel, M., Jr (1959). Performance as a joint function of amount of reinforcement and interreinforcement interval. *Journal of Experimental Psychology*, **57**, 115–120.

Collier, G. and Willis, F. (1961). Deprivation and reinforcement. *Journal of Experimental Psychology*, **62**, 377–384.

Collier, G., Vogel, J., and Rega, F. (1966). Two-bar sucrose preference. *Psychonomic Science*, **6**, 203–204.

Contrucci, J. J., Hothersall, D., and Wickens, D. D. (1971). The effects of a novel stimulus introduced into a DRL schedule at two temporal placements. *Psychonomic Science*, **23**, 97–99.

Crossman, E. K., Heaps, R. S., Nunes, D. L., and Alferink, L. A. (1974). The effects of number of responses on pause length with temporal variables controlled. *Journal of the Experimental Analysis of Behavior*, **22**, 115–121.

Cruse, D. B., Vitulli, N., and Dertke, M. (1966). Discriminative and reinforcing properties of two types of food pellets. *Journal of the Experimental Analysis of Behavior*, **9**, 293–303.

Davey, G. C. L., Harzem, P., and Lowe, C. F. (1975). The aftereffects of reinforcement magnitude and stimulus intensity. *Psychological Record*, **25**, 217–223.

Davis, H. and Iriye, C. (1973). Effects of a brief novel stimulus during temporally spaced responding: evidence for external inhibition? *Conditional Reflex*, **8**, 67–79.

Dethier, V. G. (1966). Insects and the concept of motivation. In *Nebraska Symposium in Motivation* (D. Levine, ed.), pp. 105–136, University of Nebraska, Lincoln, Neb.

Douglas, R. J. (1967). The hippocampus and behavior. *Psychological Bulletin*, **67**, 416–442.

Dove, L. D., Rashotte, M. E., and Katz, H. N. (1974). Development and maintenance of attack in pigeons during variable-interval reinforcement. *Journal of the Experimental Analysis of Behavior*, **21**, 563–569.

Dunham, P. (1977). The nature of reinforcing stimuli. In *Handbook of Operant Behavior* (W. K. Honig and J. E. R. Staddon, eds), pp. 98–124, Prentice-Hall, Englewood Cliffs, N. J.

Eibl-Eibesfeldt, I. (1975). *Ethology*, Holt, Rinehart, and Winston, New York.

Farmer, J. and Schoenfeld, W. N. (1964). Effects of a DRL contingency added to a fixed-interval reinforcement schedule. *Journal of the Experimental Analysis of Behavior*, **7**, 391–399.

Farmer, J. and Schoenfeld, W. N. (1967). Response rates under varying probability of reinforcement. *Psychonomic Science*, **7**, 173–174.

Felton, M. and Lyon, D. O. (1966). The postreinforcement pause. *Journal of the Experimental Analysis of Behavior*, **9**, 131–134.

Ferster, C. B. and Skinner, B. F. (1957). *Schedules of Reinforcement*, Appleton-Century-Crofts, New York.

Flanagan, B. and Webb, W. B. (1964). Disinhibition and external inhibition in fixed interval operant conditioning. *Psychonomic Science*, **1**, 123–124.

Gentry, W. D. (1968). Fixed-ratio schedule-induced aggression. *Journal of the Experimental Analysis of Behavior*, **11**, 813–817.

Guttman, N. (1953). Operant conditioning, extinction, and periodic reinforcement in relation to concentration of sucrose used as a reinforcing agent. *Journal of Experimental Psychology*, **46**, 213–224.

Harzem, A. L. and Harzem, P. (1981). Effects of reinforcer magnitude: an enigma in the literature, its variations, and a resolution. *Unpublished manuscript under review*.

Harzem, P. (1968). Temporal orientation of behaviour, Doctoral dissertation, University of Wales.

Harzem, P. (1969). Temporal discrimination. In *Animal Discrimination Learning* (R. M. Gilbert and N. S. Sutherland, eds), pp. 299–333, Academic Press, London.

Harzem, P., Lowe, C. F., and Bagshaw, M. (1978). Verbal control in human operant behavior. *Psychological Record*, **28**, 405–423.

Harzem, P., Lowe, C. F., and Davey, G. C. L. (1975a). Two-component schedules of differential reinforcement of low rate. *Journal of the Experimental Analysis of Behavior*, **24**, 33–42.

Harzem, P., Lowe, C. F., and Davey, G. C. L. (1975b). After-effects of reinforcement magnitude: dependence upon context. *Quarterly Journal of Experimental Psychology*, **27**, 579–584.

Harzem, P., Lowe, C. F., and Priddle-Higson, P. J. (1978). Inhibiting function of reinforcement: magnitude effects on variable-interval schedules. *Journal of the Experimental Analysis of Behavior*, **30**, 1010.

Harzem, P., Lowe, C. F., and Spencer, P. T. (1978). Temporal control of behavior: schedule interactions. *Journal of the Experimental Analysis of Behavior*, **30**, 225–270.

Hearst, E., Besley, S., and Farthing, G. W. (1970). Inhibition and the stimulus control of operant behavior. *Journal of the Experimental Analysis of Behavior*, **14**, 373–409.

Hilgard, E. R. and Marquis, D. G. (1935). Acquisition, extinction and retention of conditioned lid responses to light in dogs. *Journal of Comparative Psychology*, **19**, 29–58.

Hinrichs, J. A. (1968). Disinhibition of delay in fixed-interval instrumental conditioning. *Psychonomic Science*, **12**, 313–314.

Hovland, C. I. (1936). Inhibition of reinforcement and phenomena of experimental extinction. *Proceedings of the National Academy of Sciences of the U.S.A.*, **22**, 430–433.

Hurwitz, H. M. B., Walker, S. F., Salmon, B. A., and Packham, D. (1965). The effects of two sucrose solutions on rate of response under a fixed-ratio schedule. *Psychological Record*, **15**, 145–150.

Hutchinson, R. R., Azrin, N. H., and Hunt, G. M. (1968). Attack produced by intermittent reinforcement of a concurrent operant response. *Journal of the Experimental Analysis of Behavior*, **11**, 485–495.

Hutt, P. J. (1954). Rate of bar pressing as a function of quality and quantity of food reward. *Journal of Comparative and Physiological Psychology*, **47**, 235–237.

Kelleher, R. T., Fry, W., and Cook, L. (1959). Interresponse time distribution as a function of differential reinforcement of temporally spaced responses. *Journal of the Experimental Analysis of Behavior*, **2**, 91–106.

Keller, R. T. and Schoenfeld, W. N. (1950). *Principles of Psychology*, Appleton-Century-Crofts, New York.

Kello, J. E. (1972). The reinforcement-omission effect on fixed-interval schedules: furstration or inhibition? *Learning and Motivation*, **3**, 138–147.

Kello, J. E., Innis, N. K., and Staddon, J. E. R. (1975). Eccentric stimuli on multiple fixed-interval schedules. *Journal of the Experimental Analysis of Behavior*, **23**, 233–240.

Killeen, P. (1969). Reinforcement frequency and contingency as factors in fixed-ratio behavior. *Journal of the Experimental Analysis of Behavior*, **12**, 391–395.

Kimble, D. P. (1968). Hippocampus and internal inhibition. *Psychological Bulletin*, **70**, 285–295.

Kimble, G. A. (1961). *Hilgard and Marquis' Conditioning and Learning*, Appleton-Century-Crofts, New York.

Kling, J. W. and Schrier, A. M. (1971). Positive reinforcement. In *Experimental Psychology* (J. W. Kling and L. A. Riggs, eds), pp. 615–689, Methuen, London.

Knutson, J. F. (1970). Aggression during the fixed-ratio and extinction components of a multiple schedule of reinforcement. *Journal of the Experimental Analysis of Behavior*, **13**, 221–233.

Lachter, G. D. (1971). Some temporal parameters of non-contingent reinforcement. *Journal of the Experimental Analysis of Behavior*, **16**, 207–218.

Lattal, K. A. and Bryan, A. J. (1976). Effects of concurrent response-independent reinforcement on fixed interval schedule performance. *Journal of the Experimental Analysis of Behavior*, **26**, 495–504.

Lowe, C. F., Davey, G. C. L., and Harzem, P. (1974). Effects of reinforcement magnitude on interval and ratio schedules. *Journal of the Experimental Analysis of Behavior*, **22**, 553–560.

Lowe, C. F., Davey, G. C. L., and Harzem, P. (1976). After-effects of reinforcement magnitude on temporally spaced responding. *Psychological Record*, **26**, 33–40.

Lowe, C. F., Harzem, P., and Spencer, P. T. (1979). Temporal control and the power law. *Journal of the Experimental Analysis of Behavior*, **30**, 255–270.

Lund, C. A. (1976). Effects of variations in the temporal distribution of reinforcements on interval schedule performance. *Journal of the Experimental Analysis of Behavior*, **26**, 155–164.

Mackintosh, N. J. (1974). *The Psychology of Animal Learning*, Academic Press, London

Malott, R. W. and Cumming, W. W. (1964). Schedules of inter-response time reinforce ment. *Psychological Record*, **14**, 211–252.

Meltzer, D. and Brahlek, J. A. (1968). Quantity of reinforcement and fixed-interval performance. *Psychonomic Science*, **12**, 207–208.

Meltzer, D. and Brahlek, J. A. (1970). Quantity of reinforcement and fixed-interval performance: within-subject effects. *Psychonomic Science*, **20**, 30–31.

Mowrer, O. H. (1960). *Learning Theory and Behavior*, John Wiley, New York.

Mowrer, O. H. and Jones, H. M. (1943). Habit strength as a function of pattern of reinforcement. *Journal of Experimental Psychology*, **35**, 293–311.

Neuringer, A. J. and Schneider, B. A. (1968). Separating the effects of inter-reinforcement time and number of inter-reinforcement responses. *Journal of the Experimental Analysis of Behavior*, **11**, 661–667.

Nevin, J. A. (1973). The maintenance of behavior. In *The Study of Behavior: Learning, Motivation, Emotion and Instinct* (J. A. Nevin and G. S. Reynolds, eds), pp. 201–233, Scott-Foresman, Glenview, Ill.

Pavlov, I. P. (1927). *Conditioned Reflexes*, Oxford University Press, London.

Powell, R. W. (1968). The effect of small sequential changes in fixed-ratio size upon the post-reinforcement pause. *Journal of the Experimental Analysis of Behavior*, **11**, 589–593.

Powell, R. W. (1969). The effect of reinforcement magnitude upon responding under fixed-ratio schedules. *Journal of the Experimental Analysis of Behavior*, **12**, 605–608.

Richards, R. W. and Rilling, M. (1972). Aversive aspects of a fixed-interval schedule of reinforcement. *Journal of the Experimental Analysis of Behavior*, **17**, 405–411.

Schneider, B. A. (1969). A two-state analysis of fixed-interval responding in the pigeon. *Journal of the Experimental Analysis of Behavior*, **12**, 677–687.

Scull, J. W. (1973). The Amsel frustration effect: interpretations and research. *Psychological Bulletin*, **79**, 352–361.

Sevenster, P. (1973). Incompatibility of response and reward. In *Constraints on Learning* (R. Hinde and J. Hinde, eds), p. 265–284, Academic Press, London.

Sherman, J. G. (1959). The temporal distribution of responses on fixed-interval schedules. Doctoral dissertation, Columbia University.

Shull, R. L. (1970a). A response-initiated fixed-interval schedule of reinforcement. *Journal of the Experimental Analysis of Behavior*, **13**, 13–15.

Shull, R. L. (1970*b*). The response-reinforcement dependency in fixed-interval schedules of reinforcement. *Journal of the Experimental Analysis of Behavior*, **14**, 55–60.

Shull, R. L., Guilkey, M., and Witty, M. (1972). Changing the response unit from a single peck to a fixed number of pecks in fixed-interval schedules. *Journal of the Experimental Analysis of Behavior*, **17**, 193–200.

Sidman, M. (1956). Time discrimination and behavioral interaction in a free operant situation. *Journal of Comparative and Physiological Psychology*, **49**, 469–473.

Singh, D. and Wickens, D. D. (1968). Disinhibition in instrumental conditioning. *Journal of Comparative and Physiological Psychology*, **66**, 557–559.

Skinner, B. F. (1938). *The Behavior of Organisms*, Appleton-Century-Crofts, New York.

Staddon, J. E. R. (1970*a*). Effect of reinforcement duration on fixed-interval responding. *Journal of the Experimental Analysis of Behavior*, **13**, 9–11.

Staddon, J. E. R. (1970*b*). Temporal effects of reinforcement: a negative 'frustration' effect. *Learning and Motivation*, **13**, 227–247.

Staddon, J. E. R. (1972). Temporal control and the theory of reinforcement schedules. In *Reinforcement: Behavioral Analyses* (R. M. Gilbert and J. R. Millenson, eds), pp. 212–263. Academic Press, New York.

Staddon, J. E. R. (1974). A note on behavioral contrast and frustration. *Quarterly Journal of Experimental Psychology*, **26**, 285–292.

Staddon, J. E. R. and Innis, N. K. (1966). An effect analogous to frustration on interval reinforcement schedules. *Psychonomic Science*, **4**, 287–288.

Staddon, J. E. R. and Innis, N. K. (1969). Reinforcement omission on fixed-interval schedules. *Journal of the Experimental Analysis of Behavior*, **12**, 689–700.

Starr, B. C. and Staddon, J. E. R. (1974). Temporal properties of periodic schedules: signal properties of reinforcement and blackout. *Journal of the Experimental Analysis of Behavior*, **22**, 534–545.

Stebbins, W. C., Mead, P. B., and Martin, J. M. (1959). The relation of amount of reinforcement to performance under a fixed-interval schedule. *Journal of the Experimental Analysis of Behavior*, **2**, 351–355.

Terrace, H. S. Stimulus control. In *Operant Behavior: Areas of Research and Application* (W. K. Honig, ed.), pp. 271–344, Appleton-Century-Crofts, New York.

Thorpe, W. H. (1963). *Learning and Instinct in Animals*, Methuen, London.

Van Hartesveldt, C. (1973). Size of reinforcement and operant responding in hippocampectomized rats. *Behavioral Biology*, **8**, 347–356.

Walker, S. F., Schnelle, J., and Hurwitz, H. M. B. (1970). Rates of concurrent responses and reinforcer duration. *Psychonomic Science*, **21**, 173–175.

Wilkie, D. M. (1974). Stimulus control of responding during a fixed-interval reinforcement schedule. *Journal of the Experimental Analysis of Behavior*, **21**, 425–432.

Wilson, M. P. and Keller, F. S. (1953). On the selective reinforcement of spaced responses. *Journal of Comparative and Physiological Psychology*, **46**, 190–193.

Zeiler, M. D. (1979). Output dynamics. In *Advances in Analysis of Behavior, Vol. 1; Reinforcement and the Organization of Behavior* (M. D. Zeiler and P. Harzem, eds). John Wiley, Chichester.

Zimmerman, J. and Schuster, C. R. (1962). Spaced responding in multiple DRL schedules. *Journal of the Experimental Analysis of Behaviour*, **5**, 497–505.

Predictability, Correlation, and Contiguity
Edited by P. Harzem and M. D. Zeiler
© 1981 John Wiley & Sons Ltd

Chapter 4

Contingency, Contiguity, Correlation, and the Concept of Causation

A. Charles Catania and Kenneth J. Keller

> The bird behaves as if there were a causal relation between its behavior and the presentation of food, although such a relation is lacking. (B. F. Skinner, 1948, p. 171)

> Man's first experience with causes probably came from his own behavior: things moved because he moved them. (B. F. Skinner, 1971, p. 7)

Introduction

The term *cause*, in the sense of an event that has an effect, came to us, through Middle English and Old French, from the Latin *causa* (Onions, 1966; Partridge, 1958). In its legal usage, as a motive, ground, or reason for action, it also had the sense of a thing, leading to *chose* in contemporary French and *cosa* in contemporary Spanish and Italian (cf. the German *die Sache* and the Russian *delo*). The word *because* is probably a contraction of *by cause that*.

The technical usages of *cause* in philosophy (Brand, 1976) have ranged from the constant conjunction of Hume (1748) to accounts in terms of conditional counterfactuals (e.g. Lewis, 1973) or combinations of necessity and sufficiency (e.g. Mackie, 1965). The role of causal concepts in scientific accounts has been stated as follows:

> . . . laws of probable sequence, though useful in daily life and in the infancy of a science, tend to be displaced by quite different laws as soon as a science is successful. The law of gravitation will illustrate what occurs in any advanced science. In the motions of mutually gravitating bodies, there is nothing that can be called a cause, and nothing that can be called an effect; there is merely

a formula. . . . No doubt the reason why the old 'law of causality' has so long continued to pervade the books of philosophers is simply that the idea of a function is unfamiliar (Russell, 1912–1913).

In dealing with the concept of cause, some philosophical treatments recognize that the concern is more with what determines the language of causation than with its logical implications (e.g. Gasking, 1955): under what circumstances do we say that X caused Y, or that we caused Z to happen? The problem is one of verbal behaviour (Skinner, 1957), and is exemplified by studies of the conditions under which the language of causation develops and is maintained (e.g. Lesser, 1977; Mendelson and Shultz, 1976; Michotte, 1963; Piaget, 1927). Similar issues are implicit in research on attribution (e.g. Kelley, 1973; Nisbett, Caputo, Legant, and Marecek, 1973) and on locus of control (e.g. Lefcourt, 1976; see also de Charms, 1968).

The responding that may follow observations of conjunctions of events is not limited to verbal behaviour; the literature of conditioning documents the behavioural effects of stimulus–stimulus contingencies (cf. Rescorla, 1967). But cases in which responding has consequences may have a special status. Here too it is appropriate to distinguish between verbal behaviour and other types of responding (the relation between behaviour changes produced by response consequences and what we say about those behaviour changes is at the root of the controversy over learning with and without awareness; cf. Eriksen, 1962; Hefferline and Keenan, 1963; Reynolds, 1966). When an experimenter arranges consequences for responding, however, behavioural effects rather than the epistemological status of the causal relation are at issue.

In the analysis of behaviour, the issue of causation is implicit in the description of contingency relations between responses and their consequences. Such relations determine contiguities of events at particular moments and correlations among events over extended time periods. The common features of these terms are demonstrated by the prefix that they share, from the Latin root *com-* (together). *Consequence*, as a thing resulting, is derived from the Latin root *sequi* (to follow), and through the Latin *socius* (a companion or follower) is linked to another behaviourally significant term, *association*. *Correlation*, as a correspondence or changing together, is derived from the Latin *relatus*, a past participle of *referre* (to carry back). *Contingency*, as a possibility or as something incidental to something else, comes from the Latin *contingere* (to touch on all sides, to happen). Like *contact*, its prefix is combined with a derivative of the Latin *tangere* (to touch). *Contiguity*, the condition of touching or being in contact, has the same origins. Thus, the distinction between *contingency* and *contiguity* in our technical usage is paradoxical: *contingency* stresses how one event may affect the likelihood of another, whereas *contiguity* implies the juxtaposition of events in space or time, without regard to causation.

To arrange a contingency is to arrange a causal relation. When we create an environment for a hungry pigeon in which its key-pecks operate a feeder, the statement that its pecks cause food deliveries is little different from the statement that its pecks produce food. The study of operant behaviour is easily entangled in questions of causes and purposes simply because its fundamental concern is the sensitivity of behaviour to its consequences. The research that follows examines the limits of this sensitivity: what relations must behaviour have to its consequences for the behaviour to be maintained by those consequences? The role of temporal contiguities and of the distribution of events in time are among the dimensions of behaviour that can be explored by relaxing the relation between responses and the reinforcers they produce. (A related issue, the discrimination of response–reinforcer contingencies, is not included among the present concerns (cf. Killeen, 1977; Lattal, 1975).)

Response-dependent and Response-independent Reinforcers

The behavioural effects of a contingency are assessed by comparing the responding maintained when the contingency operates with that maintained when it does not (Catania, 1979, Chapters 4 and 8). A prototype case is the transition from reinforcement to extinction. Assume, for example, that a pigeon's key-pecks produce food according to a variable ratio 20 schedule (VR 20: on the average, one of every 20 pecks operates the feeder). This schedule maintains substantial rates of responding, but when it is discontinued, rates decrease to near-zero levels. The decrease in responding demonstrates the temporary effects of the contingency; it is not maintained indefinitely after the contingency ceases. This difference between behaviour with and behaviour without the contingency is the basis for the vocabulary of reinforcement. We say that responding has been reinforced by an event or that a particular event is a reinforcer if more responding occurs when that event is its consequence than when it is not.

The transition from reinforcement to extinction, however, is only one way to terminate a contingency, and it may involve two behavioural effects. In the preceding example, not only do the pigeon's pecks in extinction no longer produce food; the pigeon that was occasionally eating during reinforcement is now no longer eating. Thus, the general effects of removing food may be superimposed on specific effects of the contingency relating pecks to food. It may therefore be argued that the appropriate way to study the effects of response–reinforcer contingencies is to arrange transitions from response-produced to response-independent reinforcers. For example, with a VR 20 schedule that maintains about 120 pecks/min, food deliveries will occur on the average every 10 s. If the VR schedule is followed by one in which food is delivered independently of responding on the average every 10 s (variable time or VT 10 s) (Zeiler, 1968), then the contingency between pecks and food will be terminated but the pigeon will eat about as often as when the contingency operated.

This transition too may involve complications. If a response-independent reinforcer follows closely upon a response, its behavioural effect may be no different from that of a reinforcer produced by a response. In fact, to assume that contingencies operate through summation of the effects of individual temporal conjunctions between responses and reinforcers is also to assume that no difference in behavioural effect is even possible. These assumptions are the basis for accounts in terms of temporal contiguity. The argument then is that the transition from response-produced to response-independent reinforcers cannot be used to assess the effects of the response–reinforcer contingency, because responding after the transition will be maintained to some extent by accidental contiguities between responses and reinforcers.

The literature of superstition (Skinner, 1948) is explicitly concerned with such effects (e.g. Catania and Cutts, 1963; Henton and Iversen, 1978; Jenkins, 1970; Lachter, 1973; Lachter, Cole, and Schoenfeld, 1971; Lattal, 1972, 1973, 1974; Neuringer, 1970; Schoenfeld, Cole, Lang, and Mankoff, 1973; Staddon and Simmelhag, 1971; Zeiler, 1972):

> In superstitious operant behavior, . . . the process of conditioning has miscarried. Conditioning offers tremendous advantages in equipping the organism with behavior which is effective in a novel environment, but there appears to be no way of preventing the acquisition of non-advantageous behavior through accident. Curiously, this difficulty must have increased as the process of conditioning was accelerated in the course of evolution. If, for example, three reinforcements were always required in order to change the probability of a response, superstitious behavior would be unlikely. It is only because organisms have reached the point at which a single contingency makes a substantial change that they are vulnerable to coincidences. (Skinner, 1953, pp. 86–87).

(Note that *contingency* in this quotation refers to a particular temporal conjunction rather than to a continuing probability relation between responses and reinforcers.)

If evolutionary contingencies generated the effects of single contiguities between responses and reinforcers, they may also have generated other behavioural processes that counteract these effects (cf. Skinner, 1966, 1975). Presumably the organism whose responding is differentially affected by events that are consequences of its behaviour and events that are accidentally contiguous with its behaviour will have a survival advantage over one whose behaviour is not.

> Is it possible that the accidental correlations in time among responses, stimuli, and reinforcers do not exert control over behavior? . . . One of the characteristics of accidental correlations between behavior and environmental events is *variability*. Every aspect of behavior may vary and yet be

contiguous with a reinforcer that is independent of the behavior. In contrast, behavior that is instrumental must have at least one aspect that has a more or less fixed correlation with the reinforcer. Were animals sensitive to this difference, they could detect those events over which their behavior has no real control. (Herrnstein, 1966, pp. 42–43)

The problem, therefore, is not whether accidental contiguities have their effects, but rather the range of conditions over which such effects occur. In other words, the issues are at least in part experimental.

Transitions to Response-independent Reinforcement and to Extinction

The rates of key-pecking maintained during VR 20 reinforcement and in subsequent sessions of VT 10 s reinforcement are shown for three pigeons in Figure 4.1. Four successive transitions from VR to VT were arranged; details of procedure are presented below (cf. Table 4.1). For each pigeon, VT response rates decreased over sessions relative to those maintained by VR reinforcement, in some cases perhaps toward non-zero asymptotes. In general, response rate decreased more rapidly in later than in earlier transitions from VR to VT. (The high-rate sessions 16–20 in the first transition for pigeon 1 occurred when the Plexiglas chamber ceiling accidentally dropped into the pigeon's area, trapping it away from the key; the pigeon was run again, and responded at unusually high rates in that and the next couple of sessions.)

These data are consistent with those from other studies. After the change from response-dependent to response-independent reinforcement, response rate falls, usually to near-zero levels (Lachter, 1971; Lachter et al., 1971; Skinner, 1938, Figure 52; Zeiler, 1968). The decrease is sometimes slower than that during extinction, with the difference attributed either to accidental contiguities of responses and reinforcers or to discriminative and eliciting functions of the reinforcer (Lattal, 1972; Rescorla and Skucy, 1969). Nevertheless, response-independent reinforcement and extinction have in common the property that responding declines more rapidly with successive exposures to each (e.g. Anger and Anger, 1976; Bullock, 1960; Bullock and Smith, 1953; Jenkins, 1961; Perkins and Cacioppo, 1950; Schaeffer, Salzberg, Birkle, and Ryan, 1967).

The similarity of the response decrements produced by transitions from response-dependent reinforcement either to response-independent reinforcement or to extinction is illustrated in Figures 4.2 and 4.3. Figure 4.2 shows the final VR-to-VT transition for each of the pigeons of Figure 4.1. Figure 4.3 shows transitions from variable interval (VI) reinforcement to extinction (EXT) averaged across a group of four pigeons; these functions differ on the basis of the reinforcement schedule that operated on a second key (Catania, 1969). Despite the several differences (e.g. VR vs. VI schedules, single pigeons vs. group data), the functions are all reasonably linear with roughly the same range of slopes

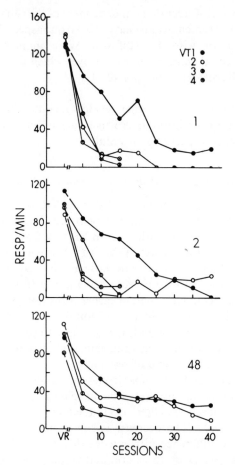

Figure 4.1. Response rates in four successive transitions from response-dependent reinforcement (VR 20) to response-independent reinforcement (VT 10s) for each of three pigeons (conditions 1–4, Table 4.1). Sessions lasted for 60 reinforcer deliveries. The leftmost point on each function is the mean of the last five of the preceding VR sessions

(exponents) in the semilogarithmic coordinates of these figures. To a first approximation, responding declines exponentially over sessions of both VT reinforcement and EXT (but cf. Killeen, 1979; Nevin, 1974; Shettleworth and Nevin, 1965).

It is at least appropriate to conclude that the effects of terminating a response–reinforcer contingency can be studied either in transitions to EXT or in transitions to VT reinforcement. But the decrement in responding with VT reinforcement has some puzzling implications. If accidental contiguities are involved in the form of the decrement, why is the rate of decline roughly proportional to the current response rate (i.e. the exponential functions of Figure 4.2)? Accidental contiguities ought to decrease as response rates drop,

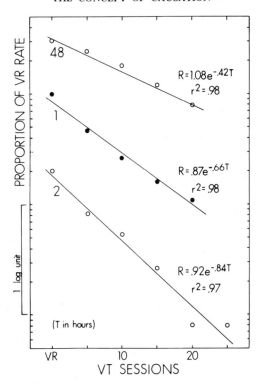

Figure 4.2. Relative response rates in the last transition from VR 20 to VT 10 s for each pigeon (condition 20 for pigeons 1 and 48 and condition 10 for pigeon 2, Table 4.1). The best-fitting exponential equation and r^2 accompany each function; R is in responses per minute and T is in hours. The functions are displaced vertically to avoid crowding

thereby contributing less and less to response maintenance and thus producing an accelerating decrement rather than a proportional or exponential one. Furthermore, if the relatively slow decline in responding during early transitions to VT (e.g. first VT in Figure 4.1) depends to some extent on the maintenance of responding by accidental contiguities between responses and reinforcers, why does the decrement occur more rapidly during subsequent transitions? Is the pigeon becoming sensitive to the different properties of a response–reinforcer contingency and its absence, in a kind of learning set (cf. Sidman, 1960, pp. 101–103 on repeated acquisitions and extinctions)? If so, on the basis of what sorts of higher-order contingencies might this learning occur?

The present research approaches these issues by examining performances maintained when the relation between responses and their reinforcers is relaxed. For example, responses may produce variably delayed rather than immediate reinforcers. To the extent that the variable delays generate a distribution of times between responses and subsequent reinforcers that approximates that obtained during VT responding, such a procedure duplicates a behavioural property of the

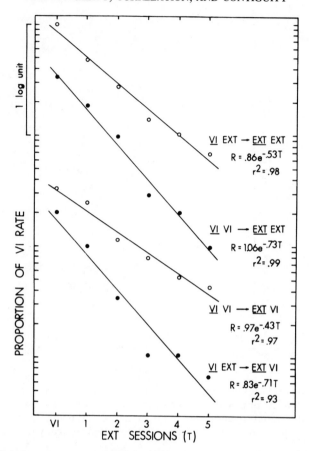

Figure 4.3. Relative response rates in transitions from VI 180 s reinforcement to extinction (EXT) on one key, concurrent with various schedule transitions on a second key, averaged across three pigeons. The relevant schedule is underlined in the schedule pairs that label the four functions. The best-fitting exponential equation and r^2 accompany each function; R is in responses per minute and T is in hours. The functions are displaced vertically to avoid crowding. (From Series 3 in Catania, 1969, Figure 2)

VT schedule without discontinuing the dependency of reinforcers on responses. In the next section, we examine some methodological features of various response-dependent and response-independent reinforcement schedules, including arrangements with fixed and variable delays of reinforcement.

Response-independent Reinforcers and Delayed Reinforcers

Consider some of the properties of transitions from response-produced to VT reinforcers. Because the VT schedule delivers reinforcers unsystematically over time and without reference to behaviour, the time between any reinforcer and the most recent preceding response will be variable. The VT schedule imposes no maximum on these response–reinforcer intervals, except incidentally in that none can exceed the duration of the longest interreinforcer time. The form of the distribution of response–reinforcer intervals will depend on that of the distribution of interresponse times (IRTs), and the mean of the distribution will increase as the rate of responding decreases (cf. Sizemore and Lattal, 1977). For any definition of response–reinforcer contiguities in terms of an arbitrary minimum duration of the response–reinforcer interval, the rate at which such contiguities occur also will vary with the rate of responding. Furthermore, a reinforcer may occasionally be delivered just as a response is initiated, so that the reinforcer onset briefly precedes a response instead of following it. These conjunctions too will be more likely with high than with low rates of responding.

Responses will often occur during the time between two successive reinforcers, but because reinforcers no longer depend on them, two or more successive reinforcers may be delivered without any intervening responses. For the same reason, response rate and reinforcement rate will not ordinarily be correlated over any extended time periods except by chance; any temporary correlations that occur by chance are as likely to be negative as positive (cf. Baum, 1973).

Some of these variables can be manipulated within reinforcement schedules in which reinforcers are response-dependent rather than response-independent. For example, as will be explored in what follows, various delay-of-reinforcement procedures can be used to alter the distribution of response–reinforcer intervals. In at least one case, however, the variable is tied by definition to the difference between response-dependent and response-independent reinforcers. If any correlation between responding and reinforcers is arranged, the responding and the reinforcers cannot be independent of each other. Whatever the status of the other variables, differences in the correlation between responses and reinforcers will always be implicated when different performances are maintained by response-dependent and response-independent reinforcement. The role of these correlations in maintaining the effects of contingencies is therefore to some extent a logical rather than an empirical issue.

Resetting and Non-resetting Delays of Reinforcement

Delays of reinforcement have been arranged in different ways. In one set of procedures, a response immediately produces a stimulus and the reinforcer is delivered in the presence of that stimulus at some later time (e.g. Chung, 1965; Chung and Herrnstein, 1967; Ferster, 1953; Neuringer, 1969; Rachlin and Green, 1972). Because the immediate stimulus onset may function as a conditioned reinforcer, related procedures have arranged sequences of stimulus trials in which reinforcers in some trials depend on the responses in earlier trials (e.g. Jenkins, 1970; Kendall and Newby, 1978; Williams, 1975).

Resetting t-sec delay.

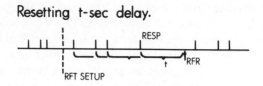

Non-resetting t-sec delay.

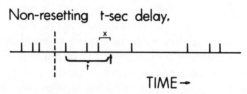

TIME→

Figure 4.4. Resetting and non-resetting delays of reinforcement. Dashed lines show reinforcement setups, solid
vertical lines show responses, and arrows show reinforcers. With resetting delays, responses reset the
delay timer, so that the time between the last
response and a reinforcer always equals the delay, t. With
non-resetting delays, the first response after the setup
initiates the delay, t; the time between the last response
and a reinforcer, x, can never exceed t, but it will be
shorter than t if other responses follow the one that
initiated the delay within less than t seconds

In another class of delay procedures, a response initiates a delay that
terminates with a reinforcer delivery but no exteroceptive stimulus is added
during the delay. Figure 4.4 provides two examples. In both cases, the delay is
shown arranged for the first response after a reinforcer has become available in
an interval schedule. In one version (Figure 4.4, top), any subsequent responses
during the delay reset the delay timer, so that the time between the most recent
response and the reinforcer always equals the scheduled delay (e.g. Azzi, Fix,
Keller, and Rocha e Silva, 1964; Dews, 1960). In another (Figure 4.4, bottom),
subsequent responses do not affect the delay, so that the time between the most
recent response and the reinforcer can be shorter than the scheduled delay,
though it cannot exceed it (e.g. Sizemore and Lattal, 1977, 1978; Williams, 1976).

For the purposes of studying the functional relation between responding and
delayed reinforcers, both procedures have disadvantages. The former differentially reinforces a response followed by a minimal period of no responding. Thus,
the responding maintained by such schedules may depend more on the
differential reinforcement of the spacing of responses in time (e.g. Anger, 1956;
Catania, 1970; Staddon, 1965) than on the temporal separation between the
response and the reinforcer. In the latter procedure, on the other hand, the actual
response–reinforcer intervals will often be shorter than the scheduled delays (x
rather than t in Figure 4.4, bottom), and they will typically also be variable

whereas the scheduled delays are fixed. For the present purposes, however, non-resetting delays may have an advantage. When interresponse times or IRTs are short relative to the scheduled delay, the distribution of response–reinforcer intervals generated with such delays is likely to resemble the distribution generated with response-independent reinforcers.

Fixed and Variable Delays of Reinforcement

Both resetting and non-resetting delays of reinforcement have typically been arranged as fixed delays. Either could also be arranged as variable, but only variable non-resetting delays are likely to be of behavioural interest for the present purposes. This is because the longer delays of the distribution would probably be the primary determinant of the differentiation of periods of no responding with variable resetting delays, and because neither a minimum nor a maximum response–reinforcer interval is established by variable non-resetting delays. Only non-resetting delays will therefore be considered in what follows.

With schedules of immediate reinforcement, the distribution of response–reinforcer intervals is narrow, and is determined primarily by the latency with which the scheduling apparatus reacts to a response. Distributions with high and with low rates of responding maintained by immediate variable interval (VI) reinforcement are illustrated at the upper left in Figure 4.5. At intervals, the schedule makes the next response eligible to produce a reinforcer. The time from this reinforcement setup to the response may vary, but once the response occurs the reinforcer is delivered promptly. The distribution of response–reinforcer intervals does not vary with rate of responding. Both with VT reinforcement and with fixed or variable non-resetting delays of VI reinforcement, the distribution of response–reinforcer intervals depends on the distribution of IRTs and varies with rate of responding. These relations are illustrated in the remaining quadrants of Figure 4.5.

In VT schedules, reinforcers are delivered without reference to responding. With high rates of responding the mean response–reinforcer interval will be shorter than with low rates of responding (Figure 4.5, upper right). The distribution of response–reinforcer intervals generated by a given distribution of IRTs can be estimated by assuming that reinforcers will be uniformly distributed over time within any IRT class. For example, if IRTs in the class interval centred at 5 s take up one-tenth of the total session time, one-tenth of the total VT reinforcers will be delivered on the average during these IRTs. If these reinforcers are uniformly distributed between zero and 5 s, then about one-fifth will produce 0–1 s response–reinforcer intervals, about one-fifth will produce 1–2 s response–reinforcer intervals, and so on. A summation across the intervals similarly derived from the remaining IRT classes will then approximate the overall distribution (cf. Dews, 1969, p. 195).

The major effect of VI reinforcers delivered after fixed non-resetting delays is

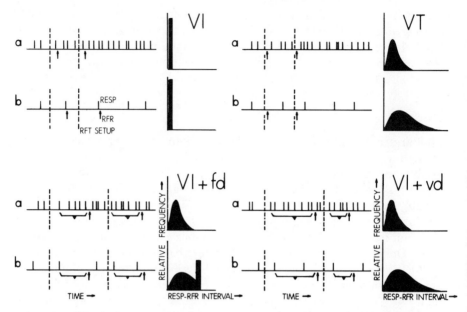

Figure 4.5. Hypothetical effects of four schedules on the distribution of response–reinforcer intervals. Each example includes event records for high rate (a) and low rate (b) responding with corresponding distributions. Dashed lines show reinforcement set-ups, solid vertical lines show responses, arrows show reinforcers, and brackets show reinforcement delays. With immediate reinforcement (variable interval or VI, upper left), the distribution of response–reinforcer intervals is not affected by a change from high rate to low rate responding. With response-independent reinforcers (variable time or VT, upper right), a change from high rate to low rate responding affects the mean but not necessarily the form of the distribution (in practice, these and the remaining distributions would vary with the form of the interresponse time or IRT distribution). During VI reinforcement with fixed non-resetting delays (VI + fd, lower left), the high rate distribution resembles that with VT, but with lower rates a peak appears because no response–reinforcer interval can exceed the scheduled fixed delay. With variable non-resetting delays (VI + vd, lower right), both the high rate and the low rate distributions resemble those with VT, because this arrangement does not limit the maximum response–reinforcer interval

that they impose a maximum response–reinforcer interval: any reinforcer must have been produced by a response that preceded it by no more than the scheduled delay. In the illustration (Figure 4.5, lower left), this property of VI schedules with fixed delays is shown in the case of low rate but not high rate responding. With high rates in which virtually all IRTs are shorter than the scheduled delay (a), the distribution of response–reinforcer intervals may be indistinguishable from that with VT reinforcement. With low rates (b), however, the distribution of response–reinforcer intervals may correspond to that with VT reinforcement up to the duration of the scheduled delay, but the portion of the distribution that would otherwise have extended beyond it is instead concentrated at this maximum value.

In practice, the response–reinforcer intervals generated with fixed delays would also depend on other features of responding. For example, superimposing a 3 s fixed delay on a performance consisting predominantly of 2 s IRTs would generate many 2 s IRTs followed by 1 s response-reinforcer intervals. The sequential patterning of responses might have effects following from the higher probability of reinforcement after long than after short IRTs in VI schedules. For example, the grouping of responses in high rate bursts separated by pauses might make responses early in a burst more likely to initiate a delay than later responses, and the subsequent delivery of the reinforcer during the burst would then favour short response–reinforcer intervals (cf. Anger, 1956; Skinner, 1938, p. 275).

The development of consistent relations between IRTs and delays can be prevented by arranging variable rather than fixed non-resetting delays. Some properties of variably delayed VI reinforcement are illustrated in Figure 4.5 (lower right). These schedules impose no maximum response–reinforcer interval, and they operate so that response–reinforcer intervals vary even over those cases in which the most recent response is the one that initiated the delay (e.g. as for the second reinforcer in the low rate record (b)). As in the preceding cases, the form of the response–reinforcer distribution will depend on the IRT distribution and its mean will vary with the rate of responding. But as long as response rate is sufficiently high that some responding occurs even within the shortest interreinforcer interval of the VI schedule, the distribution of response–reinforcer intervals generated by this schedule may be indistinguishable from that generated by VT reinforcement.

Timing Intervals from Reinforcers or from Reinforced Responses

In the technical vocabulary of schedules (Ferster and Skinner, 1957), VI reinforcement with fixed non-resetting delays as so far described may be referred to as a tandem variable interval fixed time (tandem VI FT) schedule: the completion of the VI component initiates the FT component, with no corresponding stimulus change. With this arrangement, however, a new interval of the VI schedule cannot begin until the delayed reinforcer initiated by the last one has been delivered. Thus, as illustrated in the top record (a) of Figure 4.6, two reinforcers cannot occur in succession without an intervening response. In this respect, VI reinforcement with non-resetting delays differs from VT reinforcement, in which reinforcers may occur in succession without intervening responses.

The bottom record (b) of Figure 4.6 illustrates how this property of VT reinforcement can be incorporated into VI schedules with non-resetting fixed delays. The timing of the interreinforcer intervals of the VI schedule begins with

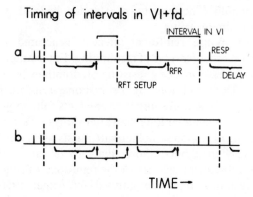

Figure 4.6. Two procedures for timing intervals in VI
schedules with non-resetting fixed delays of reinforcement. Dashed lines show reinforcement setups, solid
vertical lines show responses, arrows show reinforcers,
upper brackets show VI intervals, and lower brackets
show delays. In the first procedure (a), intervals are timed
from successive reinforcer deliveries (technically these are
tandem VI FT schedules); two successive reinforcers
cannot be delivered without at least one response intervening. In the second procedure (b), timing of a new
interval begins with the response that initiates a reinforcement delay; two or more delays may operate together,
and therefore two successive reinforcers may sometimes
be delivered without an intervening response

the response that initiates the delay rather than with the reinforcer that
terminates it. Thus, once one response has initiated a delay, a response after the
end of the next scheduled interval may initiate another delay that operates
together with the first. If these delays both end during a period of no responding,
their respective reinforcers will be delivered without an intervening response (cf.
the first two reinforcers of (b) in Figure 4.6). The same arrangement may also be
applied to variable non-resetting delays. (Note that the tandem vocabulary is
inappropriate for these varieties of fixed and variable delays.)

Relaxing the Relation between Responses and their Reinforcers

During the early stages of the present research, one goal was the design of a
schedule in which responses produced reinforcers but in which responding was
maintained no more effectively than by VT schedules. Our assumption was that
response–reinforcer contingencies that did not maintain behaviour would tell us
something about the critical features distinguishing response-dependent from
response-independent reinforcers. But an experiment to demonstrate that such
contingencies exist is not necessary. If the reinforcers today depend on a pigeon's

responses in a session yesterday, its performance will probably differ little from that maintained by VT reinforcement; even if this were not the case, we would only extend the delay to 2 days or a week or even more. What is more important is to compare the behavioural as well as the procedural properties of various response-dependent and response-independent reinforcement schedules, and to determine which properties of contingencies are sufficient to maintain behaviour.

Procedure

Two adult male White Carneaux pigeons (1 and 2) and one adult male Silver King pigeon (48), each with extensive histories in a variety of operant procedures, were maintained at 80 per cent of free-feeding weights. Pigeon 2 became ill during the study and was omitted from later conditions.

In a standard two-key experimental chamber with 20 mm diameter pigeon keys separated by 40 cm, schedules were arranged for the right key. This key was operated by a minimum force of about 0.15 N, and was lit during sessions while

Table 4.1. Sequence of conditions for pigeons 1, 48 (all), and 2 (A and B only)

Condition	Preceding sessions of VR 20	Sessions of schedule
A. *Variable ratio (VR) to variable time (VT) transitions*		
1. VT 10 s	10	40
2. VT 10 s	10	40
3. VT 10 s	10	15
4. VT 10 s	10	15
B. *Variable ratio and variable interval schedules with variable delays (tandem VR VT and VI VT)*		
5. Tandem VR 13.3 VT 4 s	7	25
6. Tandem VI 10 s VT 4 s	None	20
7. Tandem VR 13.3 VT 4 s	None	20
8. VT 20 s	None	10
9. VT 10 s	10	15
10. VT 10 s	10	25
C. *Variable ratio schedules with fixed delays (tandem VR FT)*		
11. Tandem VR 13.3 FT 4 s	13	40
12. Tandem VR 13.3 FT 2 s	10	40
13. Tandem VR 13.3 FT 1 s	16	20
14. Tandem VR 13.3 FT 1 s	9	20
15. Tandem VR 13.3 FT 3 s	8	20
16. Tandem VR 20 FT 0.67 s	6	25
17. Tandem VR 13.3 FT 1.33 s	None	15
18. Tandem VR 13.3 FT 3 s	None	20
19. Tandem VR 13.3 FT 5 s	None	20
20. VT 10-sec	7	20

the left key remained dark. A 6 W white lamp at the upper right of the panel served as houselight. Reinforcers were 3 s presentations of either mixed grain (conditions 1 through 15) or Purina checkers (conditions 16 through 20) in a standard Gerbrands feeder centred below the keys. During its operation, the feeder was lit and the other lights were off. A ventilating fan provided masking noise. Standard electromechanical scheduling and recording equipment was located in an adjoining room.

The procedure included three experimental sequences. The first examined repeated transitions from VR to VT reinforcement (cf. Figure 4.1). The second examined response rates maintained by VR and VI reinforcement with non-resetting variable delays (tandem VR VT and tandem VI VT schedules). The third examined VR responding over a range of non-resetting fixed delays (tandem VR FT schedules). The sequence of conditions, summarized in Table 4.1, was preceded by 16 pilot sessions of VR and tandem VR FT schedules. Daily sessions lasted 60 reinforcers through condition 16. They were then reduced to 40 reinforcers, because the pigeons began to gain weight within sessions after the change from mixed grain to Purina reinforcers.

Some of the data for transitions from VR to VT reinforcement have already been presented (Figure 4.1); additional data are presented below. For convenience of exposition, the findings with fixed delays will then follow. The presentation of data obtained with variable delays will be deferred until after treatment of the fixed delay data and a discussion of some additional types of fixed delay procedures.

Transitions to response-independent reinforcement. In conditions 1 through 4, sessions of VR 20 reinforcement were followed by sessions of VT 10 s reinforcement. The VR 20 schedule was arranged by a Lehigh Valley Electronics probability generator set to select pecks for reinforcement with a probability of 0.05. For the response-dependent schedule, VR was chosen rather than VI because VR reinforcement rate varies directly with VR response rate. Given the possibility that sensitivity to correlations between reinforcement rates and response rates might depend on experience with relevant schedules, it seemed reasonable to provide these pigeons with appropriate histories. In addition, the high and relatively constant response rates maintained by the VR schedules favoured more frequent accidental response–reinforcer contiguities after the transition to VT reinforcement than would be generated after lower VI rates.

In sessions of VT 10 s, pulses at a rate of one per second were selected to operate the feeder at a probability generator setting of 0.10. This mean interreinforcer interval approximated that generated during VR sessions (with VR 20, a rate of 120 responses/min produces about one reinforcer every 10 s; cf. Figure 4.1). Reinforcement durations were excluded from all timing and rate calculations. Four transitions from VR to VT were arranged.

Distributions of response–reinforcer intervals were recorded during sessions of condition 1. During the 2 s preceding each reinforcer, pulses at a rate of 10 per second operated a stepper that distributed responses to independent decades of a print-out counter. The last response in each print-out therefore located the beginning of the response–reinforcer interval for that reinforcer. Equipment limitations precluded the recording of response–reinforcer intervals greater than 2 s, and the separate counting of these long intervals and those interreinforcer intervals without responses. Within the recorded range, response–reinforcer intervals were resolved to 0.1 s. Responses occurring after the onset of feeder operations were also recorded; such cases were, in effect, response-reinforcer intervals with negative values. Any feeder operation that included at least one peck was included in this category, but instances of continued responding through a reinforcer delivery were infrequent. Most cases involved one or two pecks during the first second of reinforcement.

Variable delay reinforcement. The VR 20 sessions that preceded those with variable delays were arranged as in the preceding conditions. With variably delayed VR reinforcement (tandem VR VT), a probability generator setting of 0.075 selected responses to initiate delays according to a VR 13.3 schedule. Once a delay had been initiated, a second probability generator set at 0.25 selected one-per-second pulses to operate the feeder, thus producing variable delays with a mean of 4 s. Responses during the delay had no scheduled consequences. Response rates were such that actual responses per reinforcer ranged from about 16 to about 20 when these responses were added to those for which the VR 13.3 schedule operated. Because the one-per-second pulses were independent of responses, this arrangement generated an effectively continuous distribution of variable delays.

With variably delayed VI reinforcement (tandem VI VT), a probability generator setting of 0.10 selected one-per-second pulses to make the next response eligible to initiate a delay, thereby establishing a VI 10 s schedule. Once a delay had been initiated, the second probability generator arranged variable delays with a mean of 4 s as above. In this arrangement, the scheduling of a new interreinforcer interval could begin only after a reinforcer delivery (cf. (a), Figure 4.6); thus, with the delay, minimum interreinforcer intervals averaged about 14 s.

The sequence of conditions consisted of VR reinforcement, variably delayed VR reinforcement, variably delayed VI reinforcement, a return to variably delayed VR reinforcement, and then VT 20 s. The VT schedule was arranged by selecting one-per-second pulses to operate the feeder with a probability of 0.05. Two repetitions of the transition from VR 20 to VT 10 s then followed. The mean intervals arranged by the VT 20 s and VT 10 s schedules bracketed the actual interreinforcer intervals generated during the tandem VR VT and the tandem VI VT conditions. The additional repetitions of the VR-to-VT transition were included to examine the possibility that, given the potential similarities of variably delayed and VT reinforcers (e.g. Figure 4.5), the exposure to the schedules with variable delay might have reduced sensitivity to the difference between response-dependent and response-independent reinforcers.

Fixed delay reinforcement. The first part of this sequence examined transitions from VR 20 reinforcement to VR 13.3 reinforcement with fixed delays of 1, 2, 3, or 4 s (tandem VR 13.3 FT *t* s). The schedules were arranged as in the preceding conditions, except that a timer set for the delay of *t* seconds was substituted for the probability circuit. Pigeon 2 was dropped from the experiment at the end of condition 12 because of illness. The remainder of the sequence successively examined VR schedules with fixed delays of 0.67, 1.33, 3 and 5 s, and terminated with another transition from VR 20 to VT 10 s reinforcement. As in the earlier conditions, VR 13.3 was arranged in the tandem VR FT schedules so that actual responses per reinforcer would approximate those of the VR 20 sessions; with the shortest fixed delay, 0.67 s (condition 16), the ratio component remained VR 20.

, During conditions 16 through 20, responses and reinforcers were recorded on a 3 mm/s event record. This method permitted the measurement of all response–reinforcer intervals and the separate counting of VT interreinforcer intervals without responses, but it allowed intervals to be resolved only into 0.33 s class intervals.

Response–reinforcer Intervals and Responses Initiated
During Reinforcer Deliveries

Figure 4.7 presents distributions of response–reinforcer intervals for each pigeon from sessions 1 to 5 and session 15 in the first transition to VT 10 s (condition 1). In the first VT session, when response rates were high, reinforcers that followed within 0.1 s of a response made up the largest proportion of response–reinforcer intervals, and this proportion was exceeded by negative response–reinforcer intervals (those in which the most recent response occurred during the feeder operation itself). Together, these two classes constituted almost half of the distributions of response–reinforcer intervals in session 1. In other words, almost half of the reinforcers were closely contiguous with responses.

In subsequent VT sessions, as response rates fell, the distribution shifted to the right. By session 5 and continuing to session 15, the largest class interval was that for response–reinforcer intervals greater than 2 s (this class also included interreinforcer intervals without a response). Even in session 15, however, the two shortest class intervals (negative and 0 s to 0.1 s) together constituted almost one-fifth of the distribution. The continued occurrence of negative response–reinforcer intervals implies that there is a time period between the initiation and the completion of a response during which the response will not be interrupted by feeder operations (probably because responding to the feeder stimuli must include some latency).

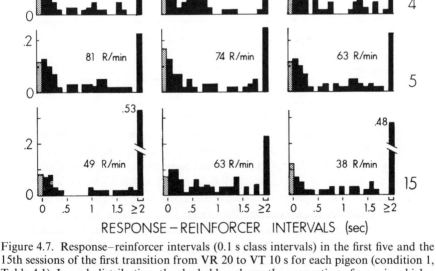

Figure 4.7. Response–reinforcer intervals (0.1 s class intervals) in the first five and the 15th sessions of the first transition from VR 20 to VT 10 s for each pigeon (condition 1, Table 4.1). In each distribution, the shaded bar shows the proportion of cases in which a response occurred after feeder operation had been initiated, and the rightmost bar includes in its proportion both response–reinforcer intervals greater than 2 s and interreinforcer intervals without an intervening response. Mean session rates (in responses per minute) accompany each distribution

The role of negative response–reinforcer intervals is difficult to assess. On the one hand, an account in terms of temporal contiguity might appeal to these intervals as contributing to the maintenance of VT responding. On the other, it might be assumed that the differential occurrence of negative response–reinforcer intervals in response-dependent and response-independent schedules provides a basis for the more rapid decline in responding with successive VR-to-VT transitions. To counter the argument that responses sometimes run over into reinforcer deliveries even with immediate response-produced reinforcers, it could be noted that such responses will always be preceded by the earlier reinforced response, which has a fixed temporal relation to the reinforcer, whereas such consistencies will not occur with VT reinforcers (but cf. Lattal, 1974).

The technical problem with negative response–reinforcer intervals is that it is difficult to see how they can be manipulated experimentally. We cannot predict the occurrence of individual responses with sufficient certainty consistently to deliver reinforcers just before rather than just after them. Statistically reliable differences could probably be produced given detailed measures of IRT distributions and of sequential dependencies among IRTs, but results from this statistically controlled variable might be hard to interpret. For example, if a response were about to occur at a particular moment and the reinforcer were delivered too early, the reinforcer might interrupt the response in progress instead of intercepting it at its completion. Inevitably, differential reinforcement would operate on precursors of the response rather than on the response itself, and would probably lead to frequent incipient but uncompleted responses. It would be inappropriate to assume that a decrease in responding produced in this way was necessarily related to the decreases produced by transitions to VT reinforcement.

Fixed Delays

Response rates during transitions to VR reinforcement with non-resetting fixed delays are shown in Figure 4.8. Whereas the decrease in response rate after the change from VR to VT (Figure 4.1) was roughly monotonic over successive sessions, the change in responding with fixed delays was more variable. After the initial decrease in responding, accompanied by a proportional decrease in reinforcement rate, response rates fluctuated over a range of values. In some cases, the decrease was followed by a recovery to higher rates (e.g. pigeon 1 at 3 s delays, pigeon 48 at 4 s delays).

Response rates relative to VR baseline over the last five sessions at each delay are shown in Figure 4.9. Relative response rates decreased more with longer delays for pigeon 1 than for pigeon 48, but the replication with Purina chow reinforcers roughly duplicated the functions obtained with mixed-grain reinforcers. Rates generated with VT reinforcement (conditions 10 and 20) and with

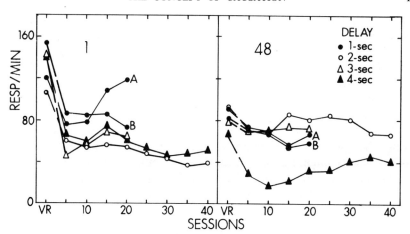

Figure 4.8. Response rates in transitions from VR 20 to VR schedules with non-resetting fixed delays (tandem VR FT: conditions 11–15, Table 4.1), for pigeons 1 and 48. The two exposures to 1 s fixed delays are respectively shown as A and B

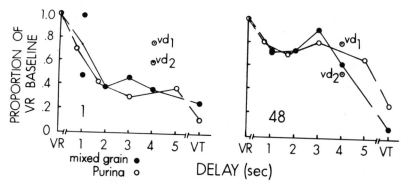

Figure 4.9. Rates of VR responding, relative to baseline VR rates, as a function of non-resetting fixed delays, for pigeons 1 and 48. Means over the last five sessions at a given delay include both those with mixed grain reinforcers (conditions 11–15, Table 4.1) and those with Purina chow reinforcers (conditions 16–19). For comparison, relative rates maintained by non-resetting variable delays (vd_1 and vd_2: conditions 5 and 7) and by response-independent reinforcers (VT 10 s: conditions 10 and 20) are included

variable delays (conditions 5 and 7) are included for comparison. At all delays, relative response rates were higher than those maintained by VT reinforcers. For pigeon 1, higher rates were maintained with 4 s variable delays than with 4 s fixed delays, but for pigeon 48 the rates were within comparable ranges.

Maximum response–reinforcer intervals and responses within interreinforcer intervals. Figure 4.10 shows distributions of response–reinforcer intervals for the last session at each fixed delay in conditions 16 through 19. The shortest class interval included negative response–reinforcer intervals (responses during the feeder operation). Fixed delays impose a maximum response–reinforcer interval (cf. Figure 4.5, lower left), but only for pigeon 1 at the 5 s delay was there a mode at the longest class interval. A secondary mode at this class interval occurred for pigeon 48 at the 1.33s delay. The resolution of the class intervals at the 0.67 s delay was not fine enough to allow a judgment, but there is no evidence for a peak at the longest class interval in the remaining distributions; for pigeon 1 at the 3 s delay, the relative frequency for this class interval was zero. Responding may have been affected by the maximum response–reinforcer interval in early fixed-delay sessions, when it might have contacted this maximum more often, but the event is of sufficiently low frequency in the sessions of Figure 4.10 that it is not likely to be the basis for the difference in maintained responding with fixed-delay and VT reinforcement.

Figure 4.11 shows comparable distributions of response–reinforcer intervals from every fifth session of the last transition from VR to VT (condition 20); these distributions, shown in 0.67 s class intervals, were recorded in the same way as those of Figure 4.10. The limit on response–reinforcer intervals imposed by VT scheduling is the time between reinforcers. When IRTs are sometimes longer than the interreinforcer intervals of the VT schedule, two reinforcers may occur

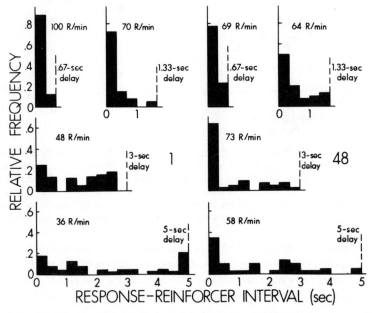

Figure 4.10. Distributions of response–reinforcer intervals (0.33 s class intervals) from the last session with each of four non-resetting fixed delays (condition 16–19, Table 4.1), for pigeons 1 and 48. Mean session rates (in responses per minute) accompany each distribution

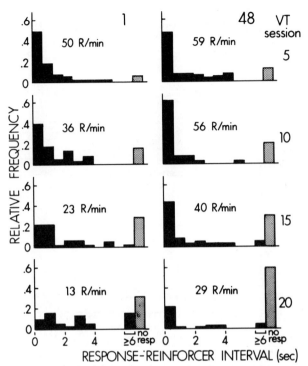

Figure 4.11. Distributions of response–reinforcer intervals (0.67 s class intervals) from every fifth session of the final transition to VT 10 s (condition 20, Table 4.1), for pigeons 1 and 48. The shaded bars show the proportion of interreinforcer intervals that included no response. Mean session rates (in responses per minute) accompany each distribution

in succession without an intervening response. As response rate decreased over VT sessions, the relative frequency of interreinforcer intervals without a response increased while that of the shortest response–reinforcer interval decreased.

Response–reinforcer contiguities. Figure 4.12 compares some properties of fixed delay VR schedules with those of VT schedules. Response–reinforcer contiguities are here arbitrarily defined as responses within 0.33 s of a reinforcer delivery. In the figure, the proportion of contiguities is shown as a function of delay for the fixed delay VR schedules and as a function of sessions for the VT schedule; the VT data also include the proportion of interreinforcer intervals without a response (cf. Figure 4.11). A different temporal criterion for contiguity would primarily affect the level rather than the form of the functions.

Response–reinforcer contiguities are mathematically dependent on response rates and reinforcement rates (cf. Dews, 1969). Figure 4.12 demonstrates this dependence empirically with both fixed delay VR schedules and VT schedules. Accounts of response maintenance in terms of contiguities must deal with the

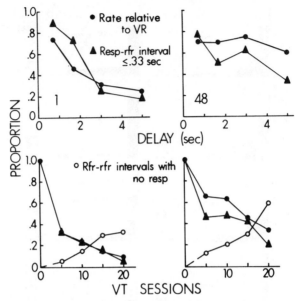

Figure 4.12. Response rates relative to baseline and response–reinforcer contiguities (response–reinforcer intervals shorter than 0.33 s) with non-resetting fixed delays (conditions 16–19, Table 4.1), and with successive sessions of VT 10 s (condition 20), for pigeons 1 and 48. The VT data also show the proportion of interreinforcer intervals that included no response. All data are from single sessions

finding that VT response rates were lower by session 20 than those maintained by any fixed delay VR schedule, even though the proportion of contiguities in the early VT sessions exceeded those at the longer fixed delays (e.g. for both pigeons, the proportion of contiguities through the first 10 sessions of VT exceeded those at the 5 s fixed delay). In other words, response rates cannot be determined by contiguities alone; if contiguities affect response rate, they must do so in conjunction with other variables. (A related finding is the decrease in responding that occurs when some reinforcers in a VI schedule are made response-independent, even though the remaining reinforcers continue to be contiguous with responses (Lattal, 1974).)

The Reinforcement of Other Behaviour

With both VT and delayed reinforcement, periods without responding may occasionally be followed by a reinforcer. One interpretation of the response decrement produced in transitions from immediate reinforcement either to VT reinforcement or to delayed reinforcement is in terms of the contiguity of reinforcers with other behaviour during pauses. To the extent that these reinforcers act on the other behaviour rather than on the responses for which they were scheduled, response rate will decrease. This decrease will further increase the likelihood that reinforcers will be contiguous with behaviour other than these responses.

If not implausible, this account is at least imprecise. Both response–reinforcer contiguities and contiguities of reinforcers with other behaviour can be invoked in some combination to explain why VT responding either continues at a low level (e.g. Herrnstein, 1966) or disappears (e.g. Lachter, 1971). The importance of each variable in generating the rate decrease is unclear, because criteria are lacking for judging how often the organism's behaviour comes into contact with these variables, or at what stage each comes into play.

Some two-key experiments on delayed reinforcement are relevant to these issues. A peck on one key initiates the delay, at the end of which a peck on a second key produces the reinforcer. In this procedure, the peck on the second key stands in a similar relation to the one that initiated the delay as that of other behaviour to the single response of the standard delay procedure: in both cases, the response contiguous with the reinforcer is not the one that produced it. Because fixed delays were included among these procedures, it is appropriate to consider them here before moving on to the treatment of variable delays.

Two-key procedures and the delay gradient. Figure 4.13 summarizes the data from an experiment on the reinforcement of pigeons' sequences of responses on two keys (Catania, 1971). Reinforcement was arranged according to a VI 60 s schedule for a sequence consisting of a single peck on one key (B) followed by a specific number of consecutive pecks on the second key (A). When an interval of the VI schedule had ended, a B peck initiated the sequence, but any subsequent B pecks reset the count of A pecks to zero; thus, each reinforcer followed a single B peck followed by exactly n A pecks. To assess the effect of the fixed ratio (FR) contingency on response rates, performances maintained by tandem VI 60 s FR 2 and VI 60 s FR 12 schedules for A pecks were also examined. In these sessions, B pecks continued to reset the count of A pecks, and rates of B responding were low.

The left column in Figure 4.13 shows the sum of the rates on both keys and the rate on key B for each of four pigeons. The total responding increased as the required consecutive A responses increased, and B responding decreased as the number of A responses that separated it from the one producing the reinforcer increased. A delay-of-reinforcement gradient for B responses can be estimated from these data by multiplying the mean IRT for a given condition by n, the number of required A responses. The rate of B responding is plotted against these estimated delays in the right column in Figure 4.13 (note the different scale of response rates). The function was estimated by visual fits of the data plotted on reciprocal-ruling paper; the same constants were used for each pigeon.

The function is consistent with an assumed inverse relation between responding and delay of reinforcement (e.g. Chung and Herrnstein, 1967; Rachlin and

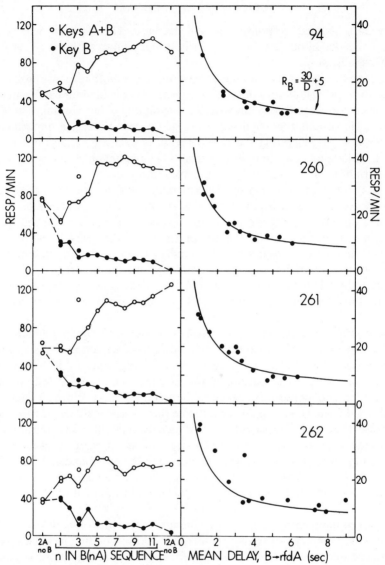

Figure 4.13. Response rates in a two-key procedure with VI reinforcement arranged for one B peck followed by n A pecks, for four pigeons. The A-peck count was reset to zero by each B peck. Left graphs show sums of rates on both keys (A + B) and rates on B as a function of n. The leftmost and rightmost points respectively show rates with two (two determinations) and 12 A pecks and no B pecks required. Two determinations with $n = 1$ preceded higher values of n; the unconnected points at $n = 3$ show a redetermination after the rest of the procedure was completed. Time and responses from reinforcement setups to reinforcer deliveries were excluded from all rate calculations. Right graphs show B responding as a function of the mean delay between B pecks and reinforced A pecks, calculated from obtained A + B response rates. The solid curves are fits to the data from all birds, where R_B is B rate (in responses per minute) and D is mean delay (in seconds).
(Adapted from Catania, 1971, Table 2)

Table 4.2. Sequence of sessions and mean data over the last five sessions of each condition in two-key, fixed delay procedures

Delay (s)	Sessions	Pigeon 15 B	Pigeon 15 A+B	Pigeon 15 CO	Pigeon 15 Set-up	Pigeon 20 B	Pigeon 20 A+B	Pigeon 20 CO	Pigeon 20 Set-up	Pigeon 22 B	Pigeon 22 A+B	Pigeon 22 CO	Pigeon 22 Set-up
2.0R	15	18.0	95.1	10.5	5.0	27.4	51.1	11.5	5.7	10.5	101.2	9.0	6.7
3.0R	13	12.8	102.9	7.8	7.5	13.4	31.7	8.2	9.1	5.8	70.5	4.4	14.7
10.0R	27	3.5	66.1	1.9	29.7	3.7	35.6	2.7	57.1	1.0	46.9	0.8	68.4
10.0N	22	6.0	77.8	3.8	19.6	59.6	92.0	17.9	10.7	4.4	95.5	3.2	22.7
5.0N	19	18.6	114.7	14.9	9.0	64.1	102.2	18.9	6.7	5.3	78.7	4.6	16.4
3.0N	13	24.2	109.3	20.3	5.7	70.7	110.7	28.0	4.2	7.4	76.2	5.3	9.8
2.0N	15	28.6	109.1	25.3	4.4	76.2	117.0	29.6	3.4	10.8	69.3	7.2	8.8
1.0N	10	27.5	108.6	25.1	4.4	63.1	101.9	28.2	3.0	15.2	82.2	12.1	4.3
0.5N	11	32.1	121.9	29.8	2.2	68.2	102.2	27.1	2.5	22.9	90.2	22.0	2.7
0.1N	21	37.9	96.4	32.2	1.7	62.7	95.4	26.7	1.9	13.8	47.4	13.5	4.4
0.1R	13	26.4	76.2	22.6	3.2	70.6	104.4	30.4	1.7	17.1	43.8	15.7	3.9
0.5R	17	25.8	94.0	23.5	3.0	51.4	98.1	23.9	2.5	28.4	101.8	27.6	1.8
0.75R	21	31.2	98.4	16.5	3.1	40.7	86.8	24.2	3.3	16.3	75.6	16.0	3.9
1.0R	14	30.3	75.1	10.9	4.5	29.6	89.3	18.7	5.1	12.3	79.7	11.5	5.2
1.5R	14	21.1	76.8	9.0	5.2	16.5	75.9	9.7	7.9	10.2	74.7	8.4	6.3
2.0R	29	10.0	61.6	6.2	8.1	16.0	86.5	8.0	8.5	5.5	68.8	4.8	10.5
3.0R	49	4.2	57.5	3.1	18.9	17.4	62.1	7.1	11.4	4.2	30.0	3.0	18.7
Other Procedures													
—	61												
0.1N	13	26.5	89.5	28.6	2.7	48.3	79.8	22.8	5.5	31.3	51.8	15.6	3.5
0.5N	15	32.8	108.6	27.2	2.4	47.8	90.0	25.2	3.1	32.3	68.9	20.4	2.8
0.75N	17	39.3	106.6	27.0	2.7	73.0	119.7	26.9	3.5	31.4	83.6	17.0	2.8
1.0N	12	34.4	104.3	25.8	3.2	53.7	82.1	21.4	11.5	24.7	77.1	13.6	3.8
1.5N	13	38.3	100.1	28.6	3.4	59.9	84.7	21.0	11.8	18.5	64.6	10.3	6.4
2.0N	15	26.8	102.4	22.0	4.7	61.8	88.3	22.2	18.4	11.3	57.1	7.2	8.4
3.0N	20	17.3	84.2	14.7	8.3	47.7	75.3	21.2	15.1	6.8	46.8	4.4	15.2
5.0N	31	23.3	90.7	19.6	8.4	30.0	68.6	15.8	9.7	8.2	32.2	3.4	14.6
10.0N	17	10.6	63.5	8.4	24.6	4.7	10.4	2.5	36.2	4.2	38.1	1.8	33.7

Notes: R, resetting; N, non-resetting; B, B pecks/min; A + B, total pecks/min; CO, changeovers/min (one direction); setup, time from reinforcer availability to reinforcer delivery in seconds per reinforcer. All rates exclude time and responding between reinforcer availability and reinforcer delivery.

Green, 1972). The rate of B responding, however, approaches an asymptote of 5 responses/min with increasing delays. One interpretation of the asymptote might be in terms of a summated effect of the B responses that preceded the one initiating the reinforced sequence; another might be in terms of induction from A responses.

The delay gradient of Figure 4.13 was obtained indirectly. A two-key procedure was therefore initiated to obtain the gradient more directly. Again a sequence of responses on keys A and B was reinforced according to a VI 60 s schedule. When an interval of the VI schedule had ended, a B peck initiated a delay at the end of which an A peck could produce food. In one procedure (resetting delay), once a B peck had initiated the delay, subsequent B pecks reset it; early A pecks had no effect. In a second procedure (non-resetting delay), neither A pecks nor B pecks reset the delay once it had been initiated. Other details of the procedure were as described in Catania (1971). Sessions lasted 1 h, exclusive of the time from reinforcement set-ups to reinforcer deliveries; the latter times were also excluded from all rate calculations. Sequences of delays and summary data are presented in Table 4.2.

For three pigeons, data with resetting delays are shown in the left column of Figure 4.14; those with non-resetting delays are shown in the right column. As in Figure 4.13, rates are shown for both keys together and for key B. The function from Figure 4.13 is reproduced in each graph to facilitate comparisons within and across the two figures. Rates of B responding generally decreased with increasing delay, and B rates at a given resetting delay were typically lower than those at the same non-resetting delay.

One feature of the data in Figure 4.14 is the variability both within functions and across pigeons relative to those in Figure 4.13. With resetting delays, the low rates of B responding are consistent with the differential reinforcement arranged by this schedule. With non-resetting delays, the differences among the data for the three pigeons are consistent with the different distributions of intervals between the most recent B response and the reinforcer that this schedule can generate. It might be argued that the delay gradient should be bracketed between the data with resetting delays and those with non-resetting delays, but there is too much room between the two sets of data to justify the fitting of a function. Another difficulty was that responding was not consistently well maintained by these schedules, especially at the longer delays (cf. Table 4.2). It therefore may be that the indirect procedure of Figure 4.13 is the more appropriate one for studying delay gradients. Because both A response rates and B response rates were able to vary even while the numerical requirements of that schedule were being met, the degrees of freedom available for B responding to come into a particular temporal relation with reinforcers while it was maintained at a particular rate might have allowed a gradient to develop independently of the differential reinforcement of temporal properties of responding.

Our primary concern, however, is not with the delay gradient, but rather with

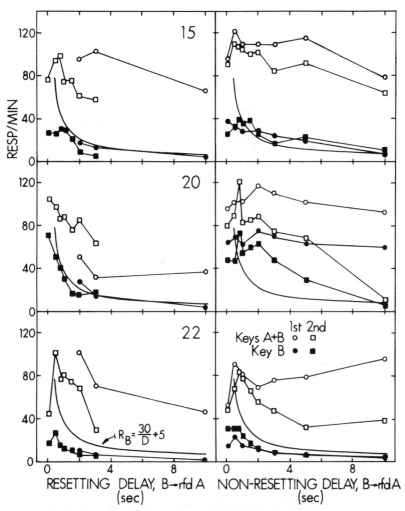

Figure 4.14. Response rates in a two-key procedure with VI reinforcement arranged for a B peck followed by an A peck, for three pigeons. A B peck initiated a delay at the end of which an A peck could be reinforced; early A pecks did not reset the delay. In one procedure, after a B peck had initiated the delay, subsequent B pecks reset it; in another, subsequent B pecks did not reset the delay. Two sequences of delays (circles and squares) were arranged with each procedure (cf. Table 4.2). Graphs show sums of rates on both keys (A + B) and rates on B as a function of resetting (left) and non-resetting (right) delays. Time and responses from reinforcement setups to reinforcer deliveries were excluded from all rate calculations. The solid curves duplicate the function in Figure 4.13

what these performances imply about accounts of response decrements in terms of the reinforcement of other behaviour (cf. Herrnstein, 1970, on r_0). In the schedules of Figures 4.13 and 4.14, every reinforcer was contiguous with an A response, and no B response could be in closer contiguity with a reinforcer than a reinforced A response. Even though performances were more variable in the delay procedures of Figure 4.14 than in the response-number procedures of Figure 4.13, B responding was a function of delay in both cases. In VT schedules and in single-key delay procedures such as those of Figure 4.8, the contiguity of reinforcers with particular samples of other behaviour would have been less consistent than that of reinforcers with A responses in the two-key delay procedures. If the rate of B responding was not determined by the contiguities of the two-key procedures, it is inappropriate to attribute decrements with VT and delayed reinforcers to contiguities with other behaviour in the single-key procedures. Given the demonstration that responding is weakly maintained by response-independent reinforcers, it would in any case be paradoxical to attempt an account of this process in terms of an equivalent independence between reinforcers and other behaviour.

Variable Delays

We have demonstrated that VR schedules with non-resetting fixed delays maintain higher response rates than VT schedules. It is appropriate now to turn to schedules with variable delays, because some properties of these schedules can provide closer approximations to the properties of VT schedules. For example, schedules with variable delays, like FT schedules, need not impose a maximum response–reinforcer interval. We will examine both variable delay schedules in which at least one response must occur between successive reinforcers and those in which interreinforcer intervals may occur without responses in them (cf. the fixed delay example of Figure 4.6).

Figure 4.15 shows data for the transition from immediate VR 20 reinforcement to VR 13.3 and VI 10 s reinforcement with non-resetting variable delays (Table 4.1). The mean of the variable delays was 4 s; with VR reinforcement, responses during delays did not count toward the ratio. The changes in response rate were consistent across pigeons. Responding decreased after the change from the VR to the tandem VR VT schedule, and again after the change to the tandem VI VT schedule. With a return to tandem VR VT reinforcement, responding increased slightly, and then declined during sessions of VT 20 s.

The figure also includes data from two subsequent transitions from VR 20 to VT 10 s, shown within the shaded envelope of the first VR-to-VT transition (cf. Figure 4.1). After the variable delay schedules, the decreases in VT rate for pigeon 1 were only slightly different from those in the initial transition. The VT rate had declined more rapidly in later transitions (conditions 2–4) than in the initial transition. Thus, if the several VR-to-VT transitions had made this

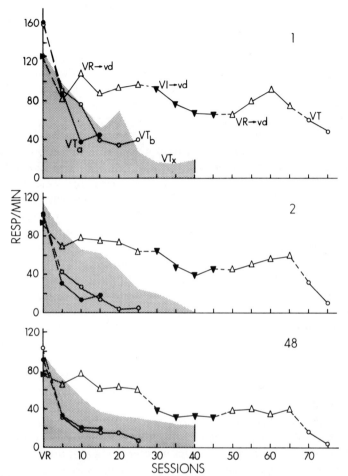

Figure 4.15. Response rates in the transition from VR 20 to VR and VI schedules with non-resetting variable delays (vd) and to VT 20 s (conditions 5–8, Table 4.1), for three pigeons. The leftmost points of each function are means over the last five sessions of VR 20. The shaded area (VT$_x$) shows response rates in the first transition from VR to VT (condition 1); repetitions of this transition (conditions 9 and 10) are shown respectively as VT$_a$ and VT$_b$

pigeon's behaviour sensitive to the difference properties of response-dependent and response-independent reinforcers, the variable delay procedures may have reduced this sensitivity. For pigeons 2 and 48, however, the decreases in VT rates were comparable to those in the most recent VR-to-VT transitions; they remained more rapid than those in the initial transition. Whatever the basis for the sensitivity of these pigeons' behaviour to the difference between VR and VT schedules, it was unaffected by exposure to variable delay schedules.

Ratio and interval contingencies with delayed reinforcement. Some accounts of the higher response rates maintained by VR than by VI schedules have appealed to the differential reinforcement of IRTs (e.g. Anger, 1956; Catania and Reynolds, 1968). Reinforcement probability is independent of time since the last response in VR schedules, but it increases as the time since the last response increases in VI schedules. Thus, the relative frequency of reinforced long IRTs in VR performances is typically lower than that in VI performances.

The effects of delayed VR and VI reinforcement shown in Figure 4.15 raise difficulties for an IRT interpretation, because the IRTs that were differentially affected by VR and VI contingencies in these schedules were the ones that initiated the variable delays, and were not contiguous with the reinforcers delivered at the end of the delays. Given that the delays were variable rather than fixed, it is unlikely that these IRTs were even in a consistent temporal relation to the later reinforcers that they had produced.

Figure 4.16 illustrates another delay experiment relevant to an IRT analysis. A VR 30 schedule operated for a pigeon's pecks in one chamber; each reinforcer produced by this pigeon's pecks made the next peck of another pigeon in a different chamber eligible for reinforcement. The second pigeon's pecks were therefore reinforced according to a VI schedule the intervals of which were determined by the interreinforcer times generated by the first pigeon (yoked schedules: Catania, Matthews, Silverman, and Yohalem, 1977; Ferster and Skinner, 1957). The VR and yoked VI schedules were occasionally reversed for the two pigeons, and after several reversals a 2 s non-resetting fixed delay of reinforcement was added to both schedules.

Without the delay (Figure 4.16, top panel), VR rates increased relative to yoked VI rates after the introduction of yoking (solid circles vs. open triangles); when the schedules were reversed, rates of responding also reversed, so that VR rates again became higher than VI rates (solid triangles vs. open circles); and so on. When the 2 s delay was added (Figure 4.16, bracketed segments of bottom panel), VR response rates at first decreased (solid circles to solid triangles), but then increased relative to the yoked VI rates for the other pigeon. The delay was removed for five sessions and then reinstated, after which three reversals of the direction of yoking were arranged. Overall response rates were lower, rate changes were slower, and the differences between VR and yoked VI rates were smaller with the delay than they had been without it, but VR rates still became high relative to yoked VI rates over successive sessions of a given direction of yoking.

As in the schedules of Figure 4.15, VR rates exceeded VI rates even though delays separated IRTs temporally from the reinforcers they had produced. Data are not presented for a second pair of pigeons for which yoked scheduling was also arranged. For those pigeons, response rates were generally low, rate

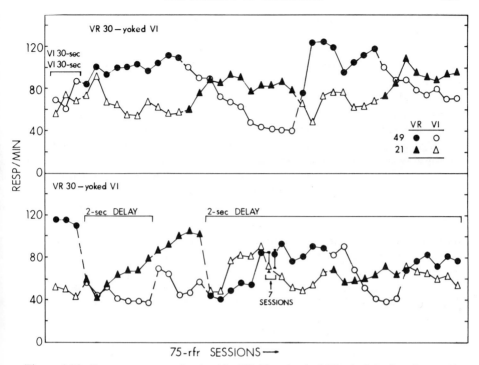

Figure 4.16. Response rates maintained by VR 30 and yoked VI schedules for pigeons 49 and 21. After baseline sessions with VI 30 s schedules, yoked sessions were arranged with no delay and with non-resetting 2 s delays of reinforcement. The direction of yoking was occasionally reversed. Both with and without the 2 s delay, higher rates were generally maintained by VR reinforcement (solid symbols) than by yoked VI reinforcement

reversals with changes in the direction of yoking were inconsistent even without delays, and responding was not well maintained after the delay was introduced. The experiment, however, is a kind of feasibility study. Its point is that VR and VI rate differences can sometimes emerge even with delayed reinforcers, and not that these differences must always emerge. Thus, the consistent rate reversals for pigeons 49 and 21 of Figure 4.16 are a sufficient demonstration that VR and VI rate differences need not depend on the differential contiguity of IRTs with the reinforcers they produce.

Correlations between response rates and reinforcement rates. Another property that differentiates ratio schedules from interval schedules is the correlation between response rates and reinforcement rates. In VR schedules, reinforcement rates vary directly with response rates. In VI schedules, reinforcement rates are somewhat independent of response rates, as long as the time between responses is short relative to the duration of the shortest scheduled interreinforcer interval.

One account of performances maintained by schedules is in terms of sensitivity to such correlations between rates (Baum, 1973). These correlations cannot be reduced to contiguities, because rates can be determined only by integrating events over some extended time period. If this is a difficulty, however, it applies as well to IRT analyses, because IRTs and their differential reinforcement can only be assessed by sampling responses and reinforcers over some extended time period (cf. Shimp, 1976, on molar and molecular accounts of behaviour). The problem of sampling over periods of time would also be relevant to accounts of contingency sensitivity that might appeal to changes in distributions of response–reinforcer intervals or their means.

The present research arranged strong correlations between response rates and 1 einforcement rates in its VR schedules, and allowed such correlations to emerge with relatively small decreases in response rates in the high reinforcement density of its VI schedules (VI 10 s). Although the introduction of non-resetting delays may have diminished the correlations, they would nonetheless have remained high, whereas those within VT schedules were on the average zero. The problem with relating these correlations to maintained rates of responding is that of specifying the dimensions on which the correlations are based, such as the differential features of various reinforcement contingencies and the range of time periods over which rates can be integrated (cf. Williams, 1976).

Transitions to variable delays from high rate and from low rate baselines. The variable delay schedules so far considered were arranged so that two successive reinforcers could not be delivered without an intervening response (cf. Figure 4.6). Figures 4.11 and 4.12 demonstrated that even with VT response rates as high as 50 responses/min, interreinforcer intervals without responses were events that might have distinguished VT reinforcement from response-dependent reinforcement. In addition, the preceding research was primarily concerned with transitions to VT and to delay schedules from relatively high rates of VR responding. Because the effects of a schedule may depend on the performance that first contacts the schedule contingencies, the following procedures examined responding with VT and with variable delay reinforcement after transitions from VI 10 s and from EXT baselines.

Two adult male Silver King pigeons (88 and 87) with brief experimental histories were added to pigeons 1 and 48 of the earlier studies. The first sequence of procedures consisted of VI 10 s reinforcement (26 sessions), EXT (10 sessions), VI 10 s reinforcement (13 sessions), VI 10 s reinforcement with variable delays (14 sessions), and VT 10 s (18 sessions); an additional 14 sessions of VI 10 s reinforcement with variable delays included an interruption caused by equipment failures. Reinforcer deliveries were 2.5 s and sessions were 10 min.

The VI 10 s schedule was arranged by a probability generator that selected one-per-second pulses with a probability of 0.10. When the variable delay was added, the response to be reinforced stepped an add–subtract stepper in one direction; the delivery of a reinforcer at the end of the variable delay stepped the stepper back in the other direction; thus, delays operating for different reinforcers could be accumulated. When a single delay operated, the variable delay was arranged by a probability generator that selected one-per-second pulses to operate the feeder with a probability of 0.20 (mean delay of 5 s). The pulse rate to this single probability generator was doubled when two delays operated together, tripled when three operated, and quadrupled when four operated, in effect maintaining independent mean delays of 5 s for each of the accumulated reinforcers. The pulse rate could not be increased further for accumulations of five reinforcers or more, but that large an accumulation of delays was a rare event.

In practice, this arrangement generated a VI 10 s schedule in which responses produced reinforcers after variable delays of 5 s, and in which successive interreinforcer intervals were scheduled from these responses rather than from reinforcer deliveries; the frequency of interreinforcer intervals that did not include responses varied with response rate, but at least one such interval occurred in most sessions of this schedule for each pigeon. (Note that a range of interreinforcer intervals was generated by the sampling of the one-per-second pulses.) The VT 10 s schedule was arranged by a probability generator that selected one-per-second pulses with a probability of 0.10 for initiation of the delay circuit. Because the times between successive initiations of the delay circuit averaged 10 s, the average interreinforcer interval remained 10 s. This procedure was used so that the combination of variable interreinforcer intervals with variable delays would be common to both the VT and the variably delayed VI schedules.

A second sequence of conditions, after 37 sessions of other procedures, consisted of EXT (12 sessions); VT 10 s reinforcement (11 sessions), EXT (13 sessions), and VI 10 s reinforcement with variable delays (11 sessions for pigeon 1, ten sessions for the remaining pigeons). The operation of the delayed VI and the VT schedules was as in the preceding sequence, except that the mean variable delay was 10 s (one-per-second pulses selected with a probability of 0.10). Reinforcer deliveries were 2.5 s and sessions were 10 min.

Data from the first sequence are shown in Figure 4.17. After the change from immediate to variably delayed VI reinforcement, response rates decreased for all pigeons. The low rates for pigeons 1 and 48 were followed by a recovery to higher levels (cf. the fixed delay 4 s data for pigeon 48 in Figure 4.8). For pigeon 88, a transient decrease was followed by increasing rates. For pigeon 87, the slight decrease in the first session was followed by relatively stable rates. The change to VT reinforcement then produced decreasing response rates for all pigeons. (For comparisons with earlier figures, note that single sessions rather than blocks of five sessions are plotted.) Higher response rates were again obtained in a later return to variably delayed VI reinforcement, except for pigeon 88; with this pigeon's rates of about 100 responses/min maintained by both schedules, it is

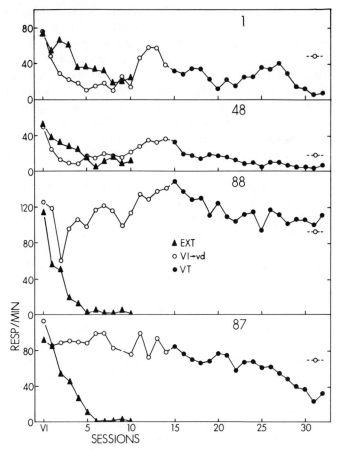

Figure 4.17. Response rates maintained in transitions from VI 10 s to extinction (EXT), to non-resetting variable delays (vd), and to response-independent reinforcement (VT 10 s), for two pigeons from earlier procedures (1 and 48) and for two new pigeons (88 and 87). With variable delays, interreinforcer intervals were timed from the responses that initiated delays rather than from reinforcer deliveries (cf. Figure 4.6); mean variable delays were 5 s. Sessions were 10 min. The first point on the EXT function and on the variable delay function is a mean over the last hour of the preceding VI sessions. Open circles at the right show mean rates over the last hour of 14 later sessions of VI reinforcement with variable delay

unlikely that the different contingencies of the VT and the variably delayed VI schedules had any differential behavioural consequences.

The decrements over the initial sessions of variably delayed VI reinforcement for pigeons 1 and 48 were probably comparable to those that would have been obtained in transitions to VT reinforcement. For these pigeons, responding in EXT declined more slowly. Thus, differences in the rate declines with VT and

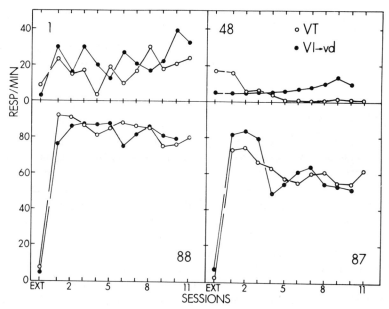

Figure 4.18. Response rates in transitions from extinction (EXT) to response-independent reinforcement (VT 10 s) and to VI 10 s reinforcement with non-resetting variable delays, for four pigeons; mean variable delays were 10 s. With variable delays, interreinforcer intervals were timed from the responses that initiated delays rather than from interreinforcer intervals (cf. Figure 4.6). Sessions were 10 min. Leftmost points in each graph are means over the last three of 12 (open circles) or 13 (solid circles) preceding sessions of EXT

with EXT (cf. Figures 4.2 and 4.3) may depend in part on the organism's history with respect to these transitions. A comparison after repeated transitions to both EXT and VT might be more appropriate than a comparison after a single transition to each (cf. Rescorla and Skucy, 1969).

Figure 4.18 shows data for transitions from EXT to VT and to variably delayed VI reinforcement for each pigeon. A differential effect of the schedule contingencies was evident only in the responding of pigeon 48: a low rate was maintained by variably delayed VI reinforcement, whereas rate fell to near zero with VT reinforcement. For the relatively low rate responding of pigeon 1 and the relatively high rate responding of pigeons 88 and 87, variably delayed VI rates and VT rates were not consistently different.

In retrospect, it should not be surprising that response-dependent and response-independent reinforcers had differential effects in some conditions and not in others, and that these effects were more substantial for pigeons with longer histories in these types of procedures. The data for pigeons 1 and 48 in Figure 4.17 and for pigeon 48 in Figure 4.18 show that variably delayed reinforcement can differentially maintain responding relative to VT reinforcement even when both schedules include interreinforcer intervals without responses in them. Other patterns of results might have been obtained at different parameter values of our various schedules, but the present data have at least demonstrated the maintenance of behaviour over a range of conditions within which the relation between responses and their reinforcers was relaxed.

The Concept of Causation

Let us first summarize our findings. The decrease in pigeons' rates of pecking after the change from response-dependent to response-independent reinforcement occurred more rapidly with successive exposures to this transition. With non-resetting fixed and variable delays of reinforcement, various schedules of response-dependent reinforcement were then arranged within which some of the behavioural properties of response-independent reinforcement were duplicated. Included among these properties were distributions of response–reinforcer intervals and frequencies of interreinforcer intervals without responses. Although the delay schedules reduced the contiguity between responses and reinforcers relative to that with immediate reinforcement, they typically maintained higher rates of responding than response-independent reinforcement schedules.

Because some of the behavioural properties of schedules are likely to differentiate between response-independent and response-dependent reinforcers when response rate is high (e.g. relative frequency of negative response-reinforcer intervals), and others are likely to do so when response rate is low (e.g. local correlations of response rate and reinforcement rate), it may be reasonably to conclude that the sensitivity to contingencies can be based on any of a variety of different properties of contingencies. Different variables may therefore come into play at different points in a given transition from one type of schedule to another.

We may argue that organisms are sensitive to those features of the environment that are correlated with the presence or absence of response–reinforcer contingencies. But this argument remains vague if we do not specify the features. For example, what features differentiate variably delayed reinforcement from response-independent reinforcement so that the former usually supports responding whereas the latter usually does not? By themselves, contiguities are inadequate. If local asynchronies between responses and consequences could not be tolerated in contingencies, only automated environments would be capable of maintaining behaviour. Instead, organisms must be able somehow to integrate events over time and to respond on the basis of correlations among reinforcement rates and response rates. But they must also make contact with other simpler schedule dimensions correlated with contingencies. If an organism acquires a history with respect to the various correlates of contingencies, responding may begin to decline as in extinction when these correlates are absent.

It would be inappropriate, strictly speaking, to call the correlates discriminative stimuli or the process discrimination, because the usual definition of these terms does not apply. These correlates are features correlated with contingencies, and not stimuli in the presence of which contingencies operate. Furthermore, it is not clear what differential contingencies could be the basis for the discrimination of the contingencies themselves. If we argue that some properties of contingencies must be learned, to what contingencies can we appeal as the basis for that learning?

Contingency features, then, are those features of reinforcement schedules that provide the basis for differential control by response-dependent and response-independent reinforcers. Variables that might be candidates for this role include many of the schedule properties that have already been considered: distributions of response–reinforcer intervals, including their forms, their means, and the negative intervals that occur when responses follow closely after the onset of a reinforcer; interreinforcer intervals without responses; and various rates, delays, and correlations among events, integrated over periods of time. Some of these features will be more likely to be present in some contexts than in others. Thus, it is unlikely that any one alone will be either a necessary or a sufficient feature to control differential responding.

In human behaviour, too, the features of contingencies may enter into judgements of causation. If a lobby elevator does not have a floor indicator, the only consequence of pressing the elevator button may be the arrival of the elevator after a variable delay. But the elevator might also arrive because someone earlier had already pressed the button and then had taken the stairs instead, or because someone already in the elevator had pressed the button for the lobby floor, or because this elevator always returns to the lobby after a call to another floor. (Under such circumstances, accidental contiguities might maintain behaviour that in other contexts would be called superstitious.) One day the elevator doors might open just as someone reached out to press the button. On another, the elevator might arrive and leave and arrive again, even though the button was for some reason not pressed in the intervening time. With respect both to verbal behaviour and to pressing the button, the concept of causation will here depend not on any constant conjunctions of events, but rather on some sample of the complex of features correlated with contingencies. If causation is a unitary concept, its unity rests on the nature of contingency. In any case, some of the features of the elevator examples are the same as those we explored earlier with pigeons, and therefore may justify our regarding the pigeons' pecks as worthy causes.

We began with a reference to superstitious behaviour. Our account does not imply that response-independent events will not generate superstitious behaviour; the differentiation between response-independent and response-dependent events cannot be guaranteed. Certainly single response–reinforcer contiguities have behavioural effects (Skinner, 1938; Henton and Iversen, 1978,

Figures 3.22 and 3.23). The account does suggest, however, that the range of conditions within which superstitious behaviour will be generated is narrower than was once supposed. In particular, behaviour will be more likely to be maintained by accidental contiguities over short than over long periods of exposure to particular contingencies. In other words, pigeons are more likely to behave as if there were a causal relation between their behaviour and the presentation of food when the causal relation exists than when the causal relation is lacking. And given that pigeons as well as humans can be sensitive to the features of contingencies, it may be appropriate also to paraphrase the other quotation with which this treatment began. An organism's first experience with causes probably comes from its own behaviour: things move because it moves them.

Note

Research supported by NSF Grant BNS76-09723 and NIH Grant MH-33086 to the University of Maryland Baltimore County. The data in Table 4.2 and Figure 4.14 were obtained in collaboration with Terje Sagvolden; those in Figure 4.16 were obtained in collaboration with Robert Epstein. For assistance in the conduct of the experiments, thanks go to several UMBC students, and especially to Kenneth Thurston, Marla Caplan, Susan Vennari, Mary Fox, Gary Reich, and Ira A. Katz.

References

Anger, D. (1956). The dependence of interresponse times upon the relative reinforcement of different interresponse times. *Journal of Experimental Psychology*, **52**, 145–161.

Anger, D. and Anger, K. (1976). Behavior changes during repeated eight-day extinctions. *Journal of the Experimental Analysis of Behavior*, **26**, 181–190.

Azzi, R., Fix, D. S. R., Keller, F. S., and Rocha e Silva, M. I. (1964). Exteroceptive control of response under delayed reinforcement. *Journal of the Experimental Analysis of Behavior*, **7**, 159–162.

Baum, W. M. (1973). The correlation-based law of effect. *Journal of the Experimental Analysis of Behavior*, **20**, 137–153.

Brand, M. (ed.) (1976). *The Nature of Causation*, University of Illinois Press, Urbana.

Bullock, D. H. (1960). Repeated conditioning-extinction sessions as a function of the reinforcement schedule. *Journal of the Experimental Analysis of Behavior*, **3**, 241–243.

Bullock, D. H. and Smith, W. C. (1953). An effect of repeated conditioning–extinction upon operant strength. *Journal of Experimental Psychology*, **46**, 349–352.

Catania, A. C. (1969). Concurrent performances: inhibition of one response by reinforcement of another. *Journal of the Experimental Analysis of Behavior*, **12**, 731–744.

Catania, A. C. (1970). Reinforcement schedules and psychophysical judgments. In *The Theory of Reinforcement Schedules* (W. N. Schoenfeld, ed.), Appleton-Century-Crofts, New York.

Catania, A. C. (1971). Reinforcement schedules: the role of responses preceding the one that produces the reinforcer. *Journal of the Experimental Analysis of Behavior*, **15**, 271–287.

Catania, A. C. (1979). *Learning*, Prentice-Hall, Englewood Cliffs, N. J.

Catania, A. C. and Cutts, D. (1963). Experimental control of superstitious responding in humans. *Journal of the Experimental Analysis of Behavior*, **6**, 203–208.

Catania, A. C., Matthews, T. J., Silverman, P. J., and Yohalem, R. (1977). Yoked variable-ratio and variable-interval responding in pigeons. *Journal of the Experimental Analysis of Behavior*, **28**, 155–161.

Catania, A. C., and Reynolds, G. S. (1968). A quantitative analysis of the behavior maintained by interval schedules of reinforcement. *Journal of the Experimental Analysis of Behavior*, **11**, 327–383.

Chung, S. H. (1963). Effects of delayed reinforcement in a concurrent situation. *Journal of the Experimental Analysis of Behavior*, **8**, 439–444.

Chung, S. H. and Herrnstein, R. J. (1967). Choice and delay of reinforcement. *Journal of the Experimental Analysis of Behavior*, **10**, 67–74.

de Charms, R. (1968). *Personal Causation*, Academic Press, New York.

Dews, P. B. (1960). Free-operant behavior under conditions of delayed reinforcement: I. CRF-type schedules. *Journal of the Experimental Analysis of Behavior*, **3**, 221–234.

Dews, P. B. (1969). Studies on responding under fixed-interval schedules of reinforcement: the effects on the pattern of responding of changes in requirements at reinforcement. *Journal of the Experimental Analysis of Behavior*, **12**, 191–199.

Eriksen, C. W. (ed.) (1962). *Behavior and Awareness*. Duke University Press, Durham, N. C.

Ferster, C. B. (1953). Sustained behavior under delayed reinforcement. *Journal of Experimental Psychology*, **45**, 218–224.

Ferster, C. B. and Skinner, B. F. (1957). *Schedules of reinforcement*, Appleton-Century-Crofts, New York.

Gasking, D. (1955). Causation and recipes. *Mind*, **64**, 479–487.

Hefferline, R. F. and Keenan, B. (1963). Amplitude-induction gradient of a small-scale (covert) operant. *Journal of the Experimental Analysis of Behavior*, **6**, 307–315.

Henton, W. W. and Iversen, I. H. (1978). *Classical Conditioning and Operant Conditioning*, Springer-Verlag, New York.

Herrnstein, R. J. (1966). Superstition: A corollary of the principles of operant conditioning. In *Operant Behavior: Areas of Research and Application* (W. K. Honig, ed.), pp. 33–51. Appleton-Century-Crofts, New York.

Herrnstein, R. J. (1970). On the law of effect. *Journal of the Experimental Analysis of Behavior*, **13**, 243–266.

Hume, D. (1748). *Enquiry Concerning Human Understanding*, London (reprinted by Open Court, Chicago; 1912).

Jenkins, H. M. (1961). The effect of discrimination training on extinction. *Journal of Experimental Psychology*, **61**, 111–121.

Jenkins, H. M. (1970). Sequential organization in schedules of reinforcement. In *The Theory of Reinforcement Schedules* (W. N. Schoenfeld, ed.), Appleton-Century-Crofts, New York.

Kelley, H. H. (1973). The processes of causal attribution. *American Psychologist*, **28**, 107–128.

Kendall, S. B. and Newby, W. (1978). Delayed reinforcement of fixed-ratio performance without mediated exteroceptive conditioned reinforcement. *Journal of the Experimental Analysis of Behavior*, **30**, 231–237.

Killeen, P. (1977). The pigeon's perception of causality. Paper delivered at the Midwestern Association of Behavior Analysis, Chicago, III., May 1977.

Killeen, P. (1979). Arousal: its genesis, modulation, and extinction. *Advances in Analysis of Behavior*, **1**, 37–78.

Lachter, G. D. (1971). Some temporal parameters of non-contingent reinforcement. *Journal of the Experimental Analysis of Behavior*, **16**, 207–217.

Lachter, G. D. (1973). Response–reinforcer relationships in variable delay and non-contingent schedules of reinforcement. *Psychological Reports*, **33**, 627–631.

Lachter, G. D., Cole, B. K., and Schoenfeld, W. N. (1971). Response rate under varying frequency of non-contingent reinforcement. *Journal of the Experimental Analysis of Behavior*, **15**, 233–236.

Lattal, K. A. (1972). Response–reinforcer independence and conventional extinction after fixed-interval and variable-interval schedules. *Journal of the Experimental Analysis of Behavior*, **18**, 133–140.

Lattal, K. A. (1973). Response–reinforcer independence in multiple and mixed schedules. *Journal of the Experimental Analysis of Behavior*, **20**, 265–271.

Lattal, K. A. (1974). Combinations of response–reinforcer dependence and independence. *Journal of the Experimental Analysis of Behavior*, **22**, 357–362.

Lattal, K. A. (1975). Reinforcement contingencies as discriminative stimuli. *Journal of the Experimental Analysis of Behavior*, **23**, 241–246.

Lefcourt, H. M. (1976). *Locus of Control*, Lawrence Erlbaum, Hillsdale, N. J.

Lesser, H. (1977). The growth of perceived causality in children. *Journal of Genetic Psychology*, **130**, 145–152.

Lewis, D. (1973). Causation. *Journal of Philosophy*, **70**, 556–567.

Mackie, J. L. (1965). Causes and conditions. *American Philosophical Quarterly*, **2**, 245–264.

Mendelson, R. and Shultz, T. R. (1976). Covariation and temporal contiguity as principles of causal inference in young children. *Journal of Experimental Child Psychology*, **22**, 408–412.

Michotte, A. (1963). *The Perception of Causality*, Methuen, London.

Neuringer, A. J. (1969). Delayed reinforcement versus reinforcement after a fixed interval. *Journal of the Experimental Analysis of Behavior*, **12**, 375–383.

Neuringer, A. J. (1970). Superstitious key pecking after three peck-produced reinforcements. *Journal of the Experimental Analysis of Behavior*, **13**, 127–134.

Nevin, J. A. (1974). Response strength in multiple schedules. *Journal of the Experimental Analysis of Behavior*, **21**, 389–408.

Nisbett, R. E., Caputo, C., Legant, P., and Marecek, J. (1973). Behavior as seen by the actor and as seen by the observer. *Journal of Personality and Social Psychology*, **27**, 154–164.

Onions, C. T. (ed.) (1966). *The Oxford Dictionary of English Etymology*, Oxford University Press, London.

Partridge, E. (1958). *Origins. A Short Etymological Dictionary of Modern English*, Macmillan, London.

Perkins, C. C. and Cacioppo, A. J. (1950). The effect of intermittent reinforcement on the change in extinction rate following successive reconditionings. *Journal of Experimental Psychology*, **40**, 794–801.

Piaget, J. (1927). *The Child's Conception of Physical Causality*, Geneva (English edition published by Routledge and Kegan Paul, London, 1951).

Rachlin, H. and Green, L. (1972). Commitment, choice and self-control. *Journal of the Experimental Analysis of Behavior*, **17**, 15–22.

Rescorla, R. A. (1967). Pavlovian conditioning and its proper control procedures. *Psychological Review*, **74**, 71–80.

Rescorla, R. A. and Skucy, J. C. (1969). Effect of response-independent reinforcers during extinction. *Journal of Comparative and Physiological Psychology*, **67**, 381–389.

Reynolds, G. S. (1966). Discrimination and emission of temporal intervals by pigeons. *Journal of the Experimental Analysis of Behavior*, **9**, 65–68.

Russell, B. (1912–1913). On the notion of cause. *Proceedings of the Aristotelian Society*,

13, 1–26; reprinted in *Readings in the Philosophy of Science* (H. Feigl and M. Brodbeck, eds), Appleton-Century-Crofts, New York, 1953.

Schaeffer, R. W., Salzberg, C. L., Birkle, R. A., and Ryan, F. J. (1967). Resistance to extinction as a function of reinforcement patterns. *Psychological Record*, **17**, 353–358.

Schoenfeld, W. N., Cole, B. K., Lang, J., and Mankoff, R. (1973). 'Contingency' in behavior theory. In *Contemporary Approaches to Conditioning and Learning* (F. J. McGuigan and D. B. Lumsden, eds), Winston, Washington, D. C.

Shettleworth, S. and Nevin, J. A. (1965). Relative rate of response and relative magnitude of reinforcement in multiple schedules. *Journal of the Experimental Analysis of Behavior*, **8**, 199–202.

Shimp, C. P. (1976). Organization in memory and behavior. *Journal of the Experimental Analysis of Behavior*, **26**, 113–130.

Sidman, M. (1960). *Tactics of Scientific Research*, Basic Books, New York.

Sizemore, O. J. and Lattal, K. A. (1977). Dependency, temporal contiguity, and response-independent reinforcement. *Journal of the Experimental Analysis of Behavior*, **27**, 119–125.

Sizemore, O. J. and Lattal, K. A. (1978). Unsignalled delay of reinforcement in variable-interval schedules. *Journal of the Experimental Analysis of Behavior*, **30**, 169–175.

Skinner, B. F. (1938). *The Behavior of Organisms*, Appleton-Century-Crofts, New York.

Skinner, B. F. (1948). 'Superstition' in the pigeon. *Journal of Experimental Psychology*, **38**, 168–172.

Skinner, B. F. (1953). *Science and Human Behavior*, Macmillan, New York.

Skinner, B. F. (1957). *Verbal Behavior*, Appleton-Century Crofts, New York.

Skinner, B. F. (1966). The phylogeny and ontogeny of behavior. *Science*, **153**, 1205–1213.

Skinner, B. F. (1971). *Beyond Freedom and Dignity*, Knopf, New York.

Skinner, B. F. (1975). The shaping of phylogenic behavior. *Journal of the Experimental Analysis of Behavior*, **24**, 117–120.

Staddon, J. E. R. (1965). Some properties of spaced responding in pigeons. *Journal of the Experimental Analysis of Behavior*, **8**, 19–27.

Staddon, J. E. R. and Simmelhag, V. L. (1971). The 'superstition' experiment: a reexamination of its implications for the principles of adaptive behavior. *Psychological Review*, **78**, 3–43.

Williams, B. A. (1975). The blocking of reinforcement control. *Journal of the Experimental Analysis of Behavior*, **24**, 215–225.

Williams, B. A. (1976). The effects of unsignalled delayed reinforcement. *Journal of the Experimental Analysis of Behavior*, **26**, 441–449.

Zeiler, M. D. (1968). Fixed and variable schedules of response-independent reinforcement. *Journal of the Experimental Analysis of Behavior*, **11**, 405–414.

Zeiler, M. D. (1972). Superstitious behavior in children: an experimental analysis. *Advances in Child Development and Behavior*, **7**, 2–29.

Predictability, Correlation, and Contiguity
Edited by P. Harzem and M. H. Zeiler
© 1981 John Wiley & Sons Ltd

Chapter 5

Contiguity, Response Strength, and the Delay-reduction Hypothesis

Edmund Fantino

Introduction

The delay-reduction hypothesis states that the strength of a stimulus as a conditioned reinforcer is a function of the reduction in time to reinforcement correlated with the onset of that stimulus. Thus, the reinforcing strength of a stimulus (A′) is determined by both the length of the interval (A) between the onset of A′ and the onset of primary reinforcement and the length of the interval (B) measured from the onset of the preceding stimulus (B′) to the onset of A′. The reinforcing strength of A′ should be a function of the reduction in delay correlated with the onset of A′, $(A+B) - A = B$, divided by the original delay $(A+B)$ or:

$$\text{Reinforcing strength of A}' = f\left(\frac{B}{A + B}\right). \tag{5.1}$$

Every viable theory of conditioned reinforcement (cf. Fantino, 1977) requires that the reinforcing strength of a stimulus be enhanced the smaller the average interval between the onset of the stimulus and the onset of reinforcement. Thus, a stimulus associated with a variable interval or variable time 30 s schedule of reinforcement (VI 30 s or VT 30 s[2]) should be a stronger (conditioned) reinforcer than one associated with a VI 60 s or VT 60 s. But the delay-reduction hypothesis also requires that the contribution of contiguity to the conditioned reinforcing strength of the stimulus must be considered in the context of how remote primary reinforcement has been *prior* to the onset of the stimulus (or the interval $(A+B)$). The greater the percentage improvement, in terms of contiguity to primary reinforcement, correlated with the onset of the stimulus, the greater its conditioned reinforcing strength. Thus, a stimulus associated with a VI 30 s schedule (or an FI 30 s schedule) should be a stronger reinforcer if it is preceded by a 60 s period of non-reinforcement than if it is preceded by a 10 s period of non-reinforcement, since in the first case the onset of the 30 s interval is correlated with a two-thirds reduction in time to reinforcement whereas in the second case the onset of the 30 s interval is correlated with only a one-fourth reduction in time to reinforcement.

In this paper we review some strengths and limitations of this hypothesis and then point to some new directions where we feel it can make a contribution. First, however, we review the development of the hypothesis.

The Concurrent Chains Procedure

The delay-reduction hypothesis was developed in the study of choice for schedules of reinforcement. These studies utilized the concurrent chains procedure, developed by Autor (1960, 1969) and Herrnstein (1964). This procedure not only permits the study of conditioned reinforcement but is also an effective procedure for the study of choice that is in several respects superior to the use of simple concurrent schedules. The measure of choice on simple concurrent schedules is confounded with the rate of responding produced by the schedules themselves. For example, as Fantino and Logan (1979) have noted:

> Suppose we encounter a young man who goes hiking once every weekend and who also spends his lunch hour jogging as part of a weight-regulation program. We could not infer that he prefers jogging to hiking simply because the response is made more frequently (five times a week rather than one) and more vigorously. Rather, the demand characteristics and intrinsic nature of the activities require that jogging be more frequent and vigorous. Taking a different example, a young married couple will probably spend more time eating than making love (frequency of eating in meals per week greater than making love in intercourses per week) but may actually enjoy making love more (especially if the couple is inept in the kitchen) (p. 227).

Presumably this type of confounding is maximal when schedules of reinforcement controlling different rates and patterns of responding—such as FI and VR—are compared for choice. Response rates on typical VR schedules tend to be much higher than those on FI schedules. Hence it cannot be determined whether responding is controlled by the nature of VR and FI schedules or reflects choice for one schedule over another. Such a measure of choice would be more obviously inappropriate if the comparison involves schedules that require particular rates of responding (such as DRH, DRL or DRO) but is also potentially flawed when the schedules are more comparable (such as two VI schedules providing different rates of reinforcement and which control different rates of responding in isolation). The concurrent chains procedure avoids this difficulty. In this procedure, diagrammed in Figure 5.1, the subject responds on two concurrently available alternatives (the initial links or 'choice phase'). Generally, the procedure has been used with pigeons pecking at two concurrently available keys, each illuminated by the same stimulus. Responses on each

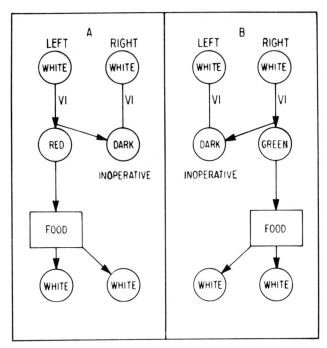

Figure 5.1. The concurrent chains procedure. (A) the sequence of events when responses on the left key are reinforced. (B) The analogous sequence on the right key. Responses in the presence of the coloured lights, the stimuli of the terminal links, are reinforced with food according to some schedule of reinforcement (typically, the independent variable). The measure of choice is the relative rate of responding to the concurrently available white lights. (After E. Fantino (1969b). Choice and rate of reinforcement. *Journal of the Experimental Analysis of Behavior*, **12**, 723–730. Copyright © 1969 by the Society for the Experimental Analysis of Behavior, Inc)

alternative occasionally produce another stimulus, correlated with entry into the terminal link of the chain on that key (the 'outcome phase'). When the subject produces one terminal link the other key becomes dark and inoperative. Responses in the outcome phase are reinforced with food. In the typical experiment, after the subject obtains a single reinforcement the choice phase (initial links) is reinstated. The measure of choice is the distribution of responses in the initial links. For example if the subject responds 100 times on the left key and 50 times on the right key during the initial links its 'choice proportion' is $100/(100 + 50) = 0.67$. The independent variable has generally involved some difference in the conditions arranged during the two terminal links.

Since entry into the two terminal links generally occurs at the same rate, the concurrent chains procedure has the additional advantage of keeping the number of primary reinforcements for responding on each key close to the number intended by the experimenter over a wide range of choice proportions. For example, if a subject responded exclusively on one key no primary reinforcements would be delivered on the other key. Owing to the nature of concurrently available VI schedules, however, the subject produces a higher rate of entry into the terminal links if it responds on both keys. For example, if the subject responded on only one key with concurrent VI 60 s VI 60 s initial links, it would enter a terminal link every 60 s, on the average. By responding on both keys, however, the subject enters a terminal link every 30 s, on the average. In usual practice this assures that the subject enters the terminal links of each key equally often. Thus, the effects of number of reinforcements are not confounded with those of the intended independent variable. Exceptions may occur, however, when choice proportions vary markedly from indifference, e.g. beyond the range of 0.15–0.85 (or 0.10–0.90). Since the delay-reduction hypothesis predicts when the subject should respond exclusively to one key, this is not a generally serious problem for our purposes. There is, however, a means for ensuring that terminal-link entries are equal no matter how high (or low) the choice proportions. This involves use of a forced-choice procedure, modelled after Stubbs and Pliskoff (1969). Use of this procedure has interesting implications for choice, discussion of which we defer to a substantive section.

Finally, the concurrent chains procedure is useful for studying conditioned reinforcement for two additional reasons. First, since schedules of primary reinforcement are maintained in the outcome phase of concurrent chains, the conditioned reinforcers (the stimuli associated with the terminal links, typically key lights) do not undergo extinction. Second, choice procedures are known to be quite sensitive to manipulations of independent variables, thus promoting experimental differentiations among the strengths of different conditioned reinforcers (e.g. Catania, 1963, 1966; Herrnstein, 1961).

Development of the Delay-reduction Hypothesis

Early work with the concurrent chains procedure suggested that pigeons match their choice proportions to the proportions of reinforcements available during the two terminal links. Specifically, both Autor (1960) and Herrnstein (1964) varied the rates of reinforcement available for responding on VI and VR schedules presented in the terminal links. They found that pigeons' choice proportions were well described by the following equation:

$$\frac{R_L}{R_L + R_R} = \frac{1/t_{2L}}{1/t_{2L} + 1/t_{2R}}, \tag{5.2}$$

where R_L and R_R represent the number of responses during the choice phase on the left and right key, respectively, and t_{2L} and t_{2R} specify the average time to reinforcement in the corresponding terminal links ($1/t_{2L}$ and $1/t_{2R}$ being the rates of reinforcement during the terminal links).

According to equation (5.2), choice should not vary with the length of the initial links, which are not represented in the equation. According to the delay-reduction hypothesis, however, choice should vary systematically with initial link length since, in equation (5.1), the longer B, the greater the putative reinforcing strength of A'. Specifically, Fantino (1969a, b) suggested the following quantitative alternative to equation (5.2) which was also consistent with Autor and Herrnstein's data:

$$
\frac{R_L}{R_L + R_R} = \begin{cases} \dfrac{T - t_{2L}}{(T - t_{2L}) + (T - t_{2R})}, & t_{2L} < T, t_{2R} < T, \\ 1, & t_{2L} < T, t_{2R} > T, \\ & t_{2L} > T, t_{2R} < T, \\ 0, & \end{cases} \tag{5.3}
$$

where T, the only new term, represents the average delay to primary reinforcement from the onset of the initial links. Thus, $(T\text{-}t_{2L})$ represents the delay reduction correlated with the onset of t_{2L} and $(T\text{-}t_{2R})$ represents the delay reduction correlated with the onset of t_{2R}. Note that when entry into either terminal link produces an increase in average waiting time to primary reinforcement (either $t_{2R} > T$ or $t_{2L} > T$), equation (5.3) requires the organism to emit all of its choice responses to the other alternative. In other words, equation (5.3) specifies when the subject should prefer one outcome exclusively (obviously t_{2L} and t_{2R} cannot *both* be greater than T). Equation (5.3), like equation (5.2), requires matching, but it stipulates matching to different quantities than equation (5.2). In words, equation (5.3) specifies that the subject's choices should match the delay reductions correlated with each outcome. Expressed differently, the greater the improvement, in terms of temporal proximity to reinforcement, correlated with the onset of one stimulus, the more effective that stimulus will be as a conditioned reinforcer. Equations (5.2) and (5.3) both stipulate that the conditioned reinforcing effectiveness of a stimulus will depend upon its proximity to primary reinforcement (t_{2L} and t_{2R}). Only equation (5.3), however, requires consideration of the temporal context in which this proximity is embedded.

Fantino (1969b) tested the two equations by varying the length of the choice phase (thus varying T) while holding t_{2L} and t_{2R} constant. This was accomplished by using three different pairs of VI schedules to arrange entry into the two terminal links, which were always VI 30 s and VI 90 s. The data strongly supported equation (5.3). For example, in 15 of 16 cases in which the two equations required different choice proportions, equation (5.3) more closely fitted the data. In addition, for each of these 16 points, equation (5.3) accounted for the direction of the deviation of data from equation (5.2). The effects of the length of the choice phase upon choice were also demonstrated in subsequent studies (including Wardlaw and Davison, 1974; Hursh and Fantino, 1974).

Another implication of equation (5.3) concerns the duration of the terminal links (t_{2L} and t_{2R}). For a given duration of the choice phase, say, with VI 60 s initial links, how should choice vary as t_{2L} and t_{2R} are varied while maintaining a constant ratio to one another? For example, assume the following four pairs of outcome values are studied: (1) $t_{2L} = 5$, $t_{2R} = 10$; (2) $t_{2L} = 10$, $t_{2R} = 20$; (3) $t_{2L} = 20$, $t_{2R} = 40$; (4) $t_{2L} = 40$, $t_{2R} = 80$. Equation (5.3) requires choice proportions of 0.54, 0.58, 0.67, and 0.83 in (1), (2), (3), and (4), respectively. Increasing the duration of the terminal links relative to the choice phase should, therefore, have the same effect as decreasing choice phase duration relative to that of the outcome phase: Preference for the favoured alternative should increase, Equation (5.2), on the other hand, requires a constant choice proportion of 0.67. The results from several studies of choice for either VI or FI schedules show that preference increases when the duration of the outcome phase is increased while a constant ratio is maintained between them (e.g. MacEwen, 1972; Williams and Fantino, 1978).

Another implication of equation (5.3) appeared doubtful, however. A choice proportion of 0.50, or indifference, is required whenever $t_{2L} = t_{2R}$, regardless of the initial link values, since the two terminal link stimuli are correlated with the same degree of reduction in average waiting time to reinforcement. This is so even when the initial link values are quite different, e.g. VI 15 s and VI 60 s. Squires and Fantino (1971) tested this implication and found it wanting. Instead, preference varied with the relative values of the initial links in the manner expected if rate of primary and conditioned reinforcement affected choice, i.e. a higher rate of responding occurred to the initial link stimulus associated with the higher rate of terminal link entry (the shorter VI). Squires and Fantino suggested that an additional variable be added to equation (5.3) which takes into account the rate of primary reinforcement on each key separately. These rates may be simply stated as r_L and r_R, the rates of primary reinforcement on the left and right keys, respectively. (These equal the reciprocal of the respective initial and terminal link times or $1/(t_{1L} + t_{2L})$ and $1/(t_{1R} + t_{2R})$). Thus, the new equation is

$$\frac{R_L}{R_L + R_R} = \begin{cases} \dfrac{r_L(T - t_{2L})}{r_L(T - t_{2L}) + r_R(T - t_{2R})}, & t_{2L} < T, t_{2R} < T, \\ 1, & t_{2L} < T, t_{2R} > T, \\ 0, & t_{2L} > T, t_{2R} < T, \end{cases} \quad (5.4)$$

Equation (5.4) describes all of the data discussed thus far as well or better than equation (5.3). Moreover, it has the important additional value of requiring matching in choice with simple concurrent VI schedules (Herrnstein, 1961, 1970), i.e. when $t_{2L} = t_{2R} = 0$. Nonetheless, for the sake of clarity, we shall discuss the simpler unmodified version, equation (5.3), in this chapter. This is acceptable since equations (5.3) and (5.4) make roughly comparable predictions with equal initial links, and since all the studies we discuss henceforth use equal initial links.

Although all of the work discussed thus far has used the standard concurrent chains procedure with pigeons, there are other data which permit an assessment of the delay-reduction hypothesis in different situations and with at least one other organism, the rat. The final and major section of this chapter reviews some current research from our laboratory which further extends the hypothesis as it relates to conditioned reinforcement, but also examines the utility of the hypothesis to account for elicited and discriminative responding. We conclude the present section by noting the relevance of two areas of research for the delay-reduction hypothesis of conditioned reinforcement: the study of optimal feeding strategies and self-control.

Collier's Study of Optimal Feeding Strategies

Recent work with rats from Dr George Collier's laboratory at Rutgers University constitutes an experimental analysis of the entire behaviour chain involved in feeding, from search through identification, procurement, handling, and consumption (Collier, 1977; Collier and Kaufman, 1976). In one set of studies the rat was shaped to respond to two levers located in an apparatus in which it lived continuously. When an FR schedule was satisfied on one lever—the 'search lever'—the light below the lever extinguished and one of two

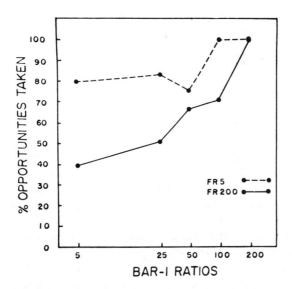

Figure 5.2. Percentage of opportunities taken from the low-cost (FR 5) (●---●) and high-cost (FR 200) (●—●) meals as a function of the search cost (the ratio required on the search bar, Bar-1). (After Collier (1977) as appearing in Fantino and Logan (1979). From *The Experimental Analysis of Behavior: A Biological Perspective* by Edmund Fantino and Cheryl A. Logan. W. H. Freeman and Company Copyright © 1979)

lights under the second lever—the 'procurement lever'—lit up. If the rat made a single response on the procurement lever within 7.5 s of light onset, it was committed to completing the ratio. If no response was made for 7.5 s, however, the procurement light was turned off and the search light was reilluminated.

In one study the ratios on the procurement lever were held at 5 and 200 (depending upon which light was on) while the ratio required on the search lever varied from 5 to 200 across conditions. As the search ratio increased, corresponding to longer initial links, was the rat more likely to accept opportunities on the larger procurement ratio? Figure 5.2 gives an affirmative answer. For example, when the search ratio was 200, essentially all opportunities to obtain food were taken on both procurement ratios. This result makes good sense from the rat's point of view, at least in terms of maximizing food intake. In the language of the delay-reduction hypothesis, the occurrence of either procurement light is correlated with a reduction in time to reinforcement so long as search time is sufficiently great. With sufficiently shorter search times, however, only the FR 5 procurement schedule brings the rat closer to reinforcement. Collier's results are therefore at least qualitatively consistent with the delay-reduction hypothesis.

Self-control

Self-control generally reduces to a choice between a large delayed reward (for example, better health) and a small immediate reward (for example, a cigarette for a chain smoker). As Rachlin and Green (1972), Ainslie (1974) and others have argued, self-control and impulsiveness (choice of the small immediate reward) are governed by the same general laws that govern all choice behaviour. Here we review briefly two of the studies that have demonstrated self-control in the pigeon and then two whose results have suggested that self-control may be understood in the context of the delay-reduction hypothesis.

Probably the first study of self-control in the pigeon was conducted by Fantino (1966). In this study food—followed by a period of extinction—could be obtained immediately by pecking a red key. If the pigeon waited until the key turned green, however, a peck would produce food without a subsequent penalty. The advantage to delay was greatest when the extinction period was 30 min and the pigeon could earn three reinforcements if it waited for the green light. The advantage to delay was least when impulsive pecks produced only a 1 min extinction period and when self-control resulted in only one reinforcement. As Figure 5.3 shows, pigeons delayed most often when the advantage to delay was greatest. These data also show, however, a rather limited degree of self-control, and even these results were obtained only after several months of exposure to the procedure.

A more robust degree of self-control has been demonstrated in some subjects by an ingenious commitment procedure developed by Ainslie (1974). He gave

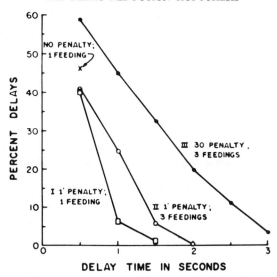

Figure 5.3. The greater the advantage to delay, the greater the percentage of delays. Hence the curve for condition III is highest and that for condition I lowest. Each point represents the average for the three birds over the last three sessions under each test situation. (After Fantino (1966). Reproduced by permission of the Psychonomic Society, Inc)

pigeons the opportunity to commit themselves in advance to waiting for the larger delayed reinforcer. This commitment procedure mimics a time-honoured self-control technique employed by humans at least as far back as Homer's time. Recall the example of Ulysses, who avoided the Sirens' temptation by tying himself to the mast of a ship. At a distance it was easy to see that the advantage of avoiding shipwreck outweighed the positive aspects of the Sirens. By tying himself to the mast Ulysses committed himself to his original decision. Many people follow the same logic when they put an alarm clock out of easy reach so that they will not be able to turn it off without rising from bed the following morning. This is done when the consequences of one behaviour—getting up on time—are valued more highly than the consequences of another—getting more sleep. In the morning this preference may be reversed; the out-of-reach alarm, however, forces one to get out of bed. Ainslie's experiment was similar conceptually to Fantino's except that the occurrence of the red key light (which set the occasion for impulsive pecks) could be avoided by pecking a different colour light prior to the scheduled onset of the red light. Some of Ainslie's pigeons (actually a minority of them) consistently avoided red in this procedure, thereby demonstrating self-control.

The rationale behind the commitment strategy envisaged by Homer and Ainslie is that as the rewards become temporally close, a reversal of preference occurs: immediacy of reward becomes more important than magnitude (*see*

Fantino and Navarick, 1974, pp. 148–149, for a discussion). If commitment occurs because preference changes with time, then it should be possible to get comparable preference reversals by having the subject choose at different times—that is, at different temporal distance from reinforcement—between two rewards. Thus, in Rachlin and Green (1972) preference for the small immediate reward over the large delayed reward was reversed by adding a constant amount of delay to both rewards: when the added delays were both long, subjects chose the larger (more delayed) reward; when the added delays were short, they chose the more immediate (smaller) reward. Rachlin and Green interpreted their results in terms of Baum and Rachlin's (1969) matching model, in which

$$\frac{V_1}{V_2} = \frac{A_1}{A_2} \times \frac{D_2}{D_1} = \frac{R_1}{R_2} \qquad (5.5)$$

where V represents the value of an alternative, A the amount of reinforcement, D the delay of reinforcement, and R the number of choice responses.

We first note that such a model is consistent with the phenomenon of preference reversal. For example, let $A_1 = 6$ s of reinforcement, $A_2 = 3$s, $D_1 = 10$ s, and $D_2 = 0$ s. In that event, $V_1/V_2 = 0$, and the subject should behave impulsively (select A_2). In other words, all or most of the organism's choice responses should be those producing the immediate smaller reward ($R_2 > R_1$). Now add 30 s to each delay so that $D_1 = 40$ s, and $D_2 = 30$ s (A_1 and A_2 remain 6 and 3 s, respectively). Equation (5.5) now requires that the subject choose A_1 (display self-control) since $V_1/V_2 = 2(3/4) = 1.50$, that is $R_1 > R_2$. Rachlin and Green acknowledged that equation (5.3) was also consistent with these results. (Actually, modification of equation (5.3) is necessary to apply it with differing reinforcer magnitude. The details, which need not concern us here, are in Navarick and Fantino (1976).) Moreover, Navarick and Fantino (1976) noted that a simple procedural variation could differentiate between the adequacy of equations (5.3) and (5.5): Let the delays of reinforcement (D_1 and D_2) associated with A_1 and A_2 (with $A_1 > A_2$) be *equal* and vary the size of these equal delays. Now equation (5.5) requires a constant preference for the larger reward (since $D_1 = D_2$, $R_1/R_2 = A_1/A_2$), whereas equation (5.3) requires *increasing* preference for the larger reward as the absolute size of the equal delays is increased. Navarick and Fantino's results conclusively supported equation (5.3).

Although the delay-reduction hypothesis appears to account for self-control in the same way it accounts for choice in concurrent chains schedules, it should not be understood that the hypothesis offers a complete account of self-control. Clearly there are dynamic aspects of training (e.g. Mazur and Logue, 1978) that can affect the degree of self-control obtained but which are not reflected in static accounts such as those suggested by equations (5.3) and (5.5). In addition we expect that self-control depends critically upon the nature of the stimuli setting the occasion for impulsive and self-control pecks. For example, investigations of self-control in the pigeon have utilized a procedure that may be heavily biased in the favour of impulsiveness. Specifically, in the typical self-control experiment, a keylight paired with the immediate availability of food is presented to the pigeon; self-control is demonstrated if the pigeon does not peck at this keylight. But the literature on autoshaping (e.g. Brown and Jenkins, 1968) suggests that many pecks in the typical self-control situation are not operant pecks but, rather, are elicited by the stimulus differentially correlated with positive reinforcement. Thus, the typical self-control paradigm requires the pigeon to withhold a key-peck in a situation which optimizes the elicitation of that peck. If our analysis is correct, it should be possible to demonstrate a much greater degree of self-control by utilizing stimuli and responses that do not lend themselves so readily to elicited responding. For example, if a tone were used instead of a keylight, elicited pecks would be minimized.

Our initial results suggest that the use of auditory stimuli as the stimuli setting the occasion for 'impulsive' pecks, i.e. pecks which produce a relatively immediate but small reward, greatly enhances the likelihood of self-control, i.e. the likelihood that the subject will wait for a stimulus setting the occasion for pecks producing a larger reward. For example, when the impulsive period duration was 2 s, subjects with the auditory stimulus exhibited self-control on 81 per cent of the trials, while those with visual stimuli exhibited self-control on only 36 per cent of the trials (five session means at the end of a condition; no overlap between auditory and visual birds). The large difference between the degree of self-control obtained with an auditory stimulus and the more typical keylight stimulus supports our hypothesis that elicited key pecking may interfere with self-control. We are presently assessing the possibility that pigeons, although capable of discriminating the tones used—as ascertained by pilot work, i.e. we selected only subjects who could use tones as the basis for a discrimination—learn to ignore them, thereby facilitating self-control.

Despite these intriguing complexities the delay-reduction hypothesis offers an adequate account of the preference-reversal phenomenon which remains the cornerstone of self-control. We now turn to some potential limitations of the delay-reduction hypothesis as a general account of choice.

Potential Limitations

The delay-reduction hypothesis makes accurate quantitative predictions only when the schedules chosen are VIs. The formulation is useful only in making ordinal predictions for binary choice, i.e. whether one schedule will be preferred to another, when the terminal links consist of schedules other than VIs. This restriction depends upon fundamental characteristics of choice and has been discussed extensively by Fantino and Navarick (1974). We concern ourselves in this section with three other potential limitations.

The Forced-choice Procedure

As noted, the delay-reduction hypothesis was developed in the context of the concurrent chains procedure. In this procedure independent VI schedules arrange access to the terminal links. Thus the subject, in principle, may respond exclusively on one key. Moreover, equations (5.3) and (5.4) stipulate when the organism should *restrict* its responding to one key. In that sense, the use of non-independent VIs would not appear appropriate to assess the delay-reduction hypothesis.[3] Put another way, the delay-reduction hypothesis should make accurate quantitative predictions only with independent VIs. Although there is little data on this point, one published experiment shows that the forced-choice procedure yields lower choice proportions than the independent procedure. These data from MacEwen (1972), shown in Table 5.1, are from the only two subjects in the study exposed to choice with independent VIs as well as a forced-choice procedure. They underscore the importance of using comparable procedures in making between-experiment comparisons.

Percentage Reinforcement

Kendall (1974) reported that pigeons preferred a schedule of reinforcement that provided food delivery intermittently to one providing twice the rate of food delivery. His results are not readily incorporated within quantitative models of choice behaviour such as that represented by equations (5.2)–(5.5). Specifically, Kendall compared two periodic schedules, 15 s in duration, which differed in that one reliably ended in reinforcement (probability of reinforcement, $p = 1.0$) while the other ended in reinforcement half the time ($p = 0.5$) and otherwise ended in blackout. Kendall found preference for the reliable schedule only when differential stimuli were not correlated with the intermittent outcomes, i.e. impending reinforcement or blackout. When stimuli were correlated with the

Table 5.1. Choice proportions predicted by equation (5.3) compared with data from MacEwen (1972)

Pigeon	Schedule		Choice proportion	
			Predicted	Obtained
M3	VI 20–40	Forced choice	0.97	0.85
M5	VI 20–40	Forced choice	0.97	0.81
Mean			0.97	0.83
M3	VI 20–40	Independent	0.97	0.93
M5	VI 20–40	Independent	0.97	0.96
Mean			0.97	0.94

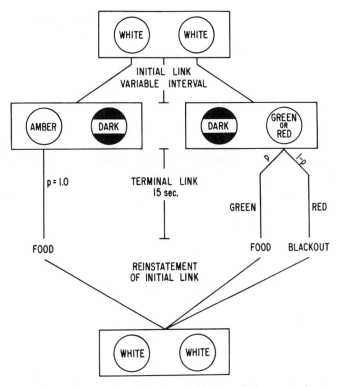

Figure 5.4. The sequence of events in the concurrent chains procedure used in the percentage reinforcement procedure. Circles within the boxes represent the stimuli on concurrently available response keys. The sequence on the left key always ends in food delivery. The sequence on the right key ends either in food delivery or blackout. (After E. Fantino, R. Dunn, and W. Meck (1979). Percentage reinforcement and choice. *Journal of the Experimental Analysis of Behavior*, **32**, 335–340. Copyright © 1979 by the Society for the Experimental Analysis of Behavior, Inc)

intermittent outcomes, pigeons preferred the intermittent outcome, even though this outcome provided only half the rate of reinforcement available during the reliable outcome.

We have recently completed a study that removes the thorn in the side posed by Kendall's results (Fantino, Dunn, and Meck, 1979). In our study, pigeons responded on the procedure shown in Figure 5.4. As indicated, pigeons' responses in the choice phase produced outcomes of either periodic reinforcement schedules always terminating in reinforcement (reliable schedules) or otherwise identical schedules providing reinforcement on only a percentage of instances (percentage reinforcement schedule). In all cases preference occurred for the outcome providing the higher rate of reinforcement. Specifically, each of three subjects was exposed to four conditions, with a reversal in each to control for key bias, in which the percentage reinforcement schedule provided reinforcement on between 25 and 75 per cent of trials, depending upon the condition. In all 24 cases (including reversals) preference was found for the reliable schedule with the average choice proportion over conditions being at least 0.60 for each subject. Comparable results were obtained when both outcomes consisted of percentage reinforcement schedules: subjects all chose the schedule providing the higher percentage. Similarly, when four new subjects were tested in conditions which pitted reliable schedules against percentage reinforcement schedules in which the more negative outcome was a leaner schedule of reinforcement (rather than non-reinforcement), the reliable schedule was chosen by each subject, although in this case preferences were somewhat less reliable and were somewhat lower (the average choice proportion, over conditions, was 0.59 for each of three subjects and 0.58 for the remaining subject).

We are left to explain the discrepancy between our results and those of Kendall (1974). To this end Roger Dunn decided to incorporate an unusual feature of Kendall's concurrent chains procedure into ours: keys in the initial links were unlit (as was the key associated with the *inoperative* terminal link when the other terminal link was operative). We had eschewed this feature in our prior work since our initial aim was to assess the generality of Kendall's findings with a conventional concurrent chains procedure. Now we exposed six subjects to this procedure. In both the initial comparison and the reversal, key bias now appeared to account for most of the variance. Averaging across comparisons, two of six subjects showed a preference for the outcome providing percentage reinforcement (choice proportions of 0.55 and 0.54). When the inoperative terminal link was lit in a subsequent condition, however, each of the six subjects preferred the outcome with the higher rate of reinforcement, just as the seven other subjects had in the previous procedures.

It now appears that Kendall's anomalous results depended on the physical equivalence of the initial link stimulus and that of the inoperative terminal link in his procedure. In order to appreciate how this procedural feature may have influenced the results, consider the pigeon's likely behaviour during the terminal links. When the terminal link stimulus preceded food delivery the subject should peck at the lit key and presumably not attend to the unlit inoperative key. Indeed, responding to the dark, terminal link stimulus occurred only when the concurrent stimulus preceded blackout on the percentage reinforcement key. Responding to an unlit key in the terminal links was limited therefore to the key correlated with the outcome providing the higher rate of reinforcement. The functional length of the initial link leading to the more reliable outcome would therefore have increased to the extent that the subject generalized between the dark terminal link and the dark initial link stimuli in this chain. Moreover, such an increase should enhance choice for the alternative, percentage reinforcement outcome as equation (5.4) requires. This argument is, of course, strengthened by the results from the final portion of our study in which the inoperative, terminal link stimulus was made distinct from those in the initial links and in which all subjects preferred the outcome providing the higher rate of reinforcement. In any case, none of our results support the notion that a schedule of intermittent reinforcement is preferred to one providing reinforcement on every trial.

Segmentation of the Interreinforcement Interval

It has been our contention that choice may not be described accurately by considering simply the temporal characteristics of the scheaules being chosen (e.g. Duncan and Fantino, 1972; Fantino, 1969a, 1977). Instead, events during the interreinforcement intervals (IRIs) may affect choice as well. Specifically, segmentation of the IRI into two or more parts should increase the 'psychological distance to reward' and have an adverse effect upon choice. If so, models such as those based on the equations above are necessarily incomplete. Although our initial tests of the segmentation notion supported our view unequivocally (e.g. Duncan and Fantino, 1972; Fantino and Duncan, 1972; Wallace, 1973), equally convincing tests produced compelling negative results (Schneider, 1972). Thus, the issue remains somewhat unresolved.

All of the prior research had employed relatively homogeneous chains (e.g. Hull, 1952) in the terminal links of concurrent chains, i.e. the links of the chain were arranged on the same key. Bill Whipple, Ginny Richards, and I are conducting an experiment using heterogeneous chains which produces more pronounced effects on choice. Thus, we compared choice for tandem FI X s FI X s with that for chain FI X s FI X s in which each link of the chain (but not the tandem) was associated with a different key. (A tandem is a control condition for a chain in which the schedule requirements are the same but no stimulus change occurs between links.) The basic procedure (with values from the first condition studied) is

LEFT	RIGHT
Initial Link	Initial Link
VI 60 s Key A	VI 60 s Key C
↓	↓
Terminal Link	Terminal Link
Tandem	Chain
FI 15 Key B	FI 15 Key D
FI 15 Key B	FI 15 Key E
↓	↓
Food	Food

Table 5.2 presents the results for each of six subjects (pigeons) in the original determination and in a reversal (keys A and C reversed above). The actual (obtained) temporal length of the tandem schedule proved to be equal to that of the chains so that no adjustment of tandem schedule values proved necessary.

Table 5.2. Choice proportion for tandem

Subject	Original	Reversal
1	0.838	0.822
2	0.926	0.816
3	0.850	0.772
4	0.714	0.684
5	0.924	0.842
6	0.922	0.788
	$\bar{X} = 0.862$	$\bar{X} = 0.789$

The data show a large preference for the tandem over the heterogeneous chain. We repeated this procedure, segmenting the chain in ways requiring different motor movements relative to the location of the food source and varying the relative locations of the keys pecked in different segments. In all cases we obtained preference for the unsegmented schedule. In addition we have obtained such preference even when the component schedules are VIs instead of FIs. Mean choice proportion for two subjects reaching stability on VIs thus far was 0.81. This preference is particularly important since Schneider (1972) found no preference with tandem and chain VIs in homogeneous chains.

These results confirm our earlier findings with homogeneous chains that segmentation of the IRI has a weakening effect on responding—consistent with Gollub's (1958) pioneer work with extended chain schedules—and choice. Thus the delay-reduction hypothesis set forth in equations (5.1), (5.3), and (5.4) is limited to describing choice when only the mean size of the IRI is manipulated. While the mean IRI is a crucial determinant of choice, events *during* the IRI must also be considered in any complete account of choice. While we have discussed only segmentation here, other events during the IRI affect choice and have been discussed elsewhere (e.g. Fantino, 1977; Fantino and Logan, 1979). Despite such limitations, the delay-reduction hypothesis is consistent with most of the research on choice for reinforcement schedules. As such it has promising generality. The final section assesses its potential generality in several different areas.

New Directions and Some Predictions

In this section we discuss four areas in which extensions of the delay-reduction hypothesis can be assessed. These areas range from the study of observing behaviour, in which we have completed an extensive study, to the study of choice in a three-key procedure, in which we have yet to collect data. The other areas, in which we have collected some interesting pilot data, involve new extensions of the delay-reduction hypothesis that may account for elicited and discriminative responding in the presence of a stimulus and in describing choice for aversive schedules.

Extension to Three-key Choice and Luce's Axiom

Although the delay-reduction hypothesis has been tested extensively with two-key choice procedures it has not been extended to more complex choice sets. For example, a test of the delay-reduction hypothesis in a three-choice situation has the interesting side benefit of testing Luce's choice axiom as well (Luce, 1959, 1977; Tversky, 1972). Indeed, as we shall show, the delay-reduction hypothesis and Luce's constant ratio rule make widely diverging predictions. Although recent experiments have addressed the constant ratio rule, with at least one supporting it (e.g. Davison and Hunter, 1976) and at least one refuting it (Prelec and Herrnstein, 1978), no systematic attempt has been made to clarify the circumstances under which it adequately describes choice in non-human subjects.

According to our extension of the delay-reduction hypothesis to the three-key case, choice proportions may be calculated as shown in equation (5.6). (We simplify our presentation by omitting the case in which only one t is greater than T. In such cases, all responding should be distributed to the remaining alternatives and delay-reduction for the third alternative is set at zero, i.e. if $t_{2C} > T$, then $(T - t_{2C}) = 0$.)

$$\frac{R_A}{R_A + R_B + R_C} = \begin{cases} \dfrac{T - t_{2A}}{(T - t_{2A}) + (T - t_{2B}) + (T - t_{2C})}, & t_{2A}, t_{2B}, t_{2C}, \text{ all} < T, \\ 1, & t_{2A} < T, t_{2B}, t_{2C} > T, \\ 0, & t_{2A} > T, t_{2B}, \text{ and/or } t_{2C} < T, \end{cases} \quad (5.6)$$

where R_A, R_B, and R_C represent the number of responses during the initial links on the three keys, t_{2A}, t_{2B}, and t_{2C} represent the average durations of the three terminal links, and where T represents the average delay-to-primary reinforcement from the onset of the initial links.

Consider first an experiment where the choice is for the following terminal link schedules: VI 9 s, VI 30 s and VI 60 s, and the initial links are (two or three) concurrently available VI 90 s schedules. In the first condition, only two keys are operative (the centre key is taped over) and the subjects choose between VI 30 s and VI 60 s terminal link schedules. In this event, $T = 90$ s and equation (5.3) requires choice proportions of 0.67 and 0.33 for the VI 30 s and VI 60 s schedules, respectively, or a ratio of 2 : 1. After stable responding is achieved the three-key choice is introduced by adding a third VI 90 s schedule on the centre key, associated with the VI 9 s terminal link. Luce's 'constant ratio rule', also known as the 'independence from irrelevant alternatives' of formal choice theories in both psychology and economics (Luce, 1959, 1977) states that adding (or subtracting) alternatives should not affect the distribution of choices between two alternatives. According to this rule, choice responses to the VI 30s and VI 60s schedules should continue to be distributed so as to approximate a ratio of 2 : 1. The three-choice delay reduction equation (5.6), however, requires the following choice proportions:

for VI 9 s   0.60,
for VI 30 s   0.37,
for VI 60 s   0.03.

Note that according to the delay-reduction hypothesis choice responses to the VI 30 s and VI 60 s schedules should now be distributed in a ratio of better than 12:1, a predicted violation of the constant ratio rule.

Although the study described above has not been completed, some support for our prediction comes from two data points in a study by Davison and Temple (1974). Their study primarily involved three-alternative choice in a concurrent chains procedure, but they did examine an initial condition in which only two terminal links were being chosen. Thus, we can compare choice for FI 25 s vs. FI 15 s with choice for FI 25 s vs. FI 15 s vs. FI 20 s. Since addition of the FI 20 s schedule lowers T (primarily because the choice phase is shortened) we would expect that the distribution of choice responses between FI 15 s and FI 25 s should increase for the FI 15 s. In fact, the mean choice proportion increased from 0.74 to 0.85 (individual data are not presented in the article), supporting our expectation. Unfortunately, introduction of the third key appeared to result in a systematic bias away from the FI 25 s schedule which was always arranged on the centre key. Thus, this support for our view is limited. In addition, this bias makes the rest of Davison and Temple's data of limited utility in assessing additional predictions made by the delay-reduction hypothesis in three-alternative choice. (The purpose of the Davison–Temple experiment was unrelated to either the delay-reduction hypothesis or the constant-ratio rule, neither of which were cited.)

It is also important to study conditions in which the added (third) choice is the least preferred alternative. Here, the delay-reduction hypothesis requires small deviations from the constant ratio rule, and in the opposite direction from that noted above, i.e. choice proportions for the two preferred alternatives should converge somewhat towards indifference relative to their values in the two-alternative case. We will conduct such a study and illustrate this principle in an extreme case which is of particular interest since it has dynamic properties which may result in support for the constant ratio rule with sufficient exposure (after initial deviations). In any case, this condition will prove important in assessing how delay-reduction principles make contact with behaviour. In particular, consider the following choices:

Two-key terminal links: VI 5 s and VI 30 s.
Three-key terminal links: VI 5 s, VI 30 s, and VI 450 s.
Initial links: All VI 60 s.

In the two-key case, delay-reduction requires a choice proportion of 0.71 for the VI 5 s (and 0.29, of course, for VI 30 s). When VI 450 s is introduced in the three-key case, equation (5.6) now requires the following choice proportions: VI 5 s, 0.54; VI 30 s, 0.46; VI 450 s, 0.0.[4] Again, this violates the constant ratio rule. Assuming the outcome is consistent with delay-reduction—and results from two-key studies suggest it will be (e.g. Fantino, 1969b)—an interesting situation would develop. If no responding occurs on the key leading to VI 450 s for some time, does the functional or effective value of T change? If all three keys are considered, $T = 182$ s. But given that the subject responds only on two keys, one might suppose that the situation has reverted functionally to the two-key case and that T now equals 47.5 s. If the latter holds, then choice proportions should approximate those in the two-key case (i.e. 0.71 and 0.29 instead of 0.54 and 0.46), thereby supporting the constant ratio rule. Our *guess* is that this indeed will occur, i.e. choice proportions will initially be consistent with those required by equation (5.6) but will then increase to those required by the constant ratio rule (and by equation (5.3)) for those subjects which fail to sample the 450 s alternative at least occasionally, say once every few sessions. If this is incorrect, however, it would mean that the mere presence (or possibility) of the third alternative—contacted, of course, in prior sessions—is sufficient to maintain T at its scheduled value.

The addition of a third alternative should affect the distribution of responses between the other two to the extent that T is altered. If the third alternative provides the highest rate of reinforcement, T will be lowered substantially. But the lower T, the less delay-reduction time will be correlated with each of the original alternatives. In other words, the closer in time the subject is from primary reinforcement at the onset of a trial, the less improvement (in terms of reduction in time to reinforcement) may be correlated with a given outcome. This, in turn, should enhance preference. For example, in the standard two-key, concurrent chains procedure, lower Ts are translated into larger preferences for the preferred outcome (e.g. Fantino, 1969b, 1977; Hursh and Fantino, 1974; Wardlaw and Davison, 1974). But the same principle should be operative with three outcomes instead of two. Thus, the distribution of responses to the preferred of two alternatives should increase as T decreases. In the context of such experiments, this means that choice for the preferred of two outcomes should increase when T is lowered by the addition of a third, highly preferred, outcome. Seen in this light our predicted results are a special case of outcomes produced by lowering T. Indeed a similar shift in the distribution of choice responses should occur in the three-key case when the three initial link schedules are halved in temporal size (e.g. to VI 45 s schedules), producing a more divergent distribution of choice proportions, or are doubled (e.g. to VI 180 s). producing a more convergent distribution.

We do have some interesting data from an unrelated experiment (Whipple, 1979) which provides indirect support for our outlook. Whipple studied choice for several pairs of fixed interval (and fixed time) schedules presented for choice in a pairwise fashion within a single session. He found that a given pair would generate systematically different choice proportions depending upon the composition of other pairs being offered in the session. For example, consider two different sessions in which the pair concurrent FI $3X$ s FI $4X$ s is available for choice. In one session a shorter pair, concurrent FI X s FI $2X$ s, is also available. Preference for the FI $3X$ s in the first pair would be reliably higher on the session in which the shorter pair was also available. Although these results have important implications for matching and choice behaviour in general, for our present purposes we must see how they are consistent with our analysis of the effects of the size of T upon choice: the presence of the shorter interval pair effectively lowers the value of T, thereby increasing preference for the other preferred schedules in the session.

Although we expect that tests of the delay-reduction hypothesis in a three-choice paradigm will produce violations of the constant ratio rule, we also expect the rule would be confirmed if the same choices were presented to the same subjects in simple concurrent schedules. With simple (two- and three-choice) concurrent schedules, the delay-reduction hypothesis requires matching to the relative distribution of reinforcements for each choice (Squires and Fantino, 1971). Thus, our explanation for the expected violations of the constant ratio rule with concurrent chains is not relevant in the case of simple concurrent VI schedules. Our explanation would thus gain plausibility if the same choice alternatives that violated the constant ratio rule in the concurrent chains case satisfied the constant ratio rule when presented as simple concurrent schedules. Taking, for example, the following pairs and triad of concurrent schedules—in different conditions—our account would predict stable choice proportions approximating those shown on the right:

Concurrent schedules	*Expected choice proportions*
(A) concurrent VI 9 s VI 30 s	VI 9 : 0.77 VI 30 : 0.23
(B) concurrent VI 30 s VI 90 s	VI 30 : 0.75 VI 90 : 0.25
(C) concurrent VI 9 s VI 30 s VI 90 s	VI 9 : 0.71 VI 30 : 0.21 VI 90 : 0.07

Note also that subjects' choice proportions should approximately 'match' the relative distribution of reinforcements schedules for each choice (Herrnstein,

1970; Squires and Fantino, 1971; de Villiers, 1977). If matching occurs as predicted, the constant ratio rule will be satisfied. For example, the ratio of choice proportions in the second condition is 3:1; when VI 90 s is added in the third condition the ratio of choice proportions between VI 30 s and VI 90 s remains 3:1. The results of Miller and Loveland (1974) and Davison and Hunter (1976) using five-alternative and three-alternative concurrent VIs, respectively, suggest that under these conditions approximation to matching will occur and, therefore, the constant ratio rule will be confirmed. Thus, the same subjects will confirm or violate the constant ratio rule with identical alternatives, depending on whether they are presented in simple concurrent or in a concurrent chains procedure. Such an outcome would constitute strong support for the delay-reduction hypothesis.

We should point out that our expectations regarding the constant ratio rule are framed primarily by our confidence in both the delay-reduction hypothesis of conditioned reinforcement and the matching relation for describing behaviour on simple concurrent schedules (as noted above, the delay-reduction hypothesis reduces to matching when no terminal links are involved). That is, necessary by-products of confirming the delay-reduction hypothesis are violation of the constant ratio rule in our three-key, concurrent chains experiments, and confirmation of it in our simple concurrent VIs experiment. At the same time, it is necessary to point out that confirmation of the constant ratio rule with simple concurrents is not generally expected when schedules other than VIs are studied. In other words we do not expect that the 'ratio of the likelihood of choosing a to the likelihood of choosing b is a constant irrespective of the number or composition of other alternatives in the set presented for choice' (Atkinson, Bower, and Crothers, 1965, p. 140). Indeed there is evidence that the 'composition' of the alternatives is critical. Prelec and Herrnstein (1978) recently reported a violation of the constant ratio rule when comparing response rates on concurrent, variable ratio (VR) VI schedules. Specifically, they studied concurrent VR VI VI and concurrent VR VI. When the second VI was removed a much larger increase in response rates occurred on the VR schedule than in the remaining VI, thereby violating the rule. This outcome makes good sense in terms of maximizing rate of reinforcement: higher rates of responding increase rates of reinforcement directly on ratio schedules; higher rates of responding, within limits, have little effect on rates of reinforcement on interval schedules. If this is correct, then the constant ratio rule should be *upheld* if the VR schedule were removed from a concurrent VI X VI Y VR 50 schedule, converting it to a concurrent VI X VI Y. In other words the distribution of extra responses made to the VI X VI Y when the VR 50 is removed should approximate the distribution made when VR 50 is present (e.g. if 0.20 for VI X and 0.30 for VI Y in the three-key case, then 0.40 and 0.60 in the two-key case). *In general we expect confirmation of the rule when the redistributed responses are to be allocated between variable interval schedules, but not necessarily when the redistributed responses are to be allocated between ratio schedules or between different schedule types*, e.g. a VI and a VR as in Prelec and Herrnstein. At present, experiments testing this are being conducted in our laboratory. These experiments will permit us to assess this rule and thereby provide boundary conditions for the applicability of the constant ratio rule to concurrently available schedules of reinforcement.

Extension to Schedules of Aversive Control

We have already discussed the advantages of the concurrent chains procedure in the study of choice. This procedure, in the form typically employed with appetitive schedules, however, is not suitable for studying choice between aversive schedules. Responding in the initial links is not maintained when the terminal links consist solely of shock schedules. Farley and Fantino (1978) and Schuster and Rachlin (1968) surmounted this difficulty by superimposing food schedules on the shock schedules in the terminal links. An implicit, and as yet untested, assumption of this procedure, however, is that relative response rate in the initial links is determined solely by the differential shock schedules in the terminal links and is not affected by possible food–shock interactions. Indeed it seems highly plausible that superimposed schedules of primary reinforcement (even equal ones) affect choice for differential shock schedules. To take a hypothetical extreme case, for example, if food were available on equal, high-frequency schedules while shocks occurred on unequal but low frequency schedules, we would expect choice proportions to reflect more indifference than when food was less frequently available.

Paul Royalty, working in our laboratory, has developed a modified concurrent chains procedure for measuring choice between aversive schedules that will maintain responding in the initial links without the necessity of superimposing food schedules on the terminal link shock schedules. The procedure, diagrammed in Figure 5.5, is basically similar to the typical appetitive concurrent chains procedure with the addition of a high rate of inescapable, unavoidable, response-independent shocks to the initial links. Identical but independent variable interval schedules arrange access to the terminal links which also consist of response-independent, inescapable, unavoidable shock schedules. The shock schedules in the initial and terminal links are chosen so that a substantial reduction in shock frequency is possible by responding on the VI schedules. After a fixed exposure to a terminal link shock schedule, the initial links are automatically reinstated.

To assess the feasibility of this procedure, we have used an FT 5 s shock schedule in the initial links and studied one pair of shock schedules (including a reversal) in the terminal links with four rats serving as subjects. The schedule associated with one terminal link was FT 5 s, with the other FT 60 s. According to shock frequency-reduction theory (e.g. de Villiers, 1972, 1974), the relative

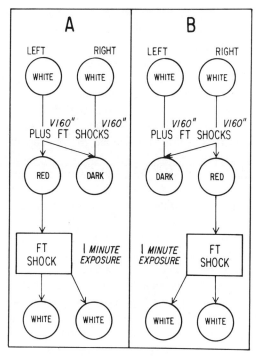

Figure 5.5. Pictorial representation of the concurrent chains procedure modified for studying choice between aversive schedules. The sequence of events in the experimental chamber is similar to the sequence depicted in Figure 5.1 with two exceptions: (1) a high rate of response-independent, inescapable, unavoidable shock is added to the initial links; (2) the terminal links consist of response-independent shock schedules (or other aversive schedules)

rate of responding in the initial links on this procedure should match relative shock frequency reduction. The degree of shock frequency reduction is calculated for each of the alternatives by subtracting the shock rate in the left and right terminal links, respectively, from the shock rate in the initial links. Relative shock frequency reduction is simply the shock frequency reduction for one alternative divided by the sum of shock frequency reductions for both alternatives. According to the delay-reduction hypothesis (which, in its extension to the aversive case, might better be termed the delay-increase hypothesis since increases rather than decreases in delay to the next aversive event maintain responding in an aversive situation), the relative response rate should equal the increase in delay to the next shock for one alternative divided by the sum of the delay increases for both alternatives. The amount of delay increase for an alternative is calculated by subtracting the average time to the next shock in the initial links from the average time to the next shock in the terminal link for that alternative.

The mean choice proportion for the four rats was 0.92 and 0.90 for the FT 60 s terminal link in the original condition and the reversal, respectively, which conforms reasonably well to the predicted relative rate of 1.0.[5] Note that with this pair of schedules, the two formulations make identical predictions. However, with other pairs of schedules, the predictions based on delay reduction and shock frequency reduction diverge, and the range of schedule values we are now studying should allow us to determine which of these formulations best accounts for the data. More generally, we are interested in assessing whether the same conceptions that accurately describe choice in the appetitive case are also adequate in the aversive case.

Finally, it should be noted that the present procedure, although apparently similar to a procedure employed by Baum (1973) and Hutton, Gardner, and Lewis (1978), in which access to periods of time-out from response-independent shock is arranged by concurrently available VI schedules, is actually different in two significant regards. First, the simple concurrent procedure confounds the measure of choice with the rates of responding maintained by the respective VI schedules, as noted earlier. Since the modified concurrent chains procedure utilizes equal initial links, this difficulty is avoided. More importantly, responding on the simple concurrent procedure gains access to time-out periods (usually blackouts), while responding on the concurrent VIs in the modified concurrent chains procedure gains access to response-independent shock schedules. Thus, in the simple concurrent procedure, the independent variable is the relative value of the schedules controlling access to blackouts while the independent variable on the concurrent chains procedure is the relative value of the shock schedules in the terminal links. Thus, only the modified concurrent chains procedure assesses choice between aversive schedules of reinforcement.

Extension to Observing Behaviour

As noted in prior sections, stimuli which are correlated with an *increase* in time to reinforcement (or a decrease in time to an aversive event) should not be conditioned reinforcers. We have collected some data in support of this notion in the context of an observing paradigm. Moreover, these results are consistent with an extension of the delay-reduction hypothesis of conditioned reinforcement to observing. An observing response is one the only consequence of which is the production of stimuli correlated with the availability or non-availability of reinforcement. Experiments on observing have assessed whether stimuli are reinforcing because they reduce uncertainty (the 'uncertainty-reduction hypothesis') or because they are correlated with a reduction in time to reinforcement (the 'delay-reduction hypothesis'). Research—reviewed by Fantino (1977)—has clearly supported the delay-reduction hypothesis.

In the typical experiment observing responses change a mixed schedule, in which no exteroceptive stimulus is correlated with the alternating schedules, into a multiple schedule in which distinctive stimuli are correlated with each of the components. When two schedules alternate—the number used in prior studies of observing—only the stimulus associated with the schedule providing the more immediate reinforcement is correlated with a reduction in time to reinforcement. Since the mean time to reinforcement on the mixed schedule is intermediate to that associated with its two component schedules, it follows that the stimulus of the schedule providing the less immediate reinforcement is correlated with an increase, not a reduction, in time to reinforcement. Hence, according to the delay-reduction hypothesis only the more positive stimulus (i.e. that correlated with the schedule providing the more immediate reinforcement) should maintain observing. This prediction is consistent with data from many studies of observing (Fantino, 1977).

When more than two components are alternated, should the intermediate component maintain observing? For example, if the alternating schedules are FI 20 s, FI X s, and FI 180 s, where $20 < X < 180$, will a stimulus correlated with the FI X s schedule maintain observing? The delay-reduction hypothesis makes explicit predictions about observing here. These predictions were confirmed in a recently completed study by David Case and me. We found that a stimulus correlated with an intermediate delay reduction would maintain observing only when it is correlated with a reduction in time to reinforcement (e.g. when $X = 40$ s, but not when $X = 120$ s). At the same time, however, low rates of observing were also maintained by stimuli not representing delay reduction. A control experiment determined that these low rates of observing were less than that attributable to sensory reinforcement. These results support a symmetrical version of the delay-reduction hypothesis that accounts for the effects of a signal correlated with an increase in time to reinforcement (a 'delay-increase') in terms of conditioned punishment.

Although the uncertainty-reduction hypothesis had already been refuted in two-component procedures, the possibility remained that uncertainty might be more likely to reinforce observing in more complex situations, such as our three-component procedure. Instead, our results were inconsistent with hypotheses stressing the reinforcing potency of uncertainty reduction: whereas all three stimuli reduced uncertainty, only those correlated with a reduction in time to reinforcement maintained observing.

Extensions to Elicited and Discriminative Responding

Perhaps this is our most ambitious extension of the delay-reduction hypothesis. Up to now we have been concerned with extensions of the hypothesis in which we attempt to account for the rate of responding maintained by the production of a stimulus (a conditioned reinforcing function) whether the situation involves two- or three-key choice, schedules of aversive control, self-control, or observing. The hypothesis is also potentially applicable to account for the rate of responding *in the presence* of a stimulus (an eliciting and/or discriminative stimulus function). We consider this possibility briefly here, including some encouraging data.

Elicited Responding

A stimulus following a long intertrial interval is correlated with a greater reduction in time to reinforcement than the same stimulus following a shorter intertrial interval. Will such a stimulus also maintain a higher rate of responding in its presence? Some data from autoshaping procedures suggest an affirmative answer. For example, Terrace, Gibbon, Farrell, and Baldock (1975) found that higher rates of key-pecking were maintained the longer the intertrial interval (ITI) in both acquisition and maintenance with an autoshaping procedure. Jenkins and Barnes (1976) reported a similar acquisition effect. In a more extensive study, however, Gibbon, Baldock, Locurto, Gold, and Terrace (1977) found no *maintained* effect of ITI upon response rates. Moreover, under certain conditions *shorter* ITIs may enhance maintained responding (Williams, 1976, and personal communication). Finally, Schwartz (1978) studied multiple schedules consisting of a VI 30 s (or VT 30 s) schedule alternating with extinction (EXT). Thus, the schedules were either Mult EXT VI 30 s or Mult EXT VT 30 s. The primary independent variable was the length of the extinction period, which was either 1 s or 60 s. Schwartz found higher maintained rates of responding when the VT (or VI) alternated with the 60 s EXT period than with the 1 s EXT period. Although this result supports our extension of the delay-reduction hypothesis, two qualifying points should be made:

(1) The study examined only two values. A parametric study would provide a more rigorous test of our hypothesis.

(2) As Schwartz notes, 1 s is functionally like 0 s, further underscoring the importance of a parametric study.

Our primary interest in these data is in their relevance for the delay-reduction hypothesis. It would appear that the simple extension of this hypothesis to autopecking studies varying ITI size accounts in a general way for acquisition but not always for steady state performance. Since these studies were not conducted as tests of the delay-reduction hypothesis, however, their data are not ideally appropriate for evaluating it. Moreover, as we shall show, there are conditions under which the length of the ITI can be expected to affect sustained responding, even after many sessions of exposure. Specifically, we have completed a series of pilot experiments in our laboratory which provide a direct test of an extension of the delay-reduction hypothesis to account for the degree of responding maintained in the presence of a stimulus. We discuss this work briefly before proposing a prototypical experiment designed to adequately test our extension of the delay-reduction hypothesis. We will then list some important additional questions this line of research may answer. All of this work is consistent with the emphasis of this laboratory and several others on the crucial role played by the temporal context in which reinforcement occurs.

Assume two stimuli bear the same absolute temporal relation to reinforcement (a 30 s interval between stimulus onset and response-independent delivery of reinforcement, i.e. an FT 30 s schedule). The two stimuli are correlated with different reductions in time to reinforcement, however, since they follow non-reinforcement periods of different length. Will equal or different rates of responding be maintained in their presence? To answer this question certain salient aspects of the normal concurrent chains procedure are reversed: the terminal link (outcome) stimuli are now associated with identical schedules whereas the initial link stimuli are now unequal (and not available concurrently). Twelve pigeons were exposed to two chain schedules on a single key and within a session. In one chain an FI 120 s schedule, correlated with a purple keylight was followed by an FT 30 s schedule, correlated with a green keylight. Following completion of this chain FI 120 s FT 30 s, food was made available for 4 s (reinforcement). The other chain was FI 10 s FT 30 s, also followed by reinforcement (keylight colours, purple and red, respectively). A given chain—each ending in food—was presented five times in succession. Following completion of this block of five chains, the alternative chain was presented five times in succession. The chains thus alternated, in blocks of five, until 30 reinforcements had been obtained in a session. Sessions were conducted daily for a minimum of 15 sessions (depending upon the condition). The main result is shown in Figure 5.6. Note that a substantially higher rate of responding was maintained in the presence of the FT 30 s schedule when it was preceded by FI 120 s (i.e. in chain FI 120 s FT 30 s) than when it was preceded by FI 10 s (i.e. in chain FI 10 s FT 30 s). A paired t-test shows this difference to be significant, $t(11) = 2.79$, $p < 0.05$. This result is consistent with our extension of the delay-reduction hypothesis, but it is ostensibly inconsistent with the more extensive and systematic work done by Gibbon et al. (1977). We say 'ostensibly' because there are several potentially crucial differences between our procedure and that of Gibbon et al. The three most obvious differences, in order of increasing likelihood of importance are: (1) our keylights were lit during the initial link of the chain, whereas Gibbon et al.'s were dark during their ITI; (2) our comparisons were made within-subjects and within-session, whereas Gibbon et al.'s were made across subjects; (3) we required responding during our initial link (FI schedule), whereas little or no responding occurred during the ITI in Gibbon et al.

In fact, we chose the procedural aspects which produced the results shown in Figure 5.6 in part on the basis of pilot data which implicate the importance of the third factor. When we used FT schedules, instead of FI schedules in the initial links, we obtained no effect of ITI length upon rate of responding in the presence of the terminal link stimuli in four subjects. At the same time we had found a clear

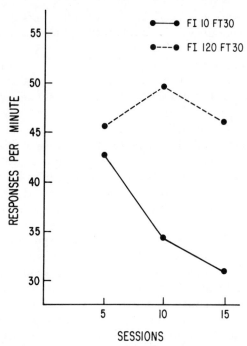

Figure 5.6. Mean response rate for 12 pigeons during terminal links following either 120 s (●---●) or 10 s (●—●) initial links

effect with four other subjects and using identical values and procedure, but with FIs in the initial links. These results were obtained immediately prior to those shown in Figure 5.6. At that point we decided to switch the four subjects that had shown no effect with FT to FI. Each of the four now showed at least a modest effect of initial link length upon rate of responding. We then reversed key colours in the terminal links for our eight experienced subjects, now all in the FI condition and added four naive birds. These are the data shown in Figure 5.6. Not shown in the figure is the fact that responding in the FI 10 s schedules is at a higher rate than on the FI 120 s schedule. Thus, to the extent responding on FT 30 s constitutes responding induced by (or carried over from) responding in the preceding FI, response rate in the FT 30 s schedule should be *higher*, not lower after FI 10 s. The delay-reduction hypothesis, of course, requires the opposite.

These data, together with the results of Gibbon *et al.* (1977), tentatively suggest the following generalization: the effect of ITI length (or the length of the initial link of a chain schedule) upon response rate maintained in the presence of a stimulus correlated with a response-independent schedule depends upon whether or not responding is required during the ITI (or in the initial link of the chain). Our data thus support the importance of the third of the 'obvious differences' between the procedure used to obtain the results in Figure 5.6 and those of Gibbon *et al.* (1977) in terms of the apparently inconsistent sets of results. These data also suggest that our extension of the delay-reduction hypothesis can account for data only when responding is required in the initial link (or ITI). An obvious question involves the mechanism accounting for the different results with FI and FT in the initial links. Our present hypothesis is a simple one involving attention. Attention may be maximized when responding is required, thus enhancing temporal control by the length of the initial link.[6]

Discriminative Responding

The studies in the prior subsection all measure response strength in the presence of response-independent schedules of reinforcement (e.g. VT and FT schedules). Response strength may also be assessed in the presence of response-dependent schedules (e.g. VI and FI). For example, an analogous extension of the delay-reduction hypothesis to response-dependent schedules requires the following: a stimulus associated with a VI 30 s schedule should occasion a higher rate of responding in its presence when preceded by a 60 s period of non-reinforcement than when preceded by a 10 s period of non-reinforcement (following the 60 s period, the stimulus of the VI 30 s schedule is correlated with a two-thirds reduction in time to primary reinforcement; following the 10 s period only a one-fourth reduction in time). The results of several experiments support this prediction of the delay-reduction hypothesis (e.g. Byrd, 1971; Gollub, 1958; Taus and Hearst, 1970). In Taus and Hearst (1970), for example, five groups of pigeons received equal numbers of presentations of a 30 s stimulus in which key-pecking was intermittently reinforced, but the duration of the blackout periods that separated these stimulus presentations was different for different groups (0–30 s). Response rate during the stimulus was found to be a direct function of the duration of the intervening blackouts. We have begun a more direct assessment of this extension of the delay-reduction hypothesis in parametric studies using a within-subjects design. In these studies it will be interesting to determine the extent to which our obtained effects are mediated by operant and respondant pecks. Specifically, assuming that our extension of the delay-reduction hypothesis does account for responding in the presence of a stimulus to what extent does it appear to do so for elicited and discriminative responding considered separately?

Conclusion

We have reviewed the delay-reduction hypothesis of conditioned reinforcement including extensions to studies of optimal feeding strategies and self-control. Although the hypothesis is limited to making precise quantitative predictions in restricted circumstances, and although other factors are certainly involved in the phenomena of conditioned reinforcement and choice, the hypothesis does have encouraging generality, especially at the ordinal level. Moreover, the hypothesis has promising applicability to areas such as elicited and discriminative responding, observing behaviour, choice for schedules of aversive control and three-alternative choice. One merit of the hypothesis is that it can be rigorously tested by experiments that approach it from several different directions, as suggested in the chapter. The prospect of further assessing its applicability in the laboratory is an exciting one to us. I hope some of that excitement has been imparted to you.

Notes

1. Research and preparation of this chapter were supported by NIMH Grant No. 20752 to the University of California, San Diego. I thank all those who made suggestions on a prior draft, especially Roger Dunn, Paul Royalty, and Ben Williams.
2. A variable time (VT) schedule is the same as a VI schedule except that no response is required for reinforcement.
3. The use of non-independent VIs was pioneered by Stubbs and Pliskoff (1969) for use with simple concurrent schedules. When applied to concurrent chains, once one VI arranges a terminal link entry, entry into the other terminal link is not possible until the first terminal link has been entered and the initial links subsequently reinstated. Thus subjects must respond on both keys or soon be in perpetual extinction.
4. T here sums to 182 s. The 450 s schedule thus brings the subject further temporally from reinforcement and should not maintain choice responding. In calculating the values of the other choice proportions we assign 0.0 to the degree of delay reduction correlated with the VI 450 s alternative ($T - t_{2c}$) in the denominator). The VI 30 s outcome represents a delay reduction of $182 - 30 = 152$ s while the VI 5 s outcome represents a reduction of $182 - 5 = 177$ s. Thus, the choice proportion for the VI 5 s outcome is $177/(177 + 152 + 0) = 0.54$, and for the VI 30 s outcome is $152/(177 + 152 + 0) = 0.46$.
5. The choice proportions for individual rats were 0.90, 0.88, 0.93, and 0.99 in the original condition and 0.86, 0.94, 0.87, and 0.92 in the reversal.
6. This type of account is also consistent with the effects of ITI length upon acquisition found by Terrace et al. (1975) and Gibbon et al. (1977). On early trials the subject comes to attend to the response key illumination. Subsequently, however, the subject may come to ignore the key during the ITI. Admittedly this explanation is speculative and should be tested.

References

Ainslie, G. W. (1974). Impulse control in pigeons. *Journal of the Experimental Analysis of Behavior*, **21**, 485–489.

Atkinson, R. C., Bower, G. H., and Crothers, E. J. (1965). *An Introduction to Mathematical Learning Theory*, John Wiley, New York.

Autor, S. M. (1960). The strength of conditioned reinforcers as a function of frequency and probability of reinforcement. Doctoral dissertation, Harvard University.

Autor, S. M. (1969). The strength of conditioned reinforcers as a function of frequency and probability of reinforcement. In *Conditioned Reinforcement* (D. P. Hendry, ed.), Dorsey Press, Homewood, Ill.

Baum, W. M. (1973). Time allocation and negative reinforcement. *Journal of the Experimental Analysis of Behavior*, **20**, 313–322.

Baum, W. M. and Rachlin, H. C. (1969). Choice as time allocation. *Journal of the Experimental Analysis of Behavior*, **12**, 861–874.

Brown, P. L. and Jenkins, H. M. (1968). Auto-shaping of the pigeon's key-peck. *Journal of the Experimental Analysis of Behavior*, **11**, 1–8.

Byrd, L. D. (1971). Responding in the pigeon under chained schedules of food presentation: the repetition of a stimulus during alternative components. *Journal of the Experimental Analysis of Behavior*, **16**, 31–38.

Catania, A. C. (1963). Concurrent performances: a baseline for the study of reinforcement magnitude. *Journal of the Experimental Analysis of Behavior*, **6**, 299–300.

Catania, A. C. (1966). Concurrent operants. In *Operant Behavior: Areas of Research and Application* (W. K. Honig, ed.), Prentice-Hall, Englewood Cliffs, N. J.

Collier, G. (1977). Optimal feeding strategies in animals: laboratory simulation. Paper presented at the meetings of the Eastern Psychological Association, Boston.

Collier, G. and Kaufman, L. W. (1976). The patchy environment: a laboratory simulation. Paper presented at the meetings of the Psychonomic Society, St. Louis.

Davison, M. C. and Hunter, I. W. (1976). Performance on variable-interval schedules arranged singly and concurrently. *Journal of the Experimental Analysis of Behavior*, **25**, 335–345.

Davison, M. C. and Temple, W. Preference for fixed-interval terminal links in a three-key concurrent chain schedule. *Journal of the Experimental Analysis of Behavior*, **22**, 11–19.

de Villiers, P. A. (1972). Reinforcement and response rate interaction in multiple random-interval avoidance schedules. *Journal of the Experimental Analysis of Behavior*, **18**, 499–507.

de Villiers, P. A. (1974). The law of effect and avoidance: a quantitative relationship between response rate and shock-frequency reduction. *Journal of the Experimental Analysis of Behavior*, **21**, 223–235.

de Villiers, P. A. (1977). Choice in concurrent schedules and a quantitative formulation of the law of effect. In *Handbook of Operant Behavior* (W. K. Honig and J. E. R. Staddon, eds), Prentice-Hall, Englewood Cliffs, N. J.

Duncan, B. and Fantino, E. (1972). The psychological distance to reward. *Journal of the Experimental Analysis of Behavior*, **18**, 23–24.

Fantino, E. (1966). Immediate reward followed by extinction versus later reward without extinction. *Psychonomic Science*, **6**, 233–234.

Fantino, E. (1969a). Conditioned reinforcement, choice, and the psychological distance to reward. In *Conditioned Reinforcement* (D. P. Hendry, ed.), pp. 163–191, Dorsey Press, Homewood, Ill.

Fantino, E. (1969b). Choice and rate of reinforcement. *Journal of the Experimental Analysis of Behavior*, **12**, 723–730.

Fantino, E. (1977). Conditioned reinforcement: choice and information. In *Handbook of Operant Behavior* (W. K. Honig and J. E. R. Staddon, eds), Prentice-Hall, New York.

Fantino, E. and Duncan, B. (1972). Some effects of interreinforcement time upon choice. *Journal of the Experimental Analysis of Behavior*, **17**, 3–14.

Fantino, E. and Logan, C. A. (1979). *The Experimental Analysis of Behavior: A Biological Perspective*, W. H. Freeman, San Francisco.

Fantino, E. and Navarick, D. (1974). Recent developments in choice. In *The Psychology of Learning and Motivation*, Vol. 8 (G. H. Bower, ed.), Academic Press, New York.

Fantino, E., Dunn, R., and Meck, W. (1979). Percentage reinforcement and choice. *Journal of the Experimental Analysis of Behavior*, **32**, 335–340.

Farley, J. and Fantino, E. (1978). The symmetrical law of effect and the matching relation in choice behavior. *Journal of the Experimental Analysis of Behavior*, **29**, 37–60.

Gamzu, E. and Schwartz, B. The maintenance of key pecking by stimulus-contingent and response-independent food presentation. *Journal of the Experimental Analysis of Behavior*, **19**, 65–72.

Gibbon, J., Baldock, M. D., Locutro, C., Gold, L., and Terrace, H. S. (1977). Trial and intertrial durations in autoshaping. *Journal of Experimental Psychology: Animal Behavior Processes*, **3**, 264–284.

Gollub, L. R. (1958). The chaining of fixed-interval schedules. Doctoral dissertation, Harvard University.

Herrnstein, R. J. (1961). Relative and absolute strength of response as a function of reinforcement. *Journal of the Experimental Analysis of Behavior*, **4**, 267–272.

Herrnstein, R. J. (1964). Secondary reinforcement and rate of primary reinforcement. *Journal of the Experimental Analysis of Behavior*, **7**, 27–36.

Herrnstein, R. J. (1970). On the law of effect. *Journal of the Experimental Analysis of Behavior*, **13**, 243–266.

Hull, C. L. (1952). *A Behavior System*, Yale University Press, New Haven, Conn.

Hursh, S. R. and Fantino, E. (1974). An appraisal of preference for multiple versus mixed schedules. *Journal of the Experimental Analysis of Behavior*, **22**, 31–38.

Hutton, L., Gardner, E. T., and Lewis, P. (1978). Matching with a key-peck response in concurrent negative reinforcement schedules. *Journal of the Experimental analysis of Behavior*, **30**, 225–230.

Jenkins, H. M. and Barnes, R. A. (1976). Analysis of the effect of trial spacing in autoshaping. Paper presented at the meetings of the Eastern Psychological Association, New York.

Kendall, S. B. (1974). Preference for intermittent reinforcement. *Journal of the Experimental Analysis of Behavior*, **21**, 463–473.

Luce, R. D. (1959). *Individual Choice Behavior: A Theoretical Analysis*, John Wiley, New York.

Luce, R. D. (1977). The choice axiom after twenty years. *Journal of Mathematical Psychology*, **15**, 215–233.

MacEwen, D. (1972). The effects of terminal-link fixed-interval and variable-interval schedules on responding under concurrent chained schedules. *Journal of the Experimental Analysis of Behavior*, **18**, 253–262.

Mazur, J. E. and Logue, A. W. (1978). Choice in a 'self-control' paradigm: effects of a fading procedure. *Journal of the Experimental Analysis of Behavior*, **30**, 11–17.

Miller, H. L. and Loveland, D. H. (1974). Matching when the number of response alternatives is large. *Animal Learning and Behavior*, **2**, 106–110.

Navarick, D. J. and Fantino, E. (1976). Self-control and general models of choice. *Journal of Experimental Psychology: Animal Behavior Processes*, **2**, 75–87.

Prelec, D. and Herrnstein, R. J. (1978). Feedback functions for reinforcement: a paradigmatic experiment. *Animal Learning and Behavior*, **6**, 181–186.

Rachlin, H. C. and Green, L. (1972). Commitment, choice and self-control. *Journal of the Experimental Analysis of Behavior*, **17**, 15–22.

Schneider, J. W. (1972). Choice between two-component chained and tandem schedules. *Journal of the Experimental Analysis of Behavior*, **18**, 45–60.

Schuster, R. and Rachlin, H. (1968). Indifference between punishment and free shock: evidence for the negative law of effect. *Journal of the Experimental Analysis of Behavior*, **11**, 777–786.

Schwartz, B. (1978). Stimulus–reinforcer contingencies and local behavioral contrast. *Journal of the Experimental Analysis of Behavior*, **29**, 297–308.

Squires, N. and Fantino, E. (1971). A model for choice in simple concurrent and concurrent-chains schedules. *Journal of the Experimental Analysis of Behavior*, **15**, 27–38.

Stubbs, D. A. and Pliskoff, S. S. (1969). Concurrent responding with fixed relative rate of reinforcement. *Journal of the Experimental Analysis of Behavior*, **12**, 887–895.

Taus, S. E. and Hearst, E. (1970). Effects of intertrial (blackout) duration on response rate to a positive stimulus. *Psychonomic Science*, **19**, 265–267.

Terrace, H. S., Gibbon, J., Farrell, L., and Baldock, M. D. (1975). Temporal factors influencing the acquisition and maintenance of an autoshaped keypeck. *Animal Learning and Behavior*, **3**, 53–62.

Tversky, A. (1972). Elimination by aspects: a theory of choice. *Psychological Review*, **79**, 281–299.

Wallace, R. F. (1973). Conditioned reinforcement and choice. Doctoral dissertation, University of California, San Diego.

Wardlaw, G. R. and Davison, M. C. (1974). Preference for fixed-interval schedules: effects of initial-link length. *Journal of the Experimental Analysis of Behavior*, **21**, 331–340.

Williams, B. A. (1976). Elicited responding to signals for reinforcement: the effects of overall *versus* local changes in reinforcement probability. *Journal of the Experimental Analysis of Behavior*, **26**, 213–220.

Williams, B. A. and Fantino, E. (1978). Effects on choice of reinforcement delay and conditioned reinforcement. *Journal of the Experimental Analysis of Behavior*, **29**, 77–86.

Whipple, W. (1979). Delay of reinforcement studied in a multiple-choice situation. Doctoral dissertation, University of California, San Diego, 1979.

Predictability, Correlation, and Contiguity
Edited by P. Harzem and M. D. Zeiler
© 1981 John Wiley & Sons Ltd

Chapter 6

The Several Roles of Stimuli in Negative Reinforcement

Philip N. Hineline

Introduction

The point of departure for this chapter lies in a rather separate sub-discipline of the study of behaviour, identified with a set of phenomena called 'avoidance'. For years, within psychology this label was applied primarily to one procedure, a procedure that embodies only a small part of what the vernacular word suggests. The procedure seemed straightforward, so it was treated as identifying avoidance as a basic, distinct phenomenon. Further, 'avoidance' has been treated as a distinct theoretical domain, apparently for the following reason: In most forms of operant or instrumental conditioning the manipulated events are made to occur contiguously with the behaviour under study. Avoidance, on the other hand, is behaviour that prevents some event that is not currently present, which necessarily prevents contiguity between the conditioned behaviour and the consequences that maintain it. Avoidance theory, then, has been mostly theory about how to interpret this non-occurrence in terms of plausible events that could be assumed to contiguously to follow the behaviour, thus mediating between observed behaviour and its environmental consequences. The typically proposed interpretation for avoidance has been a linear concatenation of two processes: Pavlovian conditioning has been said to provide the basis for instrumental, or operant conditioning. Through this, avoidance conditioning has been brought into a network of principles derived from other conditioning paradigms, with assumed contiguity as a ubiquitous feature. The assumption of avoidance as a basic phenomenon well represented by the 'classical' avoidance procedure, and the attendant 'two-process' or 'two-factor' interpretation, are still featured in both basic and advanced textbooks on conditioning and learning. (For historical reviews of avoidance and two-process theory, *see* Hernstein (1969) and Bolles (1973).)

Yet clear-cut evidence has long been available showing that the classical avoidance procedure is anything but straightforward in terms of behavioural process. The procedure confounds two key primary variables, and it masks several important processes or variables that contribute to the behaviour, but that are ignored by two-process theory. The evidence also indicates that the role of contiguity has been vastly overrated. In addition, it is now amply clear that the relationships between Pavlovian and operant processes are not well enough understood to support two-process theory as 'explaining' avoidance in any rigorous sense. My initial task here, after presenting some basic definitions, will be to present some of the evidence that supports the above assertions. My remaining task will be to present a different rubric for organizing and interpreting the facts that include avoidance. Concepts of negative reinforcement and of discriminative stimulus control will provide the outline. There will be an emphasis on continua, but aside from boundary cases a distinction will be maintained between reinforcement by change of situation, and reinforcement by change in frequency or quality of events within a situation. Thus, in this account, *avoidance* is neither a basic phenomenon nor an organizing concept. Finally, I shall identify some features of the present analysis that address current issues in general behaviour theory that relate to the relativity, the definition, and the measurement of reinforcement.

Basic Definitions

Negative reinforcement is the shaping or maintaining of behaviour through removal, reduction, postponement, or prevention of stimulation. The stimulation is defined as *aversive*, through this relation with behaviour. Traditionally, 'avoidance' refers to cases of negative reinforcement where the reinforced behaviour occurs in the absence of the aversive stimulus—thus, to avoid is to prevent or postpone aversive stimulation rather than to remove it. In the study of free-operant behaviour there are two basic types of procedures for arranging negative reinforcement: one type involves *deletion*; the other type involves *postponement*. In deletion, the timing of events proceeds independently of the behaviour under study, and the behaviour can prevent the occurrence of an event when it comes due. Thus, a watchman makes regular or irregular rounds, and a thief's actions may prevent detection of the crime without altering the watchman's routine of making the rounds. With respect to the thief's behaviour, detection is a likely aversive event whose deletion maintains that behaviour. In the case of postponement, the time of events is anchored upon the behaviour under study. The thief's actions might interrupt the watchman's routine, postponing his arrival at the scene of the crime. In the past, I and others have often used the term 'delay' in this context, instead of 'postponement'. While it is a bit unwieldy, I am adopting the latter term, since the former can be ambiguous. 'Delay' can refer passively to the interval from one event to another, or actively to a *change* in time when an event is due. 'Postponement' refers only to the active case, which applies here. Typically, in basic research on negative reinforcement electric shock is the manipulated event, rather than the arrival of a watchman, so

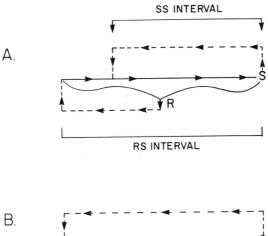

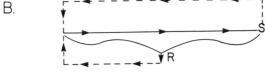

Figure 6.1. Flow diagrams indicating relations between events of Sidman's shock-postponement procedure. Passage of time is indicated by solid lines with duration represented by distance from left to right. Dashed lines indicate transitions that occur instantaneously. Brief shock is denoted by S; a response, indicated by R, can be effective during any part of the interval, as indicated by the brackets. In part A, the response–shock (RS) and shock–shock (SS) intervals are unequal. Part B portrays a comparable procedure in which the two intervals are equal

the remainder of this discussion will refer to shock postponement, and shock deletion. The behaviour under study will be that of rats, monkeys, and pigeons, rather than that of thieves.

The oldest free-operant procedure for negative reinforcement, the one devised by Sidman (1953a, b), provides a straightforward case of shock postponement. It is diagrammed in Figure 6.1, which is best understood by following the arrows with a pointer. In the absence of responding, brief shocks occur periodically, scheduled by a 'shock–shock' interval as indicated by the top loop in the figure. (Typically this interval ranges from 5 to 20 s but is constant within a given experiment.) The first response aborts this timing cycle and initiates a new timing interval, the 'response–shock interval' (typically 15–30s), that schedules the next shock. This interval can be reset to zero by a response (indicated by the bottom loop in Figure 6.1) so if the response–shock interval is never allowed to elapse without an intervening response, no shocks will occur. If the interval does elapse without a response, the periodic shock-delivery schedule resumes, as specified by the shock–shock interval. The response–shock and shock–shock intervals are independently manipulable and their systematic variation has produced orderly results (Sidman, 1953b; summarized by Sidman, 1966, Hineline, 1977).

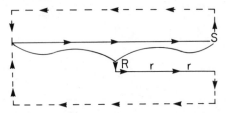

Figure 6.2 Flow diagram indicating relations between events in a shock-deletion procedure. Passage of time is indicated by solid lines, with duration represented by linear distance from left to right. Dashed lines indicate transitions that occur instantaneously. Brief shock is denoted by S; occurrence of a response (arbitrarily placed, for purpose of example) is indicated by R. As indicated by the brace, responses can be effective in any part of the interval; however, only the first response in a given cycle is effective. Additional responses, as indicated by r, have no effect

A simple example of a shock-deletion procedure was also provided by Sidman (1962a, 1966). Here, a repeated timing cycle (e.g. 15 s) proceeds inexorably. If no responses occur a brief shock is delivered at the end of each cycle, which is also the beginning of the new cycle, as indicated by the upper loop in Figure 6.2. A response cancels the shock due at the end of the cycle in which the response occurred. Additional responses during that cycle are without effect; if at least one response occurs within each cycle, no shocks will be delivered. This, too is an effective conditioning procedure, although it has not been studied so extensively as Sidman's shock-postponement procedure.

These examples of shock postponement and shock deletion are both based on fixed time intervals. Indeed, fixed intervals have been studied most often, perhaps because they are easily arranged in an experiment. They are also plausibly handled by conventional, two-process theorizing, for with fixed timing cycles the passage of time can plausibly be treated as a sequence of conditionable stimuli (Anger, 1963). Temporal regularities in a procedure can be given an interpretive role, analogous to that of external cues. However, the regularity of timing cycles is not related to the effectiveness of shock-deletion and shock-postponement procedures for the shaping and maintaining of behaviour. de Villiers (1974) used a procedure resembling Sidman's shock-deletion procedure described above, but based upon variable timing cycles. In the absence of responding a brief shock was delivered at the end of each cycle; the duration of any given cycle was independent of that on preceding cycles such that the probability of shock was roughly constant from moment to moment. The first response in a cycle deleted that cycle's shock; additional responses within the cycle were ineffective. de Villiers established responding in rats, with a mean cycle length of 15 s, and then varied this mean interval over blocks of sessions. Initial conditioning was readily accomplished and the subsequent manipulations of average cycle length produced orderly effects on rates of responding.

With shock-postponement procedures, variable timing cycles have been studied less systematically, but sufficiently to show that effectiveness of the procedure does not depend upon temporal regularities (Bolles and Popp, 1964; Sidman and Boren, 1957a). I shall return later to issues derived from these basic experiments on postponement and deletion but first will consider the role of certain added cues.

Warning Stimuli

'Warning stimuli'—that is, lights or sounds that reliably precede impending aversive events—have often been included in negative reinforcement experiments. Indeed, the addition of a warning stimulus to the shock-deletion procedure described above converts that procedure into the classical procedure that started the tradition of research on avoidance. However, it is shock-postponement procedures that best reveal the role of these added stimuli in the control of behaviour. In one such experiment, Sidman (1955) superimposed stimulus presentations on his basic shock-postponement procedure, using a light as the stimulus for rats, and a tone in an analogous procedure with cats. Initial training was accomplished without the warning stimuli, using his standard shock-postponement procedure, with equal response–shock (RS) and shock–shock (SS) intervals of 20 s. Then the warning stimuli were introduced, as diagrammed in part A of Figure 6.3. As before, in the absence of responding, brief shock occurred every 20 s; lever-press responses postponed shocks exactly as before, by resetting the 20 s timer. The procedure differed in that a light or tone

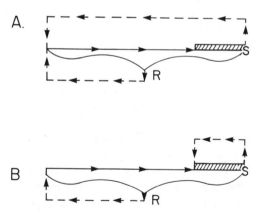

Figure 6.3. Flow diagrams indicating relations between events in shock-postponement procedures with added warning stimuli. The presence of a warning stimulus is indicated by the hatched area. As indicated by the braces, responses anywhere in the timing cycle restart the cycle. In so doing, responses prior to the onset of the warning stimulus postpone the onset of that stimulus. Responses in the presence of the stimulus terminate the stimulus while restarting the timing cycle. Part A describes the procedure used by Sidman (1955); part B describes the procedure used by Ulrich et al. (1964)

came on at 15 s, and terminated with the shock. Responses in the presence of the warning stimulus terminated that stimulus. Responses in the absence of the stimulus postponed its onset, resetting the 15 s response-tone (for cats) or response-light (for rats) interval just as they reset the 20 s response shock interval.

Traditional two-process theory predicts that the light or tone in this procedure would become a conditioned aversive stimulus through its pairing with shock. However, detailed examination of the results does not support this prediction. Figure 6.4 illustrates this fact, showing the momentary probabilities of responding at various times within the RS and RL intervals. At the left in the figure are data from sessions without warning stimuli; at the right are data from sessions with warning stimuli; the shaded areas correspond to times when the warning stimulus was present. The top left part of the figure shows that during the first 13 sessions of training on the shock-postponement procedure, before the light had ever been introduced, responding was distributed throughout the interval with only slightly increased probability in the final few seconds before shock was due. When the light was added, in session 14, the probability of responding decreased early in the interval. Session 15 shows a partial reversal of this effect—and subsequent reversals of the procedure, illustrated by lower parts of the figure, indicated that while adding a warning stimulus contributed to the development of temporal discrimination, the increased probability of responding late in the interval, with decreased probability early in the interval, was substantially due to the stimulus itself rather than to mere extended training. The development of behavioural control by the warning stimulus was distinguishable from the development of temporal discrimination independent of the warning stimulus. Overall, the greatest effect of the warning stimulus was to *reduce* the probability of responding early in the interval. The probabilities computed for different parts of the interval are independent of each other (unlike, for example, measures of relative frequency or percentage measures), so this reduced probability is not a statistical by-product of increased responding in the presence of the warning stimulus (which was relatively slight, if it occurred at all). If the light had acquired aversive properties through its pairing with the shock, one would expect, to be sure, that responding in its presence would increase, reinforced by response-contingent removal of the light. However, one would also predict that responding *earlier* in the interval, that could prevent the onset of the light, would also increase. Instead, the probability of such responding *decreased*.

Related experimental procedures that might be expected to enhance the likelihood of the animals' postponing the onset of warning stimuli provide further evidence that opposes an emphasis upon conditioned aversive properties of these stimuli. For example, Ulrich, Holz, and Azrin (1964), added a buzzer to a shock-postponement procedure, in a manner similar to Sidman's procedure described just above, but with more shock paired with the stimulus, as diagrammed in part B of Figure 6.3. Whenever their animals failed to postpone a

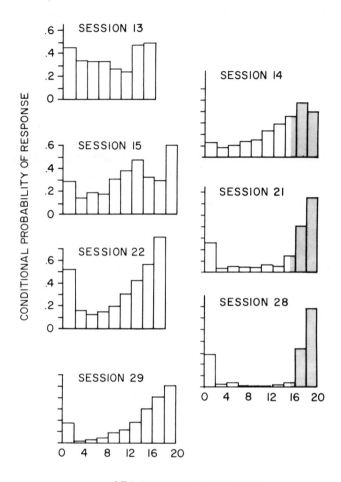

Figure 6.4. Momentary (conditional) probability of response as a function of time within the response–shock interval, during several phases of a rat's training with and without a 5 warning stimulus. The warning stimulus (flashing light) was first introduced in session 14; it was also present in sessions 17–21 and 23–28. The data were selected to show performance immediately before and immediately after procedure changes, from no-stimulus to stimulus, and vice versa. The probabilities were computed by dividing the percentage of responses in a given 2 s class interval, by the percentage of interresponse times that exceeded the lower limit of that class interval. For a detailed discussion of this measure and its rationale, *see* Anger (1963) or Hineline and Herrnstein (1970). The data are derived from Sidman (1955, Figure 5 *Journal of Comparative and Physiological Psychology*, **48**, 444–450. Copyright 1955 by the American Psychological Association. Reprinted by permission). Probabilities of responding in the presence of the stimulus are indicated by stippled areas; note that stimulus onset occurred midway in a 2 s class interval

shock, subsequent shocks occurred once every 5 s, with the buzzer on continuously, until another response reinstated the shock-postponement procedure. This contrasts with Sidman's (1955) shock–shock intervals of 20 or 30 s in which the warning stimulus terminated with shock, as diagrammed in part A of the same figure. In Ulrich, Holz, and Azrin's experiment, the rats responded even less in the absence of the warning stimulus. Instead of postponing the buzzer they consistently waited for it, and then responded, turning if off as they postponed shock.

Field and Boren (1963) devised an experiment that provided 'warning stimuli for warning stimuli', using a shock-postponement procedure in which rats could accumulate varying amounts of shock-free time (diagrammed in Figure 6.5). In the absence of responding, brief shocks occurred every 5 s, determined by a conventional shock–shock interval. A single lever-press interrupted this sequence, initiating a 10 s response–shock interval. Additional responses, instead of merely restarting the RS interval, accumulated additional 10 s periods as well, up to a maximum accumulation of 100 s. Thus, by responding once in every 10 s, the rat could maintain shock at a constant temporal distance; more rapid responding would increase that 'distance', up to ten 10 s increments away; slower responding would result in loss of the 10 s increments until, if it persisted, it resulted in shock delivery and reinstatement of the 5 s shock–shock interval. During initial training the procedure was accompanied by both visual and auditory stimuli. The visual stimuli were lights spaced evenly in a row on the wall where the lever was mounted. During the 5 s shock–shock interval, the lamp directly above the lever was lighted. The other lamps were ordinally related to the 10 s accumulations of shock-free time, such that when 100 s had been accumulated the most distant lamp was lighted; each 10 s pause in responding lighted the lamp next closer to the lever. The analogous auditory stimulus was a clicker, which produced 58 click/s at the 100 s accumulation, decreasing geometrically

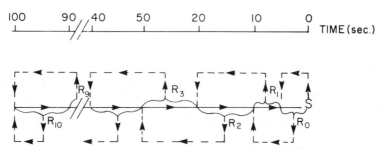

Figure 6.5.   Flow diagram indicating relations between events in Field and Boren's (1963) shock-postponement procedure. Passage of time is indicated from left to right along the solid line. Dashed lines indicate instantaneous transitions initiated by shocks (S) or responses (R). Subscripts identify the 10 s intervals in which responses occurred, with R_0 referring to responses in the 5 s shock–shock interval. Amounts of accumulated shock-free time are indicated by the time above the flow diagram

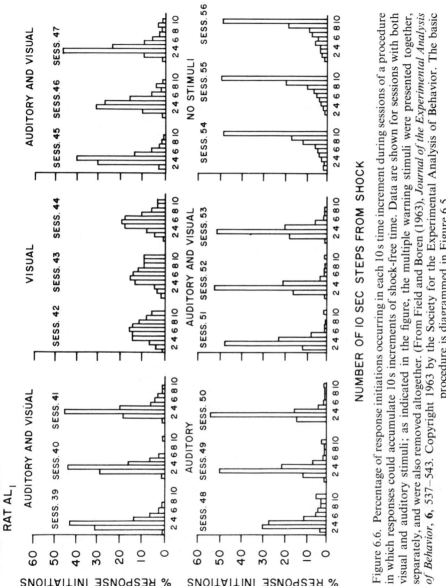

Figure 6.6. Percentage of response initiations occurring in each 10 s time increment during sessions of a procedure in which responses could accumulate 10 s increments of shock-free time. Data are shown for sessions with both visual and auditory stimuli; as indicated in the figure, the multiple warning stimuli were presented together, separately, and were also removed altogether. (From Field and Boren (1963), *Journal of the Experimental Analysis of Behavior*, **6**, 537–543. Copyright 1963 by the Society for the Experimental Analysis of Behavior. The basic procedure is diagrammed in Figure 6.5

to zero at shock delivery. Figure 6.6 shows data for one rat as the stimulus combinations were systematically changed; it indicates the relative frequencies of responding for each 10 s increment of temporal distance from shock. Probability measures comparable to those shown in Figure 6.1 could not be computed since in Field and Boren's procedure a given class interval could be entered from either side, and the total time spent in each interval was not reported. Sessions 39, 40, and 41 were the final three sessions of initial training, with the combined warning stimuli. Responses occurred most frequently in the third increment— corresponding to an accumulated period of between 20 and 30 s—with substantially less responding in the adjacent increments. When the auditory stimuli were removed, in sessions 42, 43, and 44, responses were more widely distributed across the various increments, with the distribution centered on the fifth or sixth increment. Reinstating the combined auditory and visual stimuli in sessions 45–57 produced a return to responding mostly during the third increment. Removal of the visual stimuli (sessions 48–50) produced little change, with responding still concentrated on the third increment. When both lights and tones were removed, in sessions 54–56, the distribution of responding shifted dramatically. The animals accumulated 100 s, and persistently responded, maintaining the 10-increment distance from shock.

In sum, the addition of warning stimuli for warning stimuli did not result in the animals maintaining an increased temporal distance from shock. Further, if we can assume that light and clicker combined are more discriminable or salient than light alone, we can conclude that increased saliance of warning stimuli resulted in the animals tolerating stimuli that were more closely paired with shock. This result, along with Sidman's (1955) and Ulrich et al.'s (1964) examinations of warning stimuli, suggest something other than a conditioned aversive function of the pre-shock warning stimuli. If the primary function of a warning stimulus were that of a conditioned aversive stimulus, and if the procedure permitted responses to prevent it, one would expect responding to be maintained by its prevention. The results, then, soundly contradict standard, traditional two-process avoidance theory.

Two alternative interpretations are suggested by these results. One of these could be viewed as a revised, or 'inverted' version of two-process theory, for it builds upon recent developments in the study of Pavlovian conditioning. Following Rescorla's reanalysis of Pavlovian conditioning in terms of contingent relationships as opposed to mere contiguous relationships between stimuli (Rescorla, 1967), several researchers have demonstrated that stimuli *inversely* correlated with shock, which are termed inhibitory stimuli within the Pavlovian paradigm, can reinforce behaviour that has been maintained by shock postponement. Weisman and Litner (1969) established the inverse correlation outside the shock-postponement situation, and then used response-contingent presentations of the Pavlovian conditioned inhibitor to reinforce either increases or decreases in rate of responding that was all the while maintained by shock postponement.

Dinsmoor and Sears (1973) used dimensional control, demonstrating generalization gradients, to reveal controlling effects of stimuli paired with shock-free intervals. Thus, in the experiments by Sidman (1955), by Ulrich *et al.* (1964), and by Field and Boren (1963), lack of responding to prevent the warning stimulus could have resulted from the fact that the *absence* of that stimulus (itself a stimulus configuration) was inversely correlated with shock. The warning stimulus itself, then, would be functioning not as an aversive motivator of behaviour, but rather as a contrasting stimulus that permits another stimulus to be correlated with the *absence* of shock.

The second interpretation of the effects of warning stimuli emphasizes the discriminative properties of those stimuli, focusing not upon the correlation of these stimuli with shocks *per se*, but rather upon the relation between these

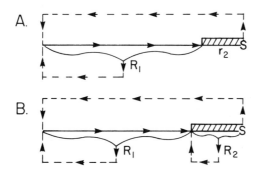

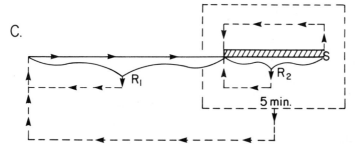

Figure 6.7   Flow diagrams indicating relations between events in three shock-postponement procedures that incorporated warning stimuli. Time is indicated from left to right along the solid lines. Dashed lines indicate instantaneous transitions initiated by shocks or by responses. R_1 designates a response prior to the onset of the warning stimulus, whose presence is indicated by a hatched area. R_2 designates a response in the presence of the warning stimulus when such a response is effective; r_2 designates such a response on a procedure where it is ineffective. Diagram A describes a procedure from Sidman and Boren (1975*b*). Diagrams B and C describe procedures from Sidman and Boren (1975*c*)

stimuli and the contingencies between responses and shocks. By this view, the warning stimuli delineate the occasions upon which responses are especially effective in postponing or deleting shocks. The responding, reinforced directly by its effects on the shock schedule, comes under discriminative control of the warning stimulus. This discriminative function is clearly revealed by a series of experiments reported in 1957 by Sidman and Boren. In one of these (Sidman and Boren, 1957*b*), seven rats were first trained on a shock-postponement procedure without warning stimuli, with shock–shock (SS) and response–shock (RS) intervals equal at 20 s as diagrammed in part B of Figure 6.1. Three animals were then placed on the procedure described by Sidman (1955), diagrammed above in part A of Figure 6.3, in which a light came on 5 s before shock was due. Responses in the presence of the light turned it off while resetting the 20 s response–shock interval. Responses in the absence of the light postponed its onset as well as the onset of the shock; that is, there was a RL interval of 15 s as well as the response–shock interval of 20 s. As in Sidman's earlier experiment, these rats seldom prevented the onset of the light; rather, they responded primarily in its presence. The four remaining rats were placed on a procedure with a 4 s warning stimulus, diagrammed in part A of Figure 6.7. A RL interval of 16 s provided for responses to postpone its onset. However, for these subjects responses could not terminate the light; once the light came on a shock was inevitable 4 s hence. An example of an ineffective response is designated as r_2 in the diagram. On this procedure, three of the four animals showed increased response rates in the absence of the light; response rates of all four rats decreased in the presence of the light. Sidman and Boren then manipulated the durations of the warning stimuli for the three animals described above whose responding could terminate the warning stimuli. These manipulations verified that the difference between outcomes on the two procedures was not attributable to differing durations of warning stimuli. These results clearly illustrate the role of the warning stimulus as a discriminative stimulus: if its presence correlates with occasions when responses can produce maximal postponement of shock, responding occurs frequently in its presence. If its presence correlates with occasions when responses are ineffective, the frequency of responding in its presence decreases. This is analogous to the conventional appetitive S^d/S^Δ discrimination, where responses can produce food in the presence of a stimulus but not in its absence.

The discriminative role of warning stimuli is more interesting and conceptually powerful than this, however, as illustrated by more of Sidman and Boren's experiments reported in 1957. One of these (Sidman and Boren, 1957*c*) began as in the experiment described by part B of Figure 6.1, with initial training on a shock-postponement procedure with SS and RS intervals of 20 s. Then, as before, a light was introduced whose onset could be postponed by responses, according to a 15 s RL interval. Once the light was allowed to come on, however, the situation was different; the response–shock interval was 5 s, so the shock could still be postponed, but only by a higher response rate. As diagrammed in part B of Figure 6.7, the light was not terminable by responses; rather, it stayed on until a shock was received, which reinstated the 20 s RS and the 15 s RL intervals. On this procedure, responding early in the RS interval (that is, responding that could postpone the onset of the light) increased slightly for three of the four animals, as shown with filled data points in Figure 6.8. In contrast, responding in the presence of the light (indicated with open data points in Figure 6.8), increased only briefly, and then decreased to levels below the corresponding response rates during initial training. That is, when behaviour had

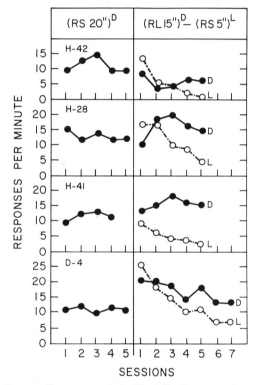

Figure 6.8. Rate of responding on a conventional shock-postponement procedure and on a subsequent chained postponement procedure. On the left are data for four individual rats during initial training on the procedure with response–shock and shock–shock intervals of 20 s, with no added stimuli (D = dark). On the right are response rates for the same animals, shown separately for the presence and absence of a light. The light accompanied a response–shock interval of 5 s and terminated if a shock was allowed to occur. In the dark, responses could postpone the onset of the light by 15 s and, at the same time, postpone the next shock by at least 20 s. (From Sidman and Boren (1957c), *Journal of Abnormal and Social Psychology*, **55**, 339–344. Copyright 1957 by the American Psychological Association. Reprinted by permission.) The latter procedure is diagrammed in part B of Figure 6.7

stabilized on this procedure, the animals frequently waited out the light when it came on, took the shock, and then resumed responding, postponing both light and shock. Note that this result contrasts with results of Sidman's earlier procedure (Sidman, 1955) and the similar one by Ulrich *et al.* (1964), diagrammed in Figure 6.3; when responses in the presence of the light had produced the same RS interval as those in the absence of the light, responding had predominated in the presence of the light.

If it were allowed to operate alone, a short RS interval could readily maintain responding in the presence of a warning stimulus. However, in the experiment that I have just reviewed, the short RS interval did not strongly maintain responding. Non-responding resulted in shock, but it also led to an additional consequence that over-rode the short-term control by that shock, and produced the decrements in responding portrayed in Figure 6.8. This fact is revealed by an additional experiment that Sidman and Boren reported, where they compared procedures in which the light, and its accompanying short RS interval, did or did not terminate with the shock. They began by replicating the results of the experiment described just above, but using slightly longer RL and RS intervals. The contingencies were as in part B of Figure 6.7, but the relative time periods were as in part C of Figure 6.7. Responses could postpone the onset of the light by 20 s (RL = 20), and if the animal's performance permitted the light to come on, a RS interval of 10 s was in effect. So long as 10 s did not elapse without a response, the shocks were postponed and the light stayed on. On this procedure, the light terminated when a shock occurred, reinstating the 20 s RL interval. As in the prior analogous procedure with a 5 s RS interval, the animals tended to wait out the light once it came on, and then respond again when the 20 s RL interval had been reinstated. These performances are portrayed in Figure 6.9, in the sections labelled 'shock terminates stimulus'. The second procedure in this experiment, diagrammed in part C of Figure 6.7, was identical, except that the duration of exposure to the light and its accompanying 10 s RS interval, was independent of the animal's behaviour. As before, responses in the absence of the light could postpone its onset, as specified by the RL interval. If the animal allowed the light to come on, however, it stayed on for 5 min with accompanying RS and SS intervals of 10 s. In this condition, response rates were high in the presence of the light. As shown by the data for two animals in Figure 6.9, the order in which the two procedures were imposed had little effect on the outcome. Sidman and Boren reported that additional animals gave comparable results with a RL interval of 20 s and a RS interval of 5 s in the presence of the light. Thus, the likelihood of responding in the presence of a warning stimulus depends not only upon the temporal proximity of shock (and discriminability of that proximity), but also upon the contingency whereby responding in the presence of the stimulus can postpone shock, and even upon the relation of that contingency to the contingency (or 'work requirement') in the absence of the warning stimulus, especially if the subject's behaviour can produce or prevent access to that

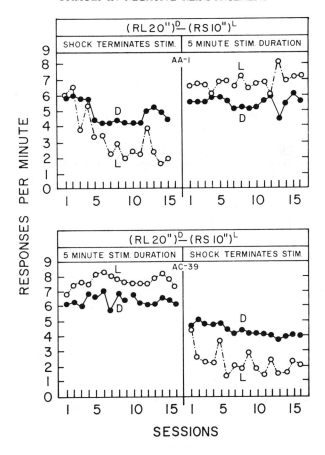

Figure 6.9   Rates of responding in the presence (L) and in the absence (D) of a light that denoted a 10 s response–shock interval, for two rates, each exposed to two conditions. In one condition (diagrammed in part B of Figure 6.7), the light terminated as soon as the animal permitted a shock to occur. The other condition is diagrammed in part C of Figure 6.7; once the animal permitted the light to come on, it stayed on for 5 min (along with the accompanying 10 s RS interval), irrespective of the animal's behaviour in its presence. Sessions occurred consecutively as shown from left to right, for each animal. (From Sidman and Boren (1957c), *Journal of Abnormal and Social Psychology*, **55**, 339–344. Copyright 1957 by its American Psychological Association. Reprinted with permission)

alternative work requirement. This is a complex statement, and a description of relationships that lie beyond the purview of traditional avoidance theory. Nevertheless, these relationships are orderly ones, and they appear to have substantial generality, as illustrated by the following two experiments: one with rats, the other with monkeys.

The principles to be illustrated are the following:

(1) The relative degrees to which responding will be maintained, in the presence vs. absence of various warning stimuli, are partly determined by the relative stringency of the contingency in the presence of each—with the animal sometimes waiting out a shock (the very shock whose postponement maintains the entire performance) when that permits access to a less stringent contingency for the postponement of subsequent shocks.

(2) The relative frequencies of responding will also be affected by the contingencies that directly enable the responding to be effective. (That is, if he responds at all on a contingency that requires a high rate, he will tend to respond rapidly).

(3) There is a slight bias toward remaining in the situations closer to shock, all other things being equal; this may reflect Pavlovian relationships whereby stimuli are correlated with shock-free intervals.

The first experiment illustrating these principles is yet another from Sidman's 'vintage year' of 1957. The basic procedure was one that I have described above, and diagrammed in part B of Figure 6.7, but the experiment entailed more extensive parametric manipulations. Once again, the warning stimulus was a light. Responding in the absence of the light (designated as R_1 in the diagram) postponed its onset by resetting a RL interval. If the animal allowed the light to come on, a response–shock interval became operative; responding (designated as R_2 in the diagram) postponed shocks but did not eliminate the light. Only a pause exceeding the RS interval—with the attendant shock delivery—turned off the light, reinstating the RL interval. As the main manipulations, the RS interval was varied while the RL interval was held constant for a given animal, and then the RL interval was varied while the RS interval was held constant.

Figure 6.10 shows the results of both kinds of manipulations for an individual rat. In panel B, we see the response rates in the presence and absence of the light (identified as L and D, respectively), when the RS interval was held constant (10 s; operative in the presence of the light) while the RL interval (operative in the dark) was manipulated. Interestingly, the greatest change of response rate occurred in the *presence* of the light, which denoted a *constant* RS interval of 10 s. When the RL interval was equal to the RS interval the rat typically waited out the RL interval, and then responded at a high rate, postponing shocks in the presence of the light. In contrast, when the RL interval was long (20 s) relative to the RS interval, response rates were much lower in the presence of the light; the rat responded at a higher rate in the absence of the light, postponing onset of the situation that included the 10 s RS interval. This result indicates that the relation between 'work requirements' in the two stimulus conditions was an extremely potent feature, for curve D in Figure 6.10 is the *inverse* of the function one usually obtains when manipulating the postponement interval in a schedule of aversive control (e.g. Sidman, 1953*b*; Clark and Hull, 1966). Panel A of

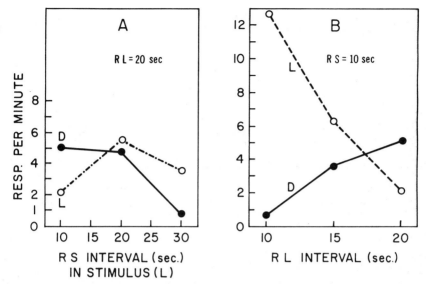

Figure 6.10. Response rates in the presence of a light (L) and in the absence of the light (D), for an individual rat, on a light- and shock-postponement procedure (diagrammed in part B of Figure 6.7). Responding in the dark postponed the onset of the light by restarting the RL interval. Responding in the presence of the light postponed shock by restarting the RS interval. The light terminated with shock delivery. Panel A shows effects of varying the RS interval while holding the RL interval constant at 20 s. Panel B shows effects of manipulating the RL interval while the RS interval was held constant at 10 s. (From Sidman (1957))

Figure 6.10 shows the effect of manipulating the RS interval while holding the RL interval constant at 20 s. Responding in the dark, which was during the constant RL interval, was strongly affected by the value of the RS interval, complementing the results described just above. The response rates in the presence of the light during this phase of the experiment were especially interesting. The response rates that accompanied RS intervals of 20 and 30 s showed the usual relationship for a shock-postponement procedure (Sidman, 1953*b*; Clark and Hull, 1966): the shorter interval produced the higher rate. However, when the RS interval was reduced to 10 s there was a substantial decrease instead of a further increase. The animal frequently waited out the interval, taking the shock which produced access to the larger RL interval. Thus, while it was in some sense the postponement of shocks that maintained these performances, a major determinant of response rate in a given situation was the effect of that responding upon the subsequent contingencies that affected responding—the 'alternative work requirement', to describe it informally.

The second experiment that illustrates these principles is one with Rhesus monkeys, reported by Krasnegor, Brady, and Findley (1971). Theirs was a shock-deletion procedure based on a 90 s timing cycle, with coloured lights denoting successive components of the cycle. The sequence is diagrammed in

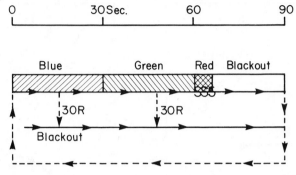

Figure 6.11. Flow diagram indicating relations between events in a chained shock-deletion schedule incorporating ratio requirements accompanied by distinctive visual stimuli. Passage of time is indicated from left to right along the solid lines. Dashed lines indicate instantaneous transitions. The procedure is that of Krasnegor *et al.* (1971)

Figure 6.11. In the absence of responding, a blue stimulus was on for 30 s, followed by 30 s with a green stimulus, followed in turn by a 3 s red stimulus accompanied by three brief, inescapable shocks. These were followed by a 27 s blackout, which completed the 90 s cycle. Ratio schedules were in effect, whereby if 30 lever-press responses occurred within either the 30 s 'blue period' or the 30 s 'green period' (with the count starting from zero at any stimulus change), the 30th response would abort the sequence, producing blackout for the remainder of the cycle, and deleting the shocks from that cycle. Two monkeys were run on this procedure, and each of them took very few shocks once initial training was achieved. Their performances differed in that one monkey completed the ratios about equally often in the blue and green components, while the other monkey completed the FR 30 in the blue (distal with respect to shock) component in roughly a fourth of the cycles, completing the ratio in the green (proximal to shock) component about three times as often. The two monkeys gave closely similar results when the ratio requirements were manipulated, however, as shown in Figure 6.12. When the ratio requirement in the presence of the proximal stimulus was manipulated over blocks of sessions while the ratio accompanying the distal stimulus remained constant at 30, the monkey continued to delete nearly all shocks, but tended to do so by responding disproportionately in the component requiring fewer responses in its 30 s period. For both monkeys there was still a substantial number of ratio completions in the proximal 'green' component when that ratio was double the ratio in the 'blue' component, which was more distal from shock. Only when the ratio in the proximal component was increased to 120, making it four times greater than the ratio in the distal component, did virtually all responding shift to the distal component. On the other hand, when the ratio in the proximal component was held constant at 30 while that in the distal component was varied, a more limited

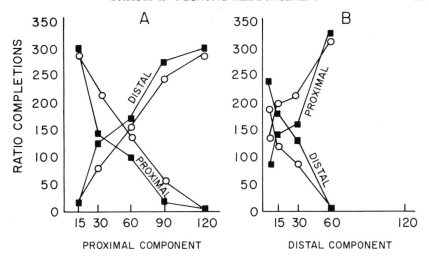

FIXED RATIO REQUIREMENT

Figure 6.12.   Performances of two Rhesus monkeys on variants of the procedure diagrammed in Figure 6.11. Panel A shows effects of varying the ratio requirement in the component proximal to shock, which was accompanied by a green stimulus. Panel B shows effects of comparable manipulations in the distal (blue) component. Each data point (open circles for one monkey, solid squares for the other) shows the mean number of ratio completions for the last five sessions on a given pair of ratios. When the fixed-ratio requirement in one component was varied, the ratio requirement in the other component was held constant at 30. (Adapted from Krasnegor *et al.* (1971), *Journal of the Experimental Analysis of Behavior*, **15**, 181–187. Copyright 1971 by the Society for the Experimental Analysis of Behavior. Inc)

range of ratios sufficed to produce the analogous changes in responding, as shown in part B of Figure 6.7. Again, responding tended to increase in the situation with the smaller ratio, while decreasing in that with the larger ratio. For both monkeys, then, there was a bias toward responding in the situation closer to shock, although only one had shown this bias when the two ratios were equal. This bias is interpretable in Pavlovian terms, emphasizing the role of stimuli *negatively* correlated with shock. However, the major features of the function are attributable to *operant* contingencies. Once again, the maintenance of behaviour in one situation depended not only upon the contingent relations between responding and shock reduction in that situation, but also upon the contingencies operative in an alternative situation, as well as the superordinate contingencies that controlled the occurrences of those situations.

The alternate contingencies described above might be loosely characterized as 'work requirements', since in both Sidman and Boren's experiment and that by Krasnegor *et al.*, relatively non-preferred situations were those with contingencies requiring high response rates. In one case this was the product of a short postponement (RS) interval; in the other case it was the product of a large ratio schedule coupled with a 'limited hold' requirement. However, it is possible that some contingencies requiring low response rates (such as DRL contingencies) would prove equally aversive; a systematic assessment of the relative preferences for the various types of negative reinforcement contingency remains to be done.

In the experiments described above, the relative aversiveness of the stimuli that delineated the various situations depended relatively little upon the pairing of stimuli and shocks. Given this, one might ask: 'What of the massive literature on Pavlovian conditioning, and its relation to negative reinforcement?' To be sure, contingent relations between stimuli are embedded in negative reinforcement procedures, and Pavlovian conditioning can be expected to accompany the operant conditioning. Correlation-based Pavlovian relationships appear in the delineating of shock-free periods, as I will be discussing below. However, the energizing/mediating functions of Pavlovian conditioning, as posited in traditional avoidance theory, are no longer viable for explanatory use. As Black (1971) spelled out in exhaustive detail, many logical and empirical pitfalls lie between the recognition of embedded Pavlovian contingencies and an accounting of operant behaviour in terms of Pavlovian process. Further, Brady, Kelly, and Plumlee (1969) found, with concurrent measures of autonomic activity and standard skeletal measures of Pavlovian conditioning, that the behaviours tapped by these measures are doubly dissociable. Each could occur without the other. Kamin, Brimer, and Black (1963) used a skeletal measure of Pavlovian conditioning to assess the conditioned properties of warning stimuli during various stages of classical avoidance training. The Pavlovian measures, even though based upon skeletal behaviour, correlated poorly with the skeletal avoidance responding. As I have argued in detail elsewhere (Hineline, 1973), it is gratuitous to assume a unitary Pavlovian, emotional process that could in some sense 'explain' avoidance. As I have noted, some of the facts arising from Pavlovian manipulations are understandable in terms of stimulus functions that will be outlined below. However, in the present exposition an analysis of negative reinforcement without added stimuli must be presented first.

Two Primary Dimensions of Negative Reinforcement

The Density Continuum, and Shock-frequency Reduction

As I noted earlier, negative reinforcement procedures do not require supplementary tones and lights to make them effective. In fact, where shock is delivered continuously the addition of such cues to denote the presence of shock would be superfluous, since shock itself is highly discriminable. This, of course, applies to the standard 'escape' procedure where responses are said to be reinforced by termination of shock. But shock continuously delivered is not always continuously received. The animal may tread rapidly or jump up and down. Further, the experimenter may schedule a train of pulses occurring several times per second. Still we would describe an interruption as removal, or discontinuation of shock. But if shock pulsing several times per second is characterized as continuous, why not two per second? Or one per two seconds? Or one per five seconds? At some point we begin referring to the postponement or deletion of individual shocks. The point at which our description changes depends partly upon whether we are starting with regularly or irregularly spaced pulses of shock. Our description is also affected by the relation between intershock time and the duration for which the sequence is interrupted. In this, it is important to remember that our qualitative change of description may not correspond to a qualitative change in controlling variables. 'Escape from continuous shock' is on a continuum with 'avoidance of intermittent shocks'. Thus, the labels 'escape' and 'avoidance' do not necessarily identify a discontinuity between different types of behavioural control.

This is borne out by experiments that have pointed to overall shock-frequency reduction as a controlling variable in negative reinforcement procedures that are based on intermittent brief shocks. It was Sidman (1962b), who first suggested this as the effective variable in shock-postponement. His inference was based on a procedure that permitted two effective responses, on two separate levers, each controlling an independent shock schedule. While the animals could have prevented all shocks by distributing responding on both levers, they tended to respond exclusively on the lever that produced the greater reduction in shock frequency, even though it produced smaller postponements of individual shocks. While the same shock-frequency interpretation could apply to the simpler, single-lever procedures, it cannot be effectively assessed there since overall shock frequency and short-term shock delay are redundant in conventional shock postponement. New procedures were needed for examining the potency of shock frequency as a controlling variable. One such procedure was devised by Herrnstein and Hineline (1966), who provided for shock deletion on a probabilistic basis, allowing for direct manipulation of shock frequency without producing predictable shock-free periods. As diagrammed in Figure 6.13, the procedure was based upon a repeating 2 s timing cycle. A pair of independent probabilistic decisions was made at the end of each cycle, resulting in potential deliveries of brief shocks, indicated by 'S' and 's' in the diagram. In the absence of responding, the higher probability decisions, represented on the centre line of Figure 6.13, controlled the delivery of shocks. A response transferred the control of shock delivery to the lower probability decisions, represented on the bottom line of the figure. When a shock was delivered, control was transferred back again. Thus the procedure can be summarized in terms of two random distributions of shock over time—a 'post-response' distribution, and a 'post-shock' distribution. As their labels suggest, at any given moment selection of the operative distribution was determined by whether a shock or a response had

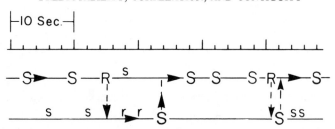

Figure 6.13. Flow diagram indicating the relations between events in a procedure for probabilistic shock-frequency reduction. Passage of time is represented linearly from left to right as indicated by the top horizontal line, which also indicate the 2 s timing cycles. The two other horizontal lines indicate probabilistic scheduling of shocks, with 'S' indicating shocks that would be delivered, and 's' indicating shocks that would not be delivered, given the hypothetical sequence of responses that is indicated. Effective responses are indicated by 'R'; ineffective responses are indicated by 'r'. As can be deduced from placement of the dashed arrows that indicate transitions, the centre line represents the post-shock distribution of shocks, while the bottom line represents the post-response distribution of shocks. The procedure is that devised by Herrnstein and Hineline (1966)

occurred more recently. On this procedure, responses did not postpone individual shocks or produce reliable shock-free intervals, for, as illustrated near the right of Figure 6.13, a response could be followed immediately by shock. Responses merely reduced the likelihood of shocks—that is, responding reduced the overall shock frequency. Nevertheless, this procedure reliably produced both acquisition and maintenance of lever-press responding. Seventeen out of 18 rats showed acquisition, some with two probabilities as close a 0.3 vs. 0.2, corresponding to mean shock frequencies of 9 and 6 shocks/min, respectively. Maintenance of responding under varied conditions was not studied extensively, for the experiment was focused upon acquisition. However, the plot with solid circles in Figure 6.14 shows that to the extent that various combinations of shock probability were examined, response rates varied *directly* with the magnitude of the probability that specified the post-shock distribution. de Villiers (1974) verified this relationship in a variable time shock-deletion procedure in which responses could delete all shocks. The plot with open circles in Figure 6.14 shows that response rates varied *inversely* with the probability that specified the post-response distribution, with these rates decreasing to zero when this probability was increased to the point of equaling that of the post-shock distribution. This indicated that, indeed, it was shock-frequency *reduction* that constituted reinforcement on this procedure. Logue and de Villiers (1978) provided further evidence for shock-frequency reduction as a controlling variable, with a two-lever shock-deletion procedure based on variable timing cycles. The control sequence relating responses to shocks for each lever was independent of the other. Also, each was equivalent to that diagrammed above in Figure 6.2, except that the timing cycles were variable, using a distribution of intervals developed by

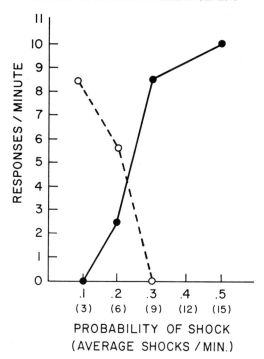

Figure 6.14. Response rate as a function of shock probabilities (and equivalent shock rates) on a probabilistic shock-deletion schedule. The open circles show rates obtained when the post-shock probability was 0.3, combined with the post-response probabilities indicated on the abcissa. The filled circles represent response rates obtained when the post-response probability was 0.1, combined with the post-shock probabilities indicated on the abcissa. Each point is a mean of the performances of at least two rats, and, in most cases, of four or five rats. The mean rates for individual rats were taken over the final 7 days of stable performance on each set of probabilities. (From Herrnstein and Hineline 1966), *Journal of the Experimental Analysis of Behavior*, 9, 421–430. Copyright 1966 by the Society for the Experimental Analysis of Behavior Inc

Fleshler and Hoffman (1962) that provided for roughly constant probability of shock from moment to moment. Logue and de Villiers used special preliminary procedures to facilitate continued responding on both levers, starting with a multiple schedule in which each lever was operative for alternate 5 min periods, followed by concurrent schedules in which both levers were simultaneously operative, each with its own shock-deletion schedule. They found that the relative rate of responding on a given lever matched the relative degree of shock-frequency on the two schedules. This is indicated in the upper part of Figure 6.15, by the approximately linear distribution of points on a log–log plot. Logue and de Villiers found that the animals' relative time allocations, as measured by the times between changeovers in the two directions (from left lever to right lever,

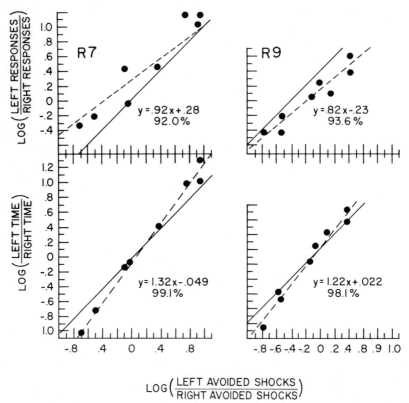

Figure 6.15. The ratios of left to right lever-press responses and left to right cumulated interchangeover time as a function of the ratios of left to right avoided shocks. Results are shown for the two rats, R_7 and R_9, and for all eight conditions, which used eight pairs of VI schedules in which responses on each lever cancelled shocks arranged by its own VI. The solid lines represent ideal matching of relative response rate to relative shock-frequency reduction, with a slope of 1.0 and an intercept of zero. The dashed lines are those that best fit the data according to the method of least squares. The equations for these lines and the percentage of the variance they account for are shown in each panel. (From Logue and de Villiers 1978), *Journal of the Experimental Analysis of Behavior*, **29**, 61–66. Copyright 1978 by the Society for the Experimental Analysis of Behavior Inc

and vice versa) matched the relative reductions in shock frequency even more closely; a linear fit to the relevant log–log plots accounted for more than 98 per cent of the variance for the two animals. Analogous matching relationships have been found for behaviour in positive reinforcement situations (reviewed by de Villiers, 1977), and in the present study response rates were high enough so that the observed matching relation cannot have been produced trivially by post-shock responding. Thus, the results of Logue and de Villiers point to shock-frequency reduction as a parsimonious characterization of the controlling variable. The demonstration would be even more convincing if each of their two independent schedules allowed only partial reductions in shock frequency, as in Herrnstein and Hineline's procedure. Such a study remains to be done.

In some respects, the term *shock density* may be better than shock frequency for characterizing the set of variables that defines negative reinforcement. 'Density' can include not only shock frequency, but also specifications of shock intensity and shock duration, which have also been shown to be effective dimensions for producing negative reinforcement. For example, Powell and Peck (1969) showed that intensity reduction was effective as negative reinforcement on a procedure that used evenly spaced shocks. Bersh and Alloy (1978) demonstrated comparable effects with a quite different procedure that used randomly spaced shocks and reinforced particular sets of interresponse times. Bersh and Alloy (1980) have also shown that reduction of the durations of brief, unpreventable, randomly spaced shocks is also a potent basis for negative reinforcement. Hence, in general discussions below I will use the term 'density', to include the implications of all of these dimensions. Specific discussions will refer to 'frequency', since it was the specific aspect of density that was manipulated in the experiments to be described.

Shock-frequency Reduction vs. Shock Delay: Interpretations

Some students of aversive conditioning have resisted the defining of reinforcement in terms of a change in density over time of events such as shocks or food deliveries. The nature of that resistance, and of its underlying assumptions, are fairly well characterized by Dinsmoor's (1977) objections:

> . . . it is difficult, logically, to see how a reduction in shock density could, by itself, serve as a reinforcing event. It has no locus in time. . . . If the reduction in estimated shock density is a continuous process, not localized in time, how can it become correlated with any specific item of behavior? If follows all behavior, but none more closely or more consistently than any other. (p. 90)

The last sentence quoted here is in error: if a specified response class uniquely affects the density of shocks distributed over time, the shocks are consistently related to the specified responses. If the shocks are variably distributed, the relation is consistent to the extent specifiable by the density changes. The earlier parts of the quoted passage, however, identify an interesting question, but one that is crucial only for conceptions of reinforcement that require its occurring at specified discrete moments in time. The fact of successful conditioning with negative reinforcement based on intermittent shocks has forced a preoccupation with theory, even within the field of behaviour analysis, where emphasis is usually upon environmental variables that can be directly measured and manipulated. The theorizing has usually taken the form of inferring plausible events that could provide immediate, discrete, reinforcing consequences contiguous with the behaviour to be reinforced. The theorizing has emphasized the question, 'How do they do it?' instead of emphasizing controlling variables. 'It', in this case, is the preventing of shocks not yet present; 'How', is translated either as the supplying of stimulus traces or internal conditioned aversive stimuli, or as the positing of more complex processes inside the behaving organism. As Lacy and Rachlin (1978) have described in detail, lack of external, contiguously causal events is often treated as justifying cognitive theorizing; and dependence upon temporal contiguity for explanation of behaviour is a cornerstone both of associationist and of cognitive theories. However, this is a weak form of justification, for adequate explanation of behaviour need not be based upon contiguous causation.

Looking again to Dinsmoor's discussion, we find the following as a suggestion of what contiguity-based theory requires if it is to accept shock-density reduction as an operative variable:

> To preserve the shock-density formulation, it might be argued that the subject can average the rate or density of shock over several successive samples of postresponse time and can then compare the resulting value with density of shock at other times during the experimental session. . . . Average shock densities are computed by tallying the number of shocks over certain selected periods of time, and dividing the first term by the second. . . . The animal must sort out samples of time, assigning some to the denominator of the fraction and rejecting others. . . . (Dinsmoor, 1977, p. 90)

Dinsmoor clearly finds these hypothetical cognitive activities to be: (a) necessarily implied by the imputing of shock frequency as the basis for reinforcement, and (b) implausible as inferred activities of laboratory rats. In short, Dinsmoor's assumption that a molar reinforcement principle implies complex digital machinations leads to his finding a molar reinforcement principle to be untenable.

The alternative interpretation that Dinsmoor offers for experiments on probabilistic shock deletion, focuses upon average time from response to shock. This approach derives partly from Anger's (1963) two-process account of performances on unsignalled shock-postponement procedures, and partly from his own demonstrations of behavioural control by response-produced stimuli (Dinsmoor and Sears, 1973). He points out that if responses produce a lower frequency of randomly spaced shocks, there must be a longer average time from response to shock than from any other event to shock. It follows, then, that even though shocks sometimes occur immediately after responses, the responses produce *relatively* shock-free periods. Whatever response-produced cues are available, then, become 'relative safety' signals, reinforcing the response.

In assessing Dinsmoor's arguments it should be noted first that 'average delay to shock' is precisely the reciprocal of shock frequency. Thus in terms of functional relationships a change in average time to shock is equivalent to a change in shock frequency; neither form of specification has a predictive advantage over the other. Second, it is premature to assert that if an organism is sensitive to the frequency of random events it must be computing digital sums and quotients. Most likely such sensitivity can, even in the rat, be based on any of a variety of computation methods, both analogue and digital. They need not even be mediated primarily by the nervous system, as illustrated by the following slightly whimsical argument: Passing electrical current through a resistance produces heat. The thermal mass of that resistance, and the rate of heat dissipation determine the integral of temperature over time. The feet of a laboratory rat have both electrical resistance and thermal mass; perhaps the changes in shock density make contact with the animal through the temperature of its feet. Lever-pressing results in cooler feet. This is at least as plausible as the method that Dinsmoor described, and it allows for shock density to be integrated without dependence on individual delays to shock.

Short-term vs. Long-term Controlling Variables

Fortunately, shock-density reduction and changes in average delay to shock need not be treated as mutually exclusive characterizations of negative reinforcement. Further, the two interpretations suggest a distinction between two controlling variables that, however confounded in traditional procedures, can be manipulated independently and thus dissociated. To the extent that they are both found effective, the determinants of their relative potency can be assessed as well. The first such dissociation was accomplished by the present author (Hineline, 1970), with experiments that permitted rats' responding to produce short-term postponement of shock while the overall shock frequency was held constant or even increased. As shown by the diagrams in Figure 6.16, the procedures were based upon 20 s cycles; each cycle began with insertion of a retracting lever into the chamber. If no response occurred, a brief shock was delivered at 8 s, and the lever retracted at 10 s, remaining inaccessible for the remainder of the cycle. A response produced immediate retraction of the lever. In one procedure (part A of Figure 6.16) a response within the first 8 s postponed the shock from being given at 8 s to being given at 18 s; there still was one shock per 20 s cycle, so shock frequency remained constant at three per minute. (Responses between 8 s and 10 s resulted in two shocks per cycle, at 8 and 18 s; however, these seldom occurred.) This proved to be an effective procedure; it produced and maintained stable lever-press responding in each of five laboratory rats, three of which were experimentally naive, and two of which had been previously trained on conventional shock-postponement procedures.

Part B of Figure 6.16 shows a procedure in which responses postponed shocks

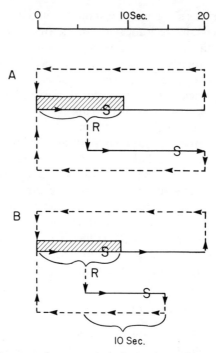

Figure 6.16. Flow diagrams for two procedures that allowed shock postponement without shock-frequency reduction. Passage of time is indicated by solid lines, linearly from left to right. Dashed lines indicate instantaneous transitions. In the absence of responding, the procedures were identical, and based on a 20 s timing cycle, as shown by the upper loops of the two digrams. A response lever was available only during the first 10 s, as indicated by the hatched areas. Brief shocks are indicated by 'S'; responses are indicated by 'R', with braces indicating the period over which responses could occur. Part A describes a procedure in which there were three shocks per minute, irrespective of responding; part B describes a procedure in which responses increased the shock frequency by shortening the timing cycle. The procedures are from Hineline (1970)

but, in so doing, produced increases in shock frequency. As before, in the absence of responding a shock occurred at 8 s and the lever retracted at 10 s. A response within the first 8 s postponed the shock until exactly 8 s after the response, and a new cycle was begun 2 s after that. Since there was still one shock per cycle, responding increased the shock frequency, even though it produced short-term shock-postponement. This procedure did not sustain responding. The two animals with previous training on conventional shock-postponement procedures which had responded persistently in the constant frequency procedure described just above, ceased responding within nine sessions of exposure to the present procedure. Eleven naive rats placed directly on this second procedure responded sufficiently to encounter the consequences of responding, but their response rates dropped to zero without ever having exceeded 30 per cent of the cycles in any session. A simple interpretation of these experiments is that short-term postponement of shock tended to maintain responding in both, and that this was effective so long as overall shock frequency was constant. When the short-term postponement was achieved only at the expense of an *increase* in shock frequency, the short-term consequence was insufficient to maintain responding. However, there are additional differences between the two procedures. The magnitude of shock postponement was greater in the procedure that maintained responding, and the time from response to shock was variable in one procedure (where it depended upon response latency), while this response–shock interval was fixed at 8 s in the other.

Subsequent experiments have permitted wider ranges both of short-term shock postponement and of change in overall shock frequency. The procedures for two of these, diagrammed in Figure 6.17, were based on 60 s timing cycles, which permitted a greater magnitude of short-term shock postponement. These procedures also provided for a fivefold change in overall shock frequency as opposed to the maximum of a twofold change in the experiment described above. As shown in part A of Figure 6.17, one shock occurred each minute, if no response had occurred during the 10 s opportunity to respond. Responses

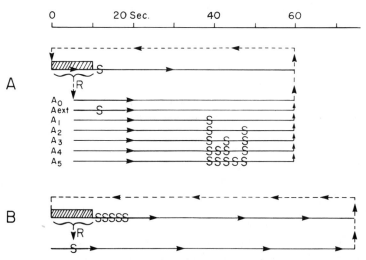

Figure 6.17. Flow diagrams for two procedures for dissociating shock postponement from shock frequency. Passage of time is indicated by solid lines, linearly from left to right. Dashed lines indicate instantaneous transitions. Availability of the response lever is indicated by the hatched areas; responses are indicated by 'R' with the accompanying braces indicating the period in which responses could occur. Brief shocks are indicated by 'S'. The procedure of part A is from Hineline (1969, 1977); that of part B is from Lambert *et al.* (1973). Several variants of procedure A are indicated by A_0 through A_5, whereby the response that deleted shock at 11 s produced one or more shocks between 39 and 47 s of the cycle. A_0 and A_{ext} portray preliminary training and extinction procedures

produced immediate retraction of the lever from the chamber and deletion of the shock that was due at after 11 s of the cycle. In the first experiment with this procedure (Hineline, 1969), initial training for five rats was accomplished with procedure A_0, in which responses could delete all shocks. After performances stabilized the extinction procedure (A_{ext} in the figure) was imposed, whereby a response produced immediate retraction of the lever, but shock still occurred after 11 s of the cycle. When responding had decreased to less than 5 per cent of the cycles, procedure A_1 was begun, wherein a response deleted the shock at 11 s, but produced an identical shock at 39 s. For the animals that responded on this procedure, additional shocks were then added, by procedures A_2, A_3, A_4, and then A_5, with stability of performance assessed before each procedure change. Thus, on the final procedure of this experiment, a response deleted the shock at 11 s, but produced five shocks distributed between 39 and 47 s of the cycle. Five of six rats reached stable performance on the shock-deletion procedure, A_0, responding an approximately 90, 80, 75, 76, and 20 per cent of the cycles, respectively. All of these animals ceased responding on procedure A_{ext} where responses no longer affected the placement of shocks. With exposure to the shock-postponement procedure A_1, only two animals resumed stable responding, those that had previously responded most frequently. For these two, however, shock postponement was apparently a potent consequence for maintaining behaviour, for their high levels of responding continued as the response-produced shock frequencies were increased via procedures A_2 through A_5. Subsequent work with these procedures in collaboration with G. D. Smith (reported in Hineline, 1977) suggested that the initial training with shock deletion (which provides shockfrequency reduction as well as shock-free post-response intervals) contributes to the potency of shock postponement as a reinforcer, but that shock postponement is still somewhat effective without a prior history of shock-frequency reduction.

The relative effectiveness of shock-frequency reduction and of shock postponement is partly a matter of their relative magnitudes, as illustrated by an experiment by Lambert, Bersh, Hineline, and Smith (1973). One of their procedures is diagrammed in part B of Figure 6.17, showing a 75 s cycle initiated by a 10 s response opportunity, making it similar to the procedure described just above. However, instead of 'one shock soon vs. five shocks later', the procedure of Lambert et al. could be characterized as 'five shocks soon vs. one shock now'. With no response in a given cycle, five brief shocks were delivered, one per second, starting after 11 s. A response during the first 10 s deleted those five shocks, but produced one immediate shock. In other variants of this procedure, the response opportunity period was extended to permit responses to abort the five shock sequence once it had begun. Studying both lever-press and shuttle responses with these procedures, Lambert et al. found that shock-frequency reduction had discernible but weak reinforcing effects when it was produced at the expense of reductions in short-term shock delay.

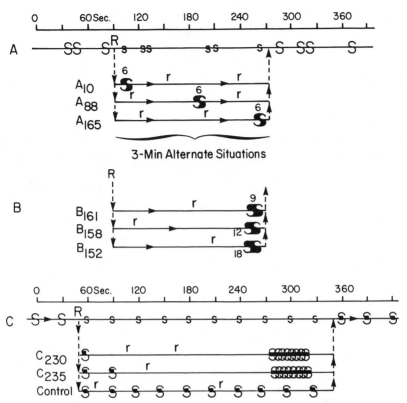

Figure 6.18. Flow diagram showing three variants of a free-operant procedure for dissociating shock postponement from shock-frequency reduction. Passage of time is indicated by solid lines, from left to right; dashed lines indicate instantaneous transitions. Shocks actually delivered are indicated by S; those eliminated due to an effective response (R) are indicated by s; superfluous, ineffective responses are indicated by r. Lines A_{10}, A_{88}, and A_{165} indicate the spacing of shocks in three separate procedures, showing in each case the events that occurred in the 3 min response-produced 'alternative situation'. Part B indicates the spacing of shocks in the 'alternative situations' of three procedures in which responses produced increases in shock frequency. The subscripts (161, 158, 152) indicate time to shock onset, corresponding to trains of 9, 12, and 18 shocks, respectively, at a rate of 1 shock per second. In each case the train of shocks ended 10 s before the transition back to the VT 30 s imposed situation. The procedures are from Gardner and Lewis (1976). Part C shows three procedures with all shocks preceded by 4.5 s tones, indicated by the rectangular shaded areas. In the imposed situation shocks were delivered on a FR 30 s schedule, with an effective response producing the transition to a 5 min alternative situation. In the control procedure shock deliveries were unaffected by responding, as shown in the bottom line. In the other two procedures, the FT schedule remained in effect for one or two shocks in the alternative conditions as shown, with the remaining shocks postponed until late in the interval. Responses in the alternative condition were without effect, as were responses within 5 s following the onset of each shock in the imposed condition. These procedures are from Lewis et al. (1976)

In each of the experiments just described, two variables, shock-frequency reduction and short-term shock postponement, were dissociated by restricting the opportunities to respond to specific parts of a timing cycle. Responses then affected placements of shocks throughout the cycle. Recently, a series of experiments has been reported that further elaborates the dissociation between these two variables, while demonstrating their effects upon free-operant responding. The new procedures appear to illustrate a remarkably sensitive measurement technique for detecting effects of these variables. The basic procedure, first reported by Gardner and Lewis (1976) is characterized in terms of two situations that can alternate within the experimental setting. The first is an 'imposed situation' which remains in effect so long as there is no responding. Responses in the imposed situation can produce the second, or 'alternative situation', which is accompanied by distinctive cues, and which has a fixed duration, typically 3 min. Responses in the alternative situation can occur and are recorded, but are without effect. In their first experiment, Gardner and Lewis delivered brief shocks in the imposed situation according to a variable time schedule whereby the probability of shock was roughly constant from moment to moment. As shown in part A of Figure 6.18, a response produced an alternative situation of 3 min duration. For three rats the alternative situation was that identified as A_{10} in the figure; six shocks were delivered, one per second, starting 10 s after the alternative situation had been initiated. For an additional three animals the six shocks began 88 s into the alternative situation (see line A_{88}); for a third group, the shocks began after 165 s (see line A_{165}). Since on the average the imposed situation provided two shocks per minute, the transition to a 3 min alternative situation, each with its six shocks, provided no change in overall shock frequency. The transitions did prove reinforcing, however, provided there was sufficient short-term postponement of shock; the apparent potency of reinforcement was directly related to the magnitude of the postponement. As shown in Figure 6.19, transitions to the situation with 165 s postponement maintained sufficient responding to keep the alternative situation in effect for more than 90 per cent of the total session time. The 88 s postponement resulted in responding that maintained the alternative situation for approximately 80 per cent of the time; transitions to the situation with 10 s postponement maintained very little responding. In the same report, Gardner and Lewis (1976) described a second experiment, in which responses could produce short-term shock postponement only at the expense of an overall increase in shock frequency. Selected aspects of these procedures are shown in part B of Figure 6.18, which indicates the placement of trains of 9, 12, and 18 shocks within the 3 min alternative conditions. In most respects the procedure was the same as that shown in part A: with no responding brief shocks were delivered on a VT 30 s schedule, which constituted the 'imposed situation'. A response initiated the 3 min alternative situation (delineated by accompanying clicker and lights), which entailed a short-term delay until the onset of a train of shocks at a rate of one per

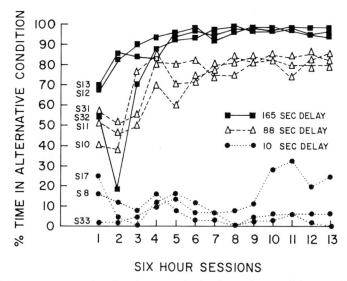

SIX HOUR SESSIONS

Figure 6.19.   Percentage of session time spent in the alternative condition, as a function of consecutive 6 h sessions, for groups of three rats, each exposed to one of the three procedures portrayed in Figure 6.18. Data are plotted separately for each rat, with the rat's designations indicated to the left of the first session points. (From Gardner and Lewis 1976), *Journal of the Experimental Analysis of Behavior*, **25**, 3–14. Copyright 1976 by the Society for the Experimental Analysis of Behavior

second that always ended 10 s before the transition back to the imposed situation. The three variants of this procedure, with trains of 9, 12, and 18 shocks respectively, are diagrammed in part B of Figure 6.18. The times to shock onset were adjusted slightly to accommodate the differing lengths of the sequences of one shock per second: hence the designations B_{161}, B_{158}, and B_{152}.

Stable responding was produced and maintained in all three animals on the procedure that entailed a 50 per cent increase (B_{161} in Figure 6.18) and in all three on the procedure that entailed a twofold increase in shock frequency (B_{158} in Figure 6.18). Only one of three animals responded appreciably on the procedure that entailed a threefold increase in shock frequency (B_{152} in Figure 6.18). Gardner and Lewis also included control procedures that employed the same changes in shock frequency, but with shocks distributed throughout the alternative conditions. These procedures did not maintain stable responding.

These experiments support the earlier demonstrations that short-term postponement of shock can override an increase in overall shock frequency. Yet they are not entirely immune to alternative interpretations, for some animals showed evidence of shock-elicited responding. Further, the transitions to the 'alternative situations' could perhaps be interpreted as enstating highly discriminable shock-free periods, contrasted with the unpredictably spaced shocks in the imposed situations. The reinforcing effect of transitions from situations with unpredictable shocks to situations where shocks (and thus shock-free periods) are predictable, has been repeatedly demonstrated by Badia and his colleagues, who have used pre-shock stimuli to render shocks predictable (e.g. Badia and Culbertson, 1972; Badia, Coker, and Harsh, 1973). These alternative interpretations have been shown to be implausible for the present context, however, by a pair of experiments reported by Lewis, Gardner, and Hutton (1976), whose experiments also elucidate further the roles of short-term shock postponement, and overall shock-frequency reduction.

The procedure for one of these is diagrammed in part C of Figure 6.18. In this procedure, all shocks were preceded by 4.5 s tones, which provided clearly discriminable shock-free periods within both situations that comprised the procedure. During the imposed situation brief shocks were evenly spaced, 30 s apart. Responses were made ineffective within 5 s following the onset of shock, to ensure that shock-elicited responding would be ineffective. Other responses within the imposed situation were effective in producing immediate transitions to 5 min exposures to the alternative situation with its accompanying light and clicker. However, this transition did not immediately affect the shock sequence. Rather, in one condition (designated C_{230} in Figure 6.18) the next shock scheduled by the 30 s schedule was delivered just as it would have been if no response had occurred; the remaining nine shocks for that instance of the alternative situation were delivered in a series of one shock every 5 s, starting 230 s after the onset of the alternative situation. As noted above, each shock was preceded by a 4.5 s tone; there was a 30 s interval between the last shock of this series and the transition back to the imposed situation. A second condition is portrayed on line C_{235} of Figure 6.18. Here, the response-produced transition to the alternate situation was followed by two shocks delivered according to the FT 30 s schedule; the remaining eight shocks scheduled for that situation occurred in a series that began 235 s after the response-produced transition. In both of these conditions, as well as in a control condition where shocks occurred every 30 s irrespective of responding, the overall shock frequency remained constant. The effects of these procedures are summarized in Figure 6.20. Four naive rats were exposed to the C_{230} procedure, and all four responded sufficiently to keep the alternate situation in effect between 80 and 90 per cent of the time Their response rates dropped consistently to low levels with subsequent exposure to the control procedure; these procedures, C_{230} followed by Control, were then repeated, with similar results. Then three of these subjects, along with three naive rats, were exposed to the C_{235} procedure, where two unpostponed shocks occurred in the alternative situation. Two of the three rats with previous training resumed responding, and maintained the alternative situation in effect approximately 80 per cent of the time. The three naive rats did not respond appreciably on this procedure. With this experiment, Lewis et al. (1976). demonstrated

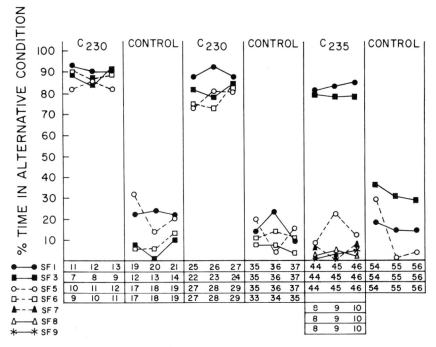

SIX HOUR SESSIONS

Figure 6.20. Percent of session time in the alternative situation for the last three sessions of each series of exposures to each of three procedure. The procedures designated C_{230}, C_{235}, and Control, are identified and diagrammed in Figure 6.18; they are presented here in the order administered. Data are shown for eight rats; SF 1, SF 3, and SF 5 were exposed to all three procedures; SF 6 was exposed only to procedure C_{230}. Rats SF 7, SF 8, and SF 9 were exposed only to procedure C_{235}. (From Lewis *et al.* 1976), *Journal of the Experimental Analysis of Behavior*, **26**, 379–386. Copyright 1976 by the Society for the Experimental Analysis of Behavior Inc

negative reinforcement effects that depended neither upon a change in time to the first shock nor upon an overall reduction in the number of shocks per unit time. Their report also included an experiment that I have not described here, showing that even with a variable time schedule for shock delivery the effectiveness of the procedure was not attributable to discriminability of shock-free intervals.

In subsequent work, Gardner and Lewis (1977) demonstrated similar negative reinforcement effects with the pigeon's key-peck instead of the rat's lever-press response. They used special procedures to initially establish key-pecking, transferring control of the response from positive reinforcement to shock deletion, as has proved necessary even in the case of more conventional negative reinforcement procedures; however, after initial training they were able to verify for maintenance of key-pecking in pigeons, a set of relationships similar to those

I have described above for the lever-pressing of laboratory rats. One experiment demonstrated the maintenance of responding by short-term postponement in the face of substantial increases in shock frequency. This confirmed with a different procedure, response, and organism the findings of my laboratory (Hineline, 1969, 1977) and, with a different response and organism, their own earlier findings (Gardner and Lewis, 1976). Another experiment reported by Gardner and Lewis (1977) also extended in similar fashion the results of Lambert *et al.* (1973), showing that shock-frequency reduction could maintain a response that produced immediate shock, and their own results regarding delayed reductions in shock frequency (Lewis *et al.*, 1976).

In sum, it is abundantly clear that an adequate account of negative reinforcement must include the role of changes in overall shock density and the short-term distribution of shocks. With respect to the maintenance of behaviour the systematic effects of these variables are apparently not limited to particular organisms or to particular experimental settings. Some special considerations may apply to the initial shaping of a response, but, as I have discussed elsewhere (Hineline, 1977, pp. 404–410), these do not invalidate the relationships described here.

Behavioural Situations, Integration Over Time, and the Several Roles of Added Cues

I have pointed out above that continuous shock is on a continuum with intermittent brief shocks. The research that I have just reviewed suggests that, analogously, there are cases where integrated delays to shock shade over into shock frequency. This latter, at first blush, may seem to be merely a rediscovery of the reciprocal relation between shock frequency and average time between shocks. However, the relation is more subtle than that. It is the relation between short-term shock-density and long-term shock-density; it concerns the periods over which shock densities are effectively integrated.

One key role of added cues such as tones or lights in negative reinforcement procedures is to help delineate this integration. This role can be illustrated by a visual analogy, such as that in Figure 6.21. In the centre of the figure is a collection of dots, distributed on an underlying matrix with a probabilistic decision determining whether there is a dot at any given point, but with a slowly increasing probability of dots from left to right, perceptually, it appears to be just that—a gradient of randomly placed dots, with density increasing from left to right. The upper and lower parts of the figure illustrate effects of superimposed stimuli with distinct boundaries. They produce a tendency to perceive the gradient as two distinct areas, a dense one and a sparse one. I suggest that with irregularly spaced shocks or other brief events, the abrupt onsets and offsets of accompanying stimuli of longer duration affect the effective groupings of the brief events.

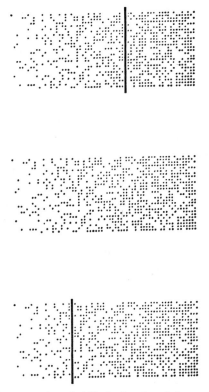

Figure 6.21.   Identical arrays of probabilistically placed dots, with and without added boundaries. The arrays were generated on the basis of an underlying matrix; in generating the pattern, the probability of a dot appearing was constant for each column; that probability was incremented by a constant amount as each new colum was generated, giving a linearly increasing density of dots, from left to right. The vertical lines were added to the top and bottom arrays, to induce the perceived grouping of the dots into sparse and dense areas of differing sizes

The resulting boundary effects facilitate behavioural analysis, by delineating the periods over which particular events or relations between events are effective. In a terminology introduced by Baum (1973), these boundary effects help to delineate *behavioural situations*, which relate to the defining of both positive and negative reinforcement, as well as to a distinction between punishment and extinction. 'A behavioral situation consists of a set of possible activities, a set of possible events or stimuli, and a set of feedback functions (that is, contingencies) determining the effects of activities on the events.' (Baum, 1973, p. 150). As Baum has pointed out, a clearly delineated transition from one situation to another can be a powerfully reinforcing event. Applying these notions to experiments such as I have described above, two modes of reinforcement emerge: reinforcement by change in density of events within a behavioural situation, and reinforcement by change of situation. This distinction is easily made in many cases. It is difficult to make in others, and one transition from clear to ambiguous distinction is illustrated by the continuum of shock density that I described above. If shock is presented continuously, accompanied by a contingency whereby a response can terminate it, the change from presence to absence of shock constitutes a distinct transition from one behavioural situation to another. If the shocks occur briefly and probabilistically, accompanied by a contingency whereby responses can change that probability, the resulting change in shock frequency will most likely constitute reinforcement by change in density of events within a situation. Adding distinct cues that accompany the change in probability can aid in converting the mode of reinforcement to one of distinct change of behavioural situation—just as the added lines in Figure 6.21 tend to convert a gradient of dots into dense and sparse groups.

It is important to recognize, however, that a change in density of events is only *one* feature that contributes to the defining of a transition between situations. Equally important to the defining of a situation is the *contingency operative in that situation*. Thus, when a response terminates continuously delivered shock for an extended time, an immediate additional response cannot have the same effect because absent shock cannot be removed. The shock's termination necessarily constitutes a change of behavioural situation. If the shocks are brief and intermittent, and each response resets the time that schedules the next shock, then the contingency has remained substantially unchanged, and the behavioural situation endures as well. If there is a substantial change in the effect of responses on intermittent shocks, this will constitute a change of situation. Thus, in Sidman's shock-postponement procedure, if the response–shock interval differs greatly from the shock–shock interval, the two intervals define different behavioural situations. Sidman (1966) has reported that, in such cases, the animals' performances differ in the two situations, giving clearly distinguishable distributions of interresponse times. Of course with changes of response contingency there are ambiguous boundary cases, just as with changes of the frequency of events. Thus, as McLeish and Martin (1975) have pointed out, the distinction between one kind of extinction and one kind of punishment (punishment by response-contingent removal of a rewarding stimulus) is subject to this kind of ambiguity in boundary cases. The most common extinction procedure is described as the *withholding* of reinforcement; responses no longer produce the consequences that they produced previously. A type of punishment is defined as the response-contingent *removal* or withdrawal of a positively reinforcing stimulus. However, if the positively reinforcing events have been occurring frequently but not continuously, does their cessation constitute punishment or extinction? There will always be cases that lie on the boundary of ambiguity, but the analysis can often be clarified by assessing whether there has been a change of behavioural situation—in this case, definable more clearly in terms of change in contingency, rather than of change in frequency. Thus, the onset of extinction punishes the behaviour that preceded it; continuation of extinction constitutes a different behavioural situation, and the behaviour within that situation is best analysed separately. So, too, in applied settings the behaviour that *produces* a time-out situation must be analysed separately from behaviour *during* the time-out situation.

Usually the contingency between behaviour and events, and the density of those events, are both changed together in the transition from one behavioural situation to another, which accounts for contingency and frequency or density not having been clearly distinguished in the past. Thus, in the classical discrete-trial avoidance procedure, the situation transition included both change from shock to no-shock and a change from responses being effective to responses having no effect. D'Amato, Fazzaro, and Etkin (1968) came very close to distinguishing the two concepts when discussing an ingenious experiment that compared the effectiveness of response-produced onset of cues with that of response-produced termination of warning stimuli. Noting that the response-produced cue facilitated responding even though it had never been paired with shock, they suggested that both kinds of stimulus changes serve as 'discriminative cues for the shock having been avoided'. However, they did not quite draw the distinction between cue denoting absence of shock and cue denoting absence of contingency.

A change of contingency can produce a change of behavioural situation without the accompanying change in density of shock that is the usual product of the contingency. This has been shown by Bersh and Lambert (1975), who accomplished the training of a discrimination between presence vs. absence of light. Using Herrnstein and Hineline's (1966) probabilistic shock-deletion procedure (described above) for reinforcement in the presence of the light, and delivering shocks randomly at the same high probability in the absence of the light, they obtained differential responding in the two situations. Complementing this demonstration are studies of extinction with non-contingent shocks in which shock frequencies and distributions were matched to those produced during the days of conditioning that immediately preceded extinction (Coulson, Coulson, and Gardner, 1970; Smith, 1973, described in Hineline, 1977).

The combined role of added cues and contingencies between responses and shocks, for defining behavioural situations, is most clearly evident in the various experiments reported by Sidman and Boren (Sidman, 1957; Sidman and Boren, 1957b, c), and the experiment by Krasnegor *et al.* (1971), all of which I have described in detail above. In each of these, the change in a response contingency—whether a change in size of a ratio requirement or a change in the amount by which each response could postpone the next event—strongly determined the reinforcing effect of the transition from one situation to another. Recall that in one case, the change of response contingency for shock postponement resulted in a reinforcing effect of the transition from one situation to another, even though the transition entailed the delivery of a shock identical to those to be postponed. The other main group of experiments described above, dealing with short-term delay vs. long-term shock frequency, are similar to these, in combining added cues with response contingencies to delineate behavioural situations. Visual and auditory stimuli were used to enhance the situation change that accompanied a change of response contingency; the reinforcing effects of the transitions were used to assess the effective grouping of brief shocks *within* the situations, thus dissecting out the various aspects of shock frequency. The essentials of this strategy are especially evident in the experiment by Lewis *et al.* (1976), where responses produced immediate lights and clickers delineating the new situations, while the ongoing shock schedule did not change until some seconds later.

Added cues can help to delineate behavioural situations in at least one other way: they may be correlated simply with an opportunity to respond. As I have noted elsewhere (Hineline, 1977), this is one of the possible functions of the warning stimulus in the classical discrete-trial avoidance procedure, where intertrial responses were prevented by the experimenter. In some respects this function may appear redundant with the correlation between a stimulus and the contingency between response and its consequence. However, in any procedure where not every occurrence of the response affects a shock (intermittent negative reinforcement—e.g. *see* Dinsmoor, 1968), the two correlations are clearly distinguishable. Interestingly this feature, the opportunity to respond that partly defines a behavioural situation, is suggestive of Premack's concept for defining reinforcement (Premack, 1959). There, the opportunity to engage in high probability behaviour is said to reinforce lower probability behaviour upon which it is made contingent. The converse probabilities can be used to define punishment (Premack, 1971). In most applications and demonstrations of Premack's concept, the opportunities to respond have been manipulated, rather that the responses themselves. Further, these opportunities have often been made clearly discriminable through use of added cues; the role of these cues bears examining. Also, the present rubric suggests a further analysis of Premack-type relationships, by distinguishing *transitions to the opportunities* to emit high probability responses from actual occurrence of those responses.

Premack's formulation has been refined and extended by Allison and Timberlake (1974), who showed that the baseline frequencies and momentary response probabilities had to be taken into account. Like Premack's their formulation defines a behavioural situation primarily in terms of the opportunity to engage in behaviour of a given relative probability. However, Allison (1978) has recently argued that more than relative response probabilities enter into a response-based definition of reinforcement:

A more satisfactory predictive model must incorporate not only the baseline level of the instrumental response and that of the contingent response, but also the schedule requirements, the character of each response in relation to the other, and the behavior required in simply switching from each to the other. (Allison, 1978, p. 557)

The analysis that Allison suggests is closely akin to the one that I have sketched above. Some of the relevant experiments would resemble those that I have described here, but with shock deliveries replaced by food deliveries, water deliveries, and clutch releases in running wheels.

Clearly, the study of negative reinforcement is merging with the mainstream of modern behaviour theory. 'Avoidance', as a distinct phenomenon to be explained, loses its separate identity when we analyse the controlling variables that are embedded, often redundantly, in its classical defining procedure. 'Warning stimuli' are seen not as providing Pavlovian props for bridging gaps in time, but rather as correlating with several variables that contribute to the maintenance of behaviour. To be sure, warning stimuli can have Pavlovian characteristics; I would describe these as helping to delineate changes of shock distribution or density. But their effects an operant behaviour, like those of other added cues, appear to occur mainly through discriminative functions. They delineate changes of contingent relations between responses and shocks, and between responses and other consequences. In their multiplicity, these several variables contrast with the apparently elegant smplicity of two-process avoidance theory. However, the complexity is comprehensible when these variables are organized in terms of behavioural situations, with transition between situations identified as one class of reinforcing events. Further, these variables account for a range of experiments well beyond the purview of traditional avoidance theory. They show promise for orderly descriptive analysis of complex behaviour of complex organisms, in both simple and complex environments.

Note

I wish to thank Philip J. Bersh for his helpful comments on a preliminary version of this manuscript, and Charles F. Reed for his assistance in preparing a computer-generated figure. Some of the research reported herein was supported by grants from the National Institute of Mental Health, and from Temple University.

References

Allison, J. (1978). Beyond the relational principle of reinforcement. *Journal of the Experimental Analysis of Behavior*, **29**, 557–560.
Allison, J. and Timberlake, W. (1974). Instrumental and contingent saccharin licking in rats: response deprivation and reinforcement. *Learning and Motivation*, **5**, 231–247.
Anger, D. (1963). The role of temporal discriminations in the reinforcement of Sidman avoidance behavior. *Journal of the Experimental Analysis of Behavior*, **6**, 447–506.
Badia, P., Coker, C., and Harsh, J. (1973). Choice of higher density signalled shock over lower density unsignalled shock. *Journal of the Experimental Analysis of Behavior*, **20**, 47–55.

Badia, P. and Culbertson, S. (1972). The relative aversiveness of signalled vs. unsignalled escapable and inescapable shock. *Journal of the Experimental Analysis of Behavior*, **17**, 463–471.

Baum, W. M. (1973). The correlation-based law of effect. *Journal of the Experimental Analysis of Behavior*, **20**, 137–153.

Bersh, P. J. and Alloy, L. B. (1978). Avoidance based on shock intensity reduction with no change in shock probability. *Journal of the Experimental Analysis of Behavior*, **30**, 293–300.

Bersh, P. J. and Alloy, L. B. (1980). Reduction of shock duration as negative reinforcement in free-operant avoidance. *Journal of the Experimental Analysis of Behavior*, in press.

Bersh, P. J. and Lambert, J. V. (1975). The discriminative control of free-operant avoidance despite exposure to shock during the stimulus correlated with nonreinforcement. *Journal of the Experimental Analysis of Behavior*, **23**, 111–120.

Black, A. H. (1971). Autonomic aversive conditioning in infra-human subjects. In *Aversive Conditioning and Learning* (R. F. Brush, ed.), pp. 3–104, Academic Press, New York.

Bolles, R. C. (1973). The avoidance learning problem. In *The Psychology of Learning and Motivation*, Vol. 6 (G. H. Bower, ed.), pp. 97–145, Academic Press, New York.

Bolles, R. C., and Popp, R. J. (1964). Parameters affecting the acquisition of Sidman avoidance. *Journal of the Experimental Analysis of Behavior*, **7**, 315–321.

Brady, J. V., Kelly, D., and Plumlee, L. (1969). Autonomic and behavioural responses of the Rhesus monkey to emotional conditioning. *Annals of the New York Academy of Sciences*, **159**, 959–975.

Clark, F. C. and Hull, L. D. (1966). Free-operant avoidance as a function of the response–shock = shock–shock interval. *Journal of the Experimental Analysis of Behavior*, **9**, 641–647.

Coulson, G., Coulson, V., and Gardner, L. (1970). The effect of two extinction procedures after acquisition on a Sidman avoidance contingency. *Psychonomic Science*, **18**, 309–310.

D'Amato, M. R., Fazzaro, J., and Etkin, M. (1968). Anticipatory responding and avoidance discrimination as factors in avoidance conditioning. *Journal of Experimental Psychology*, **77**, 41–47.

de Villiers, P. A. (1974). The law of effect and avoidance: a quantitative relationship between response rate and shock-frequency reduction. *Journal of the Experimental Analysis of Behavior*, **21**, 223–235.

de Villiers, P. A. (1977). Choice in concurrent schedules and a quantitative formulation of the law of effect. In *Handbook of Operant Behavior* (W. K. Honig and J. E. R. Stadden, eds), pp. 223–287, Prentice-Hall, Englewood Cliffs, N. J.

Dinsmoor, J. A. (1968). Escape from shock as a conditioning technique. In *Miami Symposium on the Prediction of Behavior: 1967; Aversive Stimulation* (M. R. Jones, ed.), University of Miami Press, Coral Gables, Fla.

Dinsmoor, J. A. (1977). Escape, avoidance, punishment: where do we stand? *Journal of the Experimental Analysis of Behavior*, **28**, 83–95.

Dinsmoor, J. A. and Sears, G. W. (1973). Control of avoidance by a response-produced stimulus. *Learning and Motivation*, **4**, 284–293.

Ferster, C. B. and Skinner, B. F. (1957). *Schedules of Reinforcement*, Appleton-Century-Crofts, New York.

Field, G. E. and Boren, J. J. (1963). An adjusting avoidance procedure with multiple auditory and visual warning stimuli. *Journal of the Experimental Analysis of Behavior*, **6**, 537–543.

Fleshler, M. and Hoffman, H. S. (1962). A progression for generating variable-interval schedules. *Journal of the Experimental Analysis of Behavior*, **5**, 529–530.

Gardner, E. T. and Lewis, P. (1976). Negative reinforcement with shock-frequency increase. *Journal of the Experimental Analysis of Behavior*, **25**, 3–14.

Gardner, E. T. and Lewis, P. (1977). Parameters affecting the maintenance of negatively reinforced key pecking. *Journal of the Experimental Analysis of Behavior*, **28**, 117–131.

Herrnstein, R. J. (1969). Method and theory in the study of avoidance. *Psychological Review*, **76**, 49–69.

Herrnstein, R. J. and Hineline, P. N. (1966). Negative reinforcement as shock-frequency reduction. *Journal of the Experimental Analysis of Behavior*, **9**, 421–430.

Hineline, P. N. (1969). One shock now or five shocks later. Paper read at the Annual Meeting of the Eastern Psychological Association, Philadelphia.

Hineline, P. N. (1970). Negative reinforcement without shock reduction. *Journal of the Experimental Analysis of Behavior*, **4**, 259–268.

Hineline, P. N. (1973). Varied approaches to aversion; a review of Aversive Conditioning and Learning, edited by F. Robert Brush. *Journal of the Experimental Analysis of Behavior*, **19**, 531–540.

Hineline, P. N. (1977). Negative reinforcement and avoidance. In *Handbook of Operant Behavior* (W. K. Honig and J. E. R. Staddon, eds), pp. 364–414, Prentice-Hall, Englewood Cliffs, N. J.

Hineline, P. N. and Herrnstein, R. J. (1970). Timing in free-operant and discrete-trial avoidance. *Journal of the Experimental Analysis of Behavior*, **13**, 113–126.

Kamin, L. J., Brimer, C. J., and Black, A. H. (1963). Conditioned suppression as a monitor of fear of the CS in the course of avoidance-training. *Journal of Comparative and Physiological Psychology*, **56**, 497–501.

Krasnegor, N. A., Brady, J. V., and Findley, J. D. (1971). Second-order optional avoidance as a function of fixed-ratio requirements. *Journal of the Experimental Analysis of Behavior*, **15**, 181–187.

Lacy, H. M. and Rachlin, H. (1978). Behavior, cognition and theories of choice. *Behaviorism*, **6**, 177–202.

Lambert, J. V., Bersh, P. J., Hineline, P. N., and Smith, G. D. (1973). Avoidance conditioning with shock contingent upon the avoidance response. *Journal of the Experimental Analysis of Behavior*, **19**, 361–367.

Lewis, P., Gardner, E. T., and Hutton, L. (1976). Integrated delays to shock as negative reinforcement. *Journal of the Experimental Analysis of Behavior*, **26**, 379–386.

Logue, A. W. and de Villiers, P. A. (1978). Matching in concurrent variable-interval avoidance schedules. *Journal of the Experimental Analysis of Behavior*, **29**, 61–66.

McLeish, J. and Martin, J. (1975). Verbal behavior: a review and experimental analysis. *Journal of General Psychology*, **93**, 3–66.

Powell, R. W. and Peck, S. (1969). Persistent shock-elicited responding engendered by a negative-reinforcement procedure. *Journal of the Experimental Analysis of Behavior*, **12**, 1049–1062.

Premack, D. (1959). Toward empirical behavior laws: I. positive reinforcement. *Psychological Review*, **66**, 219–233.

Premack, D. (1971). Catching up with common sense, or two sides of a generalization: reinforcement and punishment. In *The Nature of Reinforcement* (R. Glaser, ed.), pp. 121–150, Academic Press, New York.

Rescorla, R. A. (1967). Pavlovian conditioning and its proper control procedures. *Psychological Review*, **74**, 71–80.

Sidman, M. (1953*a*). Avoidance conditioning with brief shock and no exteroceptive warning signal. *Science*, **118**, 157–158.

Sidman, M. (1953b). Two temporal parameters in the maintenance of avoidance behavior by the white rat. *Journal of Comparative and Physiological Psychology*, **46**, 253–261.

Sidman, M. (1955). Some properties of the warning stimulus in avoidance behavior. *Journal of Comparative and Physiological Psychology*, **48**, 444–450.

Sidman, M. (1957). Conditioned reinforcing and aversive stimuli in an avoidance situation. *Proceedings of New York Academy of Sciences*, **19**, 534–544.

Sidman, M. (1962a). Classical avoidance without a warning stimulus. *Journal of the Experimental Analysis of Behavior*, **5**, 97–104.

Sidman, M. (1962b). Reduction of shock frequency as reinforcement for avoidance behavior. *Journal of the Experimental Analysis of Behavior*, **5**, 247–257.

Sidman, M. (1966). Avoidance behavior. In *Operant Behavior: Areas of Research and Application* (W. K. Honig, ed.), pp. 448–498, Prentice-Hall, Englewood Cliffs, N. J.

Sidman, M. and Boren, J. J. (1957a). The use of shock-contingent variations in response–shock intervals for the maintenance of avoidance behavior. *Journal of Comparative and Physiological Psychology*, **50**, 558–562.

Sidman, M. and Boren, J. J. (1957b). A comparison of two types of warning stimulus in an avoidance situation. *Journal of Comparative and Physiological Psychology*, **50**, 282–287.

Sidman, M. and Boren, J. J. (1957c). The relative aversiveness of warning signal and shock in an avoidance situation. *Journal of Abnormal and Social Psychology*, **55**, 339–344.

Smith, G. D. (1973). Extinction of free-operant avoidance in rats. Doctoral dissertation, Temple University.

Ulrich, R. E., Holz, W. C., and Azrin, N. H. (1964). Stimulus control of avoidance behavior. *Journal of the Experimental Analysis of Behavior*, **7**, 129–133.

Weisman, R. C. and Litner, J. S. (1969). Positive conditioned reinforcement of Sidman avoidance behavior in rats. *Journal of Comparative and Physiological Psychology*, **68**, 597–603.

Predictability, Correlation, and Contiguity
Edited by P. Harzem and M. H. Zeiler
© 1981 John Wiley & Sons Ltd

Chapter 7

Effects of Experience of Electric Shock upon Subsequent Conditioning of an Emotional Response: Associative and Non-associative Accounts

Vincent M. LoLordo and Alan Randich

The UCS Pre-Exposure Phenomenon: Two Perspectives

In recent years the theory of Pavlovian conditioning has been enriched by several innovative characterizations of the conditions which promote associative learning. Rescorla's (1967) contingency view of Pavlovian conditioning was a fundamental reformulation of the necessary conditions for excitatory and inhibitory conditioning. Because it emphasized the importance of the contingency between CS and UCS rather than their temporal contiguity, this viewpoint stimulated the development of a variety of Pavlovian procedures in which there was not simply an invariant sequence of conditioned stimuli (CS) and unconditioned stimuli (UCS). Later, the Rescorla–Wagner (1972) model successfully predicted the outcomes of many of the sorts of experiments which arose from the earlier contiguity-and contingency-based positions on the basis of the discrepancy between the maximum associative strength which a given UCS would support and the combined associative strengths of all cues present on a trial. It explicitly recognized the importance of associations between background or static cues and the reinforcer, and suggested that because of competition for a fixed amount of associative strength, such associations would affect the formation of other associations between discrete CSs and the reinforcer.

These two theories of associations in Pavlovian conditioning generated interest in a host of new arrangements of conditioned and unconditioned stimuli, arrangements whose outcomes would have strong implications for the nature of conditioning. One such arrangement entailed presentations of the UCS alone prior to excitatory conditioning. Typically, exposure to a UCS prior to pairings of a CS with the UCS results in attenuation of the rate of acquisition of an excitatory conditioned response (CR) (*see* Randich and LoLordo, 1979a, for a review of studies of UCS pre-exposure). The contingency view would explain this outcome in terms of degradation of the contingency between CS and UCS, whereas the Rescorla–Wagner model would attribute it to the interfering effects of prior conditioning to background stimuli upon conditioning of a response to the discrete CS (*see* Tomie, 1980).

Although study of the UCS pre-exposure procedure gained impetus from new theories of association in Pavlovian conditioning, the procedure had been used a few times prior to the development of those theories, and had been viewed from a non-associative perspective (e.g. Kamin, 1961; Taylor, 1956). Generally, the authors of these earlier studies suggested that repeated presentations of the UCS resulted in habituation of some emotional response elicited by the UCS, and thereby attenuated conditioning of responses to stimuli subsequently paired with that UCS.

The UCS pre-exposure procedure, which has arisen independently from associative and non-associative perspectives, will be the focus of the present chapter. This procedure is an exciting and difficult one to study because both associative and non-associative factors may be contributing to its effect upon behaviour, especially when the UCS is electric shock. Thus far, the effects of prior exposure to an electric shock UCS upon subsequent Pavlovian conditioning have not been studied systematically, or with the aim of understanding the relative contribution of associative and non-associative factors, although several investigators (e.g. Anisman, 1975; Maier and Jackson, 1979) have discussed associative and non-associatives effects of prior experience with electric shock upon subsequent instrumental behaviour. In the present chapter, we have approached this goal by analysing systematically the effect of prior exposure to an electric shock UCS upon the subsequent acquisition of the conditioned emotional response (CER) (Estes and Skinner, 1941). Several associative accounts of the effects of prior exposure to the UCS upon conditioning will be evaluated in light of the outcomes of these experiments. Then we shall propose a non-associative account, based on the opponent-process theory of motivation (Solomon and Corbit, 1974). Finally, we shall discuss the implications of this account for several phenomena of aversive conditioning.

Basic Outcomes

Our first task was to ascertain the effects of prior exposure to varying numbers of electric shock UCSs upon the subsequent acquisition of a CER. The experiment had three phases: baseline training, pre-exposure to shock, and conditioning of an emotional response to a signal paired with shock. In the baseline training phase, five groups of food-deprived rats ($N = 8$ per group) were trained to press a lever for food reinforcers delivered on a VI 1 min schedule. Then four groups were pre-exposed to unsignalled electric shocks for 1, 3, 5, or 10 days. A fifth group of rats was not pre-exposed to shock. Electric shocks were nominally, 0.8 mA in intensity and 0.5 s in duration. Three shocks were presented during each daily 1.5 h session. The intershock interval ranged from 18 to 36 min.

The VI 1 min schedule of reinforcement was not in effect during the pre-exposure phase, and the response lever was removed from the chamber. Rats in the 0-day group (no pre-exposure controls) were simply placed in the chambers during each of 10 sessions, but received no shock. Rats in the 1-day group were placed in the chambers for 9 days with no shock, and were shocked on day 10. Rats in the 3-day and 5-day groups received shocks during the last three and five pre-exposure sessions, respectively. Rats in the 10-day group were pre-exposed to shock during 10 consecutive sessions.

Twenty-four hours after the last pre-exposure session, the response levers were reinserted in the chambers, the VI 1 min schedule of food reinforcement was reinstated, and the CER procedure was initiated. There were no baseline recovery sessions. During six consecutive daily sessions all groups received presentations of a 3 min white noise conditioned stimulus which terminated with presentation of a 0.8 mA, 0.5 s electric shock. Three CS–UCS pairings occurred during each 1.5 h session.

Figure 7.1 presents mean trial-by-trial suppression ratios for the various groups over the 6 days of the CER procedure. Suppression ratios were calculated as $(B/(A + B))$, where B is the number of responses emitted during the 3 min CS and A is the number of responses emitted during the 3 min period immediately preceding the CS (Annau and Kamin, 1961). Figure 7.1 indicates that the

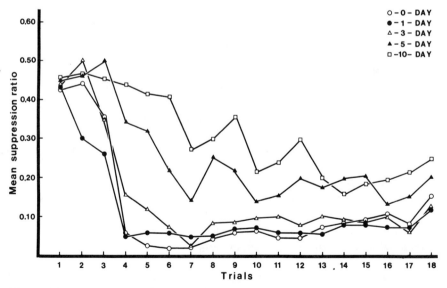

Figure 7.1. Mean trial-by-trial suppression ratios during CER conditioning for the various groups of Experiment 1

magnitude of the effect of prior exposures to shock upon acquisition of the CER does not increase as a simple, direct function of the number of days of pre-exposure. The 1-day group acquired conditioned suppression at a significantly faster rate than the 0-day group, whereas the 3-, 5-, and 10-day groups acquired conditioned suppression at a significantly slower rate than the 0-day group. Moreover, the magnitude of the attenuation of CER acquisition produced by multiple sessions of pre-exposure to shock increased as the number of pre-exposure sessions increased. These results are not confounded by between-groups differences in baseline rates of lever pressing during the CER sessions (cf. Randich and LoLordo, 1979b).

Thus, acquisition of the conditioned emotional response is enhanced by limited prior exposure to electric shock. However, as the number of sessions of pre-exposure to shock increases, acquisition of the CER is progressively retarded with reference to a no pre-exposure control group. The first outcome is novel, since only attenuation of conditioning has been observed when the number of prior presentations of the UCS has been varied in studies of the eyelid response in humans (Hobson, 1968), the nictitating membrane response in rabbits (Mis and Moore, 1973), and taste aversions in rats (Braveman, 1975; Cannon, Berman, Baker, and Atkinson, 1975; Elkins, 1974; Goudie, Thornton, and Wheeler, 1976; Vogel, 1974).

The non-monotonicity of the function relating the number of prior exposures to shock and the rate of acquisition of the CER suggests that two processes are affecting the emotional impact of the UCS, as reflected by its ability to produce conditioned suppression. This suggestion is plausible in the light of studies which have assessed time-dependent changes in aversively motivated behaviours following exposure to uncontrollable electric shock (Anisman, 1975, 1977; Anisman, de Catanzaro, and Remington, 1978; Pinel and Mucha, 1973a). These studies, which differ from our first experiment in many respects, have demonstrated that one of the after-effects of the first exposure to either signalled or unsignalled electric shock is an increased propensity to react to subsequent electric shocks or signals for shocks with strong suppression of locomotor activity. In contrast, when electric shock has been reintroduced and repeatedly presented at some time after the initial exposure to shock, suppression of activity is attenuated. If these effects on reactivity to shock are relevant for the changes in conditioned suppression observed in our experiment, then some aspect of the rat's behaviour following shock presentations should also reveal a non-monotonic effect of the number of prior exposures to shock.

Figure 7.2 presents an analysis of mean post-shock suppressiom ratios for the groups of Experiment 1. Post-shock suppression ratios were calculated as $(C/(C+A))$, where C is the number of responses during the 3 min period immediately following the UCS presentation on CER trials, and A is the number of responses during the 3 min period immediately preceding the CS presentation. Each data point represents the mean post-shock suppression ratio for the three

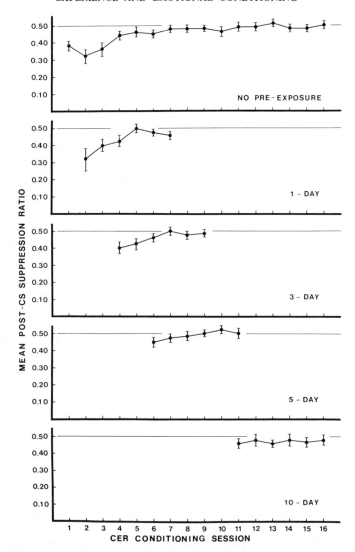

Figure 7.2. Mean session-by-session post-shock suppression ratios for the various groups
of Experiment 1

conditioning trials in a daily session (standard errors of the mean are denoted by
vertical bars). The post-shock suppression ratios for the groups pre-exposed to
electric shock are displaced on the abscissa to match the number of exposures to
electric shock with that of the 0-day (no pre-exposure control) group.

This figure shows that there is a marked increase in post-shock suppression of
responding during the second day of conditioning for the 0-day group (24 h after

their initial exposure to shock) and during the first day of conditioning for the 1-day group (24 h after their initial exposure to shock). The strong post-shock suppression of responding in these groups does not simply reflect carry-over of response suppression from the during-CS period. The 0-day group showed strong suppression of responding during the CS after day 2, but no post-shock suppression of responding on those days. More importantly, the 1-day group showed the greatest post-shock suppression of responding after their *first* CER trial, a trial on which there was no suppression of responding during the CS. For all groups, the magnitude of post-shock suppression of responding decreased as a function of the number of exposures to shock. Notice that for all groups combined, the magnitude of post-shock suppression of responding on a given trial is best predicted by the number of prior exposures to shock.

In Experiments 2 and 3, we attempted to learn more about the two phenomena observed in Experiment 1 by pre-exposing groups of rats to a wide range of intensities of electric shock and then conditioning with a common, intermediate intensity. Experiment 2 investigated the facilitation of CER conditioning obtained after a single session of pre-exposure to electric shock when the intensity of electric shock was varied between groups. Three groups of rats ($N = 8$ per group) were pre-exposed to three unsignalled, 0.5 s electric shocks of 0.5, 0.8, or 3.0 mA intensity during a single, off-baseline session. A fourth group of rats was not pre-exposed to shock. Twenty-four hours after the pre-exposure session, the response levers were reinserted into the chambers and a previously established VI 1 min schedule of food reinforcement for lever-pressing was reinstated. Then four pairings of the 3 min white noise stimulus with the 0.8 mA electric shock were superimposed on the baseline maintained by the VI 1 min schedule for all groups.

Figure 7.3 presents mean trial-by-trial suppression ratios for the various groups of Experiment 2 over the single CER conditioning session. This figure shows that all groups pre-exposed to a single session of electric shock presentation acquired the CER at a faster rate than the no pre-exposure control group, and that the magnitude of this facilitation effect generally increased as a direct function of the intensity of the shock used during the pre-exposure phase. Since all groups showed comparable levels of unconditioned responding to the novel white noise stimulus on the first CER trial, it is unlikely that pre-exposure to shock resulted in sensitization. As in Experiment 1, these outcomes were not confounded by between-groups differences in baseline rates of responding.

The facilitation effect obtained in Experiment 2 is formally similar to an outcome reported by Rescorla (1974). In the latter experiment, groups of rats received limited prior exposure to shocks of 0.5, 1.0, or 3.0 mA intensity, with each shock signalled by a salient, discrete CS. Subsequent acquisition of the CER to a novel CS paried with the 0.5 mA electric shock was a direct function of the intensity of shock used during the pre-exposure phase.

One possible explanation of these facilitation effects is that fear is conditioned

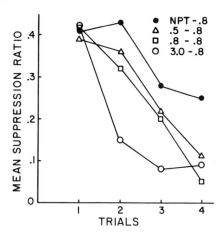

Figure 7.3. Mean trial-by-trial suppression ratios during CER conditioning for the various groups of Experiment 2

to contextual stimuli during the pre-exposure phase and subsequently summates with fear being conditioned to the discrete CS during the CER phase. This explanation has some force, given the direct relationship between UCS pre-exposure intensity and the rate of CER acquisition. However, the demonstration of the facilitation effect with a signalled pre-exposure treatment (Rescorla, 1974) and the absence in the present experiment of any changes in baseline rates of responding following pre-exposure to shock (which might be expected to reflect fear conditioned to contextual stimuli) raise doubts about the importance of the contribution of responses conditioned to contextual stimuli to these outcomes. Moreover, it is unclear how prior conditioning of fear to contextual stimuli would interact with conditioning of fear to a discrete CS in the presence of those contextual stimuli. For instance, there is evidence to suggest that fear conditioned to contextual stimuli might also interfere with or block (Kamin, 1969; Rescorla and Wagner, 1972) conditioning of fear to a discrete CS in the pre-exposure environment, thereby reducing the magnitude of the facilitation effect obtained in these experiments. Thus, the context conditioning hypothesis has a great deal of intuitive appeal, but loses force in the absence of any guidelines for predicting when fear conditioned to contextual stimuli will summate with and when it will interfere with, conditioning of a discrete CS.

On the other hand, if there is a progressive increase in the organism's emotional response to an electric shock following limited prior exposure, and that increase in emotional responsiveness is directly related to UCS intensity, and greater emotionally results in greater immobility, then one would also expect the pattern of results obtained in Experiment 2. Accordingly, post-shock suppression of responding during CER conditioning should also reflect such changes in emotional responsiveness to electric shock.

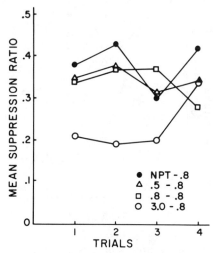

Figure 7.4. Mean trial-by-trial post-shock suppression ratios for the various groups of Experiment 2

Figure 7.4 presents mean trial-by-trial post-shock suppression ratios for the various groups of Experiment 2 during the single CER conditioning session. This figure shows that on the first two trials the magnitude of post-shock suppression of responding is a direct function of the intensity of shock used during the pre-exposure phase, as should have been the case if the initial exposure to intense electric shock resulted in a stronger tendency to suppress activity in response to shock than did the initial exposure to a weaker shock. It is important to note, however, that post-shock suppression ratios were determined from a 3 min time sample following shock presentation. Post-shock suppression of responding is maximal during the initial portion of this time sample and minimal during the terminal portion, thus a shorter interval would have permitted finer discrimination of the effects of the various treatments.

Experiments 3 and 3A investigated the attenuation effect obtained after repeated prior exposures to electric shock presentation, and thus varied the intensity of electric shock between groups during 10 sessions of pre-exposure to shock. The rats received 10 sessions of pre-exposure to shock because this parameter value resulted in a large attenuation effect in Experiment 1. In Experiment 3, three groups of rats ($N = 7$ per group) were pre-exposed to unsignalled, 0.5 s shocks of 0.5, 0.8, or 1.3 mA intensity presented at the rate of three shocks per 1.5 h session. A fourth group of rats was not pre-exposed to shock. In Experiment 3A, two groups of rats were pre-exposed to unsignalled, 0.5 s shocks of either 0.3 or 0.8 mA intensity presented at the rate of three shocks per 1.5 h session. A third group of rats was not pre-exposed to shock. Experiment 3A was conducted because we were unable to differentiate the rate of CER

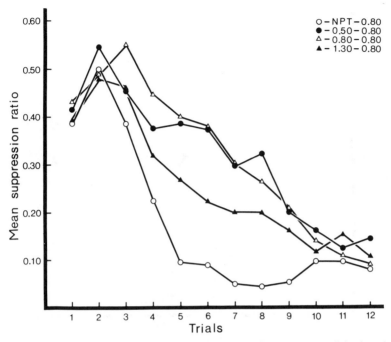

Figure 7.5. Mean trial-by-trial suppression ratios during CER conditioning for the various groups of Experiment 3

acquisition for the 0.5 and 0.8 mA conditions of Experiment 3. After the pre-exposure phase, a previously established VI 1 min schedule of reinforcement was reinstated, and all groups received repeated trials on which a 3 min white noise stimulus followed by an 0.8 mA electric shock were superimposed on the baseline maintained by the VI 1 min schedule. Three CER trials were presented in each daily 1.5 h session.

Figures 7.5 and 7.6 present mean trial-by-trial suppression ratios for the various groups of Experiment 3 and 3A, respectively. These figures show that all of the groups pre-exposed to electric shock acquired the CER at a slower rate than the no pre-exposure control groups. Moreover, the greatest attenuation of CER conditioning occurred in the groups both pre-exposed and conditioned with the same shock intensity, i.e. groups 0.8–0.8. Any shift in shock intensity between pre-exposure and CER conditioning promoted faster acquisition of the CER relative to the non-shifted group, and this effect was independent of the direction of the shift in shock intensity. This summary statement also correctly describes results obtained by Kamin (1961), who pre-exposed groups of rats to electric shocks of 0, 0.28, 0.49, or 0.85 mA intensity for 10 sessions, and found that the rate of acquisition of conditioned suppression to a CS subsequently

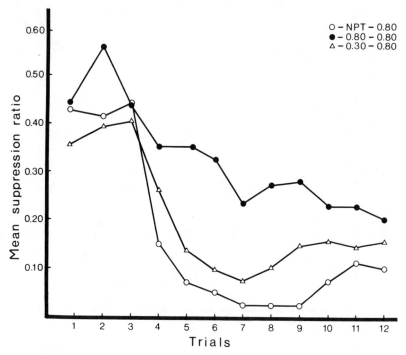

Figure 7.6. Mean trial-by-trial suppression ratios during CER conditioning for the various groups of Experiment 3A

paired with a 0.85 mA shock was inversely related to the shock intensity in pre-exposure.

Thus, not only are there two different effects of prior exposure to electric shock on CER acquisition, i.e. facilitation and attenuation, but shifts in shock intensity between pre-exposure and CER conditioning phases have different effects in the two cases. The facilitation effect is directly related to UCS pre-exposure intensity, whereas the attenuation effect is an inverted U-shaped function of UCS pre-exposure intensity.

Several experiments using UCSs and response systems other than foot shock and the CER also have examined the effects of the intensity or concentration of the UCS during pre-exposure upon the magnitude of the attenuation effect. In studies of human eyelid conditioning with an air puff UCS (Taylor, 1956), conditioning of the rabbit's nictitating membrane response to para-orbital shock (Mis and Moore, 1973), and conditioning of an aversion to a taste paired with lithium chloride in rats (Cannon *et al.*, 1975) the magnitude of the attenuation effect was directly related to UCS intensity or concentration during pre-exposure, even when all groups received a low or intermediate UCS intensity or concentration during conditioning. These findings contrast with the inverted U-shaped function relating the UCS intensity during pre-exposure to the magnitude of the attenuation effect obtained in Experiments 3 and 3A.

The different functions yielded by different response systems have important implications for understanding the mechanisms of the attenuation effect. A context conditioning account, for instance, would hold that pre-exposure to 1.3 mA electric shocks should condition the context to a greater extent than pre-exposure to 0.8 mA electric shocks. This should result in slower acquisition of the CER in group 1.3–0.8 than in group 0.8–0.8 because there should be less associative strength available for conditioning to the added element, i.e. the CS, in the former group. Thus, the context blocking hypothesis predicts the pattern of results obtained in experiments using the eyelid response in humans, the nictitating membrane response in rabbits, and taste aversion learning in rats. However, such a view would have to be modified to account for the inverted U-shaped function obtained in Experiments 3 and 3A, by assuming that shifts in UCS intensity between pre-exposure and CER conditioning result in stimulus generalization decrement of the associative strength of contextual stimuli (where the UCS is considered a salient aspect of the context). Such a decrement in the associative strength of context should result in a decrease in context blocking. However, granting this possibility, why is stimulus generalization decrement only manifested in the CER paradigm, and not in the other conditioning paradigms?

Since shifts in UCS intensity between pre-exposure and CER conditioning promoted faster acquisition of the CER relative to the non-shifted group in Experiments 3 and 3A, it might be expected that such shifts enhanced emotional responsiveness. Thus, post-shock suppression of responding in UCS intensity shifted groups should be relatively greater than post-shock suppression of responding in a non-shifted group, but all UCS pre-exposed groups should show less post-shock suppression of responding than a no pre-exposure control group. Figure 7.7, which presents mean trial-by-trial post-shock suppression ratios for the various groups of Experiment 3 during the CER conditioning sessions, tends to confirm these predictions. This figure shows that UCS intensity-shifted groups, i.e. groups 0.5–0.8 and 1.3–0.8, shows greater post-shock suppression of responding during the initial CER conditioning trials than the non-shifted group, i.e. 0.8–0.8. Thereafter, UCS intensity-shifted groups rapidly recover and show virtually no post-shock suppression of responding. Generally, the no pre-exposure control group shows greater post-shock suppression of responding than groups that were pre-exposed to shock. However, on the first two trials the no pre-exposure controls actually show less post-shock suppression than group 1.3–0.8. Later in conditioning, the no pre-exposure control group gradually recovers and shows little post-shock suppression of responding (see Figure 7.2 for comparable outcomes in the 0-day and 10-day groups). Thus, one might tentatively conclude that shifts in UCS intensity between pre-exposure and CER conditioning result in a transient increase in emotional responsiveness to electric

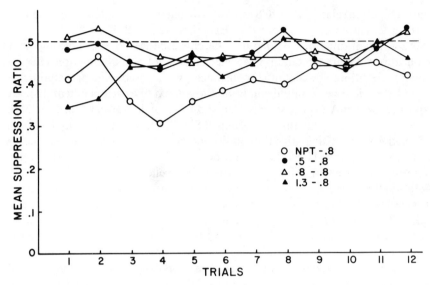

Figure 7.7. Mean trial-by-trial post-shock suppression ratios for the various groups of Experiment 3

shock which promotes faster acquisition of the CER than in a non-shifted group, but that the rats rapidly adapt to the new UCS intensity and do not attain the level of emotional responsiveness of the no pre-exposure controls.

A Context Blocking Account of the Attenuation Effect

One associative explanation of the attenuating effect of repeated prior exposure to shock upon subsequent acquisition of the CER has been mentioned earlier in this chapter. According to this context blocking hypothesis (Tomie, 1976, 1980), prior exposure to the UCS results in the conditioning of fear to some aspect, call it stimulus X, of the experimental environment. Stimulus X may be some static cue provided by the characteristics of the experimental environment, or perhaps some cue provided by the handling procedure which precedes the experimental session. Prior conditioning of fear to stimulus X blocks conditioning of fear to the discrete CS (A) when that CS is repeatedly paired with the UCS in the same environment (i.e. when AX is followed by the UCS). This result is said to occur because the UCS can support only a limited amount of associative strength, and most of the associative strength has already been acquired by stimulus X (Rescorla and Wagner, 1972), or because context (X) is a better predictor of the UCS than is the CS, causing the latter to lose salience and acquire associative strength more slowly than a non-pre-exposed control (Mackintosh, 1975).

We have performed three experiments which assess the contribution of context blocking to the attenuation effect we have observed. Experiment 4 was similar in design to Experiments 3 and 3A, except that all shocks were preceded by a salient, visual stimulus during pre-exposure. This stimulus should overshadow the presumably less salient contextual cues during pre-exposure, resulting in little, if any, fear conditioning to context. If pre-exposure to signalled shocks yields weak fear conditioning to context, then according to the context blocking account such pre-exposure should not result in a robust attenuation effect.

Four groups of rats ($N = 8$ per group) were pre-exposed to electric shocks of either 0 mA (no pre-exposure controls), 0.5 mA, 0.8 mA, or 1.3 mA. Each shock was preceded by a 3 min visual stimulus, illumination of a white houselight. The no pre-exposure control group received presentations of the visual stimulus alone. All other aspects of the pre-exposure and CER phases of the experiment were as in Experiment 3. Twenty-four hours after the last trial of CER conditioning all rats received a single presentation of the white noise CS, and a single presentation of a compound stimulus composed of the white noise used during the CER phase and the visual stimulus used during pre-exposure.

Figure 7.8 presents mean trial-by-trial suppression ratios for the various groups over the 5 days of CER conditioning. This figure shows that all groups

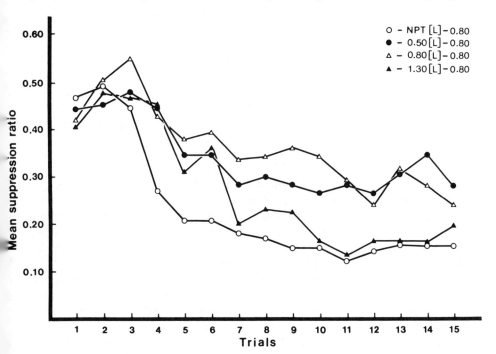

Figure 7.8. Mean trial-by-trial suppression ratios during CER conditioning for the various groups of Experiment 4

pre-exposed to signalled shocks acquired the CER at a slower rate than the group pre-exposed to the visual CS alone. Moreover, as in Experiment 3, the largest attenuation effect was observed in rats both pre-exposed and conditioned with 0.8 mA shocks. There is some suggestion that the magnitude of the attenuation effect was reduced by signalling shocks during pre-exposure. However, the magnitude of the difference between pre-exposed and control groups of the present experiment may instead reflect slower acquisition of suppression in the no pre-exposure control group of this experiment than in the control groups of the earlier experiments. That is, perhaps prior exposure to light alone retarded the formation of a CER to a white noise stimulus.

In the summation test which followed conditioning, the suppression ratios for white noise alone did not differ significantly among groups, but the suppression ratios for the compound declined as intensity of the pre-exposed shock increased, demonstrating that the magnitude of the emotional response conditioned to the visual CS during pre-exposure was directly related to the intensity of the UCS.

If it can be assumed that there was little conditioning of a response to context in this experiment, then the marked attenuation of conditioning which resulted from pre-exposure to signalled shock suggests that some process other than blocking is making a major contribution to the attenuation effect observed in our experiments. Several features of the experiment bear on this assumption. First, the absence of any changes in baseline response rate between the last day of VI 1 min training and the first day of the CER procedure, coupled with the absence of between-groups differences in baseline response rate on the first CER day, suggests that if a fear response was conditioned to the context, it was not directly revealed in performance. Second, other data from our laboratory indicate that when the visual CS which was used in the pre-exposure phase of this experiment is repeatedly paired with a 0.8 mA shock, there is rapid acquisition of the CER. In fact, the visual stimulus is roughly as salient as the white noise stimulus used in these experiments and will block conditioning to the white noise in a standard (Kamin, 1969) blocking design. Moreover, the summation test revealed that an emotional response had been conditioned to the visual stimulus during pre-exposure and that the magnitude of this response was directly related to UCS intensity. Third, the sheer infrequency of UCS occurrence during pre-exposure sessions (three times in 90 min) suggests that fear should not have been strongly conditioned to context, because, in the terms of the Rescorla-Wagner model, only one presentation in 10 of contextual cues was reinforced, whereas every presentation of the visual CS was followed by the UCS. Finally, since the rats received 10 sessions of lever-press training prior to the introduction of shock, latent inhibition of contextual cues should have occurred (Tomie, 1980). These considerations suggest that contextual cues should have been strongly over-shadowed by the visual stimulus during pre-exposure, and thus that conditioning of an emotional response to contextual stimuli is unlikely to be a major contributor to the attenuation effect observed in this study.

In Experiment 5 we conducted a second test of the context blocking account of the attenuation effect, using a design similar to that of Blanchard and Honig (1976). In their experiment, pigeons were pre-exposed to free food presentations in the presence of one stimulus (S +), but not in the presence of another stimulus (S −). Half the pigeons then received pairings of a key-light CS and food in the presence of S + whereas the other half received similar autoshaping trials in the presence of S −. The pigeons pre-exposed to food in S + and autoshaped in S − acquired the key-peck response significantly faster than pigeons both pre-exposed and autoshaped in S +. These results could be explained by context blocking, in which prior exposure to free food in the presence of S + conditions the S + context, and interferes with subsequent autoshaping of the key-peck to a discrete CS only when autoshaping trials occur in the presence of S + (see Tomie. 1980).

In Experiment 5 rats were trained to lever-press for food reinforcement as in the earlier experiments, but spent alternating 15 min periods in the dark (to-be-S +) and in the presence of an illuminated houselight (to-be-S −). Next pre-exposure was conducted off-baseline as in the earlier experiments. However, S + and S − continued to alternate as before. Two groups of rats received no shocks during this phase, but two others received a 0.8 mA shock sometime during each 15 min dark (S +) period. Thus these rats received three shocks during each of 10 pre-exposure sessions. Finally, the VI schedule of food reinforcement for lever-pressing was reinstated, and the CER phase of the experiment began. One group pre-exposed to shock and one control group received pairings of the white noise CS and a 0.8 mA shock only during S +, whereas the other pre-exposed and control groups received pairings of noise and shock only during S −. Only one conditioning trial was presented during a component, thus there were three trials per session.

The baseline rates of responding during the component in which CER trials were presented did not differ among groups. Moreover, none of the groups showed a reduction in response rate in the S + component on the first day of the CER phase, relative to their rate on the last day of baseline training. Such a reduction would have suggested that an emotional response had been conditioned to the S + context during pre-exposure to the UCS.

Figure 7.9 presents mean trial-by-trial suppression ratios for the various groups during the CER phase. This figure shows that the non-pre-exposed groups (NPT/S + and NPT/S −) acquired conditioned suppression at the same rate, but significantly faster than the two groups that were pre-exposed to shock (S +/S + and S +/S −), which were also equivalent.

Thus there was no independent evidence of changes in baseline rates of response to suggest that an emotional response had been conditioned to the S + context during pre-exposure to electric shock. Moreover, conditioned suppression was acquired equally rapidly by a group which received noise–shock pairings in the context in which it had previously been shocked and by a group

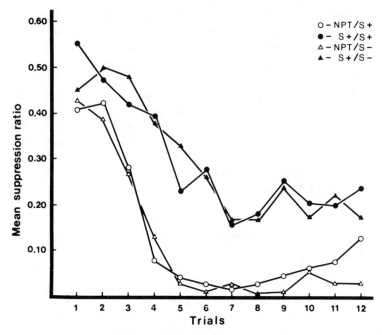

Figure 7.9. Mean-trial-by-trial suppression ratios during CER conditioning for the various groups of Experiment 5

which was pre-shocked and conditioned in different contexts. These results suggest that conditioning of a response to context during pre-exposure is not a necessary condition of the attenuation effect we have observed. Of course a counter-argument might state that although light and darkness were the most valid predictors of the occurrence of shock during pre-exposure, and are generally salient stimuli for the rat, they failed to overshadow some contextual cue that was common to S+ and S−, and that subsequently blocked conditioning of an emotional response to the white noise CS in both pre-exposed groups. Such a claim cannot be ruled out, although it must be pointed out again that baseline rates revealed no evidence of conditioning of an emotional response to any aspect of the pre-exposure environment.

It might be argued that Experiment 5 would have been more decisive if independent evidence of conditioning of an emotional response to context had been obtained, in the form of suppressed baseline rates in the S+ context on the first CER day. Had such an outcome been observed, and had the rates of CER acquisition of the two pre-exposed groups still been equivalent, it would have been reasonable to conclude that prior conditioning of an emotional response to context is not sufficient to retard acquisition of conditioned suppression to a discrete CS paired with the UCS in that context. It should be noted, however, that we are not claiming that context blocking never contributes to the attenuation effect. Rather, we are claiming that with the parameters used in our experiments the attenuation effect is largely the result of some other mechanism. The results of our next experiment were compatible with the latter claim.

The context blocking account predicts that the attenuation effect obtained after repeated prior exposure to electric shock should be diminished as the interval between pre-exposure and CER conditioning increases, if the rat is maintained in the presence of contextual stimuli to which the emotional response had been conditioned. This prediction is based upon extinction of the emotional response to contextual stimuli because they are repeatedly presented but not reinforced. If conditioning of contextual stimuli is reduced to near zero at the start of CER conditioning, then no blocking should occur (Rescorla and Wagner, 1972). The essential control comparison involves a group of rats that are also pre-exposed to electric shock, but which spend the delay period in the absence of the contextual stimuli. On the context blocking account, these rats should show no loss of the attenuation effect because there is no opportunity for extinction to occur. On the other hand, if these rats show a substantial loss of the attenuation effect, then it is reasonable to assume that a non-associative factor is important for producing the attenuation effect.

In Experiment 6, three groups of rats ($N = 8$ per group) were pre-exposed to three unsignalled, 0.5 s, 0.8 mA electric shocks in each of 10 sessions. One of these groups then received non-shocked placements in the experimental chambers for ten 1.5 h sessions prior to CER conditioning. A second group of rats which had been pre-exposed to shock spent a comparable delay interval in the home cages prior to CER conditioning. A 10 day delay period was selected after an earlier experiment showed that 3 days of non-reinforced placements in the chambers failed to produce any reduction in the magnitude of the attenuation effect produced by prior exposure to shock. A third group of rats which had been pre-exposed to shock received CER conditioning on the day following the pre-exposure phase. Finally, a fourth group of rats received no prior exposure to electric shock and was conditioned at the same time as the third group.

Figure 7.10 presents mean trial-by-trial suppression ratios for the various groups of Experiment 6 during the course of CER conditioning. This figure indicates that both the 10-day context extinction group and the 10-day home cage control group show a loss of the attenuation effect when compared to the group of rats conditioned immediately after pre-exposure to shock. However, both of the former groups still show some attenuation of CER conditioning relative to the no pre-exposure control group, e.g. on trial 3. More importantly, the 10-day context extinction group shows slightly greater conditioned suppression of responding than the home cage control group on CER trials 4–6.

These outcomes indicate that inserting a 10-day delay interval between pre-exposure to electric shock and CER conditioning results in a substantial loss of the attenuation effect, and that this loss can be enhanced by exposing the rats to

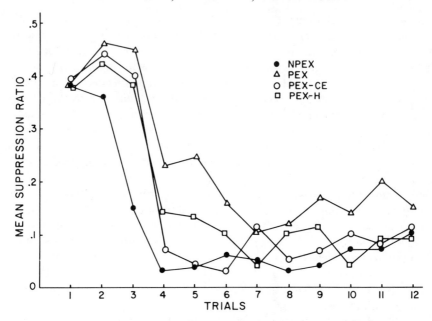

Figure 7.10. Mean trial-by-trial suppression ratios during CER conditioning for the various groups of Experiment 6

contextual stimuli. Thus some non-associative process seems to be important for producing the attenuation effect, and this process dissipates with the passage of time. In addition, there is evidence to suggest a role for contextual stimuli in producing the attenuation effect, although its precise nature cannot be specified by this experiment. For example, it is possible that a fear response was conditioned to contextual stimuli during pre-exposure to shock and was subsequently extinguished during non-shock placements in the chambers. Alternatively, one must consider the possibility that the additional handling received by the context extinction group in some fashion potentiated the loss of the non-associative factor, e.g. by acting as a dishabituator or altering arousal levels.

There are several published experiments which bear on the context blocking account of the attenuation effect. One of these experiments has used the CER procedure. Baker and Mackintosh (1979) observed a marked attenuation of the acquisition of the CER to an auditory CS paired with 1.25 mA shock following six 50 min pre-exposure sessions, in each of which the rats received eight 0.5 s, 1.25 mA unsignalled electric shocks. However, the attenuation effect was markedly reduced in a group which had received a visual CS prior to each shock during pre-exposure.

The basis of the discrepancy between this result and the results of our fourth experiment is not well understood. Baker and Mackintosh noted that with relatively weak shocks they obtained an attenuation effect even when shocks were signalled during pre-exposure. Since in our groups which did not receive intensity shifts shocks were 0.8 mA in intensity, as compared with 1.25 mA in the published experiment by Baker and Mackintosh, their suggestion that shock intensity was the basis of the discrepancy is a plausible one. However, the theoretical basis of the discrepancy is not at all clear.

Randich and LoLordo (1979a) have reviewed data from experiments on other response systems that bear on the context blocking account of the attenuation effect, and these data will not be reviewed here. To summarize the implications of these data, context blocking is a plausible account of the attenuation effect of free food upon later autoshaping (Tomie, 1976, 1980), and of prior injections of an emetic drug upon subsequent conditioning of an aversion to a taste paired with that drug (Cannon et al., 1975; Mikulka, Leard, and Klein, 1977), although it may not be the only source of the latter effect (Mikulka et al., 1977). Willner (1978) has provided evidence that cues associated with drug injections can be the cues that are responsible for the blocking effect; the normal attenuation effect produced by prior injections of a drug can be reduced by degrading the correlation between injection cues and the drug during the pre-exposure phase.

The context blocking account predicts that an animal pre-exposed to the UCS should eventually attain the same level of excitatory conditioning as an animal not pre-exposed to the UCS. This should happen because the UCS is presented only in the presence of the nominal CS during excitatory conditioning, and never in its absence. Thus the previously conditioned contextual cues should gradually lose associative strength, which should be gained by the discrete CS. Pre-exposed and control groups have attained the same level of conditioning in several studies which have presented a large number of CS–UCS pairings during excitatory conditioning (Holman, 1976; Kremer, 1971; Mis and Moore, 1973). However, a few studies have failed to obtain any conditioning of a drug-based taste aversion following pre-exposure to the drug, even with repeated CS–UCS pairings (Berman and Cannon, 1974; Braveman, 1975; Brookshire and Brackbill, 1976; Cappell, LeBlanc, and Herling, 1975; Cappell and LeBlanc, 1977). These are notable exceptions, however, because all but Braveman's study involved the use of UCSs which an animal will self-administer, i.e. D-amphetamine, morphine, or ethanol.

Finally, it is noteworthy that, as Baker and Mackintosh (1979) have suggested, the analogy drawn between the context blocking analysis of the UCS pre-exposure procedure and the typical blocking procedure using discrete CSs (e.g. Kamin, 1969) is not so straightforward. In the latter procedure, pairings of CS A and the UCS are followed by pairings of the compound CS AB with the UCS, and then the associative strength of CS B is assessed in a theoretically neutral context. If the context blocking analysis is applied to the UCS pre-exposure procedure, however, then the amount of associative strength acquired by CS B, the discrete CS in the second phase, is being assessed in the presence of A, the putatively conditioned contextual cue. From this perspective, it is surprising that summation of conditioned responses to context and the CS does not occur after a few trials, leading to a larger CR than in a non-pre-exposed control group.

Schull (1979) has recently proposed another associative account of the attenuation effect. Briefly, Schull maintains that the attenuation of conditioning of suppression to a discrete CS does not result from the prior conditioning to contextual cues of the same sort of conditioned response that usually results in suppression, but instead results from the prior conditioning of an opponent (compensatory) response to the contextual cues. During the subsequent conditioning phase this opponent response summates with, and thus at least partially cancels, the affective response to the UCS, thereby attenuating acquisition of conditioned suppression in response to the discrete CS. Although Schull's hypothesis and the context blocking account are different at a mechanistic level, the two accounts make identical predictions about the outcomes of Experiments 4–6.

Lack of Control Over the Pre-exposed UCS and the Attenuation Effect

Vogel (1974) proposed that an organism which is pre-exposed to an aversive UCS learns that the stimulus is uncontrollable. Moreover, this learning produces an associative deficit which transfers to the excitatory conditioning phase and interferes with the learning of the relationship between CS and UCS. This hypothesis is an extension of the 'learned helplessness' notion (Maier and Seligman, 1976), which would argue that the organism perceives the termination of the UCS during the pre-exposure treatment as uncorrelated with any of its behaviour. Perhaps learning that the UCS is uncontrollable interferes with formation of the association normally established by an excitatory classical conditioning procedure, thereby producing the attenuation effect.

Experiment 7 tested the controllability hypothesis by comparing the effects of pre-exposure to escapable and inescapable shocks upon subsequent acquisition of conditioned suppression.

After baseline training as in the earlier experiments rats were assigned to seven groups ($N = 8$ per group) for the pre-exposure phase. For four of the groups a chain-pull manipulandum was inserted through the centre of the Perspex ceiling. One of these groups was the no pre-exposure control group. These rats were simply placed in the chambers for 10 sessions.

Three experimental groups were pre-exposed to repetitive trains of electric shock of 0.5, 0.8, or 1.3 mA intensity. Each train consisted of 0.5 s shocks presented every 3 s for a 3 min period. Three trains of electric shock were presented during each 1.5 h pre-exposure session. The rats could perform a chain-pull response after the initial shock in a train in order to escape the remaining shocks in that train. Twelve sessions of escape training were adminis-

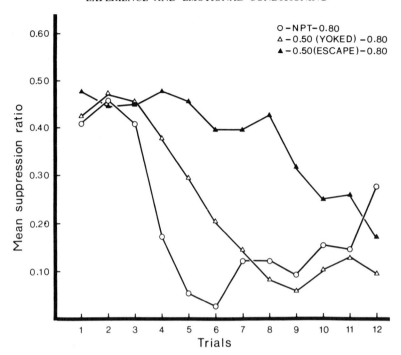

Figure 7.11. Mean trial-by-trial suppression ratios during CER conditioning for the no pre-exposure group of Experiment 7 and the groups that were pre-exposed to 0.5 mA electric shocks

tered, and the criterion for successful acquisition was a chain-pull response on every trial of the last five sessions of the pre-exposure treatment.

Each rat in an experimental group was assigned a yoked partner which received the same number, intensity, and temporal pattern of shocks, but could not perform a response to terminate the train of shocks.

The CER procedure, which began on the day after the last pre-exposure session, was as used in the earlier experiments. The UCS was 0.8 mA in intensity for all groups. The chain was not in the chambers during the CER phase.

Three rats in the 0.5 mA escape condition and one each in the 0.8 mA and 1.3 mA escape conditions failed to acquire the escape response. The remaining rats showed significant reductions in the mean number of shocks before an escape response.

Figures 7.11, 7.12, and 7.13 present mean trial-by-trial suppression ratios for the various groups in the 0.5, 0.8, and 1.3 mA pre-exposure conditions, respectively. Data from the no pre-exposure control group have been reproduced in each figure.

Regardless of the shock intensity used during pre-exposure, both the escape

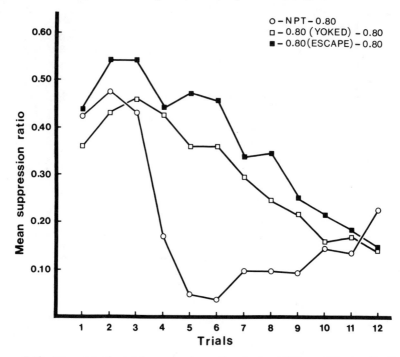

Figure 7.12. Mean trial-by-trial suppression ratios during CER conditioning for the no pre-exposure group of Experiment 7 and the groups that were pre-exposed to 0.8 mA electric shocks

and yoked groups showed a marked attenuation of conditioning relative to the no pre-exposure control. Furthermore, at each shock intensity the attenuation was greater in the group which had been pre-exposed to escapable electric shock. In the 0.5 and 1.3 mA conditions the latter difference is not confounded with differences in baseline rates of responding, whereas in the 0.8 mA condition rats in the yoked group did have a higher baseline rate of lever pressing than rats in the escape group.

It is noteworthy that the yoked rats in this experiment received many more inescapable shocks (50–70 per session) during the pre-exposure phase than rats in the previous experiments, yet the magnitude of the attenuation effect was roughly the same in the various experiments. This outcome suggests the possibility that the number of shocks administered within a session may not be as critical a parameter as the number of days over which those shocks are administered.

Allowing rats to escape shock by pulling a chain during the pre-exposure phase did not mitigate the attenuation of subsequent excitatory Pavlovian conditioning. In contrast, the data indicate that rats which had learned to *terminate* shock tended to acquire the CER at an even slower rate than did their yoked partners

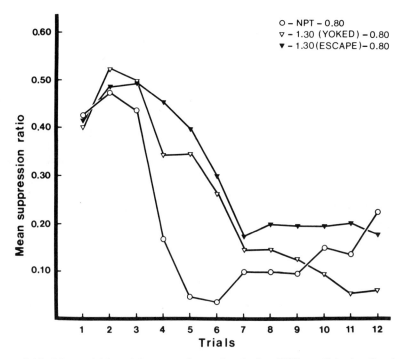

Figure 7.13. Mean trial-by-trial suppression ratios during CER conditioning for the no pre-exposure group of Experiment 7 and the groups that were pre-exposed to 1.3 mA electric shocks

which had been exposed to inescapable shock. These data indicate that Vogel's (1974) controllability hypothesis cannot account for the UCS pre-exposure phenomenon obtained with an electric shock UCS and the CER procedure.

The greater attenuation of conditioning produced by prior exposure to escapable shock cannot be explained by stimulus generalization decrement because there should be more stimulus generalization decrement following the transition from escapable to inescapable shock than in the yoked groups which received inescapable shock throughout. Thus, if stimulus generalization decrement were operating as a factor, then faster CER conditioning would have occurred in the escapable shock groups than in the inescapable shock groups. Similar logic would apply to an extension of an argument advanced by Lubow, Schnur, and Rifkin (1976), who found that the latent inhibition effect resulting from pre-exposure to a CS was reduced if that CS had been controllable. The argument would be as follows: the transition from controllable to uncontrollable shock would rearouse the organism's diminished attention to the UCS, and thereby promote faster conditioning compared to a group which received no such transition, i.e. the yoked group. Again, this view predicts a result opposite to that obtained.

Other accounts which can be brought to bear on the present phenomenon all entail the notion that escapable shocks are less aversive than inescapable shocks. Desiderato and Newman (1971) trained one group of rats to jump up to escape signalled shocks, whereas a yoked control group could not escape signalled shocks. When the signal was subsequently presented in a different environment while rats were bar-pressing for food, it produced greater response suppression in the rats which had received inescapable shocks. Desiderato and Newman (1971) concluded that stimuli paired with inescapable shock are more aversive than stimuli paired with escapable shock. If one incorporates this argument within a context blocking interpretation, then a stronger emotional response should have been conditioned to context in the inescapable shock group than in the escapable shock group, resulting in slower CER conditioning in the inescapable group than in the escapable group. Again, this was the opposite of the observed result. Osborne, Mattingly, Redmon, and Osborne (1975) also presented groups of rats with escapable or inescapable signalled shocks. Subsequently, the rats were placed in a hurdle box and allowed to escape the signal. Rats which had been exposed to escapable shocks in phase 1 had shorter latencies to escape the signal than rats which had been exposed to inescapable shocks in phase 1. Osborne et al. (1975) maintained that if the latency of hurdle-jumping is an index of conditioned fear, then the longer latencies of the rats given inescapable shock indicate less fear for this group. They offered two alternative accounts which would reconcile their results with those of Desiderato and Newman (1971). If either a greater freezing response was conditioned to a signal for inescapable shock than to a signal for escapable shock, or a tendency to respond actively was conditioned to a signal for escapable shock, but a tendency to respond with inactivity was conditioned to a signal for inescapable shock, then the greater conditioned suppression and the longer hurdle-jump latency of the inescapable shock group would be expected. This argument might be extended to the present situation by assuming that presentation of escapable shock resulted in a disposition to respond actively to shock or signals for shock, whereas presentation of inescapable shock resulted in a disposition to respond inactively to shock or signals for shock (cf. Anisman et al., 1978).

Although this argument accounts for the slower acquisition of the CER in the escapable shock group than in the inescapable shock group, it does not account for the fact that pre-exposure to inescapable shock retards acquisition of the CER relative to the no pre-exposure control group. Thus, this argument can only serve as a supplement to some more fundamental account of the attenuation effect.

The Fear Antidrive CR and the Attenuation Effect

One final associative explanation of the attenuation effect obtained following repeated prior exposure to an electric shock UCS can be derived from Konorski's

(1967) views on defensive conditioning. Konorski argued that the fear drive UCR elicited by an electric shock UCS is gradually antagonized by a fear antidrive CR which is formed as the organism learns that the occurrence of the UCS signals a period of time in which the UCS is unlikely to be presented again. In this view, the UCS is transformed into a CS eliciting a fear antidrive CR which summates with, and thereby reduces the magnitude of, the fear drive UCR simultaneously elicited by the UCS. This view predicts that a stronger fear antidrive CR should be established when the organism can use the UCS to predict a reliable shock-free period of time. For example, electric shocks presented on a fixed time (FT) basis during a pre-exposure treatment should result in a stronger fear antidrive CR than shocks presented on a variable time (VT) basis, especially when the distribution of VT intervals includes some very short intervals. Therefore, rats pre-exposed to electric shock on a VT basis should show less attenuation of CER conditioning than rats pre-exposed to shock on a FT basis.

In Experiment 8, two groups of rats were pre-exposed to unsignalled, 0.5 s 0.8 mA electric shocks for 10 sessions. Three shocks were presented in each session. For one group of rats, shock presentations occurred every 22.5 min. For the second group of rats, shock presentations occurred on a VT basis according

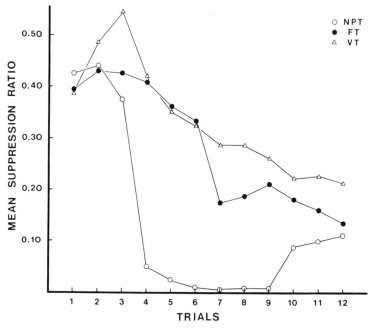

Figure 7.14. Mean trial-by-trial suppression ratios during CER conditioning for the various groups of Experiment 8

to an exponential function with a range of intervals between 0.5 and 87.0 min. A third group of rats was not pre-exposed to shock. All groups then received CER conditioning in which a 3 min white noise stimulus was repeatedly paired with the 0.8 mA shock as in the earlier experiments.

Figure 7.14 presents mean trial-by-trial suppression ratios for the various groups of Experiment 8 during CER conditioning. In general, this figure shows that both groups of rats pre-exposed to electric shock acquired the CER at a slower rate than the no pre-exposure control group, and that there were no major differences between the FT and VT treatments. If any difference between the FT and VT groups is suggested by Figure 7.14, it is that the VT group tended to show greater attenuation of CER conditioning than the FT group during the later stages of CER conditioning. Thus, it would appear unlikely that the attenuation effect obtained following repeated prior exposure to an electric shock UCS results from the formation of a fear antidrive CR, at least as hypothesized by the associative account of Konorski (1967).

The Basic Model

The outcomes of the experiments reported in this chapter suggest that the facilitating and attenuating effects of prior exposure to an electric shock UCS on the acquisition of a CER primarily reflect non-associative changes in emotional reactivity to shock, as expressed in suppression of appetitive responding. Among the various associative hypotheses we have considered, all of which bear on only the attenuation effect, only conditioning of contextual cues may contribute to the present outcomes. However, this factor does not appear to be the primary determinant of the attenuation effects observed with the parameters used in our experiments.

A modified version of the opponent-process theory of acquired motivation (Solomon and Corbit, 1974) can be used to account for the effects of prior exposure to an electric shock UCS on the subsequent acquisition of a CER. Although this account is primarily derived from the opponent-process theory of acquired motivation, the aggregate formulation represents an amalgam of information provided by studies assessing time-dependent changes in aversively motivated behaviours following exposure to electric shock (Anisman, 1975, 1977; Anisman et al., 1978) and experiments on the incubation of fear phenomenon and the Kamin effect (Anisman, 1975, 1977; Brush, 1971; Kamin, 1963; McMichael, 1966; Pinel, Corcoran, and Malsbury, 1971; Pinel and Mucha, 1973a,b; Robustelli, Geller, and Jarvik, 1970).

In this formulation, the magnitude of the organism's propensity to react to an electric shock UCS with behavioural response suppression changes as a non-monotonic function of its history of exposure to electric shock. An initial exposure to an electric shock UCS elicits a process, call it an *a-process*, which during the course of maturation increases the organism's propensity to react to subsequent shock presentations with strong behavioural response suppression (cf. Pinel and Mucha, 1973*a, b*). The strength of this a-process increases monotonically as a function of time after the initial shock exposure. Once the a-process attains an asymptotic value, it presumably remains asymptotic for at least several days, in the absence of any additional shock presentations (cf. McMichael, 1966). Since this a-process requires time to attain an asymptotic value after the initial shock exposure, it differs from the a-process which Solomon and Corbit (1974) characterized as being asymptotically large upon the first occurrence of the UCS. The present formulation of the a-process is more closely allied to Konorski's (1967) notion of a preparatory emotional UCR which must cross a critical threshold before an association is mapped into performance. Finally, the present formulation holds that once the a-process has been elicited, and has increased in strength with the passage of time, the organism will react to a shock presentation with *relatively* greater behavioural response suppression than was elicited by the *initial* shock presentation. The envelope of the a-process is depicted in the upper portion of Figure 7.15. Several features of this a-process may vary as a function of the UCS parameters. For instance, we would expect the a-process to reach asymptote within a matter of minutes with very intense electric shocks, but possibly require hours to reach asymptote with very weak electric shocks.

The present formulation also holds that a secondary process, call it a *b-process*, is activated with *each* electric shock presentation. This opponent b-process has the property of counteracting or antagonizing the response-suppressing property of the a-process. In this sense, the b-process can be viewed as an inhibitory process, but unlike the time-dependent a-process, is postulated to increase in strength as a function of the number of shock presentations. Independent evidence for these characteristics of the b-process is derived primarily from studies showing that (1) the rising portion of the U-shaped active avoidance retention function following a few escape/avoidance trials is not obtained unless shock occurs during the retention test (Pinel and Mucha, 1973*a,b*), and (2) the rising portion of the U-shaped activity retention function following exposure to either signalled or unsignalled shocks is not obtained unless shock occurs during the retention test (Anisman, 1977; Pinel and Mucha, 1973*a*). In the present formulation, repeated exposure to an electric shock UCS results in the formation of a strong b-process which, by counteracting the underlying a-process, restores the organism's propensity to react to subsequent shock presentations with a response similar to that observed on the initial exposure to shock. The b-process is also postulated to decay passively at a constant rate when the electric shock UCS is not presented (cf. Solomon and Corbit, 1974), thereby revealing relatively more of the underlying a-process. However, both the strength and the passive decay time of the b-process are increased by repeated exposure to electric shock. The envelope of the b-process is depicted in the lower portion of Figure 7.15. A few important features of this b-process should be noted. First, a

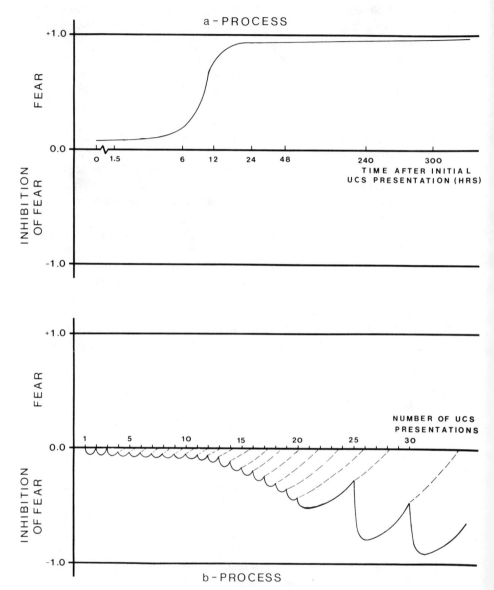

Figure 7.15. Functions depicting the hypothesized a-process (upper panel) and b-process (lower panel) of the modified opponent-process theory

b-process is elicited on the first presentation of electric shock. We assume that the magnitude of the b-process is weak at this time and the passive decay time is extremely short. However, with a sufficient number of shock presentations during an initial conditioning session the b-process may gain enough strength and passive decay time to influence the a-process after some extended delay interval, e.g. 24 h.

Thus, the a- and b-processes can be summarized as follows. The a-process (1) is elicited by an initial exposure to electric shock, (2) requires only time to attain an asymptotic value (minutes to hours depending on UCS parameters), (3) retains an asymptotic value for long periods of time, and (4) increases the organism's propensity to react to electric shock with strong behavioural response suppression. The b-process (1) is elicited by each electric shock presentation, (2) requires repeated exposure to electric shock to increase in strength, (3) decays passively when the UCS is withheld, but the passive decay time is lengthened with repeated exposure to shock, and (4) antagonizes the response-suppressing property of the a-process.

The resultant overall propensity to react to the electric shock UCS simply reflects the summation of the strengths of the a- and b-processes. The sum of these two processes describes a non-monotonic function because of the different variables postulated to be important for their formation. The resultant propensity to react to an electric shock UCS with response suppression is depicted in Figure 7.16.

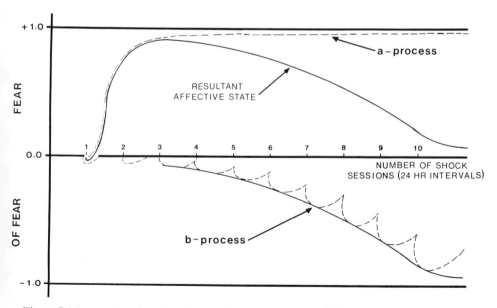

Figure 7.16. Function depicting the hypothesized resultant affective state for a rat given a typical pre-exposure treatment used in these experiments

This formulation of the opponent-process model can now be used to account for the data reported in the preceding experiments. First, consider the normal rate of CER acquisition in the no pre-exposure control groups. Typically, there is little or no conditioned suppression of responding during the initial CER trials of day 1 followed by a marked increase in conditioned suppression of responding on the initial CER trial of day 2 (24 h later). The absence of conditioned suppression of responding on day 1 is attributable to three factors: (1) the organism must form an association between the CS and the UCS, which requires at least one CER trial; (2) the a-process, elicited by the occurrence of electric shock following the first CER trial, has not had sufficient time to increase to any substantial value; (3) a weak b-process is elicited by each shock presentation. Thus, even if an association is established after a single CER trial, the model holds that it cannot be mapped into performance of conditioned suppression of responding until the strength of the a-process is greater than the strength of the weak b-process. The marked conditioned suppression of responding observed on the first CER trial of day 2 is also attributable to three factors: (1) the formation of an association on the preceding day; (2) an a-process of near asymptotic strength; and (3) a negligible b-process which has decayed with the passage of time. Hence, the rat reacts to the signal associated with shock as it would react to shock itself, i.e. with strong behavioural response suppression.

Several other features of the normal CER acquisition process should be noted. First, the marked increase in conditioned suppression of responding typically observed on the first CER trial of day 2 would be expected to occur on any similar trial administered after the a-process has attained asymptote. For example, if the rate of growth of the a-process increases as a function of UCS intensity, then substantial conditioned suppression of responding should occur within a short period of time after the initial conditioning session, or even within the initial conditioning session, if the UCS is quite intense. Second, extended CER conditioning should result in a loss of conditioned suppression of responding. This should occur because both the strength and the decay time of the b-process will be incremented with each CER trial, thereby counteracting the underlying a-process. Figure 7.17 presents mean trial-by-trial suppression ratios for a no pre-exposure control group extended CER conditioning with a 0.8 mA electric shock. This figure shows that there is a substantial loss of conditioned suppression of responding with extended CER conditioning.

The facilitation of CER conditioning obtained after limited prior exposure to an electric shock UCS (Experiments 1 and 2) can be accounted for in a similar fashion. In the present formulation, a group of rats which has received limited prior exposure to an electric shock UCS will react to the shock during CER conditioning with relatively greater behavioural response suppression than a group of rats which has not received prior exposure to shock. Thus, the association being established by CS–UCS pairings will be more directly mapped into performance of conditioned suppression of responding in a group

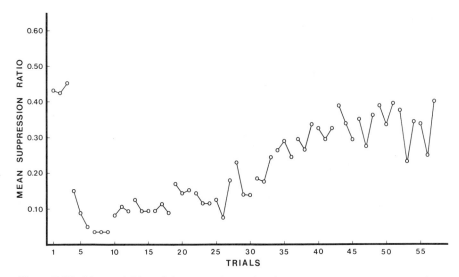

Figure 7.17. Mean trial-by-trial suppression ratios for a no pre-exposure group given extended CER conditioning

of rats which had received limited prior exposure to shock because the a-process will be stronger in this group.

Finally, the attenuation of CER conditioning observed following repeated prior exposure to an electric shock UCS is due to the antagonism between the underlying a-process and a strong b-process with a long decay time. Hence, the rats pre-exposed to repeated shock presentations are reacting to the CS being associated with shock as they would react to shock itself, i.e. with relatively less response suppression than in the no pre-exposure control group. The magnitude of the attenuation effect increases as a function of the number of prior shock exposures, since both the strength and passive decay time of the b-process are postulated to increase as a function of the number of shock exposures.

In Experiments 3 and 4, groups which received shifts in shock intensity between pre-exposure and CER conditioning phases showed faster acquisition of the CER than the non-shifted groups, but attenuation of CER conditioning relative to the no pre-exposure control groups. The present account includes no ready explanation of these effects of shifts in shock intensity, but would have to assume that the magnitude of the a-process, which carries over from the pre-exposure to CER conditioning phases, is directly related to the intensity of shock during pre-exposure. In order to account for the equivalent effects of shifts in shock intensity in opposite directions, we are forced to assume that the magnitude of the b-process is weaker in the shock-intensity shifted groups than in the non-shifted group at the start of CER conditioning. The implication of this assumption is that the a-process is ballistic in nature, whereas the b-process is an adaptational process in response to current conditions.

Some Implications for Aversive Conditioning

Changes in responsiveness to an electric shock or signals associated with shock may contribute to behaviours observed in a variety of aversive conditioning procedures. We will show how the formulation presented in the previous section may be able to account for some of these changes.

Warm-up in Avoidance Learning

The acquisition of discriminated avoidance behaviour is often characterized by between-session decrements and within-session increments in performance of the avoidance response. These effects are referred to as warm-up effects, and can be seen in Figure 7.18, from Hoffman and Fleshler (1962). Hoffman (1966) stated that the decrement in performance at the start of each avoidance session represented a motivational phenomenon; 'apparently as shocks occur, their motivational aftereffects persist and summate to creat an emotional state which somehow facilitates avoidance' (p. 513).

In contrast, the course of CER acquisition, particularly in an organism with some prior history of exposure to shock, is often characterized by between-session increments and within-session decrements in the magnitude of conditioned suppression. Figure 7.19 presents mean trial-by-trial suppression ratios for the 10-day group of Experiment 1. In this figure between-session intervals are denoted by the absence of lines connecting data points. Figure 7.19 shows the aforementioned characteristics of CER acquisition.

Thus, both between-session and within-session changes in discriminated avoidance are opposite in direction to changes in CER, but both are consistent

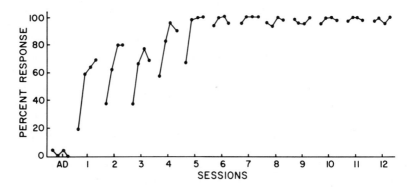

Figure 7.18. Percentage of avoidance responses per block of five trials throughout the course of acquisition of discriminated avoidance behavior. AD refers to the final session of tone adaptation when tones were presented without an accompanying shock. (Data are from H. S. Hoffman and M. Fleshler (1962) The course of emotionality in the development of avoidance. *Journal of Experimental Psychology*, **64**, 288–294. Copyright © 1962 by the American Psychological Association. Reprinted by permission)

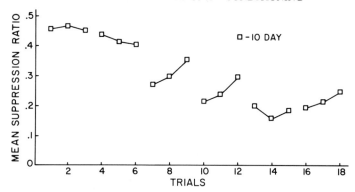

Figure 7.19. Mean trial-by-trial suppression ratios during CER conditioning for the group given 10 days of pre-exposure to electric shock in Experiment 1. Connected points represent performance on trials within the same session

with our expectations about the influence of non-associative changes in responsiveness to an electric shock UCS on these behaviours. In terms of the opponent-process model, any delay interval intervening between exposures to an electric shock UCS, e.g. 24 h separating conditioning sessions, will result in passive decay of a b-process, thereby revealing the underlying a-process at the start of each conditioning session. In the avoidance situation, this would result in a between-session decrement in the active avoidance response, since the organism will have a relatively greater propensity to react to the signals preceding the initial shocks of a conditioning session with enhanced response suppression. In the CER situation, this would result in a between-session increment in conditioned suppression, since the organism will have a relatively greater propensity to react to the signal associated with shock with enhanced response suppression. However, the magnitude of the between-session changes in performance of the avoidance response and the CER should be progressively diminished as the organism is repeatedly exposed to shock, since the b-process is postulated to increase in both strength and passive decay time under such conditions.

Similarly, the strength of the b-process should be maximally incremented during a conditioning session in which shocks are presented. In the avoidance situation, the growing b-process, which is increasing in magnitude with each occurrence of shock, would counteract the a-process and thus produce within-session increments in performance of the active avoidance response. In the CER situation, the same interaction of the a- and b-processes would result in a within-session decrement in the CER (*see* Ayres, Berger-Gross, Kohler, Mahoney, and Stone, 1979).

Hoffman (1966) reported that the between-session decrement in avoidance responding could be eliminated by presenting 40 unsignalled, inescapable shocks immediately prior to the normal avoidance session. This outcome can be seen in

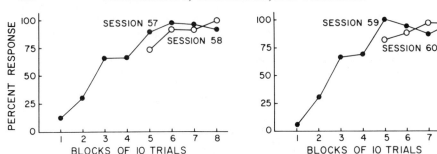

Figure 7.20. The reduction of warm-up by the delivery of unsignalled and inescapable shocks. The open circles show percentage avoidance responses during sessions (58 and 60) when the tone was disconnected and the lever was inaccessible for the first 40 trials. The solid circles show percentage avoidance responses during control sessions (57 and 59) when tones were presented on all trials and the lever was continually accessible. (Data are from H. S. Hoffman, M. Fleshler, and H. Chorny (1961). Discriminated bar-press avoidance. *Journal of the Experimental Analysis of Behavior*, **4**, 309–316. Copyright © 1961 by the Society for the Experimental Analysis of Behavior. Reprinted with permission)

Figure 7.20, from Hoffman, Fleshler, and Chorny (1961). In terms of the opponent-process model, shocks presented prior to the avoidance session would be expected to at least overcome the decrement in the b-process which had occurred between sessions. Thus, the warm-up deficit resulting from a between-session delay interval, and attributed to the manifestation of the underlying a-process, should be reversed by exposure to shock.

Punishment

Responding maintained by VI schedules of reinforcement is suppressed following a response contingent presentation of shock (e.g. Camp, Raymond, and Church, 1967; Church, Raymond, and Beauchamp, 1967). Although the response contingency plays a major role in the effectiveness of the punishment procedure, session-to-session changes in the pattern of response suppression resulting from a punishment procedure suggest that changes in responsiveness to the shock also contribute to the effectiveness of a punishment procedure. Figure 7.21 presents session-by-session suppression of lever-pressing for groups of rats responding on a VI 1 min schedule of reinforcement and punished with a 2.0 s duration electric shock UCS of various intensities according to an FR schedule (where one shock was delivered per minute if response rate remained unchanged) (the data are from Camp et al., 1967).

It is noteworthy that groups of rats punished with weak shocks show the same general pattern of response suppression as was observed in the no pre-exposure control groups of the present experiments. There is little or no suppression of lever-pressing during the initial punishment session followed by a

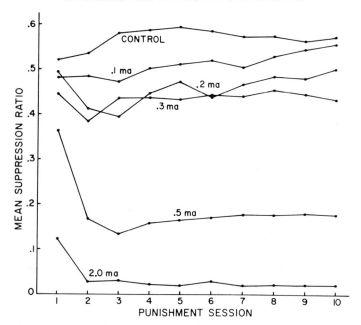

Figure 7.21. Mean suppression ratio as a function of intensity of punishment. (Data are from D. S. Camp, G. A. Raymond, and R. M. Church (1967). Temporal relationship between response and punishment. *Journal of Experimental Psychology,* **74,** 114–123. Copyright©1967 by the American Psychological Association. Reprinted by permission)

marked increase in suppression of lever-pressing during the next few punishment sessions. Finally, with repeated exposure to the punishment contingency there is a gradual recovery of responding maintained by the schedule of food reinforcement. The same explanation advanced to account for the normal acquisition of a CER in the basic model section can be applied to these results. In essence, it suggests that punishment will be most effective when the a-process has attained an asymptotic value, e.g. some time after the initial exposure to shock, and the b-process is relatively weak. In general, Figure 7.21 shows that the punishment procedure had its greatest response-suppressing effect during the second conditioning session.

A few other features of this figure should be noted. First, with intense electric shock, responding is reduced substantially during the initial punishment session. This could arise if the rise-time of the a-process increases as a function of UCS intensity (*see* 'Basic model' section). Second, groups of rats exposed to weak shock recover from the response-suppressing effects of the punishment procedure, whereas groups of rats exposed to shocks of high intensity do not recover. Perhaps groups of rats exposed to strong electric shock do not recover from the punishment contingency because they have received an insufficient number of shocks for the development of a strong b-process.

Blocking and Unblocking

This formulation of the opponent-process theory has implications for the blocking phenomenon (Kamin, 1969). Blocking refers to the situation in which prior conditioning of one stimulus (A) markedly attenuates conditioning of a second stimulus (B) in the compound stimulus (AB). A common assumption in all explanations of blocking is that if the added stimulus B provides no new information about the occurrence of the UCS, beyond that already provided by stimulus A, a response will not be conditioned to stimulus B (Rescorla and Wagner, 1972; Mackintosh, 1975). Although attentional factors may contribute to the blocking phenomenon, a reduction in the net affective A-state resulting from the formation of an opponent b-process during conditioning of stimulus A may also contribute to blocking. For example, if the opponent b-process is present in a reasonably strong form after conditioning of an emotional response to stimulus A, then conditioning of an emotional response to stimulus B in the compound AB would be retarded independently of the presence of stimulus A in either phase of conditioning. This view suggests that a group of animals receiving reinforced presentations of stimulus C followed by reinforced presentations of stimulus AB(C+/AB+) would show some degree of blocking relative to a group that received no treatment followed by reinforced presentation of the compound stimulus AB (no treatment/AB+). The results of Experiment 4, in which prior conditioning of a visual stimulus retarded the acquisition of a CER to a white noise stimulus, support such an interpretation.

It has been demonstrated that unblocking or conditioning of the added stimulus B in the compound stimulus AB does occur when the intensity of shock used to reinforce the AB compound is increased relative to the intensity of the shock used to condition stimulus A (Kamin, 1969). Dickinson, Hall and Mackintosh (1976) also showed that unblocking occurs when stimulus A is reinforced with two shocks in succession and the compound stimulus AB is subsequently reinforced with only one shock. These unblocking effects are typically attributed to the 'surprise' value of the novel shock used to condition stimulus AB, although the mechanism of surprise remains unstated. It is possible, however, that the use of a novel shock to condition the compound stimulus AB produces a temporary disruption in the opponent b-process, which permits conditioning of the added stimulus B (Randich and LoLordo, 1979a; Schull, 1979). This view of unblocking predicts that a group of animals receiving conditioning of stimulus A followed by a delay to conditioning of stimulus AB (e.g. 1 week) should also show unblocking or conditioning of the added stimulus B in the compound stimulus AB, because the opponent b-process should decay passively during the delay interval.

Note

Portions of this research were presented by the first author in partial fulfilment of the Ph.D. requirements at Dalhousie University. Some of these experiments were presented at the Psychonomic Society meeting, 1978 (San Antonio, Texas) and the Eastern Psychological Association meeting, 1979 (Philadelphia, Pennsylvania). The research was supported by grant A-9585 of the NSERC to V. M. LoLordo and by an I. W. Killam Scholarship to A. Randich.

We thank R. Klein, W. K. Honig, R. A. Rescorla, B. Schwartz, P. Urcuioli, and J. Willner for their constructive criticism of this research.

References

Anisman, H. (1975). Time-dependent variations in aversively-motivated behaviors: non-associative effects of cholinergic and catecholaminergic activity. *Psychological Review*, **82**, 359–385.

Anisman, H. (1977). Time-dependent changes in activity, reactivity, and responsivity during shock: effects of cholinergic and catecholaminergic manipulations. *Behavioral Biology*, **21**, 1–31.

Anisman, H., de Catanzaro, D., and Remington, G. (1978). Escape performance following exposure to inescapable shock: deficits in motor response maintenance. *Journal of Experimental Psychology: Animal Behavior Processes*, **4**, 197–218.

Annau, Z. and Kamin, L. J. (1961). The conditioned emotional response as a function of the intensity of the US. *Journal of Comparative and Physiological Psychology*, **54**, 428–432.

Ayres, J. J. B., Berger-Gross, P., Kohler, E. A., Mahoney, W. J., and Stone, S. (1979). Some orderly nonmonotonicities in the trial-by-trial acquisition of conditioned suppression: inhibition with reinforcement? *Animal Learning and Behavior*, **7**, 174–180.

Baker, A. G. and Mackintosh, N. J. (1979). Pre-exposure to the CS alone, US alone, or CS and US uncorrelated: latent inhibition, blocking by context or learned irrelevance? *Learning and Motivation*, **10**, 278–294.

Berman, R. F. and Cannon, D. S. (1974). The effect of prior ethanol experience on ethanol-induced saccharin aversion. *Physiology and Behavior*, **12**, 1041–1044.

Blanchard, R. and Honig, W. K. (1976). Surprise value of food determines its effectiveness as a reinforcer. *Journal of Experimental Psychology: Animal Behavior Processes*, **2**, 67–74.

Braveman, N. S. (1975). Formation of taste aversions in rats following prior exposure to sickness. *Learning and Motivation*, **6**, 512–534.

Brookshire, K. H. and Brackbill, R. M. (1976). Formation and retention of conditioned taste aversions and UCS habituation. *Bulletin of the Psychonomic Society*, **7**, 125–128.

Brush, F. R. (1971). Retention of aversively motivated behavior. In *Aversive Conditioning and Learning* (F. R. Brush, ed.), pp. 401–465, Academic Press, New York.

Camp, D. S., Raymond, G. A., and Church, R. M. (1967). Temporal relationship between response and punishment. *Jounal of Experimental Psychology*, **74**, 114–123.

Cannon, D. S., Berman, R. F., Baker, T. B., and Atkinson, C. A. (1975). Effect of preconditioning unconditioned stimulus experience on learned taste aversions. *Journal of Experimental Psychology: Animal Behavior Processes*, **1**, 270–284.

Cappell, H. and LeBlanc, A. E. (1977). Parametric investigations of the effects of prior exposure to amphetamine and morphine on conditioned gustatory aversion. *Psychopharmacology*, **51**, 265–271.

Cappell, H., LeBlanc, A. E., and Herling, S. (1975). Modification of the punishing effects of psychoactive drugs in rats by previous drug experience. *Journal of Comparative and Physiological Psychology*, **89**, 347–356.

Church, R. M., Raymond, G. A., and Beauchamp, R. D. (1967). Response suppression as a function of intensity and duration of punishment. *Journal of Comparative and Physiological Psychology*, **63**, 39–44.

Desiderato, O. and Newman, A. (1971). Conditioned suppression produced in rats by tones paired with escapable or inescapable shock. *Journal of Comparative and Physiological Psychology*, **77**, 427–431.

Dickinson, A., Hall, G., and Mackintosh, N. J. (1976). Surprise and the attenuation of blocking. *Journal of Experimental Psychology: Animal Behavior Processes*, **2**, 313–322.

Elkins, R. L. (1974). Bait-shyness acquisition and resistance to extinction as functions of US exposure prior to conditioning. *Physiological Psychology*, **2**, 341–343

Ester, W. K. and Skinner, B. F. (1941). Some quantitative properties of anxiety. *Journal of Experimental Psychology*, **29**, 390–400.

Goudie, A. J., Thornton, E. W., and Wheeler, T. J. (1976). Drug pretreatment effects in drug-induced conditioned taste aversions: effects of drug dose and duration of pretreatment. *Pharmacology, Biochemistry, and Behavior*, **4**, 629–633.

Hobson, G. N. (1968). Effects of UCS adaption upon conditioning in low and high anxiety men and women. *Journal of Experimental Psychology*, **76**, 360–363.

Hoffman, H. S. (1966). The analysis of discriminated avoidance. In *Operant Behavior: Areas of Research and Application* (W. K. Honig, ed.), Appleton-Century-Crofts, New York.

Hoffman, H. S. and Fleshler, M. (1962). The course of emotionality in the development of avoidance. *Journal of Experimental Psychology*, **64**, 288–294.

Hoffman, H. S., Fleshler, M., and Chorny, H. (1961). Discriminated bar-press avoidance. *Journal of the Experimental Analysis of Behavior*, **4**, 309–316.

Holman, E. W. (1976). The effect of drug habituation before and after taste aversion learning in rats. *Animal Learning and Behavior*, **4**, 329–332.

Kamin, L. J. (1961). Apparent adaptation effects in the acquisition of a conditioned emotional response. *Canadian Journal of Psychology*, **15**, 176–188.

Kamin, L. J. (1963). Retention of an incompletely learned avoidance response: some further analysis. *Journal of Comparative and Physiological Psychology*, **56**, 713–718.

Kamin, L. J. (1969). Predictability, surprise, attention and conditioning. In *Punishment and Aversive Behavior* (B. A. Campbell and R. M. Church, eds,), pp. 279–298, Appleton-Century-Crofts, New York.

Konorski, J. (1967). *Integrative Activity of the Brain*. University of Chicago Press, Chicago.

Kremer, E. F. (1971). Truly random and traditional control procedures in CER conditioning in the rat. *Journal of Comparative and Physiological Psychology*, **76**, 441–448.

Lubow, R. E., Schnur, P., and Rifkin, B. (1976). Latent inhibition and conditioned attention theory. *Journal of Experimental Psychology: Animal Behavior Processes*, **2**, 163–174.

Mackintosh, N. J. (1975). A theory of attention: variations in the associability of stimuli with reinforcement. *Psychological Review*, **82**, 276–298.

McMichael, J. S. (1966). Incubation of anxiety and instrumental behavior. *Journal of Comparative and Physiological Psychology*, **61**, 208–211.

Maier, S. F. and Jackson, R. L. (1979). Learned helplessness: all of us were right (and wrong). Inescapable shock has multiple effects. In *The Psychology of Learning and Motivation*, Vol. 3 (G. Bower, ed.), Academic Press, New York.

Maier, S. F. and Seligman, M. E. P. (1976). Learned helplessness: theory and evidence. *Journal of Experimental Psychology: General*, **105**, 3–46.

Mikulka, P. J., Leard, B., and Klein, S. B. (1977). Illness alone exposure as a source of interference with acquisition and retention of a taste aversion. *Journal of Experimental Psychology: Animal Behavior Processes*, **3**, 189–200.

Mis, R. W. and Moore, J. W. (1973). Effects of preacquisition UCS exposure on classical conditioning of the rabbit's nictitating membrane response. *Learning and Motivation*, 4, 108–114.

Osborne, F. H., Mattingly, B.A., Redman, W. K., and Osborne, J. S. (1975). Factors affecting the measurement of classically conditioned fear in rats following exposure to escapable versus inescapable signaled shock. *Journal of Experimental Psychology: Animal Behavior Processes*, 1, 364–373.

Pinel, J. P. J., Corcoran, M. E., and Malsbury, C. W. (1971). Incubation effect in rats: decline of footshock produced activation. *Journal of Comparative and Physiological Psychology*, 77, 271–276.

Pinel, J. P. J. and Mucha, R. F. (1973 a). Incubation and Kamin effects in the rat: changes in activity and reactivity after footshock. *Journal of Comparative and Physiological Psychology*, 84, 661–668.

Pinel, J. P. J. and Mucha, R. F. (1973b). Activity and reactivity in rats at various intervals after footshock. *Canadian Journal of Psychology*, 27, 112–118.

Randich, A. and LoLordo, V. M. (1979a). Associative and nonassociative theories of the UCS pre-exposure phenomenon: implications for Pavlovian conditioing. *Psychological Bulletin*, 86, 523–548.

Randich, A. and LoLordo, V. M. (1979b). Pre-conditioning exposure to the unconditioned stimulus affects the acquisition of a conditioned emotional response (CER). *Learning and Motivation*, 10, 245–277.

Rescorla, R. A. (1967). Pavlovian conditioning and its proper control procedures. *Psychological Review*, 74, 71–80.

Rescorla, R. A. (1974). Effect of inflation of the unconditioned stimulus value following conditioning. *Journal of Comparative and Physiological Psychology*, 86, 101–106.

Rescorla, R. A. and Wagner, A. R. (1972). A theory of Pavlovian conditioning: variations in the effectiveness of reinforcement and nonreinforcement. In *Classical Conditioning II: Current Theory and Research* (A. H. Black and W. F. Prokasy, eds), pp. 64–99, Appleton-Century-Crofts, New York.

Robustelli, F., Geller, A., and Jarvik, M. E. (1970). Biphasicity of the incubation curve. *Psychonomic Science*, 20, 129–130.

Schull, J. (1979). A conditioned opponent theory of Pavlovian conditioning and habituation. In *The Psychology of Learning and Motivation* (G. Bower, ed.), Academic Press, New York.

Solomon, R. L. and Corbit, J. D. (1974). An opponent-process theory of motivation: I. Temporal dynamics of affect. *Psychological Review*, 81, 119–145

Taylor, J. A. (1956). Level of conditioning and intensity of the adaptation stimulus. *Journal of Experimental Psychology*, 51, 127–130.

Tomie, A. (1976). Interference with autoshaping by prior context conditioning. *Journal of Experimental Psychology: Animal Behavior Processes*, 2, 323–334.

Tomie, A. (1980). Effects of unpredictable food upon the subsequent acquisition of autoshaping: analysis of the context blocking hypothesis. In *Autoshaping and Conditioning Theory* (C. M. Locurto, H. S. Terrace, and J. Gibbon, eds), Academic Press, New York.

Vogel, J. R. (1974). Prior exposure to a drug (US) attenuates learned taste aversion. Paper presented at the meeting of the Psychonomic Society, Boston, November.

Willner, J. (1978). Blocking of a taste aversion by prior pairings of exteroceptive stimuli with illness. *Learning and Motivation*, 9, 125–140.

Predictability, Correlation, and Contiguity
Edited by P. Harzem and M. D. Zeiler
© 1981 John Wiley & Sons Ltd

Chapter 8

Information Theory: A Solution to Two Big Problems in the Analysis of Behaviour

Michael B. Cantor

> The term 'information' in information theory is not "... syno-
> nynous with 'meaning.' Only the *amount* of information is
> measured—the amount does not specify the content, value, truth-
> fulness, exclusiveness, history, or purpose of the information. The
> definition does not exclude other definitions and certainly does not
> include all the meanings implied by the colloquial usages of the
> word." (Miller, 1953)

Introduction

The challenge to the learning theorist is to predict and control behaviour on the basis of a schematization of important events that occur in space and time. The achievement of this goal in the field of conditioning and learning is presently hampered by two big problems. The first is that the field is dominated by a false dichotomy between Pavlovian and instrumental learning. Each paradigm organizes the learning environment in its own special language. We have conditioned stimuli vs. discriminative stimuli; conditioned responses vs. operants; and unconditioned stimuli vs. reinforcers, to name a few. We have higher order conditioning vs. response chaining; inhibition of delay vs. fixed interval scallop; etc. The results are a language barrier that greatly hampers comparison among procedures and a data base wherein there are almost as many 'phenomena' as there are procedures.

The second major problem hampering the learning theorist is the metric of association, the means by which the relationship among important events in the environment is organized. The old view is that association between two stimuli (Pavlov, 1927) or between a response and a stimulus (Skinner, 1938) depends upon the contiguity between events, i.e. the time or distance between them. The newer view is that it is not the contiguity but the contingency between events that determines behavioural output. Rescorla (1967), for example, has said that

Pavlovian conditioning comes about when there is a positive contingency between conditioned stimulus and unconditioned stimulus and that contiguity is not sufficient. Similarly, Baum (1973) has said that it is the molar relation between responses and reinforcers and not contiguity that governs operant behaviour. What shall we take as the necessary and sufficient condition for controlling behavioural output? Contiguity, contingency, or some combination of the two?

The two problems can be solved and a synthesis forged if conditioning and learning experiments are conceptualized in the language of information theory (Cantor and Wilson, 1981, Shannon and Weaver, 1949). Information theory provides a single quantitative metric for specifying the information that one event provides about another regardless of whether the events are stimuli or responses. As such, it solves the double language problem of Pavlovian vs. instrumental learning by providing a common language and thus paves the way for a synthesis. Second, information theory can quantify with a single ratio scale both the temporal information of contiguity and the probabilistic information implied by the notion of contingency.

The problems outlined above will be addressed in the context of two main topics. In the first, I will argue that the Pavlovian vs. instrumental learning dichotomy is false by showing that the Pavlovian conditioning experiment engenders primarily instrumental behaviour in keeping with the preparatory view of Prokasy (1965) and Perkins (1968). As the second topic, I will show that the synthesis can be forged in terms of information theory. Pavlovian and instrumental learning experiments, then, will be thought of as experiments in communication between the experimenter and the subject where the focus of the communication exchange is an important event such as those stimuli that serve as an unconditioned stimulus or a primary reinforcement (Cantor and Wilson, 1981). The goal will be to show how information about important events is quantified and then show some of the underlying principles governing the relationship between information and behaviour that operate independently of the historically defined paradigm in which the experiment is performed.

Preparatory Response Theory

The preparatory response theory states that the conditioned stimulus predicts the moment of occurrence of the unconditioned stimulus and sets the occasion for the preparatory instrumental response which heightens the magnitude of reinforcement surrounding unconditioned stimulus presentation. An example of this process is the dog's conditioned salivary response which renders the meat powder, the unconditioned stimulus, more digestible and presumably more palatable. Another example is the conditioned eyelid closure which attenuates the effects of the aversive unconditioned stimulus. The preparatory response argument was first presented by Pavlov (1927) and later modified and extended by Schlosberg (1937), Prokasy (1965), and Perkins (1968). Gormezano and Coleman (1973) have recently reviewed the literature.

A crucial aspect of the preparatory view is the timing of the preparatory conditioned response. That is, for conditioned responses to be adaptive and reinforcing they must occur at the moment of unconditioned stimulus onset—not too early in the interstimulus interval and not after the unconditioned stimulus has already occurred. To simply wait until the unconditioned stimulus occurs rather than time its onset would not be effective, since unconditioned stimuli are usually very brief—about 100 ms in eyelid conditioning—and would terminate by the time that the subject reacts. That the conditioned response is timed was recognized by Pavlov (1927) as the 'inhibition of delay' phenomenon: the conditioned response occurs later and later in the interstimulus interval until it merges or overlaps with the unconditioned stimulus (see Levey and Martin, 1968). Pavlov's (1927) assumption was that the inhibition of delay phenomenon reveals that the animal makes the conditioned response at the optimal time for salivation and digestion, and thus argued for the operation of the law of effect in his procedure.

Tests of the preparatory/adaptive view have taken a number of forms. Some authors, for example, have offered animals a choice between signalled and unsignalled unconditioned stimuli such as shock (e.g. Perkins, 1968) or rewarding electrical stimulation of the brain (Cantor and LoLordo, 1970, 1972; Cantor, 1979). If the animal chooses to receive the signalled unconditioned stimuli it may be concluded that the signal somehow increases the rewarding value of stimulation either by decreasing the valence of negative stimulation or increasing the valence of positive stimulation. Only the choice response, e.g. percentage time in one choice or the other, is measured in such experiments, so the occurrence of a preparatory response can only be inferred. This literature has recently been reviewed by Badia, Harsh, and Abbott (1979). Other methods of testing the preparatory view have been reviewed and criticized elsewhere (Gormezano and Coleman, 1973; Cantor and Wilson, 1981)

Operant Simulation of Pavlovian Conditioning

Cantor and Wilson (1981) have developed a new way to test the adequacy of the preparatory response notion which has the following rationale: If Pavlovian conditioning engenders timing and instrumental preparation for the unconditioned stimulus, then a simulation of the hypothesized reinforcement contingencies using not a Pavlovian conditioned response but a traditional lever-press response should generate behaviour that is in minute detail like that generated by a Pavlovian contingency.

In the basic procedure, rats pressed a lever to turn on a light which coterminated t seconds later with a 150 ms train of reinforcing electrical brain

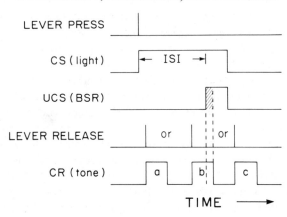

Figure 8.1. Operant simulation of Pavlovian conditioning according to the preparatory response view. The trial is initiated by the press of the lever. Overlaps (b) of the lever release-initiated duration (the simulated conditioned response) and the simulated unconditioned stimulus (brain stimulation) resulted in increased brain stimulation intensity during the time represented by the hatching. Early (a) or late (c) lever releases did not overlap the unconditioned stimulus and did not increment the brain stimulation intensity. (From Cantor and Wilson, 1981)

stimulation; this representated a self-administered Pavlovian delay conditioning trial. The lever release, the simulated conditioned response, was programmed to turn on a 150 ms tone. If the lever release was timed so that the simulated conditioned response and the simulated unconditioned stimulus overlapped (as depicted by hatching in Figure 8.1), then for the period of the overlap the brain stimulation reinforcement doubled in intensity (demonstrably increasing the reinforcing value). A time-out followed lever release, after which a discriminative stimulus came on to herald the opportunity to initiate another trial. Five hundred trials occurred in one session.

The first experiment asked what interstimulus interval is optimal for bringing about the acquisition of overlaps of the simulated conditioned response with the simulated unconditioned stimulus. If the optimal interstimulus interval in the simulation is 500 ms, as it is in conventional Pavlovian conditioning (Gormezano and Moore, 1969), then it supports the claim that the Pavlovian simulation captures the essential reinforcement contingencies inherent in Pavlovian conditioning according to the preparatory view. Three different interstimulus intervals of 500, 1000, and 2000 ms were tested with two rats each for 10 sessions. The results were that only animals with a 500 ms interstimulus interval managed to acquire the overlap of the conditioned response and unconditioned stimulus. One animal with the 1000 ms interstimulus interval showed some signs of acquisition. Animals with the 2000 ms interstimulus interval almost never came into contact with the overlap contingency by chance and thus never acquired the behaviour.

This experiment showed, then, that the operant simulation of Pavlovian conditioning may be correct. That is, an optimal 500 ms interstimulus interval is not peculiar to the Pavlovian procedure but more generally to a set of reinforcement contingencies of which Pavlovian conditioning is an example. The contingency requires that a subject withold a response and then make it within a very short time window. In operant terms, the reinforcement contingency is a trials-type differential reinforcement of low rates, limited hold schedule where the interstimulus interval is the differential reinforcement of low rates value and the duration of the limited hold is the duration of the unconditioned stimulus. In the usual Pavlovian paradigm, reinforcement is a modulation of the reinforcer magnitude rather than the all-or-none that occurs in differential reinforcement of low rates.

As a further test of the preparatory response notion, the operant simulation of Pavlovian conditioning was carried out with longer than optimal interstimulus intervals. If, as in traditional eyelid conditioning, response shaping (Prokasy, Ebel, and Thompson, 1963) would facilitate performance at longer than optimal interstimulus intervals, it would add further evidence that the simulation is an accurate portrayal of the reinforcement contingencies inherent in Pavlovian conditioning. Following Prokasy et al. (1963), the interstimulus interval in the simulation was gradually increased to its final value of 500, 700, 1000, or 2000 ms from an initial value of 500 ms. Paralleling Prokasy et al.'s (1963) finding in human eyelid conditioning, gradual 'response shaping' facilitated acquisition of overlaps of conditioned response and unconditioned stimulus in the simulation at interstimulus intervals as long as 2000 ms. Asymptotic overlaps with 500 ms interstimulus intervals were in the range of about 80 per cent, whereas 2000 ms interstimulus intervals yielded asymptotes of approximately 45 per cent. Thus, when the conditioned response is shaped. i.e. when the interstimulus interval is increased gradually, interstimulus intervals longer than the optimal 500 ms can support conditioning. Since this is true in both traditional eyelid conditioning and in the simulation, it lends further support to the claim that the simulation does indeed mirror reinforcement contingencies inherent in Pavlovian conditioning.

The next operant simulation of Pavlovian conditioning concerned partial reinforcement, a comparison that has defied the integration of Pavlovian and operant learning (Kimble, 1961; Schwartz and Gamzu, 1977). Long ago, Skinner (1938) showed that partial reinforcement facilitates the strength of an operent. A variable ratio schedule, for example, greatly increases the response rate in comparison to continuous reinforcement. Partial reinforcement is said to have just the opposite effect on Pavlovian conditioned responses (Spence, 1966). Ross (1959), for example, first established asymptotic conditioned eyelid performance with P (unconditioned stimulus|conditioned stimulus) = 1.00. Subsequently, he shifted this probability to 0.50. The result was a rapid and drastic fall-off in performance. The same paradoxical effect occurred in our operant simulation of

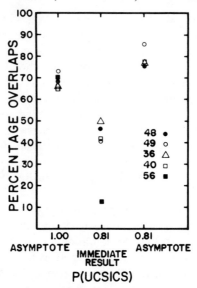

Figure 8.2. After asymptotic overlaps occurred in the simulation, the value of p (unconditioned stimulus|conditioned stimulus) was reduced. Percentage overlaps dropped sharply. After more training with $p = 1.00$, overlaps rose to an asymptote that was higher than the original asymptote with $p = 1.00$. (From Cantor and Wilson, 1981)

Pavlovian conditioning. Figure 8.2 shows asymptotic overlap performance of about 70 per cent by five rats with a 500 ms interstimulus interval and a p(unconditioned stimulus | conditioned stimulus) = 1.00. After performance stabilized, the p value was reduced first to 0.90 for two sessions and then to 0.81. The immediate result was a drop in overlap performance to about 45 per cent. One animal that did not have the two intermediate sessions at 0.90 dropped to 13 per cent when the p value was reduced to 0.81. Thus, the rapid fall-off in performance is not peculiar to Pavlovian conditioning *per se*, but rather to a certain set of reinforcement contingencies of which Pavlovian conditioning is an example. Since the simulation was a distinctly operant procedure, Spence (1966) was incorrect in his assertion that partial reinforcement has fundamentally different effects on Pavlovian and instrumental learning.

In summary, when the reinforcement contingencies described by the preparatory response view are simulated with a distinctly operant lever-press response, the optimal interstimulus interval for response acquisition is 500 ms; 'response shaping' facilitates acquisition of the overlap at longer than optimal interstimulus intervals; and 'partial reinforcement' has an immediate deleterious effect on performance. The success of the Pavlovian simulation supports the preparatory view that the conditioned response is in fact a timed instrumental preparatory response which is reinforced by its coincidence with the unconditioned stimulus. These observations suggest that the Pavlovian–operant language dichotomy is unnecessary and unparsimonious. Before proposing that information theory move in to subsume both paradigms, I will address two related issues: timing and the problem of 'voluntary' vs. 'involuntary' responses.

Timing

A key assumption of the preparatory view and a cornerstone of the simulation is that the effectiveness of the preparatory response crucially depends upon when it occurs in the interstimulus interval. Asymptotic performance has the conditioned response almost co-occurring with the unconditioned stimulus, thus the Pavlovian procedure by nature produces timing behaviour. That being the case, what is the significance of the optimal 500 ms contiguity between conditioned stimulus and unconditioned stimulus that is so often found in Pavlovian skeletal conditioning (Gormezano and Moore, 1969)?

The answer follows directly from the preparatory response notion: it predicts that the optimal temporal contiguity is also the most accurately timed interval, i.e. the interval where variance of the conditioned response latency is minimal. Studies of the optimal interstimulus interval have typically not measured the variance of the response latency but related evidence is available for both rats and humans.

The question becomes, 'What is the error in timing short intervals?' Woodrow (1930) asked this very question using a temporal reproduction task with humans. The subject was first given an interval bounded by clicks, and his task was then to reproduce it. Woodrow calculated the standard deviation and the mean at the various intervals tested (200–30 000 ms). The ratio of these statistics (standard deviation/mean) is variously named the gamma function or the coefficient of variation. The rationale for its use is that since both mean and standard deviation increase with the interval timed, t, the ratio has the effect of removing variability due to the increase in t and reflects relative timing sensitivity. In this sense the ratio is also a measure of the Weber fraction ($\Delta I/I$). The standard deviation of the distribution of timed responses at a given t value is a measure of the just noticeable difference (ΔI)—it is the subject's average 'deviation from the mark'. The mean, on the other hand, increasing with t in an approximately linear fashion (or as a power function with exponent between 0.8 and 0.9; e.g. DeCasper and Zeiler, 1977; Platt, Kuch, and Bitgood, 1973) becomes the standard interval (I) in the Weber ratio.

Figure 8.3 shows that the Weber fraction for time, like the Weber fraction for most sensory modalities (Woodworth and Schlosberg, 1954), is distinctly non-linear. Sensitivity is keenest at 600 ms, i.e., the Weber fraction increases above and below it. Up to about 4000 ms, the increase appears to be approximately linear, whereupon the Weber fraction remains approximately constant out to at least 30 s. A recent experiment by Getty (1975) using the method of constant stimuli also showed that the Weber fraction is non-linear. He, like Woodrow

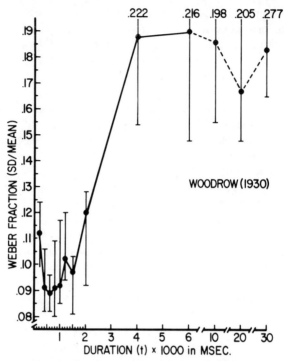

Figure 8.3. Weber fraction of human subjects (standard deviation/mean) as a function of the interval timed in a temporal reproduction task (Woodrow, 1930). Each point is a median and the vertical lines are interquartile ranges. Eight subjects timed intervals up to 10 s; five subjects timed the two longest intervals

(1930), found that the fraction was minimal between about 400 and 2000 ms and increased markedly thereafter.

According to Cantor and Wilson (1981, Experiment 1), these data are quite similar to what is found with rats. Rats received rewarding brain stimulation if and only if they held a lever longer than t_1 milliseconds but shorter than t_2 milliseconds. A time-out followed each of 1000 such trials in a session. The time window $(t_2 - t_1)$ within which lever releases were reinforced was made 15 per cent of t_1 for one animal and 20 per cent for the other. Thus as t_1 was increased parametrically at six different intervals ranging from 200 to 6000 ms, the reinforcement window was also increased as a constant proportion of the interval timed (t_1). Asymptotic performance is shown in Figure 8.4 in a plot of the Weber fraction as a function of t_1. For both animals Weber fractions were lowest between 500 and 2000 ms and increased outside this region.

What is the significance of a 500 ms contiguity? The answer seems to be that it is at about that value that both humans and rats can do their most accurate timing, i.e. can most precisely hit a 'point in time'. Timing continues to be

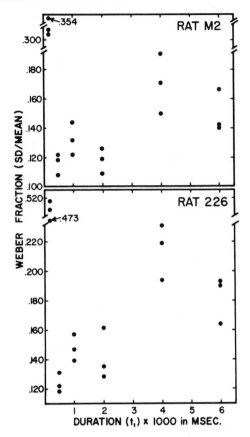

Figure 8.4. Weber fractions (standard deviation/mean) as a function of the interval timed, t_1, for two rats. Points are means of the three criterion sessions with alpha responses removed from the data. Note that timing sensitivity is keenest between 500 and 2000 ms (From Cantor and Wilson, 1980)

accurate to about 2000 ms, whereupon it takes a sharp turn for the worse. An interval of 2000 ms is the interval that Ross (1961) has said is approximately the outer limit of effectiveness of interstimulus intervals in Pavlovian eyelid conditioning. Thus, psychophysical functions for timing are very similar in their form to the interstimulus interval function in Pavlovian conditioning. And that is as it should be if the preparatory response hypothesis is correct.

Other non-experimental evidence shows that 500 ms is a special contiguity. Absolute temporal judgment involves the synchrony of behaviour with a stimulus, a task that is very well understood by musicians. One tempo that allows musicians easily to 'stay together', i.e. stay synchronized, is 'andante' (from the Italian *andare*, to walk). Andante is a tempo of about 120 beats/min or one beat every 500 ms. When a classroom of students beats coins on their desks in synchrony with andante on a metronome, they come into synchrony easily and the beats are as one. A much more difficult tempo is largo. Largo is about 30 beats/min, which is a beat every 2000 ms. Musicians find that is is quite difficult to stay together in largo. Typically the conductor beats this tempo in four so that each beat actually gets four movements of the baton. In other words, the conductor divides the long interval into easily timed intervals of about 500 ms. Try largo with the metronome demonstration; the variance will be quite obvious.

The introspection of Woodrow's (1930) subjects goes along with these findings. One subject, after reproducing a 6 s interval wrote, 'With this interval I have no certainty that the reproduction is even approximately accurate. I give the final tap ending the reproducing interval on a sort of hunch the origin of which I am unable to trace'. Another subject wrote, 'With the shorter intervals I think I always knew if I made a considerable error in the reproduction but with this interval [4 s] it was simply a lot of guesswork and I had no idea in which direction the errors were made'.

Actually, the range of 500–2000 ms appears to be optimal for many kinds of tasks. For example, reaction time is fastest when a fixed duration foreperiod is in this range (Snodgrass, Luce, and Galanter, 1967). Presumably the subject can almost perfectly time the foreperiod and anticipate the moment of occurrence of the 'go signal'. Howarth and Treisman (1961) found that the threshold for detecting a low-level stimulus is minimal when the stimulus to be detected is preceded by a 1 s warning signal and then increases linearly to an asymptote with warning intervals longer than 4 s. In an experiment by Killeen (1978), pigeons indicated that a stimulus was contingent on a response, i.e. was 'caused' by it, if the contiguity between response and stimulus was within the 500–2000 ms range.

Perhaps the basic behaviour underlying optimal performance at 500–2000 ms in Pavlovian conditioning, reaction time, the attribution of causality, and signal detection is memory. That is, timing an interval requires memory for the start of that interval (Cantor and Wilson, 1981). At least in humans, there is evidence that highly accurate short-term memory falls off markedly after about 2–3 s (Wingfield and Byrnes, 1972).

The data point to two roles of the conditioned stimulus in Pavlovian eyelid conditioning: its onset tells _if_ the unconditioned stimulus is coming and its duration (interstimulus interval) after a few repetitions tells _when_ it is coming.

Involuntary Behaviour

According to the preparatory view the conditioned response is in fact a timed, instrumental, adaptive response, or at least ends up that way after many conditioning trials. This is not to say that all responses generated by the Pavlovian paradigm are adaptive conditioned responses. Kimble (1961) described the various non-conditioned responses that find their way into the interstimulus interval. For example, the 'alpha' response occurs within the first 100 ms of a 500 ms interstimulus interval and is said to be a reflex blink to conditioned stimulus onset. The 'beta' response occurs 120–240 ms after conditioned stimulus onset and apparently results (Grant and Norris, 1947) from a visual conditioned stimulus when the eyes are not adapted to darkness. The conditioned response itself is defined as any eyeblink occurring between 250 and 500 ms and is not to be confused with a so-called involuntary blink. A particular concern is alpha responses, those short latency responses that occur long before the conditioned response even after the subject is well trained. What are they? What influences their occurrence?

Whatever they are, they are not peculiar to Pavlovian conditioning (Cantor and Wilson, 1981). Analogous responses occur in every paradigm that involves the withholding of a response until a specified time and/or event. In reaction time experiments, they occur during the foreperiod and are called 'anticipatory responses'. Typically they are regarded as an annoyance to the experimenter and are eliminated from the analysis of reaction time. Short latency responses also occur on fixed interval schedules and there they are called 'bursting'. Similarly, short latency responses occur with differential reinforcement of low rates schedules. For example, Gaddy (1979) has shown that they are more likely to occur after an interresponse time that is close to the differential reinforcement of low rates requirement, i.e. after a near miss of reinforcement. Furthermore, he found that more short latency responses were made by rats that had bilateral lesions of the neo-striatum than by those that had sham lesions. Both groups of rats otherwise did equally well in timing the differential reinforcement of low rates requirement. This experiment suggests that there may be a fundamental difference between the timed response that is reinforced and the short latency response.

Short latency responses, or 'alphas', were also prevalent in the simulation of Pavlovian conditioning. Figure 8.5 shows a distribution of responses latencies in the simulation after asymptotic performance had been attained (more than 10 000 training trials). The interstimulus interval was 700 ms and the simulated conditioned response overlapped the unconditioned stimulus in 406 of the 500 trials. The minor mode of the distribution peaked at about 150 ms. Are these the 'alpha' responses peculiar to Pavlovian paradigms or are they the short-latency 'bursting' responses peculiar to operant differential reinforcement of low rates paradigms? It obviously isn't a good question. A general principle goes beyond the Pavlovian/operant dichotomy: short latency responses result from reinforcement contingencies which require the withholding of a response. The Pavlovian paradigm is simply one of those cases.

The alpha-type responses belong to the family of adjunctive behaviours (Falk, 1971). They represent 'off-task' behaviour such as the excessive drinking (Falk, 1971; Cantor, in press; Cantor and Wilson, 1978) that occurs in the period just after reinforcement in a fixed interval or fixed time schedule. Indeed, a fixed time

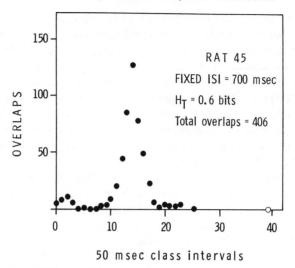

50 msec class intervals

Figure 8.5. Overlaps of the conditioned response and the unconditioned stimulus in the operant simulation of Pavlovian conditioning according to the preparatory responses view. The interstimulus interval was 700 ms. Short latency 'alpha' responses are shown as the minor mode. (Data from Cantor and Wilson, 1980)

schedule is indistinguishable from Pavlovian temporal conditioning. A number of parallels exist between 'alphas' and adjunctive behaviour. Falk (1969) found that as the duration of a fixed interval schedule for food reinforcement was increased up to about 2 min, the amount of water drunk (schedule-induced polydipsia) also increased. Similarly, short latency alpha responses increased (Cantor and Wilson, 1981, Experiment 1) and the interval to be timed, t_1, increased. Similar results have been obtained in human eyelid conditioning procedures (Grice, 1977).

What is fascinating about the finding of a mixture of two response latency classes in the Pavlovian paradigm is that exactly the same argument is being made in the operant literature! Schwartz, Hamilton, and Silberberg (1975) confirmed an earlier finding (Schwartz and Williams, 1972) that pigeon peck durations fall into two classes: short duration pecks of about 10 ms and longer ones of about 40 ms. According to their additivity theory, the short duration pecks represent reflexive 'involuntary' pecks engendered by the response–reinforcer relations such as autoshaping (indistinguishable from the Pavlovian procedure) whereas longer operant pecks of the 'voluntary' sort emerge from response–reinforcer relations. In behavioural contrast then, the facilitation in response rate in the unchanged component of a multiple schedule is said to be due to the occurrence of short duration, 'involuntary' autopecks that add to the longer duration 'voluntary' operant pecks that are controlled by the variable interval reinforcement contingency.

Those who study alpha responses in Pavlovian conditioning, brusting in fixed interval and differential reinforcement of low rates schedules, anticipatory responses in reaction time, and autopecks in multiple schedules are all 'charting the same bay'. In each case a short latency response is made at a time when contingency dictates that a response be withheld. Pavlovian and instrumental learning procedures both engender a mix of two kinds of behaviour. 'Involuntary behaviour' is not peculiar to the stimulus–reinforcer contingency of Pavlovian conditioning and 'voluntary behaviour' is not peculiar to the response–reinforcer contingency of operant behaviour.

To summarize what has been said so far, phenomena presumed to be peculiar to either Pavlovian or operant procedures are in fact common to both. We are left, then, with an unparsimonious system which stands squarely in the way of the real question at hand: how shall we organize the events occuring in space and time and thereby predict and control behaviour?

Organizing the Environment

How should relationships among stimuli and responses in the environment be described? What is needed is a single metric that quantifies if, when, and where reinforcement will occur, since the foregoing preparatory response model emphasizes that reinforcement is the all-important commodity in both Pavlovian conditioning and in instrumental learning. The associative metrics extant are contiguity and contingency. Neither fulfils the above criteria.

Contiguity

Since Aristotle it has been held that contiguity between two events—two stimuli for Pavlov (1927) and a response and a stimulus for Skinner (1938)–is at least a sufficient condition for an association to occur. In the Pavlovian conditioning of the eyelid and other skeletal responses, a 500 ms contiguity seems to be about ideal (Gormezano and Moore, 1969) and 2000 ms is about the upper limit. In instrumental paradigms, a similar function is known to describe the associative relationship between a response and a punisher (Solomon, 1964) and a response and a reinforcer (Skinner, 1936; Grice, 1948). The strength of a conditioned reinforcer also requires brief contiguity with primary reinforcement—about 0.5–1.0 s—for it to be effective (Bersh, 1951). Another example is the superstition experiment (Skinner, 1948); when any response is followed within about a second by reinforcement, the response is increased in probability. Responses are *reduced* in probability by the same contiguity principle: in concurrent schedules, the superstitious reinforcement of a response on one schedule by a reinforcer on the other is prevented if the duration of a change-over delay is made longer than about 2 s. There is also historical precedent and much empirical evidence from a variety of associative paradigms to show that temporal contiguity—*when* a consequence occurs with respect to an antecedent—is at least a sufficient condition for an association to be acquired and maintained.

Contingency

Rescorla (1967) made a fundamental change in our understanding of the necessary and sufficient conditions for an association to occur. He suggested that contiguity between conditioned stimulus (CS) and unconditioned stimulus (UCS) may be necessary, but it is not sufficient. The important determinant of association is the contingency between conditioned stimulus and unconditioned stimulus, i.e. the degree to which the unconditioned stimulus is probable in the presence and absence of the conditioned stimulus. Quantitatively, conditioning occur if

$$p(\text{UCS}|\text{CS}) > p(\text{UCS}|\text{not CS}).$$

When these terms are equal, conditioned stimulus and unconditioned stimulus are truly random with respect to each other and no conditioning occurs. Indeed, Rescorla (1967) has argued that this case is the appropriate control in Pavlovian conditioning. Tests of Rescorla's theory using primarily the conditioned emotional response paradigm have been mixed in their outcomes. Some show the predicted failure of conditioning with the random control (e.g. Rescorla, 1968) and others show some conditioning (e.g. Kremer and Kamin, 1971). The contingency view has also been tested in the autoshaping paradigm by Gamzu and Williams (1972). They found that pigeons pecked a key only when

$$p(\text{food}|\text{key light}) > p(\text{food}|\text{not key light}).$$

When the probability of food was the same in both the presence and absence of the key light, no key-pecking occurred.

While the notion of contingency makes an important contribution to our understanding of associative learning, it has at least one serious flaw: it ignores the importance of contiguity. For example, the $p(\text{UCS}|\text{CS})$ might be 0.95 and the $p(\text{UCS}|\text{not CS}) = 0.1$, but there would be no conditioning because un-specified in the contingency metric is the fact that the interstimulus interval is an hour and a half! The contingency view, then, suggests that behaviour is ruled by a molar view of the CS–UCS relationship and does not include a specification of temporal parameters.

Contingency between response and reinforcement has been suggested as the important rule governing operant behaviour (e.g. Baum, 1973; Herrnstein, 1970; Staddon and Simmelhag, 1971). Baum (1973, p. 141), for example, has said, '. . . the correlation based law of effect suggests that simple response–reinforcer contiguity cannot account for instrumental behaviour—the molar relation between response and reinforcer is crucial'. Thus, the molar correlation between a response and reinforcement is said to control operant behaviour just as the correlation between conditioned and unconditioned stimulus controls the conditioned response in Pavlovain conditioning. Again, however, a contingency metric leaves out the importance of contiguity.

The real problem is that notions of contiguity and contingency are not mutually exclusive. A decrease in correlation between two contiguous events also results in a loss of contiguity between them. Put another way, contingency features the importance of *if* something will occur with respect to an antecedent, and contiguity features the importance of *when* something will occur with respect to an antecedent. But the question 'when' is just the question 'if' asked in each successive moment. Both Pavlovian and operant paradigms, then, need a single metric that can synthesize the contingency question 'if' with the contiguity question 'when', and thereby organize the learning environment. Information theory (Shannon and Weaver, 1949) fills the bill.

Information Theory as an Associative Metric

In adopting information theory as an associative metric, any controlled learning experiment is conceptualized as a study in communication between the experimenter and the subject. The focus of the exchange is the unconditioned stimulus or reinforcement (hereinafter called S*). The experimenter provides two sorts of information about the occurrence of S* and each is quantifiable in bits: contingency information that tells if S* will occur and temporal information that tells when S* will occur. For example, the onset of S + in discriminative training tells if S* will occur and the presentation of S* after a fixed duration interval tells when. The output of the communication system and the index of information transmission is a measure of response strength such as response rate, latency or probability. Behaviour, then, is predicted and controlled by a quantitative analysis of uncertainty about the onset of S*. In that way the relationship among events in the organism's environment—be they stimuli, S*s, or responses (response-produced stimuli)—is completely and simply specified in bits, the quantitative units of information. It is possible to dispense with all manner of terms such as conditioned and unconditioned stimulus, variable and fixed interval schedule, discriminative and conditioned stimulus, among others; and replace them with a quantification of information about S* on the input side and the usual dependent measures on the output side.

I will begin by reviewing how information theory quantifies choice uncertainty, i.e. the case where one of a finite number of discrete outcomes can occur. Applications of information theory in psychology in general and conditioning and learning in particular (e.g. Bloomfield, 1972; Eckerman, 1973; Fantino, 1977; Miller and Frick, 1949) have been almost exclusively of this type. A second kind of uncertainty—one central to the present schema—is temporal uncertainty, uncertainty about when an event will occur.

Choice Uncertainty

The amount of information conveyed by the occurrence of an event is an increasing logarithmic function of the number of events that could have occurred. The basic form of the information formula (Shannon and Weaver, 1949) is given by

$$H_T = \log_2 m, \tag{8.1}$$

where H_T is the uncertainty or information expressed in bits and m is the number of equally likely alternative events that could have occurred. A fair coin, then, has 1 bit of uncertainty before it is flipped and gives 1 bit of information afterward. Drawing a spade from the deck reduces 2 bits of uncertainty; losing at Russian roulette reduces 2.58 bits. Zero bits of uncertainty about S* is reduced by lever-pressing on a CRF schedule since only one event could have occurred; but onset of S + in Pavlovian discriminative conditioning reduces 1 bit of uncertainty since the trial could have 'as easily' been an S − .

Perhaps the most impressive demonstration of the efficacy of information theory in psychology is Hyman's (1953) classic series of choice reaction time experiments. Four subjects were run in three experiments over a period of 3 months for a total of 15 000 reaction time trials per subject. Each experiment varied choice uncertainty in a different way. In the first experiment, subjects were tested in eight different choice reaction time conditions where each condition had different numbers of equally likely choices. Stimulus uncertainty varied from 0 bits (simple reaction time) to 3 bits (eight possible choices). The second experiment also tested reaction time in a choice situation, but in this case the probabilities of alternative events were not equally likely. Instead, as in one case, a signal occurred with a probability of 4/8, a second with a probability of 2/8 and a third or fourth each with a probability of 1/8. To calculate the average uncertainty reduced by the onset of these stimuli is somewhat more complicated than applying equation (8.1) for equally likely alternatives. It is necessary to calculate the weighted average of the 'surprisal' h_i of each of the four possible events according to the following formula:

$$H_T = \sum p_i h_i, \tag{8.2}$$

where H_T is information in bits and p_i is the probability of the ith event. The calculation of the surprisal of the ith event, h_i, follows directly from equation (8.1) and is given by

$$h_i = \log_2(1/p_i). \tag{8.3}$$

Thus, Hyman's second experiment also tested choice reaction time as a function of uncertainty, but the manner of producing the uncertainty was fundamentally different from the method used in the first experiment. In the third experiment, different numbers of equally likely alternatives were used; but the probability of an alternative occurring depended upon the immediately preceding event. For

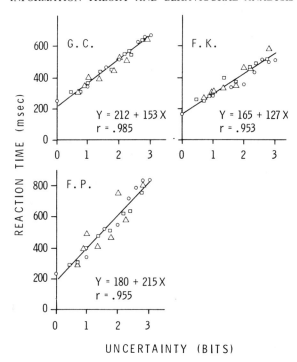

UNCERTAINTY (BITS)

Figure 8.6. Reaction time as a function of uncertainty about stimulus onset. Uncertainty was produced in three different ways: by equally likely events, by unequally likely events, and by sequential dependencies in the events. (From Hyman, 1953)

example, in one of the eight conditions three different 'go' signals were used. For one stimulus the $p(b|a) = 8/10$ and for the other two stimuli $p(a|b) = p(c|a) = 1/10$. Average uncertainty, H_T, based on the weighted surprisals of the stimuli, was calculated for all eight conditions.

Each subject's average reaction time as a function of H_T in the three experiments is presented in Figure 8.6. The functions are linear in all cases and the amount of variance accounted for by the straight line, r^2, ranges from 91 to 97 per cent among subjects. That the regression lines associated with the three experiments were identical could not be rejected at the 5 per cent level of confidence. In other words, Hyman could come to the very substantial conclusion that it does not matter how choice uncertainty about stimulus onset is manipulated—with equally likely alternatives, with unequally likely alternatives, or with sequential dependencies—reaction time is a direct function of uncertainty about the stimulus. The linear relation between reaction time and H_T, particularly in choice reaction time procedures with equally likely alternatives, has come to be known as Hick's law in recognition of its first demonstration (Hick, 1952).

Temporal Uncertainty

It is also possible to quantify the information inherent in a continuous stimulus such as direction, frequency, amplitude, and time. Recently, time and timing behaviour in learning experiments have aroused considerable interest (e.g. Cantor and Wilson, 1981; Church, 1978; DeCasper and Zeiler, 1977; Gibbon, 1977; Platt, 1979; Stubbs, 1979). The treatment of time in terms of information theory has special advantages because it allows one quantitatively to integrate the notion of when an event will occur with the notion of if it will occur, i.e. integrate contiguity between events with contingency between them.

A subject's ability to anticipate the exact moment when a stimulus will occur is hampered by two sorts of temporal uncertainty (Klemmer, 1957). One is the inability of the subject to time a fixed duration with the accuracy of a clock—this is quntified as subject's uncertainty, s_s. The other kind of temporal uncertainty is experimenter's uncertainty, s_e, and stems from the inability to time an interval made variable by an experimenter, e.g. as in a variable interval schedule.

The calculation of temporal uncertainty differs from choice uncertainty in a fundamental way. Choice uncertainty is easy to calculate because the possible outcomes are discrete and the number that could happen are known. Temporal uncertainty is somewhat more difficult to calculate because it is based on the subject's error in timing the onset of an event. Error (here a standard deviation of a normal distribution of temporal productions) is a continuous distribution, so there are technically infinite alternatives and consequently infinite bits of temporal uncertainty. This problem is solved by specifying a 'grain' for time and quantizing the error continuum into a finite number of non-overlapping 'alternatives' or choices. Stroud (1955) called these quantal units 'psychological moments'. The assumption is that events occurring within the same 'moment' are perceived as simultaneous.

Once a meaningful 'moment' is chosen, the temporal uncertainty of a stimulus is easily calculated. The standard deviation of the distribution of responses aimed at timing the interval is divided by the duration of the 'psychological moment'. This gives the number of temporal moment 'alternatives' associated with the interval timed. The $\log_2$ of that number is temporal uncertainty in bits. The formula for this relative uncertainty is:

$$H_T = \log_2 s_{s:t} - \log_2 s_{s:moment}$$

or

$$H_T = \log_2 (s_{s:t}/s_{s:moment}), \tag{8.4}$$

where $s_{s:t}$ is the subject's uncertainty for a given t and $s_{s:moment}$ is the duration of the 'psychological moment'. The derivation of this formula from Shannon and Weaver's (1949) formula for uncertainty in a normal distribution,

$$H_T = \log_2 (\sqrt{2\pi e}\sigma)$$

has been shown elsewhere (Cantor and Wilson, 1980; Klemmer, 1957).

Equation (8.4) is like a 'decibel scale' for time. Instead of relative sound pressure we calculate relative temporal uncertainty about an event. As with the decibel scale, the meaningfulness of the zero point and, for that matter, the units of the scale, depend upon the meaningfulness of the 'psychological moment', i.e. the standard. For the decibel scale, the standard is the absolute auditory threshold (0.0002 dynes/cm^2). Thus 0 db is not an absence of sound pressure; rather it is sound pressure at the threshold. Similarly for temporal uncertainty, the temporal grain used by Cantor and Wilson (1981) is the standard deviation of the most accurately timed interval (500 ms, *see below*). Zero temporal uncertainty is not the absence of time between events but rather the interval that is most easily timed.

These considerations were applied to Cantor and Wilson's (1981, Experiment 1) temporal production data. Since 500 ms was the most accurately timed interval, its uncertainty, $s_{s:500}$, was taken as the 'psychological moment'; this value for two animals was 63 and 64 ms. Stroud (1955) estimated the same value for human subjects at between 50 and 100 ms using very different methods. Figure 8.7 shows temporal uncertainty for two animals as a function of the intervals timed. Note that a 500 ms interval has zero uncertainty by definition. That is, there is zero uncertainty in timing a 500 ms interval to within one

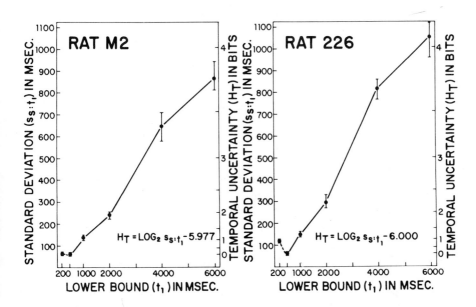

Figure 8.7. Average standard deviation over three criterion sessions in which reinforcement was delivered if a lever press was longer than t_1 milliseconds but shorter than t_2 milliseconds. Vertical lines show the range at each point. The right ordinate is a transformation of the standard deviation into the information measure, bits, from the formula given at the lower right. (From Cantor and Wilson, 1981)

'psychological moment' since the moment is based on the standard deviation of timing that 500 ms interval. Note also that the average temporal uncertainty associated with a 2000 ms interval is about 2.1 bits. That is to say, the temporal uncertainty in timing a 2000 ms interval ($s_{s:2000}$) is about 4.3 times the value of the moment, $s_{s:500}$. This finding suggests three related points.

The first is that rats showed almost exactly the same ratio of $s_{s:2000}/s_{s:500}$ as did humans in timing experiments by Woodrow (1930) and Getty (1975), 4.4 and 4.0, respectively.

Second, for rat and man, 2 s or 2.1 bits is temporal channel capacity (Cantor and Wilson, 1981), the greatest amount of information that the subject can transmit about a temporal stimulus, t, without becoming confused. This is a reasonable conclusion from the fact that rat and human Weber functions take a sharp turn for the worse at intervals greater than 2 s and human subjects at this point start to complain of having difficulty 'remembering the start of the interval'. What makes this finding particularly interesting is that a temporal channel capacity of 2.1 bits or about 4.3 chunks (actually 'alternatives') is well within the 7 ± 2 (Miller, 1956) or 5 ± 2 (Simon, 1974) chunks that have been proposed as human channel capacity in other information input modalities. That is, when humans have to make absolute discriminations along a single dimension of pitch, loudness, odour intensity, or numerosity, they can make only about 5 ± 2 or 7 ± 2 (between 3 and 9, in any case). If the assumptions about quantifying temporal uncertainty in bits are true, then time can now be added to the list.

Since both rat and man have the same temporal channel capacity, maybe the 2 s duration—associated as it is with short-term memory and optimal contiguity—is basic to the insectivore from which mammals diverged. Perhaps it is more basic than that. The simplest organism displaying timing and synchrony that I am aware of is the synchronous firefly of Thailand (Buck and Buck, 1968, 1976). These fireflies alight in trees and flash synchronously starting at dusk as part of a mating ritual. Apparently, a male wins a female by flashing brightly and by being in synchrony with his cohorts. Buck and Buck have studied the timing behaviour in some detail in individual organisms and have found that it operates much the same as human synchrony. What is particularly striking is that different species of firefly synchronize at different interflash intervals. The shortest known interval is about 520 ms and the longest is about 3 s. It is too tempting not to speculate that a channel capacity of about 2–3 s is determined by some basic property of nervous systems.

The third point relates to theory building. Given that error in timing a 2000 ms interval is approximately four times the error in timing a 500 ms interval, subjects may time a 2000 ms interval by counting out four easy-to-time 500 ms intervals in the way that a conductor divides one beat in a largo tempo or the American touch football player calls 'One-alligator, two-alligator, three-alligator' before rushing the quarterback. Cognition of this sort is at least implied by counting models of timing (e.g. Creelman, 1962; Getty, 1976). The rats may have been doing something like this. They developed a streotyped response topography during temporal production which appeared to build when t_1 was made longer. One rat held the lever, reared back and then released it when timing the 500 ms interval. This topography was embellished with a right side movement with the 1000 ms interval and a right and left sterotyped side movement at the 2000 ms interval. The response topography at 6000 ms appeared to build on these right–left movements by increasing the time that the rat oscillated at each segment of the dance. Similar observations of rats responding on differential reinforcement of low rate schedules were made by Laties, Weiss, Clark and Reynolds, (1965). Since rats cannot emit a heterogeneous verbal chain, e.g. 1-*Homo sapiens*, 2-*Homo sapiens*, 3-*Homo sapiens*, to tell them where they are in a sequence of equal-duration events, perhaps the sterotyped movement from one side to the other is an attempt at spatially (instead of verbally) tagging their location in the chain. Whereas counting may indeed be occurring at such overt or even covert levels, it is important to note that *this cognitive assumption is not required by the use of information theory. Information theory is simply a means of quantifying if or when an event will occur; the term 'uncertainty' need have no more cognitive overtones in psychology than it has in physics and cybernetics.* Thus, the term 'information' is not a metaphor for 'meaning', 'knowledge', etc. (e.g. Epstein, Lanza, and Skinner, 1980), but rather a technical term that quantifies the input.

The discussion of subject's temporal uncertainty can now be related to the operant simulation of Pavlovian conditioning (Cantor and Wilson, 1980). In the simulation, a lever release was reinforced if it coincided with the onset of the unconditioned stimulus, a 150 ms 'point in time' similar in duration to the proposed 'psychological moment'. The number of overlaps of conditioned response and unconditioned stimulus in 500 trials was the measure of absolute temporal judgment. The results, couched in terms of information theory, were as follows: Maximal overlaps occurred (approximately 83 per cent) when temporal uncertainty was 0, i.e. when the interstimulus interval was 500 ms. Overlaps fell to about 50 per cent accuracy when temporal uncertainty was 2.1 bits, i.e. when the interstimulus interval was 2000 ms; that is, the overlap measure (Experiment 3) fell below 50 per cent accuracy at the same time value where the Weber fraction (Experiment 1) took a sharp turn upward. The absolute number of overlaps, a dependent variable very different from the Weber fraction, then, also supports the assertion that 2000 ms or 2.1 bits is temporal channel capacity.

Another Pavlovian simulation experiment (Cantor and Wilson 1981, Experiment 4) supports this assertion in a different way and elucidates the second kind of temporal uncertainty. Whereas subject's temporal uncertainty, $s_{s:t}$, quantifies the subject's inability to anticipate the moment when a fixed duration will end, experimenter's temporal uncertainty, s_e, quantifies the inability to anticipate the end of a duration that is made variable by the experimenter. This sort of uncertainty is, of course, familiar as a variable intertrial interval in

Pavlovian conditioning, a variable foreperiod in reaction time experiments, or a variable interval in operant experiments.

To quantify the relationship between combinations of subject's and experimenter's uncertainty on the one hand and overlaps on the other, the Pavlovian simulation was run exactly as described before, except that the interstimulus interval was made variable rather than fixed. The variability was carefully defined from a Z distribution table using 21 different values that each cut off 5 per cent of the area under the curve ranging from -4 to $+4$ standard deviations. The mean of the distribution—producing subject's uncertainty—was 700, 850, or 1000 ms for three different rats and remained constant throughout the experiment. From the timing experiment we calculated that these interstimulus intervals produced subject's temporal uncertainty of 96 ms (0.6 bits), 116 ms (0.87 bits), and 145 ms (1.18 bits), respectively. Behaviour was first allowed to reach an asymptotic level of overlaps at these fixed durations. Then experimenter-produced uncertainty was introduced by making the interstimulus interval variable according to the method described above. The amount of variability about the mean interstimulus interval was incremented in 0.5 bit steps so that the total amount of temporal uncertainty—subject's plus experimenter's—ranged from the low of the fixed interstimulus interval conditions to a high of 3.0 bits. The method for doing this is based on appropriate substitution of s_e into equation (8.2):

$$s_T = \sqrt{s_s^2 + s_e^2},\qquad\qquad (8.6)$$

where s_T is total temporal uncertainty, s_s is subject's uncertainty and s_e is experimenter's uncertainty.

The results for three animals in this study can be summarized simply: the asymptotic number of overlaps was a linear decreasing function of s_T. Figure 8.8 shows the data for all subjects in the Pavlovian simulation for whom asymptotic performance was determined. It includes data points for subjects which had fixed and variable interstimulus intervals. On the basis of the fitted straight line ($r^2 > 91$ per cent) it was concluded that it does not matter how temporal uncertainty about the onset of the unconditioned stimulus was produced—either by subject's uncertainty alone or in combination with experimenter-produced uncertainty— it is temporal uncertainty that predicts and controls overlaps, i.e. synchrony with the unconditioned stimulus. Furthermore, the straight line best fitting these points crossed the 50 per cent overlap line when s_T was 279 ms (Figure 8.8). This is only 10 ms more than the average s_s in timing a 2000 ms interval as determined in the timing experiment. Our previous estimate of temporal channel capacity was thereby supported.

Information theory has the very useful ability to quantify the occurrence of events in space and time in terms of a common language. The question immediately arises as to whether one bit of temporal uncertainty has the exact same effect on behaviour as one bit of choice uncertainty. Does 'not knowing' *if*

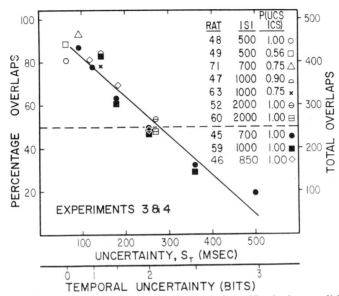

Figure 8.8. Percentage overlaps in the operant simulation of Pavlovian conditioning as a function of total uncertainty. Plotted points are maxima for all data collected at a given parameter value. The straight line was fitted by the method of least squares ($r^2 = 0.92$). The intersection of the straight line and the 50 per cent line, temporal channel capacity, occurred when $S_T = 279$ ms or 2.13 bits. (From Cantor and Wilson, 1981)

have the same effect on behaviour as 'not knowing' *when*? Surprisingly, this important question has received little attention. The easiest approach to the question is to compare the reaction time data of an experiment such as that of Hyman (1953), where choice uncertainty was manipulated, with that of, say, Klemmer (1957), where time uncertainty was manipulated. Klemmer (1957) quantified subject's and experimenter's uncertainty in a variable foreperiod reaction time task using methods that were the basis for quantifying the variable interstimulus interval in the Pavlovian simulation. He found a linear ($0.91 < r^2 < 0.97$, among subjects) relation between reaction time and uncertainty about the onset of the 'go' signal regardless of how the temporal uncertainty was produced. This, of course, was the same result that Hyman found for three kinds of choice uncertainty. The difference between the two studies, however, was that Klemmer found a slope of 18 ms of reaction time per bit of temporal uncertainty and Hyman found 173 ms/bit. This order-of-magnitude difference suggests that there may in fact be a real difference in the capacity to handle temporal and choice information. Before coming to such a conclusion, however, it would be important to assess the effects of temporal and choice uncertainty in the same subject. The important point for now is that reaction time is impressively predicted by a single number—information about onset of the 'go' signal; it doesn't matter how the information is presented.

A Preliminary Synthesis

Information theory provides a single theoretical structure that replaces the operant–Pavlovian dichotomy. The task now becomes one of showing that both Pavlovian and operant experiments are studies in communication between the experimenter and the subject, where the focus of the exchange is reinforcement and the index of information transmission is a measure of response strength.

On the basis of the simulation experiments (Cantor and Wilson, 1981) and other support for the operation of the law of effect in Pavlovian conditioning, the term 'unconditioned' stimulus is replaced with a general symbol for reinforcement. S*.

A generality emerges from the simulation snd timing experiments that has been called Postulate I (Cantor and Wilson, 1981). It states: In a Pavlovian procedure, if the measure of response strength is probability of conditioned response, percentage overlaps, or synchrony, then response strength is inversely related to temporal uncertainty, s_t, about the onset of S*. In terms of the information measure, H_T, maximal response strength occurs at 0 bits and the upper limit of response strength, i.e. the point of 50 per cent synchrony, is about 2.1 bits. This is channel capacity. In other words, absolute temporal judgment or synchrony of R and S* (as occurs in the eyelid conditioning paradigm) is only possible when variance—another name for uncertainty—involves four or five 'psychological moments'.

Postulate I can not be generated by Pavlovian experiments, but also by time-based free-operant schedules. In comparing Pavlovian eyelid conditioning with a variable interval schedule, say, one immediately notices that the time course of association is very different—a couple of seconds on the one hand and minutes on the other. The reason is that eyelid conditioning involves synchrony of a response and S* and the variable interval schedule involves vigilance, as evidenced by switch closure, for S*.

The behaviour of a pigeon pecking a key on a variable interval schedule is the same as the behaviour of a human in a watchkeeping or vigilance experiment. The human watchkeeper is instructed to detect a change in state of the visual display and to report it as fast as he can on a key; the pigeon tests for the availability of reinforcement by pecking a key. Change in state of the display may occur according to a fixed or variable interval; likewise, the schedule of reinforcement for the pigeon. The watchkeeper's behaviour (Simth, Warm, and Alluisi, 1966) is measured in terms of his latency to press the response key, which presumably depends upon his vigilance to the display, i.e. the rate at which he looks at it; the pigeon's performance on the schedule is his rate of pecking.

Given these similarities, it is not surprising that the two kinds of experiment generate exactly the same functional relation between input and output. Smith *et al.* (1966) quantified the subject's and experimenter's uncertainty about the signal

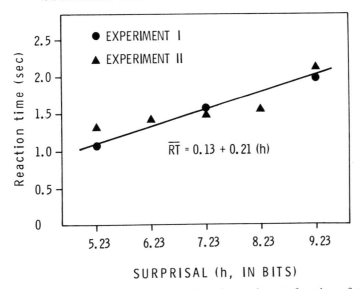

Figure 8.9. Reaction time in a human watchkeeping task as a function of temporal uncertainty about the onset of the signal to be detected. (From Smith *et al.*, 1966)

in their experiment and found a linear inverse relation with response speed (*see* Figure 8.9). The same result was found by Klemmer (1957 using a variable duration signal or foreperiod. Similarly, Cantor and Wilson (1981) quantified the uncertainty about reinforcement in variable interval and fixed interval schedules using the data of Catania and Reynolds (1968) and Schneider (1969), respectively. Uncertainty about reinforcement in a variable interval schedule, for example, is given by

$$H_T = \log_2 (R/s_{\text{s:moment}}),$$

where R is the range of the variable interval distribution and $s_{\text{s:moment}}$ is the 'psychological moment'. As with Smith *et al.*'s (1966) experiment, pigeons' response rates were inversely to uncertainty, H_T, about the onset of reinforcement (*see* Figure 8.10).

Two conclusions follow. One is that there is no essential difference between watchkeeping and variable foreperiod reaction time tasks on the one hand and time-based schedules of reinforcement of the other. Calculation of information about S* in both procedures reveals that both follow Postulate I. The second conclusion is that by first taking into account whether a response measure involves synchrony or vigilance, Postulate I describes both Pavlovian conditioning and operant time-based schedules. That is, in both paradigms the subject is sensitive to information about S*; a quantification of it predicts behaviour according to the same rule.

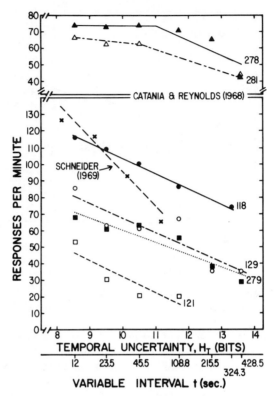

Figure 8.10. Response rate of pigeons as a function of variable interval schedule value and the information about reinforcement in bits. Straight lines were fitted by the method of least squares. (Data from Catania and Reynolds (1968) and Schneider (1969))

My treatment of simple variable interval schedules resembles that of the matching law (Herrnstein, 1970). The matching law states:

$$\text{Responses}_1 = \text{Reinforcements}_1/\text{Total reinforcements}.$$

i.e. the rate of behaviour varies directly with its relative rate of reinforcement. This predicts, for example, the hyperbolic relation that Catania and Reynolds (1968) found between response rate and reinforcement rate. Postulate I says, essentially, that those curves are logarithmic, so that instead of saying that the organism allocates responses in proportion to the rate of reinforcement, Postulate I says that organisms allocate responses in inverse proportion to the amount of uncertainty that there is about S*.

Quantifying information inherent in a reinforcement rate rather that specifying the rate itself has the important advantage of generality. For example, when reinforcement rate is quantified in terms of information about reinforcement, it becomes immediately obvious that the matching law is actually the same as

Hick's law; that is, Hick's law states that reaction latency is directly related (or reaction speed is inversely related) to uncertainty about the onset of an event in space. The matching law states that the same relation holds for response rate with respect to uncertainty about an event in time. See Figure 8.6 and 8.10. Consideration of information about reinforcement, of course, says nothing about the matter of relative rate of reinforcement, as the matching law does, but integration would be quite straightforward. Information theory, then, in going beyond the simple data language, has the advantage of rigorously synthesizing seemingly disparate phenomena.

Whereas response strength is inversely related to uncertainty about the onset of S^*, the effectiveness of stimuli informative of S^* is directly related to uncertainty about their onset; elsewhere (Cantor and Wilson, 1981) this was labelled Postulate II. Postulate II is derived from associative relationships that have been known all along: Pavlovian conditioning is facilitated when the duration of the intertrial interval is long and variable rather than short and fixed, i.e. when trials are 'spaced' rather than 'massed' (e.g. Gormezano and Moore, 1969, Terrace, Gibbon, Farrel, and Baldock, 1975). Postulate II puts this fact in general terms. It says that the subject is in a watchkeeping situation during the ITI and that the conditioned stimulus is 'noticed' or 'attended to' to the degree that it is not expected, i.e. to the degree that it is surprising. The beauty of information theory is that it allows us to dispense with the terms in quotation marks—terms that describe the subject's thought processes qualitatively—and quantify the information inherent in the temporal distribution that is the intertrial interval. From watchkeeping experiments (e.g. Smith et al., 1966) we know that the relation between temporal information and reaction time (a measure of 'surprise') is linear.

Cantor and Wilson (1981) have shown that Egger and Miller's (1963) well-known experiment also follows Postulate II. Egger and Miller presented experimental and control groups of rats with sequential stimuli, S_1 and S_2, prior to reinforcement. Unlike the experimental group, the control group received this sequence with occasional presentations of S_1 alone. The results of this training were that S_2 was effective as a conditioned reinforcer only for the control group; for the experimental group, S_2 was redundant—it simply repeated the information carried by S_1. Thus, the effectiveness of S_2 in the Egger and Miller experiment is governed by the same principle that makes long intertrial intervals more effective than short ones in simple Pavlovian conditioning. In other words, it is irrelevant whether the stimulus is informative by virtue of reducing temporal uncertainty (as in the intertrial interval effect) or by virtue of reducing choice uncertainty (as in the Egger and Miller experiment). Information controls the behaviour.

Kamin's (1969) blocking phenomenon follows from Postulate II in essentially the same way. The major difference between the two procedures is the time in the procedure when S_1 is presented. In Egger and Miller's experimental group, S_1

gained information over S_2 by its short (500 ms) precedence to S_2 (*see* Cantor and Wilson, 1980, for a discussion of this). In the blocking procedure, S_1 gained information over S_2 by being presented alone in the first stage of training. Logically, then, there is no difference between Egger and Miller's phenomenon and the blocking phenomenon, and both follow Postulate II.

An information analysis of conditioning and learning helps to break down the language barriers separating the many 'areas' of psychology and shows universal behavioural laws. Postulate II, for example, is quite well known in the perception literature. Attneave (1954) found that maximal information in a complex line drawing occurs at points where the line has greatest curvature. This was determined by connecting those points in a photograph of a cat and then showing that a naive subject could tell that the pictogram was derived from a photograph of a cat. Other evidence for the importance of sharp angles comes from studies of eye fixation. Zusne and Michels (1964) found that eye fixations are most numerous at the corners of geometric figures and at the intersections of lines; fixations were least numerous in the background field and along straight lines. These studies are supported by the classic Russian work (cited by Zusne, 1971) showing that when a subject looks at a face, the gaze is mostly concentrated around the eyes, nose, and mouth, and less around the cheeks and forehead; that is, people allocate their looking time to non-redundant, informative, complex, 'surprising' areas. That this tendency is built into the organism is suggested by studies of infants' eye fixations on geometric figures (Kessen, 1967). On the first day of life they, like adults, fixate more at the corners of geometric shapes and less in the background and along straight lines. My point is that Postulate II—that stimuli preceding S* are effective to the degree that they are preceded by intervals with temporal uncertainty, i.e. to the degree that their onset is informative—operates in visual perception just as it does in the temporal mode in Pavlovian conditioning. In general, it is the informative value of a stimulus that controls behaviour.

Other Evidence

There are two non-experimental areas in which information about the occurrence of an event in space and time is used to predict and control behaviour. The power of information theory to predict these phenomena by the same simple laws that predict behaviours in the experimental space attests to its generality. I refer to the arts of magic and comedy.

In the last several years, I have become a rather serious student of close-up magic. The essence of magic is to take advantage of the fact that the behaviour of everyday objects is known to us as we learn about the world. Objects such as silk scarves have permanence in time: we know when they will move and when they won't; they have permanence in space (generally they stay where they are put); they also have permanence in colour, shape, size, etc. Because of permanence, they are quite uninformative. The magician's job is to increase the informativeness of everyday objects by defying permanence, Silks disappear in the hand. Red silk turns yellow. Big hat becomes little hat. Rabbit comes out of hat. In each case, the ordinarily low information—actually surprisal since the possible alternative outcomes are not all equally likely—of the object is greatly increased. The best tricks use the most common of objects since their behaviour is ordinarily least informative. The magician, then, is controlling the vigilance of the audience by orchestrating information about common objects according to Postulate II. The information may occur in any number of modalities.

A magician takes a long time to learn a certain 'bit of business' beautifully and adds tricks to his repertoire slowly. A given trick is performed for many naive audiences and a common response to the magician's sudden increments in information is anger. The more common response to the trick done well though, is fascination and laughter. Under the proper circumstances, increments in information are funny (e.g. Berlyne, 1972).

Comedy occurs primarily in the sensory modalities of vision, audition, touch, and time. A scene is set and then, in the visual humour of the Vaudevillian, the comedian falls in a hole, is kicked in the behind, or perhaps a worm comes out of his *boutonnière*.

> What's the difference between
>   a psychologist and a magician?
> A magician pulls rabbits from a hat. (*Pause*)
> A psychologist pulls habits from a rat.[2]

In verbal (auditory) comedy such as this, the meaning of words ordinarily establishes a scenario of relatively low uncertainty—and then the punch-line increments it. In the joke, above, the punch-line rhymes two words from the set-up by reversing the first letters of 'rabbit' and 'hat'. The rhyme is crucial here; pulling operants from a rat wouldn't be very funny.

Tactile humour—tickling—is perhaps the most basic laugh-getter of all. Chimpanzees laugh to a tickle at an early age. The Gardners' (Gardner and Gardner, 1969) chimp, Washoe, had symbols for 'tickle' and would communicate that she wanted her trainer to come tickle and play with her. Human babies also respond to tickling at a fairly early age (about 4 months). Tickling gets a laugh because it is simply one more case of stimulation with relatively high temporal uncertainty. At its best, tickling must be somewhat unpredictable. Tickling oneself is no fun at all.

Temporal humour is one of the most interesting modes of comedy. In general, temporal uncertainty about the occurrence of an event is incremented; that is, in the punch-line the expectancy of *when* something will occur is violated. One could ask the question: How much information does it take to get a laugh? Consider an animated cartoon of a basketball player dribbling a ball. After a few normal bounces in the set-up, the ball bounces back to his hand—but first it sticks to the floor. The independent variable would be the time that the ball sticks to the floor quantified in bits, and the dependent variable would be some measure of response strength of laughter. Such an experiment would quantify what the comedian means when he says that 'timing is everything'.

To summarize, in a number of sensory modalities—vision, audition, touch, and time—things are funny when a low probability 'alternative' of what could have happened does happen, i.e. when they have relatively high surprisal. Does anyone know any good taste or smell jokes?

Conclusions

This chapter has been concerned with two primary topics. The first is the assertion that the Pavlovian vs. instrumental dichotomy causes serious problems of double language in that the phenomena generated by each paradigm are similar in minute detail. The second assertion is that neither contiguity nor contingency alone is adequate to serve as a metric that can organize the learning environment. Both problems can be solved neatly if one thinks of the learning experiment as a study in communication between experimenter (environment) and subject and organizes the environment in the quantitative terms of information theory.

In so doing, the way is opened for the many apparently diverse phenomena that make up the field to be synthesized into a few quantitative generalizations. One of the most useful aspects of this analysis is that it allows for an integration of the data of conditioning and learning and the data of other literatures such as cognition, perception, and perhaps language. All of these fields can be defined as studying behaviour as a function of information about the occurrence of important events in space and time. Quantification of the stimulus in both language and perception has been an eternal problem—it is as difficult as quantifying the information in a drawing, a joke, or a magic trick. The principles of behaviour working in these stimulus environments are the same as those governing behaviour in the Skinner box and Pavlov harness. In the latter, however, the stimuli are simpler and the quantification is easier. If one can work out the prediction and control of behaviour in the simple environments by quantifying every last bit of information about the occurrence of reinforcement, perhaps then the principles can be more easily applied in the stimulus sets that are complex.

Notes

1. I thank Dr J. J. McDowell for his helpful comments on an earlier version of this manuscript.
2. Dr Sheldon Zalkind, personal communication.

References

Attneave, F. (1954). Some informational aspects of visual perception. *Psychological Review*, **61**, 183–193.

Badia, P., Harsh, J., and Abbott, B. (1979). Choosing between predictable and unpredictable shock conditions: data and theory. *Psychological Bulletin*, **86**, 1107–1131.

Baum, W. M. (1973). The correlation-based law of effect. *Journal of the Experimental Analysis of Behavior*, **20**, 137–153.

Berlyne, D. E. (1972). Humor and its kin. In *The Psychology of Humor* (J. H. Goldstein and P. E. McGhee, eds), Academic Press, New York.

Bersh, P. J. (1951). The influence of two variables upon the establishment of a secondary reinforcer for operant responses. *Journal of Experimental Psychology*, **41**, 62–63.

Bloomfield, T. M. Reinforcement schedule: contingency or contiguity? In *Reinforcement, Behavioral Analyses* (R. M. Gilbert and J. R. Millenson, eds), pp. 165–205, Academic Press, New York.

Buck, J. and Buck, E. (1968).Mechanism of rhythmic synchronous flashing of fireflies. *Science, New York*, **159**, 1319–1327.

Buck, J. and Buck, E. (1976). Synchronous fireflies. *Scientific American*, **234**, 74–85.

Cantor, M. B. (1979). Brain stimulation reinforcement: implications of an electrode artifact. *Science*, **204**, 1235–1237.

Cantor, M. B. (1981). Bad habits: Models of induced ingestion in satiated rats and people. *Nutrition in Health and Disease*, (in press).

Cantor, M. B. and LoLordo, V. M. (1970). Rats prefer signaled reinforcing brain stimulation to unsignaled ESB. *Journal of Comparative and Physiological Psychology*, **79**, 259–270.

Cantor, M. B. and Wilson, J. (1978). Polydipsia induced by a schedule of brain stimulation reinforcement. *Learning and Motivation*, **9**, 428–445.

Cantor, M. B. and LoLordo, V. M. (1972). Reward value of brain stimulation is inversely related to uncertainty about its onset. *Journal of Comparative and Physiological Psychology*, **79**, 259–270.

Cantor, M. B. and Wilson, J. (1981). Temporal uncertainty as an associative metric: operant simulations of Pavlovian conditioning. *Journal of Experimental Psychology: General*, in press.

Catania, A. C. and Reynolds, G. S. (1968). A quantitative analysis of the responding maintained by interval schedules of reinforcement. *Journal of the Experimental Analysis of Behavior*, **11**, 327–385.

Church, R. M. (1978). The internal clock. In *Cognitive Processes in Animal Behavior* (S. H. Hulse, H. Fowler, and W. K. Honig, eds), Lawrence Erlbaum Associates, Hillsdale, N. J.

Creelman, C. D. (1962). Human discrimination of auditory duration. *Journal of the Acoustical Society of America*, **34**, 582–593.

DeCasper, A. J. and Zeiler, M. D. (1977). Time limits for completing fixed ratios. IV. Components of the ratio. *Journal of the Experimental Analysis of Behavior*, **27**, 235–244.

Eckerman, D. A. (1973). Uncertainty reduction and conditioned reinforcement. *Psychological Record*, **23**, 39–47.

Egger, M. D. and Miller, N. E. (1963). When is reward reinforcing? An experimental study of the information hypothesis. *Journal of Comparative and Physiological Psychology*, **56**, 132–137.

Epstein, R., Lanza, R. P., and Skinner, B. F. (1980). Symbolic communication between two pigeons (*Columba livia domestica*). *Science*, **207**, 543–545.

Falk, J. L. (1971). The nature and determinants of adjunctive behavior, *Physiology and Behavior*, **6**, 577–588.

Fantino, E. (1977). Conditioned reinforcement: choice and information. In *Handbook of Operant Behavior,* (W. K. Honig and J. E. R. Staddon, eds), pp. 313–339, Prentice-Hall, Englewood Cliffs, N. J.

Gaddy, J. R. (1979). Neostriatal lesion effects upon temporally-spaced operant responding in the rat. Dissertation, Emory University.

Gamzu, E. R. and Williams, D. R. (1972). Associative factors underlying the pigeon's key pecking in autoshaping procedures. *Journal of the Experimental Analysis of Behavior*, **19**, 225.

Gardner, R. A. and Gardner, B. T. (1969). Teaching sign language to a chimpanzee. *Science, New York*, **165**, 664–672.

Getty, D. J. (1975). Discrimination of short temporal intervals: a comparison of two models. *Perception and Psychophysics*, **18**, 1–8.

Getty, D. J. (1976). Counting process in human timing. *Perception and Psychophysics*, **20**, 191–197.

Gibbon, J. (1977). Scaler expectancy theory and Weber's law in animal timing. *Psychological Review*, **84**, 279–325.

Gormezano, I. and Coleman, S. R. (1973). The law of effect and CR contingent modification of the UCS. *Conditioned Reflex*, **8**, 41–55.

Gormezano, I. and Moore, J. W. (1969). Classical conditioning. In *Learning Processes* (M. H. Marx, ed.), pp. 121–269, Macmillan, New York.

Grant, D. A. and Norris, E. B. (1947). Eyelid conditioning as influenced by the presence of sensitized beta-responses, *Journal of Experimental Psychology*, **37**, 423–433.

Grice, G. R. (1948). The relation of secondary reinforcement to delayed reward in visual discrimination learning. *Journal of Experimental Psychology*, **38**, 1–16.

Grice, G. R. (1977). Information-processing dynamics of human eyelid conditioning. *Journal of Experimental Psychology:General*, **106**, 71–93.

Herrnstein, R. J. (1970). On the law of effect. *Journal of the Experimental Analysis of Behavior*, **2**, 243–269.

Hick, H. E. (1952). On the rate of gain of information. *Quarterly Journal of Experimental Psychology*, **4**, 11–26.

Howarth, C. I. and Treisman, M. (1961). Lowering of an auditory threshold by a near threshold warning signal. *Quarterly Journal of Experimental Psychology*, **13**, 12–18.

Hyman, R. (1953). Stimulus information as a determinant of reaction time. *Journal of Experimental Psychology*, **45**, 188–196.

Laties, V. G., Weiss, B., Clark, R. L. and Reynolds, M. D. (1965). Overt 'mediating' behavior during temporally spaced responding. *Journal of the Experimental Analysis of Behavior*, **8**, 106–116.

Kamin, L. J. (1969). Predictability, surprise, attention, and conditioning. In *Punishment and Aversive Behavior* (B. A. Campbell and R. M. Church, eds), Appleton-Century-Crofts, New York.

Kessen, W. (1967). Sucking and looking: two organized congenital patterns of behavior in the human newborn. In *Early Behavior* H. W. Stevenson, E. H. Hess, and H. L. Rheingold, eds), John Wiley, New York.

Killeen, P. R. (1978). Superstition:A matter of bias, not detectability. *Science*, **199**, 88–90.

Kimble, G. A. (1961). *Hilgard and Marquis' Conditioning and Learning*. Appleton-Century-Crofts, New York.

Klemmer, E. G. (1957). Simple reaction time as a function of time uncertainty. *Journal of*

Experimental Psychology, **54**, 195–200.

Kremer, E. F. and Kamin, L. J. (1971). The truly random control procedure: associative or non-associative effects in the rat. *Journal of Comparative and Physiological Psychology*, **74**, 203–210.

Levey, A. B. and Martin, I. (1968). Shape of the conditioned eyelid response. *Psychological Review*, **75**, 398.

Miller, G. A. (1953). What is information? *American Psychologist*, **8**, 3–11.

Miller, G. A. (1956). The magical number seven , plus or minus two: some limits on our capacity for processing information. *Psychological Review*, **63**, 81–97.

Miller, G. A. and Frick, F. C. (1949). Statistical behavioristics and sequences of response. *Psychological Review*, **56**, 311–329.

Pavlov, I. P. (1927). *Conditioned Reflexes: An Investigation of the Physiological Activity of the Cerebral Cortex*, Oxford University Press, London.

Perkins, C. C., Jr (1968). An analysis of the concept of reinforcement. *Psychological Review*, **75**, 155–172.

Platt, J. R., Kuch, D. O., and Bitgood, S. C. (1973). Rats' lever press durations as psychophysical judgements of time. *Journal of the Experimental Analysis of Behavior*, **19**, 239–250.

Platt, J. R. (1979). Temporal differentiation and the psychophysics of time. *Advances in Analysis of Behavior*, **1**, 1–29.

Prokasy, W. F. Classical eyelid conditioning: shaping. In *Classical Conditioning: A Symposium* (W. F. Prokasy, ed.), pp. 208–225, Appleton-Century-Crofts, New York.

Prokasy, W. F., Ebel, H. C., and Thompson, D. D. (1963). Response shaping at long interstimulus intervals in classical eyelid conditioning. *Journal of Experimental Pschology*, **66**, 138–141.

Rescorla, R. A. (1967). Pavlovian conditioning and its proper control procedures. *Psychological Review*, **74**, 71–80.

Rescorla, R. A. (1968). Probability of shock in the presence and absence of CS in fear conditioning. *Journal of Comparative and Physiological Psychology*, **66**, 1–5.

Ross, L. E. (1959). The decremental effects of partial reinforcement during acquisition of the conditioned eyelid response. *Journal of Experimental Psychology*, **57**, 74–82.

Ross, L. E. (1961). Conditioned fear as a function of CS–UCS and probe stimulus intervals. *Journal of Experimental Psychology*, **61**, 265–273.

Schlosberg, H. (1937). The relationship between success and the laws of conditioning. *Psychological Review*, **44**, 379–394.

Schwartz, B. and Gamzu, E. (1977). Pavlovian control of operant behaviour: an anlysis of autoshaping and its implications for operant conditioning. In *Handbook of Operant Behavior* (W. K. Honig and J. E. R. Staddon, eds), pp. 53–97, Prentice-Hall, Englewood Cliffs, N. J.

Schwartz, B. and Williams, D. R. (1972). Two different kinds of key-peck in the pigeon: some properties of responses maintained by negative and positive response–reinforcer contingencies. *Journal of the Experimental Analysis of Behavior*, **18**, 201–216.

Schwartz, B., Hamilton, B., and Silberberg, A. (1975). Behavioral contrast in the pigeon: a study of the duration of key pecking maintained on multiple schedules of reinforcement. *Journal of the Experimental Analysis of Behavior*, **24**, 199–206.

Shannon, C. E. and Weaver, W. (1949). *The Mathematical Theory of Communication*, University of Illinois Press, Urbana.

Simon, H. A. (1974). How big is a chunk? *Science*, **103**, 482–488.

Skinner, B. F. (1936). The effect of amount of conditioning on an interval of time before reinforcement. *Journal of General Psychology*, **14**, 279–293.

Skinner, B. F. (1938). *The Behavior of Organism*, Appleton-Century-Crofts, New York.

Skinner, B. F. (1948). 'Superstition' in the pigeon. *Journal of Experimental Psychology*, **38**, 168–172.

Smith, R. P., Warm, J. S., and Alluisi, E. A. (1966). Effects of temporal uncertainty on watchkeeping performance. *Perception and Psychophysics*, **1**, 293–299.

Snodgrass, G., Luce, D., and Galanter, E. (1967). Some experiments on simple reaction time. *Journal of Experimental Psychology*, **75**, 1–17.

Solomon, R. L. (1964). Punishment. *American Psychologist*, **19**, 239–253.

Spence, K. W. (1966). Cognitive and drive factors in the extinction of the conditioned eye blink in human subjects. *Psychological Review*, **73**, 445–458.

Staddon J. E. R. and Simmelhag, V. L. (1971). The 'superstition' experiment: a reexamination of the implications for the principles of adaptive behavior. *Psychological Review*, **78**, 3–43.

Stroud, J. M. (1955). The fine structure of psychological time. In *Information Theory in Psychology* (H. Quastler, ed.), The Free Press, Glencoe, Ill.

Stubbs, D. A. (1979). Temporal discrimination in psychophysics. *Advances in Analysis of Behavior*, **1**, 341–369.

Terrace, H. S., Gibbon, J., Farrell, L., and Baldock, H. D. (1975). Temporal factors influencing the acquisition of auto-shaped key-peck. *Animal Learning and Behavior*, **3**, 53–62.

Wingfield, A. and Byrnes, D. L. (1972). Decay of information in short-term memory. *Science*, **176**, 690–692.

Woodrow, H. (1930). The reproduction of temporal intervals. *Journal of Experimental Psychology*, **13**, 473–499.

Woodworth, R. S. and Schlosberg, H. (1954). *Experimental Psychology*, Holt, New York.

Zusne, L. (1971). Measure of symmetry. *Perception and Psychophysics*, **9**, 363–366.

Zusne, L. and Michels, K. M. (1964). Non-representational shapes and eye movements. *Perceptual and Motor Skills*, **18**, 11–20.

Predictability, Correlation, and Contiguity
Edited by P. Harzem and M. D. Zeiler
© 1981 John Wiley & Sons Ltd

Chapter 9

Economics and Operant Conditioning

James Allison

Introduction

Even a casual record would show that the daily activities of the laboratory rat, confined to an operant conditioning box 24 h each day, vary dramatically with the conditions of life arranged by the experimenter. Given free access to food pellets and water, and a lever projecting from a wall but serving no apparent function, the daily log of activities will reveal a good deal of eating and drinking, but little pressing of the lever. Remove the free pellets, wire the lever to a pellet dispenser, and the daily log may soon show several hundred or several thousand more lever-presses than before, depending on the number of responses required for each pellet, and the size of each.

Many generations of psychology students have learned, and many more will learn, a pleasingly simple account of this dramatic change in the rat's behaviour. Having gone without food for some time, food becomes a potential reinforcer for the hungry rat. Because food is now a reinforcer, the contingent delivery of food, close on the heels of the instrumental response, strengthens the tendency to press the lever again. As an operational index of this strengthening process, witness the rise in the probability of the instrumental response relative to the time when food was freely available, the lever non-functional.

This chapter proposes that the response-strengthening metaphor has become so difficult to defend, and so limited in comparison with other theoretical accounts, that it merits no further use as an explanatory concept. The chapter opens with some reasons for discontent with the notion that laboratory rewards strengthen behaviour, goes on to show why such rewards might better be viewed as economic goods or commodities, and closes with some models of instrumental performance that address the economics of operant conditioning.

Rewards as Reinforcers

In explaining why contingent food strengthens instrumental lever-pressing in the hungry rat, our associationistic rearing in the house of Pavlov, Ebbinghaus,

Locke, and Aristotle naturally leads our attention to a sequence of two events in close temporal order: the antecedent response, lever-pressing, and the consequent response, eating. Having accepted eating as a reinforcer, we ask what all such consequent events have in common. The answer defines the class 'reinforcers', and takes a first step towards a theory of reinforcement.

A sampling would reveal several possible answers, and much ingenuity. Reinforcement might occur if the consequent event were to reduce a drive, such as hunger or thirst (Hull, 1943), or any strong internal stimuli, such as those of hunger, thirst, pain, or fear (Miller, 1951). Or it might occur if the response were to bring about some pleasant state of affairs, as a sweet might do for a rat deprived of neither food nor water; indeed, any powerful consummatory response, such as the drinking elicited by saccharin, even though it lacks nutritional value, might serve as a reinforcer (Sheffield, 1966). A reinforcer might be any event that follows the response so closely as to crowd out other activities: the hungry rat eats so eagerly that no other response can easily intervene in the associative sequence between pressing the lever and eating (Guthrie, 1935). Reinforcers might be biologically adaptive; any biologically significant event might do (Bolles, 1972; Hearst and Jenkins, 1974), assuming that such events can be identified independently of their reinforcing effects. They might be species-specific approach responses (Glickman and Schiff, 1967), such as the attack the prey elicits from the predator. Or a reinforcer might simply be any consequent that would normally be more probable than the antecedent response (Premack, 1965), as eating is more probable than pressing the lever when lever and food are both freely available. Other reinforcement theorists, otherwise averse to theory, content themselves with a non-committal empirical approach: if consequence Z is known to reinforce antecedent response X, further experience may show that Z can reinforce antecedent response Y as well (Skinner, 1953; Meehl, 1950).

All of these theories would agree that for the thirsty rat living in an activity wheel, an antecedent running response, rotating the wheel through several degrees of the circle, should be reinforced if followed closely by drinking. A powerful consummatory response that can crowd out other responses, drinking may also cause a pleasant reduction in the strong internal stimuli of thirst. A biologically significant, species-specific approach to water, normally more probable than running, we already know that drinking can reinforce a variety of responses, including the response of our example (Premack, 1962). Theory and previous experiment leave us ill equipped to deal with any failure of drinking to reinforce running, but such failures exist. As reported by Premack (1965), drinking closely followed running many times throughout each experimental session, yet running failed to rise above its normal level over the course of several such sessions. Others have experienced similar failures with non-thirsty rats running for sucrose solution. With both responses freely available the rats spent more time drinking the sucrose solution than running, but under several subsequent schedules instrumental running failed to rise above its normal level

(Mazur, 1975). Such failures suggest a logical difficulty in classifying drinking as a reinforcer: the class does, but drinking does not, automatically strengthen an antecedent running response.

This is not to say that these rats learned nothing of the contingent relation between running and drinking. Further tests might have revealed some evidence of learning, even though the tests described above revealed no reinforcement of running. But the concept of response reinforcement makes no place for a distinction between learning and performance, so leaves us to conclude simply that the results revealed no reinforcement of running.

A class of events bearing the reinforcement property would serve little purpose unless we could sort other events into another class, none bearing the reinforcement property. Psychologists long accepted two such classes—reinforcing events, such as drinking, and reinforceable ones, such as running—but many now question this distinction. Much of the doubt stems from the seminal work by Premack (1962), who showed that two responses, running and drinking, could each belong to either class, depending on the experimental conditions. If rats have already gone without water for some time, while running as much as they pleased, they spend more time drinking than running when finally given free access to water in a freely rotatable wheel. In other words, in the water-deprived rat, drinking is more probable than running. If conditions are now changed, so that the water-deprived rat must run a fair amount for each little bit of contingent drinking, the rat runs more than the normal amount. Such a result would lead us to classify drinking among the reinforcing events, running among the reinforceable events. But if the rats have had plenty of water and no chance to run, they spend more time running than drinking when finally allowed to run and drink as much as they please. If the run-deprived rat must now do a fair amount of drinking for each little bit of contingent running, the rat drinks more than the normal amount. Combined with the first, this second result would lead us to conclude that either response can reinforce the other, depending on the experimental conditions. But if each response jumps from either class to the other because of a change in experimental conditions, the responses themselves defy classification. If we must have such classes, we must define each one in terms of something other than the name of a response, such as drinking. Premack (1965) suggested that the class of reinforcers comprises all responses more probable than the one being reinforced, and that all less probable responses belong to the reinforceable class.

Similar work has shown that eating may reinforce playing among children in whom the probability of eating free candy exceeds that of playing a free pinball machine, but that playing may reinforce eating among other children more likely to play than eat (Premack, 1959). This sort of experiment would be said to demonstrate the *reversibility* of the reinforcement relation: A reinforces B under one set of conditions, and B reinforces A under another set. The experiment on running and drinking illustrates the control of reversibility by experimental manipulation, depriving the rats of water in one condition, of running in the other. The experiment with children illustrates another kind of control, one that capitalizes on individual differences: some children are eaters, others are players.

As a final example, research with a monkey showed that working a horizontal lever reinforced two less probable responses, while the least probable response, pushing a plunger, reinforced neither of the others. In isolation, those results would fit the notion that some responses are reinforcers, others reinforceable. But one of the three responses, opening a hinged door, resisted such classification: because this intermediate response reinforced the least probable response, but failed to reinforce the most probable response, opening the door would have to be classed as both a reinforcer and a non-reinforcer (Premack, 1963).

We might conclude that the evidence of these experiments offers no compelling reason to discard the concept of response reinforcement; we can simply define a response reinforcer as the more probable member of any pair of responses. But we might debate this conclusion; we might conclude instead that Premack's theory makes the concept of reinforcement unnecessary in some cases, untenable in all others. If the theory is correct, we need not assume that the contingent response strengthens the other. Having seen that the contingent response has the higher probability, we need not assume any additional properties. When it does raise the other response above the normal level, we may still choose to call the contingent response a reinforcer, but the decision reflects no more than a predilection for a certain kind of metaphor—the facts themselves require no metaphor at all. In all other cases, the contingent response is not the more probable of the two, so should not raise the other above the normal level. Given no such rise, we would in those cases have no factual reason to call the contingent response a reinforcer; there, the metaphor would be untenable. We have good reason to doubt the correctness of Premack's theory (Allison, 1978; Allison and Timberlake, 1974), but that particular issue has no bearing on the argument at hand: to the extent that Premack's or any other such theory is correct, the concept of response reinforcement is unnecessary in some cases, untenable in all remaining cases.

We should note again the distinction between learning and performance. Experience with a particular contingency schedule may strengthen the rat's conviction that water depends on running, even though the schedule may not cause running to rise above its normal level. Some recent models imply that such learning might be revealed by a change in the terms of the schedule: instead of allowing 20 s of drinking for every 10 s of running, allow only 15 s. This sort of tactic has a long history in psychology. It is at least as old as the work in Tolman's laboratory on latent learning (Blodgett, 1929) in hungry rats, which revealed a dramatic improvement in maze-running to a goal baited with food, following several lackadaisical runs to the unbaited goal. Many believe that the sudden improvement showed that the rats had already learned the layout of the maze, but merely failed to display their knowledge until moved by an expectation of food in the goal.

Behaviour recorded under another sort of procedure, experimental extinction, has strengthened many psychologists in their conviction that responses too get strengthened. We return to our opening scene: After the rat has spent several days pressing the lever once for each food pellet, the experimenter raises the instrumental requirement in several small steps to 256 presses per pellet. Within limits, the rat's usual response to a rise in the instrumental requirement is a steady rise in the total number of lever-presses performed throughout the day (e.g. Teitelbaum, 1957). Next the experimenter disconnects the feeder and the lever. In the first hour of the unannounced shutdown the rat continues to press the lever in full accord with the previous rules, and much more than it did in the days when lever and food were both freely available. But the next hour shows fewer presses, the next still fewer. After several hours, lever-pressing falls to a low level at or near the original.

Setting aside such matters as spontaneous recovery and inhibition, we can interpret such facts with ease in terms of reinforcement. Because contingent food strengthened the response, subsequent omission of food—experimental extinction—will weaken the response through a simple reversal of the strengthening process. The steady decrease in responding, hour by hour, reflects the progressive weakening of the response through the repeated omission of reinforcement.

The same facts admit an alternative interpretation, as suggested by the phraseology of the example. Experimental extinction can be viewed as a clumsy method of teaching the rat the new rules of the game. Viewed in this light, it comes as no surprise if it takes the rat several hours to learn, as it finally does, that eating no longer depends on pressing the lever. If anything gets weakened or extinguished, perhaps it is the rat's conviction that pressing the lever causes the pellet to appear.

This alternative account is not entirely fanciful; close observation of behaviour under conditions resembling the shutdown of our example may cast some doubt on the notion that training strengthened, and extinction weakened, the response. As a case in point, a particular rat with food, a retractable water tube, and a retractable lever freely available typically spends about 28 s holding the lever in the daily 1 h session. After this preliminary baseline phase, the rules change. Now the rat must hold the lever a certain time—mostly 10 s, sometimes 15 s—for each opportunity to drink for a certain time. After some 17 h of training under the new rules, hold followed by drink many hundreds of times, the rat now spends 600–700 s holding the lever in a typical 1 h session. Note that the rat perforce began each of the 17 training sessions by holding the lever, moving to the tube, drinking, and returning to the lever—an enforced sequence that should have strengthened the tendency to hold the lever, as indeed it seems to have done.

Now the rules change again, back to the original baseline condition: Now the experimenter begins each session as before, introducing the lever and the tube at the same time, both remaining freely available throughout the session. If we looked at nothing but the total amount of holding recorded in each of the first few postcontingency baseline sessions, we would probably conclude that the contingent drinking had strengthened the lever-holding response. The first such session shows a total of some 48 s of holding—more than the 28 recorded originally, before training. The second session shows a slightly lower total, the third still lower. But a closer look at the behaviour shows that the rat does not accumulate these times by starting each session as it was trained to do, holding the lever for several seconds and then switching to the tube. On the contrary, the rat begins each of these postcontingency baseline sessions with several thousand licks at the water tube. Only then does the rat move to the lever, hold it for several seconds, and then resume licking, trying the lever a second or third time after a few thousand or several hundred more licks (Allison, 1976). I have seen the same pattern in many other rats in many similar experiments. The pattern is difficult to explain in terms of a simple reinforcement of instrumental responding during training. It seems rather to reflect a residual habit of responding to the lever after drinking, a sequence which occurred several hundred times during training. More fancifully, the pattern might reflect an inclination to test an apparatus that seems to have suddenly malfunctioned—a low priority test, performed much later in deference to an unexpected windfall, several free licks at the tube.

This example joins many others in which the behavioural pattern enforced over a long period of training promptly fell apart upon the removal of the contingency (Allison and Timberlake, 1975; Ayllon and Azrin, 1965; Baer, 1962; Holstein and Hundt, 1965; Wasik, 1968). We can generalize the lesson of the latent learning experiments by saying that animals may sometimes learn while showing little or no evidence of response reinforcement at the time the learning presumably occurred. The examples just cited suggest another critical generalization, that the organism may sometimes show a large rise in the amount or speed of responding while showing no evidence of reinforcement by some other measure.

Other studies reveal another critical point, that humans may learn a response that is never reinforced just as well as one that is always reinforced (Estes, 1969, pp. 75–81). Although the logic of reinforcement favours prompt application of the reinforcing agent, under certain conditions humans learn better when the reinforcer comes later than when it comes immediately (Buchwald, 1969). The parallel experiment has not been done with animals, of whom the literature generally supports the logic of prompt application, but it does appear that under certain conditions rats will learn as well when reinforcement comes as much as 8 min later as when it comes immediately (Lett, 1973). As another critical question, why should a particular reinforcer work well for some responses, but not others? If the hungry hamster digs so readily for contingent food, why so reluctant to wash its face for the same food (Shettleworth, 1975)? Finally, why may a reinforcer work so well at first, so poorly later on? Why does the boy, pressing a lever for all of his daily food, work so willingly over the first 15 days, less on the next, and not at all on the next few days, forcing a humane cancellation of the experiment (Longfellow, 1967, as described by Walker, 1969, p. 55)?

The rest of the chapter seeks answers to many of the questions raised here, but has little to say about learning. We focus rather on performance, taking refuge under the assumption that the organism somehow learns the environmental contingencies over the course of its experience with the world at hand.

I do not pretend to understand how the learning occurs, a question that belongs to another specialized field of inquiry. To the eye of a non-specialist, it might appear that the field's main achievement since Aristotle is the exposure of his errors through modern experimental method. Probably his chief contribution to principles of learning, periodically re-invented by subsequent theorists (Esper, 1964), is the principle of contiguity: 'Acts of recollection, as they occur in experience, are due to the fact that one movement has by nature another that succeeds it in regular order' (Dennis, 1948, p. 5). But modern research shows that sheer contiguity, A followed closely by B, may not suffice to teach the linkage between the two. Having already learned that shock follows noise, the rat, now shocked right after a compound signal of noise plus light, may later respond to the light as if it had never been followed by shock (Kamin, 1969). Thus, sheer contiguity may not guarantee learning. We have already seen in addition that contiguity is not necessary, that learning can occur in its absence (Buchwald, 1969; Lett, 1973; see also Revusky and Garcia, 1970). Modern research suggests further that some of the classic instances of learning by contiguity (Guthrie and Horton, 1946) might better be viewed as species-typical responses having little to do with learning or contiguity (Moore and Stuttard, 1979).

Some believe that only principle of any major promise since Aristotle is the modern principle of contingency: the organism may come to act as if A forecasts B only if A has predicted B in a statistical sense—as it has if neither warning tone nor shock ever happened without the other, but not if shock often happened without the tone (Rescorla, 1972). But once again, this is not to say that the animal learned nothing of the relation between A and B even if A did not predict B. The human observer, keeping a close tally of A and B, might later compute a measure of correlation between the two and learn that A and B were statistically independent, that A did not predict B. And some believe that if a dog gets occasional shock whatever it happens to be doing at the time—running, jumping, barking, sitting quietly, sniffing, howling, biting the cage, or wagging the tail—the dog too may learn that shock, B, was independent of any particular behaviour, A (Maier, Seligman, and Solomon, 1969). The logical conclusion would seem to agree with the premise stated before: the animal somehow learns the relations at hand, whether the relation be one of dependence or independence. The final section of this chapter assumes that the development of models of performance need not await a comprehensive understanding of learning. As one further preliminary, the next section calls attention to some affinities between psychology and economics which, with a few recent exceptions (e.g. Rachlin, Green, Kagel, and Battalio, 1976), have mostly gone unnoticed.

Rewards as Economic Goods

If food is not a reinforcer, what is it? This section shows why food, along with many other items commonly used as rewards in the laboratory study of animal behaviour, might well be viewed as economic goods or commodities.

Some define an economic good as something that someone is willing to pay for. Many definitions depend on the concept of scarcity: an economic good or commodity is relatively scarce, as food generally is, but as fresh air generally is not (Samuelson, 1976). Because scarcity itself has unexpected subtleties, we begin by identifying some of its common varieties.

When an experimental psychologist speaks of depriving the animal of food, this generally means that the experimenter has cornered the local supply of food, and has made the animal do entirely without for several hours, or has kept the animal on a daily ration so short as to cause a significant, controlled loss of body weight over a period of days or weeks. This is one kind of deprivation, and one variety of scarcity from the animal's point of view, relative to another time when food was more abundant.

A second variety also depends on the experimenter's complete control of the food supply. When the experimenter wires the feeder to the lever, making food contingent on the rat's pressing the lever, food is now scarce in a slightly different sense. Now the rat has some control over its access to food, but the access is still limited: no food comes forth unless the rat presses the lever. This is another variety of scarcity, a kind which characterizes all contingencies. The particular terms of the contingency, called the schedule, may be more generous or less. As one press of the lever for each small pellet is more generous than 10 presses for each, a large pellet for each press of the lever is more generous than a small pellet for each. But none of these schedules affords free access to an abundant supply of food; food remains scarce in the sense that it depends on the rat's pressing the lever.

The animal may encounter each of these two varieties of scarcity in the natural habitat, as well as the laboratory. In the natural habitat, food is often patchy—variable in space or time—so the animal may spend an appreciable part of its time and effort in foraging, despite which it may often have to settle for meals smaller or less frequent than the meals it would make if food were more abundant. Pressing a lever for food can be viewed as a kind of foraging behaviour, admittedly different in form from that normally seen in the animal's evolutionary habitat.

Contingency schedules in the laboratory generally involve a third variety of scarcity that probably occurs in the wild as well, but is much easier to identify under the more controlled conditions of life in the laboratory. The first step in defining this third variety is to imagine an Eden-like world with lever and food both freely available without limit. Ever present for the asking, lever and food are free goods in the lexicon of the economist (Samuelson, 1976). In the technical language of psychology, this nutritional Paradise is the paired baseline condition (Timberlake and Allison, 1974)—the lever one member of the pair, food the other. Imagine next how much the rat would eat and how little it would press the lever in the paired baseline condition. To make the case more concrete, suppose the rat eats six hundred 45 mg pellets and presses the lever five times in the typical baseline day. The baseline phase completed, the experimenter prepares for the next phase by emptying the food trough, wiring lever to feeder, and setting the terms of the contingency schedule: one press of the lever for each food pellet. Note that if the rat now presses the lever no more than it did in the typical baseline day, it would thereby earn much less food than it ate then: five pellets for five presses, considerably less than the customary 600 pellets. That condition of life is known technically as *response deprivation*, in reference to the fact that the rat would necessarily eat less than it did in baseline if it chose to perform no more than the baseline number of lever presses.

Response deprivation, our third variety of scarcity, is a most effective kind. Under the conditions of our example, it would induce the rat to do several hundred more lever presses than it did in the paired baseline condition—a result that may bear more than a superficial resemblance to productive labour in the human economy. Stripped to the bare essentials, inducing persons to labour is largely a matter of inducing them, by proper management of contingencies, to do more of the productive activity than they would if left undisturbed in Paradise. Without the kind of antecedent scarcity known as response deprivation, organisms apparently will not do more of the productive activity than they do in baseline (Timberlake and Allison, 1974). Perhaps this is why Premack's rats (Premack, 1965) failed to run any more than they had done in baseline; that particular schedule allowed so much drinking for each bit of running that the rats could do the baseline amount of drinking simply by doing the baseline amount of running. A less generous schedule probably would have induced more running, as in his earlier experiment (Premack, 1962).

As an analogue of labour in the human economy of an advanced civilization, our example may lack a crucial element: the rat works in direct exchange for the commodity, rather than an artificial token, such as a dollar, later exchanged as coin of the realm for the commodity in question. But we can surely debate the cruciality of the missing element. The father of economics himself has said that 'The real price of everything, what everything really costs to the man who wants to acquire it, is the toil and trouble of acquiring it' (Smith, 1776, p. 36). Later economists too have referred to effort as the bedrock foundation of price (Robbins, 1930). Others commenting on the economist's distinction between work and purchase (Castro and Weingarten, 1970) have called attention to experiments in which chimpanzees worked for poker chips later exchanged for peanuts or raisins (Cowles, 1937; Wolfe, 1936), and similar experiments with cats (Smith, 1939) and dogs (Ellson, 1937). Admittedly convenient in an advanced human economy, the artificial currency may play no crucial role in basic economic processes.

We have just reviewed some facts of animal behaviour that seem to justify the interpretation of laboratory rewards as economic commodities. We have also seen that laboratory experiments generally involve one or more of our three kinds of scarcity: forcing the animal to consume less than it would if the commodity were freely available, requiring some behaviour in exchange for the commodity, or making sure that the baseline amount of that behaviour would earn less of the commodity than the animal would consume if the commodity were free. What other facts might bear on the validity of this view? What have economists learned about the consumption of goods in the marketplace by the aggregate of human consumers? How does this compare with the behaviour of the laboratory animal as it buys food or other commodities at an effort price defined by the terms of the contingency schedule?

All else being equal, more beer, cars, shoes, or perfume can be sold at a low price than a higher one. Economists refer to this simple inverse relation between

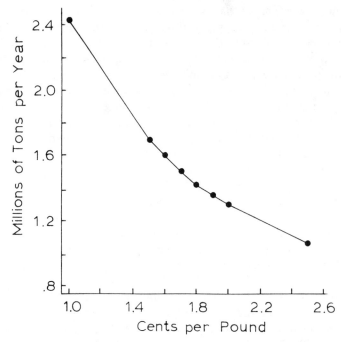

Figure 9.1. Total annual consumption of watermelons as a function of unit price. Based on data reported by Lancaster (1969)

price and total consumption as the *demand law*. Perhaps the most nearly universal law yet known to economics, practically all commodities are supposed to obey it. Figure 9.1 shows an example from the U. S. watermelon market, based on data reported by Lancaster (1969). The figure shows a steady decline in the total tonnage consumed as the unit price, in cents per pound, rises.

The relation seen in Figure 9.1 has also appeared in laboratory experiments with animals. In one such experiment, each of two rats lived in its test cage 24 h each day, with water freely available. Food, in the form of a 45 mg pellet, could be got at the price of a certain number of lever presses. The price varied across days, from as little as one press per pellet to as much as 220 presses per pellet. Figure 9.2 plots the results in logarithmic coordinates, mean number of grams consumed against the unit price of food, in responses per gram. The solid circles show that consumption generally decreased as price increased (based on Collier, Hirsch, and Hamlin, 1972, Experiment 2). The open circles show similar results from a similar experiment with seven goldfish tested in 1 h sessions; the fish got food by striking a target attached to an underwater lever (Rozin and Mayer, 1964, Experiment 3). The demand function for the fish expresses consumption as a percentage of the amount consumed at the lowest price.

A recent paper adds several examples to those of Figure 9.2 (Allison, 1979*b*; *see also* Lea, 1978). The additional examples extend the analogy in two directions, enlarging both the menagerie of laboratory consumers and the list of obedient goods: humans, monkeys, rats, fish, food, drink, heat, safety, and drugs.

As promised at the beginning of this section, we can now see several reasons why an item such as a food pellet, contingent on the performance of an instrumental response, can be viewed as an economic good or commodity. The

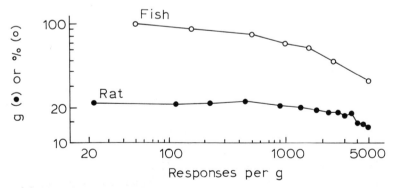

Figure 9.2. Mean food consumption by rats in 24 h sessions (solid circles, $n = 2$; adapted from Collier *et al.*, 1972, Experiment 2), and goldfish in 1 h sessions (open circles, $n = 7$; adapted from Rozin and Mayer, 1964, Experiment 3), as functions of the unit price of food. Food consumption is expressed in terms of grams for the rats, and in terms of the percentage of the amount consumed at the lowest price for the goldfish

interaction between experimenter and subject contains many basic ingredients of an economic transaction: the food satisfies one or more definitions of scarcity; the animal pays an effort price in exchange for the food, eating less as the price rises, in conformity with the demand law. Money, the missing ingredient, does not seem to be missed by either kind of consumer, animal or human, in so far as the demand law is concerned.

These particular connections between economics and the experimental analysis of behaviour depend on some basic concepts from the economics of consumer demand. Other connections depend on concepts from labour supply theory. To illustrate this second route, the next section begins by analysing some procedures commonly used in the operant conditioning laboratory in terms of the constraints they impose on the subject's behaviour.

Performance Models

Experimental Constraints

Figure 9.3 portrays some of the purely experimental constraints on the behaviour of a rat confined to an activity wheel outfitted with a brake and a retractable drinking tube, each experimental session 20 min long. Plotting total time spent drinking against total time spent running, the figure shows performance under the paired baseline condition as an open circle. The contingency schedule requires I seconds of instrumental running for each access to the tube; upon C seconds of drinking, the tube retreats and the brake releases for the next bout of running. Each of the five vectors fanning out from the origin represents one of five different schedules. The slope of each vector is the schedule ratio C/I.

Performance under a particular schedule can be represented as a point on the schedule vector: the more often the rat completes the scheduled sequence, I seconds of running followed by C seconds of drinking, the further the point moves up the vector toward a high average rate of responding. Given no overshooting of I or C, and an integral number of completions of $I + C$, the point will lie exactly on the a *priori* vector; otherwise, the point may lie a little above or below the vector. The length of each vector reflects the maximum amount of responding that could occur if the rat were to spend the whole of the session running and drinking. We would shorten each vector a little by taking into account any inability to run and drink without pause.

The broken lines through the basepoint identify four quadrants sometimes used in classifying performance under the schedule. Should performance fall into the south-eastern quadrant, the schedule would be said to have facilitated running, while suppressing drinking, relative to the paired baseline levels. The reverse effects would fall into the north-western quadrant. The two remaining quadrants define facilitation of both responses, and suppression of both. As far

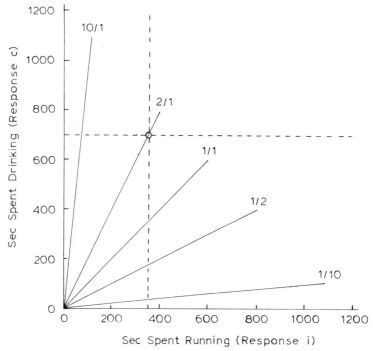

Figure 9.3. Total drink time as a function of total run time (hypothetical example). The open circle represents performance under the paired baseline condition. The slope of each vector represents the schedule ratio C/I, in seconds of drinking per second of running. The broken lines identify facilitation or suppression of performance under the schedule relative to baseline performance

as the experimental constraints are concerned, any particular schedule could produce at least one of these effects, but none could produce all, even if we lengthened each vector indefinitely by increasing the session duration.

We should pay special attention to the solitary schedule that could produce the null effect, no facilitation or suppression of either response, for its bearing on response deprivation as an antecedent condition. Because its vector passes through the basepoint, it is the one schedule that would deprive the rat of neither response: by doing the amount of running (or drinking) done in baseline, the rat could also do the baseline amount of drinking (or running). All other schedules deprive the rat of one of the two responses. Schedules whose vectors pass beneath the basepoint would deprive the rat of drinking: if the rat runs no more than the baseline amount, O_i it must settle for less than its baseline amount of drinking, O_c. Schedules whose vectors pass above the basepoint would deprive the rat of running: in doing no more than the baseline amount of drinking, the rat must settle for less than the baseline amount of running.

Labour Supply Theory

Labour supply theory provides further constraints, as illustrated by Figure 9.4. Figure 9.4 plots total daily wages against two complementary variables on the horizontal axis: daily work hours, and daily leisure hours. The example assumes a total of 15 h available each day for work plus leisure. The vectors represent five different wage rates, in dollars per hour, each analogous to the schedule ratio C/I in the example of Figure 9.3. Each point in the space represents a particular combination of daily wages, daily hours of work, and daily hours of leisure.

The theoretical constraints come from the non-intersecting curves in Figure 9.4, called *indifference curves*. All points on a particular indifference curve are supposed to be equally attractive to the worker: much leisure with little daily income is the same as a bit less leisure with a bit more income. However, the worker supposedly prefers any higher curve to any lower curve. The reason is entirely plausible: the worker will take more dollars or leisure if he can do so without sacrificing any of the other. For example, a glance at the top two curves

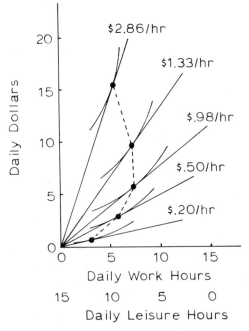

Figure 9.4. Daily income as a function of daily hours of work or leisure (hypothetical example). The slope of each vector is the wage rate, in dollars per hour. Convex curves are indifference curves. The broken line connecting the points of equilibrium is the theoretical backward bending labour supply curve

shows that at 10 h of leisure the upper curve offers more daily dollars than the lower, so the worker prefers the upper point to the lower. Because of the indifference property, the worker thus prefers any point on the upper curve to any point on the lower curve.

The theory's behavioural predictions follow directly from the same logic. Under the constraint of a particular wage rate, the worker will move up that wage rate vector until reaching the highest indifference curve attainable on that vector. This unique point of equilibrium is the point at which the vector is tangent to an indifference curve.

The broken lines that join the equilibrium points comprise the famous *backward bending labour supply* curve of labour supply theory (Awh, 1976, p. 96). It implies that if the initial wage rate is very low, a modest increase will induce the worker to work longer, trading some daily leisure for more daily dollars. But if the initial wage rate is fairly high, a further increase will induce the worker to work less, taking both more daily leisure and more daily dollars.

In theory, the curve bends backward, changing slope from positive to negative, because of a shifting balance between two opposing factors: the *substitution effect*, and the *income effect*. A rising wage rate makes work time more valuable, and leisure time more costly in terms of lost opportunity to work, so the worker would substitute more work for leisure than before. But with this additional wealth, the worker could afford more consumer goods than before, including the good known as leisure time. This income effect therefore opposes the substitution effect, and leads the worker to do less work than if governed by the substitution effect alone. If the substitution effect exceeds the income effect, the labour supply curve will have positive slope. But if the income effect exceeds the substitution effect, the curve will have negative slope. Why does the theory assume a relatively large substitution effect at an extremely low wage rate? Relative to a bit more leisure, a bit more money has more value to the poor than to the rich.

The backward bending labour supply curve implies that a large supply of labour can be had by keeping the wage rate low, but not too low. Analogously, if we want the greatest amount of lever-pressing from the rat, we must keep the fixed ratio requirement (I) large, but not too large, and the size of the food reward (C) small, but not too small. If we start with a relatively high wage rate, such as 10 food pellets ($C = 10$) for one press of the lever ($I = 1$), we can expect the response totals to show little pressing of the lever and much eating. Up to a point, we can coax more labour from the rat, while paying out fewer pellets, by raising the number of presses required for each pellet. Beyond that point, a further decrease in C/I will reverse the growth of labour supply. The reversal would appear as a progressive decrease in the total amount of instrumental lever pressing—a phenomenon known to psychologists as 'ratio strain'—and a radical drop in the number of pellets paid out. Many will see some striking similarities between the predictions of this textbook economic theory and those made by recent psychological theory from Rachlin and Burkhard (1978, Figure 17) and Staddon (1979, Figure 5), who derive the backward bending labour supply curve from rather different theoretical foundations.

Economists who specialize in labour supply claim that economic studies of the labour supply market give no evidence of a backward bending labour supply curve. Both experimental and non-experimental studies reveal no backward bend; the curve has negative slope throughout (Watts and Rees, 1977, p. 12). In other words, the economic evidence shows that an increase in wage rate generally produces a decrease in labour supply. Perhaps the reason is that countervailing pressures on organized management, from such sources as organized labour, generally keep the prevailing wage rates relatively high. So far, no such pressures have been brought to bear on laboratory experiments with animals, many of which reveal the bend that psychologists know as ratio strain.

Minimum Deviation Model

Staddon (1979) derives the backward bending curve from an admirably simple assumption about performance under the schedule relative to performance under the paired baseline condition without schedule constraint. Specifically, performance under the schedule represents a minimum deviation from the baseline levels of the two responses. In its simplest version, this model implies that a straight line drawn from the basepoint, perpendicular to the schedule vector, will intersect the schedule vector at the point of equilibrium. If four such perpendiculars were drawn in Figure 9.3, the curve connecting the five equilibrium points would look like the backward bending labour supply curve of Figure 9.4.

Although the minimum deviation model succeeds in deriving ratio strain, its basic assumption may be suspect. Experiments that allow the rat to determine C, the amount of contingent eating (Collier *et al.*, 1972, Experiment 1) or drinking (Marwine and Collier, 1979, Experiment 1), show that the rat generally deviates more than necessary from the baseline level of both the contingent response and the instrumental response. For example, such experiments show that the rat can drink some 15 ml in a single access to the water ($C = 15$ ml). Yet, under a schedule that requires 20 lever-presses for each access, the rat presses the lever more than 100 times in drinking a total of 35 ml. That many responses far exceed the 60 that would suffice: 60 responses would earn three accesses, for a total of 45 ml at 15 ml each. Because the baseline number of lever-presses generally approaches zero, the 100 presses observed deviated further from the baseline than the 60 that would have sufficed. Moreover, the number of responses actually observed would have allowed the rat to perform its baseline amount of drinking, 39 ml, rather than the 35 ml actually observed. Similar deviations may also occur under conventional variable interval schedules and concurrent fixed ratio schedules (Allison, 1979c, 1980).

Conservation

In its original form, the conservation model (Allison, 1976; Allison, Miller, and Wozny, 1979; Shapiro and Allison, 1978) also predicts a backward bending curve, but the theoretical curve may often descend too far before bending (Allison, 1979b). In other words, as the wage rate declines the actual labour supply rises at first, as the model predicts, but sometimes starts to fall before the model says it should.

To introduce this model by example, consider a captive monkey, given free access to bananas and apples, that chooses to get all of its daily calories by eating eight large bananas ($O_i = 8$) and six medium-sized apples ($O_c = 6$). Let k represent the number of apples having the same caloric value as one banana, roughly two apples ($k = 2$). We define an apple-calorie as the number of calories in one apple. It follows that the monkey takes in a total of 22 apple-calories per day, because $2(8) + 6 = 22$. In other words $kO_i + O_c = 22$.

Because apples happen to cost a good deal more than bananas, the owner would like his pet to subsist on five times as many bananas as apples. He therefore removes the freely available fruit from the cage and doles them out a few at a time, making the monkey eat a bunch of five bananas ($I = 5$) before handing over one apple ($C = 1$). Each of these packages, consisting of five bananas followed by one apple, contains 11 apple-calories: $2(5) + 1 = 11$, or $kI+C = 11$. To take in (or conserve) its usual 22 apple-calories, the monkey must eat two of these packages: $2[2(5) + 1] = 2(8) + 6 = 22$. In our example, the contingency schedule would facilitate banana-eating (10 bananas in contingency vs. 8 in baseline), and suppress apple-eating (2 apples in contingency vs. 6 in baseline). We could reverse these two effects by making the monkey eat half a banana for each apple: $11[2(0.5) + 1] = 22$, for a total of 5.5 bananas in contingency vs. 8 in baseline, and 11 apples vs. 6.

In equation form, the model for this example is approximated by

$$N(kI + C) = kO_i + O_c, \tag{9.1}$$

whose left-hand side models the contingency condition, the right-hand side the paired baseline condition, all experimental sessions having the same duration. (Conservation models for experiments that allow the session duration to vary appear in Allison (1979c).) On the left, the dependent variable N denotes the number of times the subject completes the scheduled sequence of requirements, such as I instrumental lever-presses followed by C contingent licks at a water tube. The k on both sides, a positive constant, would denote the number of licks equivalent to one press of the lever in terms of some specific dimension. For example, if the relevant dimension were energy expenditure, and one press of the lever expended twice the energy expended by one lick, k would have a numerical value of two: two licks are intrinsically equivalent to one press. Unlike k, which expresses an intrinsic rate of exchange between the two responses, the schedule ratio I/C expresses an extrinsic rate of exchange, the amount of response i the experimenter requires per unit of response c. (There is a similar multidimensional model which might be applied if the subject were to conserve on two or more dimensions, such as vitamin C as well as calories; *see* the diet problem of linear programming in Dorfman, Samuelson, and Solow (1958).)

We saw in the monkey example that we could get total banana consumption to rise from 5.5 to 10, and total apple consumption to fall from 11 to 2, simply by raising I from half a banana to five bananas. Within certain limits, explained shortly, the model predicts that the total amount of either response will decrease linearly as the total amount of the other response increases. This feature of the model thus predicts the descending part of the labour supply curve. For example, suppose NC refers to the total number of food pellets earned (daily wages) for a total of NI lever-presses (daily labour). Solving equation (9.1) for NC,

$$NC = (kO_i + O_c) - k(NI). \qquad (9.2)$$

According to equation (9.2), daily wages (NC) will decrease linearly as daily labour (NI) rises. The line will intersect the vertical daily wage axis at the intercept $(kO_i + O_c)$ and will have a constant downward slope, $-k$.

But what if we asked our monkey to eat 15 bananas in exchange for one apple? The model implies that the monkey would then get no apples at all: because 11 bananas contain 22 apple-calories, the monkey would eat no more than 11, so would never see the apple contingent on the 15th banana required by the schedule.

The model thus implies that total labour will rise with I until I becomes so large that the labourer reaches the dimensional total, $kO_i + O_c$, before completing the work requirement I even once. Because the subject will then quit responding, it will lose touch with the programmed contingency, never experiencing the contingent event—the monkey would see 15 bananas, but no apples, in session after session. After several such sessions, the monkey should come to eat the number of bananas it would typically eat in the *single baseline* condition, with bananas freely available but no apples. The model does not tell us what this new total would be, because we do not know how many apple-calories the monkey would take in if bananas were the only food available. The total caloric intake might easily depend on the types of food available. To find out, we would have to measure total caloric intake in the single baseline condition, with bananas freely available but no apples. In some cases, the single baseline of the response would probably be relatively high: the monkey, given nothing but bananas, would probably eat a relatively large number of bananas.

In other cases, the single baseline of the response would be relatively low: the rat, given nothing but a lever, will press the lever very little. For example, suppose we find that in the paired baseline condition, the rat presses the lever five times ($O_i = 5$) and eats one hundred and thirty 90 mg food pellets ($O_c = 130$). Suppose further that 0.02 pellets are equivalent to one press of the lever ($k = 0.02$). Now we make the rat press the lever I times for each food pellet. The model implies that total labour will increase with I until $kI = kO_i + O_c$; beyond that value of I, total labour will decline towards the single baseline level of lever-pressing. In our example, $kI = 0.02I$, and $kO_i + O_c = 0.02(5) + 130 = 130.1$. The critical value of I is therefore $130.1/0.02 = 6505$ lever-presses. As I increases to 6505, total labour supply should increase; beyond that point, a further increase in I should cause labour supply to fall towards the single baseline level of lever-pressing.

Note that the critical value of I is $I = (kO_i + O_c)/k$. Because O_c typically far exceeds k, the model typically predicts that the labour supply curve will descend a long way before doubling back toward the single baseline level.

Conservation and Substitution

I have already suggested several possible ways of revising the model so as to predict an earlier bend in the labour supply curve (Allison, 1979*b*). One of the suggested alternatives involves a third class of behaviours, uncontrolled by the schedule and thus freely available to the subject. The subject does little of this third class of behaviours when the instrumental requirement is relatively small, but more as the requirement rises. Much as the human substitutes tea for coffee as the price of coffee rises (Awh, 1976), the rat may engage in a passive substitution of bodily fat or water reserves as the behavioural price of external food or water rises. The alternative model can be expressed as

$$U_o + N(kI + C) = kO_i + O_c, \qquad (9.3)$$

where U_o denotes the total amount of the third class of unscheduled substitute behaviours, measured theoretically in units of response c. Because the schedule does not control response o, U_o appears outside the parentheses. Because response o does not occur with responses i and c freely available, it does not appear on the right-hand side of the equation.

The schedule ratio I/C expresses the behavioural cost of one unit of response c. In theory, response o increases systematically with I/C. We can therefore constrain response o in the manner assumed by letting $U_o = j(I/C)$, where j denotes a positive constant. All else being equal, a relatively large j would reflect a relatively great tendency to substitute response o for the behaviour controlled by the schedule. Replacing U_o, equation (9.3) becomes

$$j(I/C) + N(kI + C) = kO_i + O_c = B, \qquad (9.4)$$

where B denotes the baseline constant. This equation implies that the rat is willing to work for food if the cost of the food, I/C, is reasonably low. As the cost rises, the rat will be more inclined to substitute more internal food, food stored as body fat, for the costly external food pellets. If the fat rat were more inclined to make this substitution than the thin rat, the fat rat would have a larger value of j than the thin.

In the tests reported here, multiple regression analyses provided least-squares estimates of B, j, and k. The multiple regression equation, a rearrangement of equation (9.4),

$$NC = B - j(I/C) - k(NI),\qquad(9.5)$$

incorporates B as the intercept constant, with j and k as partial regression coefficients. Thus, an experiment reporting I/C, NI, and NC for each of nine different schedules would furnish three sets of nine pairs of scores for calculating the three correlation coefficients on which the least-squares estimates of B, j, and k depend. The model implies that the intercept B should be positive, the regression coefficients negative. The coefficient of multiple determination, R^2. would provide one further measure of the model's fit to the data. (Because NC depends on NI, R^2 provides an inflated estimate of goodness of fit. A better correlational measure is the correlation between values observed and values predicted by equation (9.5) after replacing the unknowns with least-squares estimates.) Experiments reporting the baseline measures O_i and O_c would provide a further independent test, because the model implies that the intercept B should equal $kO_i + O_c$.

The analysis was applied to an experiment with rats in which nine different schedules, tested in 60 min sessions, each required I seconds of lever-holding for

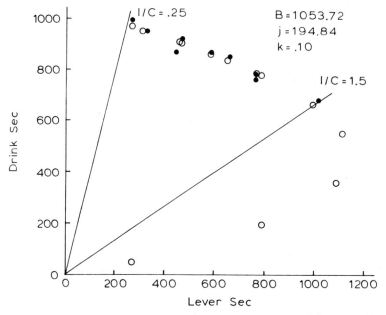

Figure 9.5. Time spent drinking as a function of time spent holding the lever (based on Allison *et al.*, 1979, Experiment 1). Open circles represent values predicted; solid circles represent values observed. The two vectors represent the two extreme schedules

C seconds of drinking (Allison *et al.*, 1979, Experiment 1). The regression equation was

$$NC = 1053.72 - 194.84(I/C) - 0.10(NI), \qquad R^2(6) = 0.96, \, p < 0.01.$$

The mean value observed for $kO_i + O_c$, 1073.20, did not differ significantly from the intercept constant 1053.72, $t(5) = 0.47$.

Figure 9.5 compares values observed under the nine schedules (solid circles) with values predicted by the substitution model. The open circle predictions represent exact values (Allison *et al.*, 1979, p. 9) calculated by setting $j = 194.84$, $k = 0.10$, and $B = 1053.72$. The fit was tested further by comparing the points predicted and observed in terms of their distance from the origin along the appropriate schedule vector. Values predicted agreed closely with values observed, $r^2 = 0.88, \, p < 0.02$.

A comparison of the correlation ratio ($e^2 = 0.71$) with the coefficient of determination ($r^2 = 0.69$), not reported originally, revealed no significant non-linear relation between the two responses over the range of schedule requirements used in that experiment. But Figure 9.5 shows in addition that we should have seen a backward bend in the curve had we gone just a little further, using I/C ratios larger than about 2.5/1. In contrast, the original model would predict of the same experiment that the curve would not bend back until I approached several thousand seconds of lever-holding, a completely different order of magnitude.

In the experiment of Figure 9.6, rats pressed a lever for food on 12 schedules in 24 h sessions (Collier *et al.*, 1972, Experiment 1). The instrumental requirement ranged from one lever-press to 5120 lever-presses, and the rat determined the size of the ensuing meal. Specifically, the food remained available until a 10 min pause in eating. The 12 resulting values of I/C, calculated after the fact, increased monotonically from 0.50 presses/g under the one-press schedule to 404.21 under the 5120-press schedule. The regression equation was

$$NC = 19.27 - 0.023(I/C) - 0.000\,25(NI), \qquad R^2(9) = 0.78, \, p < 0.01.$$

Baseline lever-presses were not reported, but had the number been negligible, say 20 or less, the model implies that the rats should have eaten about 19.3 g in baseline—not significantly different from the 22.8 g reported, $t(2) = 3.79, \, p > 0.05$. Values predicted agreed closely with values observed, $r^2 = 0.98, \, p < 0.01$.

As Figure 9.6 shows, the model predicted further that the curve would have bent back had the I/C ratios, in presses per gram, ranged higher than about 450/1—a different order of magnitude from the several thousand presses predicted by the original model. The revised model therefore suggests that the extraordinary resistance to ratio strain typically seen under this unconventional procedure (Marwine and Collier, 1979) may have little to do with the rat's freedom to control I/C by adjusting C. Instead, the animal may continue to

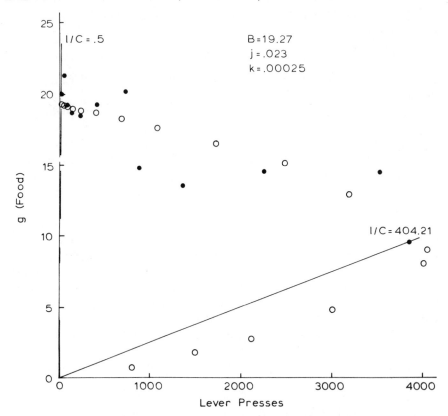

Figure 9.6. Food intake as a function of lever-presses (based on Collier *et al.*, 1972, Experiment 1). Open circles represent values predicted; solid circles represent values observed. The two vectors represent the two extreme schedules

respond at these extraordinarily high values of *I* because the procedure enables the rat to hold the *I*/*C* ratio to a relatively small value, thus keeping the wage rate, *C*/*I*, relatively high. The rat does so by increasing *C* whenever the experimenter increases *I*, whether response *c* be eating (Collier *et al.*, 1972, Experiment 1) or drinking (Marwine and Collier, 1979, Experiment 1). Comparable ratios, controlled entirely by the experimenter, might result in comparable levels of performance.

The actual curve did bend back in the experiment of Figure 9.7, which used a more conventional procedure. There, rats pressed a lever for 10 licks at an 8 per cent sucrose solution in 60 min sessions (Kelsey and Allison, 1976). The instrumental requirement ranged from 1 to 128 lever-presses. The regression equation was

$$NC = 6036.47 - 468.19(I/C) - 0.77(NI), \qquad R^2(5) = 0.98, \; p < 0.01.$$

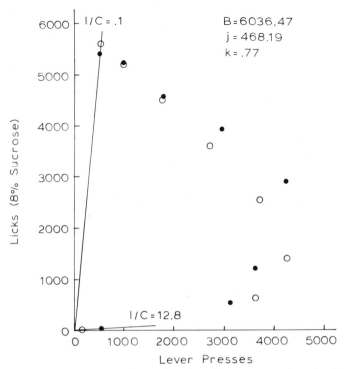

Figure 9.7. Licks (8 per cent sucrose) as a function of lever-presses (based on Kelsey and Allison, 1976). Open circles represent values predicted; solid circles represent values observed. The two vectors represent the two extreme schedules

Values predicted agreed closely with values observed, $r^2 = 0.93, p < 0.01$. Baseline measures were not reported. Given a negligible number of lever-presses in baseline, the model implies that the rats would have performed some 6000 licks in baseline, a plausible prediction. The predicted point of the bend, somewhere between 3.2 and 6.4 presses per lick, came much closer to reality than the several thousand presses predicted by the original model.

Studies of hypothalamic hyperphagia have shown that the labour supply curve bends earlier if the labourers are static obese animals, or animals still gaining weight in the dynamic stage, than it does if the labourers are normal control animals (e.g. Hamilton and Brobeck, 1964; Kelsey and Allison, 1976; Teitelbaum, 1957). The classic results of Teitelbaum (1957), replotted in Figure 9.8, illustrate these differences and show that the substitution model fits the data reasonably well, $R^2(6) = 0.84, p < 0.01$. Each group was tested in 12h sessions on schedules that required 1, 4, 16, 64, or 256 lever-presses for each 90 mg food pellet. The intercept constant B was 126.13 for the normal rats, 275.06 for the dynamic rats, and 180.85 for the obese. Baseline measures were not reported. Assuming a negligible number of lever-presses in baseline, the intercepts imply that the baseline food intake would have been about 11 g among the normal rats, 25 g among the dynamic rats, and 16 g among the obese. These predictions agree with observations often made under free-feeding conditions, where animals in the dynamic stage may eat two to three times the normal amount, but finally decrease their intake to nearly the normal amount after reaching the peak level of obesity (Teitelbaum, 1966, p. 577). Among all three groups combined, the values predicted agreed closely with values observed, $r^2 = 0.98$, $p < 0.01$.

The model revealed further that the two groups of overweight rats substituted more liberally than the rats of normal weight: The estimates of j were 0.93 for the dynamic, 0.70 for the obese, and only 0.14 for the normal rats. The inference agrees with economic theory, which supposes that consumption of a particular commodity should be more elastic—more responsive to price—when a relatively large supply of some substitute commodity is readily available. In this particular example, the substitute for food would be energy already stored as body fat.

The analysis also revealed higher estimates of k for the two overweight groups than for the normal group: 0.10 for the dynamic, 0.20 for the obese, and only 0.016 for the normal. For a speculative interpretation of these differences, suppose the underlying dimension were related to energy expenditure. Then the variations in k might mean that, relative to eating each pellet, the overweight rats expended more energy in each press of the lever than the rats of normal weight. With each press of the lever, overweight animals may work relatively hard because they must move a larger body mass in reaching for the lever, overshadowing the incidental advantage of a greater dead weight on the lever. Normal rats show a similar rise in k with a rise in the force required to depress the lever (Allison et al., 1979b, Experiment 4).

In fitting the data of Figures 9.5–9.8 the model passed its tests reasonably well. But a model that passes all of these tests could still err systematically, perhaps

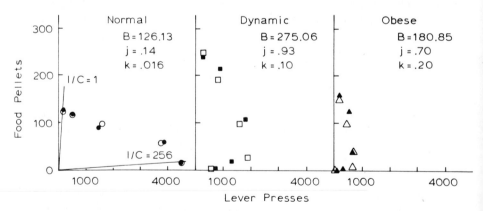

Figure 9.8. Food pellets (90 mg) as a function of lever-presses (based on Teitelbaum, 1957). Open circles represent values predicted; solid circles represent values observed. The two vectors in the left-hand panel represent the two extreme schedules

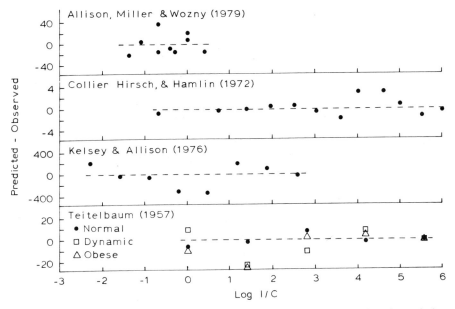

Figure 9.9. Contingent responding, predicted minus observed, as a function of the natural log of the schedule ratio I/C

underpredicting NC at one extreme value of the schedule ratio I/C, overpredicting at the other extreme. Figure 9.9 examines the model for systematic error by plotting the residual, NC predicted minus NC observed, against the natural log of I/C. Inspection of Figure 9.9 reveals no simple pattern of underprediction at one extreme, overprediction at the other. Regression analyses studied the pattern more closely, examining the residual (y) as four different functions of $I/C(x)$: the linear function $y = a + bx$; the exponential function $y = ae^{bx}$; the log function $y = a + b\log x$; and the power function $y = ax^b$. None of these analyses revealed any systematic relation between y and x; many of the coefficients of determination were zero, and the largest was only 0.10.

Taken together, the analyses show that the substitution model of equation (9.3) fits the data well, with little systematic residual error, and far better than the original model of equation (9.1).

Non-labour Income

We have already seen how labour supply theory predicts the backward bending curve often apparent in performance under fixed ratio schedules. The same body of theory has something to say about the effects of reward delivered freely during the course of the contingency session. Free licks at the water tube at the very start of the session might be conceptualized as a free dispensation of goods, or as non-labour income. (Where the animal works in direct exchange for a commodity, the commodity can be viewed as income.) The backward bending labour supply curve implies that non-labour income will increase total income, free plus earned. The basis for this prediction can be understood by returning to Figure 9.4 and imagining five new wage rate vectors, each corresponding to one of the vectors shown in Figure 9.4. Each of the new vectors would have the same slope as the old corresponding vector, but a different starting point on the vertical axis. The reason is that the free income given to one labourer would give him a head start over a less fortunate colleague who must work at the same wage rate for all he receives. Accordingly, the new intercept would be higher than the old, by an amount equal to the non-labour income. The predicted effect on total labour will depend on the wage rate: more labour if the wage rate is extremely low, less if relatively high (*see* Awh, 1976, p.96).

We can construct a conservation model for the same experimental procedure by viewing the free licks at the start of the session as unscheduled responses measured explicitly. Letting U_c signify the number of these unscheduled licks, the substitution model becomes

$$U_c + j(I/C) + N(kI + C) = kO_i + O_c = B. \tag{9.6}$$

The equation says that as non-labour income rises (U_c increases), the rat will grow less inclined to work for a living (N will decrease). A multiple regression form of equation (9.6) would be

$$U_c + NC = B - j(I/C) - k(NI), \tag{9.7}$$

where the sum on the left-hand side signifies the total number of licks in the contingency session, free (U_c) plus earned (NC).

Figure 9.10 presents a numerical example of the predictions generated by the model. The example compares two different schedules, one requiring one lever-press for 50 licks (a relatively high wage rate), the other 16 presses for 50 licks (a lower wage rate). The example assumes further that $B = 4871$, $j = 1995$, and $k = 0.11$. The solid symbol predictions apply to the conventional procedure that allows no free licks at the tube ($U_c = 0$). The open symbol predictions assume 2633 free licks at the start of the session ($U_c = 2633$). Like labour supply theory, the model predicts that free licks will increase the total number of licks. However, the effect predicted under the conditions of our example is so slight that it might be difficult to detect experimentally, especially under the one-press schedule. In contrast, the model predicts that the free licks will produce a rather large decrease in the total amount of instrumental responding, especially under the 16-press schedule, and thus a large decrease in the total number of contingent licks (NC).

Only one of these predictions has subtlety enough to merit algebraic proof, namely the predicted rise in total licks. Let N_2 refer to schedule performance in the conventional session, N_1 to performance under the same schedule in the

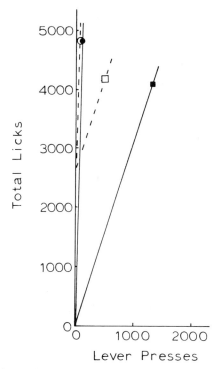

Figure 9.10. Total licks as a function of lever-presses (hypothetical example). Open circles represent values predicted for the free procedure; solid circles represent the conventional procedure. Circles represent a schedule requiring one press for 50 licks, squares 16 presses for 50 licks

session that starts with several free licks. We wish to prove the model's implication that total licks under the free condition $(U_c + N_1 C)$ will exceed total licks under the conventional condition $(N_2 C)$. According to the model,

$$U_c + j(I/C) + N_1(kI + C) = B = j(I/C) + N_2(kI + C),$$

or

$$U_c + N_1(kI + C) = N_2(kI + C),$$

which requires that N_2 be greater than N_1. Rearranging the preceding equation,

$$(U_c + N_1 C) - N_2 C = kI(N_2 - N_1).$$

Because N_2 must exceed N_1, the right-hand side of the preceding equation must be positive. It follows that the left-hand side must also be positive. The model therefore implies that total licks under the free condition will exceed total licks under the conventional condition, and that the difference will increase as I or k increases.

I recently completed an experimental test of the model with six rats in the conventional group, five in the group that got several free licks at the start of the session. The free licks numbered half of the number the individual had performed under the paired baseline condition. The experiment used three schedules: one lever-press for 50 licks, four presses for 50, and 16 for 50, tested in both ascending and descending order, each time to a rigorous stability criterion. The regression equation was

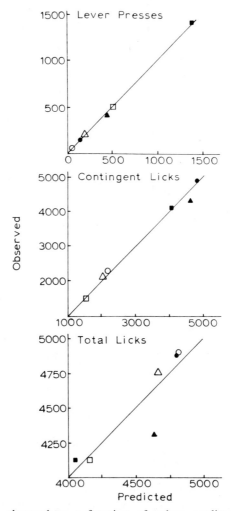

Figure 9.11. Values observed as a function of values predicted for lever-presses, contingent licks, and total licks periods. Open symbols represent the free group; solid symbols represent the conventional group. The three schedules required one press (circles), four presses (triangles), or 16 presses (squares) for 50 licks

$$U_c + NC = 4870.72 - 1999.50 \ (I/C) - 0.11(NI), \qquad R^2(3) = 0.80,$$

just short of the 0.05 level of significance. The intercept B did not differ significantly from the value observed, 5296.09, $t(10) = 1.29$, $p > 0.20$.

The three panels of Figure 9.11 show fairly close agreement between values observed and values predicted for lever-presses, contingent licks, and total licks; open symbols represent the free group, solid symbols the conventional group. Further analyses revealed statistically significant support for several qualitative predictions. The conventional group performed more lever-presses and more contingent licks than the free group. As the wage rate rose, total lever-presses fell, especially in the conventional group, while contingent and total licks rose steadily. That much of the pattern conformed fairly well to the downward sloping part of the theoretical labour supply curve. Perhaps the most important finding was that free licks failed to produce a significant increase in total licks. Because it contradicts both conservation theory and classical labour supply theory, work in progress will attempt to discover whether this important exception can be reproduced under other conditions. The work in progress incorporates a larger number of free licks, a wider range of wage rates, and a more sensitive design which tests each subject under both conditions, the free and the conventional. Further experiments will increase the force required to depress the lever, which, by increasing k, should increase the separation between the conventional condition and the free.

Conclusion

I have tried to show how economics and operant conditioning can be related in fact and theory by viewing laboratory rewards as economic goods, whether received as non-labour income or bought at a behavioural price defined by the terms of the schedule. The key empirical relations appear in the consumer demand functions of Figures 9.1 and 9.2, and the labour supply functions of Figures 9.4–9.8, and 9.10. Although not the only psychological theory that might bridge the two disciplines (Rachlin and Burkhard, 1978; Staddon, 1979), conservation theory has probably been analysed in economic terms more throughly than any other. We have seen how the substitution model of equation (9.3) predicts both the general form of the backward bending labour supply curve and several specific features of consumer demand functions, including the demand law. It serves this double purpose because the wage rate stands in a simple inverse relation to the behavioural price of response c: wage rate is C/I, price I/C. As the wage rate rises, total labour supply rises and falls while total income rises steadily. By the inverse relation, as price rises total consumption falls steadily (the demand law).

Furthermore, the same model predicts some well-established facts about the elasticity of demand—how the relative drop in consumption relates to the relative rise in price. Typically inelastic at low prices, consumption becomes more elastic as price rises, and finally becomes altogether elastic at the highest prices. If the price of gasolene doubles from $0.50 to $1.00 per gallon, consumption of gasolene might drop just a little. Were its price to double from $4.00 to $8.00, consumption might drop catastrophically.

Taking Figure 9.7 as an example, the downward sloping part of the curve is the region of inelastic demand, where the relative rise in price exceeds the relative drop in consumption. The upward sloping part is the region of elastic demand, where the relative drop in consumption exceeds the relative rise in price. The point where the curve bends is the point of transition between inelastic and elastic demand. We can predict this point by deriving from the model a point elasticity coefficient (Awh, 1976),

$$E = -\frac{kB + j}{(I/C)^{-1}[B - kj(I/C)^2] - j + kB}. \tag{9.8}$$

When the numerator on the right is less than the denominator, demand is inelastic; when greater than the denominator, demand is elastic. Because E rises as I/C rises, the model predicts a commonplace fact of life in the marketplace: elasticity of demand increases with price.

The model also provides some points of contact between economics and biological constraints on behaviour. The human who trades D dollars for a loaf of bread will trade aD francs for the same loaf, a being the rate of exchange between francs and dollars. In the conservation model, the constant k is a similar rate of exchange. Relative to eating one food pellet, one lever-press may not have the same intrinsic value as one turn of the running wheel. We can compare these organismic rates of exchange by comparing the k measured under press-to-eat schedules with the k measured under run-to-eat schedules. According to this view, many constraints on behaviour may turn out to reflect biologically determined differences in the rate of exchange. Thus, in hamsters, digging and washing the face (Shettleworth, 1975) may have different rates of exchange for food (Allison et al., 1979).

Several economists and psychologists have already argued that each of their two behavioural sciences should pay closer attention to the other (Castro and Weingarten, 1970; Hayes, 1950; Kagel and Winkler, 1972; Mitchell, 1914; Rachlin et al., 1976; Skinner, 1953). Perhaps the argument was never more cogent than now.

Note

The research reported here was supported in part by USPHS grant MH31970 from the National Institute of Mental Health.

References

Allison, J. (1976). Contrast, induction, facilitation, suppression, and conservation. *Journal of the Experimental Analysis of Behavior*, **25**, 185–198.

Allison, J. (1978). Beyond the relational principle of reinforcement. *Journal of the Experimental Analysis of Behavior*, **29**, 557–560.

Allison, J. (1979a). Remarks on Staddon's comment. *Journal of Experimental Psychology: General*, **108**, 41–42.

Allison, J. (1979b). Demand economics and experimental psychology. *Behavioral Science*, **24**, 403–415.

Allison, J. (1979c). Constraints on performance in two elementary paradigms. Paper presented at the Second Harvard Symposium on Quantitative Analysis of Behavior, Cambridge, Mass., June, 1979.

Allison, J. (1980). Conservation, matching, and the variable-interval schedule. *Animal Learning and Behavior*, **8**, 185–192.

Allison, J. and Timberlake, W. (1974). Instrumental and contingent saccharin licking in rats: response deprivation and reinforcement. *Learning and Motivation*, **5**, 231–247.

Allison, J. and Timberlake, W. (1975). Response deprivation and instrumental performance in the controlled-amount paradigm. *Learning and Motivation*, **6**, 122–142.

Allison, J., Miller, M., and Wozny, M. (1979). Conservation in behavior. *Journal of Experimental Psychology: General*, **108**, 4–34.

Awh, R. Y. (1976). *Microeconomics: Theory and Applications*. John Wiley, New York.

Ayllon, T. and Azrin, N. H. (1965). The measurement of reinforcement of behavior of psychotics. *Journal of the Experimental Analysis of Behavior*, **8**, 357–383.

Baer, D. B. (1962). Laboratory control of thumbsucking by withdrawal and representation of reinforcement. *Journal of the Experimental Analysis of Behavior*, **5**, 525–528.

Blodgett, H. C. (1929). The effect of the introduction of reward upon the maze performance of rats. *University of California Publications in Psychology*, **4**, 113–134.

Bolles, R. C. (1972). Reinforcement, expectancy, and learning. *Psychological Review*, **79**, 394–409.

Buchwald, A. M. (1969). Effects of 'right' and 'wrong' on subsequent behavior: a new interpretation. *Psychological Review*, **76**, 132–143.

Castro, B. and Weingarten, K. (1970). Toward experimental economics. *Journal of Political Economy*, **78**, 598–607.

Collier, G. H., Hirsch, E., and Hamlin, P. H. (1972). The ecological determinants of reinforcement in the rat. *Physiology and Behavior*, **9**, 705–716.

Cowles, J. T. (1937). Food-tokens as incentives for learning by chimpanzees. *Comparative Psychology Monographs*, **14** (5, whole no. 71).

Dennis, W. (1948). *Readings in the History of Psychology*, Appleton-Century-Crofts, New York.

Dorfman, R., Samuelson, P. A., and Solow, R. M. (1958). *Linear Programming and Economic Analysis*, McGraw-Hill, New York.

Ellson, D. G. (1937). The acquisition of a token-reward habit in dogs. *Journal of Comparative Psychology*, **24**, 505–522.

Esper, E. A. (1964). *A History of Psychology*, Saunders, Philadelphia.

Estes, W. K. (1969). Reinforcement in human learning. In *Reinforcement and Behavior* (J. T. Tapp, ed.), Academic Press, New York.

Glickman, S. E. and Schiff, B. B. (1967). A biological theory of reinforcement. *Psychological Review*, **74**, 81–109.

Guthrie, E. R. (1935). *The Psychology of Learning*, Harper & Row, New York.

Guthrie, E. R. and Horton, G. P. (1946). *Cats in a Puzzle Box*, Rinehart, New York.

Hamilton, C. L. and Brobeck, J. R. (1964). Hypothalamic hyperphagia in the monkey. *Journal of Comparative and Physiological Psychology*, **57**, 271–278.

Hayes, S. P. (1950). Some psychological problems of economics. *Psychological Bulletin*, **47**, 289–330.

Hearst, E. and Jenkins, H. M. (1974). *Sign-tracking: The Stimulus–Reinforcer Relation and Directed Action*, The Psychonomic Society, Austin, Texas.

Holstein, S. B. and Hundt, A. G. (1965). Reinforcement of intracranial self stimulation by licking. *Psychonomic Science*, **3**, 17–18.

Hull, C. L. (1943). *Principles of Behavior*, Appleton-Century-Crofts, New York.

Kagel, J. H. and Winkler, R. C. (1972). Behavioral economics: areas of cooperative research between economics and applied behavioral analysis. *Journal of Applied Behavior Analysis*, **5**, 335–342.

Kamin, L. J. (1969). Predictability, surprise, attention, and conditioning. In *Punishment and Aversive Behavior* (B. A. Campbell and R. M. Church, eds), Appleton-Century-Crofts, New York.

Kelsey, J. E. and Allison, J. (1976). Fixed-ratio lever pressing by VMH rats: work vs. accessibility of sucrose reward. *Physiology and Behavior*, **17**, 749–754.

Lancaster, K. (1969). *Introduction to Modern Microeconomics*, Rand-McNally. Chicago.

Lea, S. E. G. (1978). The psychology and economics of demand. *Psychological Bulletin*, **85**, 441–466.

Lett, B. T. (1973). Delayed reward learning: disproof of the traditional theory. *Learning and Motivation*, **4**, 237–246.

Longfellow, L. A. (1967). Effects of food deprivation on temporally spaced responding in moderately retarded children. Doctoral dissertation, University of Michigan, 1967.

Maier, S. F., Seligman, M. E. P., and Solomon, R. L. (1969). Pavlovian fear conditioning and learned helplessness: effects on escape and avoidance behavior of (a) the CS–US contingency and (b) the independence of the US and voluntary responding. In *Punishment and Aversive Behavior* (B. A. Campbell and R. M. Church, eds), Appleton-Century-Crofts, New York.

Marwine, A. and Collier, G. H. (1979). The rat at the waterhole. *Journal of Comparative and Physiological Psychology*, **93**, 391–402.

Mazur, J. E. (1975). The matching law and qualifications related to Premack's principle. *Journal of Experimental Psychology: Animal Behavior Processes*, **4**, 374–386.

Meehl, P. E. (1950). On the circularity of the law of effect. *Psychological Bulletin*, **47**, 52–75.

Miller, N. E. (1951). Learnable drives and rewards. In *Handbook of Experimental Psychology* (S. S. Stevens, ed.), John Wiley, New York.

Mitchell, W. C. (1914). Human behavior and economics: a survey of recent literature. *Quarterly Journal of Economics*, **29**, 1–47.

Moore, B. R. and Stuttard, S. (1979). Dr Guthrie and *Felis domesticus* or: Tripping over the cat. *Science*, **205**, 1031–1033.

Premack, D. (1959). Toward empirical behavioral laws. I. Positive reinforcement. *Psychological Review*, **66**, 219–233.

Premack, D. (1962). Reversibility of the reinforcement relation. *Science*, **136**, 255–257.

Premack, D. (1963). Rate differential reinforcement in monkey manipulation. *Journal of the Experimental Analysis of Behavior*, **6**, 81–89.

Premack, D. (1965). Reinforcement theory. In *Nebraska Symposium on Motivation*, Vol. 13 (D. Levine, ed.). University of Nebraska Press, Lincoln, Neb.

Rachlin, H. and Burkhard, B. (1978). The temporal triangle: response substitution in instrumental conditioning. *Psychological Review*, **85**, 22–47.

Rachlin, H., Green, L., Kagel, J. H., and Battalio, R. C. (1976). Economic demand theory and psychological studies of choice. In *The Psychology of Learning and Motivation: Advances in Research and Theory*, Vol. 10 (G. H. Bower, ed.) Academic Press, New York.

Rescorla, R. A. (1972). Informational variables in Pavlovian conditioning. In *The Psychology of Learning and Motivation: Advances in research and theory*, Vol. 6 (G. H. Bower, ed.), Academic Press, New York.

Revusky, S. and Garcia, J. (1970). Learned associations over long delay. In *The Psychology of learning and motivation: Advances in Research and Theory*, Vol. 4 (G. H. Bower, ed.), Academic Press, New York.

Robbins, L. (1930). On the elasticity of demand for income in terms of effort. *Economica*, **10**, 123–129.

Rozin, P. and Mayer, J. (1964). Regulation of food intake in the goldfish. *American Journal of Physiology*, **206**, 1430–1436.

Samuelson, P. A. (1976). *Economics*, 10th edn, McGraw-Hill, New York.

Shapiro, N. and Allison, J. (1978). Conservation, choice, and the concurrent fixed-ratio schedule. *Journal of the Experimental Analysis of Behavior*, **29**, 211–223.

Sheffield, F. D. (1966). A drive induction theory of reinforcement. In *Current Research in Motivation* (R. N. Haber, ed.) Holt, Rinehart & Winston, New York.

Shettleworth, S. J. (1975). Reinforcement and the organization of behavior in golden hamsters: hunger, environment, and food reinforcement. *Journal of Experimental Psychology: Animal Behavior Processes*, **1**, 56–87.

Skinner, B. F. (1953). *Science and Human Behavior*, Macmillan, New York.

Smith, A. (1776). *An Inquiry into the Nature and Causes of the Wealth of Nations*, Vol. 1, Strahan & Cadell, London.

Smith, M. F. (1939). The establishment and extinction of a token-reward habit in the cat. *Journal of General Psychology*, **20**, 475–486.

Staddon, J. E. R. (1979). Operant behavior as adaptation to constraint. *Journal of Experimental Psychology: General*, **108**, 48–67.

Teitelbaum, P. (1957). Random and food-directed activity in hyperphagic and normal rats. *Journal of Comparative and Physiological Psychology*, **50**, 486–490.

Teitelbaum, P. (1966). The use of operant methods in the assessment and control of motivational states. In *Operant Behavior: Areas of Research and Application* (W. Honig, ed.), Appleton-Century-Crofts, New York.

Timberlake, W. and Allison, J. (1974). Response deprivation: an empirical approach to instrumental performance. *Psychological Review*, **81**, 146–164.

Walker, E. L. (1969). Reinforcement—'the one ring'. In *Reinforcement and Behavior* (J. T. Tapp, ed.), Academic Press, New York.

Wasik, B. H. (1968). A postcontingency test of the effectiveness of reinforcement. *Psychonomic Science*, **13**, 87–88.

Watts, H. W. and Rees, A. (eds) (1977). *The New Jersey Income Maintenance Experiments*, Vol. 2: *Labor-supply Responses*, Academic Press, New York.

Wolfe, J. B. (1936). Effectiveness of token rewards for chimpanzees. *Comparative Psychology Monographs*, **12** (5, whole no. 60).

Predictability, Correlation, and Contiguity
Edited by P. Harzem and M. D. Zeiler
© 1981 John Wiley & Sons Ltd

Chapter 10

Correlation and Contiguity in Foraging Behaviour

Stephen E.G. Lea

Introduction

'Correlation or contiguity?' is a useful question to pose about the control of the behaviour of an individual organism. But in this chapter I shall pose it on a larger scale. I am going to look at some aspects of animals' natural behaviour, and ask whether they are maintained by the same kind of (relatively) contiguous reinforcement processes as we study in the laboratory, or whether they are special kinds of behaviour, involving special kinds of learning, maintained because of their long-run correlation with evolutionary success. Towards the end of the chapter, however, I return to the question of correlation and contiguity within the life of the individual organism.

In recent years behavioural ecologists have given a great deal of attention to naturally occurring instrumental behaviour in many different species, in the process of creating what is now virtually a subdiscipline of its own: the study of foraging. In this chapter I shall argue that there are important parallels between foraging and the kinds of instrumental performance seen in the operant laboratory, so that operant psychologists and behavioural ecologists have quite a bit to learn from each other; that the same principles seem to govern instrumental performance in the field as in the laboratory; and that, in consequence, operant psychology may be able to supply the behavioural mechanisms of some of the effects observed by ecologists, while foraging may supply the evolutionary rationale for some of the phenomena observed in the laboratory.

The layout of the chapter is as follows. I start with a brief discussion of the nature of foraging. Second, I review some of the foraging data that have been reported by behavioural ecologists, and the theories that have guided their collection. I then discuss in detail the analogy between foraging and certain kinds of experimentally produced behaviour, and conclude by discussing the strengths, weaknesses, and implications of the analogy in the light of all the data.

The Nature of Foraging

Foraging is hunting for prey. Since from an ecological point of view it matters little whether the prey is animal or vegetable, almost all animals can be said to forage. (There are exceptions, such as filter feeders or gut parasites, but these are not notable for the interest they have aroused within operant psychology; and even filter feeders have been considered as foragers by Lehman (1976).) Probably no two species of animals forage in exactly the same way, since a species' manner of foraging virtually defines its ecological niche, and Gause's (1934) principle of competitive exclusion points out that no two species can occupy the same niche for long. We can therefore expect that some aspects of any animal's foraging behaviour will be under control of their consequences for the survival of its genes, rather than their consequences within the lifespan of the individual organism. Wolves hunt in packs because they are wolves, not because they have been reinforced for doing so; cats hunt alone because they are cats, not because they have been punished for social hunting. But other aspects of foraging must involve reaction to contingencies operating at the individual level. Many animals return day after day to a fruitful hunting ground (e.g. the fruit bats studied by Morrison (1978); *see below*), and this falls within the definition of reinforced operant behaviour. Whether it has any other resemblance to laboratory operant behaviour remains to be seen.

In considering any species' foraging behaviour, there are a number of questions that it is helpful to pose.

What prey? At a crude level this is determined by the predator's species. Cows eat grass; flycatchers catch flies. But even a cow in a meadow will often have a choice between different grass types, and a flycatcher sitting on a post may let some flies go by, but go in pursuit of others (Davies, 1977*b*).

When does it forage? Again this may be determined up to a point by the nature of the species. Bats are one of the most successful of mammal groups just because they forage by night where other flying predators mainly exploit the day. Or straightforward stimulus factors may be involved, as in shore birds which must follow the tides (Evans, 1976). But either genetic or individual adaptation to track temporal variations in prey density is also conceivable.

With whom does it forage? For anyone interested in social behaviour this is one of the most important questions in ecology. Territoriality is probably closely related to foraging economics (e.g. in nectar feeders (Wolf, 1975)). It has even been argued that foraging patterns can determine the entire social structure of a species: Wrangham (1979) proposed that the gorilla's reliance on eating leaves predisposes it to a one-male group social structure, while the chimpanzee's requirement for ripe fruit encourages its large, fundamentally patrilineal, open troops; and the capacity to eat green fruit predisposes some frugivorous monkeys to a matrilineal social organization (Wrangham, 1977). But the degree of sociality need not be fixed: Davies (1977*a*) observed that wagtails hunted as individuals in the morning, when cow and horse dung were the richest insect sources available to them; later in the day, as flies collected over a nearby pool, the birds hunted there as a flock.

How does it forage? At the most basic level this may concern the question about being a sit-and-wait predator or an active forager. Given either of those styles, however, there are a number of important questions, e.g. about movement patterns as a function of prey capture (Smith, 1974a, b; Thomas, 1974, 1977).

Where does it forage? To some extent this is determined by prey type; silkworm larvae must forage on mulberry trees, kingfishers must forage along rivers, and so forth. At a more subtle level, though, this question can again lead into important sociobiological issues such as the size of the home range and whether a territory is defended (e.g. Andersson, 1978; Morrison, 1978). There is also a question about the details of the 'where' of foraging; this comes close to the 'how' question. The most discussed problem is that of 'patch use'; many kinds of prey are concentrated into circumscribed areas, which ecologists call 'patches' (for example, a pine cone containing several of the larvae hunted by tits would constitute a patch). Foraging then has two stages, hunting for patches (or at least travelling between them) and exploiting them once found. It seems obvious that the transition between these stages will depend on the animal's previous experience of the environment. To an operant psychologist it will also be obvious that there is an analogy here to a chained schedule of reinforcement.

Satisfactory answers to all these questions for a given species should lead to a good descriptive understanding of its foraging behaviour. That will leave unanswered, however, two important questions: what evolutionary pressures cause the animal to forage on its own particular prey, and when, where, how, and in the company that we observe it to forage? and what mechanisms within the individual animal implement those evolutionary imperatives? The next section of this chapter is aimed at the first of those questions; the following three sections at the second.

Ecological Theories and Data

Foraging and Natural Selection

The tradition of the experimental analysis of behaviour calls for a theory-free description of behavioural data; theory should come later, if at all (Skinner, 1950). If that ideal procedure is ever appropriate it certainly is not for describing the existing literature on foraging. Nearly all the relevant research has been carried out in the light of some theory and can only be understood in that light.

The theory that informs practically all foraging research (and, arguably, all biological research worthy of the name) is of course the theory of evolution by natural selection. It is important to foraging in two ways; first in understanding why animals forage as they do, but second in understanding the consequences of foraging for prey populations—which in a balanced ecosystem must be expected to feed back and affect the forager species. Natural selection offers to explain why animals choose the prey they do, why some animals hunt alone and others socially, and so forth. Insofar as all this concerns species-typical behaviour, it is of only marginal interest to operant psychology: it suggests certain constraints on reinforcement (cf. Breland and Breland, 1961; Stevenson-Hinde, 1973) but no more. But natural selection is also advanced as an explanation of the aspects of foraging that depend on individual experience, e.g. patch use. These clearly also involve learned instrumental behaviour and hence reinforcement principles. It is the interaction of these two principles, reinforcement and natural selection, that I shall concentrate upon.

The way in which natural selection is brought to bear on individual learned foraging behaviour seems simple in retrospect, but according to Davies and Krebs (1978, p. 2) it was not really grasped until the mid-1960s when 'the whole face of ecology was changed by R. H. MacArthur and his followers'. MacArthur and Pianka (1966) put forward the simple idea that natural selection will tend to turn each species into *optimal foragers* within the constraints of their particular niche. Evolution does not necessarily bring about the best possible solution to every problem but there are reasons to think that optimization is particularly likely in the case of foraging (food intake is often critical to individuals' survival or breeding success and foraging can often be improved by quantitative rather than qualitative change). If some aspects of a species' behaviour are relatively fixed (e.g. its perceptual capacities, range of prey types it can handle, efficiency of locomotion, etc.), much of the what, where, and how of its foraging can be predicted by considering what the logically most efficient forager would do given those constraints. The behaviour of the real and ideal animals can then be compared, an exercise that has dominated foraging research in recent years.

Because optimal foraging theory works in terms of ideal decision processes, a very common term within the field is 'strategy'. It is important, especially in the context of an experimental analysis of behaviour, to understand what is meant by a foraging strategy. It implies that the situation can be analysed into a succession of choices, and a particular strategy will specify how each choice should be made; often one strategy will be better than all others. It does not imply that the forager is consciously following that strategy (i.e. using what a Skinnerist would call 'rule-governed behaviour' (cf. Skinner, 1969, Chapter 6)). Ecologists, indeed, often rule that possibility out at the beginning (perhaps unnecessarily: *see below*). It does not even imply that the choice-points of the ideal strategy are in any way real to the animal, or recognized by it as crucial. Optimal foraging theory is neutral on all these points, because they concern mechanism rather than adaptive significance, proximate rather than ultimate causation. Radical behaviourists should beware lest a habitual reaction against terms like 'strategy', 'decision', and 'choice' restrict their grasp of foraging data (cf. Harzem and Miles, 1978). In the present section I shall follow in the ecological tradition of analysing behaviour in terms of strategies; in the following section I shall attempt an experimental analysis of the behaviour that enables animals to perform 'as if' following particular strategies.

Optimal Strategies

The literature on optimal foraging strategies divides into two parts. An increasing number of papers deal with long-term optimization, that is to say with the feeding pattern that should be shown over a day or year (e.g. Belovsky, 1978; Craig, De Angelis, and Dixon, 1979; Katz, 1974; Powell, 1979). There is an operant literature to which these studies must in due course be related, that on behaviour under 'free' behaviour regimes summarized by Lea (1978), but there is as yet little that can be said in that connection. This chapter concentrates on short-term optimization, that is, on behaviour within a period exclusively devoted to obtaining food.

Before the optimal strategy for any situation can be chosen, we must know what is to be optimized, i.e. the basis on which strategies are to be compared. The key issue here is whether foraging has one goal or many. We know, of course, that animals have many needs: for water as well as for food, and for many different kinds of food—carbohydrate, protein, fats, vitamins, minerals. But it is very much easier to prescribe the optimal strategy if we assume that just one of these needs is relevant (usually, the need for energy). This seems an implausible assumption, but it need not be. It is quite likely that all other nutrients will be present to excess in a diet that yields sufficient energy; it will be so, necessarily, where the predator has a single source of food, and even in the case of a much more complex diet it is quite likely that a single need will be dominant in a foraging bout of interesting length. As a specific example, Belovsky (1978) shows that though moose on Isle Royale must forage on energy-poor aquatic plants if they are to maintain adequate sodium intake, their behaviour is still predicted by an optimizing model which assumes energy maximization as the single goal.

Even if it has to be assumed that there is more than one relevant goal, it is still possibly to say something about the optimal strategy. That, indeed, is the entire subject-matter of microeconomics, which nowadays sets out by assuming that individuals seek to maximize some quantity, 'utility', which is undefined except that it increases with the amount of any good procured; different goods are assumed to contribute to it in different ways with no precise equivalences (*see*, for example, Simmons, 1974, Chapter 2). One or two authors have tried to translate microeconomics to deal with foraging behaviour where more than one goal is relevant (McCleery, 1978; Pulliam, 1975; Rapport, 1971), but the predictions made in ecology, as in economics, are weak and obvious, and no interesting data have yet been analysed in this way. Mainstream optimal foraging theory assumes that foragers are aiming to maximize energy intake, and insofar as observed behaviour has been near enough optimal to render the theory fruitful, that assumption is justified. More strictly, the forager is assumed to maximize net energy gain per unit time foraging; net, that is, of the energy costs of foraging, and of pursuing, catching, eating, and digesting the prey.

This assumption makes it possible to refine the 'what, where, and how' questions about foraging down to the following.

(a) Of two prey types, which is the better? It turns out that prey should be rated by the value of E_i/h_i, where E_i is the net energy gain for a prey item of the ith type, and h_i is its total handling time—the time during which the predator which has decided to pursue an item of that type is thereby not free to continue foraging after other prey.

(b) When foraging within a patch (or within a field of non-patchy prey), if a prey item of a particular type is encountered, should it be pursued? The answer turns out to depend on the E/h value for the type concerned and on the average rate of energy intake per time foraging that can be achieved if that prey type is consistently not pursued. That average, in turn, can be shown to depend on the E/h values for all *better* prey types existing within the patch, and on the frequency with which each of them is encountered. If the average intake rate achievable without including the ith prey type exceeds E_i/h_i, the optimal forager always ignores the ith prey type. But if that average is lower than E_i/h_i, the optimal forager always pursues that type of prey. It follows, as a simple corollary, that if the densities of all types of prey within the environment increase together, prey types should be dropped from the diet one by one, in reverse order of E/h: hence the richer the environment, the more selective the optimal forager should be. An important point to notice is that the average energy intake rate achievable without including the ith type, and hence the decision about including it, is independent of the rate of encountering that type of prey; it depends instead on the density of all better types of prey. The 'all-or-none' nature of optimal behaviour is also interesting, and recalls the nature of optimal behaviour in other situations better known in psychology, e.g. probability learning (*see below*).

(c) When foraging in a patch, when should that patch be left and a better one sought? The solution to this problem follows the same lines as the previous one, since there is no logical difference between a patch type and a prey type (except that a predator may be assumed to know the E and h values for a type but to have to learn them for a patch). If the energy yield per unit time of a patch is not depleting with time, the predator should leave at once if it knows of a better hole, and otherwise stay put indefinitely. In the more realistic case where patch depletion occurs (commonly as a result of the predator's activities), the optimal strategy is in dispute. The optimal forager should continue in the patch until the rate of net energy intake there falls either to the mean for the entire habitat (Charnov, 1976*b*) or until it falls somewhat below that level (Oaten, 1977). In either case, however, the criterial rate within the current patch is a function of net energy intake achievable within patches and travelling time between them. The probability of staying in a given patch should therefore depend on the density of better patches in the environment.

Derivations of these optimal strategies, and also of more complex strategies to deal with refinements of the basic questions posed above, can be found in Charnov (1976a,b), Krebs, Erichsen, Webber, and Charnov (1977), MacArthur and Pianka (1966), Pyke, Pulliam, and Charnov (1977), Oaten (1977), Royama (1976), Schoener (1971), and elsewhere. I shall spare the reader the algebra here, for the fundamental ideas involved are simple enough. The solution to problem (a) is really just a restatement of the notion of optimizing energy intake per unit time; the solutions to problems (b) and (c) consist in accepting the prey type, or staying in the patch, so long as the return for doing so exceeds the 'opportunity cost', the possible return for doing something else.

These strategies require the subject to know almost all there is to know about the environment: the net energy worth, handling time, and encounter frequency of every kind of prey in any patch, and the travelling times between patches. That makes these strategies very suitable for comparing with data from choice studies in operant laboratories, where the custom is to maintain each experimental condition until all change in behaviour has ceased. But it also makes them unrealistic, as a description of any real forager. In most cases the real forager must learn all the parameters of his environment, and although net energy worths and handling times may perhaps be stable enough for an experienced animal to reach asymptotic estimates of them (or even for genetically-based food preferences to reflect them, where prey types are qualitatively different in appearance), encounter rates at least must always be learned, in fact tracked continuously. At first sight this looks like a question that belongs under the heading of the mechanism of foraging, but it is not so entirely: it is possible to work out the optimal strategy, at least in certain simple environments, for a forager who is ignorant in specified ways. Such a forager has, in effect, two simultaneous goals: to maximize his food (energy) intake, and to learn about the environment. But the problem is not as intractable as that of a forager trying to maximize (say) energy and protein intake simultaneously, since it is easily reduced to terms of maximizing energy intake over a foraging session of fixed length. Krebs, Kacelnik, and Taylor (1978) considered the case of an animal faced with two patches each containing the same, single kind of prey at unknown, possibly different, non-depleting density. In mathematical statistics this is known as the two-armed bandit problem, and Krebs et al. (1978) showed that, if travel time between patches is ignored, optimal behaviour is to alternate between the two patches at the start of the session, and at some point to switch abruptly to staying within the one that has yielded more prey so far (note the recurrence of the 'all-or-none' theme so common in optimal behaviour). An 'optimal sampling' strategy for a more complicated environment, say including travel time, could perhaps be worked out, but that has not yet been done; Oaten (1977) offers the start of a solution.

A development along somewhat similar lines, however, is the theory of movement patterns within an environment. Random movement through an environment is rarely if ever optimal, but exactly what the optimal path is depends on the perceptibility of the prey and of any patches in which it is concentrated; these in turn depend on the sensitivity and directionality of the forager's sense organs. For example, if patch boundaries cannot be perceived, it is usually best to increase rate of turning ('tortuosity') or decrease speed of movement after encountering one prey item, as this should increase the probability of staying within a patch. Any development of an optimal path model must make assumptions about the prey's regeneration rate and the forager's information-processing capacity, of course: much depends on whether the forager can know when it is revisiting a particular area. Several optimal path models, using different assumptions, have been discussed: *see* Cody (1971), Pyke *et al.* (1977), and Smith (1974*b*). One of the most sophisticated models of this kind was Toda's (1962) 'design for a fungus-eater', but so far as I know it has had no influence in ecology.

As well as requiring the optimal forager to be all-knowing, the simpler short-term foraging models require the forager to be unconstrained by needs other than for food. Papers on long-term optimization commonly do take such constraints into account, by using linear programming to obtain the optimal solution under constraint; a recent paper by Dunstone and O'Connor (1979) is important because it introduced a constraint into a short-term optimal foraging problem, that faced by a mink foraging for fish under water, constrained by a limited oxygen supply.

Tests of Optimal Foraging Theory

Do real foragers behave optimally? I shall consider this under a series of headings corresponding to the various questions raised above. Here, as elsewhere in the chapter, I restrict my surveys to data on vertebrate predators; most of the points made could also be supported from invertebrate data, and Krebs (1978) includes them in his review of foraging.

Preference between prey items. As well as the optimal pattern, of preference determined by E/h, there are at least three other possibilities: preference might be determined by E alone, h alone, or might be random. Since E and h will generally be correlated (larger prey may be more nutritious, but they will be tougher to handle), these four possibilities should all be distinguishable. However, comparison of results between studies is complicated by the fact that different experimental techniques and different measures of preference have been used.

The simplest kind of experiment involves captive animals given either a series of two-choice tests, or unlimited access to two or more foodstuffs; even then preference can be assessed either in terms of percentage intake (by weight or calorific contribution) of the different foods, or by the percentage of feeding responses (e.g. seeds picked up) directed to each source. In field experiments there may be no alternative to assessing preference by percentage diet content, determined from analysis of excreta; sometimes, though, it is possible to compare diet content with encounter rates to give probabilities of acceptance. Another alternative is to assume that the subject drops types of prey from his diet, as overall prey density increases, in reverse order of preference; this is consistent with the theory of optimal prey type selection (*see above*), but also with common sense.

Table 10.1 lists a number of studies where food preferences have been observed, and both net energy gain (or some plausible surrogate measure: with reasonably uniform prey types, weight is often sufficient) and handling times were recorded. The results are summarized in terms of whether correlation with E/h could be assessed separately from correlation with E or h (where one of the two varied much more than the other the ratio is confounded with the dominant variable), and if so which variable gave the best prediction of performance. It would not be hard to double the length of this table, but it includes enough data to justify the following conclusions: both E and h can have an effect on behaviour; in some cases they both affect behaviour to some extent; but preference is rarely if ever determined by their ratio—in some experiments E is too important, in others h is. Here we have a picture of qualitative but not quantitative agreement with optimal foraging theory.

The decision to pursue an individual prey item. Before considering tests of the precise predictions of optimal foraging theory, it is worth considering the simple corollary that with increasing overall prey density, the constitution of the diet should change: the worse types of prey should be dropped (abruptly). This corollary was used in the previous subsection. Where optimal and observed prey preferences do not coincide, it may be desirable to replace 'worse' with 'less preferred' in making our prediction.

Increased selectivity as a function of overall prey density has been confirmed in a number of studies, including Ivlev's (1961, Chapter 4) work on carp, Davies' (1977*b*, Figures 4 and 5) on flycatchers, Gibb's (1958) on tits (for discussion of this work in terms of optimality theory, *see* Tullock (1971)), as well as in several recent studies where densities of different kinds of prey were manipulated independently. Studies of this latter type have generally confirmed the effect of the density of a preferred prey on acceptance of a less preferred type: examples include Goss-Custard's (1977*a*) field studies of redshank, and the laboratory work of Krebs *et al.* (1977) on Great tits, Werner and Hall (1974) on Bluegill sunfish and Zach and Falls (1978) on ovenbirds. However, the dropping of the

Table 10.1. Results of studies showing effects of net energy worth (E) and handling time (h) on food preferences

Author and species	Foodstuffs	Preference measure	Best predictor
(a) *Studies demonstrating an effect of E with h effectively constant*			
Krebs et al (1977) Great tit	Mealworms	Dropping from diet	
Ivlev (1961) Carp	Assorted natural foods	Dropping from diet	
Ware (1972) Rainbow trout	Amphipods	Dropping from diet	
(b) *Studies demonstrating an effect of h with E effectively constant*			
Smith (1970) American red squirrels	Pine cone seeds	Dropping from diet	
Emlen and Emlen (1975) Mice	Seeds	Choice tests	
Partridge (1976) Great tits	Mealworms in containers	Percentage of attempts to feed	
(c) *Studies in which E and h were both varied*			
Davies (1977a) Wagtails	Dungflies	Choice tests	E/h
Davies (1977b) Flycatchers	Flying insects	Percentage pursued	E/h
Goss-Custard (1977b) Redshank	Estuarine worms and crustaceans	Dropping from diet	E

	Food	Measure	Currency
Hainsworth and Wolf (1976)			
Hummingbirds	Sugar solutions	Intake rates	E
Kear			
Chaffinch	Seeds	Percentage of diet	E/h
		Percentage of seeds	E
Smith and Follmer (1972)			
Gray and fox squirrels	Nuts	Choice tests	E
Stein (1977)			
Smallmouth bass	Crayfish	Percentage of prey	E/h
Werner and Hall (1974)			
Bluegill sunfish	Daphnia	Dropping from diet	E/h
Willson (1971)			
Cardinals			E
Fox sparrows			E
Juncos			h
Song sparrows	Seeds (three to six types)	Percentage of seeds	h or E/h
Swamp sparrows			h
Tree sparrows			h
Whitethroats			E
Willson and Harmeson (1973)			
Cardinals			h
Song sparrows	Seeds	Percentage of seeds	h
Zach and Falls (1978)			
Ovenbirds	Insects naturally in diet	Percentage of prey	E/h

non-preferred type does not seem to occur abruptly, as optimality requires. Also, it often seems that the density of the less preferred type affects either the frequency at which it is taken itself (this was true of Goss-Custard's redshank, and also arose in earlier studies of foraging (e.g. Ivlev, 1961, 60*ff*; Mook, Mook, and Heikens, 1960; Tinbergen, 1970), or the frequency at which preferred items are taken. Several recent studies of predation probability as a function of density have concluded that the relative predation rate on two prey types is some symmetrical function of their relative density (Cook and Miller, 1977; Elton and Greenwood, 1970; Fullik and Greenwood, 1979; Manly, Miller, and Cook, 1972: Murdoch, Avery, and Smyth, 1975; Murdoch and Oaten, 1975). Murdoch and Oaten consider the formula

$$P_1/P_2 = cR_1/R_2, \tag{10.1}$$

where P_1 and P_2 are the numbers of two kinds of prey eaten, R_1 and R_2 are their densities in the environment, and c is a constant. They show that for the majority of cases this does not fit, and it is necessary to raise the density ratio to a power of about 2. This corresponds to excessive predation on the denser prey, a situation Murdoch (confusingly) calls 'switching'. Murdoch *et al.* (1975) demonstrated the effect in guppies fed fruit flies (which float) or Tubificids (which sink) in varying proportions; Manly *et al.* (1972) and Cook and Miller (1977) got similar results from quail searching for artificial pastry baits, though their data require an exponent of around 3; and in chicks picking up different coloured crumbs, Fullick and Greenwood (1979) find an exponent of 1.7. This range of exponents suggests a parallel to laboratory operant experiments of a very different kind: *see below*.

Because of the symmetrical effects of the two densities, this kind of behaviour seems to be inconsistent with optimality. However, additional processes such as 'search image formation' (*see below*) or digestive changes to accommodate the commonest prey type (as Krebs (1978) suggests), or increasing skill in handling it, leading to reduced handling time (*see* Hughes (1979) for a detailed model), may render it optimal. Ivlev (1961, p. 79*ff*) demonstrated that prolonged feeding on particular foods may be sufficient to make them more highly preferred; such 'trophic adaptation' may well reflect either cognitive or digestive changes.

Patch use. The distinction between a patch and a prey type is not always hard and fast. For convenience, Gibb's data on tits' foraging were included above; the tits were foraging for pine cones, which were treated as prey items, but their ultimate prey were *Enarmonia* larvae, which infest the cones, so the cone could be regarded as a patch (with perceptible borders but imperceptible prey density).

Apart from Gibb's work there are relatively few field studies of patch exploitation that go further than demonstrating that animals aggregate in richer patches, or spend a high proportion of time there, a glimpse of the obvious. (e.g. Goss-Custard (1970) with redshank; Altmann and Altmann (1970) for baboons' use of waterholes; Smith and Sweatman (1974) with tits). Note, however, that because of handling time effects, the patch of greatest prey density need not be the most profitable; in some cases the optimal density may even vary with the predator's state of hunger, as Heller and Milinski (1979) have demonstrated for sticklebacks feeding on Daphnia.

From the point of view of optimality theory the most interesting question is when an animal will abandon a depleting patch. Almost all the vertebrate data on this point come from the Oxford group's work with tits in various kinds of artificial environment, for example hunting for meal worms through sawdust in pieces of drainpipe on an aluminium tree. One related field study did show that Great tits and Blue tits usually visited each foraging site only once, but revisited sites where they had found prey unusually quickly; they abandoned them, regardless of former success, when foraging time rose to the average for 'new' sites, in accordance with optimality (Smith and Sweatman, 1974, Experiment 4). Zach and Falls (1979), give some related data from a field study of ovenbirds.) In a more formal situation Krebs, Ryan, and Charnov (1974), using chickadees (American members of the tit genus), showed that the time to abandon a patch was not significantly correlated with the density of prey within it, a result also reported in a field experiment on carrion crows (Croze, 1970). Earlier crow data (Tinbergen, Impekoven, and Franck, 1967, Tables 3 and 5) seem to show the same result. Krebs et al. (1974) also claimed to show that 'giving-up time' was negatively correlated with overall prey density in the environment, and Gill and Wolf (1977) report a corresponding result in a field study of sunbirds foraging for nectar. Cowie and Krebs (1979) suggest that the Krebs et al. (1974) result, and also, presumably, that of Gill and Wolf (1977), could have been obtained even if behaviour had been random. Zach and Falls (1976a) report a failure to confirm predictions from optimality in a laboratory study of ovenbirds foraging in depleted patches, but they used very few prey per patch, resulting in a weak test of the model. Cowie (1977) made a direct test of the effects of travel time by putting resistant lids on the 'patches' in some conditions, and showed that this increased the time that Great tits spent foraging in each patch, in accordance with optimality theory.

Dunstone and O'Connor (1979) demonstrate that the problem faced by a diving mammal, when underwater, is formally analogous to that of a forager in a patchy environment, each prey sighted corresponding to a patch and the crucial decision being when to abandon pursuit and hunt for a more easily caught prey. Dunstone and O'Connor showed that mink had a constant 'giving-up time' within a foraging bout at constant prey density, but longer giving-up times in bouts with lower density, in accordance with the prediction of the patch use model; it is not clear, however, whether Cowie and Krebs' critique would apply to their data in the same way as to those of Krebs et al. (1974).

Search paths. There are numerous demonstrations that, where there are patches with imperceptible boundaries, animals reduce the speed and increase the tortuosity of their movements after prey capture, and so stay within the vicinity.

This was termed 'area-restricted searching' by Tinbergen *et al.* (1967), who observed it in carrion crows. Their observations were extended by Croze (1970); the phenomenon has also been studied in sticklebacks (Beukema, 1966, p. 43; Thomas, 1974, 1977), sunbirds (Gill and Wolf, 1977), thrushes (Smith, 1974*a,b*), and ovenbirds (Zach and Falls, 1976*a,b,c*, 1977, 1979). Beukema showed that his sticklebacks' search paths were substantially more efficient than a random walk, but far from optimal. Thomas (1977) added the observation that after rejecting a prey item, sticklebacks' tortuosity decreased, so that they tended to leave the area.

Morrison (1978) considered a case with visible patches, fruit bats' foraging after trees with ripe fruit. The bats showed the apparently odd behaviour of commuting on several successive days to a particular tree, when equally good trees existed at a third of the distance from the home den; under plausible assumptions about range of visibility and flight directionality, however, Morrison showed that commuting could still be optimal. The time taken to find a nearer food source would be greater that the time to fly to the known one.

With clearly perceptible patch boundaries, the exact converse of area restricted searching may occur, especially if the predator can deplete the patch substantially; it is then optimal to avoid recently visited patches, a tendency that has been reported in nectar-feeding birds by Gill and Wolf (1977) and Kamil (1978), in thrushes foraging on insects by Greenwood and Harvey (1978), and in ovenbirds by Zach and Falls (1976*a,c*, 1977). Pyke (1979) has shown a similar effect in bumblebees foraging for nectar.

Optimal sampling. Morrison's work links area-restricted searching to the approach by Krebs *et al.* (1978) to patch use assuming ignorance. With Great tits exposed to different random-ratio schedules of reinforcement for perching on two different, concurrently available manipulanda, Krebs *et al.* (1978) claimed that, in accordance with the optimal strategy, the tits showed an abrupt switch from alternating between perches to absorption on the one that had proved more productive. They also claimed that this switch came at the optimal point in the session, though as they did not vary session length (which determines the optimal switch point) this finding could easily be coincidence. However, Kacelnik (1979) has since reported that longer sessions lead to more alternation before absorption, which is consistent with optimal sampling theory, and Dow and Lea (1979) have obtained the same result from pigeons.

Experimental Analysis of Foraging Behaviour

Foraging is clearly a kind of instrumental behaviour (in the sense that it has outcomes), and many components of it must be learned. This section considers whether parallel kinds of behaviour can be observed in the operant laboratory. The first subsection looks for parallels between components of foraging and orthodox effects within the conditioning literature; the second considers attempts to synthesize entire foraging sequences.

Analysis

Each of the major predictions from optimality, discussed in earlier sections, can be applied to laboratory operant behaviour as well as to field studies and ecological experiments. Two major questions can be asked: is operant behaviour optimal? and if it is not, do ecological data show similar kinds of optimality failures?

Energy worth, handling time, and their relative weighting. One preliminary issue must be dealt with before we can ask whether an experimental analysis supports the optimal foraging prediction that prey types should be ranked by E/h. The definition of E is *net* energy worth, that is, caloric gain after taking account of the energy costs of capture, and after attenuation by the probability (less than one in many cases) of capture given pursuit. Thus optimal foraging theory depends (explicitly in some cases, e.g. Charnov (1976a)) on the 'expected value' principle, in which the gain from an action is found by weighting the gain from every possible outcome by its probability, and summing. Any optimizing theory must make this assumption, of course, but there is considerable psychological evidence that it is unjustified. In instrumental learning there is usually a preference for a variable reward condition over a fixed condition with the same mean parameters (and hence the same 'expected value'); this has been shown for the intervals in fixed interval schedules of reinforcement (Davison, 1969; Herrnstein, 1964b; Killeen, 1968); for the ratios in fixed ratio schedules (Fantino, 1967); for delays of reinforcement (Logan, 1965b; Pubols, 1962); and for reward magnitude (Levanthal, Morrell, Morgan, and Perkins, 1959), though in this last case there are two exceptions to the rule—Logan (1965b) found the opposite preference in rats, and Staddon and Innis (1966b) found no preference in pigeons. It is possible to remove apparent variance preferences of this kind by rescaling the reward parameters concerned (Bernoulli, 1954), but it is one of the merits of optimal foraging theory that it has not, so far, indulged in this kind of scaling manoeuvre, since evolution is held to be affected by objective, not subjective outcomes. But as Krebs (1978) points out, if an optimality theory fails it is usually possible to find some objectively measurable alternative quantity that might, after all, be optimized; the added sophistication of subjective scaling is therefore hardly needed.

In practice, both E and h values for prey items will usually be variable, and capture probabilities will often be less than one; and both variances and probabilities may differ between prey types. Laboratory experience leads us to predict optimality failures when this occurs, but so far there are no field data that would let us test this prediction. All we can do is bear it in mind as a caution.

In the discussion on preferability above, the major issue was whether E, h, or their ratio determines preference between prey types. In the laboratory, the equivalent of E is obviously size of reward; h can be taken as the sum of delay of reward and reward consumption time (though this may be misleading in some cases, *see below*). There is no need to review here the extensive literature that shows that animals will choose the least-delaying route to a reward of invariant size, or the larger reward when all delays are equal (except to note that choice studies are in the main free from the problems that have dogged studies of its effect on response vigour: *see* Collier and Siskel (1959), Lea (1974, Experiment IV), Lowe, Davey, and Harzem (1974), and, for commentary, Catania (1963)). The important question is, what happens when magnitude and delay of reinforcement are put into conflict?

In contrast with the muddled position that emerged from the ecological studies reviewed in Table 10.1, operant work (and psychology generally) gives a clear answer to this question. Subjects from pigeons to people have a tendency to let delay of reward dominate size of reward to an extent that consistently leads to non-optimal choice (usually referred to as *irrational* in this context). This phenomenon is known as failure to delay gratification, or failure of self-control; a thorough review of data and theories, from areas as wide apart as economics, sociology, social psychology, and the experimental analysis of behaviour, is presented by Ainslie (1975). Further discussion can be found in Lea (1978) and Navarick and Fantino (1976). But this unanimous report of failure to delay gratification should be interpreted with some caution. If a child chooses a small chocolate bar now rather than a larger one tomorrow (Mischel and Metzner, 1962), that is arguably optimal in E/h terms, for the ratio of delays far exceeds the ratio of reward sizes. It is only irrational in terms of a far more sophisticated analysis that either assumes the possibility of lending and borrowing at interest (*see*, for example, Green, 1971, pp. 170–175), or recognizes that further 'foraging' is in fact possible during the delay in this case, so that it is not a handling time in the sense defined above.

Laboratory operant or maze studies with animals, in which reinforcers of different sizes are used on different schedules of reinforcement, may provide a more exact analogy. The schedules may be arranged concurrently (e.g. Todorov, 1973) or as concurrent chains (e.g. Ainslie, 1974; Navarick and Fantino, 1976; Rachlin and Green, 1972; Schwartz, 1969); or mazes may be used (e.g. Logan, 1965a). Such studies generally confirm the dominance of the time parameter, though there are exceptions (Schwartz, 1969), and the effect can be reversed with long experience of the schedules (Fantino, 1966).

Selectivity as a function of prey density. The kind of choice involved in many foraging situations, which involves a prey type available now as against an alternative that may be encountered later, does not correspond precisely to any standard operant procedure, although it occurs as a component of the 'self-control' experiments discussed above, and something like it has been used, for unrelated reasons, by Boren (cited by Catania, 1966) and Iversen (1975). Unfortunately neither of these experimenters varied anything that could serve as a surrogate for prey densities. If schedules of reinforcement are seen as analogues of prey types, however, foraging has points in common with a multiple schedule (in that two prey types are presented successively) but also with concurrent schedules (in that the subject's behaviour determines the degree of exposure to the different options). The closest analogy is probably to the kind of concurrent schedule introduced by Findley (1958), in which an explicit operant response is required to switch between schedule components; the difference remains that in foraging the precise outcome of the changeover response is undefined.

Experimental analysis shows that in both multiple and concurrent schedules the frequency of reinforcement in one component affects performance on the other. The two cases have sometimes been brought within a single theoretical or parametric framework; three attempts to do this, starting from rather different assumptions, are Henton and Iversen (1978, Chapters 3 and 4), Herrnstein (1970), and Rachlin (1973). The most usual form of schedule interaction is *contrast*; that is, the higher the reinforcement frequency in one component, the lower the response rate in an alternative tends to be. Qualitatively, at least, this is capable of explaining the dropping of unprofitable prey items from the diet as the density of better prey increases. The step function for prey-inclusion predicted from optimality would not be expected from operant work, but neither is it found in the field, as was discussed above. Similarly, asymmetry of schedule interactions, with density of better prey affecting pursuit probabilities of worse types but not vice versa, might not be expected from operant studies, and is not found consistently by the ecologists; the position is complicated by inconsistencies in both ecological and psychological data, however, and is discussed in more detail below.

Patch use. Schedules were considered as prey types above; they can also serve as an analogy for patches and this seems especially apt when the schedules are arranged on spatially separated manipulanda. Krebs (1978) explicitly compared Herrnstein and Loveland's (1975) study of pigeons under concurrent, variable ratio schedules with Krebs *et al.*'s (1978) work on Great tit patch use; indeed except for the procedural differences springing from two quite different experimental traditions, the two experiments were formally identical, since the Krebs *et al.* (1978) experiment involved learned instrumental responses rather than 'natural' foraging. As Krebs (1978) points out, however, such schedules correspond to the (relatively rare) non-depleting patch condition, and their use is therefore limited; they are more realistic as models of prey types, which are likely to change much more slowly with time than patches (in most cases: but the nectar gain a hummingbird or sunbird can expect from a particular flower type usually falls sharply as time passes within a day (Gill and Wolf, 1975; Wolf, 1975)).

Schedules that can serve as models of depleting patches have been described. Hodos and Trumbule (1967) trained chimpanzees on a complex progressive ratio schedule, in which the cost of reinforcement (in terms of button-press responses made) increased each time it was obtained. There was an alternative schedule on which reinforcement was always available for 1000 presses. In a condition where selecting this fixed ratio reduced the progressive ratio to its minimum value (100 presses), Hodos and Trumbule found that the chimpanzees switched to the fixed ratio when the progression had reached about 600, which was almost the optimal performance. This schedule is formally very close to foraging in depleting patches, with the switch ratio corresponding to a travel time. In contrast, in a related experiment using pigeons, I found no evidence for optimal behaviour (Lea, 1976). The pigeons were faced with a choice between a 'standard' fixed ratio (or interval) schedule and an 'adjusting' schedule that became leaner each time it yielded reinforcement and richer every time reinforcement was delivered on the standard schedule. The resulting behaviour kept the standard and adjusting schedule parameters the same, whereas optimal behaviour would have allowed the adjusting schedule parameter to fall to a low value and kept it there by alternating choices between the two schedules. Unfortunately I did not include a condition like Hodos and Trumbule's, where switching away from the adjusting schedule reduced its parameter abruptly to the minimum, so it is impossible to tell whether optimal behaviour depends on the subject (it is plausible for chimpanzees to be more 'rational' than pigeons) or the situation (Hodos and Trumbule's paradigm is closer to the natural depleting patch condition than mine).

As for simple aggregation in more profitable patches, innumerable operant studies show preference for the more favourable of two schedules, and these include one or two which approximate natural conditions at least as well as some of the ecologists' experiments (e.g. Baum, 1972, 1974a; Graft, Lea, and Whitworth, 1977). Experiments using 'choice boxes' (e.g. Baum and Rachlin, 1969; Morgan, 1974a), are particularly relevant. To discuss the extent of preference for the more favourable schedule involves the whole vexed question of the 'matching law' and its relation to optimality in behaviour; this is taken up below.

Search paths. Though anyone who has ever trained a rat in a maze will have seen behaviour that could be described as 'increased tortuosity following prey capture', there are few psychological experiments that provide direct parallels to area-restricted searching, and those are not, in the main, in the operant tradition. The most closely analogous result is the well-known acceleration in the second half of a double runway when reward is omitted in the first half, first reported by Amsel and Roussel (1952); analogous results have been found in operant apparatus (e.g. Staddon and Innis, 1966a), and although Amsel attributed the effect to frustration at non-reward, it could as easily be an absence of tortuosity that would normally follow reward. Further analogies to area-restricted searching can be drawn, but they are somewhat speculative, and they are therefore deferred to the section on mechanisms of optimal behaviour, below.

The converse case, of avoidance of recently visited patches, also has parallels in the literature on alternation learning, as Kamil (1978) discusses; but it also relates to questions about concurrent interval schedules, raised below.

Optimal sampling. The question of the optimal degree of exposure to two sources of reinforcement touches on a major current controversy in operant psychology, which is taken up in some detail below. An issue that has taken up a lot of attention is that of whether or not animals 'maximize', i.e. respond exclusively to the better alternative, in a situation where there are two probabilistic sources of reinforcement; and a plausible hypothesis to explain failure to maximize is the need to monitor the environment against possible changes in reinforcement probabilities. Krebs *et al.* (1978) took this reasoning out of the range of mere speculation by considering the precise kinds of ignorance of the environment that the subject has to combat, and specified the optimal behaviour under those circumstances. As an alternative to their optimization analysis, it ought to be possible for an experimental analysis to offer a conditioning model, specifying how more frequent reinforcement at one source leads to increased responding there, the inevitable consequence of this positive feedback being absorption at one source; which Krebs *et al.* found to happen by the end of each session. But models of this kind, dealing with the *dynamics* of conditioning, are rare in operant psychology, though many have been proposed in the field of probability learning in humans (*see below*). Herrnstein and Loveland (1975) pointed out that Herrnstein's (1970) 'law of effect' predicts absorption at one source under concurrent ratio schedules, but the data on which that law is based come primarily from 'steady state' conditions; it has no basis in studies of transitions between schedules, which have been curiously little studied since Ferster and Skinner's (1957) careful reporting of cumulative records of transitional performance. de Villiers' (1977) case in favour of the application of Herrnstein's law to single-operant paradigms does make use of many studies where stable behaviour, by the criteria usually accepted in the operant laboratory, was not obtained; but the aim was not to predict changing response rates.

Reasons for this concentration on the steady state are not hard to guess at. Theories like Herrnstein's are essentially *molar*; they assume that the crucial relations are between response rates and reinforcement rates computed over relatively long time periods, rather than between single responses and single reinforcements (Baum, 1973). The validity of this molar approach is, in a sense, the theme of this book. The molar emphasis is congenial to an analysis of foraging behaviour, since optimal foraging theory requires the subject to respond to overall rates of energy intake, not to individual events. But it is less helpful when dealing with a changing situation; for a dynamic environment, a dynamic analysis of behaviour is required. It is possible that more molecular approaches to concurrent performances (e.g. Hale and Shimp, 1975; Henton and Iversen, 1978, Chapter 3; Shimp, 1969; Silberberg, Hamilton, Ziriax, and Casey 1978) may come into their own here, but to date they have been more concerned with predicting steady state than variable behaviour. Even those few experiments in which 'tracking' of changing schedule parameters has been reported have involved systematic changes that could be predicted by the subject (e.g. progressive intervals (Harzem, 1969) or cyclic intervals (Staddon, 1967)).

There is therefore little operant work to set beside Krebs *et al.*'s (1978) analysis of optimal sampling, at the empirical level. The theoretical questions are taken up again below.

Simulations of Foraging

There is something unsatisfactory about 'the experimental analysis of behaviour' as an alternative title for operant psychology. Any science that deals with complex materials has two modes of enquiry, of which one is indeed analysis; the other, however, must not be forgotten: synthesis. Synthesis is in fact more likely to effect the kinds of change in people's perceptions, about behaviour as in other areas, that radical behaviourists want: compare the decisive role in the history of biochemistry traditionally ascribed to Wöhler's synthesis of urea 'without the intervention of kidney of man or dog'. Skinner himself has always been interested in synthesis (e.g. Skinner, 1948, 1962), and the example of language learning in apes shows that this kind of synthesis does catch the public imagination.

The previous section aimed to show that most of the elementary patterns of behaviour observed in studies of foraging have their analogues in laboratory studies of instrumental behaviour. But the argument is incomplete unless we can synthesize the entire pattern of behaviour in the laboratory. Behavioural ecologists themselves have come close to doing this in recent years. Although everyone justly pays tribute to the patient and often enchanting field studies of investigators like Davies (1977a,b), Goss-Custard (1977a,b), or Smith (1974a,b), the crucial tests of optimal foraging theory tend to take place in laboratory conditions at least in the first instance. These laboratory experiments usually mimic field conditions in some way (e.g. Krebs *et al.* (1974) used simulated pine cones hung on artificial trees—note, though, that mimicry of natural feeding is part and parcel of the conventional operant chamber too (Moore, 1973)), but some of the most recent are frankly operant in flavour (e.g. Krebs *et al.*, 1978). This tendency may increase as interdisciplinary contacts develop, a process that is now well under way, as this chapter, as well as recent work by Krebs (1978) and Collier (1978), for example, testifies.

From the point of view of establishing the relevance of pre-existing operant literature to the study of foraging, however, it is important to use the traditional apparatus, subjects, and procedures of the operant laboratory. Two recent experiments have done that.

Collier and Kaufman (1976). Using rats, Collier and Kaufman (reported by Collier and Rovee-Collier, 1980) attempted a simulation of the prey selectivity problem using learned instrumental responses. (They described it as a patch selection problem, but the two are formally identical for present purposes.) Each rat lived in an operant chamber (what Logan (1964) calls a 'free behaviour' situation). Presses on a lever at one end of the cage were reinforced according to a fixed ratio schedule (called the 'search ratio'), by turning on lights around another lever at the opposite end of the cage. When these lights were on, pressing the second lever was reinforced with food according to another FR schedule, which itself took one of two values depending of the particular signal lights given (these were called 'procurement ratios'). In terms of the prey selection problem, pressing on the first lever corresponded to foraging activity, and pressing on the second lever corresponded to pursuit of prey. (These analogies can equally well be stated in terms of searching for patches and hunting within them.) Collier and Kaufman kept the lower of the two procurement ratios at FR 5, but varied the higher from 50 to 200; they also varied the search ratio from 5 to 200.

If the rat did not switch to the second bar within 7.5 s of the signal lights appearing, the opportunity for food was lost (corresponding to a decision not to pursue a prey item). Figure 10.1 shows how the probability of switching varied

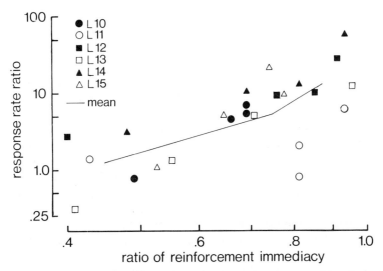

Figure 10.1. Results of a simulated foraging experiment by Collier and Kaufman (1976), showing how the probability of taking feeding opportunities given two different 'procurement' schedules varied as a function of the 'search' schedule. © Alan C. Kamil, 1980; reproduced by permission

with the search ratio, the procurement ratios being constant at FR 5 and FR 200. Clearly, all subjects became less selective as the search ratio decreased, i.e. as the overall density of food in this artificial environment decreased, in accordance with both theory and data on foraging. As Collier and Kaufman state, these results show that it is possible to simulate ecological problems within the laboratory and to derive sensible data. However, the behaviour was not strictly optimal; an optimal forager would have taken the lower cost meal at every opportunity regardless of the search ratio, and the rats in this experiment did not. But with the very low search ratios involved, and given that the geometry of Collier and Kaufman's test chamber may have imposed costs in watching out for the signals, the rats' behaviour was acceptably close to optimality.

Lea (1979). I have recently carried out a somewhat more elaborate experiment in a very similar spirit, using pigeons in a conventional operant chamber. Figure 10.2 shows a flowchart of my procedure. It differed from Collier and Kaufman's mainly in using interval schedules throughout (so as to allow quantitative predictions from optimal foraging theory to be tested) and in allowing a few extra parameters to be varied. On completion of an FI schedule on the centre key, a side key lit up red or green; the pigeons then had an effectively unlimited time to choose whether to peck the central key again, and thus reject a chance of food, or to accept it by pecking the side key, and thus initiate a second FI schedule, whose interval was correlated with the colour of the side key. This second schedule was arranged on the side key. As in Collier and Kaufman's experiment, variations in the 'search' schedule (the centre key FI, t in Figure 10.2) with the 'procurement' schedules (the side key FI values, h_s and h_L) and their probabilities (p and $1 - p$) constant led to increased selectivity as food availability became more common. The experiment used conventional fixed-length sessions (80 entries to the SEARCH state), so this optimal-foraging-like behaviour is not confined to free behaviour situations; in fact behaviour was closer to optimality than in Collier and Kaufman's study, in that when the shorter procurement schedule was offered it was always accepted.

By varying t and p it was possible to vary independently the rates at which the pigeons encountered the two different procurement schedules. I give here the results of one set of tests of this type (the procurement schedules were kept constant at FI 5 s and FI 20 s, referred to below as 'short prey' and 'long prey' respectively). Once again the FI 5 s procurement schedule was always taken when available, so the dependent variable of interest is the probability of taking the FI 20 s schedule. All six pigeons were more likely to take it when both prey types occurred 0.011 times per second than when they both occurred 0.1 times a second, again confirming Collier and Kaufman's result. The important point is different effects of reducing the 'long' and 'short' prey encounter rates while holding the other constant. Reducing the long prey encounter rate had almost no effect on average; reducing the short prey encounter rate sharply reduced the

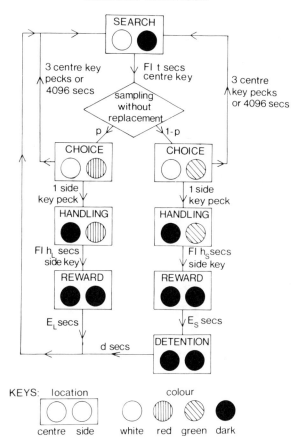

Figure 10.2. Flowchart of the schedule of reinforcement used by Lea (1979) to simulate foraging, using pigeons as subjects. Each rectangle represents a state of the schedule; the conditions for state transition are noted by the transition are written by the transition arrows. (Reproduced from Lea (1979) by permission of Balliére Tindall)

probability of accepting the long prey when it was offered. Thus the asymmetry of effect of the two prey densities, which is predicted by optimality but seemed questionable in some field studies of foraging (*see above*), appeared unambiguously in this simulation.

I also tested two other predictions from optimality theory. With all other parameters held constant, I varied the food magazine operation times (E_s and E_L in Figure 10.2) so that they cancelled out the difference in the procurement schedules: the FI 5 s schedule now led to 2 s access to food, while the FI 20 s schedule led to 8 s access. Optimal behaviour is then to accept all chances of procuring food, since in E/h terms all are now equal. Compared with a condition in which E_L and E_s were both 2.5 s, the unequal hopper times did lead to an increase in the probability of accepting the 20 s procurement interval, in accordance with optimality; but that probability did not reach 1.0 for any bird.

The second manipulation was the introduction of a 30 s detention period (d in Figure 10.2) after food had been delivered on the 5 s procurement interval schedule. This had no systematic effect on the probability of accepting either procurement interval, even though from the point of view of optimal foraging theory it made the longer procurement interval the better prey type—the post-reward interval counting towards handling time just as much as the pre-reward interval, in terms of the definition given above. Taken together these two results show that, in simulated foraging at least pigeons show the preference for immediacy that has been found in so many other conditioning experiments (*see above*).

These two simulations prove that it is indeed possible to synthesize foraging behaviour in the operant laboratory. Further results from simulated foraging are discussed below, in the sections on matching in relation to foraging.

Mechanisms of Optimal Foraging

Although the thrust of the recent ecological literature has been to investigate how far real foraging behaviour resembles what optimal foraging theory predicts, suggestions have been made about the mechanisms producing optimal or near-optimal performance within the life of the individual; indeed, an entire book devoted to this problem is due to appear shortly (Kamil and Sargent, 1980). A major purpose of the present chapter is to consider how far principles discovered in the operant laboratory can provide such mechanisms and in this section various possibilities are taken up and examined.

Rational Decision Making

Like many previous authors, before discussing optimal foraging strategies, I hastened to disclaim the idea that the subject could be carefully weighing the costs and benefits of different decisions like a true strategist. Nonetheless, conscious use of strategies can play a part in foraging, as I can testify on the basis of a marked improvement in my own blackberrying efficiency since I encountered foraging theory; and though it is hard to see how it could be done without language, even that is not logically impossible. We shall have Lloyd Morgan's canon behind us, however, if we take true rationality as an explanation of last resort.

The Search Image

Historically, the most influential idea about the mechanism of foraging to come from the ecologists has been the notion of a 'search image', a hypothetical construct whose property is to make it easier for the predator to recognize particular types of prey. The image is assumed to be strengthened by experience with the relevant prey type. The idea seems to have originated with Von Uexkull (1957), but it appears in recent work by Croze (1970), Dawkins (1971*a*), Mook *et al.* (1960), Tinbergen (1960), and others. Tinbergen, and also Dawkins (1971*b*) use the idea of 'selective attention' in discussing the same idea; as Croze points out, related ideas, often under the name of 'set', have been used in the study of human visual search (e.g. Djang, 1937; Neisser, 1966). A recent series of experiments by Shepard and his colleagues (concisely reviewed by Shepard, 1978, p. 132) have shown that the detectability of a pattern can indeed be improved merely by instructing subjects to form a mental image of it.

In foraging, the effect of such an image will be to lead to increased probability of predation on the most frequent of otherwise equally suitable prey types, and, as discussed above, this does sometimes occur, Krebs (1978) points out that this kind of concentration is adaptive if, for example, there are metabolic changes to suit the animal to its commonest prey, and such changes are known to occur in some species. The idea of a search image may be distasteful to radical behaviourists, but the underlying hypothesis need not be stated in such apparently mentalist terms: we need only point out that the absolute rate of reinforcement for frequent prey will be higher than for any other prey type to see that plausible quantitative laws of learning could readily produce the effects conventionally ascribed to search images. The link to the idea of selective attention (or, as an operant psychologist might prefer to put it, differential control by different stimulus dimensions) is also rich with possibilities for interdisciplinary investigation. Some promising work along these lines has been started: Croze (1970) and Dawkins (1971*a,b*) both showed more awareness of psychological issues than psychologists working in discrimination learning usually show of ecology, and Pietrewicz and Kamil (1977, 1979, 1980) have started a most interesting investigation of search images using an operant discrimination training procedure based on Herrnstein and Loveland's (1964) work on the 'person concept' in pigeons. Pietrewicz and Kamil exposed bluejays to coloured slides of natural prey items (Noctuid moths of three different species), varying the kind of tree trunk on which the moth was photographed, its orientation, and its distance. The birds were rewarded with food only when they pecked at slides including a moth (matched photographs with no moth present were used as negative stimuli). Results of their 1977 experiment showed that the four stimulus dimensions (prey species, substrate, orientation, and distance) affected recognition differently, and interacted to some extent. The interaction allows the possibility of search image formation, and this was demonstrated directly in the 1979 experiment. Slides of two different species of moth were used, and detection of either species was impaired following a run of eight trials with the other species.

Search images or equivalent concepts can be useful, as explained above, in accounting for density-dependent predation. They cannot easily account for phenomena predicted by optimality, however, such as the effects of density on patch use and prey selectivity. For these, other mechanisms must be postulated.

Giving-up Times

The optimal forager continues in a patch until the capture rate there has fallen to the average for the entire environment. A very simple 'rule of thumb' which produces this behaviour, or a good approximation to it, is to have a criterion time for unsuccessful foraging in a patch; after this 'giving-up time' has elapsed, the forager leaves. If the habitat is unchanging, giving-up time could be fixed; otherwise it must be adjusted to equal (or approximate) the mean interval between recent prey captures, averaged over travelling time and time within a patch. Tests of this model are therefore vexed by the need to be precise about the meaning of 'recent'. Use of a criterial giving-up time is clearly one version of the 'win–stay/lose–shift' strategy that has been discussed in many contexts (e.g. Morgan, 1974b).

Mechanisms based on giving-up time have been proposed by Hassel and May (1974), Krebs et al. (1974) and Murdoch and Oaten (1975, p. 42), and some evidence relating to it was mentioned above. In addition, Davies (1977b, Table VII) showed that a flycatcher moved to a different post if, on average, 29.1 s elapsed without a capture, regardless of how long it had been at its current perch or how many prey it had caught there; the mean intercapture interval while at a perch was 17.9 s. Davies showed that under plausible assumptions the observed giving-up time was optimal, but since he did not observe varying capture rates, we do not know whether this was coincidence.

Criterial giving-up times could also be useful in solving the prey selectivity problem. A rule such as 'reject all but the best prey types unless t seconds have elapsed since one was encountered' would produce prey selectivity that was correlated solely with the density of the best prey type, and subsidiary rules could produce optimal behaviour even in the face of quite complex prey spectra. So far as I know this possibility has not been explored in the ecological literature; preliminary inspection of the simulated foraging data from Lea (1978) shows no sign of such a rule. It would of course imply control of behaviour by local contingencies instead of, or in addition to, overall correlations with reinforcement, a point which will be taken up again later.

Area-restricted Search

Area-restricted search (decreased speed or increased tortuosity after prey capture) has been mentioned as a kind of optimal behaviour. It is also a mechanism for optimality, in the sense that it might allow a forager to stay within a patch so long as it was fruitful. But that leaves open the question of how area-restricted search itself might be brought about, and thereby opens some interesting possibilities.

One possible interpretation is that area-restricted search simply reflects the most basic principle of the entire experimental analysis of behaviour, the effect of reinforcement. On a naive analysis of reinforcement, there is something paradoxical about the stickleback or blackbird that swims or hops on when its last swim or hop failed to provide food, but twists and turns when swimming or hopping has just been rewarded. But within operant psychology, it is not supposed that reinforcement strengthens particular muscle movements: the 'response' whose probability is changed is whatever produces a particular environmental state (Skinner, 1935), a concept much closer to that of 'action' than 'movement' (cf. Taylor, 1964, Chapter III). There is no reason why the environmental state concerned should not consist in being at a given location in space, indeed some recent operant analyses (e.g. Baum and Rachlin, 1969) have defined operants in just this way. In several field experiments, 'staying in a patch' in fact consisted of returning to it on a series of consecutive occasions (e.g. Smith and Sweatman, 1974, p. 55), and this recalls the kind of place learning that, for example, laboratory rats achieve particularly easily (Tenen, 1965; Tolman, Ritchie, and Kailash, 1946).

Alternative analyses of search following prey capture are possible, however. Reinforcement does not always lead to the immediate repetition of the reinforced response; instead, it may be followed by socalled 'adjunctive' behaviours, which lead on, in a more or less orderly sequence, to the repetition of the formal operant (Henton and Iversen, 1978, Chapter 5; Roper, 1978; Staddon and Ayres, 1975; Staddon and Simmelhag, 1971). Although considerable effort has gone into proving that adjunctive behaviours are not directly maintained by accidental contingency with reinforcement (*see* the summary by Staddon (1977 pp. 127*ff.*)), the argument that the total performance is a result of straightforward conditioning effects can still be put persuasively, as Henton and Iversen (1978) show.

In the laboratory adjunctive behaviours appear bizarre and maladaptive unless they can be fitted into some normal motivational pattern (e.g. Lotter, Woods, and Vasselli, 1973). But in the field they may serve all kinds of purposes, of which retaining the subject within an imperceptibly bounded patch could easily be one.

More generally, it is worth recalling that animals can easily be trained to vary their responding explicitly, as in reinforced alternation (e.g. Petrinovich and Bolles, 1957). Discussing a more elaborate schedule that had the effect of reinforcing alternation, Morgan (1974*b*) argued that even reinforcement itself should be seen as a reinforced response strategy, brought to new situations because it had worked in old ones. If we look on progressing forward and searching the neighbourhood as two alternative responses, it may be that Smith's

(1974*a*) thrushes or Thomas's (1977) sticklebacks were exhibiting either reinforced alternation as such or the effects of a history of reinforced alternation in similar situations. That history could be either individual or phylogenetic. Morgan's paradoxical view of reinforcement is of crucial importance in understanding foraging, and I shall return to it below.

The Partial Reinforcement Extinction Effect (PREE)

Smith and Dawkins (1971), in a study of time allocation to artificial patches of different density, included a reversal condition and found that Great tits abandoned patches of diminished density slowly and incompletely. They suggested that this could be a case of the PREE (*see* Mackintosh, 1974, p. 435*ff.*), though they did not show how the quantitative form of their data could be predicted. In a similar vein, R. L. Mellgren (personal communication) has suggested that the PREE might contribute to area-restricted search, density-dependent selectivity, or patch leaving: to take the last example, if the PREE operates, the scarcer prey is in the environment as a whole, the longer it will take for extinction of searching to occur in a particular patch, and hence giving-up time might vary with the overall prey density in something like the optimal manner. Known PREE effects could also predict that giving-up time would be independent of the density of the current patch, since extinction may be prolonged by intermittent reinforcement that has occurred in the past even if continuously reinforced practice has intervened (Jenkins, 1962; Theios, 1962). In fact the more recent reinforcement schedule seems to have relatively little effect on the course of extinction, so that continuous reinforcement followed by partial produces less resistance to extinction than partial followed by continuous (Jenkins, 1962; Sutherland, Mackintosh, and Wolfe, 1965). Similarly, extinction rate in one environment is affected more by whether, during acquisition, non-reinforcements preceded it in a different environment than by whether non-reinforcement occurred there (Einon, 1975, Experiment 6; Mellgren and Dyck, 1972; Rudy, Honzie, Cox, Graeber, and Carter, 1970); this again suggests a mechanism whereby overall habitat prey density could affect patch leaving time.

The Principles of Performance

This was the title under which Tolman (1955) tried to answer the famous charge that he had left his rat 'buried in thought'. The 'principles of performance' were to be the rules that would relate various parameters of a learning situation, such as the size, delay, and probability of reward and punishment, to choice probabilities and response vigours. The difficulty is that, as Tolman (1938) had earlier recognized, the functions involved are likely to be complex and to involve multiple interactions. (In Tolman's view this was one of the chief reasons for using intervening variables in psychology.) Passage of time has given us a vastly greater data base, and modern operant methods (especially automation of test equipment) allow the collection of much more stable data. It is therefore reasonable to ask whether the principles of performance, as we now see them, can provide an adequate explanation of foraging behaviour as the ecologists observe it.

This question is the heart of the present chapter, but it can now be disposed of relatively briefly, since the relevant information has been assembled in previous sections. The aim of the experimental analysis section was to show that whatever phenomena could be found in foraging behaviour could be echoed in the operant laboratory, both in pre-existing data and by direct simulation. On the whole that was established successfully; a few points, however, require further discussion.

Anomalous preferences for immediacy. Preference for a small, immediate reward over a larger, delayed one seems to be a more consistent finding in psychology than in ecology; it is interesting that it should also turn up reliably in operant simulation of foraging (Lea, 1979). It could be that animals are better at weighing the relative importance of size and handling time when faced with prey to which they are specifically adapted; but in the first place not all the studies mentioned in Table 10.1 used natural prey, and in the second place Table 10.1 does not show consistent use of E/h as a basis for preference—most species, in fact, were influenced to a more than optimal degree by either E or h. Thus, though there is a difficulty here in the way of an operant analysis of foraging, it cannot be resolved by appealing to the naturalness or otherwise of the prey items. Possibly a crucial factor is that the handling times involved in Table 10.1 are part of what would, in an operant experiment, be counted as consummatory time rather than pre-reward delay (this is not true of all handling times, of course), and it may be that animals discount consummatory time to some extent. Indeed, the fact that pigeons prefer longer periods of access to grain to shorter periods (Catania, 1963) is a demonstration of dominance of E over h in an operant situation, for in E/h terms all durations are presumably equal.

Long- and short-term optimization. If we credit the pigeon in the Skinner box with an exceedingly short time horizon, it is of course optimal to be more sensitive to the delay of a reward (so long as it has not actually arrived yet) than to its size. Such a short horizon would be quite useless for optimal foraging, but it could be that in natural situations animals can cope with longer time periods than in arbitrary ones, as is certainly the case in avoidance learning, at least on the obvious interpretation of taste aversion experiments (Garcia and Koelling, 1966).

The failure of pigeons to take account of post-reward detention in my operant simulation of foraging (*see above*) can also be seen as a short-time-horizon phenomenon, and so can the pigeons' failure to optimize in titration (Lea, 1976): optimal behaviour there required a sacrifice of short-term advantage to secure the best return in the long run. Shimp's (1966, 1969) notion of momentary maximization is in a similar spirit. But it is of the essence of density-dependent selectivity, and of optimal patch use, that the predator should be able to reject a bird in the hand in favour of two in the bush—provided, of course, that the bush is sufficiently thickly populated. Except in the explicit simulations of foraging there are few demonstrations that animals can do this in the laboratory, though it is fair to say that they have rarely been given the opportunity.

Taken to extremes, the issue of long- vs. short-term optimization reduces to that of molar vs. molecular control of behaviour, which is discussed further below . One further point is worth making here. The integration time over which the consequences of behaviour is assessed must always be a compromise. If it is too short, excessive preference for immediacy may result. If it is too long, the subject will be unable to adjust (by varying giving-up times, for instance) to variations in overall prey density. The optimal compromise is unlikely to lead to exactly optimal behaviour in any particular situation, least of all an arbitrary operant experimental situation.

Contrast and its asymmetries. Because of the varying and inconsistent form the principles of performance tend to take, we usually treat them as qualitative rather than quantitative. Nonetheless, recent years have seen the emergence of a number of tentative quantitative forms. The best known of these is Herrnstein's (1970) 'quantitative law of effect' according to which the rate, P of a response can be predicted from the rate at which it is reinforced, R, by the formula

$$P = \frac{kR}{(R + R_0)},$$
(10.2)

in which k and R_0 are constants. Herrnstein interprets R_0 as the rate of reinforcement for alternative responses. The first application of this formula was to predict the 'matching law' for two responses with different reinforcement rates, concurrently available; using subscripts in the obvious way, (10.2) leads to

$$P_1/P_2 = R_1/R_2$$
(10.3)

(*see* Herrnstein, 1961). More recently, however, Herrnstein (1970) and de Villiers (1977) have shown that (10.2) can describe data from many other situations.

For present purposes, what sets (10.2) off from previous attempts at quantifying the principles of performance is the explicit way in which it recognizes interaction between concurrent schedules. It is therefore natural to ask whether it can be used to predict the asymmetric contrast (densities of preferred prey affect pursuit probabilities of less preferred types, but not vice versa) predicted by foraging theory and found in at least some foraging data, including my operant simulation (Lea, 1979). Superficially, matching seems to imply symmetrical contrast. Consider, however, the flowchart of simulated foraging (Figure 10.2). The point at which the subject has a choice is when a 'prey' has been presented. There are two distinct stimulus situations. Under one, when the 'short prey' colour is presented, the better option is unambiguous, and the pigeons infallibly selected it. Effectively, there is only a choice to be made when the long prey colour occurs. We have in fact no evidence that contrast does not affect this choice symmetrically; since the two possible responses were mutually exclusive, we cannot determine their rates independently. It is possible to apply the matching law to this choice: this is done below in an attempt to predict the extent of the preference for the side or centre key (that is, for accepting or rejecting the worse prey type).

There are clearly some obstacles in the way of reconciling operant and foraging data. They do not seem overwhelming; there remains a good case for considering that conditioning principles can explain foraging. It is of course an explanation of a distinctly limited type. First, it is restricted to the lifespan of the individual organism—the ecological plane remains appropriate for discussions of why such mechanisms exist and how they are maintained. Second, because of the anti-mechanism bias within operant psychology, it does no more than include foraging behaviour in a more compact and more general description of performance principles; it does not explain the mental or physiological processes that affect those principles. Some of the other mechanisms discussed above may well be more fruitful at that level, though indeed they also provide alternative and perfectly tenable accounts of some phenomena at the same level as operant conditioning.

Foraging, Matching, and Sampling

Of all the deviations from optimality in foraging data that have been reported, the most consistent is a failure to show an abrupt switch between two kinds of behaviour; failure, for example, to show 'all-or-none' preference for a particular patch or prey type. It also occurred in both the simulations of foraging discussed earlier. Wilson (1975, p. 266), noting that stochastic rather than absolute preference was involved in Herrnstein's (1961) matching law, proposed that matching or some similar process might underly foraging patterns like those seen by Altmann and Altmann (1970, p. 117–126) in baboons, where a few parts of the home range account for much of an animal's hunt but other parts are not ignored completely.

Four possibilities exist for the origins of stochastic preference. One is simple failure to discriminate (cf. Luce (1959), Thurstone (1927), and Sowter, Gabor, and Granger (1971) for development of this idea in connection with preference; Emlen and Emlen (1975) have a use of it in connection with optimal foraging). Second, the principles of learning or performance might be such that stochastic preference is the best that can be achieved. Third, a closer examination of the situation might show that stochastic preference, is, after all, optimal. Finally, and as a special case of the previous possibility, the subject may be monitoring the environment, or sampling the less favourable source, as a check that conditions have not changed.

These four possibilities are not all mutually exclusive, nor do they exhaust the questions we need to ask, but I shall emphasize the last three here, because they bring us back to the general theme of this book. In an earlier section I abandoned the matching law before considering it as a quantitative predictor of preference; that omission can now be repaired, as I move on to consider the relation between matching and optimal choice, especially in relation to foraging.

Matching Can Be Optimal

Much confusion can be caused by failing to distinguish the *matching law* from the older phrase *probability matching*. Herrnstein's matching law applies directly to concurrent interval schedules, in which two different responses are each reinforced if and only if a (usually variable) time has elapsed since that same response was last reinforced. That time may have been spent in any way, including making the alternative response, and receiving reinforcements for it. Thus the concurrent schedules are not mutually exclusive: time that counts towards the completion of one can also count towards the completion of the other. Furthermore, unless a so-called 'limited hold' is in force, once the scheduled time period for a response has elapsed, the next response of that type will be reinforced no matter how long it is delayed. Because of this 'storage' of reinforcers, optimal behaviour on such a schedule involves at least some responding to all alternatives. This is in contrast to the absorption at a single reinforcement source that is optimal in the more usual 'probability learning' paradigm where each response is reinforced with a fixed probability, and making one type of response excludes the possibility of making the other. For further discussion of the relation between these two types of matching *see* Gibbon, Berryman, and Thompson (1974) and Mackintosh (1974, pp. 190 *ff.*).

Although concurrent interval schedules obviously make stochastic preference optimal, matching of response rate to reinforcement rate need not be optimal, nor is it enforced by the schedules. Under special circumstances, however, it may be favoured.

Alternation of reinforcers. Stubbs and Pliskoff (1969) introduced a schedule which used concurrent, variable interval schedules that were not strictly independent. A single timer generated a schedule interval, and at its end a probabilistic gate was used to assign the reinforcer to one of the two possible responses. The timer was not restarted until reinforcement had been obtained. Matching is optimal under these conditions: if the frequency of reinforcement on the left is (say) three times its frequency on the right, the chances that the schedule interval has finished and set up a reinforcement since the last response of a given type will be the same for both responses if the left and right interresponse times are in the ratio 1:3, provided that they are short relative to the schedule interval. It follows that optimal behaviour is to maintain this ratio of interresponse times.

This kind of reinforcer alternation will even produce stochastic preference between ratio schedules; Morgan (1974b) used it, for example, in an experiment on concurrent random ratios. He showed that reinforcer alternation in fact favoured a degree of response alternation following non-reinforcement, and that rats were sensitive to this contingency. Similar considerations apply to discrete-trials probability learning experiments if unsignalled 'correction' trials are given whenever the subject fails to obtain a reinforcement (as in Graf, Bullock, and Bitterman, 1964).

Changeover delays. Conventional concurrent interval schedules favour switching between schedules so strongly that rapid simple response alternation often results. To prevent this banal outcome, it is usual to introduce a changeover delay (COD), such that responses made within a fixed period of time since a different response are not reinforced. Matching does not depend on any particular value of the COD (Allison and Lloyd, 1971; Stubbs and Pliskoff, 1969), but Rachlin, Green, Kagel, and Battalio (1976) have shown that as the COD becomes comparable with the schedule intervals matching becomes the best available strategy.

Qualitatively different reinforcers. Absolute preference is not the optimal strategy if the two responses yield different reinforcers and no single dimension governs the need for both. Where this happens, even when concurrent ratio schedules are used, stochastic preference is observed (e.g. Lea and Roper, 1977), though there is no evidence for matching as such.

Conditioning Principles Can Predict Absolute Preference

In a straightforward probability learning task, probability matching (making the two responses in the same proportion as reinforcers are assigned to them) is not optimal. But nor is it predicted by most conditioning theories: the matching law, for example, predicts optimal behaviour (absolute preference), as Herrnstein and Loveland (1975) and Pear (1975) point out, whether discrete trials or concurrent ratio schedules are used. Some early mathematical learning theories (e.g. Bush and Mosteller, 1955, Chapter 13; Estes, 1957) did predict probability matching, and they inspired an experimental literature, mainly using human subjects, in which it was often claimed that matching was demonstrated. But the bulk of the evidence (reviewed by Edwards, 1961) in fact shows overmatching, that is a tendency towards absolute preference for the better alternative. In work with animals this tendency is even more marked, provided that no correction is used after missed reinforcements. Cynomologous monkeys

(Wilson, 1960), rats (Bitterman, Wodinsky, and Candland, 1958; Roberts, 1966; Uhl, 1963), pigeons (Graf *et al.*, 1964; Herrnstein, 1958; Herrnstein and Loveland, 1975; Mackintosh, Lord, and Little, 1971), Great tits (Krebs *et al.*, 1978), farmyard ducks and a grey seal (H. G. Hurrell, personal communication), and the African mouthbreeder fish *Tilapia* (Behrend and Bitterman, 1961) have all shown choice proportions that overmatch reward proportions, and sometimes reach 100 per cent at asymptote. Probability matching does occur reliably in pigeons (Bullock and Bitterman, 1962; Graf *et al.*, 1964) and fish (Bitterman *et al.*, 1958; Behrend and Bitterman, 1961, 1966; Mackintosh *et al.*, 1971) if the subject is forced to repeat any choice on which he fails to obtain a possible reward; but that is not a condition with much relevance to foraging; Nature is unlikely to be so benevolent.

Matching and Optimality in Concurrent Chained Schedules

The matching law was first stated for simple concurrent schedules. But Herrnstein (1964a) claimed that it also held for concurrent chain schedules, where the response rates were calculated over the initial links of the chain, but the reinforcement rates were calculated from the schedules to which initial link responding gave rise; there was no direct food reinforcement for initial link responding, but only the initial links were concurrent—as soon as one initial link schedule had been completed, both initial links became unavailable until food had been obtained on the corresponding terminal link schedule. Autor (1969) supported Herrnstein's conclusion; and Neuringer (1969) showed that it made no difference whether the terminal link consisted of an interval schedule of reinforcement or a corresponding delay period at the end of which food was delivered non-contingently.

Subsequent work has shown that matching is much too simple a description of what happens on such schedules. Fantino (1969) and Wardlaw and Davison (1974) showed that the response rates on the initial links are a function of the initial link as well as the terminal link schedules, as is scarcely surprising considering that it is the initial links that are actually concurrent, and the matching law should apply to them as concurrent schedules.

Another way of looking at the contrast between simple concurrent schedules and concurrent chains is to use Baum's (1974b) generalization of the matching law, in which equation (10.3) is replaced by

$$P_1/P_2 = (R_1/R_2)^{a+b} \qquad (10.4)$$

The exponent *a* expresses the sensitivity of response rates to reinforcement rates. For concurrent schedules it is typically around 0.8 (Lobb and Davison, 1975; Myers and Myers, 1977), whereas matching requires a value of 1.0. Table 10.2 shows values calculated for individual birds in a number of experiments using concurrent chains (I have included only cases where the terminal link schedules

Table 10.2. Sensitivity parameter a, from several studies of choice between interval schedules or delays of reinforcement in concurrent chains

Investigation and subject no.	Initial link schedules	Terminal link schedules[a]	No. of conditions	a	$r^{2\,b}$
Herrnstein (1964a)	VI 60 s	VI 15–45 s vs. VR 40–80			
50			9	1.40	0.85
67			9	0.76	0.87
231			9	1.29	0.81
055			9	1.38	0.88
Herrnstein (1964b)	VI 60 s	VI 15 s vs. FI 4–15 s			
405			3	1.29	0.99
406			3	0.88	0.85
407			3	1.47	1.00
408			3	1.55	0.89
Chung and Herrnstein (1967)	VI 60 s				
S236		FD 8 s vs. FD 1–30 s	10	1.22	0.93
S237			10	0.84	0.77
S415			10	1.38	0.89
S416			10	0.61	0.77
S211		FD 16 s vs. FD 1–3	7	1.10	0.91
S242			7	1.18	0.81
Autor (1969)	VI 60 s				
44		VI 15 s vs. VI 3.75–60 s	5	0.69	0.94
77		VI 15 s, 180 s VI 3.75–60 s	5	0.53	0.92
267		VI 15 s, 180 s VI 15–180 s	5	0.61	0.86
Davison (1969)	VI 60 s	VI 60 s vs. mix (FI 15 s. FI 45 s)			
C			5	2.02	0.86
E			5	2.33	0.74
F			5	2.44	0.58
G			5	2.96	0.75
H			5	2.85	0.56

Table 10.2. (Cont.)

Investigation and subject no.	Initial link schedules	Terminal link schedules[a]	No. of conditions	a	$r^{2\,b}$
Duncan and Fantino (1970)	VI 60 s	FI vs. FI			
2			7	3.09	0.87
6			7	3.09	0.80
Killeen (1970)	VI 60 s	FI vs. FI			
321			4	1.81	0.99
367			4	2.03	0.99
394			4	2.28	0.87
467			4	3.39	0.99
Davison and Temple (1973)	VI 60 s	FI 1–100 s vs. FI 1–60 s			
31			13	0.92	0.88
31b			13	1.47	0.87
32			26	1.03	0.90
33			26	1.11	0.83
34			8	0.66	0.75
34b			18	1.59	0.82
35			26	1.23	0.78
36			26	1.18	0.83
Hursh and Fantino (1973)		FI 10–60 s vs. mix (FI 10–60 s, FI 10–60 s)			
S1495			7	2.12	0.17
1190			8	1.21	0.42
4251			5	1.23	0.34
7352			9	1.09	0.38
7399			8	2.74	0.72

Wardlaw and Davison (1974)					
Group means	VI 27 s	FI 5 s vs. FI 5–30 s	4	3.60	0.76
	VI 38 s		5	1.83	0.97
	VI 49 s		6	1.76	0.79
	VI 115 s		5	0.87	0.90
Cicerone (1976)					
6	VI 60 s	FD 8–32 s vs. FD 8 s	3	1.37	0.93
7			3	2.50	1.00
9			3	2.30	1.00
11			3	2.27	0.94
6		FD 8–32 s vs. mix (FD 6 s, FD 10 s)	3	2.67	0.93
7			3	1.73	0.99
9			3	2.52	0.99
11			3	2.82	0.98
6		FD 8–32 s vs. mix (FD 2 s, FD 14 s)	3	0.90	0.99
7			3	1.68	0.98
9			3	2.02	1.00
11			3	2.23	0.99
Simulated foraging (Lea unpublished)					
L10	FR 1, FR 3	FI 20 s vs. complex interval	4	4.65	0.96
L11			4	0.18	0.01
L12			4	2.27	0.83
L13			4	4.15	0.89
L14			4	3.94	0.89
L15			4	6.59	0.87

[a] In addition to the conventional schedule abbreviations, FD is used to denote a fixed delay of reinforcement.
[b] Proportion of variance accounted for by the generalized matching law.

were intervals or delays). Here sensitivity is typically greater than one, and that is in agreement with an 'approximate optimality' view of matching; for in a concurrent chain the advantage of stochastic over absolute choice results only from the initial links' being conventional concurrent schedules, with the typical 'storage' of programmed reinforcers. The terminal links are mutually exclusive, and the longer their parameters relative to the initial links the more absolute preference will be favoured (a tendency which can be deduced from the formulae that Fantino (1969) and Wardlaw and Davison (1974) produce to summarize their results).

Matching and Foraging in the Static Case

There may be a few foraging situations which approximate to concurrent interval schedules of the conventional type. Altmann and Altmann's (1970) baboons may well have faced one: slowly growing or ripening plant food in a relatively secure territory home range is a resource whose survival when ready may be long compared to the time taken for replenishment of an exhausted patch. Nectar is another case, and, as mentioned above in connection with search paths, both bumblebees and nectar-feeding birds systematically avoid flowers they have recently visited, thus allowing some extra replenishment time. In situations like these, the matching law might apply directly in the field, though no data are available to test it at present.

More usually, however, prey will appear only to disappear shortly afterwards if the predator is not in the right place at the right time. This corresponds to the $t \cdot \tau$ schedule of reinforcement introduced by Schoenfield, Cumming, and Hearst (1956), which, with a short cycle time, is logically and behaviourally equivalent to a random ratio schedule. Deviations from optimality in such situations cannot be explained in terms of matching, which also predicts absolute preference. A similar problem arises with density-dependent predation; if the denser prey becomes preferable, whether by search image formation, digestive change or whatever, preference for it ought to become absolute in a simultaneous choice.

The prey selection case is less cut and dried. It seems worth asking whether matching can explain a gradual increase in pursuit probability for one prey type as the density of a better one falls (optimality, it will be recalled, predicts a step function). In unpublished experiments continuing my foraging simulation, I have attacked this question directly. Using the schedule illustrated in Figure 10.2, but varying only t, the centre-key, fixed interval schedule, I again observed a gradual increase in the probability of accepting the worse prey type as t increased. This amounts to stochastic rather than absolute preference in the CHOICE state of Figure 10.2, on trials where the worse 'prey type' was offered. Figure 10.3 shows an analysis of the choices made in that state, with response ratios plotted (on logarithmic scales) against the ratio of delays from leaving the CHOICE state to the next reinforcement, following the two possible kinds of

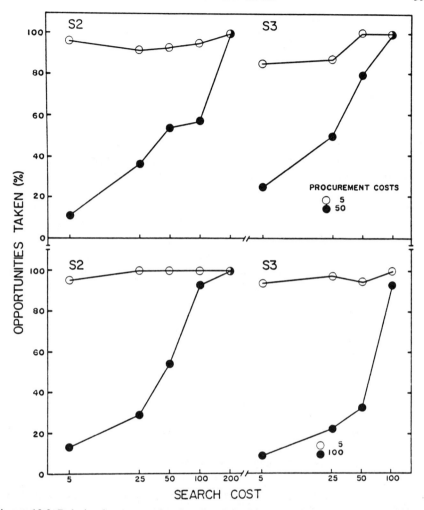

Figure 10.3. Relation between ratio of responses to the two keys in a foraging simulation to the inverse ratio of delay to reinforcement after successful pecks on those keys. Note that both axes have logarithmic scales, but that the scale on the ordinate is contracted by a factor of 10. (Unpublished data from a continuation of the experiment by Lea (1979))

response. The slope of the line gives a sensitivity parameter, comparable to those presented in Table 10.2, and data for the individual birds of this experiment are included at the end of the table. The values observed were high, but they fit into the pattern of the table, since the 'initial link schedules' were minimal (FR 1 and FR 3).

At least within this simulation, therefore, foraging fits into a pattern derived from studying concurrent schedules. But that pattern is not predicted by the matching law; as yet no theoretical formula has gained much acceptance. Taking generalized matching with an exponent of 2–3 as a rough empirical description, however, one further set of foraging data can be accommodated within this framework, the 'density-dependent predation' experiments in which subjects faced with two equally desirable kinds of prey showed an excess tendency to accept the more frequent one when it was encountered (e.g. Murdoch *et al.*, 1975; Cook and Miller, 1977). Suppose the subjects adopt highly specific search images which prevent them seeing one kind of prey while searching for the other. (There is some evidence in favour of this possibility from work on chicks (Dawkins, 1971*a*).) The probability of predation will then be directly proportional to the proportion of time for which the relevant search image is used. If selecting a search image is a response that obeys the same reinforcement laws as switching from one key to another in a concurrent chain schedule, we can expect relative predation probabilities to vary as the square or cube of relative prey densities, as is actually observed (*see above*). In passing, it may be noted that people's choice between shopping centres can also be predicted by a formula like generalized matching, with an exponent in a similar range (Huff, 1962, discussed by Graft *et al.*, 1977).

The Dynamic Case

I now want to return to the case where the predator does not know which of two patches is the better, so that absolute preference for the better is optimal only after a period of sampling. Can the reinforcement principles that underly matching predict what will happen in this situation? It is fairly clear that Herrnstein's reinforcement principle (equation (10.2)) will, like the optimal sampling model discussed by Krebs *et al.* (1978), predict little or no preference at the start of a session, but absorption at the end of it. However, the manner in which absorption is approached is different according to the two theories. Optimal sampling implies a sudden switch from stable alternation to absorption, with the switch coming immediately after a success on the absorbing source (Jones, 1975). Equation (10.2) predicts a gradually increasing probability of responding to one source, which leads to absorption by positive feedback—the greater the response rate to either source, the higher the resulting reinforcement rate there. In practice the great tits studied by Krebs *et al.* (1978) did not show alternation, but runs of responding on each manipulandum, as was reasonable given that a flight of 4 m separated the two. Unfortunately no-one has yet worked out optimal strategies for a 'two-armed bandit' with travelling costs between the two arms, but it seems reasonable to suppose that the main features of optimal performance would be preserved.

Krebs *et al.* (1978) do not say whether tits showed an abrupt switch from 'sampling' to 'exploitation'. I was interested to see whether any gradual shift would have been detectable, so I constructed a Monte-Carlo simulation of the schedule. To do this it is necessary to specify what Cowie (1977) calls the 'memory window', the interval over which response and reinforcement rates are calculated, and it turns out that the result of the simulation depends critically on the window duration. If it is too long, no absorption ever takes place. If it is too short, absorption on the less favourable source of food becomes probable. But if the right compromise is chosen to ensure reliable absorption on the better schedule, a gradual drift towards absorption is clearly observable.

If the Great tits in Krebs *et al.*'s (1978) experiment did not show any such pre-absorption non-stationarity of preference, the law of effect (and a large number of other conditioning theories) would be ruled out as a model of foraging in the two-armed bandit case. However, unpublished experiments by S. M. Dow (Dow and Lea, 1979), have extended Krebs *et al.*'s procedure, using pigeons on Findley concurrent schedules in conventional operant apparatus. We originally hoped to test more stringently for non-stationarity in the pre-absorption case, and to examine the effects of varying session length. But in fact we are finding that the situation is a great deal more complicated than Krebs *et al.*'s fairly brief experiment revealed. Much seems to depend on how often, and how much, the schedule values are varied; the pigeons seem to have substantial long-term memory capacities for past reinforcement rates. Two other interesting phenomena have come to light. One is a tendency for birds that have shown signs of satiation at the end of a session to break away from schedules on which they had apparently been thoroughly absorbed. The other is a tendency, in the pre-absorption phase, for switching to occur immediately after reward. Neither of these effects is predicted either by a conditioning analysis or by optimal sampling. Both make sense in terms of naive optimization, however. As an animal becomes sated, the opportunity costs of exploring the environment fall, and a switch away from the better schedule becomes plausible. As for switching after reinforcement, if the animal lives in a world where things often have to be obtained at the cost of a determinate amount of work, it may make sense to find out what that amount is while one is about the business of sampling the environment. (Interestingly, leaving the patch immediately after a capture is a possible consequence of Oaten's (1977) model of patch use under ignorance.) Conditioning data also furnish some parallels. Pausing after reinforcement is well known, and has led Staddon (1970) to talk in terms of 'the inhibitory effect of reinforcement'. Adjunctive behaviour following reinforcement has already been mentioned (*see above*). Schedule switching could easily be integrated into either effect.

Correlation, Contiguity, and Foraging

In this brief final section I return to the major theme of this book in order to summarize the arguments and my conclusions about the relation of foraging to operant conditioning.

Superficially, optimal foraging theory and operant conditioning principles appear to be opposed. But the opposition is only superficial, because ecologists have always recognized the need to specify a mechanism for foraging behaviour, and some kind of conditioning mechanism has always seemed a likely candidate. One of the founding fathers of modern feeding ecology wrote, 'It is clear that the only correct way of analyzing (prey) selectivity is the method indicated by I. P. Pavlov' (Ivlev, 1961, p. 49). At present, none of the mechanisms proposed earlier can be ruled out, but the very nature of foraging does create a bias towards a particular sort of behaviour theory. On the face of it, foraging requires animals to be sensitive to reinforcement rates over extended periods of time, a requirement that is most easily accommodated by a molar, correlational theory. It may also be met by a molecular theory, emphasizing contiguity, but that will require demonstration. The chief current molar theories, the variants of Herrnstein's 'quantitative law of effect' are all particularly well suited to handle foraging, because they were designed to handle contrast phenomena.

But foraging behaviour is not always optimal, or at least it does not always fit simple optimal foraging models. Is there anything in the known failures of optimality that betrays an emphasis on contiguity? One possible place to look is at food preferences. The failure of ranking by E/h to give, reliably, the best prediction of preference, implies that correlation with overall energy gain does not govern the whole of food preferences. A general tendency for dominance of ranking by handling time would have implied an emphasis on contiguity of a kind, but that is not found in all cases, although it does seem to be a feature of operant behaviour. A greater emphasis on reward size in the natural situation may reflect an enhanced effect of size when alternatives are within the perceptual field—and such perceptual effects would be very direct cases of contiguity dominating correlation.

In considering selectivity as a function of prey density, the major failures of optimality encountered were a failure of the prescribed asymmetry of contrast, and stochastic rather than absolute preference. The preceding section showed that conditioning theory is in no better case than optimal theory to explain stochastic preference, and asymmetry of contrast required something of a stretched argument. There may be scope for a molecular theory here.

Patch use, search paths, and optimal sampling all require some attention to local details of recent performance and its effects, because all deal with dynamic situations. As such they enforce an analysis with some degree of molecularity. The notion of the 'memory window', introduced to make possible a simulation of patch sampling using a molar theory, is significant here. An intermediate value had to be used: a long window (which corresponds to a truly molar theory) or a short one (truly molecular) produced nothing like the observed behaviour.

Cowie (1977) suggested that the length of the memory window might itself be optimized, presumably by evolution. It follows that the question 'correlation or contiguity in foraging?' may not be a true opposition: behaviour may be governed by principles that are just as molar as they need to be in any given situation. As

Morgan (1974*b*) suggested, even the notion of reinforcement as increasing the frequency of the preceding behaviour must itself, paradoxically, be subject to reinforcement if it is successful within the life of the individual organism, and extinction if it is not; it is even more likely to be modified by selective pressures than by the evolutionary timescale.

In the majority of cases evolution must surely favour the efficient operation of reinforcement. Those interested in operant conditioning, therefore, can reasonably draw three kinds of comfort from the material I have reviewed in this chapter. First, existing conditioning literature has proved useful in allowing at least a tentative analysis of naturally occurring behaviour. Second, the foraging literature provides a new source of evidence about instrumental behaviour, extending its scope to a wide range of new species, responses, and situations. Third, and resulting from the first two, the need to forage provides a possible explanation for the laws of conditioning being as they are. At the level of mechanism, conditioning principles may well turn out to explain why foraging behaviour is as it is. That would make it highly probable that, at the level of function, the opposite would be true. On all these grounds, the analogy with foraging provides the study of schedules of reinforcement with some sorely needed ecological validity.

Notes

Thanks are due to George Collier, Susan Dow, H. G. Hurrell. Alan Kamil, John Krebs, Roger Mellgren, and Richard Wrangham for permission to cite unpublished material, and for taking time to discuss it with me; and to Susan Dow for reading the manuscript and for a great deal of discussion of the issues dealt with here.

References

Ainslie, G. W. (1974). Impulse control in pigeons. *Journal of the Experimental Analysis of Behavior*, **21**, 485–489.

Ainslie, G. (1975). Specious reward: a behavioral theory of impulsiveness and impulse control. *Psychological Review*, **82**, 463–496.

Allison, T. S. and Lloyd, K. E. (1971). Concurrent schedules of reinforcement: effects of gradual and abrupt increases in the changeover delay. *Journal of the Experimental Analysis of Behavior*, **16**, 67–73.

Altmann, S. A. and Altmann, J. (1970). *Baboon Ecology: African Field Research*, University of Chicago Press, Chicago.

Amsel, A. and Roussel, J. (1952). Motivational properties of frustration: I. Effect on a running response of the addition of frustration to the motivational complex. *Journal of Experimental Psychology*, **43**, 363–368.

Andersson, M. (1978). Optimal foraging area: size and allocation of search effort. *Theoretical Population Biology*, **13**, 397–409.

Autor, S. M. (1969). The strength of conditioned reinforcers as a function of frequency and probability of reinforcement. In *Conditioned Reinforcement* (D. P. Hendry, ed.), pp. 127–162. Dorsey, Homewood, Ill.

Baum, W. M. (1972). Choice in a continuous procedure. *Psychonomic Science*, **28**, 263–265.

Baum, W. M. (1973). The correlation-based law of effect. *Journal of the Experimental Analysis of Behavior*, **20**, 137–153.

Baum, W. M. (1974*a*). Choice in free-ranging wild pigeons. *Science*, **185**, 78–79.

Baum, W. M. (1974*b*). On two types of deviation from the matching law: bias and undermatching. *Journal of the Experimental Analysis of Behavior*, **22**, 231–242.

Baum, W. M. and Rachlin, H. C. (1969). Choice as time allocation. *Journal of the Experimental Analysis of Behavior*, **12**, 861–874.

Behrend, E. R. and Bitterman, M. E. (1961). Probability matching in the fish. *American Journal of Psychology*, **74**, 542–551.

Behrend, E. K. and Bitterman, M. E. (1966). Probability-matching in the goldfish. *Psychonomic Science*, **6**, 327–328.

Belovsky, G. E. (1978). Diet optimization in a generalist herbivore: the moose. *Theoretical Population Biology*, **14**, 105–134.

Bernoulli, D. (1954). Exposition of a new theory on the measurement of risk. *Econometrica*, **22**, 23–36. (Originally published 1738.)

Beukema, J. J. (1966). Predation by the three-spined stickleback (*Gasterosteus aculeatus* L.): the influence of hunger and experience. *Behavior*, **30**, 1–126.

Bitterman, M. E., Wodinsky, J., and Candland, D. K. (1958). Some comparative psychology. *American Journal of Psychology*, **71**, 94–110.

Breland, K. and Breland M. (1961). The misbehavior of organisms. *American Psychologist*, **61**, 681–684.

Bullock, D. H. and Bitterman, M. E. (1962). Probability matching in the pigeon. *American Journal of Psychology*, **75**, 634–639.

Bush, R. R. and Mosteller, F. (1955). *Stochastic Models for Learning*, John Wiley, New York.

Catania, A. C. (1963). Concurrent performances: a baseline for the study of reinforcement magnitude. *Journal of the Experimental Analysis of Behavior*, **6**, 299–300.

Catania, A. C. (1966). Concurrent operants. In *Operant Behavior* (W. K. Honig, ed.), pp. 213–270, Appleton-Century-Crofts, New York.

Charnov, E. L. (1976*a*). Optimal foraging: attack strategy of a mantid. *American Naturalist*, **110**, 141–151.

Charnov, E. L. (1976*b*). Optimal foraging: the marginal value theorem. *Theoretical Population Biology*, **9**, 129–136.

Chung, S. H. and Herrnstein, R. J. (1967). Choice and delay of reinforcement. *Journal of the Experimental Analysis of Behavior*, **10**, 67–74.

Cicerone, R. A. (1976). Preference for mixed *versus* constant delay of reinforcement. *Journal of the Experimental Analysis of Behavior*, **25**, 357–361.

Cody, M. L. (1971). Finch flocks in the Mohave desert. *Theoretical Population Biology*, **2**, 142–158.

Collier, G. (1978). Ecological view of incentive and consummatory behavior. Paper read at the convention of the American Psychological Association, 1978.

Collier, G. H. and Kaufman, L. W. (1978). The patchy environment: a laboratory simulation. Paper reat at the meeting of the Psychonomic Society, St Louis.

Collier, G. H. and Rovee-Collier, C. K. (1980). A comparative analysis of optimal foraging behavior: laboratory simulations. In *Mechanisms of Foraging Behavior*. (A. C. Kamil and T. D. Sargent, eds), Garland, New York.

Collier, G. and Siskel, M. (1959). Performance as a joint function of amount of reinforcement and inter-reinforcement interval. *Journal of Experimental Psychology*, **57**, 115–120.

Cook, L. M. and Miller, P. (1977). Density-dependent selection of polymorphic prey—some data. *American Naturalist*, **111**, 594–598.

Cowie, R. J. (1977). Optimal foraging in Great tits (*parus major*). *Nature*, **268**, 137–139.

Cowie, R. J. and Krebs, J. R. (1979). Optimal foraging in patchy environments. In *Population Dynamics* (R. M. Anderson, B. D. Turner, and R. L. Taylor, eds), Blackwell Scientific Publications, Oxford.

Craig, R. B., De Angelis, D. L., and Dixon, K. R. (1979). Long and short-term dynamic optimization models with application to the feeding strategy of the loggerhead shrike. *American Naturalist*, **113**, 31–51.

Croze, H. (1970). Searching image in carrion crows. *Zeitschrift for Tierpsychologie*, Beiheft 5.

Davies, N. B. (1977a). Prey selection and social behaviour in wagtails (Aves: Motacillidae). *Journal of Animal Ecology*, **46**, 37–57.

Davies, N. B. (1977b). Prey selection and the search strategy of the Spotted flycatcher (*Muscicapa striata*): a field study of optimal foraging. *Animal Behavior*, **25**, 1016–1033.

Davies, N. B. and Krebs, J. R. (1978). Introduction: ecology, natural selection and social behavior. In *Behavioural Ecology* (J. R. Krebs and N. B. Davies, eds), pp. 1–18, Blackwell Scientific Publications, Oxford.

Davison, M. C. (1969). Preference for mixed-interval *versus* fixed-interval schedules. *Journal of the Experimental Analysis of Behavior*, **12**, 247–252.

Davison, M. C. and Temple, W. (1973). Preference for fixed-interval schedules: an alternative model. *Journal of the Experimental Analysis of Behavior*, **20**, 393–403.

Dawkins, M. (1974a). Perceptual changes in chicks: another look at the 'search image' concept. *Animal Behaviour*, **19**, 566–574.

Dawkins, M. (1974b). Shifts of 'attention' in chicks during feeding. *Animal Behaviour*, **19**, 575–582.

de Villiers, P. (1977). Choice in concurrent schedules and a quantitative formulation of the law of effect. In *Handbook of Operant Psychology* (W. K. Honig and J. E. R. Staddon, eds), pp. 233–287, Prentice-Hall, Englewood Cliffs, N.J.

Djang, S. -S. (1937). Role of past experience in the visual apprehension of masked forms. *Journal of Experimental Psychology*, **20**, 29–59.

Dow, S. M. and Lea, S. E. G. (1979). Optimal sampling in pigeons. Paper read at the meeting of the Association for the Study of Animal Behaviour, London.

Duncan, B. and Fantino, E. (1970). Choice for periodic schedules of reinforcement. *Journal of the Experimental Analysis of Behavior*, **14**, 73–86.

Dunstone, N. and O'Conner, R. J. (1979). Optimal foraging in an amphibious mammal. I. The aqualung effect. *Animal Behaviour*, **27**, 1182–1194.

Edwards, W. (1961). Probability learning in 1000 trials. *Journal of Experimental Psychology*, **62**, 385–394.

Einon, D. F. (1975). The partial reinforcement effect in animal learning. Ph.D. dissertation, University of Cambridge.

Elton, R. A., and Greenwood, J. J. D. (1970). Exploring apostatic selection. *Heredity*, **25**, 629–633.

Emlen, J. M. and Emlen, M. G. R. (1975). Optimal choice in diet: test of a hypothesis. *American Naturalist*, **109**, 427–435.

Estes, W. K. (1957). Theory of learning with constant, variable or contingent probabilities of reinforcement. *Psychometrika*, **22**, 113–132.

Evans, P. R. (1976). Energy balance and optimal foraging strategies in shorebirds: some implications for their distributions and movements in the non-breeding season. *Ardea*, **64**, 117–139.

Fantino, E. (1966). Immediate reward followed by extinction vs. later reward without extinction. *Psychonomic Science*, **6**, 233–234.

Fantino, E. (1967). Preference for mixed- *versus* fixed-ratio schedules. *Journal of the Experimental Analysis of Behavior*, **10**, 35–44.

Fantino, E. (1969). Choice and rate of reinforcement. *Journal of the Experimental Analysis of Behavior*, **12**, 723–730.

Ferster, C. B. and Skinner, B. F. (1957). *Schedules of Reinforcement*, Appleton-Century-Crofts, New York.

Findley, J. D. (1958). Preference and switching under concurrent scheduling. *Journal of the Experimental Analysis of Behavior*, **1**, 123–144.

Fullick, T. G. and Greenwood, J. J. D. (1979). Frequency dependent food selection in relation to two models. *American Naturalist*, **113**, 762–765.

Garcia, J. and Koelling, R. A. (1966). Relation of cue to consequence in avoidance learning. *Science*, **4**, 123–124.

Gause, G. F. (1934). *The Struggle for Existence*, Williams and Wilkins, Baltimore.

Gibb, J. A. (1958). Predation by tits and squirrels on the encosmid *Ernarmonia conicolana* (Heyl.). *Journal of Animal Ecology*, **27**, 375–396.

Gibbon, J., Berryman, R., and Thompson, R. L. (1974). Contingency spaces and measures in classical and instrumental conditioning. *Journal of the Experimental Analysis of Behavior*, **21**, 585–605.

Gill, E. B. and Wolf, L. L. (1975). Economics of feeding territoriality in the Golden-winged sunbird. *Ecology*, **56**, 333–345.

Gill, F. B. and Wolf, L. L. (1977). Nonrandom foraging by sunbirds in a patchy environment. *Ecology*, **58**, 1284–1296.

Goss-Custard, J. D. (1970). The responses of redshank (*Tringa totanus* (L.)) to spatial variations in the density of their prey. *Journal of Animal Ecology*, **39**, 91–113.

Goss-Custard, J. D. (1977a). Optimal foraging and the size-selection of worms by redshank, *Tringa totanus*, in the field. *Animal Behaviour*, **25**, 10–29.

Goss-Custard, J. D. (1977b). The energetics of prey selection by redshank, *Tringa totanus* (L.), in relation to prey density. *Journal of Animal Ecology*, **46**, 1–19.

Graf, V., Bullock, D. H., and Bitterman, M. E. (1964). Further experiments on probability-matching in the pigeon. *Journal of the Experimental Analysis of Behavior*, **7**, 151–157.

Graft, D. A., Lea, S. E. G., and Whitworth, T. L. (1977). The matching law in and within groups of rats. *Journal of the Experimental Analysis of Behavior*, **27**, 183–194.

Green, H. A. J. (1971). *Consumer Theory*, Penguin, Harmondsworth.

Greenwood, P. J. and Harvey, P. H. (1978). Foraging and territory utilization of blackbirds (*Turdus merula*) and song thrushes (*Turdus philomelos*). *Animal Behaviour*, **26**, 1222–1236.

Hainsworth, F. R. and Wolf, L. L. (1976). Nectar characteristics and food selection by huming birds. *Oecologia*, **25**, 101–113.

Hale, J. M. and Shimp, C. P. (1975). Molecular contingencies: reinforcement probability. *Journal of the Experimental Analysis of Behavior*, **24**, 315–321.

Harzem, P. (1969). Temporal discrimination. In *Animal Discrimination Learning* (R. M. Gilbert and N. S. Sutherland eds), pp. 299–334, Academic Press, London.

Harzem, P. and Miles, T. R. (1978). *Conceptual Issues in Operant Psychology*, Wiley, Chichester.

Hassell, M. P. and May, R. M. (1974). Aggregation of predators and insect parasites and its effects on stability. *Journal of Animal Ecology*, **43**, 567–594.

Heller, R. and Milinski, M. (1979). Optimal foraging of sticklebacks on swarming prey. *Animal Behaviour*, **27**, 1127–1141.

Henton, W. W. and Iversen, I. H. (1978). *Classical Conditioning and Operant Conditioning*, Springer-Verlag, New York.

Herrnstein, R. J. (1958). Some factors affecting choice in a two-response situation. *Transactions of the New York Academy of Sciences*, **21**, 35–45.

Herrnstein, R. J. (1961). Relative and absolute strength of response as a function of frequency of reinforcement. *Journal of the Experimental Analysis of Behavior*, **4**, 267–272.

Herrnstein, R. J. (1964a). Secondary reinforcement and rate of primary reinforcement. *Journal of the Experimental Analysis of Behavior*, **7**, 27–36.

Herrnstein, R. J. (1964b). A periodicity as a factor in choice. *Journal of the Experimental Analysis of Behavior*, **7**, 179–182.

Herrnstein, R. J. (1970). On the law of effect. *Journal of the Experimental Analysis of Behavior*, **13**, 243–266.

Herrnstein, R. J. and Loveland, D. H. (1964). Complex visual concept in the pigeon. *Science, New York*, **146**, 549–551.

Herrnstein, R. J. and Loveland, D. H. (1975). Maximizing and matching on concurrent ratio schedules. *Journal of the Experimental Analysis of Behavior*, **24**, 107–116.

Hodos, W. and Trumbule, G. H. (1967). Strategies of schedule preference in the chimpanzee. *Journal of the Experimental Analysis of Behavior*, **10**, 503–514.

Huff, D. L. (1962). A probabilistic analysis of consumer spatial behavior. In *Emerging Concepts in Marketing* (W. S. Decker, ed.), pp. 443–461, American Marketing Association, Chicago.

Hughes, R. N. (1979). Optimal diets under the energy maximization premise: the effects of recognition time and learning. *American Naturalist*, **113**, 209–221.

Hursh, S. R. and Fantino, (1973). Relative delay of reinforcement and choice. *Journal of the Experimental Analysis of Behavior*, **19**, 437–450.

Iversen, I. H. (1975). Reciprocal response interactions in concurrent variable-interval and discrete-trial fixed-ratio schedules. *Scandinavian Journal of Psychology*, **16**, 280–284.

Ivlev, V. A. (1961). *Experimental Ecology of the Feeding of Fishes*, Yale University Press, New Haven, Conn.

Jenkins, H. M. (1962). Resistance to extinction when partial reinforcement is followed by regular reinforcement. *Journal of Experimental Psychology*, **64**, 441–450.

Jones, P. W. (1975). The two-armed bandit. *Biometrika*, **62**, 523–524.

Kacelnik, A. (1979). Optimal sampling and time horizon in the Great tit. Paper read at the meeting of the Association for the Study of Animal Behavior, London.

Kamil, A. C. (1978). Systematic foraging by a nectar-feeding bird, the amakihi (*Loxops virens*). *Journal of Comparative and Physiological Psychology*, **92**, 388–396.

Kamil, A. C. and Sargent, T. D. (1980). *Mechanisms of Foraging Behavior*, Garland Press, New York.

Katz, P. L. (1974). A long-term approach to foraging optimization. *American Naturalist*, **108**, 758–782.

Kear, J. (1962). Food selection in finches with special reference to interspecific differences. *Proceedings of the Zoological Society of London*, **138**, 163–204.

Killeen, P. (1968). On the measurement of reinforcement frequency in the study of preference. *Journal of the Experimental Analysis of Behavior*, **11**, 263–269.

Killeen, P. (1970). Preference for fixed-interval schedules of reinforcement. *Journal of the Experiemental Analysis of Behavior*, **14**, 127–131.

Krebs, J. R. (1978). Optimal foraging: decision rules for predators. In *Behavioural Ecology* (J. R. Krebs and N. B. Davies, eds), pp. 23–63, Blackwell Scientific Publications, Oxford.

Krebs, J. R., Erichsen, J. T., Webber, M. I. and Charnov, E. L. (1977). Optimal prey selection in the Great tit (*Parus major*). *Animal Behaviour*, **25**, 30–38.

Krebs, J. R., Kacelnik, A., and Taylor, P. (1978). Optimal sampling by foraging birds: an experiment with Great tits (*Parus major*). *Nature*, **275**, 27–31.

Krebs, J. R., Ryan, J. C. and Charnov, E. L. (1974). Honting by expectation or optimal foraging? A study of patch use by chickadees. *Animal Behaviour*, **22**, 953–964.

Lea, S. E. G. (1974). Mathematical models and learning theory: an approach through measurement theory. Ph.D. dissertation, University of Cambridge.

Lea, S. E. G. (1976). Titration of schedule parameters by pigeons. *Journal of the Experimental Analysis of Behavior*, **25**, 43–54.

Lea, S. E. G. (1978). The psychology and economics of demand. *Psychological Bulletin*, **85**, 441–466.

Lea, S. E. G. (1979). Foraging and reinforcement schedules in the pigeon: optimal and non-optimal aspects of choice. *Animal Behaviour*, **27**, 875–886.

Lea, S. E. G. and Roper, T. J. (1977). Demand for food on fixed-ratio schedules as a function of the quality of concurrently available reinforcement. *Journal of the Experimental Analysis of Behavior*, **27**, 371–380.

Lehman, J. T. (1976). The filter feeder as an optimal forager and the predicted shapes of feeding curves. *Limnology and Oceanography*, **21**, 501–516.

Levanthai, A. M., Morrell, R. F., Morgan, E. J., and Perkins, C. C. (1969). The relation between mean reward and mean reinforcement. *Journal of Experimental Psychology*, **57**, 284–287.

Lobb, B. and Davison, M. C. (1975). Performance on concurrent variable-interval schedules: a systematic replication. *Journal of the Experimental Analysis of Behavior*, **24**, 191–197.

Logan, F. A. (1964). The free behavior situation. In *Nebraska Symposium on Motivation* Vol. 12 (D. Levine, ed.), pp. 99–131, University of Nebraska Press, Lincoln, Neb.

Logan, F. A. (1965a). Decision-making by rats: delay versus amount of reward. *Journal of Comparative and Physiological Psychology*, **59**, 1–12.

Logan, F. A. (1965b). Decision-making by rats: uncertain outcome choices. *Journal of Comparative and Physiological Psychology*, **59**, 246–251.

Lotter, E. C., Woods, S. C., and Vasselli, J. R. (1973). Schedule induced polydipsia: an artefact. *Journal of Comparative and Physiological Psychology*, **83**, 478–484.

Lowe, C. F., Davey, G. C. L., and Harzem, P. (1974). Effects of reinforcement magnitude on interval and ratio schedules. *Journal of the Experimental Analysis of Behavior*, **22**, 553–560.

Luce, R. D. (1959). *Individual Choice Behavior*, John Wiley, New York.

MacArthur, R. H. and Pianka, E. R. (1966). On optimal use of a patchy environment. *American Naturalist*, **100**, 603–609.

Mackintosh, N. J. (1974). *The Psychology of Animal Learning*, Academic Press, London.

Mackintosh, N. J., Lord, J., and Little, L. (1971). Visual and spatial probability learning in the goldfish. *Psychonomic Science*, **24**, 221–223.

Manly, B. F. J., Miller, P., and Cook, L. M. (1972). Analysis of a selective predation experiment. *American Naturalist*, **106**, 719–736.

McCleery, R. H. (1978). Optimal behaviour sequences and decision making. In *Behavioural Ecology* (J. R. Krebs and N. B. Davies, eds), pp. 377–410, Blackwell Scientific Publications, Oxford.

Mellgren, R. L. and Dyck, D. G. (1972). Partial reinforcement effect, reverse partial reinforcement effect, and generalised partial reinforcement effect within subjects. *Journal of Experimental Psychology*, **92**, 339–346.

Mischel, W. and Metzner, R. (1962). Preference for delayed reward as a function of age, intelligence and length of delay interval. *Journal of Abnormal and Social Psychology*,

64, 425–431.

Mook, J. H., Mook, L. J., and Heikens, H. S. (1960). Further evidence for the role of 'searching image' in the hunting behaviour of titmice. *Archieves Néerlandaises de Zoologie*, **13**, 448–465.

Moore, B. R. (1973). The role of directed Pavlovian reactions in simple instrumental learning in the pigeon. In *Constraints on Learning* (R. A. Hinde and J. Stevenson-Hinde, eds), pp. 159–188, Academic Press, London.

Morgan, M. J. (1974a). Do rats like to work for their food? *Learning and Motivation*, **5**, 352–368.

Morgan, M. J. (1974b). The effects of random reinforcement sequences. *Journal of the Experimental Analysis of Behavior*, **22**, 301–310.

Morrison, D. W. (1978). On the optimal searching strategy for refuging predators. *American Naturalist*, **112**, 925–934.

Murdoch, W. W., Avery, S., and Smyth, M. E. B. (1975). Switching in predatory fish. *Ecology*, **56**, 1094–1103.

Murdoch, W. W. and Oaten, A. (1975). Predation and population stability. *Advances in Ecological Research*, **9**, 1–131.

Myers, D. L. and Myers, L. E. (1977). Undermatching: a reappraisal of performance on concurrent variable-interval schedules of reinforcement. *Journal of the Experimental Analysis of Behavior*, **27**, 203–214.

Navarick, D. J. and Fantino, E. (1976). Self-control and general models of choice. *Journal of Experimental Psychology: Animal Behavior Processes*, **2**, 75–87.

Neisser, U. (1966). *Cognitive Psychology*, Appleton-Century-Crofts, New York.

Neuringer, A. J. (1969). Delayed reinforcement *versus* reinforcement after a fixed interval. *Journal of the Experimental Analysis of Behavior*, **12**, 375–383.

Oaten, A. (1977). Optimal foraging in patches: a case for stochasticity. *Theoretical Population Biology*, **12**, 263–285.

Partridge, L. (1976). Individual differences in feeding efficiencies and feeding preferences of captive Great tits. *Animal Behaviour*, **24**, 230–240.

Pear, J. J. (1975). Implications of the matching law for ratio responding. *Journal of the Experimental Analysis of Behavior*, **23**, 139–141.

Petrinovich, L. and Bolles, R. C. (1957). Delayed alternation: evidence for symbolic processes in the rat. *Journal of Comparative and Physiological Psychology*, **50**, 363–365.

Pietrewicz, A. T. and Kamil, A. C. (1977). Visual detection of cryptic prey by bluejays (*Cyanocitta cristata*) *Science, New York*, **195**, 580–582.

Pietrewicz, A. T. and Kamil, A. C. (1979). Search image formation in the bluejay (*Cyanocitta cristata*). *Science*, in press.

Pietrewicz, A. T. and Kamil, A. C. (1980). Search images and the detection of cryptic prey: an operant approach. In *Mechanisms of Foraging Behavior* (A. C. Kamil and T. D. Sargent, eds), Garland Press, New York.

Powell, R. A. (1979). Ecological energetics and foraging strategies of the fisher (*Martes pennanti*). *Journal of Animal Ecology*, **48**, 195–212.

Pubols, B. H. (1962). Constant versus variable delay of reinforcement. *Journal of Comparative and Physiological Psychology*, **55**, 52–56.

Pulliam, H. R. (1975). Diet optimization with nutrient constraints. *American Naturalist*, **109**, 765–768.

Pyke, G. H. (1979). Optimal foraging in bumblebees: rule of movement between flowers within inflorescences. *Animal Behaviour*, **27**, 1167–1181.

Pyke, G. H., Pulliam, H. R., and Charnov, E. L. (1977). Optimal foraging: a selective review of theory and tests. *Quarterly Review of Biology*, **52**, 137–154.

Rachlin, H. (1973). Contrast and matching. *Psychological Review*, **80**, 217–234.

Rachlin, H. and Green, L. (1972). Commitment, choice and self-control. *Journal of the Experimental Analysis of Behavior*, **17**, 15–22.

Rachlin, H., Green, L., Kagel, J. H., and Battalio, R. C. (1976). Economic demand theory and psychological studies of choice. In *The Psychology of Learning and Motivation*, Vol. 10 (G. H. Bower ed.), pp. 129–154, Academic Press, New York.

Rapport, D. J. (1971). An optimization model of food selection. *American Naturalist*, **105**, 575–587.

Roberts, W. A. (1966). Learning and motivation in the immature rat. *American Journal of Psychology*, **76**, 3–23.

Roper, T. J. (1978). Diversity and substitutability of adjunctive activities under fixed-interval schedules of food reinforcement. *Journal of the Experimental Analysis of Behavior*, **30**, 83–96

Royama, T. (1976). Factors governing the hunting behaviour and selection of food by the Great tit (*Parus major* L.). *Journal of Animal Ecology*, **39**, 619–668.

Rudy, J. W., Homzie, M. J., Cox, R. D., Graeber, R. C., and Carter, E. N. (1970). Effects of sequential manipulations in the within-subjects partial reinforcement experiment with rats. *Journal of Comparative and Physiological Psychology*, **72**, 105–115.

Schoener, T. W. (1971). Theory of feeding strategies. *Annual Review of Ecology and Systematics*, **2**, 369–404.

Schoenfield, W. N., Cumming, W. W., and Hearst, E. (1956). On the classification of reinforcement schedules. *Proceedings of the National Academy of Sciences, of the U.S.A.*, **42**, 563–570.

Schwartz, B. (1969). Effects of reinforcement magnitude on pigeons' preference for different fixed-ratio schedules of reinforcement. *Journal of the Experimental Analysis of Behavior*, **12**, 253–260.

Shepard, R. N. (1978). The mental image. *American Psychologist*, **33**, 125–137.

Shimp, C. P. (1966). Probabalistically reinforced choice behavior in pigeons. *Journal of the Experimental Analysis of Behavior*, **9**, 443–456.

Shimp, C. P. (1969). Optimal behavior in free-operant experiments. *Psychological Review*, **76**, 97–112.

Silberberg, A., Hamilton, B., Ziriax, J. M., and Casey, J. (1978). The structure of choice. *Journal of Experimental Psychology: Animal Behavior Processes*, **4**, 368–398.

Simmons, P. J. (1974). *Choice and Demand*, Macmillan, London.

Skinner, B. F. (1935). On the generic nature of the concepts of stimulus and response. *Journal of General Psychology*, **12**, 40–65.

Skinner, B. F. (1948). 'Supersition' in the pigeon. *Journal of Experimental Psychology*, **38**, 168–172.

Skinner, B. F. (1950). Are theories of learning necessary? *Psychological Review*, **57**, 193–216.

Skinner, B. F. (1962). Two 'synthetic social relations'. *Journal of the Experimental Analysis of Behavior*, **5**, 531–533.

Skinner, B. F. (1969). *Contingencies of Reinforcement*, Appleton-Century-Crofts, New York.

Smith, C. C. (1970). The coevolution of pine squirrels (*Tamiasciurus*) and conifers. *Ecological Monographs*, **40**, 349–371.

Smith, C. C. and Follmer, D. (1972). Food preferences of squirrels. *Ecology*, **53**, 82–91.

Smith, J. N. M. (1974a). The food searching behaviour of two European thrushes. I. Description and analysis of search paths. *Behaviour*, **48**, 276–302.

Smith, J. N. M. (1974b). The food searching behaviour of two European thrushes: II. The adaptiveness of the search patterns. *Behaviour*, **49**, 1–61.

Smith, J. N. M. and Dawkins, R. (1971). The hunting behaviour of individual great tits in relation to spatial variations in their food density. *Animal Behaviour*, **19**, 695–706.

Smith, J. N. M. and Sweatman, H. P. A. (1974). Food-searching behaviour of titmice in patchy environments. *Ecology*, **55**, 1216–1232.

Sowter, A. P., Gabor, A., and Granger, C. W. J. (1971). The effect of price on choice: a theoretical and empirical investigation. *Applied Economics*, **3**, 167–181.

Staddon, J. E. R. (1967). Attention and temporal discrimination: factors controlling responding on a cyclic interval schedule. *Journal of the Experimental Analysis of Behavior*, **10**, 349–360.

Staddon, J. E. R. (1970). Effect of reinforcement duration on fixed-interval responding. *Journal of the Experimental Analysis of Behaviour*, **13**, 9–11.

Staddon, J. E. R. (1977). Schedule-induced behavior. In *Handbook of Operant Behavior* (W. K. Honig and J. E. R. Staddon, eds, pp. 125–152, Prentice-Hall, Englewood Cliffs, .J.

Staddon, J. E. R. and Ayres, S. L. (1975). Sequential and temporal properties of behavior induced by a schedule of periodic food delivery. *Behaviour*, **54**, 26–49.

Staddon, J. E. R. and Innis, N. K. (1966a). An effect analogous to 'frustration' on interval reinforcement schedules. *Psychonomic Science*, **4**, 287–288.

Staddon, J. E. R. and Innis, N. K. (1966b). Preference for fixed vs. variable amounts of reward. *Psychonomic Science*, **4**, 193–194.

Staddon, J. E. R. and Simmelhag, V. L. (1971). The 'superstition' experiment: A re-examination of its implications for the principles of adaptive behavior. *Psychological Review*, **78**, 3–43.

Stein, R. A. (1977). Selective predation, optimal foraging, and the predator–prey interaction between fish and crayfish. *Ecology*, **58**, 1237–1253.

Stevenson-Hinde, J. (1973). Constraints on reinforcement. In *Constraints on Learning* (R. A. Hinde and J. Stevenson-Hinde, eds.), pp. 285–296, Academic Press, London.

Stubbs, D. A. and Pliskoff, S. S. (1969). Concurrent responding with fixed relative rate of reinforcement. *Journal of the Experimental Analysis of Behavior*, **12**, 887–895.

Sutherland, N. S., Mackintosh, N. J., and Wolfe, J. B. (1965). Extinction as a function of the order of partial and consistent reinforcement. *Journal of Experimental Psychology*, **69**, 56–59.

Taylor, C. (1964). *The Explanation of Behaviour*, Routledge and Kegan Paul, London.

Tenen, S. S. (1965). Retrograde amnesia from electroconvulsive shock in a one-trial appetitive learning task. *Science*, **148**, 1248–1250.

Theios, J. (1962). The partial reinforcement effect sustained through blocks of continuous reinforcement. *Journal of Experimental Psychology*, **64**, 1–6.

Thomas, G. (1974). The influences of encountering a food object on subsequent searching behaviour in *Gasterosteus aculeatus* L. *Animal Behaviour*, **22**, 941–952.

Thomas, G. (1977). The influences of eating and rejecting prey items upon feeding and food searching behaviour in *Gasterosteus aculeatus* L. *Animal Behaviour*, **25**, 52–66.

Thurstone, L. L. (1927). A law of comparative judgement. *Psychological Review*, **34**, 273–286.

Tinbergen, L. (1960). The natural control of insects in pine woods: I. Factors influencing the rate of predation by song birds. *Archives Néerlandaises de Zoologie*, **13**, 265–343.

Tinbergen, N., Impekoven, M., and Franck, D. (1967). An experiment on spacing-out as a defence against predation. *Behaviour*, **28**, 307–321.

Toda, M. (1962). The design of a fungus-eater: a model of human behavior in an unsophisticated environment. *Behavioral Science*, **7**, 162–183.

Todorov, J. C. (1973). Interaction of frequency and magnitude of reinforcement on concurrent performances. *Journal of the Experimental Analysis of Behavior*, **19**, 451–458.

Tolman, E. C. (1938). The determinants of behavior at a choice point. *Psychological Review*, **45**, 1–41.

Tolman, E. C. (1955). Principles of performance. *Psychological Review,* **62**, 315–326.

Tolman, E. C., Ritchie, B. F., and Kalish, D. (1946). Studies in spatial learning. II. Place learning versus response learning. *Journal of Experimental Psychology*, **36**, 221–229.

Tullock, G. (1971). The Coal tit as a careful shopper. *American Naturalist*, **105**, 77–80.

Uhl, C. N. (1963). Probability learning in the rat as a function of incentive, probability of reinforcement, and training procedure. *Journal of Experimental Psychology*, **66**, 443–449.

Von Uexkull, J. (1957). A stroll through the world of animals and men. In *Instinctive Behaviour*, (C. H. Schiller, ed.), Methuen, London. (Originally published 1934.)

Wardlaw, G. R. and Davison, M. C. (1974). Preference for fixed-interval schedules: effects of initial-link length. *Journal of the Experimental Analysis of Behavior*, **21**, 331–340.

Ware, D. M. (1972). Preation by Rainbow trout (*Salmo gairdneri*): the influence of hunger, prey density, and prey size. *Journal of the Fisheries Research Board of Canada*, **29**, 1193–1201.

Werner, E. E. and Hall, D. J. (1974). Optimal foraging and the size selection of prey by the Bluegill sunfish. (*Lepomis macrochirus*). *Ecology*, **55**, 1042–1052.

Willson, M. F. (1971). Seed selection in some North American finches. *Condor*, **73**, 415–429.

Willson, M. F. and Harmeson, J. C. (1973). Seed preferences and digestive efficiency of cardinals and song sparrows. *Condor*, **75**, 225–234.

Wilson, E. O. (1975). *Sociobiology*, Harvard University Press, Cambridge, Mass.

Wilson, W. A. (1960). Supplementary report: two-choice behavior of monkeys. *Journal of Experimental Psychology*, **59**, 207–208.

Wolf, L. L. (1975). Energy intake and expenditure in a nectar-feeding sunbird. *Ecology*, **56**, 92–104.

Wrangham, R. W. (1977). Paper read at the conference of the Association for the Study of Animal Behaviour, London.

Wrangham R. W. (1979). On the evolution of ape social systems. *Social Science Information*, **18**, 335–368.

Zach, R. and Falls, J. B. (1976*a*). Do ovenbirds (Aves: Parulidae) hunt by expectation? *Canadian Journal of Zoology*, **54**, 1894–1903.

Zach, R. and Falls, J. B. (1976*b*). Foraging behaviour, learning and exploration by captive ovenbirds (Aves: Parulidae). *Canadian Journal of Zoology*, **54**, 1880–1893.

Zach, R. and Falls, J. B. (1976*c*). Ovenbird (Aves: Parulidae) hunting behavior in a patchy environment: an experimental study. *Canadian Journal of Zoology*, **54**, 1599–1603.

Zach, R. and Falls, J. B. (1977). Influence of capturing a prey on subsequent search in the ovenbird (Aves: Parulidae). *Canadian Journal of Zoology*, **55**, 1958–1969.

Zach, R. and Falls, J. B. (1978). Prey selection by captive ovenbirds (Aves: Parulidae). *Journal of Animal Ecology*, **47**, 929–943.

Zach, R. and Falls, J. B. (1979). Foraging and territoriality of male ovenbirds (Aves: Parulidae) in a heterogeneous habitat. *Journal of Animal Ecology*, **48**, 33–52.

Index